THE MEN OF THE
FIRST FRENCH REPUBLIC

THE MEN OF THE FIRST FRENCH REPUBLIC

POLITICAL ALIGNMENTS IN THE NATIONAL CONVENTION OF 1792

Alison Patrick

THE JOHNS HOPKINS UNIVERSITY PRESS
BALTIMORE and LONDON

The Johns Hopkins University Press, Baltimore, Maryland 21218
The Johns Hopkins University Press Ltd., London

Library of Congress Catalog Card Number 72-4018
International Standard Book Number 0-8018-1305-0

Library of Congress Cataloging in Publication data
will be found on the last printed page of this book.

1-19-79

For

J. F. P.

and the others

and for

my mother

CONTENTS

TABLES

FIGURES

ABBREVIATIONS

C.P.S.:   Committee of Public Safety

C.G.S.:   Committee of General Security

Annales: *Annales historiques de la Révolution
              Française*

*Rev. hist.
de la R.F.:*   *Revue historique de la Révolution Française et
              de l'Empire*

PREFACE

I cannot hope to thank all the people who have made the appearance of this book possible, but I should like to acknowledge some of my greatest debts.

The generosity of The Johns Hopkins Press and the Publications Fund of the University of Melbourne has made publication financially practicable. I thank those responsible very much. I have a particular and great debt to Mr. Robert Forster of the Johns Hopkins University, who put me in touch with historians in his own country, and to Mr. J. G. Goellner of The Johns Hopkins Press. I owe acknowledgement also to the *Journal of Modern History*, in which an earlier form of the first parts of this book appeared.

Work on this subject came within my reach with the acquisition by the National Library of Australia of a large collection of French Revolutionary pamphlets. I owe more gratitude than I can express to the staff of the National Library, who were unfailingly generous and helpful to an annual visitor. Whether facilities had to be provided in the subtropical or arctic depths of the subbasement or in the uncertain splendors of a new building not yet fully completed although half-occupied, they always were provided with the greatest of courtesy and the least possible fuss, and so were microfilms, xerox copies, books on loan, and badly needed cups of coffee. Help was given over a long period, but I would mention especially, for his recent contributions, Mr. Ivan Page of the Rare Books Department. My one regret was that my stays had to be so short—a regret perhaps not altogether shared by those in Canberra who provided hospitality far beyond the call of family duty.

I thank also Miss Mary Lugton, of the Baillieu Library, University of Melbourne, who first told me of the Canberra purchase, and her colleagues, Mr. Patrick Singleton and particularly Miss Elizabeth Garran for her amazing patience, persistence, and good temper in the collection of microfilm. The *Bibliothèque Nationale*, the *Archives Nationales*, the *Archives Départementales* of the *Départment du Nord* and the *Préfecture des Yvelines*, the British Museum, the New York Public Library, and the University of Kansas Library all provided essential microfilm or xerox copies. *M. le Conservateur* of the Indre-et-Loire *Archives Départementales* kindly tried to trace for me the missing full text of the Indre-et-Loire 1792 electoral *procés-verbal*.

The W. L. Baillieu Trust and the Baillieu Library in conjunction provided funds for the purchase of material used in Melbourne. Students of Revolutionary history owe them much, as also Dr. (now Professor) Austin Gough for his initiative and enthusiasm in arranging acquisitions in Paris. The research funds of my own department provided generous help for the purchase of important microfilm.

Many individuals contributed advice and encouragement; the blunders I have made are my responsibility and not theirs. Professor Alan McBriar and Professor J. R. Poynter both read parts of the manuscript. Professor George Rudé advised me on further sources in Paris. Dr. Lloyd Robson did his best to introduce me to the use of statistical methods. Mr. Rhys Isaac provided interest, criticism, and constructive suggestions. Miss Kate Patrick gave valuable help with the sources in the British Museum, and my Melbourne computer advisor devised a program to deal with the 1795 financial statements. Mr. Frank Key made it possible for me to draft a map; Miss Joyce Wood advised me on its reproduction and expertly drew both map and diagrams.

I thank very much those who befriended me in Paris: Mr. David Bien of the University of Michigan, and particularly M. François Furet of the *VIe Section, Ecole Pratique des Hautes Etudes*, who was generous with his time and interest.

For typing, I am grateful to Mrs. Pia Lofhelm, who cheerfully wrestled with the thesis manuscript under unexpectedly difficult conditions, and to Mrs. Beverley Goldsworthy who typed the final draft of the book. And lastly, I have a domestic debt; but one which defies calculation and is beyond acknowledgement.

Melbourne
December 1971

THE GREAT DEBATE OF 1793

Il existe un parti, il existe une faction qui veut évidemment atteinter à la souverainté du peuple, et se rendre l'arbitre de sa destinée, qui se livre à la coupable ambition de dominer par la terreur la Convention nationale, et par la Convention la République entière. (A. Gensonné, deputy for Gironde, *Opinion . . . sur le jugement de Louis.*)

Pourquoi les fondateurs de la république sont-ils divisés sur la punition du tyran? (M. Robespierre, deputy for Paris, *Second discours . . . sur le jugement de Louis Capet.*)

Quant à moi, je ne connois pas cette justice qui frappe, en souriant, un coupable obscur, et qui se prosterne devant un illustre criminel. (L. Le Cointre, deputy for Seine-et-Oise, *Opinion . . . sur le jugement de Louis Capet.*)

Jugeons-le . . . en hommes qui dédaignent une vengeance inutile, qui la regardent comme la resource misérable des ames foibles et sanguinaires . . . . (J. Dusaulx, deputy for Paris, *Opinion . . . sur le jugement de Louis Capet.*)

J'ai entendu parler de factions; s'il en existe, je ne les crains pas . . . Ma vie est à ma patrie; mais ma conscience est à moi et à moi seul. (L. E. Beffroy, deputy for Aisne, *Opinion . . . 14 janvier 1793.*)

INTRODUCTION

The bulk of the literature on the political history of the French Revolution of 1789 is already so large that it seems presumptuous to suggest that there are still some areas which remain almost untouched. Yet as far as modern scholarship is concerned, blank spaces do exist, and in surprising places; and one such blank relates to the character and development of France's revolutionary legislatures, as the collective entities which they so proudly were.

The student now knows, thanks to Soboul, what sort of man might be a *sans-culotte* in the Paris of 1793–94, but if he wants a detailed analysis of the membership of the Legislative Assembly of 1791, or more than the vaguest generalities about its character in comparison with that of the Constituent Assembly of 1789, he will search in vain. General texts will tell him, in very general terms, what sort of man was elected to the States-General in 1789; they will not refer him to any modern study of the composition of the Third Estate, nor tell him which of its members became Patriot, which *monarchien*, and which found it difficult to decide. Any textbook will tell him how many (though not which) of the members of the Legislative Assembly joined the Jacobin Club and how many the Feuillants, in October 1791; no one will tell him how these men voted in the *appels nominaux* of 1792, nor which from each group and which men from the rest of the Legislative were still sitting at the end of August 1792. Such questions have at present no answers, because they require a careful consideration of the whole membership of the legislature, and even the best of the discussions of revolutionary politics have hitherto been focussed on one or other particular group of politicians; thus, while Michon writes of the Feuillants, Sydenham of the Girondins, and Palmer of the Committee of Public Safety, their work gives no detailed analysis of the membership of the Constituent, the Legislative, or the Convention as a whole. The pictures presented are of absorbing interest, but as parliamentary history they lack depth; they are all foreground and no background.

It may seem that the detail of the background is not important, since after all it was the leaders who made the crucial decisions and determined the direction of political developments. But even if this is true to a point, it is not the whole truth. The leaders needed followers. Sometimes, indeed, the concentration solely on the leadership leaves central questions unanswered. For instance, it has never been exactly clear by what development of majority attitude the Legislative Assembly, which in May–June 1792 passed the three Revolutionary Decrees, refused in August to impeach Lafayette; the pressures operating within the Assembly and the degree of consistent behavior among the deputies can be determined only by looking at the members as individuals. Generalizations, whether they concern parliamentary behavior, factional allegiance, social origin or experience of political life, can only ultimately be acceptable if they are shown to be firmly based on examination of the evidence. The generalizations about France's revolutionary legislatures are still impressionistic, because the evidence which is always quoted about their composition and behavior has never been systematically analyzed, and that part of it relating to the obscurer deputies who made up the bulk of the membership has hardly been looked at at all.

This study represents an attempt to analyze some of the well-established evidence concerning the deputies of the National Convention of 1792. It has always been assumed that this evidence supports the accepted generalizations about the Convention's character and outlook. An examination of the Convention as a whole, rather than of any of the various groups of deputies in particular, suggests that a number of these generalizations may have to be reconsidered. An enquiry of this kind, which is concerned primarily with the close examination of limited and specific evidence on a very large subject, cannot hope to provide any final answers, but it may perhaps indicate within what limits the final answers are most likely to be found.

PART I

THE PROBLEM OF POLITICAL DIVISIONS IN THE CONVENTION

Soyez unis, et nous serons invincibles.

Jeanbon Saint-André,
deputy for Lot, to the
National Convention,
January 1793

CHAPTER 1

THE PROBLEM
AND THE EVIDENCE

On 25 September 1792, four days after the formal repudiation of the Bourdon monarchy in France, the newly elected deputies of the National Convention proclaimed their country a republic, "one and indivisible." From the point of view of the deputies the republic was unavoidable, the need for unity against the divisive forces of provincialism and counterrevolution was overwhelming, and the decree was a propaganda move as well as an affirmation of principle. The hope which it embodied was not realized in the larger sense; within six months France was torn apart by civil war; and ironically it was unrealized also within the Convention itself, which became the first of the revolutionary legislatures to decimate its own membership in the name of revolutionary unity. A bitter clash of opinion among the deputies, obvious before the end of September, became more envenomed with time, with two factions contending for an authority which neither could exercise without the acquiescence of the other. By mid-summer 1793 a sharp, and for many of the protagonists a fundamental, cleavage had clearly taken place: a cleavage between those who were willing, with whatever ill-grace, to accept and possibly to further Jacobin control over national policy, in spite of its corollary of compromise with Parisian extremism, and those who were willing to take the risks involved in disputing that control.

The division of the Convention is a fact accepted by historians as it was accepted at the time; no one has yet queried the reality of the feud between Montagnards and Girondins. But in assessing the numbers involved on either side, and the attitude of those deputies who remained uncommitted, the contenders expressed two opposing views. The leaders of the Gironde maintained from the outset that they did not represent a "party," a "faction," or a minority element of any sort. The quarrel, according to them, was not between themselves as one "faction" and the Montagnards as another, but between the Mountain, an aggressive minority representing Parisian radicalism, and the overwhelming majority in the Convention, representing the nation as a whole, which this minority wished to dominate and of which the so-called Girondins were merely the most conspicuous representatives. As Gensonné put it in December 1792: "Il existe un parti, il existe une faction qui veut évidemment atteinter à la souveraineté du peuple, et se rendre l'arbitre de sa destinée, qui se livre à la coupable ambition de dominer par la terreur la Convention nationale, et par la Convention la république entière."[1]

Robespierre, as a leading spokesman for the Mountain and the target of the Girondins' most splenetic attacks, did not deny that in one sense at least the Montagnards were a minority. In an overquoted speech of 28 December 1792, he said that "*la vertu fut toujours en minorité sur la terre*." He did not however mean by this, as the right-wing press implied at the time, that the Montagnards were a permanent minority in the Convention. On the contrary, he maintained that among the deputies permanent majorities and minorities were unknown, since the majority, "*celle des bons citoyens*," had no special allegiance and tried to take its decisions in the public interest; thus when, from time to time, the assembly recognized that it had made a mistake, the former minority immediately became a majority as the mistake was corrected.[2] He did claim that the Gironde was certainly a minority, "*une faction puissante*," formed during the period of the Legislative Assembly and now working against the interest of the Revolution to lead the Republic to disaster.[3] Even if he had wished to do so, he could not have denied the existence of the Jacobins, the "*députés patriotes*," nor asserted that the bulk of the Convention belonged to or consistently supported the Jacobin Club. The distinction between his point of view and Gensonné's was rather that whereas Robespierre tacitly recognized the existence of a substantial middle group in the Convention, amenable to leadership and frequently, in his eyes, misled, but not permanently committed to any political line, Gensonné and his colleagues steadily asserted that such a middle group did not exist. To them, the Convention as a whole was unitedly anti-Montagnard, and all that the Girondins were doing in attacking the Mountain in general, or Robespierre or Marat or Paris more particularly, was expressing a general point of view which only intimidation could force the deputies to abandon. Thus when victory went clearly to the Mountain, as over the king's trial, this was interpreted as the result of illegal pressure from Montagnard deputies backed by the Paris mob.

The conventional interpretation adopted by historians has been an amalgamation of these two points of view. On the one hand, the Montagnards have

---

1. A. Gensonné, *Opinion . . . sur le jugement de Louis.*
2. See M. Robespierre, *Second discours. . . sur le jugement de Louis Capet*, in *Oeuvres*, IX, ed. M. Boiloiseau et al. (Paris, 1958), p. 198. The report of this speech contained in *Le Patriote Français* (ibid., pp. 201–2) is very revealing.
3. See, e.g., his speech *Contre Brissot et les Girondins* (10 April 1793) *Oeuvres*, IX: 376–99, in which, however, he admitted the persistent domination of the Convention (the king's trial excepted) by the Girondins and those who accepted their lead.

been accepted as a small group centering on the Parisian delegation, whose main source of strength lay outside the Convention, in the Commune and radical sections of Paris. On the other hand, the Girondins also have been accepted as a minority, though a minority having the fairly constant support of a large number of the deputies newly elected in September 1792. Between the two, as admitted reality, lies Robespierre's middle group, that of the uncertain and unwilling, of those, in short, who did not intend to get involved. Thus Cobban:

> In 1792 open conflict began between the two small factions which the Convention had inherited from the Legislative Assembly. On one side were the Brissotins and Rolandists, to whom a number of new members joined themselves; on the other, the Jacobin deputation from Paris . . . . The mass of the deputies formed the Plain, or *Marais*, and were uncommitted to either faction. . . .[4]

Older historians are rather less specific about the limited base of Montagnard influence,[5] but the general line of comment is very similar. The stereotype is rather closer to the Girondin version of the situation than to the Montagnard, since emphasis tends to be placed on the smallness of the Montagnard "faction" rather than on that of the Gironde, and it is assumed that the sympathies of the Plain were likely to lie with the Gironde. The existence of this amorphous mass of deputies, sometimes known also as the Marsh or the Belly, one would have thought could hardly have been denied, since it was taken for granted in 1792-93.[6]

This usual view of the Convention's political alignments has been challenged in the only book which has so far analyzed any of the groups of *conventionnels*, Sydenham's careful discussion of the Gironde.[7] After an exhaustive consideration of a large number of individual histories, Sydenham has approved that view of the situation in the Convention which was first presented by the Girondin leaders in 1792. He concludes that the Girondin "party" or "faction" was for the most part a political myth manufactured by the small Jacobin group for its own purposes and that the real antagonism lay, as the Girondins consistently claimed, between the aggressive, intransigent, and ambitious minority of Montagnards (described by him as "Robespierre's élite"[8]) and the bulk of their colleagues who, led by the so-called "Girondins," refused to accept their domina-

4. A. Cobban, *A History of Modern France*, 2 vols. (London, 1962), I: 203.
5. See, e.g., A. Thiers, *History of the French Revolution* trans. F. Shoberl, 5 vols. (London, 1881), II: 104; A. Aulard, *The French Revolution, a Political History*, trans. B. Miall, 4 vols. (New York, 1965) III: 37-43; G. Pariset, *La Révolution Française 1792-1799* (Paris, 1920), pp. 6-8; P. Sagnac, *La Révolution Française 1789-1792* (Paris, 1920), p. 414. Thiers's comment on the provincial support for the Mountain is noteworthy; cf. Sagnac (above).
6. It acquired one of its nicknames from an acid reference by Vadier to *"les crapauds du marais."* (A. Tournier, *Vadier, président du Comité de sûreté générale* [Paris, n.d.], p. 83.)
7. M. J. Sydenham, *The Girondins* (London, 1961).
8. Ibid., p. 212.

tion.[9] According to Sydenham, the Gironde was not in any sense a united "party," nor did it operate as one; its sole point of unity was the hostility to Parisian (and Montagnard) presumption which was common to the Convention as a whole. The argument is developed in detail with considerable care and is clinched by a reference to the enforced expulsion of the Girondin leaders from the Convention on 2 June 1793:

> The only distinction between [the Girondins] and their principal opponents which has any consistent validity is that of their divergent attitudes towards Paris, and in this essential matter the attitude of the so-called Girondin deputies was that of the majority of the Convention. Had it not been so, the insurrection of 2 June 1793 would not have taken place, for it would not have been necessary.[10]

Strangely enough, it is Sydenham's very industry in examining the activities of the Girondins which highlights the difficulty of accepting his or any other generalizations about the nature and extent of the Convention's political divisions. He has analyzed very carefully indeed the membership of the traditional Girondin "party"—but as far as the rest of the Convention is concerned we know as much as we did before; which is very little indeed, since his was a pioneer work. Hence it is not possible either to accept or reject his assertions about general attitudes in the Convention, since they are based almost entirely on information about the behavior of a special group of 200 deputies out of a total of 749. No basis for a general judgment exists. What is needed is an analysis of the Convention as a whole, of a kind that seems never to have been made. Political labels have been tossed about freely, by historians, by Jacobins and Girondins themselves, by other *conventionnels* of all shades of opinion, but, apart from what Sydenham has gathered together, elementary information is almost nonexistent. Who should be included among the Montagnards; where one should draw the boundaries of the Plain; the number, even approximately, of those who dropped temporarily out of politics after 2 June; even the way in which members of the Jacobin Club actually did vote in the trial of Louis XVI—the detail of all this remains totally obscure.

A complete and detailed analysis of the political history of 749 politicians would obviously take several lifetimes. It may, however, be possible to aim at something simpler which will still be useful as far as it goes. To explain political behavior is a delicate and complicated business, to describe it is not quite so difficult. If 2 June 1793 be taken as a dividing point, there does exist biographical evidence covering *all* the deputies, not just some or most of them, which should make it feasible to describe in very general terms their political behavior in 1793–94. This would establish at least those who seemed to accept Montagnard rule and those who did not, and the extent of the cooperation which was offered. With the assistance of the six *appels nominaux* of 1793 and the printed

9. Ibid., p. 205.
10. Ibid., pp. 205–6.

speeches on the king's trial it should be possible to look back over three of the major parliamentary crises of 1793 and, in general, over the first eight months of the Convention's history, to establish the pattern of behavior for every deputy during that time. This should allow some discrimination between those whose behavior on crucial occasions was consistently radical and those who merely accepted the Mountain once its victory was assured. This examination of behavior should also allow an estimate of support for the Gironde by disclosing evidence of it in what deputies did or said, thus excluding use of the term "Girondin" as a form of mere political abuse for the opponents of the Mountain.

It must, of course, be remembered that deputies were not elected for single-member constituencies on an individual basis. They were members of departmental delegations. If it is possible to group them at all accurately according to their political sympathies as individuals, it should also be possible to consider the plausibility of the judgments arrived at by reassembling them into the groups in which they were elected; the character of each departmental delegation should make sense in terms of its local background and the circumstances of its election. Here again a complete investigation would be an enormous task, but some check can be applied by analyzing the proceedings of the electoral assemblies of 1792 and by placing a sample selection of these in the context provided by local histories of the areas in which they sat. If the conclusions seem to survive this test, it may then be possible to arrive at some tentative generalizations about the distribution of departmental support, at the parliamentary level, for the contending "factions."

If it proves possible to establish political categories among the deputies, the biographical evidence may then be used in rather a different way, to test some of the common assumptions about the social character of the Convention and the social differences, or lack of them, between deputies taking one or another line in politics; differences not only of age, occupation, and environment, but of earlier experience or lack of experience of revolutionary political life. (It is frequently said, for example, that "local officials" elected to the Convention in 1792 were Girondin in sympathy, but no evidence bearing on this point has yet been produced.) This rather widens the perspective, in that generalizations about the character of political groups will naturally depend for their validity on the accuracy with which political categories have been established, but the social character and previous experience of the membership of the Convention as a whole is a separate question about which, also, far too little is at present known.

What is the evidence from which such a comprehensive picture of the Convention might reasonably be compiled?

Since the object is to establish comparable information about all deputies rather than very detailed information about some of them, the analysis must be developed from a close examination of the limited number of comprehensive sources available. For the description of political behavior, these will be Kuscinski's *Dictionnaire des Conventionnels*; Aulard's *Société des Jacobins*; the *Moniteur*; the *appels nominaux* of 1793 on the trial of Louis XVI, the impeachment of Marat, and the reinstatement of the Commission of Twelve; the *Table Analytique* of the Convention's *Procès-Verbaux*; and the collection in the *Bibliothèque nationale*, with some additions, of the printed speeches on the king's trial. This is the fundamental evidence, and though there has been a temptation to go beyond it into the endless labyrinth of speeches, memoirs, articles, biographies, and specialist works, the temptation has been as far as possible resisted. The aim here cannot be the compilation of an encyclopedia on the Convention's membership, but merely the sorting out of some of the basic material which has for fifty years and more been accepted as definitive.

The official evidence speaks for itself. The *appels nominaux*[11] were the accepted record of the voting, or lack of it, of every deputy on six critical occasions in 1793, with such additional explanations as many of them supplied at the time, and the several hundred speeches on the king's trial may be used collectively to establish which decisions were most in dispute, as well as for evidence of individual points of view.[12] The republished records of the Jacobin Club, imperfect though they are, can be used for much of the period as a check on membership, and on the names of those expelled.[13] For general proceedings in the Convention, the *Table Analytique* provides a convenient means of access to the Convention's own record of committee appointments, assignments to work *en mission*, arrivals, resignations, and applications for leave.[14] For day-to-day debates, the *Moniteur* is the most satisfactory source; the Convention's *procès-verbaux* must also be consulted, but, especially in the crucial last weeks of the king's trial, they are less detailed than the *Moniteur*, do not give the names of speakers, and at some points give the impression that they have been edited for political reasons.[15] Access to a report of debate is important for

11. *Appels nominaux sur le jugement de Louis XVI* (Paris, 1793) *Appel nominal . . . Y a-t-il lieu à accusation contre Marat?* (Paris, 1793). *Appel nominal . . . "Le décret qui a cassé la Commission des Douze, sera-t-il rapporté, oui ou non?"* (May 28, 1793) *in* Mavidal et Laurent, *Archives parlementaires de 1787 à 1860*, 82 vols. (Paris, 1867–1914), LXV: 496, 520ff.

12. Since the trial of the king was the only occasion in the history of the Convention on which some of the backbenchers made their views known, and since for very many the decisions then made seem to epitomize their political attitude under the Terror, it seemed important to read as many of the speeches as could be found. There is a large collection in the National Library in Canberra; this has been supplemented by the addition of all the speeches in the *Bibliothèque nationale* which are not in Canberra (Canberra has some which are not in Paris) and by a few from other sources in England and the United States. The collection may not be quite complete but covers a large proportion of the deputies. For the impeachment of Marat, the *appel nominal* itself contains a considerable number of comments made by deputies as they voted, some of them extremely important.

13. A. Aulard, *La Société des Jacobins: Recueil des Documents*, 6 vols. (Paris, 1889–97).

14. M. Boiloiseau, M. Reinhard, and G. Lefebvre (eds.), *Procès-Verbaux de la Convention nationale: Table Analytique*, 3 vols. (Paris, 1959–63).

15. *Réimpression de l'ancien Moniteur*, 31 vols. (Paris, 1854), vols. XIV–XVI especially; *Procès-verbaux de la Convention nationale, imprimé par son ordre*, 72 vols. (Paris, 1792–94), vols. I–V especially. Note the reporting in the *Moniteur* (XV: 228) and in the *Procès-Verbal* for January 17, 1793, of the scene when Duchastel came in to cast his vote on

information about the process of election to office in the Convention, for the constant duel of discussion, and for estimating the members most active in getting decrees put through—a matter of major interest when the struggle for leadership was going on.

For the deputies individually, Kuscinski[16] must remain the indispensable source, and no apology is offered for the considerable use made of his information, though it must be emphasized that a number of checks have been applied and that the analysis of the political balance in the Convention which is to be offered here is nowhere suggested by him, although when he does give an opinion on the political stance of any deputy this has been very carefully considered. For present purposes, the material to be found in the *Dictionnaire des Conventionnels* may be conveniently divided into three categories. In the first place, Kuscinski was interested in the parliamentary careers of his subjects, and therefore gives information about work on committees, about missions, about major speeches, and about major or minor political controversies. Since his passionate affection for the Convention was spread over all its members, he recounts as much as he could discover about those who were least known, and gives many relevant anecdotes. He also comments irritably on any striking lack of activity. He does not, unfortunately, give dates of committee appointments, but these can be derived from other sources, which establish his accounts as in general fairly reliable, though they sometimes go astray on points of detail.[17]

Second, Kuscinski deals with the personal background of the deputies. Here again the generality of his interest is invaluable, since he supplies the same basic information about every deputy and so makes comparisons possible. For the purposes of Chapter 8, below, it has been accepted as it stands except for a few obvious emendations.[18] The interest of the present study is in a general survey of the Convention's membership, and it seems unlikely that apart from the slips pointed out by Mathiez, other errors are wholesale enough to make a general picture derived from Kuscinski's evidence seriously misleading.[19]

---

the sentencing of the king, and of the proceedings on January 19 when the secretaries' report of the voting was queried (*Moniteur* XV: 235).

16. A. Kuscinski, *Dictionnaire des Conventionnels*, 4 vols. (Paris, 1916–19). Hereafter referred to in footnotes as *Conventionnels*.

17. He would not be a good final guide for anyone wanting to analyze in detail the membership of any particular committee; allowance must be made here for the circumstances in which the *Dictionnaire* was published. Kuscinski did not live to see it through the press, and Aulard, who edited it, said that he could not attempt to identify or correct mistakes. But if one is interested in the type of activity—committee work in general—rather than in exactly which committee, he seems to be trustworthy enough; the errors seem to be slips rather than real blunders. I have found very few deputies of any sort who sat on committees under the Terror when Kuscinski does not note the fact, and I have not found any member who did not do committee work when Kuscinski says he did. The same sort of comment may be made for work *en mission.*

18. On this, cf. Appendix I, below, and the review by Mathiez in *Annales Révolutionnaires*, XII (1920).

19. Many of the errors, e.g., in names, pointed to by Mathiez were apparently misprints, of which the *Dictionnaire* certainly has its fair share.

Finally, Kuscinski sometimes makes comments about the political outlook of the deputy under discussion. When he does this, which is by no means always, the comment sometimes arises naturally from the character of the evidence produced, and can itself be disregarded. The difficulties created when he presents a statement about political attitude without providing much supporting evidence will be considered later, but it may be noted here that they are not serious, because most of the deputies in this category were in fact active in politics and their outlook may be independently assessed in terms of what they did rather than in terms of what he says about them. Credit has, however, often been given to Kuscinski primarily, partly because, as has been indicated, he did not make a judgment of this sort as a matter of course, and partly because it must be recognized that he knew more about the members of the Convention, collectively and individually, than any other historian who has ever lived. He had a conscious sympathy for the Montagnards, but he did not idealize them, there is no sign that he tried to exaggerate their numbers, and he is generous to men of all political persuasions; though it must be admitted that he has little time for the meaner revenges of the Thermidorians.

Because so many of the *conventionnels* were graduates of the Legislative Assembly, reference has also been made to Kuscinski's other major work, that on the deputies of the Legislative, and to the *appels nominaux* of 1792.[20] For the circumstances in which the deputies were elected, the central evidence to be analyzed is that contained in the *procès-verbaux* of the 1792 electoral assemblies.[21] For any further examination of the departmental background, the field was so enormous that the choice had to be completely arbitrary: it was therefore governed partly by the material readily available, but an attempt was made to look at departments varying widely in both geographical location and revolutionary enthusiasm, and to examine very different kinds of source—biographies, right-wing and clerical histories, republican histories, as well as published and unpublished records from departmental archives. From this necessarily very selective survey, some context should emerge for the departmental delegations of 1792, and for some of the assumptions about recent events in national politics which many of the deputies seem to have brought with them to Paris in September 1792.

It is a considerable disadvantage that the method proposed will not permit any estimate of the size of political groups at any time earlier than January 1793, when the voting on the trial of the king took place. It would be interesting and important to test the validity of the assertion that during the preceding four months there was a very large anti-Montagnard majority, on which the outcome of the trial made a considerable impact. Unfortunately there seems to be no way of making a general check on Convention attitudes during this period. There was

20. A. Kuscinski, *Les députés à l'Assemblée législative de 1791* (Paris, 1900); *Tableau comparatif des sept appels nominaux fév.-août 1792* (Paris 1792).
21. *Archives nationales*, C 178 CII 1 (Ain) to C 181 C II 83 (Yonne).

no *appel nominal*, and the only obvious material would seem to be the Convention debates, in which only a minority of members spoke and in which some of those who did speak cannot certainly be identified. One cannot even use the Jacobin records for evidence of Montagnard strength, since a number of deputies (De Perret and Chambon, for example) began their Convention careers in the Club without offering or intending any allegiance to the Mountain.[22] It may be assumed that the original strength of the Gironde lay in the circle of friends and acquaintances around Brissot, Vergniaud, and the Rolands, plus any others certainly known to have gravitated toward them by the end of September—Buzot and De Perret, to name two of these; whereas the original Montagnards may have been those whose Jacobin activities, down to September 1792, can be accepted, in retrospect, as clear evidence of left-wing enthusiasm, plus any others who "sat with the Mountain" when the Convention met. Beyond this, all is surmise. It seems safer therefore to keep to the more solid ground of actual known behavior, whether under the Terror or in the *appels nominaux*, of which the first was held on 15 January 1793.

The political analysis which follows has been based on evidence about the general political behavior of the deputies in 1793–94. A large proportion of this evidence can be found in Kuscinski, but it has been checked and rechecked on all basic points from the other sources. Very occasionally it has been supplemented from individual biographies or local histories, but in general it was unnecessary to move much beyond the sources enumerated above. The concern was with the actual responsibilities which the deputies were willing to undertake, rather than with their reasons for what they did; a limitation which at once established a common basis of comparison and eliminated the difficulty which must otherwise arise in comparing behavior in an assembly in which some members are famous and others virtually unknown. It seemed useful to begin by dividing the Convention among the political groups into which it appears to fall after 2 June 1793, and then to look back over the first half of 1793 to see whether these groups were merely the sum of individual reactions to a crisis, or whether the actions of their members during previous crises suggest some fundamental similarity of political outlook.

---

22. A. Aulard, *Jacobins*, IV: 328, 338. cf. Buchez et Roux for Brissot's attitude at the time (October 1792) when he was expelled. P. J. B. Buchez and P. C. Roux-Lavergne, *Histoire Parlementaire de la Révolution depuis 1789 jusqu' en 1815*, 40 vols. (Paris, 1834–38), XIX: 301–2.

CHAPTER 2

THE POLITICAL ATTITUDES OF 1793–1794

During the period between the expulsion of the Girondin leaders from the Convention, on 2 June 1793, and the fall of Robespierre, on 27 July 1794, the deputies may be roughly divided, according to their political attitude, among the following groups:

a) Those who were actively involved in sharing the responsibilities of government under the Jacobin régime, or were willing to appear as representatives of it, and whose record and/or reputation *before* 2 June 1793 seems consistent with this attitude; these may be called Montagnard.[1]

b) Those who opposed the régime, either in alliance with Brissot, Vergniaud, and their associates or by showing sympathy with their protest against it; these may be called Girondin.

c) Those who, while co-operating with the government under the Terror, had refused occasionally or consistently to accept the Montagnard line in politics before 2 June.

d) Those who, as far as can be seen, withdrew completely from politics under the Terror, or who (a handful only) opposed the Mountain without associating themselves with the Gironde.

These last two groups together we may call the Plain. It may be argued that the Girondins represented only a more active wing of the last group; nevertheless, a prima facie case exists for drawing a line between those who were willing to support a given type of protest and those who were not. We may discover whether it is sensible to make this distinction when the records of the different groups *before* 2 June are systematically compared.

---

1. The term "Jacobin régime" is too well established to be abandoned. But I have avoided using the term "Jacobin" for any deputy of the Left unless there is evidence that he was a member of the Jacobin Club of Paris. Some prominent figures of the Jacobin régime (Carnot was one) would not go to the Club in Paris, and it would seem misleading to call these men Jacobins even if they were or had been members of a popular society at home.

Some initial qualifications must be made. If the Convention is to be divided in terms of the political attitudes of mid-1793 and later, the deputies concerned must have remained in the Convention for a sufficiently substantial period after 2 June for some assessment of their attitude to be made. Similarly, to have an adequate check on the consistency of political behavior, any deputy should have been present in the Convention during the first half of 1793 and have had some experience of the controversy over the issues which produced the *appels nominaux*; in particular, his voting record in the *appels* should be available as evidence, unless indeed he was so busy with the nation's affairs that he could not come to vote. Those who were not involved in politics during the first half of 1793 and for some time after the June crisis cannot be considered on the same footing as the rest of the deputies and will have to be eliminated from the analysis.

There were a few deputies, apparently of all shades of opinion, who never had to make a final decision, since they had no part in national politics after the early weeks of 1793. Caila collapsed and died during the voting on the king's trial; Le Peletier was murdered by a royalist on 20 January; Guillermin died on the 16th and Verdollin on the 17th of April; Villette, who died on 9 July, had not been seen in the Convention since January; Daubermesnil, sick and on leave throughout January, failed to return and in June was forced to resign; and Hugo was an invalid who never took his seat at all, forfeiting it without protest in September.[2] Five more men, Larroche, de Houlières, Balla, Fockedey, and Mennesson, retired, went on leave or withdrew before the first week in June; none of these was in evidence after the trial of the king.[3] Mellinet remained active up to the *appel* of 28 May, in which he voted against the Mountain, but he died on 7 June and his political position remains uncertain.[4] Philippe-Egalité and Sillery were under suspicion and had faded out of politics by the middle of April, and Quinette, Lamarque, Camus, and Bancal des Issarts were handed over to the Austrians by Dumouriez at the beginning of April and were all interned.[5] None of these men was engaged in politics for long enough to be considered in a general analysis. It is perhaps inconsistent not to add to the list Manuel and Kersaint, who stamped out of the Convention in a rage after the voting on the

2. See Kuscinski, *Conventionnels*, p. 99 (Caila), pp. 399-400 (Le Peletier), p. 318 (Guillermin), pp. 597-98 (Verdollin), p. 608 (Villette), pp. 177-78 (Daubermesnil), and p. 334 (Hugo).

3. Ibid., pp. 376 (Larroche), p. 186 (de Houlières), p. 19, (Balla), pp. 259-60 (Fockedey), and p. 447 (Mennesson). De Houlières is listed as having voted on 13 April in favor of the Marat impeachment, but this vote may be spurious, as Hugo's and Second's certainly were. For the circumstances of this *appel*, see p. 113, below.

4. Ibid., p. 447.

5. Ibid., pp. 239-42, pp. 568-69 (Philippe-Egalité and Sillery), pp. 513-14 (Quinette), pp. 356-57 (Lamarque), pp. 109-10 (Camus), and p. 20 (Bancal des Issarts). Bancal was of the group of 60 deputies more or less associated with Brissot, Vergniaud, and the Rolands; Quinette and Lamarque had Montagnard connections; Camus's exact position is hard to determine.

king's sentence and would not come back, and Rebecqui, who resigned on 9 April, but the withdrawal of each of these men was in its way a political manifesto, and each delivered a parting broadside of such vehemence as to make it absurd not to place him with the inner group of Girondins with whom all three had close personal associations.

It seems equally proper to omit from the analysis men who arrived in Paris after the end of January, either as *suppléants* or as deputies for the new departments or the colonies, since such members were only involved in politics for a comparatively short time before the June crisis erupted and had no share in the catalytic experience of the king's trial. We shall therefore make no additions to the total January membership of the Convention, which was 749,[6] but delete the 19 deputies listed above, because of their illness or incapacity by the middle of the year. This leaves 730 deputies. How are they to be divided?

There is only one of the Convention's political groups whose members have ever been systematically listed by name or examined in detail. A start should therefore be made with the Gironde.

THE GIRONDE

The overt opposition to Jacobin rule, from the deputies loosely linked together as "the Gironde," varied in form from parliamentary protest to the fomenting of civil war. As Sydenham points out,[7] the whole question has been much confused because in 1793 the government did not concern itself with careful discrimination among those whom it believed to be the enemies of the Republic, and the label "Girondin" was thus sometimes attached to people for whom it was quite inappropriate. The list of two hundred deputies which Sydenham has compiled contains most, though not all, of those who have ever been called "Girondin" by anybody; apart from distinguishing with great care those individuals who were in some way personally linked with each other and also with Brissot, Vergniaud, or the Rolands, he has not attempted to estimate how many of those included really had any active interest in the Girondin cause. (On the premise that there is little point in trying to draw a line between the "Girondins" and the rest of the Convention, such an estimate is, of course, unnecessary.) Thus, although this list must remain the basis for any discussion of the Girondins, it will probably need to be modified to exclude any deputy placed on it for apparently insufficient reason; and, for the methodological reasons explained above, any deputies excluded from this political analysis

6. Bertezène, the younger Malhes, and Lafon were late arrivals. Lafon was a *suppléant* replacing Germignac (d. 18 December); the others replaced men who had refused election. But all appeared before a decision on the king's fate had been reached, and Bertezène actually took part in the voting; the others, perhaps wisely, abstained. Lafon arrived on 7 January, Bertezène on the 13th, and Malhes on the 17th. See Kuscinski, *Conventionnels*, p. 52 (Bertezène), p. 425 (Malhes) and p. 362 (Lafon). Cf. Appendix VIII, below.

7. Sydenham, *The Girondins* (London, 1961), pp. 29–30.

because of their inadequate experience of the Convention's politics will also have to be removed. On the other hand, some additions may be required. Since Sydenham's intention was to examine the traditional Girondin "party," rather than to search the Convention for those who sympathized with the Girondin leaders,[8] it may be that Kuscinski's evidence will disclose additional obscure supporters who have been overlooked.

Using Sydenham's careful analysis[9] as a foundation, and on the strength of Kuscinski's evidence and that in the Convention's general records concerning political behavior after 2 June, it seems reasonable to classify as Girondin any deputy who falls into one of the categories below (some will, of course, be eligible for more than one reason):

i) The "inner group" named by Sydenham as more or less personally associated with Brissot and his friends. This includes 60 deputies, but the omission of Bancal des Issarts as an Austrian prisoner and Minvielle as a *suppléant* who did not arrive until April reduces the total to 58.[10]

ii) Those not of this group who signed public protests against the decree of 2 June, or who publicly objected in other ways to the expulsion of the Girondin leaders (94 deputies).[11]

iii) Those suspected in 1793-94, on apparently adequate evidence, of having deliberately or negligently aided the federalist revolts (8 deputies).

iv) Those who are credibly reported as having expressed sympathy for the Gironde, whether or not this got them into trouble at the time, and who were apparently in opposition under the Terror (18 deputies).

The total figure, rather lower than Sydenham's, involves both deletions from and additions to his original list. As well as Bancal, 4 other alleged Girondins (Daubermesnil, Larroche, Mennesson, and Sillery) have been excluded because they were out of politics before June 1793; as it happens, none of these 4 seems to have had specifically Girondin leanings. As well as Minvielle, 2 other *suppléants* (Blaviel and Viger) and 3 representatives of the new department of Alpes-Maritimes (Blanqui, Dabray, and Massa) fail to qualify because they did not join the Convention until the spring of 1793. The total number of potential Girondins excluded from consideration is thus 11. Seventeen other deputies on Sydenham's list have been dropped because, whatever their views may have been, there is no sufficient indication of specific sympathy for the Girondins' resistance to Montagnard domination; for some of these (Moreau and Chénier, for example) Sydenham himself suggests that the claim is baseless.[12] Six names have

8. Ibid., chap. III.
9. Ibid., Appendix A, List XI.
10. Ibid., List C. This total includes Manuel, Kersaint, and Rebecqui.
11. Ibid., Appendix A, List VII-IX for most of the names. Some have been added on the strength of Kuscinski's information. All those who protested are identified in Appendix IV, below.
12. Ibid., pp. 51, 53. It must be emphasized that whereas Sydenham's aim was to show the diversity and incoherence of a supposed "party," the present object is simply to discover

been added because of Kuscinski's description of their behavior in 1793: Dandenac *jeune* and Delaunay *jeune,* from Maine-et-Loire, and Engerran (Manche), Barthélemy (Haute-Loire), Marcellin-Béraud (Rhône-et-Loire), and Poullain-Grandprey (Vosges). The original total of 200 deputies is thus reduced for present purposes to 178. These men, whatever their other differences, which were both numerous and easily demonstrable, were linked together by a common antagonism to the illegal, Paris-dominated rule of the rump of the Convention as it remained after 2 June. What they did was various, but their hostility was shared and explicit.

The Girondins were thus, it is suggested, self-identified by the fact of their opposition. This was to some extent a negative bond of union. Since the expelled deputies were the most conspicuous opponents of Montagnard leadership, their attempts to resist it attracted support from quarters not otherwise sympathetic to the general political aims of men like Brissot and Vergniaud. For example, Giroust and Cussy[13] joined the fugitives in Brittany for reasons which remain unknown, and Delahaye, an active and persistent rebel, may well have been a royalist.[14] It seems probable that the signatories of the June protests, and the associates and sympathizers in categories (iii) and (iv), include a number of men who rallied to the cause for anti-Parisian rather than pro-Brissotin reasons. Nevertheless, all have been left as "Girondin," because the stand they took, whatever its motive, did in fact imply support for those expelled and rejection of the Parisian campaign against them—or, at the minimum (in the case of Despinassy, say[15]) encouragement for the provincial assertiveness against Paris which leading Girondins had been urging since September 1792.

The potentially great diversity of motive for sympathy with the Girondin cause may, of course, mean that the "Girondins" had virtually nothing else in common—that they were little more than a cross-section of the whole Convention, as Sydenham seems to imply. It is certainly apparent that at least one dividing line within the group should be drawn from the start. The 60 men of the inner circle (or, for our purposes, 58) are known, from Sydenham's investigations, to have been loosely but genuinely—in some cases, quite closely—drawn together by personal friendship, and it was the most conspicuous of these deputies who were the targets of Parisian denunciations and received the full

---

who backed the Gironde after 2 June; when this has been done it will be time to see whether such deputies had anything else in common as far as their political or other history is concerned. Sydenham's rejection of, e.g., Saladin as no Girondin because he was converted to the cause only after 2 June is, therefore, interesting but beside the point at present. The names of those who, on Kuscinski's evidence, cannot be established as Girondin are: Antiboul (Var), Andréi (Corse), Audrein (Morbihan), Chénier (Seine-et-Oise), Coren-Fustier (Ardèche), Devars (Charente), Dupin (Aisne), Forest, Michet, Patrin, and Vitet (all from Rhône-et-Loire), Magniez and Personne (both from Pas-de-Calais), Moreau and Tocquot (both from Meuse), Sanadon (Basses-Pyrénées), and Solomiac (Tarn).

13. Kuscinski, *Conventionnels*, pp. 297, 166.
14. Ibid., p. 189.
15. Ibid., p. 204.

weight of Robespierre's attacks in the Convention. The remaining 120 of our 178 deputies were apparently linked only by the similarity of their attitude toward the events of 31 May-2 June. When the behavior and background of the "Girondins" is being examined in more detail, it seems logical to maintain a distinction between leaders and sympathizers, if only to see how far the leaders attracted support from men similar to themselves.[16]

THE MOUNTAIN

When we turn to the Convention's other "faction," it is harder than might appear to decide who should and who should not be placed with the Mountain. Even if the Parisian delegation should turn out to be Montagnard to the last man, the most cursory of glances at the executive committees of the Terror makes it clear that one must look far beyond Paris, even beyond the membership of the Jacobin Club, to discover the full range of deputies who supported the Jacobin régime. This is a subject about which historians have written surprisingly little, and when one tries to make practical use of the few concrete assertions that are put forward, difficulties appear on every side.

The two twentieth-century general historians with most to say—no one says very much—about the origins and numbers of the Montagnards in the Convention are Sagnac and Pariset. Sagnac draws attention to the dispersal of Girondin support, to the fact (he claims) that in almost one department in three there were no Girondins at all, and to the alleged great strength of the Mountain, particularly in the north and east.[17] He may be right; but the old province of Franche-Comté, which according to him was entirely dominated by the Mountain, contained the department of Jura in which six of the eight deputies signed a protest against 2 June. This makes one wary of accepting his generalizatons as the basis of even a tentative listing of potential Montagnards. Pariset adopts a different approach and forms his estimates on the ground of behavior in the

16. See Sydenham, *The Girondins*, Appendix C, for the names of the "inner sixty," divided into 3 groups according to the closeness of their relationship with Brissot and his intimate friends. (Names also in Appendix IV, below.) This "inner sixty" has been accepted as forming a political group primarily because of Sydenham's description of their behavior, which indicates (a) consistent personal association for some time, which marked off those concerned in it from the rest of the Convention, and (b) some attempt in 1792-93 to draw together these deputies for political action against the Left. See ibid., chap. IV. Professor Sydenham understandably dislikes the use of the term "Girondin," as though those to whom it applied were members of an organized body with a defined and consistent policy, which they of course were not. But the "Montagnards" were not united in this sense either, as the friction in the Jacobin Club and elsewhere in 1793-94 more than demonstrates. The confusion of terminology over the "Gironde" (references to "Brissotins," "Rolandins," etc.) may indicate not confusion over what was meant, but trouble in finding an umbrella term to cover men who had no club or other label that could be conveniently used. In any discussion of revolutionary history at this period, there will be less muddle if it can be agreed that both "Girondin" and "Montagnard," and any other labels, are terms used to indicate political tendencies, and not tags designating membership of an organization.

17. Sagnac, *La Révolution 1789-1792* (Paris, 1920), p. 414.

Convention. He specifies as Girondin all the protesters against 2 June, all those without exception who were proscribed or condemned, and all those who voted in favor of the impeachment of Marat; and as Montagnard all those who opposed Marat's impeachment, plus all those who later cooperated with the government of the Terror by serving on either of the great executive committees or by going *en mission* between March 1793 and July 1794.[18] Some of the difficulties of this procedure, as it affects the identification of the Girondins, have already been noticed. The trouble with using the *appel-nominal* on Marat as prima facie evidence is that those who supported the impeachment included among others Précy, an attested Jacobin who survived the purge of the Jacobin Club at the end of 1793,[19] and those who opposed it included Lanthénas, a member of the Girondin "inner sixty" who was certainly not Montagnard; and those *en mission* from March 1793 included Carra and Grégoire, both also of the "inner sixty," whom it is very difficult to see as Montagnard in any sense. Blanket criteria will not suit the need; these deputies, like the Girondins, will have to be assessed individually. But what standards should be applied?

What we are after is the basis of support in the Convention for Montagnard control of national policy, and this means that we should include as "Montagnards" not only those who firmly and publicly aligned themselves with the leaders of the Mountain but also those who, without parading their opinions, consistently acted in support of Montagnard measures. Consider the case of a man who in 1793-94 took on his share of parliamentary responsibility in the form of committee work, or missions in the departments, or simply (in the absence of other evidence) public appearance as a representative of the régime. Is this mere trimming? Not, surely, if it is associated with steady hostility to the king during his trial, and with a refusal to support the Gironde in the *appels nominaux* of April and May; in this situation, it suggests a consistent political attitude. Since the Convention had no party organization, it seems possible that we may find some deputies who nominally "sat with the Plain," but who, when forced to choose, knew which side they were on and chose the same side consistently from January 1793 to Thermidor. These men will have to be considered as part of the backing for the Mountain.[20]

Let us begin, however, with those whom the Convention's collective biographer saw, rightly or wrongly, as definite supporters of the Mountain.

An analysis of Kuscinski produces a considerable number of men said by him simply to have "sat with the Mountain"—presumably from the time the Convention assembled. (For various other deputies, e.g., Robert Lindet, he scrupulously notes changes of allegiance as and when they occurred.) Since in such cases he

18. G. Pariset, *La Révolution 1792–1799* (Paris, 1920), p. 8.

19. Kuscinski, *Conventionnels*, p. 506.

20. To call these men "Montagnard" does not necessarily create too much confusion, since they are not necessarily labeled at all; sometimes they have been placed with the Plain. For present purposes they will be called Montagnards "by attribution." Cf. below, pp. 20–25.

rarely if ever cites his sources or gives reasons for his statement, a methodological problem presents itself. However, on closer examination this turns out not to be serious. What we are here concerned with is the attitude of deputies under the Terror, and all but a small handful of those men who allegedly "sat with the Mountain" were also engaged in 1793–94 in giving open support to the government, usually *en mission* or on committees of the Convention or both. There are only 4 exceptions: Legot (Calvados), Dandenac (Maine-et-Loire), Cambor-Borie (Dordogne), and Jacomin (Drôme), of whom only Cambor-Borie surfaced briefly during the year of the Terror, when he asked in ventôse, an II, for a spell of leave. The other 3 remained completely invisible, as far as one can see, until after Thermidor. Why Kuscinski considered these 4 to be Montagnard is not clear, but it does not seem to have been a casual decision; for example, he makes it clear that he considers Cambor-Borie a time-server, and he remarks that Legot was one of the few Montagnards who voted against the death of the king. The 4 present so small a minority that we may perhaps let his opinion stand.[21] It is incidentally interesting to note in the opening weeks, when the Mountain was more openly a minority than it later became, several deputies with earlier Girondin connections who abandoned them to move to the Left. So Robert Lindet and Jeanbon Saint-André; so also Baille, whose friend Barbaroux was deeply resentful.[22] To these Montagnards, certified as such by Kuscinski and by other evidence, we may add those others with histories of active political service under the Terror who are described as "loyal Montagnards after Thermidor," or as offering help and comfort to colleagues victimized by the Thermidorian reaction.[23] There were altogether 153 deputies who "sat with the Mountain" or remained loyal to it in difficult times.

Of these 153, 80 are also traceable in the Jacobin Club of Paris, that obvious source of information about left-wing deputies. Unfortunately the Club's membership lists have not survived, and the best substitute for them, the enumeration of the members whose credentials were gone over in the purge at the end of 1793, peters out in December 1793.[24] From this point, the minutes are no longer available, and the newspapers do not report proceedings in detail; where one might expect to find a rewarding list of names, the *Moniteur* says baldly that "several" who were members of the Club had their membership confirmed[25] —which leaves the central question still unanswered. A number of dep-

21. Kuscinski, *Conventionnels*, pp. 394–95 (Legot), p. 167 (Dandenac), p. 108 (Cambor-Borie), and p. 342 (Jacomin).
22. Ibid., p. 16.
23. See, for example, Artaud-Blanval, Huguet, and Michaud (ibid., pp. 11, 334, 459). All were regicides; none voted with the Gironde in either April or May; all took on government jobs and went *en mission* under the Terror; any parliamentary government would have had to consider them as functioning members of the majority.
24. Aulard, *La Société des Jacobins*, 6 vols. (Paris, 1889–97), V: 551. According to Aulard, the minutes are missing after 12 December 1793.
25. *Moniteur* XIX: 40 (23 December 1793); cf. XIX: 337, for a similar report.

uties can be identified in the earlier stages of the purge and at various points in the debates. The total of these, not otherwise identified as Montagnard (for a good many the identification is hardly necessary) is 62.

Included among both Jacobins and those "sitting with the Mountain" are a few men who kept their political independence but who can hardly be placed elsewhere because of the character of their political behavior. A member of the "great" Committee of Public Safety, for instance, showed rather more than implicit support for the Jacobin régime. Yet the "great" Committee included at least two men whose membership of the Left might be disputed. Barère was a member of the Jacobin Club from its very early days and a speaker there again after his prodigal return from a divagation to the Feuillants. He has however been expressly described as being "of the Plain"; and he would have welcomed, and in fact tried to promote, a reconciliation of the opposing factions.[26] Could it not be argued that his Committee membership was simply going with the tide? Again, what of Carnot? He would not go to the Jacobin Club in Paris[27] and, in June 1793, attached to the Army of the North, he refused to distribute to the troops the proclamation giving the official version of the events of 31 May - 2 June, thus providing a notable instance of the right to private judgment which he preserved throughout his career.[28] Yet he was one of the Committee's strongest and most useful members, as Barère was one of its outstanding orators. Because of their share in the events of 1793-94 these men must be accepted as Montagnard.

The uneasiness disappears if we look more closely at their activities before 31 May. Barère's great speech of 4 January on the referendum[29] was evidence enough that he had little sympathy with Girondin ambitions or strategy, and on 28 May he came out against the Gironde. Both he and Carnot were firm and unworried regicides. Each had chosen his side not once but several times before 2 June, and in big decisions it was always the same side. They were not the only ones of their kind. There were altogether perhaps half-a-dozen of these "independents," whose existence is yet another sign that in revolutionary France organized "party" was unknown. All sorts of people backed the Gironde; all sorts backed the Mountain as well.

The total of "Montagnards" and Jacobins is 215. It is when we look at the rest of the Convention that the problem appears which the *appels nominaux* may help to provide an answer. How can those who deliberately chose to support the Mountain be distinguished from those who merely tolerated it or, faced with a fait accompli, put aside prejudice to save the Republic? There were in the Convention in 1793-94 altogether 219 men who, without having any very obvious political views, in different ways and to different degrees were serving the

26. Cf. L. Gershoy, *Bertrand Barère* (Princeton, 1962), chaps. VII-VIII.

27. M. Reinhard, *Le grand Carnot*, 2 vols. (Paris, 1950-52), I: 195; see also S. J. Watson, *Carnot* (London, 1954), p. 45.

28. Reinhard, *Carnot*, I: 300.

29. B. Barère, *Discours . . . sur le procès de Louis Capet (4 janvier 1792)* [sic] [Paris].

existing government. Very few of them ever reached top rank and their precise political affiliations will probably never be known, but it can at least be said that they were politically active. How much or how little did that activity mean?

The Convention as a body took its duties seriously. It was unusual for a deputy *not* to serve at some stage of his career either *en mission* or on some committee—sufficiently unusual for Kuscinski to comment on it when the fact appears. Very many deputies did both; witness the activity of ten of the twelve members of the "great" Committee of Public Safety. The committees were numerous because there was a great deal of business and, in September 1793, alarmed at the thinning attendance at meetings, Gossuin suggested that the Committee of Public Safety be empowered to replace any deputy absent from his duties for a week or more.[30] It was at this time that Hugo finally lost the seat he had never bothered to fill. (Gossuin, incidentally, was not a Montagnard.) There was too much to do for complete passivity to be encouraged. On the other hand, as long as deputies were about, their failure to be of very much use might be overlooked; they might come around later and be more helpful.[31] So committee service was a general feature of the Convention, but its timing was uneven; if you did not like the régime or felt that the régime did not like you, employment would wait until the weather changed. Many deputies who served under the Terror continued to be active throughout the session, but after Thermidor there was a considerable influx into the committees (largely reorganized in August) of men who had had good reason to lie low during the preceding year but whose withdrawal from politics, though complete while it lasted, was only temporary. Whatever these men were, they were not Montagnard. But there were 127 men, opinions uncertain, who did serve on committees under the Terror. Some of these may have done so from choice and others from prudence; how can one tell which were which?

Activity *en mission*, less general than committee membership, was also widespread, and perhaps suggests the possibility of a deeper commitment to the existing government. To go *en mission* under the Terror was usually arduous and might be exceedingly dangerous. It is illuminating to consider just what some of the dangers were.

One might, for instance, be engaged in actual battle; Claude-Dominique Fabre was killed in action in December 1793.[32] One might be surrounded by a howling mob threatening massacre unless one conceded total price control, or

30. Kuscinski, *Conventionnels*, p. 300.

31. Thus Girard, who had had Girondin associations, was sent *en mission* in late 1793. (The government's attitude to all but the most conspicuous Girondins was surprisingly pragmatic; witness Delecloy's escape from all retribution for activities in Amiens in June 1793 which could have had very dangerous results; see Kuscinski, *Conventionnels*, p. 194.) Admittedly he was difficult to handle, fell in with a female companion of distinctly dubious character, would not return on order, and finally had to be firmly dragged back "for meddling in things which did not concern him"; one of his colleagues insinuated that he was mildly insane. He remained active in the Convention. Ibid., p. 294.

32. Ibid., p. 248 for details.

some other measure equally at variance with official policy. (In the activities of those *en mission*, the suppression of rioting comes up with some regularity.) Kuscinski comments scornfully on the craven conduct of Birotteau and his colleagues, who gave in to such pressure in November 1792—even so, they barely escaped with their lives—and compares them unfavorably with other deputies who, he says, at a later stage in revolutionary history committed suicide rather than capitulate to the mob.[33] The assumption that any public-spirited deputy should immediately have opted for death rather than the most fleeting shadow of dishonor seems a little extreme; it is nevertheless true that Tellier and Brunel did later commit suicide becuase they felt that, under very trying circumstances, they had failed in republican firmness,[34] and it is also true that in October 1793 the Committee of Public Safety guillotined Antiboul for "conduct unworthy of a representative of the people" in dealing with the Marseillais.[35] Anyone going into a civil war area ran the risk of being captured by the rebels, and several deputies temporarily detained faced moral dilemmas as a result, but no deputy *en mission* could be sure that he would not unexpectedly be confronted by a similar sort of emergency.

Even if all went well, and the local population was both loyal and enthusiastic, it was easy to fall foul of some section of it which might send damaging reports back to Paris, and it was all too easy to fall foul of one's colleagues. Then there were the practical difficulties of the job itself. One might have to grapple, as Ferry did in the Bourges area, with bad roads, inadequately fed workers, lack of men and equipment, impossible requisitions, and the failure of those in Paris to answer one's letters;[36] or one might merely find, as Bar did at Neusaarwerden, that hardly anyone could understand French or grasp what they were supposed to be doing, so that all key officials had to be imported.[37] And there was purely physical wear and tear. Sautayra died in September 1793, after maltreatment by a group of rebels; Petitjean, Vidalin, and Anthoine all fell ill and died *en mission*; Gillet died at the end of 1795 as a direct result, it was said, of his exertions on the Republic's behalf. Cochet had his property looted by the enemy.[38] It is true that opportunities of another kind, for corruption, peculation, sadism, and the venting of ordinary spite, were almost endless, and that persons like Fréron and Carrier did not waste them. But the number of deputies attracted by them was

---

33. Ibid., p. 42.
34. Ibid., pp. 581, 95.
35. Ibid., pp. 8–9. He was said to have talked too freely under interrogation.
36. Ibid., p. 258.
37. Ibid., p. 20. Or consider Esnuë-Lavallée's position. He was in Rennes helping to organize the repression of rebellion in the West, and puzzled that instructions from Paris were not arriving. He did not know that his colleague Garnier, athwart his line of communication and intercepting his mail, was to end by pilfering the credit for the arrest of one of the rebel leaders. Ibid., pp. 245–46.
38. Ibid., p. 558 (Sautayra), p. 489 (Petitjean), p. 605 (Vidalin), p. 8 (Anthoine), p. 293 (Gillet), and p. 143 (Cochet). Cochet asked for 4,000 *livres* compensation; it is not clear how much he got. Gillet was only 29 when he died.

far smaller than is sometimes believed, and should be set against the frustration, exhaustion, and discomfort which were often the lot of anyone trying to stimulate and direct departmental patriotism. Among our 219 deputies there were 92 who were prepared to carry out duties of this sort.

The simplest way to separate the early converts from those who were merely *ralliés* to the Montagnard cause is to eliminate all those who showed *any* public sign of doubt in the *appels* of the first half of 1793, when the outcome was still uncertain. In order to use the *appels* in this way, some assumptions must be made about the general character of Montagnard voting.[39] It must be taken for granted that it was the normal thing for a Montagnard to vote against the king throughout the trial, and in the later *appels*, if he voted at all, to oppose both the Marat impeachment and the Commission of Twelve. If any one of his six possible votes was on the moderate side, the potential Montagnard must be placed instead with the Plain.

This is a far more rigorous rule than seems to have been applied by the Jacobin Club of Paris itself. Only in December 1793 did the Club go so far as to insist that any member who as a deputy had voted against the death of the king must be expelled. (In spite of vigorous *sans-culotte* assaults earlier on the supporters of the *appel au peuple*, this was ignored, as were the *appels* of April and May.) Under this provision Casa Bianca lost his membership, though not, apparently, his influence in the Club.[40] But investigations do not seem to have been very thorough. Précy, who voted in every *appel* and every time with the Right, remained a member and survived the purge of February 1794.[41] If, therefore, we set, as a minimum standard, consistent radical voting during the trial and a refusal to vote with the Gironde thereafter, we are asking more than the Jacobins did; but better, for this purpose, too much than too little.

But *is* too little being asked? Should not any possible Montagnard have as credential a vote *against* the Gironde in April or May—if not over Marat, at least over the Commission of Twelve? This would establish a positive loyalty, whereas a regicide line over the trial and support of the Mountain after June, with no definite evidence between, may show only cooperation with the winning side or acceptance of *sans-culotte* intimidation.

There are no easy answers here.[42] It must however be said again that we are not concerned with the motives of political behavior, but only with its consistency. From this point of view, anyone who in January was cowed into radicalism, provided he remained in that condition, was if not as useful to the

39. It will later appear how far these assumptions are justified. It seems fair to make them now, because they are those which have traditionally governed the attitude both of contemporaries and of historians to the conflicts of opinion embodied in the *appels*.

40. Kuscinski, *Conventionnels*, p. 117; cf. *Moniteur* XVIII: 665.

41. Kuscinski, *Conventionnels*, p. 506.

42. The question of support for the "winning side" is discussed briefly in note 22, p. 97, below. This may have existed in January 1793, but the evidence for it is hard to find.

Mountain at any rate as lost to the Gironde as the most dedicated Montagnard. On the immediate issue, it is important that even in the *appel* of 28 May, which was obviously a great political crisis, less than 70 percent of the Convention was present to vote. Many deputies were, of course, away *en mission*, but even of those in Paris a number did not bother to attend. Without party discipline, and without the virtually compulsory voting enforced by the Convention itself during the trial, this situation was inevitable. (The personal unpopularity of Marat, on the left as well as on the right, meant that voluntary absences on 13 April were more numerous still.) The deputies we are considering, who showed their political sympathies tacitly rather than explicitly, may fairly be seen as the element to be found toward the right wing of most radical parties, and it would be unreasonable to impose on them a standard not reached by the acknowledged Left. Among the 215 deputies already placed with the Mountain, 12 ignored both the April and May *appels*. It seems illogical to impose a higher level of interest on men who were less frankly partisan.

When the actual situation is examined, the problem becomes, in any case, partly theoretical. Out of our 219 candidates, 87 qualify by the minimum standard; 55 of them combined *en mission* duties in 1793–94 with radical voting in the trial and an absence of moderate voting afterwards, and another 32 had the same sort of voting pattern plus committee activity in 1793–94. But of the 87, 67 did vote in favor of the Mountain in April or May or both, and of the 20 who failed to do this, 11 were away *en mission* for the whole two months and could not. There were only 9 voluntary double absentees. The general impression is one of considerable political involvement. Only 23 of the whole 87 failed to take on a mission of some kind between September 1792 and Thermidor. The half-dozen or so who were, as Kuscinski says of Guermeur, "completely overwhelmed by events,"[43] and were swept along with the tide, may be regarded as the most lukewarm supporters of the Mountain, but they were too continuously submissive to its influence to be placed with the Plain.

One significant point may be noted. Our 87 have been selected from among 219 deputies of unstated political views who co-operated with the Mountain under the Terror. For the 219, that cooperation was in the proportion of about 58 percent committee members to 42 percent who went *en mission*. Among those whom we have accepted as Montagnards, because they were regicides who refused to back the Gironde, these proportions were more than reversed: over 63 percent *en mission*, less than 37 percent doing committee work only. In other words, for these men at least, a decision to share Montagnard attitudes during the Mountain's rise to power carried with it an inclination to shoulder the heavier burdens of responsibility later on.

Some of these 87 Montagnards "by attribution," of whom the outstanding case is Cambon, have sometimes been placed with the Plain, and may seem by

---

43. *Conventionnels*, p. 314.

some criteria to be very dubiously Montagnard. Cambon opposed the establishment of the Revolutionary Tribunal, he was angry over the events of 31 May-2 June, he was often at odds with the Jacobin Club, and he was hostile to Robespierre. Nevertheless, Kuscinski describes him as "the true finance minister" from 10 July 1793 to Thermidor,[44] and he was an unswerving regicide. He was certainly not a legendary radical (though he had his radical moments, especially concerning the Church), but then we are not collecting Jacobins of the legendary type; we are trying to determine the deputies on whom, under the Terror, the Montagnard leadership could depend for support, and on the evidence of his behavior down to Thermidor Cambon was one of these. (He may in some ways be compared with Carnot.) He did not approve 2 June; but on 28 May he voted with the Mountain. For a lesson in the folly of establishing rigid norms for the backers of the Mountain, one need only look at the membership of the Committee of Public Safety itself.

Some of the evidence adduced to establish 1793-94 activity and approval of the Jacobin régime (e.g., public appearances to represent the Convention) may be considered to be slight to the point of being negligible; but when deputies are otherwise unknown one must work from what indications there are. No man has been placed as Montagnard unless he was (a) explicitly described as such, or (b) an active and accepted Jacobin, or (c) *both* apparently cooperative in 1793-94 *and* a Left voter before June. The combination of these two last criteria is rigid enough to make it quite possible that some genuine Montagnards may have been excluded. It has been noted above that Précy and Casa Bianca, if they had not qualified on other grounds, would have had to be excluded for deviant voting, and there were others like them; there may well have been more who have been omitted because they were too obscure to appear on any record. At the other extreme, Laguire, who voted with the Mountain throughout the trial and on 28 May, has been placed with the Plain because nothing at all is known of his activities during 1793-94. A later report that he regretted his vote for the death of the king suggests that this placing may be fair enough, but one cannot be sure.[45]

A last note may be added on the subject of the 32 "attribution" Montagnards who did committee work (or made public appearances) under the Terror, and did nothing more. Since these deputies had apparently the least investment in the Jacobin régime, their history after its collapse is interesting. Seven disappeared from view. Of the 25 who continued in politics, only 3 are described by Kuscinski as Thermidorians, and he classes one of these, Garos, as a *Thermidorien de gauche.*[46]

44. For this, and the facts above, ibid., pp. 106-7.
45. See Kuscinski, ibid., p. 362.
46. Ibid., p. 281. The 32 were not entirely static in 1793; 9 of them had been *en mission* before the end of May. At least one of them, Dubreuil-Chambardel, had a reasonable excuse for not going *en mission*, being aged 65 (ibid., p. 216).

The total of Montagnards, in the broad sense, is now 302, made up thus:

i) Jacobin Club
   Described as "sitting with
   the Mountain"   80
   Others   <u>62</u>   142

ii) "Sat with the Mountain," or
    equivalent, not traceable in
    the Jacobin Club   <u>73</u>   215*

iii) Regicide—no moderate votes
     En mission 1793 -94   55
     Committee members, or
     otherwise in evidence,
     1793 -94   <u>32</u>   <u>87</u>
                                                    302

*The voting record of these deputies has been ignored.

THE PLAIN

We are now left with 250 members who by the definitions so far adopted do not qualify for either the Gironde or the Mountain. If opposed to Jacobin rule, they gave no positive help or admitted encouragement to those struggling against it: if inclined to cooperate with it once it was established, they had had reservations about voting with the Left in critical divisions before 2 June.

Historians have treated the Plain as an entity which simply disliked taking sides; indeed, Pariset has argued that the comparatively small number of men who moved from the Plain to either Gironde or Mountain indicates that to be a member of the Convention's Center was a matter of deliberate choice, the taking up of a positive position, and not just a matter of terrified caution.[47] Since consistent voting in the *appels nominaux* was likely to land them in de facto 'support of one side or the other, one might infer that members of the Plain were likely to vote first one way and then the other, according to their assessment of the issues. During the king's trial they might waver between mercy and severity, or alternatively between justice and expediency; in April and May, if Mathiez is to be believed, they should have backed the Gironde against Paris;[48] but over the whole series of *appels* one might expect consistency in either direction to be exceptional. Under the Terror, one would expect—what? reluctant acquiescence? resigned cooperation? temporary withdrawal from politics?

47. Pariset, *La Révolution*, p. 8.
48. A. Mathiez, *The French Revolution*, trans. C. Phillips (New York, 1965), pp. 314-15.

Under the Terror, these deputies in fact fall into three groups:

i) Men who acted for the government *en mission* in the departments, though they cannot be shown to have supported the Montagnard line before June, or on one or more occasions actually opposed it.

ii) Men with a similar attitude before June, who confined themselves to committee work afterward.

iii) Men who, as far as can be seen, abandoned all responsibility by withdrawing from political activity completely; with these may be placed a very few who expressed distaste for the Jacobin régime without associating themselves in any way with the Gironde.

The deputies in group (i), 37 in all, were busy and useful during the Terror, as half of them had already been in the spring of 1793. None of them seems to have been either venal or especially vindictive. Some were more bigoted, some less conscientious than others, but the general impression is of a solid average. Perhaps half-a-dozen, including the unlucky Antiboul, failed in some way to meet the demands imposed upon them, but the great majority seem to have been both diligent and reasonably successful in carrying out duties which, after all, they need never have undertaken. Though hardly any are even tolerably well known, and their work naturally varied in quality, the firmness and common-sense of someone like Godefroy in Seine-et-Marne or Malhes in Lozère,[49] the efforts of Lambert to get more arms produced in Haute-Marne and Côte d'Or, Ehrmann's blunt condemnation of a proposal to enforce the use of French in Rhineland schools (*"c'est comme si vous vouliez enseigner à Paris les arts et les métiers en grec"*), even Duval's struggles to see that enough paper was manufactured to print the Convention's decrees and propaganda[50]—all this, however unspectacular, was the sort of thing that had to be done if the Republic were to continue to function. If not Montagnards, these deputies *en mission* were at least very valuable fellow-travelers. (Beauchamp, intermittently in the provinces for fifteen months, might not have appreciated the pun.[51])

In group (ii) from the Plain there were 95 deputies who, whatever their opinions of the events of 31 May-2 June, went on taking part in the business of government. In the year of the Terror, they did not go out *en mission*, as some did both in earlier and later periods, but they did belong to the committees of the Convention or make public appearances on its behalf. On the Education Committee, or the Public Relief Committee, or whatever it might be, they helped to carry on the routine labor of the Republic without fighting the Mountain's battles in the departments. Of these men, four died before the end of 1794, and 14 seem to have faded out of parliamentary life after Thermidor, but the remaining 77 continued their committee work or even went *en mission* in

49. Kuscinski, *Conventionnels*, pp. 298, 425. Malhes resigned after this mission, to look after (he said) his sick wife and 11 young children.
50. Ibid., p. 367 (Lambert), p. 242 (Ehrmann), p. 237 (Duval).
51. Ibid., p. 42.

1794-95. From Kuscinski's accounts they do not emerge as a collection of turncoats, indeed the vast majority of them had no outstanding political color. They were as near as the Convention could come to nonparty members who spent the entire session simply doing the jobs that came to hand.[52] In 1794-95 the surviving 91 included 15 who gave more or less support to the Thermidorian reaction; as against these, there were nine firmly upholding republican principles, some of them doggedly battling *en mission* to strike a balance between royalism and a return to Terror, and 53 who seem to have avoided taking sides at all.

In the third and last group from the Plain there were 118 deputies who, as Kuscinski puts it, held themselves *à l'écart* from June 1793, or thereabouts, until Thermidor. A man *à l'écart* lay low and said little or nothing during this time, waiting until in happier circumstances he was able, if he wished, to take ample revenge for the months of silence. This did not necessarily mean that he was absent from Paris, or even from the Convention's debates. Gilbert Chevalier, for instance, made no discoverable contribution to national politics during the Terror, and very little afterward; but he refused to consider reelection in 1795 on the not unreasonable ground that he had sat from 1792 without leave of any kind and was not in good enough health to carry on. (He complained of dizziness, numbness of the left side, and "symptoms of apoplexy." He was also, in 1795, sixty years old.[53]) This statement of his seems to be all that is available in the Convention's records to show that in 1793-94 he considered himself a diligent deputy, or indeed that he functioned as a deputy at all; but function he possibly did, as others may have done whose presence was equally unremarked. As we have already seen, complete absence was something that the Convention might notice and act upon. Leave from one's parliamentary duties could not simply be taken, it had to be asked for and granted, and applications of this kind from obscure sources which appear in the *procès-verbaux* from time to time are reminders that consistent absenteeism was an offense that might cost the sluggard his seat—and, if it mattered, eighteen livres a day.

One could of course be a cipher in politics without being actually missing. Of the 118 deputies *à l'écart* in 1793-94 there were 72, or about 60 percent, who neither applied for leave nor were listed as absentees nor did anything else that appears on the record. Their political history in the Republic's year of crisis is a perfect blank. After Thermidor 60 of them returned to action; 20 served *en mission*, the others at least sat on committees or made some recorded contribution to debate. Only 2 of the whole 72 had gone *en mission* before Thermidor,

52. Cf., however, La Revellière-Lépeaux's scathing description of the *modéré* as the man who "*se laisse toujours entraîner par le parti le plus menacant, sans ôser meme examiner si c'est le parti le plus juste.*" Too many deputies from the Plain had voted against the Mountain down to 31 May for this to be quite fair; and afterwards they had to choose between accepting a *fait accompli* or accepting the possibly suicidal gamble (for the Republic) of civil war. But see A. Meynier, *Un représentant de la bourgeoisie angévine; La Revellière-Lépeaux* (Paris, 1905), pp. 355, also 309-10.

53. Kuscinski, *Conventionnels*, pp. 136-37.

even in the emergency of the spring of 1793; the political climate of the Thermidorian period was obviously much more congenial . . . What of the 12 who seem to have done nothing after Thermidor, as they had done nothing before? These were the real nonentities, the men who can hardly be said to have withdrawn from activity since they never really shared in it. They lacked the personality to attract a denunciation from the local Jacobin Club, they lacked even the spirit to go home. Kuscinski might well have said of them, as he quotes Carrier as saying of the Girondin Penières-Delzors, that during their parliamentary lives they were "known only to the cashier of the Convention."[54] One of them, Gertoux, frankly admitted that in his whole term of office he had never sat on a committee nor carried out a mission; "he thus" comments Kuscinski sourly "proclaimed his perfect nullity."[55] This did not prevent his reelection. In 1795 one had to be like Joseph Fabre of Pyrénées-Orientales, somewhat exceptionally *nul*, to be rejected for that reason alone.[56]

One deputy among those *à l'écart* died in November 1794, and a further 8 left the Convention before the end of 1793, either by resignation or on indefinite leave which became exclusion; of these only 2 later returned. The 2 Rhône-et-Loire deputies Michet and Forest seem to have done nothing in particular until they were arrested as federalists—unjustly in their own eyes; they stayed in confinement until they resumed their seats with a number of the Girondins in December 1794. There were 32 deputies who took on no responsibilities in 1793-94, but who were demonstrably *there*, even if all they did was to ask for a brief spell of leave from whatever they considered their duties to be. Finally, there were at least 3 deputies—there may well have been many more among the silent—who were not Girondins, but who were both hostile to the Mountain and present at times in the Convention. With the 26 Girondins who also continued to sit, these formed a nucleus for a parliamentary opposition quite apart from any opposition which might develop from splits within the Mountain itself. Their attitude was cautious (as Durand-Maillane is reported to have said to Tallien and Bourdon before Thermidor, "*nous vous seconderons si vous êtes les plus forts; non, si vous êtes les plus faibles*"[57]), but they took their chance when it came, and in taking it they might even perhaps hope for support from their still more reticent colleagues.

Between 2 June and Thermidor, the deputies *à l'écart*, taken as a group, said very little and could not do much, but some of them were significant figures in the intrigues leading up to the fall of Robespierre. It is hard to place any of them as members of the Plain in the traditional sense, since their temporary inactivity was hardly a sign that they were politically neutral; more accurately, they were

---

54. Ibid., p. 479. This was, however, true of Penières-Delzors only under the Terror, when he had real excuse for his retirement, having freely spoken his mind in June 1793.
55. Ibid., p. 293; cf. A. N. C353 C1838 (Hautes-Pyrénées).
56. Ibid., p. 248.
57. Ibid., p. 233.

opposition deputies who accepted the inevitable while refusing all cooperation with it. The number of them who reappeared in politics after Thermidor is suggestive; 60 from the 72 who were totally silent, and 25 more from the 35 who were present but uncooperative in 1793-94; a total of 85 out of 118, or more than 72 percent. Instead of the meager 7 who had carried out missions down to June 1793, 29 went *en mission* for the Thermidorians. If the Convention had a right wing, it must surely be looked for here.

The conclusions of this discussion may be summarized in Table 1.

Table 1. Suggested political groups of 1793-94

GIRONDE—those in open protest against Jacobin rule during or after June 1793		
i) Sydenham's "inner sixty" (excluding Bancal and Minvielle)		58
ii) June and post-June petitioners and protesters, other than those of the "inner sixty"		94
iii) Others: subversive activity 1793-94	8	
sympathizers 1793-94	18	26
	Total:	178
MOUNTAIN—supporters of Jacobin régime, excluding *ralliés* after June 1793		
i) *Jacobin Club of Paris*		
Described as "sitting with the Mountain"	80	
Others	62	142
ii) "Sat with the Mountain" or equivalent, not traceable in the Jacobin Club		73
		215
iii) Regicide—no moderate votes		
en mission 1793-94	55	
Committees 1793-94	32	87
	Total:	302
PLAIN		
i) *en mission* 1793-94		37
ii) Committee activity or equivalent, 1793-94		95
iii) *à l'écart*—withdrawn from politics 1793-94		118
	Total:	250
		730
Total number of deputies:		
Add deputies withdrawn from politics by June 1793		19
Deputies eligible to vote in the trial of Louis XVI		749

There are two obvious ways in which the credibility of this division of the Convention may be tested. The first involves looking at the deputies in a different context, this time not as members of a parliamentary body but as members of the delegations chosen by the various departments in September 1792; the

aim being to see whether the balance of political feeling attributed to the delegation elected by a given department is compatible with what can be discovered
about the electoral situation of 1792. This test will be applied as part of the
investigation into the background of the deputies, in Part III of this study. The
second test relates more directly to the politics of the Convention itself. If the
different groups which have been postulated had more than an accidental cohe-
sion; if their members shared to any significant degree a common outlook on the
political problems of 1793, the groups should be distinguishable by their distinctive reactions to the crises of 1793 which preceded the expulsion of the
Girondin leaders.

The division of the Convention under examination has been made almost
entirely on the evidence of the behavior of the deputies concerned under the
Terror. Only for a minority of Montagnards has any evidence from the first half
of 1793 been considered, and even for these deputies no positive sign of loyalty
after January has been required. For all other deputies, behavior after June 1793
has been the sole criterion, and the *appels nominaux* have not been relevant. If a
man chose to stand *à l'écart* in 1793-94, or to back the Gironde, he has been
classified accordingly no matter how he voted or what he did before June, and
similarly if he is reported to have "sat with the Mountain," or to have been a
member in good standing of the Jacobin Club, his voting has been ignored. In
the six *appels nominaux* the voting, or lack of it, of every deputy was duly
recorded; apart from what is contained in Kuscinski, and in the other records of
the Convention itself, this is the only evidence in existence which covers the
whole membership of the Convention, and it relates to three occasions on which
the contending "factions" of 1793 were in open and bitter conflict.

How good a test of political consistency, for deputies of all shades of opinion, are the *appels nominaux* likely to be?

As between groups, we might expect a good deal of inconsistent or cross-
voting for several reasons. In the first place, in sorting out the "Montagnards"
from the Plain a single moderate vote was allowed as the decisive factor. Since
Ducos, Carra, Lasource, and others became regicides without disrupting their
links with their Girondin colleagues, clearly the regicides were not all Montagnard; and if it is true that Sydenham's "noisy minority," the "extreme element
which dominated the Convention on this occasion,"[58] forced the majority into
unwilling acquiescence with the Mountain over the fate of the king, it might be
expected that a number of men who voted with the Left in January would swing
back to their natural position fairly quickly. Even if they lacked the courage to
back the moderates, there was nothing to stop their registering a muted protest
by joining the deputies *à l'écart*. There seems no reason why there should not be
quite large numbers of regicides outside the Mountain. Given the long Girondin
campaign against the king and Sydenham's emphasis on Girondin disunity, one
might even expect this among the Girondins.

58. Sydenham, *The Girondins*, p. 142.

Second, there is Mathiez's argument, already referred to, that "the centre ... voted with the Mountain when it was a question of taking strong measures for the salvation of the Republic. But almost every time a vote was taken on a personal matter or on one affecting Parisian affairs, they sided with the Gironde."[59] The trial was a national concern; the Marat impeachment and the Commission of Twelve were personal and local. Third, Hampson's very cursory treatment of the trial suggests that he does not consider it in any way an important indication of political opinion.[60] Finally, all the *appels* of 1793 raised crucial questions of political and moral principle over which even close associates might disagree; and, in practice, disagreement was made easier by the very great importance attached to individual conscience and by the complete absence at the time of any form of party discipline. (December 1793 was perhaps rather late for the Jacobin Club to concern itself with the way its members had voted on 15-19 January.) Even under the Terror, it was very rare for men to be penalized simply for political independence.

Such difficulties of interpretation are likely to be even more noticeable in considering the other evidence related to the *appels nominaux*: the speeches published by the Convention, both before and during the king's trial and in the record of the *appel nominal* on the impeachment of Marat. These speeches are very valuable, illuminating for many deputies the decisions which appear in the voting lists; on the other hand, as evidence they lack the comprehensiveness of the *appels* themselves, since they report only the views of those deputies who wanted to make public statements, and such men were probably more politically committed than their less vocal colleagues. The speeches should give some idea at least of the range of attitudes which men were willing to take up in public, but since they were all produced by individual deputies to state personal points of view, they may through their selectiveness be of very dubious value as a guide to the outlook of any group of deputies, even if the members of the group were personally quite closely associated and followed the same political line.

What if it be objected that it is illogical to use the *appels nominaux* as a check on the consistency of the deputies' political behavior, because they have already been used to decide whether a man was Montagnard or whether he was not? The limitations of this argument, as it affects the present classification, have already been indicated. To expect a man to be likely to behave in a particular way, because he is believed to be Montagnard in sympathy, is not the same thing as to assume that he was Montagnard simply because he behaved in that way. For classification purposes, "Montagnard" voting in the *appels* has been irrelevant unless it was followed by support for the government of the Terror.[61]

59. A. Mathiez, *The French Revolution*, pp. 314-15.
60. N. Hampson, *A Social History of the French Revolution* (London, 1963), p. 162.
61. It seems unlikely that Kuscinski used the *appels* as a basis for his classification either. He is scrupulous to note the January and April voting, but he does not classify all

Nevertheless, if the political groups which have been postulated have any reality, their members should show some similarity of approach to the great questions raised by the *appels nominaux*, and the voting of any one group should have some relevance to the presumed outlook of its members; and so should the arguments which members of the group put forward in order to persuade the rest of the Convention. The *appels*, and the speeches relating to them, may not be ideal as evidence; but if we are looking for evidence of political behavior which gives a perspective of the Convention as a whole, they are all that we have.

* * * *

Whatever their other virtues or deficiencies, this much at least can be said of the *appels nominaux*: they provide evidence of the state of opinion in the Convention on questions over which fundamental divergences of political attitude, as well as of principle, could hardly fail to appear. In general, during its first months of life the Convention managed the day-to-day business of government without too much difficulty. Clashes both of personalities and of policies, however acrimonious, did not prevent the emergence of a reasonable consensus on such matters as economic policy, church policy, foreign policy, or the conduct of the war. But all of the questions raised in the *appels nominaux* touched raw nerves, and all of them intensified in some way or other those political tensions which had been present in the Convention since the time of its election. To see why this was so, it is necessary to recall the political situation in France in the autumn of 1792.

When the Convention took over responsibility for the government of France—not then officially a Republic—on 20 September 1792, the difficulties confronting it were formidable: foreign war, religious schism, growing inflation, social unrest, and an administrative and taxation system not yet two years old and still feeling its way. The political structure itself was not yet established; this was what the Convention had been elected to determine. Republican? If so, in what sense?

On the face of it, a Republic seemed publicly acceptable. The fall of the monarchy on 10 August had been brought about in the main by the Parisian *sans-culottes*, but they had had valuable help from the *fédérés* who had arrived in Paris, on their way to the frontier, from many parts of France. The almost total absence of royalist activity during the Convention elections suggested that royalism was for the time being quiescent and no serious threat to the establishment of a new régime. Nevertheless, although the franchise had been broadened to include all adult males, only a small minority of voters had taken part in the

---

regicides, or all opponents of the Marat impeachment, as Montagnard, and he does not mention the 28 May *appel* at all.

elections, and if even France's national politicians had only become converted to republicanism within the previous year or so, there was every chance that many ordinary Frenchmen were still consciously or unconsciously attached to the idea of monarchy. There was no opposition to the creation of a Republic, but whether the Republic could maintain itself would depend largely on whether it could prevent its enemies from making use of the inevitable grievances of a revolutionary period to undermine its position: the economic and military hardships imposed by war and revolution, the dislocation of traditional religious life, the resentments of those who had failed to arrest the progress of the revolution and also of those who had so far failed to profit from it, might all be exploited in the interest of the supporters of the old régime, or even in the interest of the constitutional monarchists who had just been reclassified as counterrevolutionaries. Under these circumstances, what sort of republicanism would the Convention adopt, and what was to be done with the royal prisoners in the Temple, in whose fate many Parisians had an angry personal interest?

There were problems also about the relationship between the Convention and the city of Paris in which it sat. It was the newly established Paris Commune, not yet even formally legalized in September 1792, which had dethroned Louis XVI after the Legislative Assembly had failed to take the lead against him. During the six weeks which had elapsed between the fall of the monarchy and the meeting of the Convention, the Legislative Assembly had been in de facto control of the government of France; but the Commune had tended to behave as though it, and not the Legislative, were entitled to act as spokesman for the nation. This attitude was excusable in view of the refusal of the majority in the Legislative, down to 10 August, to support the Parisian radicals against the king, but after 10 August, the mainly republican rump of deputies which had at last taken charge was enraged and sometimes humiliated by a Parisian arrogance for which they saw no shade of constitutional justification. Once the Convention had established itself in office, the Commune became less presumptuous, but pride in Parisian leadership remained, and so did the hard core of *sans-culotte* political activism, retaining an organizational framework through the popular clubs, and more formally through the sectional assemblies and committees which were now an integral part of Parisian municipal government. And apart from its radicalism and its political independence, Paris had serious economic problems which led to endemic social unrest; in addition, the underlying current of violence, which in the first week of September had swept through the prisons to cause over a thousand deaths, was still there just below the surface, and the city was not well policed. What policy should the Convention adopt toward Parisian demands, Parisian unrest, Parisian opinions on matters of national policy? Later events were to show that even under great provocation the *sans-culottes* would still respect the persons of the deputies, as representatives of the nation, but many *conventionnels* did not feel even physically secure; the massacres had blackened the name of Paris all over France. The relationship between national legislature and national capital could not help but be uneasy, at least for a time.[62]

To complicate the whole situation almost unbearably, there was the fact that the Convention itself contained a number of men already publicly entangled in the problems which they were supposed to help in solving. Some of the most conspicuous of these, Brissot and Vergniaud in particular, were seen by the Parisian radicals as traitors to the revolutionary cause, because after having led the attack on the monarchy during the first half of 1792 they had chosen to abandon it during July, just as the war crisis was mounting and the agitation in Paris reaching fever pitch. It was not known until 3 January 1793 that Vergniaud, Guadet, and Gensonné had actually written to the king late in July, offering to cooperate with him in government if he would give assurances that he would be loyal to the constitution, but Brissot's and Vergniaud's open discouragement of Parisian republicanism immediately before the August revolution was public property and had cost the Girondins their former popularity in Paris. They got their seats without difficulty, being well known through their own activities and the widely circulated newspaper which they controlled; but their presence in the Convention meant that their personal feud with Paris was likely to be perpetuated, and broadened by their use of their considerable influence with newly elected provincial deputies who had heard of them through the press.

Within the Convention, also, were the new deputies for Paris, almost entirely anti-Girondin and on good terms with the Commune, as well as a number of other deputies more or less identified with the Jacobin Club of Paris. The most conspicuous of these men were Robespierre, Marat, and Danton: Robespierre, at odds with Brissot since December 1791, critical of the Girondin war policy, bitterly hated since his attempt to get Brissot and Roland arrested during the September massacres; Marat, closely associated with the massacres, the symbol of Parisian violence, blood-thirstiness and irresponsibility; Danton, popular in Paris, the minister of justice in the provisional government of August/September, who was giving up his ministerial portfolio for a parliamentary seat. They represented very different tendencies among the Convention's left-wing deputies; but the Girondins did not distinguish, and drove them together by subjecting them to brutal personal attacks. Robespierre and Marat especially were presented to the Convention as monstrous extremists aiming at the destruction of the Convention's authority for the sake of their own ambition. The massacres, and the Commune's toleration of them, made it relatively easy to create among the generally more conservative deputies still inexperienced in national government an atmosphere markedly unsympathetic to anyone who could be identified with a Parisian point of view. The majority in the Convention would not take sides in a purely personal squabble, as it showed when Louvet launched an envenomed

62. For Paris at this time, see G. Lefebvre, *La première terreur* (Paris, *Cours de Sorbonne*), pp. 141–204, where the causes, progress, and aftermath of the massacres are discussed.

attack on Robespierre at the end of October. On the other hand, the Paris of late 1792 was sufficiently disorderly, demanding, and undisciplined for prejudice to be fairly widespread against both the Parisians and anyone in the Convention who tried to defend them.

In this way, the personal and political rivalries and animosities of the summer of 1792 took root in the Convention. The Girondin interpretation of the situation was clear. With their justified distrust of Paris, their dislike and fear of Robespierre, their repudiation of Marat and his unprincipled violence, they spoke (they said) for the whole Republic, and nearly all the Convention agreed with them, except for a small group of obstructive and "factious" Montagnards. The Mountain also claimed to speak for the Republic, but in a different sense. The Montagnards were more genuinely ready than the Girondins to recognize the achievements of the Parisians—though this did not mean that they wholeheartedly approved of *sans-culotte* demands, or even understood them. They did not claim to have the whole Convention on their side; they said that the majority was often misled by slander and intrigue. (The Girondin reply to this was to say that the radicals were a minority who could only control the Convention by intimidation, using the mob as a threat in the background.) The Montagnards did claim, as Robespierre explained in his impassioned speech of 28 December, to speak for "the people" who had made 14 July and 10 August possible, and on whom the real strength of the Republic rested.

The *appels nominaux* of 1793 concerned the fate of the king, part of the problem which had first estranged the Girondin leaders from Paris; the impeachment of Marat, as a symbol of Parisian agitation against the Girondin leaders personally; and the reinstatement of the Commission of Twelve, a body originally set up to investigate allegations that a purge of the Convention was being planned in Paris. These were issues on which variations of political attitude between the Gironde, the Mountain, and the less committed Plain should be easily discernible. It should be possible to see from the voting patterns and the lines of argument put forward by various deputies in support of them whether there was indeed any substantial difference in the behavior of the Gironde, the Mountain, and the Plain, or whether the Girondins were right in asserting that the only real difference was that between the Mountain and the rest of the Convention. This is not how the Convention seems to have been divided during 1793-94; but perhaps the attitudes of 1793-94 represented merely a temporary accommodation to the Jacobin dictatorship, and the 1792-93 situation was quite different.

PART II

THE DEPUTIES, THE *APPELS NOMINAUX*, AND THE POLITICS OF 1792–1793

Je ne parlerai ici que d'après ma conscience.

A. N. de Bellegarde,
deputy for Charente,
January 1793

CHAPTER 3

THE TRIAL OF LOUIS XVI
(i): THE ISSUES

Even in revolutionary times there are relatively few occasions during which those involved can consciously say to themselves: "This is a turning point in the history of my country. By what happens now, the shape of the future will be decided." It is even rarer for the decision to be so personal that individuals can be separately aware of their responsibility and its possible consequences for themselves, and can know as they take time to make up their minds that they will be answerable to history for what they decide. The trial of Louis XVI was such an occasion. It was the only event between 1789 and 1799 which set an almost impassable barrier between men of the Revolution and the government of the Restoration, and while it was happening those taking part were openly assessing the significance of its outcome. It is very well for later historians to say that "the trial . . . was a mere formality";[1] it is hard to believe this after reading the speeches, some very brief, others more than thirty pages long, in which more than 70 percent of the deputies recorded their views on one or more aspects of the trial.[2] The debate reached into the farthest corners of the Convention and provoked into public statement some men whose parliamentary lives are otherwise completely obscure.[3] Some of the speeches were statesmanlike, some were

1. C. Brinton, *A. Decade of Revolution* (Harper, 1963), p. 113.
2. For the purposes of this study I have read 406 speeches printed at the Convention's expense and written by 292 individual deputies. Twenty-five others made explanations when delivering their votes on the questions of guilt or the *appel au peuple*, and many more made comments as they voted on the sentence; in all, at least 3 in every 4 deputies who took part in the voting made some announcement about their attitude and the reason for it. Some and perhaps a number of printed speeches may not have survived; e.g., A. Martin and G. Walter, *Catalogue de l'histoire de la Révolution française*, 5 vols. (Paris, 1936–43), lists a *Quatrième discours* by C. N. Osselin, but only 2 others (III: 519).
3. Cf. the statement made by Boyaval in the *appel-nominal* on the *appel au peuple*: "*Au cas que les assemblées primaires aient lieu ici par la majorité des voix, je demande qu'assemblées elles delibèrent et prononcent si ceux de ses Députés qui se refusent de juger*

demagogic, some showed great anxiety, and a few were bizarre, but all give the impression that the authors were wrestling as best they could with a problem which many would gladly have been spared, but which all recognized as raising major matters of principle. When one comes to Lozeau, a conscientious middle-ranker from the Plain, and finds him explaining that he feels he owes a statement of his views to himself, to his constituents, to foreigners, and to posterity, one accepts his sincerity and shares his feelings.[4]

I

Why was Louis XVI put on trial? Lefebvre argues that the aim of the Girondins was to shelve the problem of bringing him to judgment, since they had no desire to see him executed and they believed that once the trial began his fate was almost inevitable.[5] There were, however, both emotional and practical considerations which made the trial unavoidable. In the first place, if Louis were not in some sense implicated in counterrevolutionary activity, the insurrection of 10 August and the existence of the Convention itself had no justification. It was not possible to remove Louis from the spotlight for any length of time, because of the evidence of his activities which kept turning up in the papers which were now under public investigation, and which was presented to the Convention in the very form which it was least possible to ignore.[6] In the second place, the Paris Commune, which had reft the royal family from the untrustworthy hands of the Legislative Assembly on 10 August and had guarded it jealously ever since, was not only insistent that justice be done but was also finding the duty of securing safe custody for the leading criminal a heavy burden.[7] In the third place, as the debates were to show, other deputies besides those in the Parisian

---

souverainement Louis Capet, n'ont pas, de fait, abdiqué leurs fonctions." He then firmly voted *non.* As one of only 2 recorded expressions of opinion by an otherwise totally unknown deputy, this has something of the impact of a sniper's shot from close range. (His second comment, at Carrier's impeachment, was similarly noteworthy.)

4. P. A. Lozeau, *Opinion . . . sur le jugement de Louis Capet . . . .*

5. G. Lefebvre, *The French Revolution to 1793* (London, 1962); see N. Hampson, *A social history of the French Revolution* (London, 1963), p. 162; and A. Goodwin, *The French Revolution* (London, 1966), p. 127, for variations on this interpretation.

6. Both on 1 October, when the Commune secured the appointment of the Commission of Twenty-four to investigate the documents in their charge, and on 20 November, when Roland's belated disclosure of the existence of the *armoire de fer* produced the Commission of Twelve, what stirred the Convention to immediate activity was the allegation that papers had been discovered relating to the king's attempts to suborn members of the Legislative. *Moniteur* XIV: 96-97, 530-31.

7. See G. Lenôtre, *The Dauphin (Louis XVII)* trans. F. Rees (London, 1922), Chaps. I-II. Despite the violent bias of Lenôtre's description, the very real difficulties encountered by the Commune are clear. What the Commune was frightened of—and naturally enough, when one considers the crowds of people who apparently went regularly in and out of the Temple—was another Varennes for which it would be held responsible. (This is of course apart altogether from feelings which the members individually had about the king.) The danger could be guarded against by trying to prevent possible planning (thus the king was separated from his family), by keeping to a minimum the chances of communicating with

delegation believed that justice should take its course; and in the fourth place, the trial was a useful weapon for the opponents of the Gironde, the Girondins being more influential in the Convention in its early weeks than they were ever to be again. The one thing it was impossible for Buzot, Brissot, Vergniaud, and the others to do was to oppose the trial; but by failing to press for it themselves, and by their attitude to those who did, they involved themselves in endless equivocation and gave away an initiative which they never again recovered for any length of time.

The main stages of the trial may be summed up as (1) the examination of the evidence, initiated by the Legislative Assembly on 10 August and accelerated by the appointment on 1 October of the Commission of Twenty-Four; this was reported on by Dufriche-Valazé on 6 November;[8] (2) the examination of the legal position begun by the Legislation Committee on 5 October, reported on by Mailhe on 7 November and debated intermittently from 7 November until 3 December; (3) the preparation of an indictment, initiated by the decree of 6 December which represented the Convention's final decision to try the king itself, and completed by the presentation of Robert Lindet's draft on 10 December; (4) the king's defense—his appearance before the Convention on 11 December and de Sèze's formal presentation of his case on the 26th; (5) the debate on the possible ratification of the sentence by the primary assemblies, which raged from 27 December to 4 January; and (6) the actual voting, which took place from 15 to 19 January 1793.

Over the evidence itself there was very little argument, although it seems clear that there was not enough time, and perhaps not enough inclination, for it to be properly sifted.[9] As was clear when the final vote was taken, no one in the

---

those outside the Temple, and by keeping the prisoners in sight, more or less, for 24 hours a day. This was wearying for the jailers as well as for the jailed.

For the complete unwillingness of the anti-Commune deputies in the Convention to grasp the problems of guarding the king, see the debate of 14 December (*Moniteur* XIV: 746–47) over the admittedly very ham-handed methods suggested to ensure that he would not use his defense counsel as a means of communication.

8. Another report from the Commission of Twelve, on the contents of the *armoire de fer*, was presented by Rühl on 3 December. This was the immediate cause for the final move toward actual indictment, since Rühl's evidence, read out in the assembly, could hardly be glossed over or ignored.

9. In a preliminary report to the Convention on 4 October, dealing mainly with the search for proofs that members of the Legislative had been bribed, Valazé stated that the committee was listing the contents of 95 cartons, 6 boxes (one of 54 cubic feet), 20 portfolios, 34 registers, 7 files, and several thousand pages stored in wheat sacks. Since they had been at work only 3 days, his assertion that there was no evidence incriminating the Legislative was obviously premature, as Marat immediately pointed out. (However, if the Commune had seen this evidence as was said on 1 October, presumably the Commission should have been able to see it too fairly quickly. The source of this confusion, if there was one, has never been made clear.) Valazé said at this time that it would take several months to work through all the documents; it is hard to believe that the job could have been properly completed during the 5 weeks which were actually spent on it. See E. Seligman, *La justice en France pendant la Révolution (1791-1793)* (Paris, 1913), pp. 391–92, for a comment on the work of this committee, which he thinks rather incompetent, and

Convention was really willing to dispute the king's guilt or to challenge the facts adduced to establish it. Those who came nearest doing so were probably Girault and Kersaint, both of whom claimed that a man born and brought up to be a king could hardly be expected to behave like other men and was not therefore really accountable for his actions, and neither of whom would admit that Louis's future was a matter of much significance.[10] Both of these deputies, interestingly enough, tried to divert attention from the king's person to the more general questions of royalism, public security, and (in Kersaint's case particularly) the dangers of illegitimate pressure from "*des poignards des assassins du 2 septembre.*" These speeches are very unusual in that they do show some sympathetic interest in the king's predicament. The matter of Louis's oath to the Constitution and his sincerity in taking it, of course, loomed large in the minds of most *conventionnels*, but Girault was exceptional in pointing out that since, to Louis, the Constitution simply overturned his rights and he had little choice but to swear allegiance to it, he was in his own eyes quite free to break his oath; there was thus no point in distinguishing between his public and private behavior, which were all of a piece.[11]

The only person to dispute any substantial part of the facts was Louis himself, who in his interrogation on 11 December showed considerable intelligence in professing utter ignorance whenever an awkward question was raised. He made a good witness, and the deputies, more than half of whom had never seen him before, were impressed; but he may have gone too far when he claimed to know nothing of the *armoire de fer*, the key to which was on a bunch he had handed over to a servant after his arrest. This was the only matter on which he was cross-examined on 26 December, after de Sèze had finished his address for the defense, and may have been reckoned a good test of his truthfulness; his evasiveness on that occasion lies like a cloud over the page in the *Moniteur* which dispassionately records it.[12] But what he with all his neat side-stepping and de Sèze with his careful concentration on the law were alike unable to do was something simple, but crucial. They could produce not the smallest sign that any action which Louis had ever taken had been designed in the interest of the "free France" set up in 1789-91. The incompatibility of attitude between king and revolutionaries was summed up in a single exchange on 11 December:

Sydenham, *The Girondins* (London, 1961), pp. 134-35, for a few words in defense. The general attitude of the Committee is suggested by the behavior of one of its members, Birotteau, on 4 October; he took the opportunity not to indicate the material bearing on the activities of the king, but to attack the Commune for alleged incompetence which was said to have led to the deaths of innocent persons in the September massacres. (*Moniteur* XIV: 96-98, 121-22, 128-31.)

10. C. J. Girault, *Opinion . . . sur le jugement de Louis XVI*; A. G. S. Coetnempren de Kersaint, *Seconde opinion . . . sur le jugement du ci-devant roi*, and also *Opinion . . . sur cette question: Quel parti la Convention nationale doit-elle prendre touchant le ci-devant roi et sa famille?*

11. Girault, *Opinion.*

12. *Moniteur* XIV: 720-24, 848.

LE PRESIDENT: Le corps législatif avait rendu, le 20 janvier, un décret contre les prêtres factieux; vous en avez suspendu l'exécution. Qu' avez-vous à repondre?

LOUIS: La constitution me laissait la sanction des décrets.[13]

De Sèze might later maintain to the Convention that the veto had been honestly imposed in the public interest, since more Frenchmen opposed the decree than supported it;[14] the king saw no need to explain or justify his actions. The Constitution left him free ... It was over this issue that the first of the disputes of principle among the deputies began. While the Commission of Twenty-four was toiling through cartons, boxes, portfolios, registers, files, and wheat-sacks to compile a report about whose details no one really cared, the Legislation Committee, with a leading jurisconsult as its *rapporteur*, was facing a question which pierced to the foundation of the revolutionary régime: how and by whom may a king be tried?

The great stumbling block in the way of what nearly all the deputies saw as revolutionary justice, whatever the penalty they wished to impose, was the Constitution of 1791. Article 2 of Chapter II said explicitly "The person of the king is inviolable and sacred," and Article 5 specified only three ways in which he could lose his throne: (a) by not taking an oath to the constitution within a designated period, or by retracting it after he had taken it; (b) by leading an armed force against the nation, or by failing to oppose such an undertaking in his name; or (c) by leaving the kingdom and failing to return. Any of these offenses was equivalent to abdication, and *after* one of them was committed he could, having abdicated, be tried as an ordinary citizen for offenses committed after the abdication—but not for those committed earlier, for which the only penalty prescribed was the loss of the throne.

Twenty members of the National Convention, including Girault and Kersaint, asserted that these provisions made the trial of the king for the acts for which he was admittedly responsible a legal and moral impossibility. His inviolability had been established with the Constitution, and he had lost it only with the throne on 10 August, since when he had self-evidently been unable to do anything which might justify a trial; or alternatively, he could not be tried because there was no law in existence applicable to a man in his position. He could not be tried by existing law because this law did not cover kings; none could be created for the purpose because it would then be retroactive and therefore essentially unjust; and to try him by "the law of nature," as many

13. *Moniteur* XIV: 723.
14. Ibid., p. 843. For the full text of the defense, see *Convention nationale. Défense de Louis ... par le citoyen de Sèze ...* (Paris, 1792). De Sèze did the best he could over the evidence; otherwise he stressed Louis's rights under the Constitution, with many telling hits at the legal status of the Convention in the trial.

deputies suggested, would be to put him in a situation where no rules existed, and would result, like the September massacres, in simple murder.[15] A trial could only be the application of a preexisting law; Dandenac *jeune* claimed to have searched for a relevant law without being able to find anything except provisions in the Constitution: "cette loi est le code civil et criminel de la royauté; c'est la seule loi antérieure au délit; C'est donc la seule applicable à l'accusé, au moins qu'on ne veuille effacer de nos coeurs les principes d'éternelle justice."[16] "Pour le juger," wrote Devérité, "il faut le faire légalement ... ce mot roi ne m'impose pas ... mais la sainteté des lois me frappe et m'étonne."[17] Bouchereau summed up even more forcibly the case against any form of trial: "Ce serait transporter l'état social dans l'état de nature, ce serait vouloir décider par le droit civil ce qui n'est que du ressort du droit des gens; en un mot ce serait un assassinat juridique et non un jugement légal, parce qu'il ne peut exister de jugement légal quand il n'y a ni loi applicable au délit, ni tribunal compétent pour en faire l'application."[18] Duchastel merely underlined the anomalous situation which he felt must nevertheless be accepted: "Louis le traître a égorgé son peuple. Aussi qu'ont-ils prouvé? ce que ... la loi était absurde, mais non qu'elle n'a pas été faite."[19] These deputies did not deny that in the public interest something might have to be done about Louis—prison until the end of the war, then exile, probably; what they did unanimously deny was the propriety or even possibility of any sort of judicial process: "je vais maintenant prouver," wrote Guiter, "que la personne du roi échappe à toute espèce de récherche, à toute espèce de jugement."[20] For one of them at least, it was a matter of personal integrity as well as of public good faith. Jacques Chevalier, a poor farmer from Sarthe who had owed his election as mayor to the respect of his fellow citizens,[21] had taken his duties seriously and could not forget that like all other citizens he had taken an oath of loyalty to the nation, the law, and the king. Those who believed themselves to be bound only by part of the Constitution might try the king for crimes committed before his fall; Chevalier was bound by his oath and could not.[22]

The twenty put their case and lost it, but some of them continued to argue it to the last. Eight made two, three, or four recorded speeches on the subject, shifting their ground a little as the tide went against them, but restating their basic points again and again. The rejection of the idea of a trial carried with it an automatic rejection of any police action against Louis more severe than tempo-

15. C. F. G. Morisson, *Seconde opinion . . . concernant le jugement de Louis XVI.*
16. J. Dandenac, *Opinion . . . dans l'affaire de Louis XVI.*
17. L. A. Devérité, *Mon opinion sur le jugement de Louis XVI.*
18. A. F. Bouchereau, *Opinion . . . sur cette question: Louis XVI peut-il être jugé?*
19. G. S. Duchastel, *Opinion . . . sur cette question: Quelle est la peine que le Peuple Français doit infliger à Louis? . . . .*
20. J. A. S. Guiter, *Discours . . . sur la question suivante: Louis XVI peut-il être mis en jugement?*
21. Kuscinski, *Conventionnels*, p. 137.
22. J. Chevalier, *Opinion . . . sur l'affaire du ci-devant roi . . .*

rary imprisonment; hence, a common theme in these speeches, besides the impropriety of the Convention's procedure, was the unworthiness—sometimes, the ulterior motive—of those pressing for his execution; as Albouys rather crudely put it: "c'est parce que de tels hommes demandent sa mort, que je dis moi que l'intérêt de la République est qu'il vive."[23] There was evident anti-Parisian bias:[24] and there was also, especially toward the end, some justifiable personal bitterness. Morisson, a moderate man who presented his views in two speeches, without abuse and in a very reasoned tone, let slip in his third what was probably fair comment on some of his adversaries: "ces hommes qui portent l'injustice au point de traiter d'infâmes ou de scélérats ceux qui n'ont pas leur coeur . . . ou leur esprit. . . ."[25]

When the point of decision was reached, with the voting on the trial, all of these twenty deputies showed their consistency by opting steadily for mercy; three of them abstained from the first vote, on the king's guilt, and Morisson abstained throughout. Eight of their colleagues who had not previously expressed an opinion now came forward to support them. The total number of deputies prepared to argue that whatever Louis had done he was immune from legal penalty (though security measures against him might be needed) was thus twenty-eight, a very small minority of the whole Convention. But because of the way the debate over the trial was conducted, a disproportionate amount of the Convention's time was spent on listening to exponents of their point of view. The feeling that the moderates were gaining an improper advantage in publicity may well have contributed to the angry scorn of which Morisson was finally driven to complain.

II

A normal method of debate in the Convention was to hear speeches alternately for and against a proposed decree. The debate on the king was formally launched on 13 November, after the presentation on the seventh of the Legislation Committee's report, drafted by Mailhe, which had proposed a decree providing that (i) Louis could be tried; (ii) the Convention could try him; (iii) it would not be necessary to have the Convention's decision ratified by the people at large. These were separate issues. On the first, there was very little disagreement, on the second a good deal; the third became the occasion of a major political conflict. The rational method would have been to dispose of them one at a time, but this the Convention never did and, as Montgilbert later pointed out, got itself into a considerable muddle because decisions were made without its being precisely clear what was being settled or intended.[26] (Thus the matter of inviolability could still be an admissible subject of discussion during the

23. B. Albouys, *Opinion . . . sur le jugement de Louis Capet.*
24. J. M. Rouzet, *Opinion . . . concernant le jugement de Louis XVI.*
25. C. F. G. Morisson, *Troisième opinion . . . sur le jugement de Louis XVI.*
26. F. A. Montgilbert, *Motion d'ordre . . . .*

debate on the *appel au peuple*.) Pétion suggested on 13 November that the question: "Can the king be tried? " be discussed first; but two days later, after four speeches had been heard, Buzot and Danton got this decree rescinded to widen the scope of the debate and none was ever put through to replace it. The result was that the supporters of inviolability got an early priority which they never formally lost.[27] Between 13 November and 30 November, when Legendre secured permission for all deputies to hand in their speeches to the *bureau* for printing at public expense, only nine speeches had been heard altogether, four in favor of inviolability and five against it of which two were by convinced anti-regicides.[28] The frequent and unavoidable interruptions by other business, together with a certain lack of enthusiasm on the part of the *bureau*, combined to string out a not very productive discussion until 3 December, when Rühl's report, followed by Robespierre's forceful demand that the king be sentenced forthwith, produced a flurry of activity that culminated in the decree of 6 December, providing for trial by the Convention. During the whole period 7 November–6 December only twenty speeches were heard altogether, four of them from Morisson and his associates, who spoke at considerable length.[29] In the sporadic discussion between 6 and 26 November the Left played a considerable part, but this concerned principally detail and procedure and included no major speeches on the issues of the trial, with the exception of Robert Lindet's summary of the charges against the king, which dealt mainly with the evidence.[30] And in the debate over the *appel au peuple*, which wound up the whole procedure, it was November/December all over again: thirty speeches in all, six from the extreme right, and a weighting of the remainder toward the moderates rather than the radicals.[31] This is not at all the story of the speeches which were published, and except for very attentive readers, the balance of opinion in the Convention as a whole may well have been very hard to gauge.

This point is worth some emphasis, because on the evidence of the Convention's debates alone, the speed and comparative ease with which the major decisions were made between 3 and 6 December is somewhat puzzling. The virtual unanimity on the need to settle with the king, which became evident in those four days, contrasts oddly with the apparent conflict of opinion in the desultory argument of the previous three weeks. But the printed speeches suggest that this was indeed a matter on which a debate need hardly have been held,

27. For Pétion's decree, *Moniteur* XIV: 464; for its abandonment, ibid., p. 483.

28. For Legendre's decree, *Moniteur* XIV: 620. The unequal balance of speeches to this point occurred because Paine's speech was read to the Assembly by a secretary (ibid., p. 535).

29. It is also interesting that although Morisson spoke first of all, on 13 November, and must have had an attentive audience, he was apparently anxious to have this speech printed; it is numbered 9 on a list of several hundred (*Opinion . . . concernant le jugement de Louis XVI . . .*).

30. J. B. R. Lindet, *Attentat et crimes de Louis, dernier roi des Français.*

31. The *Moniteur* (XIV: 880) notes 6 speakers in the debate on the *appel au peuple* on 29 December; all but one favored the *appel.*

let alone prolonged over such a period. There were almost as many ways of rejecting the doctrine of inviolability as there were pamphlets in print.

In Turreau's view, to ask: "Can Louis be tried? " was equivalent to asking: "Is a king a man? "[32] Sévestre said that the defenders of inviolability were willing to leave the people unprotected against a king who could do as he liked.[33] Prost gave a neat twist to the argument by commenting that if all that could happen to Louis was his compulsory reduction to the status of an ordinary citizen, ordinary values would be completely reversed—"d'autres montent à ce rang par l'heroïsme et la vertu, tu peux y descendre par un cascade de forfaits."[34] If legal quibbles meant that a self-evident criminal was safe from retribution, then it was felt that the quibbles were irrelevant and the Declaration of the Rights of Man took over; the Declaration after all antedated the Constitution and stood at its head as a summary of the principles it was designed to secure. Article VI, "Law . . . must be the same for all, whether it protects or whether it punishes," crops up in speech after speech as by inescapable logic the provision which had swept away the basis of privilege was turned against the king himself.[35] The difficulty of finding law to cover the case was got over by reference to the law of nature, which was anterior and superior to the "relative" law enforced by normal judicial institutions.[36] The constitutional contract between king and people was held to be void because the king had never accepted it; as Lecointe-Puyraveau said: "le lien qui nous attachoit à Capet est rompu . . . Il n'a pas rempli ses devoirs, ses droits sont nuls." And why should his ministers take responsibility for what he had done behind their backs? [37] Lacombe Saint-Michel summed up for one aspect: if Louis were not guilty, the whole Convention was, and either he must be punished, or the Declaration destroyed; and Mazade-Percin on another: "Louis étoit en même temps homme, citoyen et roi; homme par nature, citoyen par le pacte social, et roi par accident. Comme homme, il étoit sujet aux lois naturelles; comme citoyen, il étoit soumis à la loi civile; comme roi, la loi politique est au-dessus de lui"—and therefore, though his

32. L. Turreau de Linières, *Opinion . . . sur Capet.*

33. J. M. F. Sévestre, *Opinion . . . sur le jugement de Louis Capet.* One problem was that the Constitution specified only 3 types of offense by a king, for which he could suffer no worse than dethronement. Did "inviolability" mean that he could do with impunity anything else he chose?

34. C. C. Prost, *Opinion . . . sur l'inviolabilité de Louis XVI.*

35. See, e.g., E. B. Asselin, *Opinion . . . sur la question: Si le Roi peut être jugé?* ; J. B. Salle, *Déclaration . . . dans l'affaire du ci-devant roi*; B. J. G. B. Ribet, *Opinion . . . sur le jugement de Louis Capet*; L. F. Portiez, *Opinion . . . sur cette question: Le roi des Francais étoit-il jugeable?* ; and P. Paganel, *Opinion . . . sur le jugement de ci-devant roi* for a variation. None of these deputies was Montagnard, and Portiez was the only regicide.

36. C. A. Rudel, *Opinion . . . sur le jugement de Louis Capet.* It was pointed out rather repetitively that a crime might still be a crime even if law-makers had failed to foresee it. Solon's alleged failure to envisage parricide was the stock illustration here. (Cf. Portiez's speech above.)

37. M. M. Lecointe-Puyraveau, *Opinion . . . sur Louis Capet*; P. N. Philippeaux, *Opinion . . . sur le jugement de Louis XVI*; L. F. A. François, *Discours . . . sur l'article premier du Projet de Décret: Louis XVI peut-il être jugé?*

offenses as king had been dealt with when he was deposed, he was still indictable in his other capacities.[38] A few Jacobins suggested that the Constitution was vitiated from the start, since it had never been accepted by the people of France.[39] Some deputies were dispassionate, some violently biased, some long-winded and cautious, and some ingeniously rhetorical;[40] but they concurred on two points. The king was guilty, and he must be made to answer for what he had done. They were the only points of near-unanimous agreement that the trial was ever to produce.

III

So Louis was to be tried. By whom? By the Convention in the name of the sovereign people, said Mailhe's report;[41] and so said the Convention itself a month later. Yet this was a conclusion which many deputies felt to be inherently wrong, and some would never accept at all. What were the alternatives, what were the objections, and why was a decision reached with such apparent precipitation carried with reasonable ease and maintained despite the feeling against it?

The visible alternatives in dealing with Louis were four. The first was to treat him as an ordinary conspirator against the community and send him before an existing court—either an ordinary criminal court, such as the criminal court of Paris within whose jurisdiction he presumably came, or a court such as the High Court of Orléans, recently established for crimes against the state.[42] The second was to create a special court to deal with him, either from the existing judiciary (frequently popular election of judges and jurors was specified) or from the membership of the Convention itself.[43] The third was to recognize that he stood, in effect, outside the law and must be dealt with as a political prisoner or prisoner of war by executive decree.[44] The fourth was to recognize a wholly exceptional situation, politically as well as legally, and arraign him before the

38. J. P. Lacombe Saint-Michel, *Opinion . . . sur le jugement de Louis Hugues*; J. B. D. de Mazade-Percin, *Opinion . . . sur l'affaire de Louis Capet* [no. 1.].

39. See, e.g., E. J. B. Milhaud, *Opinion . . . sur le jugement de Louis Capet, dit Louis XVI.*

40. E.g., P. L. Pons, *Opinion sur l'inviolabilité de Louis Capet . . .* (Louis as a treacherous servant), and C. F. Oudot, *Opinion . . . sur le jugement de Louis XVI* (the king as the trusted captain of the ship of state).

41. J. Mailhe, *Rapport . . . et projet de décret . . . présentés . . . le 7 Novembre 1792. . . .*

42. J. A. Penières-Delzors, *Opinion . . . sur le jugement de Louis XVI*; P. A. Dartigoeyte, *Opinion sur la question de savoir, si Louis XVI peut être jugé; comment et par qui il doit être jugé? . . . .*

43. This solution overlaps to some extent the one suggested by Dartigoeyte; but Dartigoeyte, unlike some others, was chiefly concerned with the Convention's reputation. There are many variations on the theme; see, e.g., B. Gertoux, *Opinion . . . sur le forme de jugement de Louis XVI*; F. S. Bézard, *Opinion . . . sur le procès du ci-devant roi.* Condorcet has a long and interesting pamphlet: M.J.A.N. Caritat de Condorcet, *Opinion . . . sur le jugement de Louis XVI.*

44. So for example, to take two ends of the political spectrum, see S. P. Lejeune, *Opinion . . . sur Louis Capet, ci-devant roi de France*, and F. Rivaud, *Opinion . . . sur le jugement de Louis XVI.*

representatives of the people, embodied in the membership of the Convention itself.

The proposal that Louis be disposed of by executive decree, without a trial of any sort, was brushed aside not only by Pétion[45] but by majority opinion. Robespierre's argument that to try the king was to put 10 August on trial[46] was logically unassailable but morally inadmissible; he could not be condemned unheard. The suggestion that this be done was put forward by the brothers Robespierre, but, as far as one can gather from the documents, by very few others. Saint-Just did not suggest on 13 November that no trial should take place; he argued that an ordinary civil or criminal court was inappropriate—"On ne peut pas juger un roi selon les lois du pays . . . on le juge selon le droit des gens . . . C'est vous qui devez le juger . . . ."[47] It has been said that the Mountain "proclaimed it the obvious duty of the Convention to condemn the king without delay."[48] But how many Montagnards did so proclaim it? Sixteen of the twenty-four deputies from Paris produced pamphlets concerning the trial. Of these, those by the two Robespierres, Raffron and Beauvais urged summary justice; eleven others seem to have accepted, explicitly or implicitly, trial by the Convention—Desmoulins and Robert argued, in so many words, that this was a task which the deputies had been elected to carry out; and Osselin wanted trial by the ordinary courts. Outside Paris, fewer than a dozen Montagnards took Robespierre's line; these included Robert Lindet, but not, among other well-known members of the Jacobin Club, Couthon, Hentz, J. B. Lacoste, Le Cointre, Merlin of Douai, or Pierre-Louis Prieur.[49] How far Robespierre himself would really have wanted to insist on it seems in doubt. It may have been, as Walter seems to imply, largely a shock tactic, used on 3 December to get matters at last under way.[50] If this was indeed the intention, it succeeded, since Pétion's imme-

45. *Moniteur*, XIV: 650.
46. M. Robespierre, *Oeuvres* IX: 122.
47. *Moniteur* XIV: 467.
48. Sydenham, *The Girondins*, p. 136.
49. See M. Robespierre, *Oeuvres* IX: 12–30; A. B. J. Robespierre, *Opinion . . . sur le procès de Louis XVI*; N. Raffron, *Sentiment . . . sur le jugement de Louis XVI*; C. N. Beauvais, *Opinion . . . sur le jugement de Louis XVI, ci-devant roi des Français*; J. N. Billaud, *dit* Billaud-Varenne, *Discours . . . sur le jugement de Louis Capet*; L. S. B. C. Desmoulins, *Opinion . . . sur le jugement de Louis XVI*; P. F. N. Fabre d'Eglantine, *Opinion . . . sur l'appel au peuple . . .*; P. F. J. Robert, *Suite de l'opinion . . . sur le jugement et les crimes du ci-devant roi*; G. A. Couthon, *Opinion . . . sur le jugement de Louis Capet*; N. J. Hentz, *Opinion . . . sur le procès du ci-devant roi*; J. B. Lacoste, *Discours . . . sur le jugement de Louis XVI*; J. B. R. Lindet, *Attentat et crimes de Louis, dernier roi des Français*; L. Le Cointre, *Opinion . . . sur le jugement de Louis Capet*; P. A. Merlin, *Opinion . . . sur le procès de Louis XVI*; P. L. Prieur, *Opinion . . . sur le jugement de Louis Capet*. It must be added that 3 of the 11 Parisian deputies referred to have not been considered as Montagnard in this analysis; these are Manuel, Dusaulx, and J. J. Thomas. Of the 20 Parisian deputies who have been classed as Montagnard, 4 wanted summary justice, 9 some sort of trial, and 7 said nothing on the subject.
50. G. Walter, *Robespierre*, 2 vols. (Paris, 1961), I: 382. See also M. Robespierre, *Oeuvres complètes*, t. V, ed. G. Laurent (Paris, 1953), pp. 56–64, for an extract from his *Lettres à ses commettans*; in this, *Sur le parti à prendre à l'égard de Louis XVI*, the ideas expressed seem quite compatible with the sort of trial which was eventually conducted.

diate response was to propose the Convention trial which was very shortly provided for.[51] It may be significant that in his speech of 28 December, his other major contribution to debate, Robespierre took pains to announce his acceptance of *"le système qui a prévalu."*[52] He may have been helped toward this attitude by something which is often forgotten: the fact that rejection of the whole idea of a trial was not confined to a minority of radicals but was found also amongst the moderates. This was true not only of the supporters of inviolability but also of others like Delbrel and Pémartin, who did feel that justice required that a penalty be imposed for Louis's crimes, could not see any acceptable machinery for imposing one, and were reluctant to allow judicial responsibility to descend on the Convention, which was not a suitable body to exercise it. *"Je n'ai entendu accepter que le mandat de législateur"* was the escape clause which left the deputy who used it free to make a purely political decision.[53] The point was pressed by such men to the end, long after it had been dropped by the Left. Lanjuinais heatedly insisted on it at the opening of the *appel* debate on 26 December, and though the motion to which he was taking exception, one suggested by Couthon, had already been passed without difficulty, there was enough underlying feeling on the subject to cause the assembly to accept thankfully a nominal amendment leaving the matter still open; it seemed the only way of avoiding an interminable wrangle.[54]

This is not however an adequate analysis of the position of all those who defined their position as that of "legislators" or "statesmen" rather than judges. A large number of those who refused to be recorded as taking part in a "trial" by the Convention did so, not because they felt, like Delbrel and Pémartin, that there was no practical way of trying Louis, but because they felt that a disastrous blunder had been made over the way in which the trial had been arranged. Lanjuinais himself was repudiating the Convention's procedure only because he felt the method was wrong; the aim of *a* trial he was quite willing to accept.[55] When the decision of 6 December turned out to be irrevocable, the only action open to those who believed it to be mistaken was to state as clearly as they could the basis on which they were prepared to cooperate. A different procedure might have been acceptable; the one chosen put them in a false position which they would not accept. Beffroy argued, indeed, that the whole problem was due to haste, that the discussion had been wrongly based, and that if Mailhe's report had been more deliberately considered it would have been rejected.[56] Was this a reasonable claim?

51. *Moniteur* XIV: 650.
52. Robespierre, *Oeuvres* V: 184.
53. For this formulation, see, e.g., J. Debourges, *Opinion . . . sur le jugement de Louis XVI*; P. Delbrel, *Opinion . . . sur les questions suivantes: Louis Capet peut-il être jugé? Par qui doit-il être jugé?* ; and J. Pémartin, *Opinion . . . sur l'affaire de Louis Capet.*
54. *Moniteur* XIV: 853–54. The incident is a useful demonstration that the Mountain was not alone in resisting inconvenient majority decisions.
55. J. D. Lanjuinais, *Opinion . . . sur Louise le dernier.*
56. L. E. Beffroy, *Opinion . . . sur Louis le dernier.*

So far as the matter was ever aired in the Convention, the proponents of another form of trial never got much of a hearing. Of the five speeches up to 30 November which might have raised the subject, three accepted a Convention trial and one was not specific; only Serre argued for the ordinary courts.[57] Between 3 and 6 December, the contest was not between one form of trial and another, but, as far as could be seen, between trial by the Convention and summary execution. Despite the later protests, the trend of opinion in the pamphlets indicates that the concentration on a Convention trial was not entirely unfair, in the sense that there seems at least a clear majority in favor of the action which was finally taken. Among the printed speeches, fewer than sixty urged a trial outside the Convention, against more than twice as many who were satisfied that the Convention act for the nation; and a number did not raise the matter at all. On these figures, the Convention's acceptance of its role as an administrator of justice makes some sense. Yet the objections were very serious, they were deeply felt, and the number of deputies who stipulated, as they voted in January, their role as "legislators" or "statesmen" rather than as judges did more than give Marat the *hommes d'Etat* as a permanent target. This number registered a reservation which was shared to some extent even by someone like Vadier, who was to become intimately involved with the Jacobin régime.[58]

The most important difficulty was the one which was repeatedly summed up under the head of "this monstrous accumulation of powers," which outraged the judicial decencies, and ran counter to everything which a legalistically minded community believed itself to know about the principles of justice.[59] It did not matter how many ingenious hairs were split about the people on 10 August as the jury of accusation, the Convention as the trial jury, and the law (laying down the penalty for treason) as the judge;[60] in fact the Convention was acting as prosecutor, judge, and jury in a trial which could produce only one verdict, and the deputies knew it. All of them knew that such a trial, were it to be conducted, could be justified only by the most abstract of general principles; thus Rousseau's name flew backward and forward, being used with equal confidence by both sides.[61] And on a more practical level, they were obsessed by history. A sound classical education provided them with examples of the proper disposal of tyrants, which were quoted remorselessly when Louis's sentence was being considered; for the initial procedure they had to look nearer home, and the place where they looked was seventeenth-century England. Mr. Dick was never more haunted than were the *conventionnels*; King Charles's head rolls

57. J. Serre, *Opinion . . . contre l'inviolabilité du roi.*
58. M. G. Vadier, *Opinion . . . concernant Louis XVI.*
59. See, e.g., J. P. Rabaut, *dit* Rabaut Saint-Etienne, *Opinion . . . concernant le procès de Louis XVI*; F. J. Riffard Saint-Martin, *Opinion . . . prononcée le 17 janvier 1793*; and Condorcet's pamphlet, above (*note* 43), to which other deputies referred.
60. N. M. Quinette, *Opinion . . . sur le jugement de Louis Capet.*
61. J. Lakanal, *Opinion . . . sur la question de savoir; Si Louis XVI peut être jugé?* ; C. A. Chasset, *Opinion . . . sur l'affaire de Louis XVI addressée à la Convention nationale*; E. L. A. Dubois-Crancé, *Opinion . . . sur Louis XVI.*

almost visibly round the floor. England had given them a precedent and a warning, the difficulty being that they were not quite sure what the warning was. It was all too clear that the English republicans had made a disastrous mistake—was not George III there to prove it? —but in what did the mistake consist? Had the trial been bungled, or was it the execution that should never have taken place? Those opposed to a Convention trial could assert that the members of the Long Parliament had fatally prejudiced their case by arrogating to themselves an authority which could not rightfully be theirs; thus their "court" had no authority, and they lost the support they should have gained from associating the whole English people with the fate of their king.[62] Book-knowledge of English history was general enough for it to be common ground among all the deputies that Charles had been tried by an improperly constituted court, just as Cromwell's "tyranny" was accepted as the sort of danger against which they must be constantly on the watch; hence, any reference to 1648 and its aftermath was sure to wake an immediate response.

None of the difficulties of principle about trying the king could be solved, because there was no solution to which serious theoretical as well as practical objections could not be raised. Any decision would have to be a choice of evils, and the choice was more difficult because there were emotional complications as well. In the eyes of a good many deputies, a Convention trial would have been easier to accept if there had been any suggestion of impartiality among the prospective judges, but this was an hypocrisy which was never attempted by the Left, and the crude blood-thirstiness of the extremists was a weapon put into their opponents' hands. Contrariwise, the assumption of moral superiority by men who were quite willing to admit Louis's guilt, but who condemned as butchers all those who wished him to pay the statutory penalty for what he had done, could only breed resentment and suspicion.[63] The presence of Robespierre, Marat, Danton, Sergent and others in the Convention was a constant reminder of the September massacres, which shadowed all the debates and were far more often referred to by the moderates than were the *sans-culotte* sacrifices of 10 August; and entwined with this were the feeling of pressure from the spectators in the tribunes, the belief of some deputies that the Convention's freedom of debate was being limited, and the conviction of others that the king's

---

62. See A. M. A. Girard, *Discours... prononcé le 17 janvier 1793*; P. F. Louvet, *Opinion... sur l'affaire du ci-devant roi*; C. A. Chasset and J. P. Rabaut Saint-Etienne, *Opinions*, notes 59 and 61 above; also J. P. Chazal, *Opinion... dans l'affaire du ci-devant roi.* M. A. Guadet (*Opinion... sur le jugement de Louis, ci-devant roi des Français*) makes the same point—"*la nation ne fut pas consultée. Une faction se mit à sa place.*" The apparent currency of this line of thought among the "inner sixty" is at least interesting. Dr. D. E. Kennedy has pointed out to me that the deputies had no understanding of the theological, rather than political, way in which Charles's trial had been approached.

63. To keep the king alive purely as a hostage was, to those who suggested it, not only more expedient but far more virtuous and humanitarian than upholding the law as it stood—despite any republican principle about equality before the law. For one deputy's reaction to this kind of patronage, see P. J. M. Châles, *Opinion...* (14 Jan. 1793).

trial must not only be free but be seen to be free. The Parisian gutter-radicals were not the only problem here. It seemed undesirable for the Convention to put itself in a position where its credit might be diminished and the enemies of popular sovereignty given a chance to divert attention from Louis's crimes to the alleged injustice of his accusers.[64] (More than a third of the Convention after all consisted of members of previous legislatures, who might be expected to have their own feelings about the man they had tried to make into a constitutional monarch.) There was also a rather lower-level argument that the Convention needed to retain public respect and should not risk its credit by turning itself into a tribunal which would have to take the blame for its verdict.[65] As to who should conduct the trial if the Convention did not, the common choice was either "the ordinary courts" with or without some small variation, or a special court chosen by the departmental assemblies, sometimes from members of the existing judiciary; occasionally the people, via the primary assemblies, were to choose the form of trial.[66] One deputy urged that the Convention choose a court from among its own members; the most ingenious proposal was Enlart's, that ninety-six judges be selected from deputies chosen by the "free peoples" of Switzerland, Belgium, and Nice.[67]

A major consideration in favor of the solution finally adopted was the limited attractiveness of any of these alternatives. Those who wished Louis sent before the ordinary courts as an ordinary criminal ignored the difficulty, foreseen by Mailhe in his report, of the king's relationship to those courts and to the law which they were obliged to administer. Any such trial could only raise the problem of inviolability all over again and in an even more intractable form. Moreover, the burden placed on the judges would be heavy and the risk of bribery or intimidation a real one.[68] A further practical problem concerning the existing judiciary was that the Convention had recently accepted an allegation, by Danton, Philippeaux, and others, that these judges had shown alarming tendencies to sympathize with the *ancien régime*. For this reason a decree had been passed throwing the Bench open to laymen as well as lawyers, whose training before 1789 was said to have imbued them with the wrong principles,[69] but there had naturally not been time or opportunity for much renewal to take place

---

64. A. A. M. Thibault, *Opinion . . . sur le jugement de Louis XVI*; for other comments, C. A. Balland, *Opinion . . . sur le marche à suivre pour juger Louis Capet*; I. Brunel, *Opinion . . . sur l'affaire de Louis Capet*.

65. F. M. J. Du Bignon, *Opinion . . . sur le procès de Louis XVI* and *Réflections . . . sur le jugement de Louis XVI*.

66. M. D. Pellissier, *Opinion . . . sur le jugement de Louis XVI*; F. A. Montgilbert, *Opinion . . . sur le jugement de Louis XVI*; C. Lambert, *Opinion . . . sur le jugement de Louis XVI*; P. R. Ducos, *Opinion . . . sur cette question: Louis XVI peut-il être jugé? doit-il être jugé par la Convention nationale?*

67. J. Julien, *Opinion . . . sur le procès de Louis Capet, ci-devant roi des Français*; N. F. N. Enlart, *Opinion . . . sur le jugement de Louis XVI*.

68. M. J. Lequinio, *Opinion . . . sur le jugement de Louis XVI*.

69. *Moniteur* XIV: 14–16, 23; for further reference to this incident from another point of view, see below, pp. 221–22.

or for its effectiveness to be tested. Under these circumstances, how could any judge in office be trusted with a crucial responsibility in the administration of revolutionary justice?

If the principle of a specially constituted court was to be accepted, the argument moved on to a different plane, and one on which the superior claims of the Convention were ultimately irrefutable.[70] Mailhe's contention, in the end accepted de facto by the majority, was that the king could only be subordinated to the law if the law were applied by the sovereign people. (To illustrate this, he produced a string of anecdotes showing how the rights of private persons might be used against princes.) Some deputies contended that the Convention had in fact been elected with instructions to try the king; others indignantly denied it;[71] but whatever the facts, it was not disputed that the Convention was a body representing the whole people and could act in the people's name. It was this which, in the eyes of Mailhe and others, distinguished it from the Long Parliament. The error of 1648, it was argued, was that Parliament should have remembered that it was a merely constitutional body, elected under the old monarchial forms, and should have recognized its duty to call a Convention representing the sovereign people, which would then have had every right to deal as it wished with Charles I. Instead Cromwell had set up a special court purely on his own authority, and England had duly suffered the consequences. The Legislative Assembly, on the other hand, had secured the election of a Convention as the vehicle of the national will; and in dealing with the king, who was subordinate only to the whole people, the whole people must act—to discriminate between the members of the body politic was to reject part of the popular will. Hence, by implication, a tribunal specially selected to try the king, either from the membership of the Convention or from the judiciary or from the population at large, was improper. The Convention *was* the embodiment of the sovereign people and must function as a whole, and its decision must be final. The only possible appeal was to the whole people, which was impractical; France was not Rome or Sparta. The people could not be gathered to hear the evidence and make a joint decision. The Convention could and, as the organ of the people, it should and must.[72]

This was not ordinary justice. But the case was no ordinary case, and lay of necessity outside the ordinary forms. There was no chance that ordinary stand-

70. Whether it was politic to insist on the claims being exercised was perhaps a different matter. J. F. Ducos was reluctant to think so (*Motifs... dans le jugement de Louis Bourbon, ci-devant roi*).

71. L. Turreau de Linières, *Opinion... sur Capet*; D. Le Maréchal. *Déclaration et opinions...* (17 Jan. 1793).

72. J. Mailhe, *Rapport et projet de décret, présentés... le 7 novembre 1792.* There were a number of very interesting discussions by deputies who had obviously spent a lot of time pondering the constitutional and philosophical implications of the trial. Some random samples: E. Finot, *Opinion... sur le jugement du ci-devant roi*; P. N. Philippeaux, *Opinion... sur le jugement de Louis XVI*; J. L. Second, *Opinion politique et constitutionelle... sur le jugement de Louis, et contre l'appel au peuple*; and A. Michet, *Observations sur le procès de Louis XVI....*

ards of procedure could be met, though every effort would be made to allow the accused to present his defense. This fact would have to be faced, and to pretend otherwise was sheer self-delusion. As one clear-sighted deputy wrote: "De quelque manière que vous termineriez avec Louis, vos mesures ne pourront jamais s'excuser que comme dictatoriales ... Nulle sanction du peuple ne sauroit les légitimer dans le sens des lois de jurés."[73] It was true enough that the Convention was biased, but what part of France was not? [74] Allowing that France was whole-heartedly republican, a thing which very few deputies were willing to deny, the case for removing the trial from the Convention on the ground of bias alone became difficult to sustain; as Amar said to Lanjuinais on 26 December: "Vous êtes tous partie intéressée, vous a-t-on dit; mais ne vous dira-t-on pas aussi que le peuple français est partie intéressée, parceque c'est sur lui qu'ont porté les coups du tyran? Où donc en faudra-t-il appeler? aux planètes, sans doute."[75]

And yet—and yet . . . It was for the Convention to act, on this the majority was agreed, but did it have to take on itself the whole burden of a crushing responsibility? To those who would have wished not to be involved at all there were now added those who were willing to accept that they could not avoid being involved, but who wished to spread the burden if they could. From this combination, and from the political rivalries of the first three months of the Republic, the idea of the *appel au peuple* was born.

IV

By the last week in December, it appeared that the holding of a popular vote in connection with the trial of the king might well be expected to serve a number of different ends. It would meet the objections of most of those who were uneasy about the form of the trial, and of those who felt that the deputies alone were not qualified to make a final decision. By associating the departments with the verdict, it would satisfy those who were concerned, or said they were concerned, that the king's fate might otherwise seem to have been settled by a blood-thirsty minority of Parisians. And by emphasizing France as against Paris, the nation as against the Convention—an emphasis it would not be easy to criticize—it was a weapon ready to the hand of those deputies who had failed to take the lead over the trial, but who badly wanted to seize the political initiative.

This last point is the one most usually made; historians have long claimed that the *appel au peuple* was at bottom a political maneuver by the Gironde against the Mountain.[76] Yet the move would hardly have been made if there had not seemed likely to be ample support for it, and it was not originated by the Gironde. It had been put up at a much earlier stage by at least two non-Girondin

73. J. N. Méaulle, *Opinion . . . sur l'appel au peuple.*
74. J. B. Leclerc, *Opinion . . . sur le jugement de Louis XVI.*
75. *Moniteur* XIV: 850.
76. See, e.g., Seligman, *La justice en France pendant la Révolution 1791-1793*, 2nd ed. (Paris, 1913), pp. 434-36; Sydenham, *The Girondins*, p. 138.

deputies[77] and had been considered by the Legislation Committee, although Mailhe's report finally rejected it. It was certainly in the air in mid-December, when the rapidly approaching conclusion of the trial made the moment of choice for the deputies uncomfortably close; as evidence of this there are pamphlets from two deputies, one inclining toward the Mountain and the other firmly planted in the Plain, both dated apparently 19 December.[78] At what point the *appel* was first discussed among the Girondins it is not possible to say, but the rapid delivery on 27–29 December of a number of speeches by deputies who had some personal acquaintance with each other, all putting up the same general proposition and holding the floor to the virtual exclusion of those opposing them, suggests a certain amount of forethought and organization.[79] The move for the *appel* was proper enough in itself. If the debate which opened on 26 December was to continue until the king had been sentenced, it was of the utmost importance to persuade the Convention as soon as possible that it should not have the last word. As Sydenham points out, the *appel* had, in principle, all the right emphases: it paid homage to the sovereignty of the people, it would restore national unity by destroying the suspicion that Paris was trying to dictate to the rest of France, and it would be embarrassing for the Mountain to try to oppose it.[80] The only predictable embarrassment for the Gironde lay in their failure to raise the matter earlier, since Mailhe had dealt with it more than seven weeks before, but by ironical good fortune so few of them had contributed to the debate before 27 December that the risk was not serious.[81]

77. J. J. Regis de Cambacérès, *Observations . . . sur le jugement de Louis XVI*; B. Albouys, *Opinion . . . sur la question: Si Louis Capet, dernier roi des Français, peut être jugé?*, in which Albouys (p. 2) rather testily claims the credit for having thought of it first.

78. J. F. Loiseau, *Opinion . . . sur le jugement du ci-devant roi*; P. Marec, *Opinion . . . sur l'appel au peuple du jugement du ci-devant roi* (for the dating of this speech, see its sequel *Supplément à l'opinion . . . sur l'appel au peuple . . .*). C. Lambert, in a pamphlet dated 23 December (*Opinion . . . sur le jugement de Louis XVI*), was more interested in getting a different form of trial than in the *appel* as such. It may be assumed that most deputies were waiting to hear Louis's defense before finally sorting out their ideas.

79. On 29 December Thuriot protested against the one-sidedness of the list of speakers, which thereafter became a little more balanced, but to that point only 2 speakers out of 14 had opposed the *appel*, and 6 of the 14 had been drawn from the "inner sixty." *Moniteur* XIV: 887.

80. Sydenham, *The Girondins*, p. 138.

81. Pétion had perhaps been rather too forthright on 3 December: "*Ce jugement ne peut être porté que par la Convention nationale,*" (Moniteur XIV: 650). To follow this a month later with "*il s'agit d'une circonstance unique, non prévue, dans laquelle l'assemblée sort de ses fonctions . . . et pour laquelle conséquemment elle ne peut se passer de la ratification du peuple*" (ibid., XV: 44) was an apparent contradiction that could hardly escape unnoticed. P. A. Merlin inconveniently went back to remind Pétion of what he had said in 1791 after Varennes, at the same time pointing out that Robespierre had remained perfectly consistent (*Opinion . . . sur le procès de Louis XVI*). Dufriche-Valazé, who had accepted the recommendations of the Mailhe report virtually *in toto*, did not draw attention to his change of position by publishing another speech, which might have been awkward, but simply voted for the *appel* when the time came. C. E. Dufriche-Valazé, *Opinion . . . sur le jugement de Louis Capet*.

On the level of principle, the argument concerned the rights of the sovereign power and the occasions on which these should be exercised. There was much citing of Rousseau's doctrine on the basis and proper use of political authority.[82] It was said that since the king's rights, such as they were, derived from the Constitution, his fate was a constitutional matter and the people must decide it; that the Convention's powers were not unlimited, therefore its decision could only be provisional and must be ratified; that since the form of the trial had been irregular, its ratification was essential; that since it had been agreed that the new constitution should be subject to ratification, it was only logic to have the decision on the king subject to ratification too; and there were variations and developments of all these themes and others similar to them.[83] But for the proponents of the *appel*, almost always entangled with these questions of principle were others of more immediate relevance. There was the matter of the sentence and what it should be; there was the matter of the effect of the trial on foreign public opinion; there was the matter of bias among the deputies which might discredit the Convention's decision before it had even been made; and there was the matter of alleged radical pressure both inside and outside the Convention which implied that no decision, however arrived at, could ever appear to be free if it were made on the Convention's authority alone. The *appel au peuple* was the way out of all these entanglements. But it is fair to say, from the way the case was put, that it would not have seemed nearly such a desirable or necessary way out if an overwhelming majority of the deputies supporting it had not been strongly opposed to the sentence of death which was the legal penalty for treason.

One of the strange side-effects of the campaign over the *appel* was that the issue over which the Convention was most deeply divided was never really debated at all. Though considerable numbers of the speeches produced in late December and in January were concerned chiefly with the sentence and what it should be, the actual parliamentary debate conducted between 27 December and 4 January slid immediately away from that question, raised by Saint-Just in the opening speech, to the question of the *appel*, raised by Salle in the third, and never concentrated on the sentence for any length of time. No one argued whether Louis was guilty; no one was prepared to say that he was not. But it did not often seem possible to discuss the sentence simply in relation to the crime.

82. C. A. E. R. Blutel, *Motifs énoncés sur la troisième question: Quelle peine Louis XVI a-t-il mérité?* (In this, the last of three speeches, he explains why he voted for the *appel*—"*la souveraineté du peuple ne pouvoit être représentée ni aliénée*"); F. A. Montgilbert, *Opinion ... sur le jugement de Louis XVI*; J. Savary, *Opinion ... sur le jugement du ci-devant roi*. No one reading the speeches of 1792–93 could doubt that Rousseau had a considerable public, and the quotations (and the disagreements over their implications) suggest that many of the deputies had actually read him.

83. J. M. J. Gaudin, *Opinion ... sur le jugement de Louis*; J. B. Personne, *Opinion ... dans l'affaire ou procès de Louis*; N. Bourgeois, *Opinion ... sur le ci-devant roi et son jugement*; J. C. Poullain-Grandprey, *Opinion ... sur cette question: Le jugement qui sera prononcé par la Convention nationale contre Louis Capet, sera-t-il soumis à la ratification du peuple?*

For the proponents of the *appel au peuple,* a sentence of death was associated not with Louis's treason, but with the "cannibalism" of the *septembriseurs.* The Parisians were the best-known advocates of the death sentence, and those deputies who were prepared to draw a veil over the massacres (or worse, excuse them) were all one with the nondeputies who had committed them. By handing the final verdict on the king over to the people, the Convention could evade the stigma of association with the September murderers and clear the blood from the name of the Revolution. It was argued that a death sentence, being irrevocable, should in any case be left to the people, who alone should be responsible for a decision that could not be reversed.[84] After the *appel* was lost, the battle over the sentence went on more desperately than before, being fought out from speech to speech as the deputies cast their votes, but its association with the *appel* from the beginning was no accident.

The emotional background of the campaign over the *appel* is suggested by the fact that about half of those supporting it stiffened their case to a greater or lesser extent by an impassioned attack on the "factions" of Paris and what one deputy described as *"les fureurs indiscrettes d'un parti." "*Où est donc," wrote Gaudin, "le caractère impassible et imposant que doivent avoir des juges? Je n'y reconnois que celui d'assassins."[85] Kersaint made the point explicitly: "On vous menace de guerre civile, on vous menace aussi d'une insurrection autour de vous, et des poignards des scélérats du 2 septembre . . . On veut que vous jugiez Louis à mort, et qu'il soit exécuté"—put your trust in the nation, he advised, this at least is to be depended on.[86] Coren-Fustier was even blunter: "Mon opinion consiste dans cette proposition. Les sections de Paris ont cherché à influencer la Convention par des pétitions; pour que cette influence ne soit pas reprochée, il faut que la nation entière soit consultée."[87]

There was a case to be made for the *appel au peuple.* It was true that there was distrust between the departments and Paris and that the massacres had discredited all who could possibly have had anything to do with them. Feeling in the Convention itself was evidence of that. It might be true that the French people would be more likely to accept a sentence which it had itself imposed, instead of one coming from seven or eight hundred individuals in Paris;[88] it might be true too that the departments, having suffered quite as much as Paris from Louis's tyranny and Louis's war, were equally ablaze against the tyrant.[89] It might be true that the fate of the king in some way concerned all those who had once sworn loyalty to him, that the inviolability which had once been given

---

84. P. F. Louvet, *Suite de l'opinion . . . sur l'affaire du ci-devant roi.*
85. F. Rivaud, *Opinion . . . sur le jugement de Louis XVI*; J. M. J. F. Gaudin, *Opinion . . . sur le jugement de Louis.*
86. A. G. S. Coetnempren de Kersaint, *Seconde opinion . . . sur le jugement du ci-devant roi.*
87. *Moniteur* XV: 16.
88. E. Neveu, *Opinion . . . sur le jugement de Louis XVI, prononcée le 17 janvier 1793.*
89. C. A. Bertrand de l'Hodiesnière, *Opinion . . . sur Louis Capet.*

to him by the people via the Constituent Assembly should only be taken away by the people, and that the sovereign power should make use of its rights whenever this was possible.[90] It was true that the trial was of interest to all Europe and that the revolutionaries might themselves be judged by what they did with their king.[91] But there was more to the problem than this. The *appel* might be a gesture, perhaps in a sense a necessary gesture, to popular sovereignty, but in practice it meant that the discussion of a highly controversial and vitally important political decision would be handed over to the mainly rural, largely illiterate, and variably informed six thousand primary assemblies, and its supporters had to be extraordinarily optimistic, myopic, or deeply prejudiced to discount the dangers it involved. It seems significant that virtually none of them would even admit the existence of these dangers, let along discuss their importance. Of all the eighty-odd deputies who published speeches in favor of the *appel*, only Beffroy looked squarely at the situation and decided that on balance the potential gain justified running the risk. He felt very strongly indeed about the Parisian situation, where, he said: "des hommes égarés, se qualifiant section de Paris, se croyant en droit de dicter la loi, ont prise des arrêtés menaçans contre la Convention même."[92] He admitted that royalism was still active enough to make the *appel* risky, but it was desirable that both the republic and the abolition of royalty should be publicly accepted, and that the appearance of intimidation by Paris—he denied the reality—[93] should be removed. Beffroy is quite impressive, but he is the more impressive because he was unique. The only danger that any of his colleagues would recognize was that the primary assemblies would not confine themselves to the matter on which they were supposed to be voting, and this, it was argued, could be dealt with by precise definition of the choices open to them. It is instructive to compare the sober realism of Beffroy's speech with the oddly limited vision of Fauchet, who claimed that the royalists opposed the *appel* because it would unite the Republic, or J. B. Louvet, who thought that a referendum over a new constitution would be far more contentious than one over the fate of a mere individual.[94]

These deputies were able to ignore the potential threat of serious disturbance, very likely amounting to civil war, because when they mentioned it at all

90. J. B. Colaud la Salcette, *Opinion . . . sur les trois questions . . .* (17 Jan. 1793), for the point about exercise of sovereignty. It was stressed by a number of others.
91. The *Moniteur* regularly reports English news and parliamentary debates, as well as other foreign news, on its front page. For remarks by Sheridan and Fox, who were normally sympathetic to the revolutionaries, on the possible fate of the king, see *Moniteur* XIV: 869, 881.
92. L. E. Beffroy, *Opinion . . . sur Louis le dernier.*
93. "*Ma conscience est à moi et à moi seul.*" He said explicitly that if factions existed, they were nothing to him.
94. C. Fauchet, *Suite de l'opinion . . . sur le jugement du ci-devant roi*; J. B. Louvet, *Opinion contre la défense de Louis Capet, et pour l'appel au peuple.* For the assertion that a definition of terms would be quite enough to secure a peaceful conduct of the vote, see, e.g., J. Pétion, *Opinion . . . sur le roi.*

they saw such a threat as a *fantôme*, a scarecrow erected by the extremists to serve their own interests. As Vergniaud saw the situation, the *agitateurs* would be glad to see the *appel* defeated, as they would be glad to see the king executed, so that they would be able to hold the Convention responsible for the disasters that would follow. The *appel* was opposed, the execution demanded, by *les ambitieux*, the would-be Cromwells who were seeking to build their own tyranny on the ruins of the throne. Such men had a vested interest in disorder and disunity and since the *appel* was the way to bring Convention and people together over the trial, they conjured up mythical dangers to defeat it. That they slandered the people of France in the process was only to be expected in view of their arrogant claim, demonstrably false, that they alone truly spoke for the people; and thus the argument came around again to the central problem of Parisian attitudes.[95] It is a striking fact that those speeches favoring the *appel* which do not in some way mention the Parisian radicals—these are about half the whole number, but do not include any of those by the main spokesmen—do not mention any of the problems of holding a popular vote either, but keep closely to its theoretical justification and/or the troubles to be expected if it were *not* held. In almost all the speeches, anti-Parisian or otherwise, the spectre in the background is not exactly one of Parisian domination as such; it is one of the Convention's being pushed by Paris toward a decision which many members were not at all sure should be made. What they were frightened of was the king's execution, which might drive a wedge between those who were responsible for it and those, more likely to be found outside Paris than inside, who did not want it. Hence the desire that the Convention should not shoulder alone a responsibility which should be spread as widely as possible, if indeed it had to be borne at all. It was the pressure of "Parisian"-type republicanism in and on the Convention, not the "illegal" pressure of Paris on the Convention, which was the problem. Many future Montagnards saw this; no Girondin was quite willing to admit it.

Some of those working to promote the *appel au peuple* may genuinely have believed that it might help to secure national unity. If, as has been argued above, they also had an underlying fear of Parisian republicanism, this might explain why their campaign had some curious deficiencies. What might have been attempted was a real effort to heal the breach between Paris and the departments; perhaps a heartfelt tribute to the services Paris had rendered to the revolutionary cause, coupled with a tactful suggestion that the natural anger of the *sans-*

95. Vergniaud's speech has thinly veiled references to Robespierre and Marat which no member of the Convention could have failed to understand. The single sentence of his which is in any way complimentary to Paris compares Paris's "*courage héroïque contre les rois*," about which no more is said, with its "*ignominieux asservissement à une poignée de brigands*," which is elaborated in several contexts. Gensonné evidently felt no need to observe the conventions and filled more than half his space with violent invective to Robespierre's personal address. P. V. Vergniaud, *Opinion . . . sur le jugement de Louis XVI*; A. Gensonné, *Opinion . . . sur le jugement de Louis*.

culottes over what they had suffered at the king's hands might make it wiser to bring the whole Republic together in formal responsibility for the outcome of the trial. Reference might even have been made to the Duke of Brunswick's manifesto, which after all did plainly state that in the eyes of the allies the citizens of Paris were hostages for the safety of their king. But this sort of argument required some sympathetic understanding of the situation in Paris and the feeling which had found an outlet in September as well as on 10 August, and perhaps this was why it was never used. Those who had the understanding saw no need for the *appel*, and those who wanted the *appel* were very rarely republican in anything approaching the Parisian sense.

It must lastly be said about this campaign that it left its leaders personally very vulnerable, since it was both controversial and identifiable with a particular group of deputies.[96] The potential difficulties of conducting the *appel* had been waved away with airy assurance by those orators who were urging its acceptance. The Convention, they said, had been elected without trouble, why should there be trouble over deciding what to do with the king? As for the notion that the primary assemblies might on their own initiative reopen the whole question of the trial, Vergniaud was quietly confident—"les assemblées primaires ne delibéreront que sur l'objet que vous leur aurez soumis; une puissance irresistible les retiendra dans le cercle que vous leur aurez tracé." And as far as dissension was concerned: "Des discordes! On a donc pensé que les agitateurs exerçoient dans les départements le même empire qu'une honteuse faiblesse leur a laissée usurper à Paris?"[97] The risk of civil war, it was alleged, was the agitators' invention. The Convention would do better to consider the disastrous results which might follow Louis's execution, particularly if this were ordered by the Convention on its own authority; this was where the agitators hoped to find material to destroy the authority of the government . . . This was all very well, but it was a line of reasoning which ignored a number of danger signals (for example, the unrest in the Vendée earlier in the year, the reluctance of some departmental authorities to recognize the fall of the monarchy, the circulation of royalist propaganda in Paris) and which, to carry conviction, required respect for the judgment of those putting it forward, for most of it was sheer assertion, with no evidence to support it. This was why the "Boze incident" of 3 January, when the Vergniaud-Guadet-Gensonné correspondence with the king in July 1792 was unexpectedly revealed, was extremely unfortunate. What was at stake was the Girondin reputation for political common sense.

The opposition to the *appel* had not quite the same flavor as the campaign in support of it. For one thing, oddly enough, there was a good deal less polemic.

96. The demand for the execution of the king, though often attributed mainly to Robespierre and his immediate associates, was much more general in the Convention than the demand for the *appel*, as the speeches show, and was much less clearly the prime interest of a limited number of individuals.
97. Vergniaud, *Opinion.*

One might deduce from the language of men such as Kersaint, Lanjuinais, Birotteau, Buzot, or Savary[98] that those who disagreed with them did little but fill the Convention's time with ad hominem abuse. Yet this gives a false impression of the debate in the Convention over the *appel* and of the pamphlets attacking it. Of the ten speakers who opposed the *appel*, Dartigoeyte, Carra, Jeanbon Saint-André, Dubois-Crancé, Saint-Just, Moreau, Prost, and Lequinio kept free of all but the most indirect of personal references, and Barère steered his way so adroitly between the competing factions as to produce a tremendously skilful debater's speech, by far the outstanding performance of the whole trial. Robespierre alone was plainly fighting a personal as well as a political battle, and even he spent more time in defense than in attack, and, in addition, dealt with some thoroughness with the practical implications of the proposal to convoke the primary assemblies. Unlike Vergniaud, he did not spend much time on constitutional niceties, but he did argue forcefully that since the people had already spoken once, on 10 August, on the subject of the monarchy, it was hardly necessary to enquire again: a point to which Vergniaud might have replied, but which he significantly ignored. The speeches in the *Moniteur* against the *appel* are, on the whole, far less frankly partisan and much more politically realistic than those in favor of it, and have less party rancor; and the same is true of the printed speeches. Some were extremely bitter, but there were not very many of these, and proportionately they were only about half as numerous as their equivalents on the other side.

The objections to the *appel* may be summarized as follows: (i) it was unnecessary; (ii) it was inexpedient; (iii) some doubt had been cast on the motives of those most responsible for pressing it. The first two points in one form or another were elaborated in almost all of the speeches attacking it, sometimes at very considerable length. If Rousseau had been quoted to justify the *appel*, he was now quoted against it, and the rights of a Convention as against an ordinary legislature, the extent to which representatives of the sovereign people could exercise their delegated authority, were thrashed out again and again.[99] All this, however, was largely a rationalization of a move on which the ultimate decision would be made for other reasons. The real basis of the *appelants'* case was not the theoretically limited constitutional authority of the Convention, but the fear that its effective authority might be undermined if its verdict on Louis were felt

---

98. For Kersaint and Savary, see above (notes 86 and 82); see also J. B. B. H. Birotteau, *Opinion . . . sur le jugement de Louis le dernier*; J. D. Lanjuinais, *Opinion . . . sur Louis le dernier*; F. N. L. Buzot, *Opinion . . . sur le jugement de Louis XVI.*

99. J. F. Ducos, *Motifs . . . dans le jugement de Louis Bourbon, ci-devant roi*, put some of this more succinctly when explaining his votes. The *appel*, he said *"m'a paru subversif de tous les principes du governement représentatif sous lequel je veux vivre et mourir."* This was one of the rare occasions in Ducos's career when he aligned himself on the same side as Marat (see J. P. Marat, *Discours . . . sur la défense de Louis XVI*). Marat however was not all froth and bombast, and during the argument over the trial more than one of his colleagues reluctantly admitted that he could at times talk sense.

to be dictated by Paris. The real basis of the case against the *appel* was that whatever the uneasiness about Parisian influence, it was utter folly for the Convention to risk compromising the whole future of the Republic by providing a ready-made platform for royalist propaganda, by way of a concession which had not even been asked for by the king himself.[100]

The most effective pamphlet which completely eschewed personalities, looking instead carefully and critically at both constitutional problem and political dilemma, came from Pierre-Louis Prieur: a long and careful summing-up which is remarkable not only for its clarity and common sense but for its lack of partisan rhetoric. It was not the greatest debating achievement of the trial; that honor, as has already been noted, was unquestionably Barère's. But Prieur was not trying, as Barère was, to refute the arguments for the *appel* while saving the face of the *appelants*, to construct a position in which people could vote on the same side as Marat without feeling contaminated by doing so, to adopt the Montagnard viewpoint while gracefully complimenting the Girondins on their oratory. That Barère could achieve this, in a speech which on its own terms carried complete conviction, showed extraordinary deftness, tact, and virtuosity.[101] Prieur was not attempting virtuosity and could not have achieved it had he tried. He was setting down his views on a public issue with perhaps even a little more than his customary firmness and thoroughness, since this was, to him, the only question in the trial over which the Convention was seriously divided. The result has a tang of its own. The quality informing every tightly argued paragraph is not brilliance; it is integrity. The Constituent Assembly, after all, was used to saying that a man of high standards was *probe comme Prieur*.

Prieur argued that the Convention's powers were unlimited and intended to be so, and that by accepting without any sign of disagreement Louis's trial at the Convention's hands the people had confirmed those powers and the way in which they were to be exercised. Since the trial was to be left to the Convention, it would reverse the order of authority if the people then had to apply the penalty; furthermore, the people could not carry out this task, since it could not be informed of the evidence nor organized to consider it, and would inevitably fall prey to what he described as *une grande fermentation des esprits*, of which the outcome could not be calculated and might well be very dangerous. Such a

---

100. Several deputies pointed out that it was unusual, to say the least, for an appeal to be requested by the judges rather than by the accused. One queried the propriety of the Convention's arranging an appeal from its own verdict. See, e.g., J. N. Méaulle, *Opinion . . . sur l'appel au peuple*; Jeanbon Saint-André, *Opinion . . . sur le jugement du Roi, et l'appel au peuple*. Deleyre rather acidly noted that if the Convention decided to hold the *appel*, it also became responsible for the results, whatever these might be; Le Cointre said that it seemed a little strange to ask the intended victim to pass sentence on the murderer; and Carra enquired what was expected to happen if royalist intrigue—and money—produced the wrong popular verdict. A. Deleyre, *Opinion . . . contre l'appel au peuple, sur le jugement de Louis XVI*; L. Le Cointre, *Opinion . . . sur le jugement de Louis Capet*; J. L. Carra, *Discours contre la défense de Louis Capet, dernier roi des Français*.
101. B. Barère, *Discours . . . sur le jugement ou procès de Louis Capet*.

decision would not protect the Convention from criticism; on the contrary, it would be alleged that the people was being made the blind instrument of an injustice which the Convention itself was unwilling to commit. Prieur summed up the case for all the anti-*appelants*: the Convention should bear its own burdens. He added his own conclusion on the proper end of the trial: Louis should pay the legal penalty for treason—"En prenant ce parti, nous aurons rempli le devoir que nous ont imposé nos commettans, le tyran sera puni, la liberté et l'égalité seront sauvés, la république triomphera, et, si nous encourons une responsabilité, ce ne sera pas du moins pour avoir pris des mesures qui auroient pu compromettre la tranquillité et le salut de la patrie."[102]

Prieur's contribution is worth considering carefully, because it illustrates an independence of judgment which the *appelants* were unwilling to concede to those who disagreed with them. Prieur did not want the *appel*, but he was not intimidated by the Parisian extremists either. As he pointed out, this was the first occasion on which the Convention had become seriously divided over an issue on which some sort of decision could not be avoided. The *appelants*, while proudly proclaiming their own imperviousness to threats, suggested that others might be more vulnerable. The evidence of the speeches does not support this suggestion, which was scornfully dismissed by one of the few men of the "inner sixty" who rejected the *appel*: "N'avez-vous pas toujours," wrote Carra, "la plénitude et l'intégrité de votre propre opinion à vous-mêmes?"[103] On the contrary it gives the impression that Carra was right. Those opposing the *appel* were a more diverse group than those supporting it, as later events were to show. What they had in common was their refusal to evade the duties they believed themselves to have accepted on election.[104] As far as the matter of ad hominem argument went, it was observed at the time that the blame was more widely distributed than the *appelants* would have conceded. Lambert commented contemptuously on what he said was the *general* substitution of prejudice for argument—this sort of thing, he said, was easier than thinking—and Bourbotte noted the speed with which the advocates of the *appel* moved from the discussion of central principles to the launching of partisan attacks.[105] The ad hominem attacks from the anti-*appelants*, such as they were—and some of them were very bitter indeed—were directed at the unworthy motives and selfish ambition of those urging a course so evidently favorable to the king. Some doubts about the quality of the *appel* campaign could be suggested as part of a factual discussion of the political issues; for example Bo, Bellegarde, and Briez were fairly dispassionate.[106] But it was easy to make a connection between the

102. P. L. Prieur, *Opinion . . . sur le jugement de Louis Capet.*
103. J. L. Carra, *Discours contre la défense de Louis Capet, dernier roi des Français.*
104. E.g., L. Louchet, *Deuxième opinion . . . sur le procès de Louis XVI.*
105. C. Lambert, *Opinion . . . sur le jugement de Louis seize*; P. Bourbotte, *Opinion . . . sur le jugement de Louis Capet, dernier roi des Français.*
106. J. B. J. Bo, *Opinion . . . sur le jugement de Louis Capet*; A. N. de Bellegarde, *Opinion . . . sur le procès de Louis Capet*; P. C. J. Briez, *Vues nouvelles sur l'affaire du ci-devant roi. Opinion. . . .* Briez was very worried by what he thought was disturbingly counterrevolutionary support for the *appel.*

possible results of the *appel*, if it were held, and the motives of those who wanted it, and in this connection the open hostility of most of the *appelants* to the idea of a death sentence was suggestive evidence. Méaulle was mild enough when he described the *appel* as, in his view,*"une mauvaise chicane et une herésie bien formelle en politique,"* but Guffroy let fly with a series of dangerously detailed reminders of the behavior of leading *appelants* over the previous six months, ending with direct accusation: "s'il y a ici un parti royaliste, il est là dans ce côté droit: et s'il existe un parti fédéraliste, il est là."[107]

Guffroy's speeches were among the most extreme examples of something which was characteristic of those who criticized the *appelants* themselves, as well as the measure they were proposing. Unlike the abusive sections of the *appelants'* speeches, which were fairly precise in direction but very vague in basic content, these attacks were based on an accumulation of circumstantial evidence which did actually exist and could be shown to exist. The *appelants'* targets were *les ambitieux* (read: Robespierre, and perhaps Marat), *les factieux* (read: most of the Parisian delegation, and some other leading members of the Jacobin Club), or *cette poignée de scélérats* (read: the most persistent of the interjectors from the left side of the Convention). The evidence of the *scélérats'* ill-intent was no more specific than sustained interjection and opposition in the Convention's debates, with the massacres and the unruliness of the Paris Commune as background material. The only piece of factual evidence, and one which was used again and again, was the failure of the Parisian authorities to search out and bring to justice the authors of the massacres; and this was evidence which, however suggestive, was not actually quite as telling as it seemed, since what had happened in Paris in the first week of September had been mirrored, on a smaller scale, in many other places between July and November. Birotteau's question: "Où voit-on ces horreurs, si ce n'est pas à Paris?" could have brought from several of his friends, had he asked them, an answer he would not have wished to get.[108]

The counterattack was different. In accusing the *appelants* of inconsistency, insincerity, covert sympathy for the king, and calculated manipulation of the Convention's procedures in their own interest, men like Guffroy and Pinet did not have to generalize. They could be damagingly precise. There were many

---

107. J. N. Méaulle, *Opinion . . . sur l'appel au peuple*; A. B. J. Guffroy, *Discours . . . sur ce que le nation doit faire au ci-devant roi*; *2ᵉdiscours . . . sur la punition de Louis Capet et sur les intrigues que l'on oppose à la volonté suprême de la nation qui a condamné le tyran*; and *Discours . . . contre le sursis à l'arrêt de mort du tyran*. It is fascinating to speculate how Guffroy's diatribes would have been received if he had been able to deliver them in the Convention. A good deal of what he said was specific enough to be perfectly plausible, if anyone had been listening to him, and some part of it (e.g., the reminder that only a minority of the Legislative Assembly had been willing to accept the fall of the monarchy) was undoubtedly true even if a number of his colleagues would have been glad to forget it.

108. It is, of course, true that it was the Commune's general attitude toward the massacres which made Paris so notorious; but all the same, many deputies did talk as though such things could not happen except in Paris, which was very far from being the case. See P. Caron, *Les massacres de septembre* (Paris, 1935), part 4. For Birotteau's views, *Opinion . . . sur le jugement de Louis le dernier*.

conventionnels who could remember well enough what part Vergniaud and others had actually played in national politics immediately before 10 August, as well as immediately afterwards; for such men, the "Boze incident" merely confirmed what they might already suspect about the willingness of the Girondins to run considerable risks in the interest of their own ambition. The long delays of the trial, the efforts of Manuel and Lanjuinais to secure further delays, even after the king's defense had been completed, could all be added to the total.[109] In the *appel* debate, the evidence of the *Moniteur* substantiates Guffroy's circumstantial claim that the Girondin secretaries were arranging the order of speakers so as to keep out their opponents as far as they could.[110] In sum, the case against the *appelants* was their political ineptitude, their personal ambition which made them politically irresponsible, and their willingness to make use of parliamentary machinery to serve purely personal ends. The accusations brought against the "Parisians," by contrast, might be even more disturbing in their implications, but they were much more difficult to document. Roland's nationally circulated suggestion that a Robespierrist dictatorship was being plotted in Paris rested on coffee-house gossip and an anonymous letter,[111] whereas the Girondin correspondence with the king, whatever its intention, was attested by witnesses and admitted by the Girondins themselves.[112]

109. *Moniteur* XIV: 848-54. For one contemptuous Montagnard summing-up of the motives which had inspired the Vergniaud-Guadet-Gensonné letter to the king, see Thuriot's comment of 3 January: "*Leur système a toujours été de faire des ministres.*" Ibid., XV: 47.

110. A. B. J. Guffroy, *2ᵉ Discours... sur le punition de Louis Capet....* There were 30 speeches delivered between 27 December and 4 January, of which 16 favored the *appel*, 4 (conservative in tone) did not mention it, and 10 opposed it. This balance bears no relation to the balance of opinion in the printed speeches. Although it rapidly became clear that the main conflict in this debate was over the *appel au peuple*, its organization was peculiar. The secretaries kept two lists—those wishing to speak *for* or *against*. The *for* list, dominated by those wishing to speak *for* the *appel*, also apparently included a few who still wished to speak *for* the king's inviolability—legitimately enough, since the question of inviolability had been raised by de Sèze, and was still open to discussion; but the result was that men could put themselves down as speaking *against* (inviolability), on the same list as those speaking *against* the *appel*, make a few formal gestures on the subject, and then go on to speak *for* the *appel*, which thus got a double chance of backing (cf. the title of the pamphlet by J. B. Louvet). Thuriot complained of this (cf. note 79, above). Hotheads like Guffroy, Pinet, and Poultier were not alone in protesting against this sort of manipulation. More moderate deputies also mention their difficulty in getting a hearing. The number of men of the "inner sixty," as against leading Montagnards, who spoke in the *appel* debate (11 against 4) is at least highly suspicious. According to Guffroy, Couthon was down to speak eleventh, was moved down to fiftieth, and in the end—this at least is true—did not speak at all. See Guffroy, *2ᵉ Discours*; J. Pinet, *Réflexions sur le jugement de Louis Capet*; F. M. Poultier, *... sur le supplice de Louis Capet*; J. P. Lacombe Saint-Michel, *Opinion... sur le jugement de Louis Hugues.* There seems evidence of some self-consciousness over Couthon, in that on 7 January Guadet offered to give way to him, if the debate were prolonged (*Moniteur* XV: 80). But note that Guadet was obviously higher on the list and was confident of speaking in the near future.

111. Roland, *Rapport du ministre de l'Intérieur à la Convention nationale, sur l'état de Paris; du 29 Octobre 1792* (Paris 1792).

112. *Moniteur* XV: 46-48.

It has already been argued that the issues in the *appel* controversy were such as to make this matter of political reputation extremely important. How much weight the "Boze incident" carried in deciding the majority attitude in the Convention to the *appel*, it is impossible to say. The evidence of the speeches indicates that the *appelants'* campaign would probably have failed anyway, but as it turned out, the result was not as close as the margin between the speeches in its favor and the speeches against it would have suggested, and the "Boze incident" probably had something to do with this. The decisive blow against the *appel* is supposed to have been struck by Barère in his speech of 4 January.[113] Barère however was speaking *after* Boze had made his disclosures, and both before and after this incident his reputation was that of a man who could perfectly gauge the way the wind was blowing—not of one who could step in to determine its direction. It seems highly probable that on 4 January he was not dropping the decisive weight into the scales, but simply becoming the spokesman for a majority view which had already been determined. There seem to be indications that opposition to the *appel* was considerable before Boze appeared on the scene, but the evidence he had to offer was perfectly calculated to strengthen the case of the Left.[114]

Whatever the truth here, it was Barère's speech which ended the debate on the *appel*, and in effect the whole debate on the trial. On 7 January it was decided that final discussion should begin on the 14th, after a week's pause for reflection and the printing (and presumably it was hoped the perusal) of the final speeches. It was clear that the king must be found guilty, and probable that the Convention would decide his fate. If he were in fact to be found guilty, and the Convention were to apply the legal penalty, that penalty was death. This was the point at which the *conventionnels* knew that they had come face to face with history.

V

When Saint-Just rose to speak on 27 December, he obviously believed himself to be opening a debate on the king's guilt and sentence. Although he mentioned the *appel* ("*on a parlé d'un appel au peuple*") he gave it only a few sentences, and concluded his address with a straightforward demand for an

---

113. Gershoy, *Bertrand Barère* (Princeton, 1962), pp. 145–46.
114. The effect of the events of 3–4 January on one Montagnard can be traced through the three speeches of P. F. J. Robert. He had first pressed for a trial for the king, not for summary execution—"*ne vous dis-je pas de l'assassiner, mais de le juger.*" In a second speech, he rejected the *appel*, while willing to respect the motives of the *appelants*; but in a third, evidently written after 4 January, his angry disillusionment left him quite willing to ascribe the Girondins' acceptance of what he called "royalist propaganda" to a pro-royalist attitude which he now felt he could trace back to July 1792. It is possible to envisage a similar development in men much less politically committed than Robert. See his *Opinion . . . concernant le jugement de Louis XVI; Suite de l'opinion . . . sur le jugement et les crimes du ci-devant roi*; and *3e opinion . . . sur le jugement de Louis Capet.*

appel-nominal on the question of guilt. When Barère wound up the debate eight days later, his final words had nothing to do with either guilt or sentence, but related entirely to the problem of the *appel*, which had become almost the only matter under consideration. A good deal was said in those eight days about a possible sentence, but there was no direct confrontation of points of view, as there was over the *appel*. The confrontation took place in the printed speeches—though even there, often in reference to another question, such as the competence of the Convention—and, more tensely, in the agonizingly prolonged *appel nominal* when the last efforts were made by both sides to win over a majority. But no new arguments appeared on 16-17 January during the *appel nominal*; what was then produced was a distillation of the case for and against the execution of the king, which had been put intermittently before the deputies since the clash between Morisson and Saint-Just on 13 November.

Throughout Louis's trial considerations of principle and considerations of expediency went side by side. The actual trial itself was justified almost entirely on grounds of principle, with its expediency sometimes thrown in as a kind of make-weight; the political situation which had brought about the fall of the monarchy also made the trial almost inevitable, and the matter of expediency was seldom argued, though one or two deputies made a despairing attempt to get the Convention to consider whether something might not be gained by dropping the whole thing for the time being.[115] Over the *appel*, the two kinds of argument became inextricably entangled. The consent of the people was needed, it was said, because the people was sovereign—and also because it might not approve a death sentence passed by the Convention on its own authority; because the people had the right to show mercy—and also because an execution might provoke internal conspiracy and widening foreign war; because the whole of France, and not only Paris, had the right to join in condemning the tyrant—and also because although the views of some of the Parisians were known, those of the departments were not, and might be different, and the chance of departmental grievance must be removed. (No *appelant* seems to have thought that the deputies had been elected to express their constituents' point of view.) If people and Convention disagreed, the people's will must prevail, that was clear enough, but the real misgiving was not over constitutional impropriety; it was over the practical consequences of such a disagreement. The *appelants'* case, founded on arguments from principle, got its force chiefly from arguments of expediency. Their opponents relied also on both kinds of argument, again with heavy emphasis on the second. In their eyes, the *appel* was constitutionally unnecessary and politically very dangerous, thus it was mistaken in principle and wrong in practice.

In the course of the debate over the *appel*, the alternative sentences which might be passed on the king were considered by the *appelants* almost entirely in

115. E.g., J. F. Barailon, *Considérations sur la necessité d'ajourner le jugement de Louis Capet et de sa femme* . . . .

terms of expediency. This continued to be the line taken to the end by the opponents of a death penalty. It was almost the only way in which they could construct an argument at all, since the law on treason and conspiracy was quite unambiguous. The single objection which could be raised to a death sentence as a matter of principle, should Louis be found guilty as charged, was that capital punishment was in itself barbarous and ought to be abolished. There was enough humanitarian feeling in eighteenth-century France for this view to have some appeal, and indeed the Constituent Assembly had staged a debate on the subject only eighteen months before, in which at least four future *conventionnels* had taken part. But although the number of capital offenses had been greatly reduced, the abolitionists had lost their case. The few *conventionnels* who thought, and said, either that the Republic should immediately abandon the death penalty or that they themselves would never impose one, were greatly outnumbered by those who accepted it as fair punishment for the crimes of which Louis had been accused.[116] If the deputies were to act as judges and apply the legal penalty, no choice was open to them.

There was however an alternative, which made the law irrelevant and allowed a decision to be made purely on a basis of expediency. The arguments over the method of the trial had revealed that many deputies were very reluctant to accept the role of the Convention as a judicial body, and with every move that had been made their numbers had increased. To those who thought that Louis could not be tried at all had been added those who thought he could not be tried by the Convention, and finally those who thought that the Convention could not itself arrive at a verdict, or that its verdict could not stand unless it were ratified by a popular vote. All of these men could claim that they had been put by the decision of their colleagues in a position which they were conscientiously unable to accept, and that all they could do was to choose, as legislators, the line of action which they felt would best serve the national interest. This left them free to disregard Louis's offenses and look at the various "sentences" which might be passed on him solely in terms of their possible consequences for the Republic. His fate would be determined not by justice, nor by equity, but by *raison d'état.*

Very few such deputies considered the expediency of putting Louis to death; a death sentence could be justified on other grounds, and expediency was never mentioned except as a subsidiary factor. What had to be justified was not executing Louis, but letting him live.

116. For opposition to a death sentence which he himself was to apply, see J. B. Jourdan, *Sur la peine à infliger à Louis XVI*.... Several deputies suggested that the Convention should abolish capital punishment, and Bernard-Saint-Affrique urged that to show that the Convention was above mere vengeance, Louis, the "*plus grand coupable*," should be the first to profit; this struck Drouet as a very odd idea, and Thirion pointed out that the king's accomplices had been executed with far less ceremony than was being required for Louis—were there then two sorts of justice? See J. C. Poullain-Grandprey, *Opinion ... sur le jugement de Louis XVI*; L. Bernard, *dit* Bernard-Saint-Affrique, *Opinion ... sur le procès de Louis XVI*; D. Thirion, *Opinion ... sur le procès du ci-devant roi Louis Capet.*

The reasons for thinking that a death sentence would be unwise rested partly on historical precedent and partly on estimates of the political situation both inside and outside the Republic. As far as precedent went, Birotteau was only one of a wearying series of authors who reminded the Convention that peoples such as the Romans and the English, who had killed their tyrants, had found that they gained little by doing so. The Romans by exiling the Tarquins had rid themselves of kings, but by murdering Caesar had destroyed the Roman Republic; Charles I dead had become Cromwell's stepping stone to tyranny, and Cromwell's tyranny founded on Charles's execution had produced the restoration of Charles II. Some deputies could even note that it was the choice of exile rather than death as a suitable fate for James II which had signaled the end of Stuart rule in England. (Strangely enough, no one seems to have heard of either the Fifteen or the Forty-Five; the general assumption was that an exiled king was discredited and ineffectual.) Other tyrants were mentioned by the more erudite, but the Tarquins, Caesar, and Charles I were the stock illustrations, and the greatest play was made with the aftermath of Charles I's execution, which was familiar to all deputies; the Convention was as nervous of a possible Cromwell as the post-1917 Russians were to be of a possible Bonaparte.[117]

In the internal politics of the Republic, the possible results of an execution were seen as anarchy, the revival of royalism, and the opening of opportunity for intrigues of all kinds. The logic of this is not perfectly clear; it seems to derive partly from a feeling that because the death sentence was so loudly demanded in Paris, the granting of it might discredit the Convention in France generally, and partly from a feeling that *les agitateurs* were demanding it in their own interest—they were Cromwells-on-the-make. It was seldom that any deputy said openly that the country was still royalist enough for the king's execution to be resented, since this went against the conventional assertion that the departments were quite as fervently republican as Paris; but it is interesting that two deputies, Buzot and Lanjuinais, who had strongly favored the *appel*, felt it necessary to stress that France was not as yet thoroughly republican. "Tous les Français n'ont pas perdu l'habitude des rois," said Buzot; this meant that an execution carried out only on the Convention's authority, to which the nation had not consented, might bring real trouble. Why under these circumstances he and Lanjuinais should have thought that the *appel* could be carried out without the least disturbance is not very easy to say, but they were both certainly convinced that there was enough sympathy for the royalist cause to make extreme measures against the king inadvisable, unless the people had been consulted first.[118]

117. J. B. B. H. Birotteau, *Discours . . . sur le jugement de Louis Capet*; P. J. F. Bodin, *Mon opinion sur l'affaire de Louis Capet*; J. E. Cappin, *Opinion . . . sur le jugement de Louis XVI, et sur le ratification par le peuple*; E. J. B. Bailly, *Opinion . . . sur le jugement du dernier roi des Français*; J. P. Rabaut, *dit* Rabaut Saint-Etienne, *Opinion . . . concernant le procès de Louis XVI*; J. B. Girot-Pouzol, *Motifs de l'opinion . . . sur le jugement de Louis Capet*.

118. F. N. L. Buzot, *Opinion . . . sur le jugement de Louis XVI*; J. D. Lanjuinais, *Opinion . . . sur Louis le dernier*. Carra made the same point about the unevenness of French

Others said, rather unkindly, that Louis was the least dangerous of all his family, that once he was dead his crimes would be forgotten, and that it was pointless to remove him so that the leadership of the royalist cause could pass into more skilful hands, with the Dauphin an innocent and attractive figurehead.[119] More positively, a king dead was a king martyred, whereas a king deposed and disgraced had lost both reputation and influence. Nor might it be only the émigré princes or the alleged counterrevolutionaries who might build on the ruins of the throne. Orléanist ambition was working to make sure that Louis died, and so were the would-be Cromwells who hoped to make anarchy their path to a new tyranny.[120]

An execution would also lower the Republic's reputation and add to its enemies abroad. The French, said Neveu, did not wish to be known as a race of murderers, nor did they want to present a propaganda weapon to the despots. A number of deputies argued that alive, Louis was a useful hostage and a possible pawn for use in peace negotiations; dead, he could be used by foreign princes to persuade their peoples that the war was a just one, and his death would probably provoke England and Spain into open hostility. Louis alive was unpopular and ineffective; dead, he might serve the purposes of all the enemies of the revolutionary régime. Chaillon neatly summed up this particular aspect of the case: "Qu'il vive pour tromper l'espoir des puissances étrangères qui le dédaignent, des émigrés qui le détestent, de Rome qui voudrait déjà l'avoir beatifié, des factions qui nous entourent et des Cromwell qui les dirigent." However the war might develop, the troops of the Republic would protect their country, but who would want to take the blame for thousands of unnecessary deaths? For even one more death? "Le sang appelle le sang; il est temps d'en arrêter l'effusion," said Dusaulx.[121]

A penalty of some kind was inevitable. If it were not to be death, and could not be exile until the war was over (though Tom Paine did suggest that Louis might be allowed to rehabilitate himself in the U.S.A.), then it should be prison until exile was practicable. This was acceptable as a security measure even to men like Meynard, who felt that the Constitution made legal proceedings impossible, or those like Viquy, who refused to take responsibility for an irrevocable

republican feeling, but used it to strengthen a case *against* the *appel* and in favor of execution, which would be accepted once it was over.

119. J. B. Girot-Pouzol, *Motifs de l'opinion . . . sur le jugement de Louis Capet*; P. M. A. Guyomar, *Opinion . . . concernant le jugement de Louis Capet.*

120. F. C. P. Garilhe, *Motifs . . . sur cette question: à quelle peine Louis XVI, ci-devant roi des Français, sera-t-il condamné?* ; C. N. Tocquot, *Déclaration . . . sur le sursis du jugement de Louis Capet . . .*; J. Dusaulx, *Opinion . . . sur le jugement de Louis Capet*; F. J. Gamon, *Opinion . . . sur la question de savoir s'il est de l'intérêt du peuple de surseoir à l'exécution du jugement qui condamne Louis à mort*; J. J. Thomas, *Opinion . . . sur le jugement de Louis XVI.*

121. E. Chaillon, *Opinion . . . sur le jugement de Louis XVI*; J. Dusaulx, *Opinion . . . sur le jugement de Louis Capet*; A. G. S. Coetnempren de Kersaint, *Seconde opinion . . . sur le jugement du ci-devant roi*; E. Mollevaut, *Opinion . . . sur cette question: Quelle peine sera infligée à Louis?* ; E. Neveu, *Opinion sur le jugement de Louis XVI.*

decision, or those like Garilhe, who felt that the trial, as it had been conducted, was illegal, and who would have no part of any sentence demanded by Parisian blood lust. For some deputies, the pressure from Paris was in itself sufficient to establish grounds for some lesser punishment than the one the *septembriseurs* expected.[122]

Many of the arguments advanced against execution were well-based and all of them were plausible, and they were bound to find support in the respect for monarchy which was deeply rooted in French life. Yet though the campaign for mercy could find plenty of sympathizers, it had one notable defect: it had very limited access to the revolutionary enthusiasm from which the Republic had to get its driving power if it were to survive. Those wishing mercy for Louis could appeal to the Convention's generosity, but on this he really had little claim; otherwise the campaign was based mainly on caution, a choice of evils, and the evasion of responsibility which featured so largely in the arguments over the *appel au peuple.* It could draw only peripherally on the passions and prejudices which had so far kept the revolution in being. On the other hand, those deputies who demanded a death sentence had a great advantage in that they could appeal directly to two of the most powerful sources of revolutionary emotion: the belief in equality before the law, and the belief that the revolutionaries owed it to themselves and to mankind to set Europe an example—in this context, to show Europe that revolutionary justice treated all men alike.

Discussion of the reasons for Louis's death sometimes proceeds as though the execution in itself were in some way unjust, unnatural, or uncalled for. Reluctant the *conventionnels* certainly were. They shared the normal feelings of a murder jury, perhaps emphasized by the fact that so many of them were well read in the humanitarian literature of their century, and they had two strong additional reasons for exceptional dislike of their job: it could not be carried out within any existing or normally acceptable legal framework, and it could not be justified except by reference to highly abstract principles of natural law. Against all this, there was the evidence brought against Louis, which was not seriously questioned, and the fact that they themselves had already a solid commitment to the revolutionary cause, as their presence in the Convention showed. If Louis were to be seen as guilty of capital offenses, and very few deputies suggested that he was not, then why should he not pay the legal price for his crimes? Uncertainty over the form of the trial did not necessarily imply uncertainty over the fate that should be met by the accused, and in any case the form of the trial had in fact been accepted by a very considerable majority.[123] The numerous

122. T. Paine, *Opinion sur l'affaire de Louis Capet*; F. Meynard, *Suite de l'opinion ... sur le procès de Louis XVI*; J. N. Viquy, *Opinion ...*; F. C. P. Garilhe, *Motifs ... sur cette question: à quelle peine Louis XVI, ci-devant roi des Français, sera-t-il condamné?*; J. C. G. Delahaye, *Opinion ... sur le jugement de Louis Capet.*

123. Several deputies discussing the *appel au peuple* pointed out that though there had been plenty of time for public protests to be made about the form of the trial, no petitions had in fact appeared. It was also noted that the deputies promoting the *appel* on the ground

deputies who had taken a death sentence for granted reacted with indignant surprise when they found that it was apparently necessary to advance reasons for carrying it out. Was *this* republican justice? Or was the old "superstition" or "idolatry" of royalty still present in the Convention itself? The king was admittedly guilty, the law on treason was clear, how could any republican refuse to apply it? Nioche explained that he accepted his role as judge as being legitimated by the powers of the Convention and its decision to conduct the trial. As a judge, he had no choice but to apply the law, and as the law laid down the penalty for Louis's crimes, he had no choice over that either.[124]

Louis's death would be more than a simple act of justice. It would be a demonstration that justice did not differentiate between human beings. Here the would-be regicides picked up the moderates' arguments about the expediency of an act of mercy and turned them inside out. They would not agree that the execution of the *ci-devant* king would weaken France's position in Europe, but claimed that so far as it would make any difference at all, the revolutionary cause would only profit from it. Foreign hostility to France did not depend on what happened to the royal family, it had other and more selfish origins. If the despots had not been moved to action by the September massacres, violence in itself would not influence them; and if they could ignore the abolition of royalty, what difference would be made by the execution of a king? Osselin emphasized the importance of the way in which Louis's case had been handled: had he been murdered on 10 August, or otherwise hastily disposed of, the despots *"comprendroient encore sa mort parmi les catastrophes ordinaires"*—but a formal trial, followed by a formal death sentence and execution, was a signal to Europe that a crown was no protection against punishment for murder.[125]

---

that the Convention should not act entirely on its own authority had not raised this point at the time when a Convention trial was decreed, but had waited until the very last minute to do so; this created a strong suspicion that their real aim was simply to save Louis's life. See C. A. Pottier, *Opinion... sur le jugement de Louis XVI*; J. B. Lacoste, *Discours... sur le jugement de Louis XVI.*

124. P. C. Nioche, *Opinion....* For references to the "idolatry" or "superstition" of the past as a source of royalist sympathies, see L. F. Roux, *Opinion... sur le jugement de Louis Capet*; P. J. M. Châles, *Opinion...*; P. N. Philippeaux, *Opinion... sur le jugement de Louis XVI.*

125. C. N. Osselin, *Quatrième discours contre le sursis proposé à l'exécution du jugement de Louis.* For discussions of the attitude of the despots to Louis's possible fate, J. B. Féraud, *Opinion... sur Louis Capet*; L. M. La Revellière Lépeaux, *Opinion... sur la question de l'appel au peuple du jugement de Louis*; P. R. Ducos, *Opinion... sur cette question: Louis XVI peut-il être jugé? doit-il être jugé par la Convention nationale?* Brissot himself expounded in the Convention on 12 January a number of reasons for growing English antagonism to the Republic, none of which had really anything to do with the king or his fate. It is interesting to compare this speech, made in a foreign affairs debate, with those he made on 1 January in the debate on the *appel*, and on 17 and 19 January during the voting on the king's sentence and possible reprieve. In the one speech which had nothing to do with the trial, he does not stress the king's fate as a factor in the foreign situation at all. See J. P. Brissot, *Discours sur le procès de Louis*, and *Moniteur XV*: 127–34, 221–22, 249–52. See also L. Louchet, *Deuxième opinion sur le procès de Louis XVI*; and J. P. M. Fayau,

In all this discussion, argument from principle (kings are but men) went hand in hand with argument from principle with expediency thrown in (well for mankind and for the Republic that Europe should be shown that kings are but men). A bargain over such a life was, for the regicides, not thinkable; they could not accept the proposal that Louis would be a useful hostage or bargaining counter to be kept in reserve against peace negotiations, and they would not accept, either, the view that a Republic with its king in prison would be more popular abroad than one which had made a royal criminal face the consequences of what he had done. Pottier pushed the argument for "mercy" to its logical conclusion when he asked the Convention how far it intended to go in order to avoid provoking the Republic's royal enemies: would it consider restoring the monarchy? [126]

From the evidence of the speeches apparently written before the voting in the trial opened on 15 January, one would conclude that the deputies were as sharply divided over the matter of the sentence as they were over the *appel au peuple*, and a good deal more evenly. (In trying to estimate feeling in the Convention, statements made after 14 January must be discarded, because of the claim sometimes made that after the defeat of the *appel au peuple* many deputies, hitherto wavering, switched their support to the Mountain and therefore voted for death.) The speeches suggest the probability of a very closely divided vote, with a small regicide majority; one cannot put it any more confidently than that because of the difficulty in assessing the final views of a number of deputies who published their speeches early, before they really had to face the question of the sentence, and a number of others who supported a death penalty while making it contingent on the holding of the *appel au peuple* to ratify it. If one assumes, as most of the Montagnards did, that nearly all the *appelants* were antiregicide, whether they said so or not, and wanted the *appel* either to gain support for their views or to avoid having to take final responsibility for them, the regicide majority among the speech writers narrows, but it does not disappear.

On paper, at least, this was not a conflict between views held in Paris and those current in the rest of France. The 69 men who were willing to go on record before 14 January as frankly opposing death came from 46 different departments; if those who made their acceptance of a death sentence conditional on the holding of the *appel au peuple* are added to the total, the number of deputies goes up to 93 and the number of departments represented to 55. (Two

---

Opinion... sur le jugement de Louis Capet, ci-devant roi des Français. Louchet noted the effect of an execution on supporters of divine right monarchy.

126. C. A. Pottier, *Opinion... sur le jugement de Louis XVI.* The "hostage" argument was used frequently by the antiregicides. See P. F. Duboë, *Motifs... lors les quatre appels nominaux...*, for one deputy's explanation of his final decisions, which favored reprieve for "hostage" reasons, and J. B. D. De Mazade-Percin, *Opinion... sur l'affaire de Louis Capet* [no. 2] for an earlier speech giving a variation on the theme.

of the open antiregicides were deputies for Paris.) The 104 deputies who said firmly that Louis should die came from 50 departments, and only 12 of them had been elected for Paris. Nine in every 10 of these would-be regicides (the members for Paris excluded) had either not been in Paris since 1789, or had been there as members of the Constituent or Legislative Assemblies—bodies which have never had the reputation of being especially friendly to radical Parisian ideas. Although nearly half of the 104 had some connection with the Jacobin Club, such Jacobins were by no means all Robespierrists; Anthoine, for example, who is said by Kuscinski to have greatly disliked Robespierre, was an avowed regicide nevertheless.[127] So was Guyton-Morveau from Puy-de-Dôme, a man of personal independence who was one of the greatest chemists in France; and Vadier from Ariège, the acid old lawyer who was no friend of Robespierre; and Robert Lindet from Eure; and many more.[128] Future regicides and antiregicides had been elected throughout the length and breadth of France. The dispute over the sentence does not look like a matter of a small Paris-based group getting control of a reluctant majority; as far as the evidence of the speeches is concerned, it looks like the Convention divided against itself, with the moral advantages fairly equally balanced between the two sides. The antiregicides could denounce those demanding the king's execution as murderers, no better than *septembriseurs*; but they themselves almost always had to begin with a formal recognition of the justice of a death sentence. No wonder that the regicides often felt that they were being asked to sacrifice conscience for convenience. A man like Maure could look on appalled at what he saw as the shameful descent from the proud republicanism of November, when the Convention's decree proclaiming the brotherhood of all peoples had urged the rest of Europe to cast off its shackles and its kings. This, he said, had been "un mouvement de fierté et d'enthousiasme digne de l'ancienne Rome"; but faced with the established guilt of their own king, the French had become *"politiques, faibles et pusillanimes,"* haunted by debates in the House of Commons, threats from Spain—"Quelle est donc cette inconséquence? Ont-ils oublié leur dignité?"[129] Others shared his disillusion and his anger. But for all that, as Barère for one was willing to recognize, there were many good republicans who did not find it easy to be on the same side as Marat.

127. Kuscinski, *Conventionnels*, pp. 7–8.

128. It was Guyton-Morveau who pointed out, in the course of a very shrewd speech dealing with the *appel au peuple*, that to entrust the decision on the king's fate to the primary assemblies would not remove fear of undue influence by the clubs, but would greatly add to it. P. M. A. Guyton-Morveau, *Opinion . . . dans l'affaire de Louis Capet, dernier roi des Français.*

129. N. S. Maure, *Un mot sur l'affaire de Louis XVI . . . .* This pamphlet, which makes its single point with great vigor and effectiveness, begins with the comment that its author had been listening carefully to the debates to inform himself, so that he may give the proper verdict. He was not the only deputy who obviously took the discussion in the Convention very seriously; cf. P. A. Lozeau, *Opinion . . . sur le jugement de Louis Capet . . . .*

VI

It will by now have appeared that the deputies' views on the issues of the trial and on the way in which those issues should be resolved were highly independent in approach, even if the points made were in practice somewhat repetitive. The "debate" was less a debate in the normal sense than a series of performances, each rehearsed almost in isolation from the others. Mailhe's report was of course the starting point for a number of speeches on the feasibility and organization of the trial, but did not always even rate a mention in such discussions. It was only when the *appel au peuple* became a point of controversy that there was much in the way of cross-reference between speeches, and even then it was commoner for a man to list the speakers he agreed with, and then give his own opinion, than it was for him to make any attempt at analyzing and evaluating the proposals already put forward. The style of presentation is best illustrated by the fact that most deputies who made use of historical analogy did so as though they were the first to have thought of it, though the points to be demonstrated and the illustrations used were almost always the same.

This being the case, it is perhaps unreasonable to expect any group of deputies to have taken up a markedly similar attitude over the trial. The possible divergencies look innumerable. Yet the trial did raise, quite clearly, the questions which were to bring about the eventual split within the Convention, and it was over these questions that the clash of opinion was most bitter. Paris and its influence, the Mountain and its alleged efforts to dominate the Convention by intimidation, the cliquishness, intrigue, and political irresponsibility of the Gironde, the dangers of encouraging counterrevolution by trying to find counterweights to Parisian radicalism, all these were brought forward and feverishly elaborated. If the issues in the trial were of national importance, the measures proposed were designed to serve personal and factional interests and prejudices as well. Hence if there was indeed any community of outlook between the members of the suggested political groups of 1793–94, one might expect to see it reflected in the way these men discussed the trial, the aspects of it they thought to be important, and the conclusions to which they came.

In the period down to 14 January 1793, 240 of the 730 deputies in our political analysis, or about one in three, made speeches on various aspects of the trial. Some produced more than one speech, some wrote on more than one aspect, some confined themselves entirely to one area of debate. The speeches can be classified according to the point of view put forward on the three major questions: (a) the feasibility or otherwise of trying the king, and the form of trial proposed; (b) the holding of the *appel au peuple*; (c) the sentence to be passed on the accused. (Some speeches can of course be classified under all these headings and others under only one or two of them.) To round out the picture as far as possible, a note has been made at the foot of the table of a number of deputies who published their contributions to the debate only after it was effectively over. During the course of the actual *appels nominaux*, many deputies gave explanations, either orally as they voted or in writing to the secretaries or both, of the way in which they proposed to vote and the reasons for their choice. All these explanations were recorded in the *appels nominaux*, and it was more usual to explain than not to do so; but some men took the further step of having their statements printed afterward as separate pamphlets, and among these were a number who had not previously stated their views on the trial at all, but who evidently felt strongly enough about the conclusions they had finally reached to wish to make them generally known. Such last-minute manifestoes from the hitherto silent have not been tabulated with the earlier speeches because they were put forward in different circumstances and may have been influenced by the course of events from 15 January onward; but their total number has been shown, to give an idea of the number of deputies in each political group who chose to publicize their views on the trial.

Two important qualifications must be made about any purely statistical study of the speeches. First, the inferences to be drawn from the table must be at best very tentative, because of the lack at present of any comprehensive bibliography, the possibility that a number of speeches have not survived, and the fact that the tally recorded in the table is incomplete even as regards those which have survived.[130] Second, the speech writers cannot be considered as exactly a cross-section of the political groups in which they have been placed, being obviously more articulate and presumably more involved in political conflict than those of their colleagues who did not engage in pamphleteering, so that the results shown in the pamphlet may well exaggerate differences of attitude between groups. But here at least, if anywhere, differences of attitude should certainly show themselves if the political classification has any validity at all.

As these figures stand, they indicate that the deputies most interested in the process of the trial were the Girondin "inner sixty" and the future Montagnards of the Jacobin Club of Paris. In proportion to their numbers, both these groups contributed to the discussion far more frequently than the rest of the Convention. It is possible that the results are distorted because many of the members of these two groups were well-known politicians whose work was more likely to be preserved than that of men comparatively unknown, but by no means all of either the Girondin or Jacobin speech writers were famous, and it would take an improbable number of undiscovered contributions from the Plain and from the rank-and-file of Mountain and Gironde to redress the balance shown in the table,

---

130. J. M. Thompson (*The French Revolution* [Oxford, 1943], p. 327) refers to "some three hundred and fifty" pamphlets. The table includes deputies who produced between them a total of 391 speeches, and 12 more came from 9 of the 19 deputies who have not been politically classified, giving a total altogether of 403. I think several more have certainly been lost. Lafon and Vermon produced statements relating to their personal position, but not to the issues of the trial. J. F. Ducos's first speech is omitted, as I have not managed to see it.

Table 2. Political attitude, 1793–94, of deputies making speeches on the trial of Louis XVI, before 15 January 1793

	GIRONDE			PLAIN			MOUNTAIN				Total
	"Inner 60"	Other	Total	À l'ecart	C'ttees	En mission	Jacobin	Mont-agnard	Other	Total	Total
(a) speeches concerning the form of the trial											
Against a trial											
(a) impossible	5	8	13	3	2	2					20
(b) unnecessary				1		2	11	2	2	15	18
Trial, not by Convention	7	15	22	6	7	3	9	1	3	13	51
Convention trial	12	12	24	10	12	4	37	15	18	70	120
total	24	35	59	20	21	11	57	18	23	98	209
(b) speeches on the *appel au peuple*											
For	17	16	33	10	14	4	1		2	3	64
Against	2	6	8	4	7	3	47	15	15	77	99
total	19	22	41	14	21	7	48	15	17	80	163
(c) speeches on the king's sentence											
Against death	14	24	38	12	9	8			1	1	69
Death, but people's ratification needed	7	4	11	4	9						24
For death	4	5	9	1	4	3	49	18	20	87	104
total	25	33	58	17	22	11	49	18	21	88	197
Number of deputies making speeches before 15 January	30	36	66	22	29	14	64	19	26	109	240
Speeches printed, made 15-20 January	3	10	13	13	9	2	1	1	2	4	41
Number of deputies stating their position on the trial in print	33	46	79	35	38	16	65	20	28	113	281*
Number of deputies in the whole political group, 1793–94	58	120	178	119	94	37	142	73	87	302	730

*These figures do not tally with those on p. 39, above, because they exclude deputies from the "unclassified" group. Of these, nine men printed pamphlets before 15 January 1793; 4 were radical in tone and 5 conservative. Two radical pamphlets, and all the conservative ones, dealt with the sentence—result, 2 in favour of a death sentence and 5 against it. The only "unclassified" deputy to make a statement after 15 January which was relevant to the issues of the trial was Le Peletier, but he had already printed two pamphlets on the trial itself.

in which the activity of the groups from the Plain seems to vary in proportion to the degree of their activity in 1793-94—the *en mission* deputies producing the greatest proportionate volume of pamphlets and the *à l'écart* deputies the smallest. The problem which attracted most attention was that of the form of the trial, with the sentence running a fairly close second and the *appel au peuple* a mediocre third. The vocal members of the "inner sixty" were divided, but tending to conservatism, on the more general issues, and almost unanimous on the countermove against Paris represented by the *appel au peuple*; the Plain was also divided, with a conservative majority, but with a radical element tending to increase in size in proportion to the degree of later cooperation with the Jacobin régime. The figures are so small that this result may be quite delusive, yet it is consistent, and the unhappiness of the "committees" deputies over the question of the king's sentence is obvious. The Mountain, on this evidence, was quite astonishingly united. In proportion to their numbers, the Montagnards were not exceptionally vocal, except for the Jacobins who could be matched by the "inner sixty" at the other end of the scale; but their contribution to the debate had extraordinary impact because of its lack of ambiguity.

When the figures are looked at in detail, one fact seems clear. This is that the Montagnards were the only group of deputies strongly in favor of a Convention trial. Among the Girondins there was no consensus, and the Plain had no effective majority either, being almost equally divided between those who were willing to accept a Convention trial and those who wanted something else without being agreed as to what it should be. Since this was the subject on which the largest number of deputies felt they had something to say, the figures, such as they are, are worth careful attention. For the Mountain, it seems that the point of view expressed by Robespierre on 3 December was the exception rather than the rule even among members of the Jacobin Club. As far as the Girondins are concerned, it is interesting to note the number willing to argue a case for the king's inviolability.

With the *appel au peuple* came a straight clash of opinion between Gironde and Mountain, the Plain being a little less confident of where it stood. The "inner sixty," or those of it who expressed an opinion, decisively backed the *appel*, the Mountain was even more decisively against it. There was however what looks like an anomaly, in that although the campaign for the *appel* was a Girondin-initiated project, relatively *more* Jacobins than "inner sixty" published pamphlets dealing with it. The explanation may lie in the unrepresentative nature of the parliamentary debate, already referred to. Chances to plead a case in the Convention were very valuable because they were so limited. The Girondin "inner sixty" produced seventeen speeches in favor of the *appel*, of which nine were delivered in the Convention itself before they were printed, and of the sixteen favorable speeches from the Girondin rank and file, five similarly figured in the Convention debate. Of the Montagnards, only nine in all, including seven Jacobins, had the same chance to reach their audience directly; hence, perhaps, a stronger incentive to make use of the only means of influence which remained. To print a speech which could never be heard by a live audience was better than nothing. But it was not the same thing, as the Girondin Petit said when he despondently published his views for a second time with the comment that his colleagues were probably too swamped with reading matter to have noticed his earlier pamphlet.[131]

With the question of the sentence, the position was different. Among the Girondin pamphleteers, this attracted very nearly the same attention as the question of the trial had done, whereas the Jacobins were rather less interested. This was a matter over which a good many members of the "inner sixty" were plainly concerned, even if they could not decide what to do. In proportion to their total numbers, there were fewer Jacobins urging an immediate death sentence than there were men from the "inner sixty" arguing for mercy or delay; and those favoring a death sentence certainly did not dominate the debate in the Convention at any time. Yet it appears from the Girondin speeches, and from others, that many *conventionnels* sincerely felt that the Mountain was exerting illegitimate pressure in favor of a death sentence, and that the pressure did not come only from the spectators in the tribunes—who actually, considering what was often said about them, were surprisingly well behaved.

If it is assumed that the political groupings of the Convention have been fairly accurately estimated, the difficulty is easily recognized: it was one of total numbers. Proportionately, the Jacobins might be no more vocal than the "inner sixty," but in absolute terms they were much more numerous, and the result was a formidable body of unrelentingly regicide propaganda. The figures do indicate the absurdity of the repeated Girondin insinuation that the death sentence was being demanded by "a handful" of the extreme Left; more than half of the many speeches dealing with the sentence were from would-be regicides. But this did not mean that the result of the *appel nominal* was a foregone conclusion. The uncertainty of the whole position, and the tense atmosphere in the Convention during the voting, are foreshadowed by the comparatively small bulk of opinion which emerged from the less committed sections of the Convention. *If* the speeches provide any lead to the balance of opinion in the different groups, it *looks* as though the rank-and-file Montagnards would be solidly regicide, the rank-and-file Girondin less solidly, but quite definitely, antiregicide, the Plain divided but on the whole antiregicide too; but the figures are so slender that this is really little more than guesswork. No one before 15 January could have deduced at all confidently, from the published speeches alone, how the voting was likely to go on the sentence, if only because to trust the evidence of the speeches would have meant predicting a unity of attitude among all the various

131. E. M. Petit, *Opinion . . . sur le jugement de Louis Capet, dernier roi des Français* [no. 2]. Petit produced two speeches with the same title and virtually the same argument in many ways; the complaint about the Convention's mental indigestion comes from the second. He himself had little reason to complain, as this second speech had in fact been delivered in the Convention on 1 January.

Montagnard groups which was to be found nowhere else in the Convention. Over the *appel*, a reasonable guess might have been made, but it could hardly be said to be a certainty.

A final interesting point emerges from a consideration of the eleventh-hour contributions which are shown near the foot of the table. It will be noted that very few of these came from either the Jacobins or the "inner sixty"; in fact the Mountain as a whole produced hardly any; whereas a wholly disproportionate number were provided by the Plain and the Girondin rank and file. It is to be remembered that these particular speeches were only published (as distinct from being delivered in the Convention) after the outcome of the trial had been decided; they therefore had no practical purpose other than to justify the behavior of the deputies who wrote them. (For this reason, no attempt has been made to tabulate the last-minute offerings of men who had already made their position clear in earlier speeches. There were in fact not very many of these.) Of the total of forty-one speeches, thirty-three were antiregicide, and four of the remainder were from deputies who remained undecided to the last. Four only were from regicides, and of these one was from a member of the "inner sixty" who had ended by flatly rejecting the views of most of his friends and had perhaps mainly personal reasons for making his position clear. It is possible that since the anti-regicides had been defeated, they felt a special need to account publicly for their reluctance to accept the majority verdict, and it is also possible that the regicides were satisfied with the prospect of the official Convention pamphlet dealing with the trial and its results, but the disproportion is striking nevertheless. If the regicides had had any qualms about the public reception of what they had done, one would have expected them to be rather more active in justifying it.

* * * *

In reviewing this long and tangled controversy, one cannot help being struck by the constant recurrence of themes which were to become exhaustingly familiar in the early months of 1793. Nearly every criticism to be made by the Gironde of the Mountain, and by the Mountain of the Gironde, had been given an airing by the middle of January. True, the conduct of the war had not yet become a major issue, but the pleas of Brissot and others for Louis's life were based largely on foreign policy considerations which the Mountain—and eventually the Convention—refused to accept. The weapons which the Girondin leaders proposed to use against their opponents appeared clearly in the course of the campaign over the *appel au peuple*, and this campaign too, before it ended, provided much of the evidence on which the Montagnards were to build their future claims about Girondin "royalism" and "federalism," as well as less subjective evidence of Girondin irresponsibility.

On paper, so far as the speeches go, the Gironde lost the battle. On all the really controversial points a majority of the Girondin pamphleteers opposed the Montagnard line, but the Mountain could always scrape up enough support, including some from Girondin dissidents, to carry the day. This however was on paper only. Many of the speeches were written before the authors had to come to grips with the responsibilities of personal and perhaps irrevocable decision. Furthermore, the opinions of more than 60 percent of the deputies remained down to 15 January completely unknown. The speeches suggest that the Mountain was a far stronger force than the Gironde was willing to allow, but they provide no evidence for the balance of feeling in the Convention as a whole; they can only be suggestive. The evidence for the whole Convention, not only of what deputies said but of what they finally decided to do, lies in the *appels nominaux.*

CHAPTER 4

THE TRIAL OF LOUIS XVI (ii): THE VOTING AND ITS IMPLICATIONS

I

When the last stage of Louis's trial opened on 14 January 1793, none of the controversies aroused by it had been settled, and this although some accepted compromise seemed to be necessary if it were to reach any conclusion at all. On 14 January the deputies expected to have to vote almost immediately, but what they were to vote on and in what capacity they would be acting was still undetermined. Some would accept a quasi-judicial status and others would not, some would accept the Convention's right to make a final decision and others would not, and these disagreements were fundamental to the arrangement of the voting, since they must inevitably influence both the formulation of the questions to be voted on and the very order in which those questions were to be presented for decision.

Since the beginning of October the Convention had proceeded in an ad hoc manner, making practical decisions and leaving its members free to differ among themselves about the underlying principles involved. On 14 January some of the deputies tried for the last time to get their colleagues to make a definite ruling on the Convention's constitutional position over the trial and the exact principles on which it claimed to justify its actions; and for the last time they failed. It was clear from that day's discussion, as well as from the previous three months' debate, that the forcing of a motion on such a subject would irreparably divide the assembly before the main question, that of what to do about the king, had even been broached. The only way out was to continue as before, ignoring constitutional problems and allowing those taking part in the trial to assign to themselves whatever status they chose; and after a wearing day of confused debate which lasted until 10 P.M., this situation was finally recognized.

It is hardly surprising that the discussion of 14 January fell into a state of such utter chaos that toward the end the harassed *Moniteur* reporters completely abandoned any attempt at detailed record. Apart from what may have been said during the several hours of *"indécision tumultueuse"* noted in the *Moniteur*, each of twenty speakers made independent suggestions about the motions which should be voted on, or the order in which these motions should be presented, or both. Whether these suggestions were intended to support, to modify, or to replace other proposals already made, they were introduced in their own right; there was no formal procedure of presentation or amendment, and, as the *Moniteur* rather sourly observes, the variations were so great that it was not possible to weed them out by the elimination of alternatives. (For example, no part of Daunou's complicated scheme was ever discussed at all.)[1] In the end it was left to Boyer-Fonfrède, one of the few Girondin regicides, to collect the attention of his exhausted fellows with a few common-sense remarks and a simple straightforward set of motions to which it was hard to find reasonable objection: though it seems likely that at any earlier stage in the proceedings some deputies would certainly have tried. For the first time that day, there was immediate agreement, and the Convention thankfully went home to bed.

The thread running through the whole argument was the effort of the Right to get the Convention to define its position, or, failing that, to register an implicit doubt of its own authority by conducting a vote on the *appel au peuple* before it did anything else. The Left wished the first vote to be taken on the question of whether or not the king was guilty as charged. Since there was no serious proposal that the people be consulted about Louis's guilt or innocence, it being generally admitted that only the Convention was in a position to examine the evidence, there was really no logical reason why this should not be taken first, but the Girondin *appelants* plainly felt that the *appel* would have a better chance of acceptance if Louis were not a convicted traitor before a vote on it was held. Lehardi, who opened the debate, urged emphatically that the *appel au peuple* be given absolute priority, and all the other Girondin *appelants* who spoke on the subject agreed with him. Réal, an *appelant* from the Plain, did not, being willing to admit that the question of guilt was obviously primary; a division here appears between those who were more and those who were less concerned with purely political maneuvering which may help to explain the outcome of the debate. It is noteworthy that two of those pushing for an immediate vote on the *appel* insinuated that the king might be in danger of being lynched by the mob if he were found guilty before the matter of the *appel* had been settled. The reasoning here is not exactly clear, but the aspersion on Paris was clear enough, and, interestingly, got a cool reception.[2] Boyer-Fonfrède's final

1. *Moniteur* XV: 152. For the whole debate, ibid., pp. 144, 149-52. Daunou's contribution appears on p. 144. The *Moniteur*, presumably by a printer's error, identifies him as Danton (E. Seligman, *La justice en France pendant la Révolution, 1791-1793*, 2nd ed., [Paris, 1913], p. 460).
2. *Moniteur* XV: 149-50 (J. B. Louvet), p. 152 (Loysel). For Lehardi, ibid., p. 144; Réal, ibid., p. 150; Boyer-Fonfrède, ibid., p. 152.

motion put the voting in the following order: Louis's guilt or innocence first, the *appel au peuple* second, the nature of the sentence third; he discarded all other proposals, including those providing for a popular ratification of the Convention's power to try the king, which would in theory have been an ideal solution of the whole quarrel over the *appel*. If constitutional matters were to be put on one side, and this seemed much the easiest thing to do, then this was an order of priorities which would allow those voting on the sentence to know before they did so whether their verdict was to be final, but which began by establishing whether a sentence was necessary at all; a natural progression which was hard to challenge. As Boyer-Fonfrède pointed out, the question of Louis's guilt was not only fundamental but effectively independent of the political question raised by the *appel*, and one cannot but feel that the Girondin *appelants'* anxiety to push it into the background reveals a good deal of their whole attitude over the trial.

Monday 14 January was in itself sufficiently trying. The remainder of that week proved to be the most demanding period in the whole history of the Convention, and it is remarkable that the deputies were not reduced by it to a state of complete hysteria. The voting opened on Tuesday morning with the *appel nominal* on the question of guilt. Since 95 percent of those present could answer this with a simple affirmative, it was over comparatively quickly and could be followed at once with that on the *appel au peuple*, which also was completed the same day. In accordance with Boyer-Fonfrède's program, there came next the vote on the sentence.

For most of the deputies the *appel* on the sentence would in any case have been a highly emotional experience. The defeat of the *appel au peuple*, by leaving the king's fate entirely in the hands of those present to vote, raised the tension to an almost unbearable level, as some of the exchanges on Wednesday revealed. The voting should have begun in the morning, but was considerably delayed, first by some items of ordinary business—government had after all to continue, trial or no trial—then by an edgy quarrel over the police and security situation in Paris, and finally by a desperate effort led by Lanjuinais to make the validity of the sentence dependent on its securing a two-thirds or even a three-quarters majority.[3] This was rejected as being contrary to the Convention's usual procedures, but even legally it rested on a confusion over the capacity in which the deputies were acting: as was later said, the majority being referred to was that which the law laid down for juries, and the sentence was a matter for judges.[4] The pursuit of so forlorn a hope at so late a stage suggests, rather interestingly, that the antiregicides had begun to abandon hope and were more concerned with frustrating a regicide majority than with gaining a majority themselves, or with the dangers of the situation which might arise if they succeeded in aborting the vote.

3. *Moniteur* XV: 183–84.
4. See Seligman, *Justice en France*, p. 470; also *Moniteur* XV: 231, for P. A. Merlin on this.

The voting on the sentence thus did not actually begin until eight o'clock at night, and went on all night and all the next day, for twenty-four hours in all. By the time the votes were counted, the king's defenders heard, and their last minute pleas for a popular vote refused, it was 10:30 P.M. Next day the deputies assembled as usual, nevertheless, dealt with correspondence, conducted a checking-through of Wednesday's and Thursday's voting, and again adjourned at ten-thirty after the matter of a possible reprieve had been raised, though some of the Left wanted to hold an *appel nominal* on the reprieve forthwith, and the rather high-handed adjournment of the debate led to a scene in which perhaps half the Convention remained behind until midnight to voice a series of angry protests. On Saturday at 10:30 A.M. proceedings were resumed.[5] The project for a reprieve for the king produced a series of formal speeches, and a fourth, unscheduled *appel nominal* which caused the sitting to run for sixteen and a half hours without a break. At 3 A.M. on Sunday the final decree providing for the execution of the death sentence was passed. Later in the day the deputies were again in session, to approve the detailed arrangements and to hear also an emotional letter of resignation from Kersaint (one from Manuel having been submitted the previous day) written in furious protest against the voting of the death sentence. When Sunday's adjournment came at 5 P.M., the members had been officially off duty for only three periods of time, totaling in all somewhat less than thirty-six hours, since ten o'clock on Wednesday morning. The tone of the letters sent by Manuel and Kersaint can be explained in part by physical and emotional exhaustion as well as by moral outrage.[6] But the week's events had yet to be rounded off by an ironic postscript. On Monday, the twenty-first, almost as Louis died, the deputies were told of the murder of Le Peletier de Saint Fargeau the evening before. Those who had resisted Louis's execution had for months complained that by doing so they were running the risk of being attacked by the mob; those who had consented to it could now be gratified by evidence that they might well be assassinated by royalists as a result. It was four months to the day since royalty had been abolished in France.

II

The evidence contained in the *appels nominaux* was so obviously of national importance that it was later published by the Convention: rather curiously, in

5. The unfortunate secretaries, to all of whom the voting of the death sentence had come as a heavy personal blow, were censured for not being in their places when this sitting began. The censure was later lifted for Gorsas, who came hurrying in a few minutes afterwards to explain that having worked for 36 hours on Wednesday and Thursday, and all of Friday, on the *procès-verbal*, he had been held up on his way to the assembly by stopping to try to get from Manuel the minutes for which he had been responsible. *Moniteur* XV: 240.

6. See *Moniteur* XV: 242–43 (Manuel), p. 255 (Kersaint). Manuel had been one of the secretaries, and may well have written his letter, which was read in the Convention on Saturday, in the throes of a violent reaction after the strain of the thirty-six-hour session which ended on Thursday evening. During the tense period which elapsed between the end

three pamphlets, one giving the record of the voting on guilt, on the *appel au peuple* and on the reprieve; one entirely devoted to the sentence; and one giving all four *appels* and a note of the proceedings on Friday 18 January, when the voting in the sentence was checked over.[7] These pamphlets were, of course, compiled after the event and were not issued until February, so that what they contain is not necessarily what the Convention heard, or may have heard, on 15-19 January. The original lists of 16-17 January were amended on the eighteenth, and the record was again examined before they were printed.[8] It seems unlikely that any deputy later changed the sense of what he had already said publicly in the Convention, though a few seem to have made clearer statements of what they had intended to convey; but it must nevertheless be remembered that the *appels nominaux* as published, as also the *procès-verbaux*, are not verbatim transcripts, and that in some instances where they conflict with what is reported in the *Moniteur* there is no way of knowing which version more faithfully represents what actually took place. In one particular aspect, the Convention's pamphlets are actively misleading. The total vote for each *appel* shown in the pamphlets, itself not necessarily accurate, is in no case exactly the same as the total which was announced to the Convention at the time. For evidence of what the Convention was told about the results of the voting, as its various stages proceeded, one must rely entirely on the *Moniteur*, since the pamphlets and the *procès-verbaux* of 16-18 January were edited to provide evidence not of what the president actually did say, but of what he should have said had the secretaries more accurately reported the facts. Given the length of the proceedings, the emotional strain, and the muddled way in which many deputies stated their views, complete accuracy perhaps could hardly be expected. On the other hand, four secretaries were continually on duty,[9] to check each other's work. It is not the individual error which is in issue here. Careful checking and crosschecking, so far as this is possible, suggests that the body of evidence in the *appels nominaux* about the behavior of individual deputies is almost entirely reliable, but that some of the oddities in the secretaries' summaries of results are a little too convenient to be acceptable simply as the product of human error and fatigue. The interest arises not from the treatment of one or two men like

---

of the voting and the announcement of the result, he had been unfairly and very publicly taken to task by some of the left-wing deputies for leaving his post (ibid., p. 228). Both letters, however, voiced the same political line as that taken by their authors for weeks past.

7. *Appels nominaux dans les séances des 15 & 19 janvier, 1793 . . . sur ces trois questions . . .*; *Appel nominal . . . sur cette question: Quelle peine sera infligée à Louis?* and *Les cinq appels nominaux sur le jugement de Louis XVI.*

8. But not necessarily to the complete satisfaction of all those concerned; see A. J. Vermon, *Réclamation . . . sur le vote qui lui est attribué dans l'appel nominal . . . sur cette question: Quelle peine sera infligée à Louis?*

9. Cf. Lesage's reply to André Dumont, who claimed to have had his vote misrepresented (*Moniteur* XV: 235). The report of Dumont's vote in the *Moniteur* (ibid., pp. 208-9) is however quite unambiguous and it is hard to see how four secretaries could have got it wrong.

Dumont and Vermon, but from the way in which the secretaries chose to interpret the totals of the voting and present them to the Convention. This is a matter which will need to be considered when the implications of the voting are being discussed.

III

Each of the *appels nominaux* of the trial throws some light on the political outlook of the *conventionnels,* but each in a different way. The first *appel,* on Louis's guilt, singled out those deputies still reluctant to take even the first step toward calling their king to account. The second, on the *appel au peuple,* was largely a test of the effectiveness of Girondin leadership, but did also allow a number of deputies with strong feelings one way or the other about the king to make a separate gesture showing their opinion of the form of the trial. The last two *appels,* on the sentence and the reprieve, can be taken together as the ultimate test of the extent to which the Convention as a whole was willing to accept the Montagnard view of the king and his necessary fate—a view not in fact wholly Montagnard, as the speeches made before the voting show, but identified with the Mountain and with Paris by all those who most disagreed with it.

Analysis of the *appels* reveals that a very large majority of the Convention, nearly 80 percent of all those who took part in the voting, voted consistently either for mercy or for severity. If for mercy, they voted in favor of the *appel au peuple,* against a death sentence, and in favor of a reprieve; if for severity, they voted against the *appel au peuple,* for death, and against a reprieve. There were however some, rather more than one in seven, who voted one way on the *appel au peuple* and consistently the other way afterward, perhaps because for them the proposal to appeal to the primary assemblies raised issues of principle which had little or nothing to do with their attitude toward the king; this argument was of course part of the *appelants'* justification for their campaign. Because the conflict over the *appel au peuple* was basically a matter of political tactics, as Coren-Fustier, for one, was unwary enough to admit,[10] the voting for it will be examined separately; but in gauging opinion on the king, which was after all the crucial problem, a special classification will be provided for those men who obviously had decided feelings about him personally, which the problem of popular sovereignty, as they saw it, had forced them to put temporarily aside.

Let us now look at the voting in the four *appels.*

What, first, of the *appel nominal* on the question of guilt? The voting here has been summarily dismissed by most historians. Either they say simply, like Lefebvre, that "the vote against the king was unanimous," or, like Goodwin, they refer briefly to "a few abstentions," and let it go at that.[11] On any criterion the deputies were overwhelmingly of one mind, what else is there to say? Yet

---

10. *Moniteur* XV: 16.
11. G. Lefèbvre, *The French Revolution from its origins to 1793* (London, 1962), p. 272; J. M. Thompson, *The French Revolution* (Oxford, 1941), p. 331; cf. A. Goodwin, *The French Revolution,* 4th ed. (London, 1966), p. 127. The sole general historian to give the

the depth of feeling aroused by the style and direction of the trial, and the presence, even among the "inner sixty," of men prepared to argue that Louis could never be tried at all, indicates that the matter was not likely to be quite so simple. And, in fact, when the results of the *appel* on guilt are carefully dissected, some suggestive details emerge.

The result of this *appel* was announced to the Convention by the president, Vergniaud, as follows:

Deputies *en mission*	20
absent—ill	5
absent—reason unknown	1
submitting "*diverses déclarations*" of their views	26
voting for guilt	693
TOTAL	745[12]

This was unsatisfactory, if only because the Convention had more than 745 members, and the later official pamphlet amended it. The only totals there given are those of the deputies who voted for guilt without elaboration and of the deputies who submitted explanations of their votes, but as always in pamphlets of this sort, all deputies are listed by name and the result is fairly easy to calculate. It works out thus:

Deputies *en mission*	20
absent, ill	8
submitting explanations of their votes	37
voting for guilt	683
TOTAL	748[13]

A little research and calculation show that while some deputies have been mentioned twice in the record, others have been omitted altogether, though the errors are not numerous. When the necessary adjustments have been made, the figure of 683 can be amended to 684, and with this alteration, given that one accepts the classifications used, these figures are correct![14]

figures in detail is, as usual, Pariset, who seems to have examined the official result with some care; but he gives no reference on this and no explanation of his findings, which I think are not quite accurate. But see Pariset, *La Révolution 1792-1799* (Paris, 1920), p. 19.

12. *Moniteur* XV: 161.

13. *Appels nominaux faits dans les séances des 15 & 19 janvier 1793 . . . sur ces trois questions . . . .*

14. The figures given at different times for all the *appels nominaux* and the final conclusions reached are discussed in Appendix X. Seligman has the best discussion of the various difficulties raised by this subject (*Justice en France*, chap. XX).

There is however a concealed confusion. Both the secretaries' original summary of the vote, and the later official pamphlet, lump together under one heading a number of deputies who in fact had rather different views. The 37 men who submitted explanations of their votes fall into 3 distinct groups, in this manner:

i)	Vote of *guilty*, without qualification, but with some additional emphasis	9
ii)	Vote of *guilty*, but with a reservation about the capacity in which the voter was casting his vote	14
iii)	Abstention, i.e., refusal to vote at all	14
	TOTAL	37

On 15 January the secretaries apparently accepted one of the distinctions above when they included the men in group (i) among those voting *guilty*. (This is only an assumption, but it is the easiest and most natural way to explain the total of men voting *guilty* at which they ultimately arrived.) Seligman sees all the rest—he puts their number at 26, but the exact figure is less important than the drift of the argument—as abstaining altogether. This does not, however, seem to be a proper statement of the position. The men in group (ii) qualified their votes by saying that they were acting in the role of "legislator, not judge"; a qualification common throughout the voting later, and one which, when made by a man voting on the sentence, did not then cause his vote to be counted as an abstention. This sort of vote was in fact cast by a number of men who were willing to act in the trial so long as they could specify the capacity in which they were doing so, and it seems misleading to group them with men like Morisson or Meynard, who would not commit themselves at all. It may further be noted that even some of those who asserted to the end that Louis was legally inviolable—Kersaint and Guiter, for example—were quite prepared to admit that he was guilty, presumably because this was an acceptance of reality which in no way prejudiced their view of the Convention's authority to deal with him. A more adequate summary of the real state of opinion on Louis's guilt would therefore be:

Deputies *en mission*	20
absent or ill	8
abstained	14
voting for guilt	707
TOTAL	749

The other question which arises concerns the deputies *en mission*. When the departmental delegation from Moselle was called upon to vote, Merlin of

Thionville was passed over as absent *en mission*; on which several voices were heard to cry out "*Il a voté.*"[15] So he had. His letter proclaiming the king's guilt and asking for a death sentence, and also asking that when the time came his vote should be counted in that sense, had been read in the Convention on 11 January. But his vote was not counted, nor as far as can be seen did the secretaries ever ask the Convention for a ruling on what was to be done about such postal votes. If they had, the vote of *guilty* might have risen higher, from 707 beyond 708 even to 712, since Jagot, Simond, Grégoire, and Hérault de Séchelles also sent a joint letter supporting Louis's condemnation *sans appel au peuple*.[16]

These points are all trivial enough. Yet they seem worth noting, for the cumulative effect was to keep the record of the Convention's hostility to the king to an irreducible minimum, and in this they foreshadowed the line to be taken when the more complicated voting on the sentence had to be reported in summary form.

A majority of 707 against 14, or alternatively 693 against 28, seems substantial enough and hardly likely to be dependent on the backing of one political group in the Convention rather than another. It is however interesting to analyze the minority among the deputies; those members who could not take part in the voting because they were away on public business or ill, who would not because they could not accept the duty imposed on them, or who were reluctant because they had doubts of their constitutional position.

It appears that of the 26 members who expressed uneasiness, for political rather than personal reasons, over taking part in the trial, 3 were of the "inner sixty," 6 were deputies who later showed sympathy with the Girondin leaders, and 10 were men who were later *à l'écart* under the Terror, 6 came from the rest of the Plain, and one from the Mountain. The figures are very small, but the location of the few determined objectors seems significant and fits in well enough with the implications of the table on p. 78. The disproportionate number of Montagnards among the deputies *en mission*, even at this early stage, is interesting.

For the rest of the voting on the trial, a full analysis of the behavior of all deputies must be made, as the Convention was split from top to bottom; as in the speeches, the deputies were agreed that something must be done about their king, but on nothing else. Because the proposed political groups are so varied in size, the differences in attitude between them are more readily observable if the figures are presented as percentages of the total number of deputies in each group. This method, of course, is dangerous in the case of very small groups,

---

15. *Moniteur* XV: 160. For the reading of Merlin's letter, ibid., p. 106. The Convention immediately ordered it to be printed. See A. C. Merlin, *Lettre. . . au président de la Convention nationale* (dated 6 jan. 1793).

16. Kuscinski, *Conventionnels*, p. 309. This letter, written on 13 January, may not have arrived in time, but there seems no reason why such letters should not have figured in an appendix to the Convention's official record of the voting, published in February; as Vermon's letter did.

Table 3. Voting 15 January 1793 on the guilt or innocence of Louis XVI: Political attitude, 1793–94, of minority voters and absentees

	Abstained	Qualified vote	*En mission*	Ill
GIRONDE				
"inner sixty"	3 (1)	1	2	1
Others	3	3		
Total	6	4	2	2
PLAIN				
à l'écart	4	6	1	1
Committees	3 (1)	2	1	
en mission	1	1	4	2
MOUNTAIN				
Jacobin		1	7	1
Montagnard		no such deputies		
Others			4	
Total	nil	1	11	1
Deputies not classified			1	1
Convention total	14	14	20	7

*Note The total of "ill" includes the elder Malhes, who had refused election and whose *suppléant* nephew had not yet arrived. Of the abstainers, two, Nöel and Lafon, abstained for purely personal reasons. These two have been included in the totals, but are also indicated in parentheses as a reminder that not all those who abstained had constitutional or political objections to the trial.

when the voting, or the absence, of two or three deputies may make a considerable difference to the percentage result without being in itself statistically significant; for this reason, and others, what should be noticed as most significant is not the percentage figures in themselves but their consistency, if any, from one *appel nominal* to another. For the sake of completeness, the voting of those deputies who have not been included in the political analysis is shown at the foot of each table.

The voting on the *appel au peuple* was as shown in Table 4.

From this it appears that though no political group in the Convention unreservedly supported the *appel au peuple*, those deputies classed as Girondin came closer to doing so than anyone else. The "against" group in the "inner sixty" is a little misleading, since Grégoire, *en mission*, was certainly opposed to the *appel*, but even if both he and Lasource, also *en mission* and a regicide, are added to the "against" group it is still smaller than that to be found even among the conservative *à l'écart* deputies. Among the three groups described by Sydenham as making up the "inner sixty," that closest to Brissot was most strongly *appelant*.[17] The 215 deputies who have been considered certified

17. Voting: deputies of List A (nearest Brissot) 13 for, 3 against, 1 *en mission* (Lasource); List B (including Bancal) 13 for, 5 against; List C, 16 for, 4 against, 1 sick

Table 4. Voting in the *appel nominal* of 15 January 1793
on the *appel au peuple*

	For		Against		Abstained		En mission		Absent		Total
	No.	%	No.	%	No.	%	No.	%	No.	%	
GIRONDE											
"inner sixty"	41	70.7	12	20.7	2	3.4	2	3.4	1	1.7	58
June petitioners	65	69.2	27	28.7	2	2.1					94
Others	20	76.9	6	23.1							26
Total	126	70.8	45	25.2	4	2.2	2	1.1	1	.6	178
PLAIN											
à l'écart	79	66.9	35	29.8	2	1.7	1	.8	1	.8	118
Committees	56	58.9	35	36.8	3	3.2	1	1.0			95
En mission	11	29.7	18	48.6	1	2.7	4	10.8	3	8.1	37
Total	146	58.4	88	35.2	6	2.4	6	2.4	4	2.6	250
MOUNTAIN											
Jacobin	1	.7	133	93.7			7	4.9	1	.7	142
Montagnard	4	5.5	65	89.0			4	5.5			73
Others			87	100.0							87
Total	5	1.6	285	94.3			11	3.6	1	.3	302
Grand total	277	37.9	418	57.2	10	1.4	19	2.6	6	.8	730
Deputies not classified	9		7				1		2		19
Convention total	286	38.2	425	56.7	10	1.3	20	2.6	8	1.2	749

Montagnards showed a startling unanimity. (The 87 "Montagnards by attribu-tion" cannot be considered, since their voting was one of the reasons for their political classification.) But much of the real interest of this table is in the voting of the Plain, whose outlook before 15 January was so much of an unknown quantity. Here not even the *à l'écart* deputies could match the enthusiasm of the Gironde, but opposition apparently hardened in a direct relationship with later support for the Jacobin régime. The voting of the *en mission* group cannot be reckoned very valuable statistically, since the group was so small, but it was the only group outside the Mountain to have a majority against the *appel*—and not a marginal majority either, but one which was very nearly absolute whatever the attitude of the absentees.

(Duchastel, who would probably have voted *for*), 1 *en mission* (Grégoire, who was *against*), 2 abstained. Minvielle of course was not there. Total, 42 for (including Bancal), 12 against (with Grégoire, 13), 2 abstained, 1 *en mission*, 1 sick; the number actually favoring the *appel* was 43. But see M. J. Sydenham, *The Girondins* (London, 1961), p. 230, for a different view. Note Grégoire's attitude; as a deputy *en mission* he was more likely to be in touch with the possible views of the primary assemblies. Noël Pointe, one of the Conven-tions's handful of artisans, was strongly opposed to any idea that a popular vote should be held on the trial; see N. Pointe, *Discours . . . sur la discussion concernant le jugement de Louis.*

If these figures are compared with those for the speeches printed for and against the *appel* (p. 78), it will be seen that as far as the overall result was concerned the *appelants'* campaign turned out almost exactly as might have been predicted. In detail, however, there was a significant difference. The Mountain, which had been exceptionally vocal in pressing its views, supplied a lower proportion of the opposition in the *appel nominal* than it had in the previous controversy—about two-thirds instead of more than three-quarters—and the balance was made up by somewhat increased distrust in all other parts of the Convention. Of the now obvious dissidents among the "inner sixty," only Carra and Boilleau had spoken up before the matter actually came to be voted on; the others, whatever they thought, had held their tongues. How much the outcome was affected by the "Boze incident," how much by the character of the various departmental petitions which had come in during January, and how much by the preceding condemnation of the king, it is impossible to say. At least one deputy, Bayle from Marseille, completely changed his views on the whole matter of the trial as the debates on it proceeded, explaining that he had done so because he had come to appreciate the very real danger of royalist agitation.[18]

Let us now consider the voting on the trial as a whole.

So many of the men voting took up a consistent attitude through all the *appels nominaux* that it seems more enlightening to tabulate the overall result rather than to deal separately with the voting on the sentence and the reprieve, when separate tables would give no idea at all of how many men in each group wavered and how many stood firm. The deputies credited with three votes either for mercy or severity are those whose feelings are not really open to doubt, even if, as sometimes happened, this meant that they did not take part in all the votes. Thus Debourges—who according to the *Moniteur* queried the legality of his position on 15 January, supported the *appel au peuple*, and then abstained for the last two votes—has been credited with a consistent leaning toward mercy, an attitude consistent enough with his later career,[19] and so has Duchastel, who made his one spectacular appearance in order to vote against the death sentence; so also for Manuel and Kersaint, who absented themselves from the vote on the reprieve. Most of such assessments of attitude can be justified from the line taken by the men concerned before the trial began.

In deciding whether the voting of any deputy was consistent or otherwise, one major difficulty arises: what to do about the quite sizable group of deputies who voted for death, but qualified their votes by raising the question of a

18. M. A. P. J. Bayle, . . . *à ses collègues, sur le mode d'instruire la procédure du ci-devant roi*; and *Discours . . . contre l'appel au peuple et la proposition de faire confirmer le jugement . . . contre Louis Capet*, for the earlier and later points of view. Bayle was reproached for changing his ground, but his explanation seems convincing enough, and the trend of events in Marseille, had he heard of it, would have confirmed his attitude. See A. Vialla, *Marseille révolutionnaire* (Paris, 1910), pp. 321–22.

19. *Moniteur* XV: 161. Kuscinski (*Conventionnels*, p. 282) describes him at a later stage as *"un royaliste et un réacteur."*

possible reprieve. Forty-six such men asked for a reprieve on more or less cific conditions—until the constitution was accepted, until France was aga invaded, etc.; and another 26 voted for the Mailhe amendment, which formally supported a death penalty while also asking that the matter of a reprieve be considered. The secretaries originally counted the whole 72 as voting for mercy, but the position of those favoring the Mailhe amendment was clearly ambiguous, as it was perhaps intended to be, and on 18 January they were asked to clarify it. (Mailhe, when interrogated on 17 January, had simply repeated his vote word for word on a "take it or leave it" basis.[20]) Mailhe was not present on 18 January, but the other 25 were, and all said that their vote for death was independent of the request for a reprieve; all 26 were then accordingly placed with the regicides. However, when the *appel nominal* on the granting of a reprieve was held next day, 12 of the group, including Mailhe himself, voted in favor, implying that they were basically antiregicide. These votes have therefore been interpreted in the light of the associated votes on the reprieve: e.g., Pétion, who voted the Mailhe amendment and then the reprieve, is credited with 2 votes for mercy, wheras Vergniaud, who rejected the reprieve, has 2 votes for severity. The deputies in the first group of 46, who included Brissot, have been treated in the same way, though in their case the number not voting in favor of the reprieve was so small that the problem is relatively slight.[21]

In the rest of the Convention, deputies who certainly seem to have changed their views between the sentence and the reprieve have been left in an "undecided" category; any man, for instance, who supported the *appel au peuple*, voted for death and then backed the reprieve had indeed 2 votes for mercy, but on the face of it he must be classed as undecided. Thus the deputies with 2 votes, one way or the other, in the table, are those and only those who voted one way on the referendum and consistently the other way later—the men already referred to who found that their feelings about the *appel au peuple* forced them, for that vote only, closer to the "hard" or "soft" line than their feelings over the king would have done. For the sake of simplicity in Table 5, all those *en mission* or ill have been placed with the three consistent abstainers in a "no vote" category.

Table 5 indicates that if the *appel au peuple* was intended as an appeal to the swinging voter, it failed. Over 80 percent of those who backed it went on to vote

20. *Moniteur* XV: 228.

21. The only deputies asking for a reprieve who later voted against one were Lanthénas, who later justified his vote in unequivocally regicide terms; Blad, whose vote on the sentence was highly ambiguous and could—perhaps should—have been interpreted as a vote for death, and Monestier, whose attitude remains something of a mystery, though in his vote on the sentence he did at least admit the justice of a death penalty. See F. X. Lanthénas, *Motifs des opinions . . . sur le jugement de Louis*; E. Belhomme, "Le procès de Louis XVI à propos des lettres de Blad," *La Revolution francaise* (1896), XXX: 230–31, and *Moniteur* XV: 192. The political groups from which the reprieve and "Mailhe" voters came will be considered later.

e 5. Overall voting on the trial of Louis XVI

	For mercy		Total		For severity		Total		Unde-cided		No vote*		
			No.	%	3 votes	2 votes	No.	%	No.	%	No.	%	Total
...y	33	4	37	63.8	7	7	14	24.2	5	8.6	2	3.4	58
...ine petitioners	57	15	72	76.6	8	7	15	15.9	7	7.4			94
Others	16	2	18	69.2	4	2	6	23.1	2	7.7			26
Total	106	21	127	71.3	19	16	35	19.7	14	7.9	2	1.1	178
PLAIN													
à l'écart	77	19	96	81.4	12	2	14	11.9	6	5.0	2	1.7	118
Committees	39	24	63	66.3	6	11	17	17.9	13	13.7	2	2.1	95
en mission	9	9	18	48.6	5	2	7	18.9	4	10.8	8	21.6	37
Total	125	52	177	70.8	23	15	38	15.2	23	9.2	12	4.8	250
MOUNTAIN													
Jacobin	1	2	3	2.1	136		136	95.8			3	2.1	142
Montagnard	2	1	3	4.1	62	1	63	86.3	3	4.1	4	5.5	73
Others					87		87	100.0					87
Total	3	3	6	1.9	285	1	286	94.8	3	1.0	7	2.3	302
Grand total	234	76	310	42.5	327	32	359	49.2	40	5.5	21	2.8	730
Deputies not classified	8	2	10		5		5				4		19
Convention total	242	78	320		332	32	364		40		25		749

*Caila, of the "unclassified" deputies, is here included in the "no vote" category because, although he voted on the *appel au peuple,* he collapsed immediately afterward and did not appear again. He died on 19 January.

consistently for mercy, which suggests that the Left was correct in alleging that their main aim was to save Louis's life. A proportion of convinced regicides backed the *appel* as a matter of principle, but they were less than half as numerous as the antiregicides who would have nothing to do with it. Among 242 deputies with three votes for mercy there were certainly some who were governed almost entirely by their feelings over the *appel* and who voted against the death sentence primarily because the people were not to be consulted, and they themselves would not be party to an irrevocable decision; but such men were not very numerous. The majority of deputies, whatever their outlook, was prepared to shoulder responsibility. Such indecision as there was in the Convention was greatest over the reprieve. On 19 January 34 of the undecided deputies reversed the decisions they had made 2 days earlier, 21 moving toward a death-sentence and 13 away from it. (The other 6 of the total of 40 undecided, 2 regicides and 4 antiregicides, did not come to vote at all.) This implies, among other things, that for all the talk of mob intimidation, a number of deputies clearly felt free to the end to do as they chose. The large number, about 14 percent, who firmly changed sides after the *appel* points in the same direction.[22]

Next to the again staggering solidity of the Montagnards, one of the most noteworthy features of the overall voting is the *à l'écart* vote: here is a right-wing indeed, and with few doubts about what it should do. The next most conservative group—and a large enough one, so that the percentage is not likely to be delusive—was that of the men who less than six months later were to enter protests against the expulsion of the Girondin leaders. The discrepancy between the attitude of the "inner sixty" and that of its supporters may be explained by the protracted campaign of the Girondin leaders against the king and the beliefs which it embodied, which when allied with their views on Parisian radicalism made their position exceedingly awkward. To their great honor, after the failure of the *appel au peuple*, which would in their eyes have solved the problem of Paris, the Girondin *appelants* followed their consciences to the end: Brissot perhaps rationalizing a humane impulse by stress on the importance of foreign opinion, Vergniaud with dignity accepting the majority verdict as he had undertaken to do, Pétion in the end rejecting the death sentence which he had vainly begged the Constituent Assembly to abolish. . . .[23] Merely to examine the Girondin voting and the reasons for it leads one to reject any idea that intimidation from the tribunes decided the verdict; unless of course one is to conclude that obscure deputies, about whom one knows comparatively little, behaved quite differently from all those whose actions and feelings have been recorded in more detail. Those Girondins who claimed that they were being intimidated, repeat-

22. The question of the Convention's "freedom" to vote is too complex to be entered into here; I have discussed some of the claims about "influence" in an article, "Regicides and anti-regicides in January 1793: the problem of Fouché's vote" *Historical Studies* (Melbourne) 41 (1970). Very briefly, (1) Fouché did *not* switch to regicide at the last minute only; (2) evidence of *any* last minute regicide voting is hard to find; (3) the real problem is the size of the antiregicide vote, which, e.g., Lanjuinais apparently did not expect on 15 January. N.B. the number of deputies changing sides, 16–19 January.

23. For Brissot, *Discours sur le procès de Louis*, already referred to; for Vergniaud, the *Moniteur* (XV: 15) reports what the Convention presumably heard on 31 December: "*je déclare que, tel que puisse être le décret qui sera rendu par la Convention, je regarderais comme traître à la patrie celui qui ne s'y soumettrait pas.*" How then was he to vote on the reprieve, which was demanded in the first instance by only a minority of deputies? It should be noted that Barère and Robespierre, as well as Pétion, had contributed to the Constituent's debate on capital punishment. In 1793, Pétion stuck to his views; Barère stuck to his; and Robespierre, who changed his mind, was reproached for it more than once. (*Moniteur* VIII: 546–49, for Robespierre and Pétion; Barère was apparently not reported.) Another *conventionnel*, Le Peletier, was the *rapporteur* of the committee concerned (ibid., pp. 532–36, 544–45.) He adhered in 1793 to the views expressed in his report. As we have seen, it cost him his life. Ironically, he was murdered an hour after leaving with his printer a pamphlet arguing that the death penalty be invoked *only* for major crimes against society; the argument in this, had it become law, would not have saved his own life, since Louis would still have died, but would have preserved his murderer from the guillotine. See L. M. Le Peletier de Saint Fargeau, *Sur l'abrogation de la peine de mort*; and S. T. McCloy, *The Humanitarian Movement in Eighteenth-century France* (Lexington, 1957), pp. 204–5.

edly abused the occupants of the tribunes to their faces, and it is hard to imagine how they could well have been more provocative toward *"cette poignée de scélérats"* which, according to them, was misleading the inhabitants of Paris and seeking to dictate to the Convention. Yet nothing happened, whatever was said. Some of these references seem, in any case, beside the point, for surely it is not the Girondin *regicide* vote which needs explanation. The leading Girondins had alleged months earlier that the king was a traitor. Under the circumstances, not an acceptance but a rejection of the death penalty by about two-thirds of the "inner sixty" is the remarkable phenomenon. But either way, it was often an anguished decision. Ducos for instance really had no doubt where his duty lay, but he knew what Wandelaincourt meant when saying, on the question of guilt, that *"la douceur de [ses] moeurs"* prevented him from voting. Ducos, one feels, would have given much to have been able to come to that decision himself. "Citizens, to condemn a man to death—here, among all the sacrifices I have made for my country, is the only one that deserves to be remembered," he wrote sadly, as he explained his views.[24]

As in the pamphlets, the Convention divided sharply between those who could accept the logic which made Ducos a regicide and those who refused to do so. In considering the position of both regicides and antiregicides, the evidence of the pamphlets should be borne in mind. The antiregicides claimed consistently from the beginning that they were being subjected to intolerable pressure from the mob and from the Left generally to accept a death sentence, and their horror and repulsion at the blood lust of the gutter press and the Parisian radicals may well have helped to make their decision easier. The regicides suffered from a different kind of pressure, but one which could be equally painful, in that their critics continually insinuated that anyone arguing for the execution of the king was no better than a *septembriseur*; and this although some of the regicides had reason to believe—and after 20 January, actual evidence—that it was they, and not the king's defenders, who were risking their lives to do what they thought was right:

> Je sais, moi [said Jeanbon Saint-André on 21 January], que dans les départements on nous a fait passer pour des *maratistes* et des panégyristes des massacres du 2 septembre....Depuis quatre mois, on ne cesse de nous appeler des assassins, des hommes qui veulent se nourrir d'un pain pétri de sang; et c'est nous qu'on ménace, et c'est nous qu'on égorge! Car moi j'ai été menacé, j'ai reçu une lettre anonyme où on me dit que si je vote contre le roi, on assassinera moi et ma femme . . .

And several others added their own evidence to the same effect.[25] When to this known danger was added the fact that many of the regicides felt quite as hor-

---

24. J. F. Ducos, *Motifs . . . dans le jugement de Louis Bourbon, ci-devant roi*; A. H. Wandelaincourt, *Opinion . . . sur le jugement de Louis Capet.*

25. *Moniteur* XV: 257. On 8 January the secretaries minuted *"il n'y a lieu à délibérer"* a barely literate letter from Caën threatening death specifically to *"l'infâme Robespierre*

rified at the massacres as those who were making political capital out of them, the continued carpings and insults of the Right must have been doubly hard to endure. Those Montagnards who were indeed violent revolutionaries, or who, like Robespierre, were engaged in personal feuds, could hurl back one taunt for another; but men of this sort made up only a small proportion of the massive regicide vote. The most that many of the others could do was to state their position with as much dignity as they could muster. Otherwise, they went their way in silence.

If we return to the figures, it is interesting to compare the results with those obtained on page 78 from an analysis of the speeches on the possible fate of the king. Not only were the Montagnard voters overwhelmingly regicide; as among the speech writers, the regicide voters were overwhelmingly Montagnard. Of those firmly committed against the king, nearly 80 percent have been placed with the Mountain; of those completely committed against him, 87 percent. There were altogether 73 clear regicides outside the Mountain. Of these, 14 came from the "inner sixty," and another 24 had registered disapproval of Paris by backing the *appel au peuple*; about half of these latter were later to cooperate with the Jacobin government under the Terror. Among the 49 non-Montagnard regicides in opposition under the Terror, five in every seven were linked with the Gironde.

The traditional uncertainty and unhappiness of the Plain is illustrated by its center group, the unfortunates who so regularly staffed the Convention's committees. Absolutely as well as relatively, they had more undecided members than any other group. They did have a very decided majority for mercy, but neither those against the death sentence nor those favoring it came anywhere near agreeing among themselves about the *appel au peuple*. The committee members' 13.9 percent of real waverers were flanked by 37.2 percent of deputies who changed their minds, or put stress on different principles one way or the other, after the voting on the *appel*; the Gironde had under 21 percent in this category and the *à l'écart* deputies under 18 percent. (The number of *à l'écart* deputies who despite their conservatism could not bring themselves to stomach the *appel au peuple* is instructive; it was about one in six.) The deputies *en mission* were also in a state of muddle, though, as before, any judgment on them must be very tentative because of the high proportion of absentees.

The evidence of the *appels nominaux* thus confirms the evidence of the speeches: the outcome of the trial was a major political defeat for the Gironde, in that they were confronted with a very solid acceptance of Montagnard opinion, and over the only policy which was specifically their own—the *appel au peuple*—they had aroused considerable uneasiness among a number of deputies

---

petitfils de Damiens" and to "Chabot et Co." Doubtless it was only one of many such, but the threat was so explicit that one would like to know if Robespierre was ever told of it, before or after 20 January. The letter, edited by L. de Cardenal, is in *Annales* XIV (1937): 269.

otherwise moderate in their views. And because of the contradictory way in which Girondin policies had been justified, the defeat was more than merely political; it was moral. The approach to the *appel au peuple,* with its heavy emphasis on popular sovereignty and its refusal to discuss practical dangers, would imply that the proponents were prepared to set constitutional principle above any amount of immediate risk. Yet in opposing the death of the king, Brissot and others argued heatedly in *favor* of mere expediency against the basic republican principle of equal justice for all, and the same tactic—but with no consideration of the potentially appalling consequences—was applied over the reprieve.[26] By contrast, the Montagnard case did not obviously conflict with the previous policies of Montagnard leaders, and it had at least the advantages of simplicity, consistency, and revolutionary logic; though the crude blood-thirstiness of the gutter radicals was bound to taint any cause it touched.

IV

There are two final points about the trial. First, it was much more than a passing episode. During its course, all the fundamental complaints made by the two "factions" against each other were given an airing. The Gironde did not gain much from this, since the trial provided them with nothing to say in January that they could not as easily have said—and in general, had said—in October. For the Mountain it was different, since the events of September–January raised suspicions of Girondin "faction" and crypto-royalism which (*pace* Hampson[27]) must have seemed far more than merely plausible. The evidence which might be used to bolster up existing prejudice, or to create it where it had not previously existed, might now come from a number of different sources. The views expressed in a large number of the Girondin pamphlets; Girondin voting during the trial; and the activities, before, during, and after the voting, of the Girondin *bureau,* all had features which laid them open to suspicion at least of some bad faith in the eyes of even fairly moderate-minded regicides.

The pamphlets and the main features of the voting have already been considered. One special aspect of the voting remains, that of the deputies who on 16–17 January opted for a reprieve for the king, either by way of the Mailhe amendment or on one of a number of specified conditions. From which of our proposed political groups did these seventy-two deputies come? On 18 January,

26. Quite apart from the dangers of keeping the king as a living magnet for royalist intrigue, which no antiregicide was willing to take seriously (they might have learned something here from studying the life of Charles I), the popular formula for those urging a reprieve was to make it conditional on the cessation of hostilities against revolutionary France, or at least on France's security from further invasion. Had the reprieve been granted and a fresh invasion taken place, what kind of debate would then have been necessary? It should be added that many antiregicides argued that the royalists, and particularly the king's brothers, *wanted* him executed; on this logic, a reprieve was hardly likely to serve any useful purpose.

27. Cf. Hampson, *A Social History of the French Revolution* (London, 1963), p. 162.

all of those supporting the Mailhe amendment, with the exception of Mailhe himself who was not there, claimed that their intention was to vote for death; which of these took up the same stand the next day, when the vote on a possible reprieve was held?

Table 6. Deputies voting in favor of reprieve, 16–17 January 1793

	Mailhe amendment		Reprieve on specified terms			Number voting for death
	Total number	Number voting death, 19 Jan.	Total number	Number voting death, 19 Jan.	Total	
GIRONDE						
"inner sixty"	6	2	6	1	12	3
Others	2	2	11	1	13	3
Total	8	4	17	2	25	6
PLAIN						
à l'écart	1	1	10		11	1
Committees	7	2	9		16	2
en mission	2	1	6		8	1
Total	10	4	25		35	4
MOUNTAIN						
Jacobin	1		1		2	
Montagnard	3	2			3	2
Others	4	4	2	1	6	5
Total	8	6	3	1	11	7
Unclassified			1		1	
Convention total	26	14	46	3	72	17

The Mailhe amendment apparently attracted its very slender support from all parts of the Convention, whereas the more definite and personal commitment to the idea of a reprieve which the deputy concerned was willing to grant on known conditions came more strongly from the *à l'écart* deputies and the Gironde. If the deputies of the extreme Left were looking for scraps of evidence that leading members of the "inner sixty" wanted to save the king without making their intention too obvious, they could find them here. One of the Mailhe voters was Pétion, who on 17 January was still maintaining his support for a death sentence and yet ended by voting for the reprieve. The total number of Girondins favoring reprieve was not very high, but they were very conspicuous; they included 6 from the "inner sixty" who were drawn from among Brissot's closest associates. These were, besides Pétion, Vergniaud, Guadet, Buzot, Louvet, Dufriche-Valazé, and Brissot himself, and only Vergniaud finally rejected the reprieve. Of the 22 men whose expulsion was demanded on 1 June, only 10 could fairly be regarded as regicides in any sense, and of the 29 who were actually expelled the next day, 9 had ended by voting for Louis's death, one had abstained, and 18 had opposed it.[28]

Montagnard dislike of the policy followed by a number of leading Girondins was buttressed by resentment at the methods which were allegedly used to forward that policy in the Convention. It has already been noted that before the *appels nominaux* were held the Girondins were under fire for misuse of their positions as the Convention's elected office-holders. Historians have long accepted that between September 1792 and January 1793 the *bureau* was monopolized by the Gironde, but the practical implications of this situation for the organization of important business have not fully been explored. The monopoly was certainly apparent enough. Between 20 September 1792 and the king's execution on 21 January 1793, the Convention had 9 presidents and 27 secretaries, 35 individuals in all. Six presidents and 19 secretaries were drawn from the "inner sixty"; Vergniaud held both offices at different times. Of the 17 men named by Sydenham as closest to Brissot, 14 held office as president or secretary, and for the voting on the trial, Vergniaud was president (admittedly with Barère acting as relief from time to time) and every secretary was from the "inner sixty." Whether or not this apparent stranglehold on office was due to organization as well as to popularity, there were complaints about it at the time, and the repeated contemporary charges of "faction" had at least some ostensible basis. There was some ill-feeling well before the end of 1792, and we have seen that the arrangement of the *appel* debate, however fortuitous, left plenty of room for further criticism.[29] With the voting itself, however, came a very dangerous situation, in that the *bureau* had so clear a personal interest in the outcome that it was bound to be suspected of bias unless the secretaries were very careful indeed not only to be scrupulously impartial, but to appear to be so.

They were not as careful as they might have been, and anyone already suspicious of their behavior was likely to have had his suspicions multiplied. The

---

28. Lists in Sydenham, *The Girondins*, p. 215. *Note* that the petition of 15 April named among 22 deputies a total of 7 regicides.

29. Sydenham's conclusion that the contacts between the "inner sixty" were personal and unorganized seems sound, but is not in itself enough to rebut the "faction" accusation, or to establish that the Gironde was in this respect any different from the Jacobin Club, which housed a wide range of opinion for many months to come. In the absence of organized parties, consistent personal association, of the kind established by Sydenham's researches, was bound to create a presumption of common sympathy: it was perhaps even more likely to do so when it was purely personal and not based on the membership of a club to which many others of differing views might also belong. The combination of such association with the long run of Girondin office-holding produced from Guffroy and Poultier very detailed diatribes about the way in which the Convention's business might be stage-managed. This may have been pure invention based on prejudice, but Couthon's protest in the Convention on 29 September at what he saw as an attempt to gag opposition, followed by his better-known outburst at the Jacobins on 12 October, suggests that it had some foundation. See A. J. B. Guffroy, *Discours... contre le sursis à l'arrête de mort du tyran*; J. Poultier, ... *sur le supplice de Louis Capet*; *Moniteur* XIV: 77; A. Aulard, *La Société des Jacobins*, IV: 380–81.

recount of 18 January was held because the accuracy of the record was challenged by several deputies. André Dumont said that his explicitly regicide vote had been recorded as antiregicide; Loysel complained that the number of deputies voting "death with reprieve" was considerably understated; Gasparin and Thuriot noted errors in the total number of deputies and in the number absent *en mission*; and the problem of the exact meaning of the Mailhe votes remained unresolved. Given the length of the sitting and the ambiguity of some of the voting, it would have been natural for the secretaries to plead human error. Instead they defended themselves, to the point where Lesage asserted that the only real mistake was that which had been made over Dumont's vote—again of course passing over the Mailhe problem altogether.[30] It was agreed that a recount should be made, and this was done. But even the recount figures, as announced by Vergniaud, do not match those in the pamphlet which the Convention finally issued on this subject. The variations between the totals announced by Vergniaud on 17 and 18 January and those in the official pamphlet are shown in Table 7.

Loysel's complaint seems to be justified. It is hard to see how, or why, the secretaries separated about a dozen of the "reprieve" votes from the remainder, when all were cast in very similar terms and had much the same effect; some asked for reprieve until the Constitution was accepted by the people, some for reprieve until the war was over, and some for reprieve until all the Bourbons had been expelled or otherwise dealt with, but the effect in each case was the same, and the secretaries' case, whatever it was, was hardly strengthened by Salle's "explanation" of 18 January. It will also be noted that on 17 January all the Mailhe votes were counted as votes for mercy. It was not the secretaries but the Montagnard Garrau who asked that day for the clarification which Mailhe refused to give,[31] and these votes were not added to the "death" total, where their formulation nominally placed them, until the deputies concerned indicated on 18 January that that was where they belonged.

The effect of these maneuvers was to inflate the total of those resisting any form of death sentence and to reduce the number willing to contemplate Louis's execution to an absolute minimum—in fact to the one-vote majority which has become legendary.[32] It has of recent years become conventional to

30. The inaccuracy of the record of Dumont's vote was admitted. To Loysel, Salle said that all those voting for a reprieve until the end of the war had been classed with those voting for prison to be followed by exile, since both votes meant prison for the time being—an explanation which perhaps explained a little too much. The consistent avoidance by the secretaries of any mention of the problem of the Mailhe voting is rather striking. See *Moniteur* XV: 235.

31. *Moniteur* XV: 228.

32. Where the figure of 366 votes for death came from on 17 January will now presumably never be known; on this, see Appendix X, below. It is tempting to conclude, as one might from Conte's suggestion that a very careful check was being kept on the voting, that the secretaries knew the exact position, but after the scene of Duchastel's vote did not want to admit it; but this is mere guess-work. It is hard to credit that a group of such dedicated antiregicides could have underestimated the votes on Louis's side. For a detailed, if highly

Table 7. Voting on the sentence of Louis XVI,* 16-17 January 1793

	Vergniaud's report of 17 January	Amended report of 18 January	Figures published by Convention in official pamphlet
Imprisonment (usually exile at end of war)	319	319	286
Imprisonment with hard labor	2	2	2
Death, with reprieve (specified conditions)	11	13	46
Mailhe amendment (Convention to consider reprieve)	23	26	26
Death	366	361	361
Absent: i) ill or deceased	7	7	7
ii) reason unknown	2	1	1
iii) *en mission*	11	15	15
Abstained	4	5	5
Convention total	745	749	749
Total vote for mercy† (not stated on 17 January)	(355)	334	334

*The figures in the first two columns come from the *Moniteur* XV: 229 and 235; they fit in with the comments made at the time. Those in the third column come from the Convention's pamphlet on the sentence, . . . *quelle peine sera infligée à Louis*? The pamphlet on all 5 of the *appels nominaux* seems to contain some incidental errors.

†On 17 January, but not later, the Mailhe votes were reckoned for mercy.

accept this narrow margin as an illusion, because of the 26 Mailhe votes which were votes for death;[33] but a little reflection suggests that this is a mistake. Let us suppose that the one-vote majority of 17 January had been a majority for mercy; what then? since the meaning of the Mailhe votes was as yet unknown, Mailhe having just refused to say what it might be. (It may well be relevant that he was asked to explain himself after the voting had been concluded but before the result was known.) Twelve of the 26 Mailhe voters were to opt for mercy on 19 January anyhow. How many of the remainder would have stipulated that they were voting for death, if even one such vote would have reversed the decision on the fate of the king? Would anyone have asked them to do so? Had an apparent majority for mercy appeared, the secretaries were hardly likely to jeopardize it by asking awkward questions, since they had all voted for mercy themselves; and the regicides would have been in a most difficult position,

partisan and at times misleading, account of the voting see A. Conte, *Sire, ils ont voté la mort* (Paris, 1966).

33. See, e.g., A. Goodwin, *The French Revolution*, p. 127, where the vote is simply stated as 387 for death and 334 for mercy.

unable to raise legitimate objections to the propriety of the result without laying themselves open to charges of blood-thirstiness and intimidation which they had been trying very hard to avoid.[34]

In such a context, what conclusions might be drawn from Duchastel's sudden appearance, well past the eleventh hour? He was ill and had missed both of the first two *appels*. Whatever the validity of his own alleged explanation (that he had only just found out that he could not submit his vote in writing), it must have appeared that he had been dragged from his bed, still in his night clothes, because it was known that the result would be very close indeed. This was his only appearance during the whole of the voting on the trial; he voted for mercy, and he too was of the "inner sixty."[35]

A last feature of the voting may be remarked. We have seen that in the first *appel*, that on guilt, 14 deputies abstained. Three of these, for conscientious reasons, abstained throughout the trial: Morisson, because he refused to recognize or take part in the Convention's procedure; Lafon, because he was a *suppléant* who had arrived only on 9 January and had been able to hear none of the evidence; and Noël, because his son had been a volunteer killed in action by the Austrians, and his vote might therefore be prejudiced.[36] Of the 11 remaining, Chevalier voted once and Wandelaincourt and Barailon twice. The other 8 voted 3 times, on the side of mercy every time. It would have been natural for their colleagues to see these 8 men as active royalists. Two of the 8, Valady and Henry-Larivière, were of the "inner sixty," Henry-Larivière having the distinction of being the only deputy in the whole Convention to have been reelected after having supported the Right in the *appels nominaux* of 1792.

The second main point to be made about the trial is the significance of its outcome. This was the only occasion in the whole history of the Convention when virtually every deputy recorded his opinion on a major political issue. It was, then, a test of feeling in the whole Convention: and those deputies who

34. Note the agreement to hold an *appel nominal* on the reprieve proposal, though the number of deputies backing it was, as Couthon said, a small minority (*Moniteur* XV: 234–39). The brawl of the evening of 18 January was not over the holding of this vote, but over its delay until next day. The parting pledge of the regicides, led by Lacombe Saint-Michel, to arrive at an early hour to ensure the defeat of the reprieve is interesting. In fact, absences among antiregicides were more numerous.

35. The explanation of Duchastel's vote given above is that in Conte, *Sire*, p. 284; I have been unable to check it from other sources. The *Moniteur* does not report any statement by Duchastel. If he did in fact learn very late in the day that a written vote would not be acceptable, who told him, and on what grounds? The Convention never actually seems to have been asked for a ruling on this matter, which would, of course, have raised the question of Merlin's letter read on 11 January, and perhaps other letters too.

36. In accordance with the Convention's procedure, these 3 answered to their names at every *appel*, Morisson maintaining his detachment even when by abandoning it he might have saved Louis's life, and Noël making his opposite point with deadly meiosis. For their original statements on their reasons for abstention, see *Appels nominaux... sur ces trois questions...*, 7 (Lafon), and 8 (Noël); Morisson, having elaborated his feelings in three successive pamphlets, said simply *"je ne veux prononcer sur aucune des questions posées"* (ibid., p. 9). Lafon later published his statement as a pamphlet.

have been classified as supporting the Mountain during 1793-94 were almost unanimous in their victorious support for a line of action repudiated by two-thirds of the men who have been placed with the Gironde. In terms of the political divisions of 1793-94, as they were estimated in Chapter 2, the Convention during the trial behaved in a remarkably appropriate manner. But if these divisions are accepted as tentatively established, the Mountain was a very much larger body than is sometimes suggested: a little over 41 percent of our 730 deputies, as against just under 41 percent for its future opposition (taking the Girondin and the *à l'écart* deputies together) and an undecided center of 18 percent. The considerable number of Montagnards of course carried more weight because of their solidarity. The majority over the trial, though fairly modest, was clear, and it was gained through an acceptance of the Montagnard line by about one in six of the rest of the Convention. To get a majority on *its* side, even supposing its sympathizers held together, the Gironde was going to have to work rather harder than that. Even if we exclude the "Montagnards by attribution" as a sort of solid left wing of the Plain, we are still left with a Mountain considerably outnumbering the Gironde. The Jacobins alone, ignoring others who "sat with the Mountain," were approaching one-fifth of the deputies.

Why then the constant allegations that the Montagnards were a small minority, seeking to dominate an assembly overwhelmingly opposed to them? The answer to this question depends on one's definition of a "Montagnard" and appeared again and again in the course of the debate on the trial. The Girondin technique was to focus attention on the genuinely small and certainly very noisy extreme Left, and to insinuate that anyone pressing for radical measures, over the king or otherwise, was placing himself with this group. And in the matter of attitudes toward the extreme Left two issues were involved, both of vital concern to firm but moderate republicans: the repulsive demagogic rhetoric of men like Marat and Chabot,[37] with its supposed overtones of wildly irresponsible radicalism; and the outside pressure from Parisian extremists—conveyed partly through the Commune, partly through the tribunes, and partly it was believed through the journalistic activities of Marat—which was illegally trying to dictate the Convention's decisions and limit its freedom of debate.[38] Here lay the source of the prejudice to which the Girondins had vainly appealed in their campaign for the *appel au peuple.* It seemed that on a national level a policy might be acceptable *even if* it were urged by the extreme Left and tainted by Parisian support. But after the trial, the Parisian question became more urgent and its implications more alarming, until the Convention was faced with a threat

37. It is interesting that the anonymous letter from Caën, referred to in note 25 (pp. 98-99), was directed at only Robespierre and Chabot by name.

38. Thus Vernier's attack on Marat on 13 April, and his letter to his own commune of Lons-le-Saulnier, accusing the Paris commune of would-be despotism. See *Moniteur* XVI: 149, and Kuscinski, *Conventionnels,* p. 604.

to its own sovereignty which only a very few of its members, not including Robespierre, would willingly tolerate.

Hence the assertion, which must now be examined, that "the Convention" was on the side of the Gironde and against the extreme Left which was openly backing Paris. The Parisian problem, it may be said, exposed all the differences of opinion on the parliamentary Left, which of course existed quite independently of differences of outlook and sympathy between deputies and *sans-culottes*; Marat was easily the most unpopular man in the Convention. Contrariwise, opposition to Paris *concealed* differences of opinion among the anti-Parisians, of which the Girondins only became aware when it was far too late.[39] If "the Convention" had an overwhelming majority which was solidly anti-Parisian, then opposition to Paris would bridge the gap between regicides and antiregicides, as among the antiregicides it bridged the gap between crypto-royalists and republican-minded moderates; and our apparently impressive Mountain will melt away. The evidence relevant to this problem should appear in the April and May *appels*, which raised the matter both personally, over Marat, and in principle, over the Commission of Twelve. If the gap was in fact bridged, then votes against Marat and in favor of the Commission of Twelve should come from a large part of the alleged Mountain as well as from the rest of the Convention. An examination of the general parliamentary situation in April and May should also help in providing evidence as to whether the Mountain had members who shared the feelings of the Gironde about Paris, or whether it was, from the time of the trial onward, a fairly solid body, willing to recognize before 2 June, as during 1793-94, that the settling of accounts with the Parisian Left was not necessarily the Convention's most pressing concern.

39. Thus the dilemma for the refugees in Caën, when they found they had become implicated in a royalist revolt whose aims they indignantly repudiated. C. Barbaroux, *Mémoires*, ed. A. Chabaud (Paris, 1936). p. 231.

CHAPTER 5

THE *APPELS NOMINAUX* OF APRIL AND MAY 1793

I

The impeachment of Marat on 13 April 1793 came as a partial Girondin reply to dangerous agitation in Paris which was directed against the Girondin leaders personally, but which also touched on a very strong feeling common to the whole Convention: its proud jealousy of its own integrity.

The events of the three months which elapsed between the voting of Louis's death sentence and the *appel nominal* on Marat had brought the leaders of each of the contending "factions" to a deepening conviction that their opponents represented a mortal threat to the security and future of the Republic. For the Gironde, the Parisian grocery riots of 25–26 February were evidence that Paris was still frighteningly unruly, and the outburst of 9–10 March, when some of the Girondin presses were wrecked, might be a sign that the personal danger of which they had talked for so long was becoming a reality. In response, left-wing petitions reaching the Convention were bitterly attacked, there was much sympathy for provincial authorities trying to repress radical agitators or showing concern for the plight of the Convention in Paris, and by way of journalism and personal correspondence the Girondin view of the Parisian situation was disseminated in the departments to rally them against Parisian "anarchists."[1] To the Mountain, the Girondins seemed in this activity to be becoming more and more complacent about, if not actually encouraging toward, right-wing agitation verging on open counterrevolution, and the outbreak of civil war in the Vendée, closely followed by Dumouriez's desertion, seems finally to have persuaded Robespierre that his enemies were not far from being traitors. The parliamentary deadlock produced by this mutual enmity has been well described by Sydenham. As he points out, there was no way of breaking it within the Convention,

1. See, e.g., *Moniteur* XV: 441–44, 765–68; XVI: 4–5.

because neither side could either silence its opponents or persuade the rest of the Convention to cooperate in getting rid of them.[2] Both sides wished to preserve the independence and national reputation of the Convention, and this complicated matters for the Mountain even more than for the Gironde.[3] For the line of action being contemplated by those on whom the Gironde depended for support, there are two suggestive pieces of evidence. One was a demand made in an aggressively right-wing petition from Amiens, read in the Convention on 21 March, for "un décret d'accusation contre le parricide de Marat, contre les criminels Robespierre, Danton et leurs infâmes affiliés."[4] The other was a decree passed by the Convention on 1 April, in a wave of emotion following the news of Dumouriez's possible treason, which abandoned the principle of parliamentary immunity and made it possible to arrest deputies "contre lesquels il y aura de fortes présomptions de complicité avec les ennemis de la liberté, de l'égalité et du gouvernement républicain résultant des énonciations ou des preuves écrites . . . " This decree was moved by the savagely anti-Parisian Birotteau, who had recently shown that he was little interested in taking action over infringements of civil liberties if those affected by them were radical agitators.[5] The first deputies to be arrested after it was passed were Philippe-Egalité and Sillery, but there is said to have been a general belief that it was aimed mainly at Marat.[6] This rather implies that neither side in the struggle had much scruple about removing the opposition by any convenient means, the major problem being how this was to be achieved.

Pressure from the departments against "Paris," which was part of the Girondin tactic, might be dangerous because civil war was already under way. Pressure from the Sections on the Convention, which had become the Montagnard tactic, was dangerous because it was more obviously a threat to the Convention's independence, about which deputies of all shades of opinion cared very deeply indeed. On 8 April a deputation from the *Bonconseil* section appeared with a demand that "*les Vergniaud, les Guadet, les Gensonné, les Brissot, les Barbaroux, les Louvet, les Buzot, etc.*," be placed under arrest as accomplices in Dumouriez's treason.[7] The Marat impeachment motion was originally provoked

2. Sydenham, *The Girondins* (London, 1961), pp. 152-64. See also G. Rudé, *The Crowd in the French Revolution* (Oxford, 1959), pp. 119-20. For Robespierre's point of view, *Oeuvres* ed. M. Boiloiseau et al. (Paris, 1958), IX 376-99 (speech of 10 April 1793).

3. See the reference to Rudé, above, in which he quotes Augustin Robespierre's invitation to the Sections on 5 April (delivered in the Jacobin Club) to "*nous forcer de mettre en arrestation nos députés infidèles.*" (Aulard, *La Société des Jacobins*, 6 vols. (Paris 1889-97) V: 125-26.) Rebellion by the Sections against the Convention (instead of pressure on it) would destroy the Convention's authority, and this the Mountain was no more willing to risk than the Gironde.

4. *Moniteur* XV: 765-68.

5. For the decree, *Moniteur* XVI: 30; for light on Birotteau's general attitude, ibid., XV; 525, 723.

6. Gershoy, *Bertrand Barère* (Princeton, 1962), p. 158. See also Sydenham, *The Girondins*, p. 161, where however there is no mention of Birotteau's political sympathies.

7. *Moniteur* XVI: 87.

by a Jacobin circular in much the same sense (Marat having signed it as Jacobin president) urging the departments to recall their unworthy representatives and to rush to the defense of Paris, as the cradle of liberty, against Dumouriez and his allies.[8] Whether or not any group of deputies might be considered traitors, or as good as traitors, demands that they be expelled or recalled at the behest of outside bodies could hardly be reconciled with the Convention's freedom to function as a sovereign assembly.[9] The circular was the immediate provocation for the impeachment, and this seems important, for it represented in part a Parisian effort to turn the tables on the Gironde in the departments; but it seems also significant that it did not figure much in the final indictment of Marat, produced a week after his impeachment, which leaned almost entirely on the old charges of incitement to murder, pillage and "dictatorship," and attacks on the sovereignty of the Convention.[10] Marat had been under criticism for this sort of behavior for more than six months. The Jacobin circular however was more than his personal affair, it was an attempt to force a way out of the existing political stalemate. It was not likely that those at whom it was aimed would accept its line of action, or any other with the same end in view, as legitimate; and, as appeared from the Convention's failure to respond to Robespierre's indictment of the Girondins on 10 April, the Convention itself would not interfere substantially with its own membership: Marat was personally vulnerable, but demands for a "purge" implied surrender to a particular political outlook and were never likely to be willingly accepted.[11]

Given the persistent intransigence of Paris on the one hand and the danger of extending the civil war on the other, the only ways out of the impasse would have been for the Girondins to cease their parliamentary activity, which they refused to do, or to withdraw, as Isnard for example did after 2 June; but unless these actions were to be carried out voluntarily, which was hardly likely, the Convention's integrity would still be infringed. The apparent alternative was to

---

8. Ibid., pp. 136, 147-48. The first extract from the address, quoted in the *Moniteur* of 15 April, implies that the Jacobins were urging civil war. It was not until 17 April that the *Moniteur* printed the remainder which made the proposed line of action clearer and the emphasis rather different.

9. Some Girondins countered such Sectional demands by themselves calling for the convocation of the primary assemblies. On 21 March, in answer to a radical petition from Marseille, the future June petitioner Babey urged the summoning of the assemblies; he was hastily hushed by Barère but supported, to a point, by Barbaroux. *Moniteur* XV: 765-68. Lasource called the possible Montagnard bluff on this on 16 April (ibid., XVI: 167-68). But note Boyer-Fonfrède's disapproval in the same debate.

10. *Moniteur* XVI: 275-76 (3 May); cf. the report of the Convention's acceptance of the indictment, with no details (ibid., pp. 192, 199). All the *Moniteur* reports on this subject are very belated.

11. For Robespierre's speech and the ensuing debate, *Moniteur* XVI: 112-19, 127-36 (Vergniaud and Guadet) and note 2, above. The Parisian demand for a "purge" was evidently felt to be different in kind from, as it was clearly more dangerous than, earlier departmental suggestions that the Convention itself get rid of, e.g., Marat (ibid. XIV: 701-2).

discipline the Parisian radicals while this could still be done, and hence the impeachment, though this too might raise doubts in the minds of those who felt that Birotteau's decree had been too hasty. In the tension of early April it had slipped through without debate, and its perils were yet to be realized.

The voting on the Marat impeachment was as shown in Table 8.

From these figures it appears that the impeachment was chiefly the work of the Girondin and *à l'écart* deputies, who between them contributed more than 75 percent of the votes supporting it. Only the Gironde, however, showed anything approaching enthusiasm. This was the only group which could get even half its members to back the motion. The total vote, even allowing for the

Table 8. Voting in the *appel nominal* on the impeachment
of Marat, 13 April 1793

	For		Against		Abstained/ adjourn- ment		En mission		Absent		Total
	No.	%	No.	%	No.	%	No.	%	No.	%	No.
GIRONDE											
"inner sixty"	33	60.0	1	1.8	9	16.3	3	5.5	9	16.3	55*
June											
petitioners	59	62.8			6	6.4	3	3.2	26	27.6	94
Others	18	69.3			3	11.5	2	7.7	3	11.5	26
Total	110	62.8	1	.6	18	10.3	8	4.6	38	21.7	175
PLAIN											
à l'écart	57	48.3	5	4.2	3	2.5	3	2.5	50	42.4	118
Committees	41	43.2	4	4.2	10	10.5	9	9.5	31	32.6	95
en mission	5	13.5	1	2.7	2	5.4	12	32.4	17	45.9	37
Total	103	41.2	10	4.0	15	6.0	24	9.6	98	39.2	250
MOUNTAIN											
Jacobin	1	.7	47	33.1	9	6.3	57	40.1	28	19.7	142
Montagnard	6	8.2	18	24.6	3	4.1	20	27.4	26	35.6	73
Others			17	19.6	10	11.5	19	21.7	41	47.1	87
Total	7	2.3	82	27.2	22	7.3	96	31.8	95	31.5	302
Grand total	220	30.2	93†	12.8	55	7.5	128	17.6	231	31.8	727
Unclassified	1								7		8
Convention											
total	221		93		55		128		238		735

*Manuel and Kersaint resigned at the end of the king's trial, and Rebecqui on 9 April.

†Duval had been sick for ten days, and, he said, having spent only "quelques heures" at the sitting, had no idea of the evening's program, which he would certainly otherwise have attended. (Similar ignorance may partially explain the low vote.) Dumont, who had had a shocking cold for a fortnight, stayed 12 hours and left at 10 P.M.; he intended to vote, which is why his vote has been counted and not Duval's. The figures have been rectified as far as possible, but are suspect, since Hugo and Second certainly did not cast the votes officially attributed to them. For Duval and Dumont, see the letters annexed to the *appel nominal*.

abstentions which are often ignored, was less than half the Convention's nominal strength. The number of abstentions was striking. Of those present, more than one in seven refused to vote, and among the deputies from the Center and Left the proportion rose to nearly one in five. About one in three of the absentees were *en mission* in the departments; the others, excluding a small number who were ill, either did not choose to come or, like Duval, did not know that the *appel* was being held.

This *appel* provides no evidence that the Convention as a whole was behind this attack on Marat, nor, when the behavior of individual deputies is considered, is there much evidence of a marked swing to the right among the regicides. From the Gironde, 13 convinced regicides voted against Marat, but 8 of these had already registered disapproval of Paris by supporting the *appel au peuple*, and 2 of the remaining 5 were of the *hommes d'Etat* of the "inner sixty" who were Marat's favorite targets. The 12 regicides of the Plain who voted against Marat were more than balanced by 8 antiregicides who opposed impeachment and 7 others who abstained. The deputies undecided or ill during the trial now proved fairly conservative, more than three to one favoring impeachment, but as only 27 in all were among the voters this was hardly a large-scale movement. What happened on 13 April was not that the Convention as a whole turned decisively away from Montagnard policy, but that the Right was present in much larger numbers than the Left and had, therefore, no difficulty in taking control. Of those who in January were decided on mercy for the king, nearly 64 percent voted in April; of those decided on death, fewer than 40 percent.

Among those who were present, the number of abstentions was an eloquent commentary on Girondin political ineptitude, to put it no higher. In dealing with the king, Brissot and others had shifted between principle and expediency and had forced their followers to pick and choose among their scruples. In dealing with Marat they used methods which undermined their own moral position altogether. The abandonment of parliamentary immunity became a tactic more dubious than ever if it were intended to enable the removal of one particular deputy, but Marat's behavior and personality were such that it should have been easy to make a substantial case against him. To realize the full implications of this *appel* and the way in which it was conducted, one has to remember Marat's reputation as an irresponsible rabble-rouser, and the belief or half-belief of many of his colleagues that he was at least partially responsible not only for the September massacres but also for the recent destructive rioting of February and March. How, in these circumstances, did 55 deputies justify their refusal to vote? On Marat's first appearance at the tribune of the Convention, on 25 September 1792, he had been attacked from all sides and hardly a voice had been raised in his defense. He had defended himself with considerable skill, eloquence, and success, but the debate gives the impression that only a handful of members wished him to be heard at all.[12]

12. See *Moniteur* XIV: 49-52; L. Gottschalk, *Jean Paul Marat* (Chicago, 1967), pp. 143-45.

Some of those who abstained in April had not changed their feelings in any particular since September; they justified their abstention by saying that they had been attacked by Marat and might be considered prejudiced. This is the explanation for the at first surprisingly low vote from among the members of the "inner sixty." Six of the nine members of the "inner sixty" who abstained said nothing and did not need to say anything, their view of Marat being well known. Salle and Lasource took the chance to make their point without actually voting, the irresistible quotation being Lasource's: "Si je ne consultois que les principes de l'ordre social, les lois et ma conscience, je voterois sur-le-champ le décret d'accusation: je déclare qu'il le mérite; mais j'ai un genre de grandeur que mes calomniateurs ne connoissent pas, et que les hommes de bien seuls apprécient."[13] Only 2 of the 19 who abstained for this sort of reason were not Girondins. But the ninth member of the "inner sixty" to abstain was Isnard, and he had feelings which were shared by deputies from all over the Convention. There were in all thirty-eight deputies who, whatever they thought of Marat, could not stomach the means used for his destruction. The decree was rushed through at an all-night sitting which had begun at ten o'clock in the morning and did not finish until seven the next day, on the basis of a hasty report which was not debated and which some of those voting had not even heard. The printing of the report, an adjournment to consider it, a proper opportunity for Marat to present his defense, all were refused. Duval's letter of protest, with Dumont's, suggests that even deputies who were in the assembly during the day did not realize what was being planned.[14] To this sort of thing even Isnard took exception: he was, he said, quite ready to vote the decree, but "l'acharnement que l'on a mis à porter le décret avant toute discussion préalable, et la crainte d'être moi-même la dupe d'une intrigue" caused him to abstain.[15] And one of the future June petitioners, Dechézeaux, agreed with him. Objections were raised in various ways. Thirion was worried that Marat had been given no chance to defend himself, Couppé that the report had been neither debated nor printed. Tellier confined himself to the rights of the Convention: "Ce n'est point pour Marat, c'est pour tous les représentans du peuple que je réfus de voter avant la discussion." One of the most telling speeches came from Méaulle, the upright and dignified lawyer from Chateaubriant, who dissected the indictment with chilling precision and controlled indignation and laid it calmly aside.[16] Those favoring impeachment saw little reason to justify their conclusion, and more

13. *Appel nominal . . . contre Marat. . .*, p. 22. This applies also to those who did not attend the *appel nominal*. Brissot and Vergniaud, for instance, had made their feelings known. To help out the prosecution, Brissot helped Tom Paine arrange a strange and dubious press attack with the aim of getting Marat held responsible for an attempted suicide. A. Aldridge, *Man of Reason* (London, 1960), pp. 194–97, and *Moniteur* XVI: 276–78, for this incident, which illuminates Paine's relationahip with his Girondin friends.

14. See the remarks concerning Duval and Dumont, p. 111, above.

15. *Appel nominal. . . sur Marat. . .*, p. 23.

16. Ibid., pp. 44–45 (Dechézeaux's vote); 2 (Thirion), 4 (Couppé), 20 (Tellier); 20 (Méaulle). For the debate, such as it was, *Moniteur* XVI: 147–51; for the discussion preceding the report, only the day before, ibid., pp. 135–36, 138–40.

than 150 of them did not bother to do so. It says something for the depth of feeling aroused on behalf of a man whom few found wholly admirable[17] that almost all of those who abstained on principle explained quite forcefully why they were doing so, and all but a dozen of those on the losing side made speeches too, some of considerable length. In the result there were more speeches against the motion than for it, and by no means all of the attack came from dedicated radicals. The outcome was never in doubt, but the record leaves a strong impression that many deputies were disturbed and anxious about the conduct of a group which was too obviously willing to deny its victim the most elementary formal safeguards.

This feeling was significant, because Marat was possibly the last person in the Convention over whose fate one might have expected *any* member of the Plain to become uneasy; and if the Mountain were to hold firm, an anti-Montagnard majority could only, in the long run, be constructed with the help of equal firmness from the Plain. Over the Marat *appel*, the actual inroads on the Mountain were negligible, and the Plain showed a disquieting tendency to think for itself—so far as it attended at all.

II

During the crisis months of April and May this question of attendance was central, and the problems it raised for the Mountain, far more than for the Gironde, are plain from the April *appel*. The circumstances of the *appel*, combined with Marat's unpopularity, help to explain the small vote on 13 April when, for whatever reason, as many Montagnards did not come to vote as were unable to do so, but the figures show that had every Montagnard in Paris been in the Convention that night their numbers would still only have been a little over two hundred. There were two factors affecting the parliamentary situation at this time: a dislike of involvement in faction fights, which caused voluntary absences on crucial occasions, and service *en mission* which made attendance impossible. Tables 9, 10, and 11 show how the different groups of deputies were affected.

The political inertia of the *à l'écart* deputies was apparently already very marked before June. They had by far the highest proportion of voluntary absentees and the lowest proportion of men *en mission*. However anti-Parisian they might be, they did not seem likely to be a solid prop in the difficult spring of 1793. In the rest of the Plain, the "committees" deputies showed parliamentary diligence, but little anxiety to go *en mission*. The figures for the *en mission* deputies suggest that these men were more interested in constructive activity than in political battle, but the numbers are so small that this is really only guesswork. In the two opposing "factions" the contrast is clear.

17. See, e.g., Garran-Coulon, *Appel nominal. . . sur Marat. . .* , pp. 69–70; and Dechez-eaux's vote, above. Cf. the attitude expressed by Bréard on 25 May: *Moniteur* XVI: 476.

Table 9. Deputies absent from both April and May *appels*

	Total number of deputies	Voluntary absence		Absence *en mission*		Total absence	
		No.	%	No.	%	No.	%
GIRONDE							
"inner sixty"	55	2	3.6	3	5.5	5	9.1
Others	120	11	9.3	3	2.5	14	11.8
Total	175	13	7.4	6	3.4	19	10.8
PLAIN							
à l'écart	118	25	21.2	2	1.7	27	22.9
Committees	95	10	10.5	4	4.2	14	14.7
en mission	37	5	13.5	8	21.6	13	35.1
Total	250	40	16.0	14	5.6	54	21.6
MOUNTAIN							
Jacobin	142	6	4.2	28	20.0	34	24.2
Montagnard	73	5	6.9	10	13.7	15	20.4
Others	87	9	10.3	11	12.6	20	22.9
Total	302	20	6.9	49	16.2	69	23.1

Table 10. Deputies *en mission* between 21 January and 2 June 1793

	Total number of deputies	*en mission*	% *en mission*
GIRONDE			
"inner sixty"	55	4	7.3
Others	120	8*	6.6
Total	175	12	6.9
PLAIN			
à l'écart	118	6	5.1
Committees	95	10	10.5
en mission	37	17	45.9
Total	250	33	15.2
MOUNTAIN			
Jacobin	142	77	54.2
Montagnard	73	24	32.9
Others	87	30	34.5
Total	302	131	43.4
Convention total	730	176	24.1

*Excluding Delaunay *jeune* and Dandenac *jeune*, who do not seem to have exactly gone *en mission* in the public interest. Cf. Kuscinski, *Conventionnels*, pp. 168, 192.

Table 11. Deputies *en mission* in relation to voting over Louis XVI

	For mercy			For severity			Un-decided	No vote	Total
	3 votes	2 votes	Total	3 votes	2 votes	Total			
Voters in trial	234	76	310	327	32	359	40	21	730
Deputies *en mission*	17	8	25	131	3	134	3	12	174
% *en mission*	7.3	10.5	8.1	40.1	9.4	37.3	7.5	57.1*	23.8

*This percentage is put in merely to complete the table.

There was little to choose between Mountain and Gironde in the matter of diligence, in the two *appels* they had the lowest consistent absentee rates in the Convention; but the Gironde kept nearly all its members in Paris, whereas almost one Montagnard in six was away throughout April and May. Over the whole four-and-a-half-month period, the Mountain sent out nearly three times as many members *en mission* as the rest of the Convention put together. This, says Sydenham, "somewhat changed the balance of power in the Convention."[18] It did indeed. Table 11 shows its effect in relation to the balance of opinion which had been arrived at over the trial of the king. Those who had been firmly right-wing over the trial sent one representative in fourteen to the departments after 21 January; those who had been firmly left-wing, two representatives in five. One result of this situation was that on 13 April, out of the members of the future "great" Committee of Public Safety only Robespierre and Lindet were present to vote. Barère, perhaps inevitably, did not come, but the other nine could not have come had they wished to do so—they were all away.

III

Now let us turn to the *appel* of 28 May, over the reinstatement of the Commission of Twelve, surely an admirable test of feelings over the conflict between the Gironde and its opponents and of the solidity of opinion in the various political groups. The Commission had been appointed to investigate repeated claims that an insurrection against the Convention was being prepared in Paris. Its membership was clearly biased toward Girondin policy. Six of the twelve, Bergoeing, Boilleau, Boyer-Fonfrède, Henry-Larivière, Mollevaut, and Rabaut Saint-Etienne, were of the "inner sixty"; the eleven members who had been in Paris for the king's trial had supported the *appel au peuple* by nine votes to two (Boilleau and Boyer-Fonfrède dissenting), and nine of the same eleven had favored the Marat impeachment, with the two abstainers, Gomaire and Kervélégan, making plain their hostility to Marat. The twelfth member of the Commission was Viger, a *suppléant* who had been in the Convention only since

18. Sydenham, *The Girondins*, p. 155.

27 April, but who had distinguished himself by a violently anti-Parisian outburst within three days of his arrival.[19] There were only three regicides, Boilleau, Boyer-Fonfrède, and Bertrand la Hodiesnière, all of whom had voted against Marat. On its record to that point, the Commission was more extreme in its views than even the average of the Gironde. But the demand of the sections on 27 May that it be abolished (a demand conceded that evening by a snap vote under Montagnard auspices) could reasonably be construed as an attack on the independence of the Convention, and this was an issue which might have been expected to obliterate ordinary party divisions.

On 28 May the voting on the reinstatement of the Commission of Twelve was as shown in Table 12.

Table 12. Voting in the *appel nominal* on the reinstatement of the Commission of Twelve, 28 May 1793

	For		Against		Abstained/ absent/ unknown		En mission		
	No.	%	No.	%	No.	%	No.	%	Total
GIRONDE									
"inner sixty"	40	72.7	1	1.8	11	20.0	3	5.5	55
June									
petitioners	69	73.4	4	4.2	18	19.2	3	3.2	94
Others	19	73.0			4	15.4	3*	11.5	26
Total	128	73.1	5	2.8	33	18.9	9	5.1	175
PLAIN									
à l'écart	70	59.3	8	6.8	36	30.5	4	3.4	118
Committees	51	53.7	16	16.8	23	24.4	5	5.3	95
en mission	6	16.2	11	29.7	9	24.3	11	29.7	37
Total	127	50.8	35	14.0	68	27.2	20	8.0	250
MOUNTAIN									
Jacobin	2	1.4	86	60.6	12	8.4	42	29.6	142
Montagnard	10	13.7	42	57.5	9	12.3	12	16.4	73
Others			60	68.9	11	12.6	16	18.4	87
Total	12	3.9	188	62.3	32	10.6	70	22.2	302
Convention total	267	36.7	228	31.3	133	18.3	99	13.6	730

*This figure includes Dandenac *jeune* and Delaunay *jeune*, whose "mission" of 10 May is rather mysterious. They did nothing useful in the west, but busied themselves stirring up rebellion in Angers. (Kuscinski, *Conventionnels*, pp. 168, 192.)

There seems little in this to conflict with the pattern already established. Though a few Montagnards were justifiably worried over the implications of the Sections' behavior, on the whole the Mountain was distinguished by its unity

19. *Moniteur* XVI: 272.

and the proportion of its available members who came to vote. All the notable "moderates" who backed the Mountain in January 1793–Cambon, Barère, Bar, Bréard, Guyton-Morveau–voted, and voted Left. The success of the Mountain in getting those in Paris to take part in the vote was of course more than offset by the unavoidable absences, which told most heavily on those sections of it most definitely committed in politics: the Jacobins were harder hit than any other group in the Convention.

The Gironde behaved much as it had been behaving since January, not as a monolithic body but with a voting pattern which clearly distinguished it from both the Mountain and the Plain. Over this issue, as over Marat, those of its members who were present were much more of one mind than even the *à l'écart* deputies, and a much higher proportion came to vote. The later difference in behavior between the *à l'écart* deputies and, say, the June petitioners is mirrored in the voting: there was not much doubt about *à l'écart* conservatism, but not much doubt of their inertia either. The Plain as a whole showed signs of uneasiness which, as over Marat, appear to have increased in proportion to the degree of later cooperation with the Mountain. There does not seem to be any evidence of sweeping enthusiasm for the Girondin cause. Among the 250 deputies of the Plain the Gironde could collect fewer supporters than it got from its own 175.

These figures bear out the impression given by the *Moniteur* for the January/June period; that the Girondin "control" of the Convention, so far as it existed at all, was artifical, resting not on the overwhelming strength of those opposing the Mountain, but on the dispersal of Montagnard resources in the service of the Republic. And even this degree of "control" did not imply the exercise of political responsibility in the ordinary business of government, which in Paris as in the departments was very largely left to the Mountain. Those who assumed the burden of government after 2 June had in fact largely been carrying it since 21 January. It has long been common knowledge that when the first Committee of Public Safety was set up on 6 April, no Girondin served on it, but how this fact fitted in with the way the Convention's duties were distributed during the whole January/June period is a question which is not often raised.

IV

If one is trying to discover which deputies were entrusted with the leadership of the Convention in matters of general national policy in the months between January and June, there are two obvious sources of information. The first is the membership of the executive committees, the Committee of General Security (in its various forms), and the more junior Committee of Public Safety. The second is the record of debate contained in the *Moniteur*, from which it is possible to see, in a general way, who were the men most active and successful in formulating decrees and getting them accepted by the assembly. Other things being equal, one would expect those prominent in one direction to be conspicuous also in the other: as Brissot, for example, who was one of the leading members of the

Diplomatic Committee in 1792, made the report and introduced the decree which led to the declaration of war on England on 1 February 1793.[20] After the introduction of the executive committees with a very wide sphere of reference, the *rapporteurs* of the individual committees became less prominent, though they did not cease to function.

The Committee of General Security dated back to the Convention's earliest days.[21] As the direct successor of a similar body set up by the Legislative Assembly, it consisted at first very largely of ex-deputies from the Legislative. It was also at this stage very largely Montagnard, a fact much resented by the Gironde, who staged a long campaign to get the membership reviewed. On 9 January they succeeded, and the extent of their victory may be gauged by the reception given to the membership of the reconstituted Committee when it was announced in the Convention: there was an immediate outcry from the Left, with one deputy heard to say "A peine y trouve-t-on deux patriotes!" and Marat coming through the hubbub loud and clear–"C'est une conspiration . . . Reconnaissez-vous enfin les intrigues de la faction? "[22] It was however a purely temporary triumph. On the night of 21 January, in the aftermath of Louis's execution and Le Peletier's murder, the Mountain staged a counterattack which was completely successful. In reporting the result of this election, the *Moniteur* departed from its usual practice and noted the number of those taking part in the voting, which according to its record was 294.[23] This no doubt was to strengthen the impression that the new, almost entirely Montagnard Committee had been elected during *"une séance . . . où il ne se trouvait presque personne,"* as Buzot complained a week later.[24] But the Convention took no notice of Buzot's complaint, nor of his insistence that the Committee be once more renewed. Whether or not the *coup* of 21 January was carried out under exceptionally favorable circumstances, its results were final. An analysis of the membership of the Committee of General Security from 21 January on to 2 June is very suggestive indeed, the more so since the conclusions to be drawn from it seem to be confirmed by an examination of the more famous Committee of Public Safety.

From 21 January until the expulsion of the Girondins from the Convention, 25 deputies seem to have served at various times on the Committee of General Security, and another 9 served on the first Committee of Public Safety, set up on 6 April. The C.G.S. of 21 January had 6 *suppléants*; the C.P.S. originally had

20. For the report, *Moniteur* XV: 127–34 (session of 12 January); for the speech leading to the declaration of war, ibid., pp. 331–32 and 335, where the draft decree appears as Brissot's own.

21. For a full discussion of the membership of the Committees of General Security and Public Safety, see J. Guillaume, *Etudes révolutionnaires, 2e série* (Paris 1909), pp. 253–318. The membership is considered from one particular point of view in Appendix IX, below.

22. *Moniteur* XV: 92. On the subject of Girondin dissatisfaction with the Committee as previously constituted, see the editor's note on the same page, and Guillaume, *Etudes Révolutionnaires*, pp. 253–74.

23. *Moniteur* XV: 265.

24. Ibid., p. 300 (session of 28 January).

9, but after Brival pointed out that the decree establishing the committee did not provide for *suppléants* they were abandoned, and when De Bry refused to serve, another election was held to decide who should replace him.[25]

Among the 34 deputies who served on the 2 committees between January and June, there were 2 antiregicides, Alquier and Treilhard, both of whom however had opposed the *appel au peuple.* The rest of the membership, apart from Camus who had been out of Paris during the voting on the trial, was entirely regicide. The only man on either committee who had supported the *appel* was the "committees" deputy Lecointe-Puyraveau. In terms of the political alignment of 1793–94, both committees were overwhelmingly Montagnard. One Girondin, Jean De Bry, was elected as a titular member of both committees, but both times refused to serve; and another, Lasource, was a *suppléant* elected on 21 January who did serve on the C.G.S., and that was the total Girondin contribution. (Both these men were among the few Girondin regicides.) The nine-member first C.P.S. contained 7 Montagnards and 2 deputies from the Plain; the 25 men who served at various times on the C.G.S. comprised Lasource, one *en mission* and one "committees" deputy (Alquier and Lecointe-Puyraveau), 2 deputies not classified (Camus and Lamarque), and 20 Montagnards. In other words, those who had won the day over the trial of the king, and who had confirmed the victory with the election of the C.G.S. of 21 January, continued to man the increasingly important executive committees from that point onward. When one Montagnard lost his place on the C.G.S. because of prolonged absence *en mission,* another was chosen to replace him. The depletion of Montagnard numbers by the departure of numerous deputies on the recruiting missions of March or the army missions sent out at the end of April, or on other government jobs, seems to have made very little difference; of 12 men added to maintain the strength of the C.G.S. between 21 January and 2 June, 9 were Montagnard. By 2 June, the committee had expanded in size from the 12 members of 21 January to 16, and of its January members, only 6 were still serving; but the 10 new members were Alquier plus 9 Montagnards. Whether or not the verdict of 21 January was accidental at the time, it was continuously confirmed by the Convention thereafter.[26]

In the day-to-day debates one might perhaps expect Montagnard influence to be less noticeable, especially with the exit of deputies to the departments after the beginning of March. (The sending out of Montagnard deputies has indeed been presented as a deliberate Girondin tactic to weaken the Mountain in the Convention.)[27] Yet this does not seem to have happened. The balance of activity between one group of deputies and another might of course vary considerably from one day to another with the type of business that came up, but if the

25. *Moniteur* XVI: 83.

26. For the membership of the Committee of Public Safety, *Moniteur* XVI: 83; for the changes in the membership of the Committee of General Security, Guillaume, *Etudes révolutionnaires,* pp. 277–82.

27. J. M. Thompson, *The French Revolution* (Oxford, 1943), pp. 348–49.

debates are analyzed over a period of weeks, a pattern seems to emerge.[28] In the fortnight leading up to 13 April, a time when the Mountain was suffering heavily from absences, as the Marat *appel nominal* was to show, the *Moniteur* attributes 67 decrees on matters of national policy to motions by individual deputies. Of these, 15 were sponsored by the Gironde, 13 by the Plain, and 39 by the Mountain. A month later the balance was even more plainly in one direction. Between 1 and 27 May inclusive, there were 81 major decrees reported by the *Moniteur*. Of the sponsors, 19 were Girondin, 12 were of the Plain, and 50 were Montagnard. Many of the decrees were proposed on behalf of the executive committees, but this merely underlined the limited influence of the Gironde. The situation was, for the most part, accepted by the Plain, even on occasions when the Gironde and the Mountain directly collided; for example, both the first *maximum* of 2 May and Cambon's forced loan of 20 May were decreed in the teeth of strenuous Girondin opposition.[29]

The continued Girondin assertions that the Mountain was "a minority" are accurate but misleading. It was usually a substantial minority—in the stormy debate of 17 May, Couthon confidently set its numbers at a minimum of one hundred and fifty in a house of between three and four hundred[30]—and it was a minority that was doing, and was being allowed to do, most of the work. The members of the Plain participated, but only to a limited extent. The Girondins, and especially the "inner sixty," shared in the debates, often disproportionately, but their interest and effectiveness in the ordinary business of government seemed to be declining, even in areas which had once been their special concern. On 23 May, Collot asked that a diplomatic problem be referred to the Diplomatic Committee. This was the committee of which Brissot had been a prominent member, from which he had been elected to the abortive Committee of General Defense, and from which he had acted as *rapporteur* when war was declared on England, on 1 February. Buzot replied to Collot's suggestion by saying that the committee had been reduced to two members "and as a result no longer exists," and suggested that the Committee of Public Safety take over its work. There seems to have been no Girondin move to renew the committee's membership or revive its functions.[31] The membership of the executive committees suggests that the Plain was not eager to give the Gironde major responsibility—or, perhaps, they were reluctant to seek it.

In two directions, however, they were consistently and noticeably active. By the beginning of April, perhaps partly as a result of the exodus of deputies on recruiting missions, they had recaptured their monopoly of the Convention's

28. In examining decrees accepted by the Convention, votes of thanks and decisions concerning individuals have been ignored; so have decisions that the matter in hand be referred to the relevant committee, since these involved no commitment.

29. *Moniteur* XVI: 298, 439.

30. Ibid., p. 408. At the evening session Isnard was elected president by 202 votes out of 334—ibid., p. 411.

31. *Moniteur* XVI: 461. The committee was still active on 21 March (ibid., XV: 762–64).

official posts, which had lapsed after 21 January;[32] and they pursued their battle against Paris with every means in their power. This was a reason for their domination of the debates on the new constitution, which began on 17 April. As Vergniaud made plain in a lengthy speech on 8 May, the Gironde saw the constitution as a means of checkmating their political antagonists: "la constitution ... fera succéder le despotisme salutaire des principes à l'insupportable tyrannie des ambitions individuelles."[33] Hence the protracted attempt to limit the size of municipalities, a measure expressly directed at the Paris commune. Naturally the Left resisted, and the debates dragged on, not, as Vergniaud claimed on 21 May, because the Mountain was procrastinating, but partly because there was a good deal else to do and chiefly because there was no chance at all of an acceptable compromise on fundamentals. The Plain showed no inclination to settle the argument, to which few of its members contributed; failing external intervention, it could have gone on forever.[34]

If the Gironde did not "control" the Convention, the Mountain could not have done so either, even had its mission members all been present. The election of the Commission of Twelve, whose members had the backing of fewer than two hundred deputies,[35] might have been avoidable, but even that is problematical, since the reality of the Parisian problem was inescapable. In any case, political assertiveness did not depend on the command of a majority, as such; this of course was the perennial Girondin complaint against the Mountain. The effect of the *en mission* absences, noticed and deplored by both *sectionnaires* and Montagnard deputies,[36] perhaps excused some of the obstruction by the Left between the end of February and the end of May, but there was in fact no way of subduing irresponsible and recalcitrant elements on either side except by *force majeure*. From this arose logically, first, both the impeachment of Marat and the operations (not so much the creation) of the Commission of Twelve by the Gironde, and second, the effort of the *sectionnaires* to enforce the expulsion of the Girondin leaders.

This is not to say that the rising of 31 May-2 June was welcome to all or even to most Montagnards. Robespierre's hesitation is well known, and he was

32. Cf. *Moniteur* XVI: 181, *note*. But this effect can be seen as early as 7 March and 21 March, and may have had other causes; ibid., pp. 644-45, 765.

33. *Moniteur* XVI: 436.

34. For Buzot on municipalities, ibid., p. 455 (22 May); for Vergniaud, 21 May, ibid., p. 436.

35. Sydenham, *The Girondins*, p. 215.

36. See, e.g., the Halle-au-Blé petition read by Pétion on 10 April (*Moniteur* XVI: 100). This Pétion distorted into an attack on the "corrupt majority" of the Convention as a whole; in fact the petitioners claimed that *because of the absence of patriots en mission* the Convention was dominated by a "corrupt majority." Cf. Delacroix's speech on the Marat impeachment (*Appel nominal . . . sur Marat . . .*, pp. 54-55). Note also the way Vergniaud took up and embroidered Pétion's theme on 20 April (*Moniteur* XVI: 178); Like Robespierre's statement about the "virtuous minority," the "corrupt majority" could be cited by the Gironde with great effectiveness.

more inclined to defend the sections than many of those who voted on the Montagnard side in the *appels nominaux*. Soubrany, Romme, Du Bouchet, Grosse-Durocher, Forestier, Guyardin, Robert Lindet—the Mountain had a variety of men, many of whom distrusted Marat's judgment and were not naturally tempted to extremes. Whatever held these deputies so firmly together in the May *appel* was not subservience to Paris, nor indeed subservience to anything. But in the debates of the period two problems constantly intersected: the problem of the Convention's independence from outside pressure—specifically, pressure from Parisian radicals—and the problem of creating and enforcing an accepted national policy to win the war and establish a free republic. The Girondins repeatedly either confused the two or seized on methods to solve one problem which dangerously hindered the solution of the other. Their outlook was reflected, like the Montagnard outlook, both in the *appels nominaux* of 1793 and in the political arguments which raged throughout the first half of the year. In their attitude toward the agitation which was ostensibly in the interest of "the Republic" as against "Paris," the Girondins were consistent in one way and the Montagnards, whatever their opinion of Paris, in another; and this, it is suggested, was the hidden bond of unity on the Left.

V

In an undisciplined, highly individualized and self-conscious assembly, the boundaries of opinion were necessarily movable, and the continual tangle of argument over Paris versus the departments, local rights versus central control, civil rights versus the claims of authority, compounded the confusion. The conviction of many deputies that popular unrest, including unrest over food supplies, was created by counterrevolutionaries did nothing to help. There were moments when a dozen divergent viewpoints were being presented at once, and others when disapproval of *sectionnaire* agitation was virtually unanimous—as on 12 February and again on 12 March, when even Marat's voice (characteristically, from the report, piercing right through the general clamor) joined in the denunciations.[37] Between January and June, however, a series of revealing incidents showed a hardening line between one side of the assembly and the other.

For instance, the somewhat cavalier treatment of the Marat impeachment should have come as no surprise, since there were earlier occasions when it became clear that in the eyes of some deputies civil rights were not the same for everybody. In the absence of central control, local authorities felt obliged to deal with agitators of one kind and another, and disputes about their actions regularly reached the Convention. On 28 January, Buzot rushed to the defense of a journalist arrested by the Paris Commune. From the subsequent evidence, the man was an unrepentant royalist, but his release was supported by Prieur,

37. *Moniteur* XV: 431, 691.

Jeanbon Saint-André, and Thuriot on the principle of freedom of the press.[38] A fortnight later, when a radical agitator was similarly treated by the Finistère authorities, the Gironde opposed his release, though Châles reminded them of the precedent they had helped to set; and when on 21 February Marat pressed for the provisional freedom of a man held in Perpignan without trial or indictment since the previous November, it was again the Mountain that acted. Barbaroux observed that the accused could after all sue for wrongful imprisonment later, if he had a case, and Vergniaud eventually—and inaccurately—twisted the incident to justify far more arbitrary interference with the actions of local authorities in Paris.[39]

So too with the petitions which were the expression of public feeling most often considered in the Convention. On 21 March, an anti-Girondin petition from Marseille was lengthily and indignantly debated; but three days later another petition from Amiens demanding, among other things, the abolition of the recently established Revolutionary Tribunal was hastily passed over as "likely to cause dissension" in the Convention, and only with difficulty could Duhem and Boussion get the floor in order to obtain a formal rejection of it.[40] On 25 May, Duprat expressed concern at alleged limitations on freedom of speech in Marseille imposed by the Convention's own commissioners, against whom a Marseillais deputation had come to protest. It was clear from the general drift of the debate that few of the Girondin contributors were interested in the risk of counterrevolution, but were working on the assumption that all the troubles of Marseille were due to those whom Isnard described as "hommes de faction, sans moeurs et sans remords . . . prenant une tribune pour trône, leurs motions pour lois, un poignard pour sceptre . . ." (and much more to the same effect). When Doulcet supported a motion that popular societies be forbidden to correspond with one another, this was felt to be going a little too far; but the freedom denied to radicals in Finistère and Pyrénées-Orientales a few months before was now to be granted without condition or question to the Marseillais.[41]

The feeling behind all this was summed up by Grangeneuve, in a discussion on a radical address which was brought before the assembly on 26 March, on the eve of Dumouriez's treason. "Je m'étonne" [he said],"qu'on a déjà oublié que ce n'est point le modérantisme qui a failli nous précipiter dans l'abîme que des scélérats avaient creusé sous nos pas; que c'est au contraire ces hommes qui se couvrent avec tant d'art du masque du patriotisme . . . cette adresse . . . attribue les maux de la république au modérantisme, tandis que vous avez reconnu le

38. *Moniteur* XV: 330.
39. *Moniteur* XV: 441-44, 525, 723; Vergniaud's later remarks, ibid., XVI: 408 (17 May).
40. *Moniteur* XV: 765-68, 788. The Amiens petition was the one already referred to (p. 109, above) which demanded the indictment of Robespierre, Marat, and Danton.
41. *Moniteur* XVI: 478-79.

contraire." And Grangeneuve was an ex-member of the Legislative. He had apparently learnt nothing from his experiences of July–August 1792 which was likely to be of use to him, or to France, in 1793.[42]

The Montagnards were willing to pay at least lip-service to principles. Over the Marseille affair, Danton urged that the commissioners' side of the case be heard—this was not so much as suggested by any of the Gironde—and Barère made it clear that there were indeed two sides worth hearing, but all the same the orders of Jullien and Bourbotte in Lyon as well as those of Moise Bayle and Boisset in Marseille were quashed; free speech won a victory.[43] What even right-wing Montagnards were not willing to do was to consider local issues and local actions purely in terms of local and personal prejudice, irrespective of the national interest, and here a continuing battle was joined.

The fundamental issue came up as early as 5 January, when Choudieu begged the Convention to consider the implications of an Haute-Loire decision to raise troops on its own initiative for a possible march on Paris. Next day there were reports of similar activity in Finistère. On 11 January Couthon directly raised the matter of the authority which the departments were arrogating to themselves in raising and controlling independent military forces. On all three occasions the Gironde scornfully cried down the danger.[44] A month later, on 9 February, Cambon and Jeanbon Saint-André returned to the charge, this time in relation to Var and Lot, and some action was finally taken, though only over the angry objections of Chambon and Buzot, who with their supporters could naturally see in the departmental battalions only the counterweight against Paris of which they felt so desperately in need.[45] On 5 March Choudieu directed attention to the problem of departmental volunteers accumulating in Paris, uncontrolled by the War Office, which might not even have been told of their arrival, and suggested that they might be more useful at the front. An abusive argument followed, in which the faults of Paris were freely described, but in which, as Jeanbon pointed out, none of the Girondins concerned himself in the least with the real topic, which was the most economical and profitable use of available troops.[46]

After the recruiting campaign got under way, a new complication appeared. On 30 March a letter was read in the Convention from Levasseur and Anthoine, *en mission* in Meurthe, alleging that their work had been hampered because Salle had written to the departmental vice-president advising in effect that the deputies be assisted only as long as they behaved themselves. Salle did not deny

42. Ibid., XV: 799.
43. *Moniteur* XVI: 479.
44. Ibid., XV: 70, 71–72, 112. Chambon commented on 6 January "Je demande la mention honorable pour la conduite du département du Finistère" (ibid., p. 72).
45. Ibid., pp. 406–8.
46. *Moniteur* XV: 621–23.

the letter. On the contrary, he claimed that in view of the situation in Paris, as evinced by the riots of 9-10 March, he had a right to send it. [47]

The March riots, in wrecking some of the Girondin presses, had been aimed particularly at Gorsas's *Le Courrier des départements.* On 1 April evidence arrived from Allier that the *sans-culottes* were not alone in objecting to the tone of Girondin propaganda. Forestier and Fauvre-Labrunerie, busy with recruiting, forwarded an accusation from the departmental authorities that Gorsas's paper and Brissot's *Le Patriote français* (the other which had suffered in March) were "surrounding with suspicion" the deputies *en mission.* [48] By the end of that week, *sans-culotte* suspicion crystallized in the *Bonconseil* petition which has already been mentioned in reference to Marat's impeachment. After listing the Girondin leaders it wanted dealt with, the section had added an "etc." to cover those men, their names as yet unknown, who were circulating hostile propaganda or writing to the departments urging the arrest of those *en mission.* "Nous connaissons les crimes," said the section's spokesman, "et non les auteurs."[49] In this way the names of those who had been attacking Paris since September 1792 were directly, and not unfairly, linked by the *sectionnaires* with provincial resistance to the war effort. Barère, speaking for the Committee of Public Safety in the debate on the Marseille situation on 25 May, supplied more ammunition in parenthesis by telling of two commissioners just back from Perpignan who blamed Birotteau's letters for the chilly reception they had had. An overestimated complicity with Dumouriez was not the only count against the Girondins.[50]

Parisian petitions might be represented as the work of hot-headed *sans-culottes.* But the persistent danger from the departments was not put before the Convention by its fire-eaters. It was stressed by responsible men who cannot be regarded as blind partisans of Paris; on 30 August 1792 Cambon and Choudieu had both denounced the insurrectionary Commune.[51] The difference between Mountain and Gironde in the broadest sense, a difference which had already

47. Ibid., XVI: 4-5. Salle apparently assumed that the commisioners "represented" the Parisian rioters, since he said he had intended to convey that if the "conspirators" triumphed, as they might have done on 10 March, the commissioners should be held as hostages for the safety of the Convention. He also said that his letter had only been brought up in the Convention "*pour jeter une pomme de discorde.*"

48. Ibid., p. 30.

49. *Moniteur* XVI: 87-88, 90.

50. Ibid., p. 479. The impeachment of Marat was in many eyes as good a proof as could be desired of this complicity; cf. the interjector of 12 April: "*On demande le décret d'accusation contre Marat, parce qu'il a dénoncé Dumouriez*" (ibid., p. 136), and those in the *appel nominal* making the same point. Brissot's disclaimer of any editorial responsibility for *Le Patriote Français,* which appeared in the paper on 2 April, was so apparently belated that it was likely to reinforce rather than dispel suspicion (*Le Patriote Français* defended Dumouriez until 1 April); and his claim that he had made his position clear on 11 March still left his tacit acceptance of a pro-Dumouriez policy since that date an unresolved problem.

51. Ibid., XIII: 575.

appeared in the debate over the *appel au peuple*, lay in the assessment of the greatest potential threat to the Republic: the Gironde and the Right seeing it embodied in a Paris-centered dictatorship, and the Left, speaking through Prieur on 9 February, in possible disintegration via uncontrolled local initiatives—"*si cette conduite est tolérée, la république n'est plus qu'un vain nom.*"[52] The representatives *en mission* were the official agents of the Republic for the direction and, if necessary, the discipline of the departments, and agents for Paris only in so far as Paris was the seat of government.[53] This at least was the Montagnard line; there were indications that the Gironde disagreed.

In areas like Marseille, where personal interests were involved, some disputes might be expected. Nevertheless, it is a little startling to find Barbaroux on 12 May accusing Moise Bayle and Boisset of recruiting followers among the local paupers, to the outrage of honest working men; they were, he said, "openly preaching brigandage and murder."[54] Possibly he believed it, but why did he not press more firmly to have the deputies recalled at once? In fact they were not recalled, nor were Levasseur and Anthoine, nor Forestier and Fauvre-Labrunerie, despite the "suspicion" with which they were surrounded; someone had to do the work. With rare exceptions, the only Girondin contribution was doubt and criticism. On 7 May there was an interesting argument between Cambon on one side and Gensonné, Buzot, and Barbaroux on the other. Cambon, for the Committee of Public Safety, proposed that those *en mission* should be empowered to recruit committees from local government bodies, popular societies and the general public, to keep them informed about the available resources and economic situation of the areas for which they were responsible. To this Buzot replied, "Je ne veux donner à personne le droit de voler et de piller mon pays," and Barbaroux, seconded by Gensonné, maintained that nominations to the committee should be completely controlled by the local authorities, since otherwise the deputies would handpick the membership "*pour servir leur vengeance.*" The Convention rejected this amendment, it being all too obvious that, as Delacroix tactfully put it, a number of departments were not "*à la hauteur des circonstances.*" The exchange reveals the chasm that had opened between the future opponents of the Jacobin régime and even the more moderate of its adherents.[55]

---

52. *Moniteur* XV: 523. The immediate question was the Var department's irregular use of national tax revenues for local food purchases, but the delinquencies of Parisians and *septembriseurs* drifted into the argument at a very early stage.

53. Not that Paris was sometimes admitted as having any status at all. Cf. Guadet's snub to the secretary of the Paris department, who had made an unwise reference to the "capital" of France: "I must remind you, citizen, that in a republic there is no capital." Ibid., XIV: 252 (19 October 1792).

54. Ibid., XVI: 372.

55. For the whole debate on this subject, which was spread over two days, *Moniteur* XVI: 327–32.

VI

The significance of these incidents, however, lies not only in the antagonism which they establish, but in the attitude of those present in the Convention to the issues which they raised. On 7 May, as on a number of earlier occasions, the Convention adopted Montagnard policy. This supports Mathiez's claim that on national issues the Plain supported the Mountain. But by the middle of May the line between "local" and "national" issues was almost impossible to draw. In one sense Buzot's objection to extended powers for deputies *en mission* was a defense of local interests, in another it was a reckless refusal to accept the need for central authority. Girondin anti-Parisian propaganda was the outcome of a private feud between the Gironde and the Commune plus the parliamentary Left, but when Montagnards *en mission* found their work for the Republic obstructed because of their alleged sympathies with "Paris," a larger question arose. Departmental troops to protect the Convention were all very well, but if they were independent of government control and were kept in Paris when they were needed elsewhere for the defense of the whole Republic, their value to that Republic might be queried. Finally, the Parisian demand for a purge of the Convention and the Girondin counterattack on the Paris Commune were alike in mid-1793 suicidally dangerous, whatever the outcome: the local squabble had produced a threat to national security.

Which way did the Convention's sympathies lie? In all these matters except the last a majority came to accept the logic of Montagnard policy; and over the Parisian dispute the Mountain was itself unwilling to be aligned with the rebels until there was no alternative. But given the general direction of Girondin policy, as it developed between September and March, the hostility of Paris was predictable. For the majority to reject Girondin leadership in national affairs and yet to back the Girondin leaders against Paris was ultimately an intolerable contradiction. After 2 June the number of our 730 deputies who, with varying degrees of enthusiasm, backed the Mountain was 434, or almost exactly 60 percent. It could not be called a handsome majority. On the other hand, there seems to be no evidence that the Gironde before 2 June commanded, or could have commanded, an equal amount of support.

How good is the evidence for the conclusion that the Jacobin régime of 1793-94 had a more solid foundation than has sometimes been supposed? The Mountain, as it has been estimated, had an astonishingly united voting record in the 1793 *appels nominaux*. Were its internal divisions concealed by the fact that so many of its presumed adherents were *en mission* that spring? It may at least be noted that those Montagnards who had been *en mission* since 21 January, but returned in time to vote on 28 May, were more likely to be there to vote and less likely to support the Commission than their fellows who had remained in Paris all the time.

Table 13. Montagnards *en mission*, 21 January–2 June 1793: Voting on
the reinstatement of the Commission of Twelve, 28 May 1793

	Still *en mission*– no vote	Absent/ abstained/ unknown	For	Against	Total
Jacobin	42	2		33	77
Montagnard	12		1	11	24
Others	16	1		13	30
Total	70	3	1	57	131

If this can be taken as established, the behavior of the supposed "Mountain" before 2 June 1793 was very appropriate to the political attitude adopted by its members afterward, and those members, if a minority of the Convention, were a very considerable minority indeed.

The deputies in the remainder of the Convention also seem to have had patterns of behavior which make sense in terms of the political attitudes which have been attributed to them. The Gironde during the trial of the king was rather more united than a large part of the Plain, though with a good deal of excuse for being seriously divided, and after the trial its members consolidated; more than 60 percent of them had a record of consistently conservative voting from 16 January onward, implying that it was the strategy of the *appel au peuple* rather than the outlook embodied in it which some could not accept. This record was unmatched by any other group, including the *à l'écart* deputies, and was buttressed by the openly anti-Parisian feeling of nearly all the Girondin regicides. There were altogether 49 clear regicides who later *voted* against the Left, as distinct from opposing the Jacobin régime; 26 of these were Girondin. But the solid core of Girondin backing seems to have lain with men who were consistently moderate: men who, whether or not they favored the *appel au peuple*, would not consider executing the king, approved of the methods used to rid the Convention of Marat, and in assessing the rights and wrongs of the collision course adopted by the Commission of Twelve and the Commune, believed the Commission to be right.[56]

Most of the *à l'écart* deputies were clearly conservative, and consistently so. They were also as clearly losing interest in politics after January. The *en mission* deputies were so few that little can confidently be said about them, except that there was little in their voting record which was inconsistent with their combina-

56. In the detail of all this, of course, there were countless variations; both Gironde and Mountain were clique-ridden and individualistic. But for the Gironde, rather more than for the Mountain, the pace was set by the more violent rather than by the restrained, and all that someone like Boyer-Fonfrède could do was to try and pick up the pieces. He and Ducos were intelligent and valuable members whom the Mountain did not wish to see sacrificed on 2 June; but in the end, personal affection, local loyalty, and natural prejudice caught many deputies in a net they could not escape.

tion, in 1793-94, of considerable activity and a dislike of commitment to extremes. For hesitancy and confusion the "committees" deputies came easily first. Their 10 regicides who later voted with the Right were balanced by 7 antiregicides shifting to the Left, and they had 22 deputies who seemed unable to follow any clear line at all. (The Gironde and the *à l'écart* deputies each had 16 such undecided voters and the Mountain none.) The Convention record for uncertainty was held by Du Bignon, a "committees" deputy who voted in every *appel* and after his first 2 appearances changed sides with every vote. His unhappy progress—against the *appel au peuple*, against a death sentence, against a reprieve, in favor of the Marat impeachment, but finally against the Commission of Twelve—may serve to symbolize the series of painful choices faced by others who also accepted the Jacobin régime without either undue disturbance or much enthusiasm.

The implication of the evidence which has so far been examined is that there was in the Convention a large number of deputies prepared before 2 June 1793, as later, to accept the political line commonly associated with the Mountain, and that these deputies also did a disproportionate part of the actual work of government in the debates, *en mission*, and on the major committees, in a period during which the Gironde is said to have been politically dominant. If this implication is accepted, it would explain some of the discrepancies in conventional accounts of French parliamentary history at this time. For example, it has long been known that a large number of men went out *en mission* in the spring of 1793 and that many of these men were Montagnard. It has also been obvious that enough Montagnards remained in Paris to carry on a series of running fights with the Gironde. If these two facts are put together, it hardly seems possible that the Mountain was merely "Robespierre . . . and the delegation and city of Paris."[57] Any limitation of potential Montagnards to Robespierre's personal friends and admirers, even if the definition is extended to take in all of the left-wing deputies for Paris, makes the Jacobin régime almost unintelligible. Moreover, if the Montagnards were in fact a small minority, it is hard to explain why the expulsion of twenty-odd of their opponents should have given them "a working majority,"[58] except on the assumption that the Convention would be so cowed, and so diminished in numbers by voluntary withdrawals, that most of its members would be completely inert; and, in fact, there is no evidence of mass withdrawal immediately after 2 June, and the behavior of the June petitiioners does not support the conclusion that panic reigned supreme. Many of the deputies may well have been seriously frightened as well as being very angry. If this were so, then one would expect a dramatic falling-off in attendances at the sessions of the Convention. Yet Dodu, who has tried to estimate the average attendance at sessions from looking at the numbers voting in the regular

57. Sydenham, *The Girondins*, p. 198.
58. Rudé, *The Crowd in the French Revolution*, p. 120.

elections of the *bureau*, provides evidence that this was not quite what happened. The figures he gives for 13 June are higher than those for 25 January, when there was no military or domestic emergency to drain deputies away to the departments. From 3 August 1793 onward, he estimates the average at about 200 to 260, or about 100 less than between January and April; which, allowing for Girondin withdrawals and expulsions and *à l'écart* absences, seems reasonable enough.[59] The feelings of those who remained on duty one can only guess at, remembering however that a good many of the stories of the atmosphere come from men who had no wish to see any virtue in the Jacobin regime, and that some allowance should perhaps be made for the fact that the declared targets of the insurrection were members of a small and identifiable group.[60] As far as the attitude of the general public toward the deputies was concerned, there is the story of Lejeune, a "committees" deputy from Mayenne. On 18 June he took under his wing two delegates sent to Paris by the local authorities from his own area with a violently Girondin petition, and escorted them to his lodgings to stay the night. His reason for doing this was that whereas by themselves they might have been roughly handled—their reception in the Convention had been a stormy one—Lejeune believed that as a deputy, whatever his views, he would be respected by the crowd; and he was.[61]

It is entirely possible that the atmosphere in the Convention was indeed one of terrified acquiescence, but the trend of events after 2 June is easier to understand on the hypothesis that the Montagnard element was quite substantial and that in many fields its leadership had long been accepted. This hypothesis of accepted leadership would also make comprehensible, for instance, the choice of Saint-Just, Couthon, Hérault de Séchelles, Ramel, and Mathieu to assist the Committee of Public Safety with work on the Constitution. This took place on 30 May, before the insurrection, and was apparently accepted by the Convention with no demur at all, though of the 5, Ramel was of the "committees" and Mathieu of the *"en mission"* group and the other 3 were Montagnard.[62]

Much of this argument must necessarily center on the question of definition: who was of the Mountain and who was not? If to be Montagnard was to be

59. G. Dodu, *Le parlementarisme et les parlementaires sous la Révolution (1789–1799)* (Paris, 1911), p. 196.

60. Not that this would have been much comfort to men who thought that criticism of Paris would land them in the same position; but (a) the June petitioners were quite vocal after 2 June, and (b) the presence or absence of such men would not affect the 60 percent of the Convention which has been reckoned as its minimum for the post-June period.

61. F. Gaugain, *Histoire de la Révolution dans la Mayenne*, 2 vols. (Laval, n.d.), I: 418–19, 483. Envoys from Angers arriving a few days later were in fact manhandled. On Lejeune, see also Kuscinski, *Conventionnels*, p. 396.

62. *Moniteur* XVI: 512–15. Although the evening of 30 May heard the rumbles of the approaching storm, the morning and most of the afternoon were taken up with ordinary business. It seems interesting that in the course of this ordinary business the main speeches were made by Montagnards, and that not a single Girondin is reported by the *Moniteur* as having said anything at all. In the *appel* of 28 May, Ramel had been absent and Mathieu had

"Robespierrist," then the Jacobin régime was not Montagnard. Would Vadier have been happy to have been so described? Would Cambon or Carnot or Amar or Robert Lindet? If to be "Montagnard" was to will the death of the king, to oppose the effort to rally the departments against Paris, to make the best of 31 May-2 June, and to support the Revolutionary government of the Year Two, then on an examination of all its membership the Convention elected in September 1792 seems to have had more Montagnards than men who sympathized either actively or passively with the Gironde.

Montagnard influence was not based on a firm majority, nor even on a disciplined minority in the modern sense. The Convention had no monolithic parties, and its organization gave individualism full rein. Rather, what drew the Montagnards together may have been some sympathy with the feeling underlying Bréard's comment of 25 May: "Je crois Marat pur, mais égaré . . . Mais je crois aussi que plusieurs de mes collègues, tant de ce côté que de l'autre, sont dans l'erreur, et n'ont pas assez de courage pour faire le sacrifice de petites passions. . ."[63] The *petites passions* of the Gironde had led to the *appel au peuple*, surely the most revealing gamble that a political group ever undertook; but neither on 15 January nor later is there evidence that the Girondins had any real hope of capturing the majority of the whole Convention which over the trial had gone (but narrowly) to the Mountain.

Arguments about the size of majorities and minorities have, however, little relation to the real problem, which was that neither the more intransigent of the Girondins nor the more impassioned of their opponents saw any need to accept inconvenient decisions as legitimate, however arrived at. The conditions of ordinary parliamentary government were scarcely present in France in 1793, but the evidence suggests that from January onward the Montagnards managed to secure something which operated in effect as a working majority so far as decisions on general matters of national policy were concerned, and in this sense, and with the problem of the Parisian/Girondin feud excepted, may be regarded as having been as near to a parliamentary government as conditions and the political theory of the time would permit. Because revolutionary government was, in fact, far less coherently organized, it was possible for an anomalous situation to develop. It was possible for the executive committees to be substantially Montagnard and to be maintained thus by the choice of the Convention; it was possible for most of the Convention's executive agents in the departments to be Montagnard and to be maintained thus by the choice of the Convention; and it was possible for the Girondin leaders to exploit the real distrust of *sans-culotte* agitation to be found in all parts of the Convention, so as to maintain an influence which in other fields they had almost entirely lost. (The character of the executive committees gains added significance when it is remembered that

---

voted with the Gironde; the other 3 had voted with the Mountain. Both Ramel and Mathieu were regicides.

63. *Moniteur* XVI: 476.

"the Convention" which elected them was, after the end of February, one in which the numbers of the Left were very sharply reduced.) There is no evidence that even as far as Paris was concerned the Girondin influence ever amounted to the control of an absolute majority, but in the circumstances of 1793 it could sometimes function as if it did. In a direct confrontation over Paris, the Mountain might have won a majority—supposing it to have remained as united, or nearly so, as it was over the *appel au peuple*. The evidence of 28 May suggests that this was possible, though one cannot be sure. But this is to suppose that all the Montagnards would have been able to be present at such a confrontation, which in the crisis months of 1793 was very unlikely to be the case. On the other side, there is no evidence that when it came to a point the Gironde could rally much more support than it got over the *appel au peuple*; in April and May, nearly all the non-Montagnards were in Paris, but a number would not cooperate.[64]

The Parisian question came up often enough, but it did not stultify all the Convention's debates, nor produce continuous complaint by one side and obstruction by the other. Had it been so, government business could not have been transacted at all. But as the crisis of civil and foreign war deepened and objections from the departments to the inevitable demands of deputies *en mission* multiplied, petitions flowed back to Paris which the Girondins could not resist exploiting, and at the same time the Girondin campaign to reverse the balance of power in the Parisian sections, which was under way in May, increased the number of clashes in Paris itself.[65] Although the provincial quarrels and the Girondin attitude toward them might be taken as more evidence against the Gironde by those looking for such evidence, on such matters some compromise could be reached, as was evident from the 25 May debate on Marseille, which has already been referred to. When the incidents were Parisian and the Sections' delegates angrily appeared to plead their own case, or, as sometimes happened, the Girondin deputies themselves were being harassed, compromise was impossible, since the sections were intransigent and the Girondins would not consider conciliation. It was this sort of issue which produced most of the tumult in the Convention and the accusations that the Mountain was an obstructive minority—as on such occasions it certainly was. It is enlightening to compare the *Moniteur's* record of the session of 17 May, in which such an incident ended in uproar, with that of 11 May, when business proceeded in comparative calm and the powers of the Committee of Public Safety were, despite a Girondin challenge, renewed for another month.[66]

64. Of the 267 of our 730 deputies who backed the Commission of Twelve on 28 May, 70 percent (187) had voted for the *appel au peuple*, and 34 of the remaining 80 were convinced antiregicides.

65. Cf. Sydenham, *The Girondins*, pp. 170–72.

66. *Moniteur* XVI: 406–8, 411–13; 365–68. The *Moniteur* put the number of those opposing the renewal of the Committee's powers at about fifty (ibid., p. 367). For an example of the pin-pricking suffered by some Girondin deputies, ibid., p. 343 (8 May).

The circle here was complete. The planning to remove the Girondin leaders was a reality, which unless they would capitulate must have led to the Commission of Twelve or something like it, which in turn precipitated the insurrection. There was however another question which made some settlement of the Girondin/Parisian clash both inevitable and urgent. The Convention had been called into existence primarily to draw up a new constitution for France. The discussions during May had revealed what the Girondins intended the new constitution to achieve; but their plans apparently included more immediate action as well. In a letter to his constituents, written on 20 June, Rabaut-Pommier claimed that the attack on the Convention had been designed to forestall two decisive events. First, the Convention was about to decree that under the new Constitution a limit would be set to the size of municipalities; second, the submission of the Commission of Twelve's report would have unmasked the Parisian conspiracy against the Convention. Without the insurrection, said Rabaut, Parisian plotting would have been brought to light, and a barrier would have been set up against any such danger in the future; therefore the conspirators had to act while there was still time.[67]

Rabaut seems mistaken in saying that the Convention had formally decided to accept the Girondin proposal on a maximum size for municipalities; indeed the uncontested election to the C.P.S., as a consultant on the constitution, of Saint-Just who was a known opponent of this idea[68] may have been a favorable portent for the Mountain. But he was certainly right in implying that it was a Girondin plan, and it seems highly probable that they hoped to carry it off in the near future. It was a matter which could hardly even be discussed without reference to Paris, and had it been forced through the Convention, might have provided more than enough excuse for the antiparliamentary insurrection which the Mountain was so anxious to avoid. Yet the debate on the constitution had to continue and could not do so indefinitely without creating more trouble, since charges of obstruction and deliberate delay were already being made.[69] It is hard to see how in this particular matter Girondin policy could have led to anything but a bitter and protracted wrangle, or, a worse alternative, the provocation of Paris into a rebellion against the authority of the Convention as such. In this, as over the continuous exasperation of complaints and protests, the insurrection delivered the Convention from a cul-de-sac.

By ordinary parliamentary rules, the Gironde should have been utterly discredited in April 1793, after the failure of the *appel au peuple*, with all its implications, had been succeeded by the almost wilful misjudgment of the Dumouriez situation, over which Marat had shown such uncomfortable prescience. No one has assessed Girondin political incompetence more incisively

67. F. Rouvière, *Histoire de la Révolution dans le département du Gard*, 4 vols. (Nîmes, 1888), III: 513.

68. *Moniteur* XVI: 463–64, for his speech on the subject.

69. Cf. Henry-Larivière on 18 May (*Moniteur* XVI: 420).

than Sydenham.[70] What needs to be added to his account is the evidence that as far as the main affairs of the Republic were concerned, the Convention seems to have shared his views and acted accordingly, by entrusting responsibility to mainly left-wing deputies who were rather more numerous than he admits. Unluckily, as far as the Girondin feud with Paris and with their enemies in the Convention was concerned, there was no way of effectively avoiding the line of action which the Girondins wished to see taken without accepting the Parisian line instead, which for good parliamentary reasons most deputies not of the extreme Left were most reluctant to do. The Parisian insurrection was one way out of this dilemma, which seemed to be completely intractable, and broke the parliamentary deadlock in favor of a group of men who not only had better claims to govern than the Girondins, but had in fact been doing most of the work of government for some time.

The events of 31 May–2 June therefore do not represent a coup d'état transferring or, except remotely, consolidating government power in the larger sense. They had the effect of removing from the Convention a group of men who had already lost the power to govern, but who were making the task of government more difficult for others by forcing attention onto a problem which at that time it was not possible to solve. These men were not traitors nor counterrevolutionaries, but circumstances had placed them in a position where their only means of defense against their critics was to pile up more evidence against themselves and to push the Convention and the radicals of the capital into mutual opposition. By March 1794 it was possible to bring the Commune under control. The danger of calling on Lyon and Marseille to help in doing so in May 1793 was extreme, and the coup removed from the Convention those most active in promoting such a suicidal policy. If this had the effect of rousing dangerous opposition in the departments, it can at least be said that the most stubborn of such opposition came from those who were at bottom opposed to the Republic as well as to Paris. No majority in the Convention, however constituted, was likely to approve of the coup, but those who profited most from its results were members of a group which already had the support of a majority for the daily conduct of government.

* * * *

So far, attention has been concentrated on the deputies as members of the parliamentary body to which they belonged. The conclusions which have been reached about their political attitude will now be tested in another way, by looking at some of the electorates which sent them to Paris in September 1792.

70. *The Girondins*, p. 208. He might perhaps have stressed rather more the illogicality of any reference, on behalf of the Girondins, to "the Rule of Law and the right of the individual to resist oppression by the State" (ibid., p. 210), which was quite uncharacteristic of their own behavior at points of crisis.

Some examination will also be made of their personal characteristics and political experience, to see what sorts of men were elected to the Convention and what experience may have helped to shape their decisions as revolutionary statesmen.

PART III

THE DEPUTIES AND THEIR BACKGROUND

Le sort de la France va être décidé.
                    Electoral assembly of the
                        department of Eure,
                        3 September 1792

*La patrie en danger excite des allarmes, et fait
        renaître le courage.*
                    Electoral assembly of the
                        department of Jura,
                        8 September 1792

CHAPTER 6

THE DEPUTIES, THEIR ELECTORATES, AND THE ELECTIONS OF 1792

I

It is now time to alter the perspective, and to consider the results of the political analysis of the Convention against the background provided by the actions taken and the views expressed by the electoral assemblies of 1792 from which the different departmental delegations emerged. For there were no individual local constituencies for metropolitan France in 1792;[1] every deputy was a member of a group of representatives, usually chosen one by one to be sure, but chosen at a single election by the secondary electors of his department (or a department willing to choose him as its deputy) sitting as a body for the one purpose of settling the membership of the Convention; and there must therefore come a time at which the political views of the members of any one delegation presented in the preceding chapters must be looked at collectively, in this local electoral context, to see whether the picture still looks at all plausible.

This is a kind of inquiry which cannot be expected to produce definitive conclusions. Indeed it may be argued that there is small point in making it at all, since the crucial political conflicts of the Convention's early history could not have been anticipated when its members were elected, and the local political problems which possibly loomed large during the elections were likely to fade into the background once the deputies reached Paris. Yet responses to the events of the Revolution had already in 1792 been very different in different parts of France, and if the conflicts of 1792-93 were more than superficial, one might expect some sort of correspondence between the general outlook of a delegation and the general political atmosphere in the electoral assembly responsible for its selection. For very many of the men involved, the divisions in the Convention

---

1. Pomme (Guiane) who arrived on 10 April 1793 was the only *conventionnel* to be the sole representative of his department. The other colonies had from 2 to 6 members each. The minimum number in any metropolitan delegation was 5.

involved more than a purely personal struggle; there was a real clash over political values and the price to be paid for the survival of the Republic. If this clash of values rather than of personalities was of any serious importance, then it is relevant to examine something of the quality of a man's background as well as the line of his major political decisions. In the crudest sense, there should be at least an absence of inexplicable discrepancy between the outlooks of electors and elected. Anomalies there well may be, electors and elected may well have been mutually deceived—but it would have been to say the least unexpected had the Orne assembly bestowed one of its seats on that son of the department who in 1792 was editing *Le Père Duchêne* in Paris. The assembly was indeed looking for celebrities, local talent being apparently rather scarce—but not that sort of celebrity.[2]

The pages which follow will be concerned initially with the proceedings in the electoral assemblies which (except in Corsica) began their sessions on Sunday, 2 September 1792, and sat for periods ranging from three days in the somewhat perfunctory Pyrénées-Orientales to eighteen days in Paris, where circumstances outside the electors' control prolonged the elections to the very eve of the Convention's first meeting. The survey will be limited to a consideration of what went on at the electoral assemblies proper, that is to say at the gatherings of the electors who had been chosen by the primary assemblies, on and after 26 August, to do the work of actually selecting the deputies. A comprehensive study of the primary assemblies is long overdue, but would be in itself a very large work bearing on rather different problems. There were about six thousand primary assemblies; many seem to have met quite peacefully, some fell into actual schism, some sent no electors forward and several had presidents who refused to forward the electors' credentials, and some did not meet at all. Furthermore, of the electors they chose, not all arrived at, or were admitted to, the secondary assemblies which followed. The final decision on the composition of the secondary assemblies was taken by those assemblies themselves. It is therefore the record of the individual secondary assembly rather than that of the mass of primary assemblies which preceded it which forms the background for the choice of each departmental delegation. It was this *procès-verbal*, or some part of it, which was sent to Paris to establish that the newly arrived *conventionnels* had legal authority to take their seats; this was the official and accepted record of what went on, from the point at which the electors congregated in the town square, or in a parish or monastic church, to the point at which the assembly dispersed or (in a few cases) declared itself temporarily adjourned.

2. In its original list, Orne chose 5 deputies who later refused: André (its bishop, L.A.), Priestley, Sieyès, Gorsas, and Carra. Collombel, its only Jacobin, was elected as fourth *suppléant*. Hébert was born in Alençon, but though he had kept some connections and childhood friends in the area he was unpopular in his native department, knew it, and had no good to say of the Ornais. P. Nicolle, "Le mouvement fédéraliste dans l'Orne" (I), *Annales* XIV (1936): 504; A.N. C 180 C II 59 (Orne).

Usually the record covers all aspects of the national elections, even if the cover is sometimes rather exiguous. In the occasional case of a lively and indignant assembly, it goes further, to describe how, after finishing the national election, the electors proceeded to make a clean sweep of the local officials as well, and when this happens, more light is naturally shed on local problems and attitudes; contrariwise, in two departments (Indre-et-Loire and Haute-Vienne) the assembly's *bureau* did not think it necessary to send to Paris a full account of even the national elections, and the Legislative Assembly and the historian are left to make the best of *extraits* which describe the election of each deputy as it occurred, but tell nothing of the way the assembly had been constituted or of the other matters (if any) which it had discussed.[3]

These however are exceptional. The value of comparing the *procès-verbaux* in general is that each of them represents the record as the local assembly was willing to see it presented, and the historian is able to compare the way in which a duty common to the eighty-three departments was approached, carried out, and described by each assembly in turn. From such a study, a number of things emerge: not only the attitude of any one group of electors to the events of 10 August and to the Legislative Assembly but also the information about national politics which had reached the assembly, the interest taken locally in its proceedings, the assembly's own criteria for the admission of its members, the procedures those members chose to adopt, and the extent to which, as representatives of the sovereign people, they were or were not prepared to move beyond the duties they had been summoned to perform. Some assemblies were faced with local rioting; at least one actively concerned itself with the suppression of counterrevolution; half-a-dozen were roused to frenzied activity by the threat of invasion, and two fled *en masse* from the approaching enemy, to reassemble stubbornly in slightly safer surroundings to complete their work. Each *procès-verbal* has a flavor of its own, a flavor which comes from a consideration of all the activities it describes, taken as a whole and compared with those of other departments; and in this sense, even the meager report from Pyrénées–Orientales can yield a surprising amount.

It seems convenient to begin by considering what the assemblies were told about what they were supposed to do and why they had been asked to do it, what other information was provided for them about the national situation, and how widely this information was disseminated. We may then go on to look at the amount of local interest in the election, and outside factors (deputations, Club activity, petitions, the presence of spectators) which may have influenced the outcome; and finally, we may look at the rather different ways in which the elections were in fact conducted. It may then be possible to see whether all that

3. Indre-et-Loire sent only *extraits* of its electoral proceedings to Paris, and the departmental archives have nothing more. Haute-Vienne sent a list of those elected, with no further details; so did Nord and Seine-et-Oise, but in these two cases the full *procès-verbal* is available in the local archive.

emerges is a bewildering mass of local variations, or whether patterns of behavior can be discerned. At this point, the departmental delegations may be set in their local context, to see whether there is any apparent relationship between attitudes shown by an electoral assembly and positions later taken up by the deputies which it chose. In this respect, it must be remembered not only that some departments elected outside candidates, celebrities who had little or no direct connection with the local scene, but also that a very large number of departments elected retiring members of the Legislative Assembly, most of whom had been away from home for nearly a year when the election took place. In the first instance, it will be interesting to see which departments had the most taste for celebrities; and in the second, to examine the implications of the reelections on so large a scale.

II

Between the Legislative Assembly's acceptance of the fall of the monarchy, on 10 August, and the meeting of the electoral assemblies to choose the members of the Convention, on 2 September, the Legislative sent out to every department in France seven major documents relating to the constitutional emergency. Of these documents, three gave practical instructions to the assemblies about what they were to do; and the course of the elections was to show how sensibly these instructions had been expressed and how adequately they had been distributed. But necessary though they were, the practical directives did not comprise the bulk of the literature which the Legislative wanted to get into the electors' hands. The greater part of this literature was not intended to tell the electors what to do, but to make clear to them why they had to do it, to explain the actions taken by the Legislative and to buttress its position as the de facto embodiment of national sovereignty; and to this end, the Legislative's own decrees were filled out by circulars and printed matter, broadcast to every departmental authority both by the *comité d'inspection* as it made its way through part of the papers found in the Tuileries, and by Roland the Minister of the Interior, who was organizing the elections and was more than happy to supply covering letters for any and every batch of documents. From time to time the *commission extraordinaire* also took a hand. And to round out the picture of governmental activity, as well as for immediate action, there was the flow of decrees dealing with specific problems—arms, recruiting, and transport.

Of France's 83 electoral assemblies, fewer than half-a-dozen recorded the receipt of even most of the major items in this corpus of information. Some filled in some of the gaps with a selection of other material; some received some items more than once and others not at all; and some seem to have had virtually nothing, or to have taken so little interest that they did not think its arrival worth noting. Nevertheless, despite these variations, it is possible to see in nearly all the assemblies outside Paris a common body of assumptions about the events of 10 August and the nature of the existing emergency, and it will be argued that these assumptions reflect the views presented in the Legislative Assembly's official communications.

In looking at the material available to the assemblies, and the various attitudes adopted toward the elections, the electors' general situation must be kept in mind. The Convention elections were held a bare three weeks after the fall of the monarchy, often amidst great local confusion during which many of those who had been elected to the highest local office less than a year before were suddenly finding that their whole political outlook had become completely unacceptable. There was also a war crisis, which was all the more alarming because although the military situation was likely to worsen dramatically at any moment, its details were almost completely unknown. Communication between Paris and the departments was at best uncertain and at worst chaotic. Its unreliability is suggested by the uneven distribution of the decree directing the assemblies to add the choice of new *hauts-jurés* to their duties. This was passed on 25 August. It reached the Hautes-Alpes assembly by 6 September, the Lot assembly by 6 P.M. on the 11th, and the Oise assembly (just outside Paris) by 7 P.M. on the 7th and did not get to the Sarthe assembly at all before the electors dispersed very late on the evening of the 10th. In this instance, the very patchy distribution did not matter very much, since attention to this particular decree was mainly a matter of convenience. What was very important indeed was the dissemination of the information relating to 10 August; the more so, since a sizable proportion of the electors were not likely to have access to much more than current rumor.

One has sometimes the impression that the electoral assemblies of the Revolution were not only dominated by, but very largely made up of townsfolk. Whether or not this was true in elections before and after 1792, one cannot help being struck, in the 1792 *procès-verbaux*, by the quite considerable importance of the rural element among the electors. There is so much evident anxiety to get the business of the elections over with; sometimes, certainly, as in Loire-Inférieure or Haute-Saône, for political or military reasons, but also because in early September many of those present had other things to do.[4] *Suppléants* and/or *hauts-jurés* were sometimes elected all on one ballot, to save the time which might otherwise be consumed by repeated voting—and here one has an echo of the rural primary assemblies which insisted on choosing their electors all at once, by "relative" majority, instead of one at a time, because they had to get back to their work.[5] Some assemblies flatly refused to consider additional duties, however urgent these might appear: Lozère ignored a frantic appeal that it patch up the ranks of the departmental administration, Indre and Sarthe gladly seized on a technicality to evade the election of *hauts-jurés*, and Landes managed to ignore

4. A.N. C 179 C II 42 (Loire-Inférieure) 9 Sept.; C 180 C II 69 (Haute-Saône) 3 Sept.
5. Cf. A.N. C 179 C II 50 (Haute-Marne) 2 Sept.

altogether the collective resignation of the entire departmental council.[6] That this sort of thing might result from a real clash of priorities rather than from mere laziness or indifference is suggested by the proceedings in Côte d'Or, where a notably active and radical assembly yet suspended its activities from 9 September to 1 November, à cause (as it said) des travaux de l'agriculture.[7] This sense of urgency produced working hours which seem more suited to country people than to townsfolk; how many middle-class lawyers in eighteenth-century France habitually began work in their cabinets at 6 A.M.? Yet this was quite a common hour for electoral assemblies to start their labors, and a thirteen- to fourteen-hour day (admittedly with a two-hour break at about midday) was also usual.[8] Some assemblies started at 5 A.M., and few started later than seven. The presence of many farmers is also suggested by the obvious number of illiterates. The more extended descriptions of the electoral procedures commonly explain that the electors either wrote their ballots or got the tellers to do it for them: though there might be a certain amount of trouble even over the choice of tellers—the Nièvre secretary noted that the scrutateurs d'âge, the doyens who acted until the assembly was formally constituted, were the oldest men present who were able to write.[9] This rural element in the assemblies is worth some emphasis, because although clearly present in considerable numbers, these electors were not likely to be well-informed about national politics. In some cases, even if they could read they could not read French: in Finistère an important petition was translated into Breton for the benefit of a large part of the assembly, and in Moselle, Haut-Rhin, and Bas-Rhin it was accepted that many present knew only German, so that translation would be necessary.[10] Hence the importance of Roland's direction, sent out on 26 August, that official documents be read to the electors.[11] This was by far the safest way to get the material across, although many copies were also provided for distribution, and posters were sent to be put up in the meeting hall.[12] Some comparatively sophisticated assemblies could confi-

6. A.N. C 179 C II 46 (Lozère) 7 Sept.; C 179 C II 35 (Indre) 8 Sept.; C 180 C II 71 (Sarthe) 10 Sept.; C 179 C II 39 (Landes) 7 Sept. Landes apparently relied on the promise given by the conseil-général to stay on duty until it was replaced.

7. A.N. C 178 C II 20 (Côte d'Or) 9 Sept.

8. For an example from the many assemblies which recorded their times of meeting, cf., Haute-Saône (5 or 7 A.M. until the late afternoon ballot was finished); A.N. C 180 C II 69 (Haute-Saône). Somme sat on 3 September from 7 A.M. to 9 P.M., and daily thereafter (with a two-hour lunch break) from 6 A.M. to 9 P.M., ending with a session which ran straight through from 6 A.M. on 17 September to noon on 18 September, an average of more than 13 hours' work a day for 16 unbroken days. It seems remarkable that the bureau survived. A.N. C 180 C II 78 (Somme).

9. A.N. C 179 C II 56 (Nièvre) 2 Sept.

10. E.g., A.N. C 180 C II 66 (Haut-Rhin) 2 Sept., when proceedings began with the reading of the 13 August decree and the Exposition des Motifs, in French and in German.

11. See note 10, above, for response to this; and A.N. C 179 C II 44 (Lot) 3 Sept., for specific reference to Roland's direction that the documents be read to the electors.

12. See, e.g., A.N. C 178 C II 15 (Charente) 3 Sept.; C 178 C II 32 (Gironde) 4 Sept.

dently say that they already knew what was in the documents, or ruled that they would hear only the titles, to see whether there were any novelties, but these were the exception.[13] The Creuse assembly was more typical; on 2 September it spent all its time from 2 P.M. to 11 P.M. in combining the election of its *bureau* with the reading of decrees and proclamations *in extenso.*[14]

The basic documents which the Legislative Assembly had intended to communicate to the French electorate were: (i) its own statement of intention, of 10 August; and (ii) its more detailed decree, of 11 August, providing for the convocation of the Convention; (iii) the *Exposition des motifs d'après lesquels l'Assemblée nationale a proclamé la convocation d'une Convention nationale, et prononcé la suspension du pouvoir exécutif dans les mains du roi* (13 August); (iv) *Adresse aux Français* (19 August); (v) the resolution of 21 August guaranteeing that the Convention would meet in Paris on 20 September and that the deputies of the Legislative would stay at their posts until that date; (vi) statements by the *comité d'inspection* concerning various collections of documents relating to the king's civil list; and (vii) the decree of 25 August, ordering the election of new *hauts-jurés*, which has already been referred to. The lessons to be drawn from all this were spelled out by the *conseil exécutif provisoire*, in a proclamation about the elections sent out on 25 August.[15] The Legislative added more ammunition by issuing two pamphlets, the *Réflexions sur l'acte du corps législatif* and the *Instructions sur l'exercice de la souveraineté nationale*, the second of which had been proposed and apparently drafted by Condorcet before the fall of the monarchy.[16] Lastly, there was the Jacobin-sponsored *Tableau comparatif des sept appels nominaux fév.–10 août 1792*, sent out by the Paris Club on 29 August with a covering letter from the president, but sometimes simply accepted by the electors as official;[17] and there were proclamations and letters from the *conseil exécutif provisoire*, from the *commission extraordinaire*, and from Roland, which might or might not cover the same ground all over again.[18] The flood of paper was further swelled by the anxiety of those in Paris to make sure that the various items did in fact reach those for whom they were intended. A justified distrust of many of the men currently in departmental office had led the Legislative to decide that copies of the decrees of 11 and 13 August should be sent to districts as well as departments, so that the electors often got packets forwarded from both sources, and possibly in addi-

13. The Haut-Rhin assembly said that most of the material had been in the papers; A.N. C 180 C II 66 (Haut-Rhin) 3 Sept.

14. A.N. C 178 C II 22 (Creuse) 2 Sept.

15. Note Danton's comment on 20 August (*Moniteur* XIII: 479) that as minister of justice he had had to send out 183 decrees since 10 August, and that there would therefore be "some slight delay" in distribution.

16. Ibid., p.375.

17. A.N. C 179 C II 52 (Meurthe) 2 Sept.

18. A.N. C 179 C II 50 (Haute-Marne) 3 Sept.

tion, further consignments sent by Roland on 26 August in the belief that many assemblies might still be uncertain what they had to do.[19] The burden on the *gendarmerie* (part of which was simultaneously being mobilized for active service with the army) and on any available couriers was necessarily immense, and to it had to be added that imposed by the other decrees, such as those on recruiting. How many of the documents intended for them did the electors ever actually see?

Any answer to this question can only be approximate. For procedural reasons, if for no other, a very large number of assemblies did list more or less conscientiously the correspondence they received, but the individual items may be vaguely described, or the descriptions may be ambiguous; a few are clearly erroneous; and some assemblies fail to mention any at all, although it is clear from the context that the basic information at least had certainly arrived.[20] Except in a few special instances, it is safer to indicate the approximate number of assemblies which seem to have received various documents than to attempt to give exact figures, since precision must almost always depend on a personal estimate of the meaning of some of the evidence and the significance, if any, of gaps in the record.

With all this said, three generalizations at least can be made with some confidence. First, that what the Legislative Assembly believed to be the fundamental points relating to the elections had been thoroughly driven home in almost all departments; second, that beyond this, information even from the Legislative itself was at best very unevenly distributed; and third, that the efforts of the radicals in Paris to disseminate their view of events had met with very limited success.

For the Legislative Assembly, the essential documents were the decrees of 10 and 11 August and the *Exposition des motifs* of 13 August. These are mentioned in the overwhelming majority of *procès-verbaux* and even when not mentioned seem to have been known. The possible exceptions to this rule were the assemblies in Seine-et-Marne and in Corsica; in both these places the electors engaged in lengthy and exhausting arguments over details of procedure and the numbers of those to be elected, arguments which would, one would think, have been unnecessary had the decree of 11 August been put before them—though of course it is always possible that it was deliberately ignored.[21] All other assemblies seem to have known what they were supposed to do, even if they did not always do it, and to have been familiar with the form of the legislation, even to the point where details of wording could be cited to justify an unusual line of action. It seems that the triple safeguard of distribution to both departments and districts, plus a final broadcast on 26 August, had had the desired effect: although in Aisne this excess of caution backfired when the assembly, receiving

19. A.N. C 178 C II 31 (Gers) 5 Sept., for receipt of Roland's 26 August letter.
20. So A.N. C 180 C II 79 (Tarn), on 2 Sept.
21. A.N. C 178 C II 19 (Corse) 13 Sept.; C 180 C II 73 (Seine-et-Marne) 5 Sept.

what it thought to be a pointless further consignment of copies of the *Exposition des motifs*, simply put them back in the parcel instead of circulating them among the electors as had been intended.[22]

So far, so good. But beyond this basic information, no single item seems to have reached much more than half the assemblies, and in the case of the Legislative's documents, it was never as many as half. The Legislative circular of 25 August, about the elections, was mentioned by only about a dozen assemblies, and the resolution of 21 August by only four; even if this latter was set out again by Roland in his letter of 26 August, the Rhône-et-Loire *procès-verbal* of 7 September is evidence that Rhône-et-Loire, at least, had never heard of it.[23] The *proclamation* of 25 August seems to have had rather wider currency, but is mentioned by only about thirty assemblies; the *déclaration* of the *commission extraordinaire* probably reached only about twenty, but this was a matter of small import, since it was in any case identical with the *Exposition des motifs*. Again only about thirty assemblies mentioned the receipt of the *comité d'inspection's* evidence against the king, but this ground had been well covered in the *Exposition des motifs* and all that the committee was doing was providing detailed evidence in support of some of the accusations.[24] The failure of the *hauts-jurés* decree to circulate was more serious, since this required action, and here at least one can be definite about the evidence. The decree if received had to be implemented, and it is hard to see how its arrival could have been concealed. Of the 83 departments in France, only 28 elected *hauts-jurés* at all, and of these, 2 (Mayenne and Morbihan) proceeded provisionally on the basis of newspaper reports of the decree. As the Mayenne *procureur-général-syndic* pointed out on 7 September, the Legislative Assembly had a lot on its hands, there were bound to be delays . . . but all the same, a fairly general delay of a fortnight and more, in the circulation of a decree which had to arrive with reasonable speed if it were to be of any use whatever, seems a little excessive.[25] In the matter of additional propaganda, the Legislative need not have troubled itself, since what it sent out seems not to have got very far. The *Réflexions* was noted by 13 departments and Condorcet's *Instructions* by 5.

For the rest, assemblies here and there received scattered examples of the legislation passed in the last fortnight of August, apparently quite at random. It is sometimes suggested by historians that the decree of 26 August providing for the deportation of nonjurors was passed in order to influence the elections, presumably by removing a possible source of counterrevolutionary agitation.[26] This is an attractive and persuasive theory, but it does not quite fit the facts. The decree was first proposed on 21 August, but there was no apparent hurry to put

22. A.N. C 178 C II 2 (Aisne) 3 Sept.
23. A.N. C 180 C II 68 (Rhône-et-Loire) 7 Sept.
24. A.N. C 178 C II 15 (Charente) 3 Sept. for a typical collection of documents.
25. A.N. C 179 C II 51 (Mayenne) 7 Sept.
26. Cf. J. M. Thompson, *The French Revolution* (Oxford, 1943), p. 312.

it through, and it did not take its final form until the very day the primary elections began, although it was on this local level, if anywhere, that the non-jurors were likely to exert their influence. Nor does the news seem to have spread very fast. The only secondary assemblies to record it were those in Corrèze, Haute-Garonne, and Hautes-Pyrénées. In Calvados the arrival of batches of priests in coastal towns, evidently on their way out of the country, excited rowdy demonstrations, and the assembly intervened to protect the clergy from the risk of bodily injury, but there is no reference to any legislation on the subject. In Eure-et-Loir, where priests allegedly traveling in *voitures de luxe* were twice nearly mobbed, the electors took action to see that the local authorities could provide adequate protection, but again there is no apparent knowledge of the decree. Lastly, when the Jura assembly heard of the fall of Verdun, just as it was about to disband, it was jolted into a flurry of activity which included a direction to the departmental authorities to round up as hostages all the local nonjurors and aristocrats who could be found. It seems unlikely that this particular instruction would have taken this precise form had its authors known of the deportation order. Had this been widely known, it would surely have been widely publicized, since a number of departments (Maine-et-Loire, Ain, and Cantal, to take only three examples) were seriously worried over nonjuror activity.[27]

The emergency decrees of 26 August and later seem to have been almost unknown. Half-a-dozen departments, all, curiously, in the south, registered receipt of the legislation on the distribution of arms to inland departments (26 August) and on *visites domiciliaires* (28 August). Corrèze alone specifically mentions the decree mobilizing the *gendarmerie*. And the decree of 23 August, marking the penultimate stage in the abolition of feudalism, was referred to even by inference in only three assemblies, those of Morbihan, Dordogne, and perhaps Haute-Marne. An important decree of which the assemblies might well have been aware, though strictly speaking it was no concern of theirs, was that of 27 August, calling for an emergency levy of 30,000 men in Paris and its neighboring departments. Only Loir-et-Cher, Lot-et-Garonne, and Haute-Garonne directly record news of this, Loir-et-Cher being the only one of the three to be affected by it; and Orne provided specific evidence that in one canton, at least, on 11 September recruiting had not yet begun.[28]

Up to a point, the Jacobin attempts to inform the electorate seem at first to have fared a little better. The Jacobin-sponsored *tableau comparatif* did reach about half the assemblies, or perhaps a few more. But this is not a very high figure if one considers that this was the only evidence of the collective behavior of the members of the Legislative Assembly to be put before the electors at all.

27. A.N. C 178 C II 18 (Corrèze) 2 Sept.; C 178 C II 30 (Haute-Garonne) 3 Sept.; C 180 C II 63 (Hautes-Pyrénées) 3 Sept.; C 178 C II 27 (Eure-et-Loir) 4 Sept.; and C 178 C II 13 (Calvados) 7 Sept.

28. A.N. C 180 C II 59 (Orne) 11 Sept.

Other Jacobin documents are almost untraceable. The *Adresse aux 83 départements*, for example, was noted in only Oise, Orne, Haute-Saône, and Meurthe; one earnest elector managed to read to the Seine-et-Marne assembly the Commune's resolution of 2 September, and Somme had the benefit of Ronsin's 18 August address to the *Théâtre Français* section; and that is virtually all.[29]

This was a war crisis; what of war news? A very few assemblies (Aude, Eure-et-Loir) received a large *pacquet* of assorted printed matter, including letters from Lafayette, from *commissaires* sent to the armies, from patriot soldiers reporting from the front, etc.[30] But this was very unusual, and indeed one prominent feature of the elections was the participants' apparent ignorance of the whole military situation. Ardèche, of all places, noted receipt of the Legislative's decree on the fall of Longwy, but the fall of Verdun was a disaster of which word spread slowly and haphazardly, even through the areas most likely to be affected. The Ardennes assembly, confronting its own emergency, did not have time to hear at all. The threat to Sedan was enough to drive the electors from that city to Mézières, whence they dispersed on 5 September, apparently unaware of other events. The Meuse assembly did hear and with good reason; it was meeting in Goudrecourt, about 40 miles from Verdun, and when it appeared on 3 September that an attack in their direction was imminent, the electors fled to Châlons-sur-Marne. Among the other assemblies which recorded receipt of the Verdun news, the time-table was as follows: Marne, the third of September; Oise, perhaps the third or fourth; Vosges, the fourth; Haute-Marne, about the fourth; Yonne, the sixth; Doubs, the seventh; and Jura, the eighth. Paris, of course, had heard on the second and served as a center to funnel out information elsewhere. (It may be assumed that the Seine-et-Oise electors must have heard about the third.) It seems strange, but the state of communications made it a fact, that Yonne's information came via 4 *commissaires* from Paris and not from any more direct informant. To these 10 departments we might perhaps add on presumptive grounds Meurthe and Moselle, whose assemblies sat until the seventh and ninth respectively; it seems almost inconceivable that some rumor should not have reached them, but if so, they did not bother to record the fact or any action resulting from it. A possible total of 12 departments (among 83) directly aware of the immediate military emergency suggests that it had a rather limited impact.[31]

It seems from some *procès-verbaux* (that of Vendée, for example)[32] that many electors were keeping up with press reports, which were obviously a valuable background for their work. But access to these was uneven, limited, and subject to the delays of an erratic and overloaded postal service.[33] Perhaps for

29. A.N. C 180 C II 73 (Seine-et-Marne) 5 Sept.; C 180 C II 76 (Somme) 6 Sept.
30. A.N. C 178 C II 10 (Aude) 3 Sept.; C 178 C II 27 (Eure-et-Loir) 3 Sept.
31. This excludes Nord, which like Ardennes had its own problems to cope with.
32. A.N. C 181 C II 79 (Vendée) 5 Sept.
33. Cf. the Mayenne comment on the inevitability of delays, note 25, above.

this reason, the September massacres seem to have been known to six assemblies only outside Paris: Vosges certainly, Seine-et-Marne, Seine-et-Oise, Oise, Loiret, and Yonne almost certainly; and of the six, Vosges alone recorded its response.[34]

With all these delays and confusions allowed for, it may be supposed that whatever version provincial Frenchmen had had of the fall of the monarchy would have come to them well after the event, and with overtones of uncertainty and quite probably of local political dissension. During the elections, however, the electors had put before them a version of 10 August which was detailed, convincing, and given the hallmark of official approval. The near-universal distribution of the *Exposition des motifs* was more important than it may appear, for this was many things in one: it was an account of the crisis, a justification of the Legislative Assembly's conduct and policy since 10 August, and in addition, by inference as well as directly, a summing-up of the way in which the revolution had been achieved and the part which the Legislative had played in it.

What then did the assemblies learn from the *Exposition des motifs*?

The fall of the monarchy presented the Legislative with an extremely delicate problem. On the one hand, maintenance of its own sovereign authority as the source of the de facto government of France was essential if the country were not to slip into chaos during the interval which must elapse before the Convention could meet. On the other hand, the very calling of the elections was a recognition that sovereignty did not reside in the Legislative but in the people at large. Moreover it was not the Legislative which had dethroned the king, and the only thing which could legitimate 10 August was an assertion about the exercise of ultimate sovereignty which, if pushed to its logical conclusion, gave the revolutionary Commune a claim to greater moral authority than the Legislative could hope to possess.

In this dilemma, the deputies maneuvered with considerable skill. The decrees of 10 and 11 August were so phrased as to recognize the ultimate reality of popular sovereignty, while stressing the need to serve the common interest by keeping within the rules provided in 1791. They embodied an invitation, not an order—the Legislative well knew that it was in no position to give orders—but an invitation designed to encourage maximum obedience to the suggestions embodied in it. The technique was remarkably successful, though, as we shall see, the assemblies occasionally went their own way, and when they did, there was no sanction which could be applied. In condemning some electoral procedures as a *violation flagrante de la loi*, Mortimer-Ternaux seems mistaken, for this was a situation in which no final law existed, as the Legislative was uneasily aware.[35]

34. A.N. C 181 C II 82 (Vosges) 6 Sept.
35. Cf. Mortimer-Ternaux, *Histoire de la Terreur*, 8 vols. (Paris, 1864–1881), IV: 52, and the opening of the *Exposition des motifs*, *Moniteur* XIII: 416.

And hence in part arose the further problem, when the deputies came to justify the events which had made the elections necessary. A truthful account would have revealed the helplessness of those disillusioned with the monarchy in the face of passive resistance from those who would not abandon hope of it, and would have emphasized the fact that—as Chabot reminded the *côté droit* on 17 August—the insurrection of 10 August had been caused by the behavior of a section of the Legislative itself: "c'est vous qui l'avez faite, cette insurrection, c'est l'absolution de Lafayette qui a fait répandre le sang français aux Tuileries, et vous me paraissez couverts du sang de vos concitoyens . . ."[36] This was naturally the last thing the deputies felt inclined to record. It would have drawn attention to the dangerous conflict of opinion within the Legislative instead of creating the desired impression of strength, unity, and patriotic resolution; it would have destroyed the valuable possibility of cooperation between republican deputies and those erstwhile constitutionalists who were willing to accept the fall of the monarchy; and, most seriously, it would have provided a matchless basis for counterrevolutionary propaganda. That this last danger was both real and considerable was amply demonstrated by the reports coming in, in mid-August, from Sedan, where the constitutionalists in control were trying to convince their public that 10 August was the work of a small group of subversive Parisian scoundrels.[37] The more credit given to the Commune at the expense of the representatives of France as a whole, the more support was likely to be given to such stories. Setting aside the wounded pride of the deputies and their excusable inclination to set their own status far above that of a mere municipal administration, there were sound practical reasons for placing the Legislative and its actions in the very center of the stage, and in the rosiest possible light.

This the *Exposition des motifs* admirably succeeded in doing. In four thousand closely argued words, it did not mention the Commune of 10 August once. Attention was concentrated on the king's behavior and the Legislative's long, fruitless struggle to preserve *le salut public*, while simultaneously staying within the limits of its own constitutional authority. As the stages in the crisis were sketched in, the Legislative was presented as coming to the brink of decision, held back from precipitate action by the knowledge that it could and should move only after *un examen mûr et réfléchi* and . . . *après avoir entendu et pesé toutes les opinions.* At this point, it was explained, the people's patience was exhausted (not with the Assembly, but with the king) and in the face of intolerable provocation the attack on the Tuileries took place.[38] Thereafter the narrative could move smoothly on. Once the assembly of early August had been painted as united, resolute, and restrained solely by its respect for constitutional proprieties, the popular revolt became merely an accidental mechanism and not

36. *Moniteur* XIII: 452.
37. Ibid., p. 456.
38. Ibid., pp. 416–17.

a controlling force. The question of Paris did not arise. Of course, the question of Parisian distrust of the Legislative did not arise either, and given the alleged patriotism and devotion of the Legislative, any friction between legislature and municipality would appear to be the product of Parisian arrogance and insubordination. This situation was not suggested in the *Exposition des motifs*, but if its line of argument were accepted, very little foundation was established for any understanding of the Parisian point of view, which indeed was likely to become quite incomprehensible.

This then was what the electoral assemblies of France were told about the crisis which had produced the elections. Putting this together with the other information described above, we may say that they were in a position to know a good deal about the king and his actions, a little (all of it favorable) about the energy of the Legislative in framing policy since 10 August, virtually nothing about either the position in Paris or the military situation at the end of August, and a limited amount (perhaps) about the recent conduct of their current representatives in the legislature. The official account of the fall of the monarchy gave a sound revolutionary analysis of its causes, but a version of its actual achievement which might well be grossly misleading. If the electors had adequate information from other sources, for example from local clubs disseminating news from Paris, or from a radical press, they might be expected to show at least some recognition for the authors of the revolution—say, in the form of an address of congratulation for the Parisians, or something of that sort. But if they had no way of supplementing what the *Exposition des motifs* provided, then anyone coming to the Convention from the departments might arrive with some quite serious misconceptions. Let us now look at the assemblies themselves.

III

How wide was the range of opinion in the 1792 electoral assemblies, and what pressures were exerted on the electors to influence their decisions?

As far as the primary assemblies are concerned, it is generally accepted that only a small minority of electors, perhaps one in five, took part in the elections, and it was implied by Mortimer-Ternaux that monarchists either did not participate at all or were excluded from the electoral assemblies by the small minority of republicans who had taken charge. But detailed evidence is lacking.

The vote may well have been small, though one local historian has said that in his area there were more voters than in 1791.[39] It was less than a year since the last election; the harvest was an urgent responsibility, and if some primary assemblies telescoped their procedure so as to get back to the fields, one may imagine many voters who did not bother to come at all. In departments like Maine-et-Loire, in which the problem of the oath had made even municipal

39. L. Testut, *La petite ville de Baumont, en Périgord, pendant la période révolutionnaire*, 2 vols. (Bordeaux, 1922), I: 419.

elections a matter of bitter contention, whole communities might well not participate for reasons which had little to do with the fall of the monarchy.[40] And four departments, Ardennes, Nord, Meurthe, and Meuse, were suffering foreign invasion.

All this might depress the voting figures, but does not touch on the question of the extent to which power passed by default to a republican minority. Here again there can be no final answer, but the *procès-verbaux* indicate that supporters of a constitutional monarchy did participate, and that it was more common for monarchical resolutions to be noted in the minutes than for electors from the primary assemblies which had passed them to be forced out of secondary assemblies for that reason alone. Perhaps many monarchists had been intimidated into inactivity,[41] but the evidence suggests a different conclusion.

Out of the 83 *procès-verbaux*, 37 indicate that monarchists had been chosen as electors, and/or that primary assemblies had expressed support for a monarchy. In at least 24 of these assemblies, some electors were excluded.[42] But at least 10 assemblies certainly accepted electors with monarchical mandates, and 46 others did not exclude anyone for that reason. In at least 16 departments, what was at issue was not monarchism per se, but something much more like counterrevolution. To take two extreme examples: Ardèche's assembly cannot he called radical, but was aghast at the behavior of its elector Daizac, who fled after casting a defiant ballot for the Comte d'Artois; and Côtes-du-Nord was equally taken aback by André Caraval, who, although a municipal official, had not taken any oath since 1789 and would not take one which was not to the laws of the *ancien régime* (he said further that if he knew what the defense of liberty and equality required him to do he would not do it.[43]) The formal exclusion of men like these hardly argues rigid republican intolerance, indeed their presence in the electoral assembly implies that there was a wide spectrum of opinion among the electors. Two assemblies did follow the Parisian lead in excluding electors who had signed protests against the Tuileries demonstration of 20 June; some of the implications of this action are discussed below. But the

40. Cf., for example the struggle in some Maine-et-Loire communes in 1791 to get any valid municipal election conducted at all; as A. D. Maine-et-Loire I L 72, 19 November 1791.
41. As Goodwin claims: A. Goodwin, *The French Revolution* (London, 1966), p. 122.
42. The 24 were Aisne, Ardèche, Aveyron, Bouches-du-Rhône, Calvados, Charente-Inférieure, Côte-d'Or, Côtes-du-Nord, Creuse, Dordogne, Doubs, Drôme, Gard, Haute-Garonne, Hérault, Ille-et-Vilaine, Loire-Inférieure, Maine-et-Loire, Meurthe, Nièvre, Orne, Paris, Bas-Rhin, and Rhône-et-Loire, a likely enough list which however does not include some of the very radical assemblies of 1792. Assemblies apparently accepting electors with constitutionalist mandates were Ain, Allier, Ariège, Cher, Gironde, Lot-et-Garonne, Isère, Lot, Manche, and Vosges; there are indications of others. The figures as I have given them do not quite add up because some of the evidence is ambiguous.
43. A.N. C 178 C II 6 (Ardèche) 4 Sept.; C 178 C II 21 (Côtes-du-Nord) 9 Sept. Côtes-du-Nord had a leisurely assembly, and Caraval apparently sat as an elector for an entire week, during which 7 of the 8 deputies were chosen, before a committee finally reported on the case against him.

number of assemblies excluding electors *for any reason whatever*—including being under age—was only 31. Isère in fact accepted electors who were not only patently monarchical, but had been chosen in a manner which was illegal by any standard.[44]

It rather seems that support for the monarchy may have been lacking, because in the circumstances of 1792 this went further toward counterrevolution than most articulate Frenchmen were prepared to go. It may be, of course, that the monarchists were the inarticulate majority; but on this point there is some possibly relevant evidence from the only disputed election of 1792 of which details are recorded in an electoral *procès-verbal.* In the canton of Mauzun (Puy-de-Dôme) there was a *scission*, and one-quarter of the voters seceded to conduct a separate poll. From some descriptions of the Convention elections, one might assume that this minority would have been republican and the majority monarchist. The views of the minority of 73 are not recorded, but the victorious majority of 214, whose delegates were accepted as electors, was certainly republican.[45]

If we move from an analysis of the general political atmosphere to look at the outside influences to which the electoral assemblies were themselves subjected, the evidence is more concrete, since many of the *procès-verbaux* describe in detail the deputations, addresses, letters, and local disturbances which came the assemblies' way while they were in session. It may be noted that in 1792, the potential influence of clubs or popular groups was limited from the start by the fact that with few exceptions the elections were held in comparatively small towns. The Marne assembly did meet in Reims, the Lot assembly in Montauban, the Bouches-du-Rhône assembly in Avignon, but Saumur (Maine-et-Loire), Bernay (Eure), Chaumont (Oise), St. Jean-de-Loue (Côte d'Or) were much more typical rendezvous.[46] The smaller the town, the less likely it was to have a very numerous club or a vigorous group of radicals, and in this sense the very location of the elections tended to minimize the influence of the Left.

The easiest way to gauge the amount of active outside interest in the elections is to see, if possible, whether spectators were present and to look at the deputations and/or addresses received by the electors. These might come from many sources: from district and commune officials, judges and justices of the peace, National Guard and *gendarmerie*, contingents of regular or volunteer troops on their way to the front; and also from peripatetic *commissaires* from the Legislative Assembly or the Paris Commune, and from private citizens. If we add the local *société populaire*, if there was one, to this already lengthy list, it is a little surprising that only the Charente-Inférieure assembly had the sense to refuse admission to all deputations of any kind. (Even so, it had to sustain two military deputations and two visits from the ladies of La Rochelle taking up a

44. A.N. C 180 C II 67 (Bas-Rhin) 3 Sept.; Isère, C 179 C II 37, 2 Sept.
45. A.N. C 180 C II 62 (Puy-de-Dôme) 2 Sept.
46. In the little town of Chaumont, the electors even pleaded for better lighting in their over-crowded hall; A.N. C 179 C II 58 (Oise) 3 Sept.

patriotic collection.)[47] Here the location of most of the assemblies was probably fortunate. The unhappy Seine-et-Oise electors met in St. Germain-en-Laye, athwart one of the main roads from Paris to Rennes; this involved them not only in initiating measures to see that suspicious traffic on the roads was stopped and searched, but in extending ceremonial greetings and good wishes to 45 batches of volunteers in 13 days. Toward the end these were being welcomed three and four at a time, but the electors very soon abandoned their original courteous habit of suspending their voting to receive each fresh deputation; had they not done so they might well have been voting until November.[48]

The most obvious sources of left-wing pressure on the electors were the *sociétés populaires*, with deputations and addresses, and the spectators who might be admitted during the elections. Neither of these is very markedly in evidence. Perhaps they went unremarked, but the majority of assemblies seem to have carefully recorded their official visitors, and, in addition, it seems likely that large numbers of spectators would have presented problems of accommodation which could hardly have escaped mention. In all, there were 26 assemblies whose *procès-verbaux* establish the existence of a local *société* concerned about the elections. In 10 cases the *société* contented itself with sending an address, in 8 cases it sent a deputation, and in 6 cases it did both. The Quesnoÿ and Paris Clubs were apparently satisfied to exert any influence they might hope to have by way of those of their members who were electors, and took no formal part in the proceedings at all. Only in Lot and Finistère can one trace the story of active efforts by club members to get the electors to accept a particular point of view; in Lot they succeeded, in Finistère they were completely outmaneuvered.[49] In 57 departments out of 83, there is no evidence of club activity during the elections.

Spectators were seen even more seldom, and for good reason. The problem of finding accommodation for anything from two hundred to nearly a thousand electors, with space for the *bureau* to do the necessary paperwork and perhaps for the electors to divide into separate groups to conduct the voting, was serious enough without trying to provide for the public as well. If there was room, well and good, and care would be taken to distinguish visitors from the actual electors; but Paris was unique in moving to larger premises mainly on the ground that this would allow citizens to be present.[50] In five departments outside Paris, the assembly moved simply because the original meeting place was far too small.

47. A.N. C 178 C II 16 (Charente-Inférieure) 6–7 Sept.
48. A.D. Seine-et-Oise 1 M 361, passim. The departmental record of this assembly runs to well over a hundred pages.
49. It need not be concluded that all *sociétés* were likely to be radical. The only Ardèche club to make itself known sent a letter asking that the powers of the deputies be restricted, and the Forcalquier *société* (Basses-Alpes) surfaced only on the last day, to invite the electors to attend a Mass of thanksgiving; A.N. C 178 C II 6 (Ardèche) 8 Sept., and C 178 C II 5 (Basses-Alpes) 7 Sept. For Lot and Finistère, C 179 C II 44 (Lot) 5–6 Sept., and C 178 C II 28 (Finistère) 4 Sept.
50. It is worth noting exactly what is said in the *procès-verbal* about this; note also the return to the same problem on the last day of the elections, in search of a more permanent solution. A.N. C 180 C II 60 (Paris) 2–4 Sept. and 25 Sept.

Other assemblies that could not find better premises recorded complaints that their halls were hot and badly ventilated. The Aveyron assembly believed its quarters to be unhealthy as well as overcrowded, but retained them on finding that the only alternative, an Augustine church, was not only in a dysentery infected area but occupied by a battalion of volunteers. (What the volunteers thought of the arrangement it would be interesting to know.) The Var assembly, like that in Paris, moved to the local Jacobin Club, for the sufficient reason that it had the most spacious premises in Grasse. The usual meeting place was a church; occasionally it was the parish church because there was no alternative; and seldom indeed does there seem to have been space to spare.[51]

It is not, therefore, surprising that a number of assemblies specifically said it was impossible to admit spectators. In Loir-et-Cher the door-keepers were commended for their vigilance in keeping them out. In Nord there was an uproar over someone who had managed to sneak in; in Pas-de-Calais the admittance of the public for a brief patriotic demonstration was a major occasion. Electors were often provided with entry cards—Nord gave them ribbon armbands—and in Abbéville (Somme) the guard was so zealous that one group of genuine but belated electors who had not yet received their cards could not battle their way in.[52] Outside Paris, there were ten assemblies which accepted spectators and ten which definitely did not. Other assemblies do not mention the matter, but the general acceptance of the entry-card system and the use of the National Guard as door-keepers suggests that the presence of the public was not encouraged.[53] There was only one department in which spectators were encouraged to express their feelings. This was Bouches-du-Rhône, where Barbaroux, as president, exhorted his audience: "Appellons le Peuple autour de nous, pour que, témoin de nos élections, il nous indique, par ses aplaudissements, ou par ses improbations, si nous faisons de bien, ou de mal."[54] How the citizens of Avignon responded to this invitation to behave like the crowd at a soccer match is not recorded.

A far commoner event was the arrival of deputations from local officials or volunteers, and sometimes also from regiments quartered in the area. Even if few assemblies were as afflicted as that of Seine-et-Oise, this might cause much interruption and be unexpectedly expensive; the Hérault electors enthusiastically took up a collection for the first batch of volunteers, but found their generosity somewhat tried with the arrival of three more groups within two days.[55] The local officials usually paid their calls as the hosts of the assembly; the district had the special task of paying the electors, as well as, often, of delivering the

51. For Var, A.N. C 181 C II 78 (Var) 2 Sept.; see also C 178 C II 11 (Aveyron) 2 Sept.
52. A.N. C 179 C II 40 (Loire-et-Cher) 7 Sept.; A.D. Nord L 755, 7 Sept.; A.N. C 180 C II 61 (Pas-de-Calais) 8 Sept.; A.N. C 180 C II 76 (Somme) 3 Sept.
53. Cf., e.g., A.N. C 180 C II 61 (Pas-de-Calais) 3 Sept., 10 Sept.; C 178 C II 16 (Charente-Inférieure) 2 Sept.
54. A.N. C 178 C II 12 (Bouches-du-Rhône) 3 Sept.
55. A.N. C 179 C II 33 (Hérault) 4, 5, 6 Sept.

packets of mail from Paris. But apart from a few cases of local emergency or of friction between individual electors and members of the local commune, these outside contacts seem to have meant little beyond an exchange of good wishes. Twenty-five assemblies either had no visitors, or did not think their arrival worth mentioning in the minutes, and Maine-et-Loire and Corse, as well as Charente-Inférieure, discouraged deputations, on the ground that during the emergency they could not spare the time.[56]

One further source of outside influence must be mentioned. During the course of the elections, at least ten assemblies were visited by *commissaires* sent out by either the Legislative Assembly or the Paris Commune to stir up local enthusiasm and to promote the emergency recruiting decreed by the Legislative at the end of August. Once their credentials had been established, these men had a good deal of prestige and authority and were more likely than local volunteers or even local club officers to be articulate and forceful in expressing their points of view. The reaction to their presence will thus have to be examined. But 10 assemblies out of 83 is not really very many.[57] In general the evidence leaves the impression that outside pressures in any direction were slight; how much they mattered remains to be seen.

IV

The outcome of the elections might of course have been influenced by the electoral procedures adopted. In the circumstances of 1792, the electors were, in practice, free to modify the accepted conventions in any way they chose. For perhaps the only time in the history of France, they could, and in some cases did, assert themselves as the vehicles of popular sovereignty in action, bound by no rules they did not choose to recognize. The conventions they did accept, the opinions they did voice, the occasions on which they went beyond their brief, are therefore matters of much interest.

If we look first at the matter of procedure, that recommended by the Legislative Assembly was straightforward enough, and the confidence with which it was followed all over France indicates that after three years of revolutionary activity the routine had become well-established. The intended sequence was as follows: Once the electors had gathered ("in sufficient numbers," says an occasional record) they were to choose provisional office-holders so that formal organization could be got under way. The president and tellers were to be the four oldest men present, the secretary was nominated by the president or chosen by the assembly.[58] The credentials of the electors could then be checked, the

56. A.N. C 178 C II 16 (Charente-Inférieure) 3 Sept.; C 178 C II 19 (Corse) 17 Sept.; C 179 C II 47 (Maine-et-Loire) 4 Sept.

57. These departments were Calvados, Eure, Morbihan, Nord, Pas-de-Calais, Seine-et-Marne, Deux-Sèvres, Somme, Seine-et-Oise, and Var.

58. Cf., A.N. C 180 C II 59 (Orne) 2 Sept., when the *président d'âge*, perhaps because of his age and natural preference, made the unfortunate choice of Goupil—considered even

procès-verbaux of the primary assemblies being examined by *commissaires* acting for the whole assembly; the method of operation here varied somewhat, but the principle was always the same. Nearly all assemblies accepted that before they did anything else they had to establish their members' right to sit.[59] After the *commissaires* had reported, doubtful cases were decided by majority vote. Whether those whose rights were contested took part in the voting or not is not usually clear. Unless they had failed to attend, they were always called in to give evidence on their own behalf.[60]

After this "verification of powers," the office-holders could be chosen. To save time, these were supposed to be nominated on a single ballot-paper (*scrutin de liste*) and the five men with the most votes were elected ("relative majority"); for this election only, no absolute majorities were required. The vote was conventionally a written one, the tellers writing down the votes of the illiterate. The *bureau* having been installed and its members and the whole assembly having taken the required oath to liberty and equality, the deputies could be elected, one at a time, by absolute majority; if no one was successful after two ballots, the third ballot was a run-off between the two contestants with the most votes. When the *suppléants* (one to every three deputies) had been chosen by the same method, the assembly could state the powers it was willing to give to its representatives; rather more than half the assemblies granted the unlimited powers requested by the Legislative, the others did not bother themselves with the matter. This concluded the elections, unless the *haut-juré* instructions had arrived and had to be carried out, or occasionally where departmental officials had died or resigned and the assembly was willing to replace them. Whatever the local situation and the wishes of the electors, however strong the feeling in favor of making a clean sweep of those currently in local office, they had been given no brief for more than the national elections and few were willing to take on extra responsibility.

Many assemblies thought these conventional methods were also obligatory. However, this attitude was not universal, and had the Convention been in a position to be as exacting of formalities as some electoral assemblies were with the primary assemblies, at least fifteen departments would have been more or less in trouble and the Eure assembly might easily have had the whole election quashed. The main deviations, affecting a considerable number of departments, may be roughly classified as follows: (a) the exclusion of electors who had

---

by the Ornais to be virtually counterrevolutionary—and was asked to choose again. In Pas-de-Calais, after debate, the choice was left to the president; in Bouches-du-Rhône the assembly itself chose Barbaroux. C 180 C II 61 (Pas-de-Calais) 2 Sept.; C 178 C II 12 (Bouches-du-Rhône) 2 Sept.

59. Eure already had a printed list of electors, but this was unusual (A.N. C 178 C II 26 [Eure] 2 Sept.). Somme saved trouble and awkward questions by simply accepting the word of each district administration that all was in order (C 180 C II 76 [Somme] 2–3 Sept.), but most assemblies were more conscientious than this.

60. Cf. A.N. C 178 C II 23 (Dordogne) 4 Sept., interrogation of Laborde.

apparently been validly chosen by the primary assemblies; (b) the acceptance of electors without normal credentials, or without credentials at all; (c) the choice of deputies or *suppléants* by acclamation, by *scrutin de liste*, or by "relative" majority; and (d) the substitution of open voting (*à haute voix*) for secret ballot. Although the last of these has been the most notorious, any one of the others might in 1791 have legally invalidated the election.

Such irregularities, if widespread, would tend to support the claim that the elections were "managed" by small groups within the electoral assemblies unwilling to accept the framework of opinion sent forward by the primary assemblies, and hence willing to eliminate all who did not fall in with their own point of view. Even if the majority of assemblies were secure from club or spectator influence, a radical minority might still hope to gain control. One way of doing this was to exert illicit pressure on the voting, but a first step might be to remove as many potential opponents as possible by using, or perverting, the normal machinery to have them excluded. A "club" element could thus emerge victorious although the club itself had played no part in the election.

The case that springs to mind is of course that of Paris. But the Paris elections were unlike those anywhere else in France, except in Bouches du Rhône, and cannot be a basis for generalization. Their special features will be discussed later. As far as about 40 percent of the assemblies were concerned, there are no signs at all of overt "management" of any kind; the elections flowed smoothly from start to finish, no one was excluded, there were no irregularities.[61] The remaining 60 percent of the assemblies either excluded some members from sitting, or broke one or more of the conventional rules about procedure, or both. What did they do and how much did it mean?

The grounds on which electors were excluded were: failure to produce proof of election; failure to take the oath; being elected by a primary assembly granting its delegates only limited powers (a "monarchical" restriction which was the basis for exclusion in 2 departments); expressing support for the *ancien régime*, or *des propos inciviques*; being elected by an assembly consisting of active citizens only (2 cases, in different departments); being a member of an illegal assembly (Corsica specialized in this); being under age (half a dozen examples, in different departments) or not residentially qualified, or a domestic servant (one case of each); being elected by an assembly whose members had not taken the oath, or who had chosen their office-holders improperly; or being a redundant member of a delegation larger than the primary assembly was entitled to elect (19 cases in 18 departments, excluding Corsica where the electors' attitudes were sui generis). The first 2 grounds would always have been adequate and the second was comparatively rare as a reason in itself; most of the others were self-justifying. The contentious question was the definition of *propos inciviques*.

61. So, e.g., A.N. C 178 C II 1 (Ain), C 178 C II 22 (Creuse), C 180 C II 69 (Haute-Saône), and others.

In most cases these were clearly counterrevolutionary, but occasionally, as in Paris, there was a demand for the exclusion of all signatories of addresses sent in support of the king in June 1792. In fact, however, though many departments had forwarded addresses of this kind, the signatories were expelled in 2 departments only, outside Paris—Aisne and Ille-et-Vilaine; and in Ille-et-Vilaine, where men could withdraw their signatures if they chose, one elector explicitly confirmed his attitude and hence (one supposes) his support for *Louis le traître.* In many other places such men must have continued to sit; in Yonne, at least, the *procès-verbal* provides clear evidence that they did.[62]

Less formally justifiable than the exclusion of suspect electors was the acceptance of those with dubious credentials. In some cases the irregularities were unimportant. The Oise assembly said that given the haste and emergency character of the elections, it would not concern itself with minor formal deficiencies, and Haute-Marne and others accepted electors chosen by "relative" majority because it was plain that the voters had taken any short-cut they could find so as to get back to the harvest. The odd cases of disputed elections are too sketchily described for analysis, but it is interesting that in the only case in which figures are given, the republicans had so large a majority. Sometimes the lack of credentials was not the electors' fault; there are several cases where the president of a primary assembly failed to forward the *procès-verbal,* and so risked the disfranchisement of an entire canton. The only two flagrant cases of the admission of electors who were formally quite ineligible occurred in Isère and Eure. In Isère, one whole primary election was conducted by the *bureau d'âge,* so that the point was never reached at which the taking of the oath would have become inescapable, and in fact no one took it. Most assemblies would have condemned this transparent evasion, but Isère was not so fussy, and after a short debate the electors were admitted. In Eure may be found the one case in which a sizable number of electors never established their *bona fides* at all. This was one of three departments (Vosges and Oise were the others) in which the *bureau* was formally elected before the electors' powers had been verified—a risky thing to do, since unqualified members might take part in the election. In Oise and Vosges it did not matter much, but in Eure no fewer than twelve cantons, including two sections of the departmental *chef-lieu* Evreux, had sent forward no *procès-verbaux* whatever, and if these ever arrived their receipt was not recorded. This does raise some doubts about the methods considered acceptable by Buzot, who was not only president but in unusually firm control of the assembly.[63]

62. A.N. C 179 C II 34 (Ille-et-Vilaine) 9 Sept., (supplementary minute for 4 Sept.); C 181 C II 83 (Yonne) 4 Sept., for Le Peletier's ruling that the conduct of electors was under discussion only in relation to their possible merit as candidates.
63. A.N. C 180 C II 58 (Oise) 3 Sept.; C 179 C II 50 (Haute-Marne) 2 Sept.; C 178 C II 26 (Eure) 3 Sept.; for the placid report of the deficiencies, and 5 Sept. for an example of Buzot in control; A.N. C 179 C II 37 (Isère) 3 Sept.

In the actual conduct of the elections, it sometimes happened that deputies were elected by other than absolute majority, or by *scrutin de liste*, instead of individually by absolute majority. This usually arose from an exceptional local situation. In Yonne and Haute-Marne, the news of the enemy advance created such a sense of emergency that *scrutin de liste* was used to save time; in Somme the elections had already dragged on for over a fortnight when the exhausted electors accepted *scrutin de liste* for the *suppléants*; in Pyrénées-Orientales, by contrast, a remarkably uninterested assembly, pushing through the whole election in three days, decided that it could not be bothered with individual elections for its two *suppléants*, with the result that they were declared elected with 23 and 19 votes respectively, from a total vote of 153. In Lot and Corrèze, support for "patriotic" members of the Legislative was running high, and it was decided that it would be a waste of time to hold a ballot to elect them; they were chosen by acclamation. Very occasionally, one can trace manipulations or attempted manipulations in the interests of individuals. In Saône-et-Loire, one group of electors was apparently so annoyed when Gelin and Baudot fought out the first election ahead of Masuyer that they then secured Masuyer's election *par acclamation* as a special tribute to him. In Creuse there was a move to get Carra chosen by acclamation instead of contesting a third ballot with Jorrand, but this misfired badly when the acclamation was refused and he was then beaten on the ballot by 4 votes. (This seems to have cost him his chance of being elected there at all.) There was also occasional interference with the normal rights of *suppléants*, with new elections being held to fill the places of deputies who had refused. But this sort of thing is very rare.[64]

An interesting "irregularity" was the editing of the *procès-verbaux* themselves, so that part of the proceedings was omitted from the record. Most assemblies were careful to pass the *procès-verbal* regularly, as well as at the end of the election, so that the version reaching Paris did at least represent an account they were willing to accept, though it was necessarily highly abbreviated. But there were two occasions on which the *procès-verbal* as presented by the *bureau* was so seriously challenged that the challenge itself had to be reported in detail. The Paris *procès-verbal* of 6 September had failed to mention a proposed motion regretting that Pétion had been elected in Eure-et-Loir before the Parisian electors had had a chance to consider him. When challenged next day, the omission was explained on the ground that the motion had failed, but the complaint about it was duly recorded.[65] In Ille-et-Vilaine, the electors refused to accept a *procès-verbal*, submitted in its entirety at the very last minute, which

---

64. A.N. C 181 C II 83 (Yonne) 6 Sept.; C 179 C II 50 (Haute-Marne) 4 Sept.; C 180 C II 76 (Somme) 14 Sept.; C 180 C II 65 (Pyrénées-Orientales) 4 Sept.; C 180 C II 70 (Saône-et-Loire) 5 Sept.; C 179 C II 44 (Lot) 5 Sept.; C 178 C II 18 (Corrèze) 4 Sept.; C 178 C II 22 (Creuse) 5 Sept. For the interference with the normal rights of *suppléants*, C 179 C II 43 (Loiret); this was how J. B. Louvet got his seat.

65. A.N. C 180 C II 60 (Paris) 7 Sept.

completely omitted all reference to the exclusion of a small number of electors from the assembly. The majority held that this implied among other things that they were ashamed to stand by their decisions. Why Lanjuinais, the secretary, and Defermon, the president, should have connived at the censorship does not appear. Lanjuinais also evaded having to present the amended version, claiming that he had to leave almost immediately on urgent business; altogether a mysterious affair.[66]

Finally, the best-known so-called "irregularity" of 1792: voting *à haute voix*. This was not in the technical sense the sort of irregularity which Mortimer-Ternaux supposed, and its use in Paris has obscured one interesting earlier precedent. In the *Exposition des motifs . . .*, drawn up to be put before every elector in France, the Legislative Assembly itself had justified its choice of the Provisional Ministry, after 10 August, by explaining that this had been done in public, *à haute voix*; the Legislative, it said, "a voulu que chacun de ses membres eût pour juges ses collègues, le public pour témoin, et qu'il répondit de sa choix à la nation entière."[67] This was exactly the argument put forward by those who supported the use of *haute voix* in September 1792. In national elections it had no precedent, and its use, even its suggested use, was confined to a fairly small minority of departments, but it can hardly be called illegal; the Legislative had been careful to avoid giving orders to the sovereign people of France, and they were free to use *haute voix* if they wished. Since Mortimer-Ternaux ascribed its use outside Paris to the influence of Robespierre via the *sociétés populaires*, it must be stated that only in Lot is there any evidence at all that its use was in any way associated with club activity. The only author quoted in relation to it, anywhere, was Louvet.[68] Even in Lot, as elsewhere, the movement in its favor came from inside the assembly, not from outside.

Quite apart from the good revolutionary principle that a man should be prepared to make his choices openly, there was much to be said for *haute voix*. Its proponents always argued that it would serve *à déjouer les intrigues*, of which many revolutionaries were exceptionally wary. Cliques in an assembly might be more apparent if a trend in the voting could be sheeted home to an identifiable group among the voters. There was also a danger pointed up by the case of one Louis Chapet, thrown out of the Eure-et-Loir assembly for distributing prepared ballot-papers among his rural colleagues; in assemblies only partially literate, written ballot-papers were open to obvious abuse. (Chapet said that he himself could not read the papers he was handing out.)[69] Open voting was a safer way

66. A.N. C 179 C II 34 (Ille-et-Vilaine) 9 Sept., for the sections omitted from the *procès-verbaux* of 3, 4, 5 Sept. These related largely to the exclusion of departmental officials because they had gone electioneering in their home areas when they were held to be residentially bound to the *chef-lieu*.

67. *Moniteur* XIII: 418.

68. A.N. C 178 C II 25 (Drôme) 2 Sept.; cf. P. Mautouchet, "Le mouvement électorale à Paris en août–septembre 1792," *La Révolution française* XLIV (1903): 154.

69. A.N. C 178 C II 27 (Eure-et-Loir) 3 Sept., and report annexed.

for the illiterate to register their views, and it halved the time needed for elections because the tellers could sort out the votes as they were delivered. It could also legitimately accelerate proceedings by allowing electors to see even on the first ballot which candidates were receiving general support, thus avoiding situations like that in Charente-Inférieure, where a popular *procureur-général-syndic* repeatedly collided with the unassailable prior claims of the department's "patriotic" Legislative deputies, and quite unnecessarily prolonged the election.[70] *Haute voix* also made it much less likely that if a third ballot were needed, it would be fought out between two candidates only marginally ahead of a still crowded field. But in the 1792 electoral atmosphere, such practical points were not often directly made. If advocates of *haute voix* wanted to buttress their arguments, they made use of precedent: the Roman republic, America, England (three departments) or Paris (Corrèze and Seine-et-Oise only). A Corrèze elector pointed to the example set by the Legislative Assembly; it was an elector in Drôme who said, correctly, that the method had been recommended by Louvet.[71]

Voting *à haute voix* was urged in 20 departments outside Paris, and finally adopted in 11, not including Paris which took the method for granted. The assemblies adopting it were in Bouches-du-Rhône, Cantal, Charente, Corrèze, Drôme, Gers, Hérault, Lot, Paris, Oise, Hautes-Pyrénées, and Seine-et-Oise, and those who considered but rejected it in Aveyron, Charente-Inférieure, Finistère, Isère, Maine-et-Loire, Haute-Marne, Pas-de-Calais, Sarthe, and Seine-et-Marne.[72] There is no convincing evidence that it was forced on the majority by minority high-pressure tactics, although this may have happened. In 4 departments, Bouches-du-Rhône, Cantal, Drôme, and Hautes-Pyrénées, the suggestion was enthusiastically welcomed and carried unanimously; in Hautes-Pyrénées, this decision was tested by a second vote. Two assemblies, Gers and Charente, give no details. In 5 others, Corrèze, Hérault, Lot, Oise, and Seine-et-Oise, there was a formal debate. The Corrèze and Oise *procès-verbaux* then note only that the decision was favorable; the other 3 assemblies record a formal vote, which resulted in *une trés grande majorité* in Lot and a majority of 427 to 26 in Hérault. In Seine-et-Oise the assembly was much more evenly divided and the "yes" vote was 290 to 228. In departments which considered but rejected it, the procedure was very much the same: sometimes it was lost on the voices, once by *assis et levé* vote, and twice at least after a formal ballot. In Isère this produced a negative majority of 420 to 110; the skillful way in which the Finistère *bureau* disposed of the proposal, in a divided assembly, is discussed below in another connection.[73]

70. A.N. C 178 C II 16 (Charente-Inférieure) 4–5 Sept.
71. A.N. C 178 C II 18 (Corrèze) 2 Sept., C 178 C II 25 (Drôme) 2 Sept.
72. But cf. Mortimer-Ternaux, *La Terreur*, IV: 52; this list is incomplete.
73. A.N. C 179 C II 44 (Lot) 3 Sept.; C 179 C II 33 (Hérault) 3 Sept.; A.D. Seine-et-Oise 1 M 361 4 Sept.; A.N. C 179 C II 37 (Isère) 3 Sept.; C 178 C II 28 (Finistère) 4 Sept. C 179 C II 58 (Oise) 3 Sept.; C 178 C II 18 (Corrèze) 2 Sept.

The obvious risk in *haute voix* voting was that the result might be influenced by minority pressure working to establish a build-up of votes in a particular direction at an early stage in the voting. The electors were aware of this, and 9 of the 11 *haute voix* assemblies (outside Paris) took steps to guard against it by ensuring that electors voted in alphabetical order, or sometimes quite at random.[74] In all of these assemblies, the elections seem to have followed the general pattern of 1792, in the sense that once the self-evident choices had been made, there was no consensus, and two or three ballots were needed to settle the others. There were very few nearly unanimous votes. The two departments taking no precautions at all against possible influence on the voting were Lot and Bouches-du-Rhône. In Lot one cannot say exactly what happened, because there are no figures for the voting, but there is nothing superficially anomalous about the character of the delegation, nor does it seem to have been dominated by those who were pressing for *haute voix*.[75] The Bouches-du-Rhône results do look far too good to be true. This election, to be further discussed later, was, however, completely exceptional and there was nothing like it anywhere else in France.[76]

No verdict on possible "influences" at work in any assembly can be arrived at without far more evidence than we are ever likely to have, but it is interesting that as far as the *haute voix* assemblies are concerned, 2 departments provide scraps of material implying that the risk of "intrigue" was real and that *haute voix* might be at least a partial defense against it. In Lot, an attempt was made to get the assembly to divide into *bureaux*, or separate sections, for the actual election of the deputies. This was a way of saving time in vote counting, which was in fact adopted in 16 other departments, but it seems significant that it was proposed in Lot not only after *haute voix* voting had been overwhelmingly supported but also after Jeanbon Saint-André had been by its means elected to the presidency. The motive behind the *bureau* proposal may well have been accurately summed up in the course of the Montauban *société's* impassioned protest against it—"Que deviendra la publicité, cette sauve-garde du peuple, lorsque cette division ayant en quelque manière morcelé l'intérêt générale, le public, qui voudra être present partout, ne pourra être nulle part? . . . Le maxime des tyrans est de diviser pour régner, celle des intrigans est aussi de diviser pour parvenir . . ." and it was defeated by a combination of external and internal resistance.[77] In Seine-et-Oise, there is evidence of the existence of a highly successful group promoting the election of "men known for their writings and their patriotic views" (to quote the description given by one of their

74. So, e.g., A.N. C 179 C II 33 (Hérault) 3 Sept.; A.D. Seine-et-Oise 1 M 361 4 Sept., for another arrangement.

75. For discussion of this election from another point of view, see below, pp. 269–70.

76. The Bouches-du-Rhône election is discussed below, p. 181.

77. A.N. C 179 C II 44 (Lot) 6 Sept. This is the only occasion I have been able to find in which it is clear that club action probably influenced the course of events.

opponents) at the expense of local candidates. They achieved their aims, but not by *haute voix* in itself; it looks as though they promoted a change in the electoral procedure, a change which resulted in the successful candidature of Grangeneuve, Gorsas, and Audouin, though none of the three secured more than 40 percent of the votes cast at his election.[78] *Haute voix* alone was apparently thought insufficient—especially perhaps since the assembly had decided that the electors should vote in random order. Had *haute voix* been allowed to operate in Seine-et-Oise as it did in other departments, it seems possible that a rather more representative delegation would have emerged than the one which was actually elected.[79] The course of events in fact suggests that the intriguers, whoever they were, found that the normal operation of an *haute voix* election presented them with obstacles which could only be surmounted by a rejection of the principle of absolute majority.

Although most of the assemblies adopting *haute voix* ended by expressing fairly radical views on other questions as well, this was not necessarily the case—Hautes-Pyrénées was not a radical assembly in other ways—and conversely, there were wholeheartedly radical assemblies (for example, Dordogne), in which *haute-voix* was not so much as mentioned. It was only one possible symptom of political outlook, and its implications, if any, can be measured only by looking at it in relation to the assembly's proceedings as a whole. More significant than the machinery of elections were the purposes to which it might be put: what views the electors expressed during the elections, and what other responsibilities, if any, they felt it was their duty and right to assume.

V

The wide variations in the electoral assemblies' views of their duties, and their methods of carrying them out, may be exemplified by the contrast between the two assemblies of Hautes-Alpes and Nord. In Hautes-Alpes, every rule was observed and all the proper feelings were expressed; and within 5 days the electors neatly disposed of all that they had been told to do, asking no questions and volunteering no criticisms.[80] The Nord assembly took 10 days to choose more than twice as many deputies, but it also overhauled the local military situation and investigated possible local subversion, and having completed the national elections, adjourned itself to Lille, where it took over the entire running of the department until it had finished electing new local officials, a process which lasted until 13 October, so that the session formally extended over a

78. A.D. Seine-et-Oise 1 M 361 9 Sept., for this arrangement, which provided that on any future third ballot there should be a combination of complete freedom of choice with a first-past-the-post system. The advantages of this for an organized group which could not quite secure majority support for a given candidate seem obvious.

79. Cf. the readmission of the electors who had allegedly been trying to "influence" the vote (in favor of local candidates) *after* all the deputies had been chosen (ibid., 14 Sept.).

80. A.N. C 178 C II 4 (Hautes-Alpes) 2–6 Sept.

record 43 days.[81] Most assemblies were admittedly much closer to the Hautes-Alpes than to the Nord level of performance, and the median session lasted about a week, but 5 sessions besides that in Nord went on for a fortnight or more. The variations came partly from the varying sizes of delegations, but also and more importantly from the divisions, or lack of them, within each assembly (it took Morbihan 11 days to choose 8 deputies), from the degree of urgency (for special reasons, Marne completed the entire election in one continuous sitting lasting 96 hours), and from the degree of inclination to move on from the elections themselves to deal with other public questions. In a very general way, and other things being equal, the amount of comment on the local situation and the extent to which the electors involved themselves with general public issues are reasonable pointers to the kind of republicanism their representatives were likely to espouse, but as will appear, generalizations must be very cautiously made.

In 1792 one break with tradition was already well under way. Of the 83 assemblies, only 19 this time began the session by hearing Mass. Seven, including 4 of the 19, ended with a *Te Deum*, so that the total number holding religious services of the orthodox kind was 22. There was a portent of the future in the *fêtes civiques* attended by 8 assemblies. Three of these were held in memory of those killed on 10 August, the others seem to have been simply patriotic celebrations. The Rhône-et-Loire ceremonial took the form of a general swearing of the oath to liberty and equality around the tree of liberty—a fitting enough epitome of the atmosphere in which many of the elections were held.[82]

This atmosphere is perhaps the most notable feature of the elections, and the most difficult to re-create or to convey: a compound of pride, anxiety, conscientiousness, impatience, hope, uncertainty, and at times an extraordinary and moving exhilaration—as when cannon boomed or cheers rang out to announce the election of another deputy, or when a group of volunteers filed in to the sound of shouts of welcome and *une musique guerrière*, or when along the ranks of the assembly there came a sudden flash of brilliant color—"à l'instant la salle a présenté le spectacle d'une longue file de bonnets rouges, emblème cher à tous les amis de la liberté."[83] The Nord assembly greeted Merlin's election by singing the *Ca ira.*[84] There were of course many sides to all this. The Pas-de-Calais assembly, having invited a popular celebration by letting a woman food-rioter out of the Calais jail, had to accept a harangue from a formidable lady with the

81. A.D. Nord L 755, 2–8 Sept., 16 Sept.–9 Oct. The stay in Lille was enlivened by enemy bombardment.
82. A.N. C 180 C II 68 (Rhône-et-Loire) 10 Sept.; cf. the ceremonies in Lot and Somme, C 179 C II 44 (Lot) 8 Sept., C 180 C II 76 (Somme) 16 Sept.
83. Haute-Loire used a cannon shot to announce the election of each deputy; A.N. C 179 C II 41 (Haute-Loire) 3–5 Sept. For some *musique guerrière*, C 180 C II 68 (Rhône-et-Loire) 5 Sept.; for the *bonnets rouges* (found elsewhere as well) C 178 C II 25 (Drôme) 5 Sept.
84. A.D. Nord L 755, 4 Sept. They rang the bell as well.

local nickname of *la mère Duchêne*. Two assemblies were presented with babies for baptism: for Meurthe there are no details of what happened, except that the Bishop officiated and the father had his poverty somewhat relieved at the electors' expense, but the Orne *procès-verbal* records that Dufriche-Valazé acted as proxy for the assembly (the collective godfather) and that the mother, Madelaine Chuquet, wife of a young volunteer, was sent a collection amounting to 300 *livres*. (The baby got the names of Aluise Hyacinte Electeur.) The rather charming customary deference to age met its nemesis in Lot-et-Garonne, where the honorary president's deafness required an *adjoint*, and in Oise where his antiquity and infirmities prevented him from officiating at all; on the other hand, the Nièvre *président d'âge*, aged eighty, not only suggested but presided over an all-night sitting lasting for thirty-six hours without a break. The quality most essential to presidents was perhaps illustrated when the Seine-et-Oise assembly, having for various reasons run through a series of them, opted on 15 September for the man with the loudest voice.[85]

The extremely long hours worked by most assemblies made membership of the *bureau* as much of a burden as an honor, with the heaviest share falling to the secretary, who was occasionally given specific permission to take time off to work on the minutes. The length of the *appels* made absences frequent, and many departments tried to discipline their electors, usually by threatening to dock their pay for failure to vote; bells were also used to call them in for voting purposes, and Morbihan hired a drummer.[86] After a usually well-attended opening, attendance tended to fall off as time went on, especially after the actual deputies had been chosen, though several *procès-verbaux* indicate that the electors had not necessarily gone home; they might simply not bother to vote if not interested, just as they might not vote, or might vote informally, in a third ballot if they did not fancy either of the candidates.[87]

In considering the level of attendance, which was demonstrably very high in a number of departments, the conflicting claims on the electors must be remembered: not only anxiety over the harvest, but in the north and north-east the possibility or actuality of invasion, and in Loire-Inférieure, fear of the activity of *les malveillans*, who might use the absence of *les patriotes* to further their evil designs.[88] The pay of three *livres* a day was some compensation for the worry and inconvenience of being away from home, but in at least three towns, Bayeux

85. A.N. C 180 C II 61 (Pas-de-Calais) 8 Sept.; C 179 C II 52 (Meurthe) 6 Sept.; C 180 C II 59 (Orne) 11 Sept.; C 179 C II 45 (Lot-et-Garonne) 2 Sept.; C 180 C II 58 (Oise) 2 Sept.; C 179 C II 56 (Nièvre) 3–4 Sept.; A.D. Seine-et-Oise 1 M 361, 15 Sept.

86. A.D. Seine-et-Oise 1 M 361 3–8 Sept.; A.N. C 180 C II 78 (Somme) for arrangements about payment of electors; C 179 C II 53 3 Sept. (Meuse), use of a bell; C 179 C II 54 (Morbihan) 4 Sept., the drummer.

87. Note the resounding snub to Montégut by the Pyrénées-Orientales electors; it looks as though he got his seat largely because his opponent, a constitutional *curé*, was even less popular. A.N. C 180 C II 65 (Pyrénées-Orientales) 3 Sept.

88. A.N. C 179 C II 42 (Loire-Inférieure) 9 Sept.

(Calvados), Lectoure (Gers), and Auray (Morbihan), the electors complained bitterly about the prices of accommodation, and in St. Jean-de-Loue (Côte d'Or) they went so far as to say that the town's facilities were so inadequate that it should not be used for future elections. This complaint might more appropriately have come from the Nièvre assembly, in St. Pierre-le-Moutier, where the arrival of a battalion of volunteers for an overnight stay created such pressure on the supply of spare beds that the assembly ordered an all-night sitting so that the electors' beds could be freed for occupation by the troops.[89]

Whatever the pressure of local circumstance, there were altogether 20 assemblies which in conducting the elections kept strictly to the business in hand, and did nothing else whatever. They excluded no electors, only one of them passed a specific resolution, they committed no irregularities, they offered no criticism of the departmental administration, they did not even take up collections for volunteers; they simply did what they had been summoned to do and dispersed. Of these 20, two—Ardennes and Meuse—had had to flee from the enemy and were conducting their business in exceptional haste and difficulty; the other 18 had less obvious reason for their disinclination to take any kind of initiative. Yet even among these, the most apparently passive of all the electoral bodies, 8 among 18 took the trouble to meet the wish of the Legislative for formal approval of its policy after 10 August; and this is an indicator of the point of view generally adopted throughout France.[90]

There was in fact a striking general acceptance of the Legislative Assembly's view of 10 August. The long procession of addresses congratulating the Legislative on its courage and resolution is almost incomprehensible unless one has some understanding of what the electors had been told about the part played by the Legislative in the fall of the monarchy. Of the 83 assemblies, only seven referred directly to Paris at all: Côte d'Or, Haute-Garonne, Nord, Rhône-et-Loire, Seine-et-Marne, Seine-et-Oise, and Manche. Each of these without exception voted an address of congratulation to the Legislative for what the Manche assembly described as its *courageuse résistance* and *attitude imposante.* As far as the nation was concerned, said the Nord electors: "après l'avoir sauvée par votre courage, vous avez assuré sa gloire et sa félicité par votre sagesse."[91] In contrast, 2 only, of the 7, mentioned the sacrifices made by the Parisians on 10 August. Côte d'Or spoke of *l'insurrection nationale* during which *nos frères les*

---

89. A.N. C 179 C II 56 (Nièvre) 7 Sept. The aged, the sick, and the decrepit were allowed to use their beds, but were to do so for as short a time as possible. For complaints over prices, C 178 C II 13 (Calvados) 2 Sept., C 178 C II 31 (Gers) 2 Sept., C 179 C II 54 (Morbihan) 2 Sept.; for St. Jean de Loue, C 178 C II 20 (Côte d'Or) 9 Sept, in which the name of the place to be preferred is left blank—presumably almost anywhere else might be an improvement.

90. So, e.g., A.N. C 178 C II 4 (Hautes-Alpes) 3 Sept.; C 178 C II 10 (Aude) 3 Sept., where the assembly voted the address "*pour et metre* [sic] *son voeu relativement aux circonstances*"; C 178 C II 22 (Creuse) 8 Sept.

91. A.D. Nord L 755, 3 Sept.

fédérés des Départements et les citoyens de Paris ont versé leur sang, and the Rhône-et-Loire assembly praised the zeal and courage of the Parisians "dans la lutte terrible et sanglante à laquelle ils se sont livrés pour anéantir la tirannie et faire triompher la liberté et l'egalité."[92] But even Rhône-et-Loire expressed its admiration for the "wisdom and vigor" of the Legislative; and this was the only assembly in France which seems to have realized that the casualties of 10 August were mainly Parisian. Nowhere was the extent of the Parisian initiative appreciated. There were 41 votes of support for the Legislative, 38 of them followed by formal addresses, against one proposed address to the Parisians (Manche), the details of which have not reached the record, if indeed it was ever sent.[93]

If the electors were almost wholly ignorant of the details of events in Paris on 10 August, it is hardly surprising that they also knew little of what had happened later. There was, in any case, little time for them to be told of the September massacres, which began on the day they assembled. The massacres were referred to, even indirectly, by only half-a-dozen departments, all but one of them close to Paris. It might be argued that the Parisians were lucky not to be generally discredited during the elections, but there is another side to this coin, for it is possible to infer from the evidence that sympathetic understanding of the situation which had produced the massacres was rather more likely during the period of the elections than at any time later. The assemblies which heard the news were nearly all very worried about the military situation, and 5 of the 6 had just heard of the fall of Verdun. Not one condemned the massacres or even explicitly discussed them. The sole recorded reaction of any kind came from Vosges, a far from radical place. Here Poullain-Grandprey, the president, urged the electors to make an effort on returning to their cantons to calm down the agitation which was sure to arise from the losses caused by the cowardice of Longwy and Verdun. They should, he said, warn the people against any wish they might have to avenge these losses on the enemies of the public interest to be found in their midst; people should be encouraged to limit themselves to keeping a watch on such persons and denouncing them to the authorities.[94] This cool, intelligent appraisal of the emotional reaction underlying the massacres is an interesting contrast to the highly colored denunciations which, however excusable, became almost routine in later months, and which incidentally Poullain-Grandprey himself never seems to have made. In Vosges, in September 1792, he could understand what the Parisians had done even if he in no way approved it. But as the fear of invasion died away, all that was left visible was the brutality of the massacres and the even greater brutality of the Commune's reaction to them. Against this, the Parisians could set the sacrifices of 10 August; but the electors of France had not been told much about 10 August.

92. A.N. C 178 C II 20 (Côte d'Or) 7 Sept.; C 180 C II 68 (Rhône-et-Loire) 4 Sept.
93. A.N. C 179 C II 48 (Manche) 7 Sept. This move came from the seventh *bureau*, which seems to have been much more radical than the assembly as a whole.
94. A.N. C 181 C II 82 (Vosges) 6 Sept.

This should not be overemphasized. Without a full study of the national and provincial press in the autumn of 1792, we have no real idea of what the general public in the departments knew, or thought they knew, about events in Paris. But as far as the assemblies are concerned, a plausible enough picture does emerge which makes later proceedings in the Convention more comprehensible. If 10 August was *never* officially represented as the achievement of the revolutionary Commune, if the Legislative Assembly's role on that occasion was widely misrepresented and exaggerated, then anyone coming to Paris in September 1792 might well be bewildered at the attitude of the Parisian radicals to national politicians. If, in addition, such a man heard nothing of the massacres until the news of Verdun was past history, the report of them might well serve to bolster up his distrust of the Parisian rabble. One of the minor puzzles of the king's trial is the number of speeches which deal with "Paris" almost entirely in terms of September, ignoring 10 August altogether. After a reading of the electoral *procès-verbaux*, such speeches are easier to understand.

In these circumstances, what sort of man did the assemblies choose to elect?

If the Legislative Assembly, or at least its "patriotic" deputies, stood so high with the electors, one might expect that such deputies would have first call on the electors' sympathies; and such indeed was the case. The choice was of course selective, and tended to be absolute, in the sense that a man was either elected (and as a rule fairly high on the list) or he did not sit at all. Of 205 men from the Legislative who were offered seats as *conventionnels* (5 refused them) there were 201 chosen as *députés titulaires*, and only 4 *suppléants*.[95] How far the Jacobin *Tableau Comparatif* affected this result it is impossible to say. Even in conservative departments, there is evidence that assemblies receiving it felt bound to take it into account, and the value attached to it as a means of swaying opinion was shown in Pas-de-Calais, where the embattled radicals were able to ensure that it was specially distributed among the electors. There were also several complaints that its record was inaccurate, which suggests a belief among those concerned that their chances of reelection might be damaged. On the other hand, though nearly half the assemblies did not record its receipt at all, none seems to have had any difficulty in drawing distinctions among the department's former representatives. It may be noted however that the only two Legislatives elected with really suspect records, Tardiveau (Ille-et-Vilaine) and Henry-Larivière (Calvados) were chosen by assemblies in rather odd circumstances when it is not possible to establish how much may have been known about them and how widely the knowledge was shared.[96] The quite surprising general readiness with which

95. The *suppléants* were Méricamp (Landes), Menuau (Maine-et-Loire), de Varaigne (Haute-Loire), and Rudler (Haut-Rhin). Menuau sat from 28 September 1793; de Varaigne is the subject of a small mystery I have been unable to resolve (see Appendix I); the others did not sit. The 5 to refuse were Torné (Cher) and André (Orne) (both bishops), Tardiveau (Ille-et-Vilaine) François de Neufchâteau (Vosges) and Delaunay (Somme).

96. The Bayeux officials were very dilatory in reprinting the *Tableau Comparatif* (A.N. C 178 C II 13 (Calvados) 4–5 Sept.). The Ille-et-Vilaine *procès-verbal* says nothing at all of

right-wing members of the Legislative were rejected, even in departments like Ardèche and Lot-et-Garonne, supports Lefebvre's claim that the repudiation of the existing monarchy was not merely a Parisian affair, in fact it suggests that there was more hostility to the king than he implies.[97]

It would have been possible to accept the verdict of 10 August without necessarily endorsing the point of view of those members of the Legislative who had asserted their independence of the government before the monarchy collapsed, but here the propaganda and the de facto authority of the Legislative may be assumed to have worked together, and in an impressive vote of confidence, more than 80 percent of the left wing was returned. Reelection was not automatic, and perhaps thirty to forty (the number depending on one's definition of categories) did not secure it, but if one runs one's eye down the voting lists of 1792, the potential *conventionnels* almost select themselves. Many departments elected all or nearly all who could be considered eligible. Personal feuds, local factors, and nuances of conviction about the monarchy which could not appear on any voting list were likely to produce some rejections, but in most places these concerned one or two deputies only. The outstanding exceptions to the rule that men with sound Legislative records had a good chance of reelection occurred in Landes, which rejected 4 deputies out of a possible 6 and demoted another to the rank of *suppléant*, and in Finistère which rejected 5 out of 6, retaining only the unimpressive Bohan. It is perhaps logical that Landes had in 1793–94 only three Montagnards, and Finistère only one. The Finistère Montagnard was not Bohan, who backed the Gironde.[98]

Deputies discarded in 1792 by their own departments had to accept defeat; the only men to be rejected by their 1791 electorates and then accepted elsewhere were the famous 5 from Paris. In all, 14 departments had no Legislative members they were willing to reelect, and 6 of them (Allier, Hautes-Alpes, Indre, Orne, Isère, and Pyrénées-Orientales) chose no ex-deputies at all. These departments, however, avoided the danger of a subtle misunderstanding which might elsewhere complicate the relationship between *conventionnels* and their electorates. The political outlook of men sent into national office from local posts or from private life was presumably familiar to at least a number of those electing them; and nearly all the ex-Constituents elected had spent 1791–92 at home in their departments. But the Legislative deputies had spent that year in Paris, certainly confronting the realities of national policy, but out of touch with the way in which these might appear in the provinces. The views they had

---

what happened between the choice of the provisional *bureau* on 2 Sept. and the beginning of the elections of 4 Sept., apart from the material (on the exclusion of electors) which the assembly later insisted on reinstating, so that it is not clear what documents, if any, were put before the electors, and there is nothing on the election of the *bureau* itself. This gap is very unusual and puzzling. C 179 C II 34 (Ille-et-Vilaine) 2 Sept., 4 Sept., and see note 66, above. For Pas-de-Calais, C 180 C II 61 (Pas-de-Calais) 3 Sept.

97. G. Lefebvre, *The French Revolution to 1793* (New York, 1962), pp. 236, 241.
98. A.N. C 179 C II 39 (Landes), C 178 C II 28 (Finistère).

developed during this period might be unknown to their constituents, and they might be equally unaware of growing tensions and grievances at home. In any assessment of the political outlook of the deputies in relation to their local electorates, the chance of such a concealed conflict must be kept in mind.

Even if a minority group among the 749 *conventionnels*, the ex-Legislatives were at least a substantial minority. The ex-Constituents were far less numerous. In fact they were relatively speaking so few, 83 *députés titulaires* plus 10 *suppléants*, (eight of whom finally sat) that their success in getting as far as the Convention, and in most cases beyond it, argued a rare doggedness and flexibility. By 1792 they were the scattered survivors of a legislature whose political prestige had almost completely disintegrated within a single year. In 1791 ex-Constituents had been ineligible for reelection, and local officials had been chosen *faute de mieux*. In 1792 they were eligible, but few were still acceptable; it is revealing to see the conservative Ornais refusing to tolerate Goupil as even temporary secretary, and later ejecting him as an elector, because of his share in the right-wing reaction after Varennes.[99] Twenty-three departments would not reelect any local man from the Constituent, and 4 others chose ex-Constituents only as *suppléants*. Of the remaining departments, more than half chose only one ex-Constituent. Six assemblies (Aude, Eure, Jura, Maine-et-Loire, Haut-Rhin, and Vienne) ran counter to the general trend by electing 3 such deputies— Maine-et-Loire had 4—but it is suggestive that Haut-Rhin was the only one of the 6 which did not have an anti-Montagnard majority in its delegation in 1793–94. The choice made among these deputies was almost as final as that made among the ex-Legislatives: the 114 *suppléants* who actually entered the Convention in 1792–95 included only 8 of them.[100]

The ex-deputies comprised in all about two-fifths of the men who met in Paris in September 1792. For the rest, the electors' choice fell largely on those prominent in local politics, with men of lesser or no experience bringing up the rear. The balance of experience in the Convention resulting from this will be discussed in the next chapter; we have here to consider the matter from the electors' point of view. Their general attitude toward the Legislative was clear. Their attitude toward ex-Constituents, not categorical but individual, was greatly affected by the natural tendency of men leaving the Constituent to move into high judicial or administrative posts on their return home. Now, one major difference between the elections of 1791 and those of 1792 was the decline in the status of men in local office. Enough individual patriots could be identified to fill up the delegations, but those in office generally, and those in departmental office more particularly, were often condemned out of hand. Twenty-three departments did not elect a single departmental official. Admittedly all but one of the 23 had ex-deputies who were acceptable as candidates (5 departments

99. A.N. C 180 C II 59 (Orne) 2 Sept., 4 Sept.
100. See Appendix I, below.

had 5 such men and one had 6) but no delegation was made up entirely of former deputies, and the passing-over of those in the highest local office for men with narrower experience, or none at all, was not accidental; it implied a real rebuke. Of the remaining 60 assemblies, only 19 chose more than one departmental official. The events of 1792 had forced many administrators into showing their feelings, and now the openly monarchical among them were unhesitatingly rejected. In all, 28 departments launched direct and vehement attacks on part or all of the local hierarchy; a dozen pushed their authority to the limit by forthwith renewing the entire departmental council, and an equal number made it clear that they would follow suit as soon as possible. Local tensions varied, and might remain beneath the surface, but in places the criticism was wholesale and the action hardly less so, taking in judges, justices of the peace, and *greffiers* as well as all administrative ranks from department down to commune. It might also be darkly suggested that the postal service was in counterrevolutionary hands. It was felt that anything might happen, and sometimes it did; it would be satisfying to know who stole the Gard copy of the *Tableau Comparatif* from the Gard *bureau* before anyone had had a chance to read it.[101] As will appear in the next chapter, many local officials were of course elected—the really inexperienced deputies were comparatively few—but the process was selective and criticisms were frequent.

The electors had no official duties apart from conducting the national elections. What else did they decide to do?

As we have just seen, a substantial minority either opened the way to or actually initiated a complete overhaul of the local governmental structure. Nearly half, including nearly all of this critical minority, engaged in some sort of patriotic activity, which might range from the taking up of subscriptions (money or jewelry) for volunteers or their families (plus the provision of uniforms, weapons, and equipment) to the organization of horses, food, and transport for the army, or conducting a check on local reserves of shells for the artillery, to perhaps setting on foot the raising of volunteers or the coordination of defense in an entire department.[102] There were also local emergencies. Besides the massacres in Paris, there were at least eight cases of serious rioting in or near towns in which elections were being held. The Seine-et-Marne assembly was exceptional in refusing to concern itself with this; Calvados, Eure-et-Loir, Sarthe, and Aisne all proudly reported their success in quelling disturbances, which they attributed, perhaps rightly since they seem to have had no troops, to the respect in which the electors were generally held. In Reims (Marne) and in Paris, it has been claimed that riots and massacre influenced the outcome of the elections. The *procès-verbaux* give little direct lead on this, but from other sources it appears

101. A.N. C 178 C II 29 (Gard) 3 Sept.
102. A.D. Nord L 755, passim. For horses, see, e.g., A.N. C 178 C II 30 (Haute-Garonne) 5 Sept.; for the inquiry into stocks of ammunition, C 178 C II 16 (Charente-Inférieure) 10 Sept.

that the Reims riots may indeed have helped Armonville's chances, by allowing an assembly to which he must have been almost entirely unknown to form its own estimate of his cool behavior under stress. In Paris, the only deputies elected during the massacre period were Robespierre, Danton, and Collot, whose success needs little explanation. Evidence about the later atmosphere in the assembly is strongly partisan, but does not really suggest that the massacres as such were a major influence. The most mysterious episode is the irruption on 8 September of about two hundred new electors, bringing the numbers to almost a full house, and their equally sudden withdrawal when (apparently) they failed to get Kersaint elected. This occurrence is still unexplained; all that can be said about it in the present connection is that neither the arrival of these electors nor their apparent effect on the voting pattern suggests that the massacres had intimidated them.[103]

In dealing with disturbances the Bouches-du-Rhône assembly, under Barbaroux's leadership, went beyond mere exhortation to the mounting of a substantial military operation, complete with artillery and 1,200 troops, partly to deal with actual counterrevolutionary rebellion and partly to arbitrate in a confused quarrel among soldiers quartered in Arles. In some other places, various electors had brushes with the local authorities, who might be hostile and uncooperative (Bayeux) or openly antagonistic (Sens, where it was even suggested that the assembly move to another town), or merely disconcerted by unexpected electoral excesses of republican enthusiasm. Most assemblies met in churches, which naturally contained tombs and memorials of various kinds, and some electors became so affronted at the sight of coats-of-arms and other *vestiges de la féodalité* that they took action to have them removed or, occasionally, to remove them personally. The commune might be acquiescent or even helpful about this, but sometimes, though unable to object in principle, might see it as the vandalism which it probably was.[104]

A small minority of assemblies (10 in all) passed resolutions on constitutional questions, and 14 urged action on economic problems. The constitutional resolutions commonly reaffirmed the sovereignty of the people and the need for a ratification of the new constitution, and some provided for the recall of deputies unworthy of their trust; Dordogne, probably the most thoughtful and articulate of the radical assemblies, granted its deputies powers for only 18 months, after which they were to go back to the primary assemblies to have their authority renewed. Several departments bluntly demanded the trial of the king.

103. For Marne, G. Laurent, "Le représentation du département de la Marne à la Convention nationale," *Annales* XX (1948); for Paris, A.N. C 180 C II 60 (Paris), 5–8 Sept. especially, and P. Mautouchet, "Le mouvement électorale à Paris." The total nominal strength of the Parisian assembly was 990 (ibid., p. 142) of whom 936 appeared on 8 Sept. The Marne *procès-verbal*, AN C 179 C II 49 (Marne) is very short.

104. The Coutances commune was cooperative (A.N. C 179 C II 48 [Manche] 5 Sept). The Yonne electors ran into a good deal more hostility in Sens (C 181 C II 83 [Yonne] 4 Sept.).

Republicanism was implicit rather than openly expressed, but it must be noted that the Bouches-du-Rhône assembly not only echoed Paris in its outspoken demand for a republic, but was rather more specific: the word "Republic," said Barbaroux, "ne dit pas assès pour la garantie de la liberté, puisqu'il y a eu des Républiques telle que celle de Rome avec ses dictateurs, qu'il y en a eu d'aristo-cratiques telle que celle de Venise et de Gênes, . . . il nous faut un gouvernement républicain, mais adapté à notre Etat moral et Phisique, et qui laisse au Peuple sa souveraineté en toutes choses."[105] The economic resolutions dealt, predictably enough, with the high price and scarcity of grain; it is interesting that ten of the fourteen were passed by assemblies which also attacked the departmental admin-istration. Several assemblies felt strongly about the remnants of feudal rights, and the Morbihan electors devoted most of their address to the Legislative Assembly to speaking their minds on the subject of *domaine congéable*. This particular area of grievance might have figured more frequently in the *procès-verbaux* if knowledge of the 23 August decree had been more widespread than it apparently was.[106]

There are relatively few cases, probably fewer than a dozen, in which it is possible to say that there is evidence implying that the electors in any particular assembly were being maneuvered into decisions they might not otherwise have taken. Unsolicited advice was repudiated, as when the electors of Lozère were asked to elect at least one farmer, and the electors of Sarthe were asked *not* to do so on the ground that *cultivateurs* were unsuited for parliamentary duties. Both assemblies refused to be influenced; Lozère chose no farmers, but Sarthe almost immediately gave a seat to Jacques Chevalier, with pointed comments on "*la classe précieuse des cultivateurs*" and a remark in the *procès-verbal* that "*plus l'homme est près de la nature, plus son âme a d'énergie et moins son coeur est accessible à la corruption.*"[107] The rather engaging attempts by isolated indivi-duals to press their own claims, either by sending patriotic effusions to the assembly or, in one case, by a citizen's naively presenting himself as an example of the type of person who should be elected, met with no success whatever. The *commissaires* who visited various assemblies also seem to have had very limited impact: for example, although the Deux-Sèvres electors may have been guided by Niou and Ruamps to an attack on the departmental administration which they would not have made if left to themselves, this never got further than words, and no action followed. Ronsin and Lacroix gave the Seine-et-Marne assembly an extensive résumé of the Parisian point of view: this was enthusiasti-cally received and may have helped to provoke the famous resolution concerning the head of Louis XVI, but it did not produce any specific motion of support for the Commune or its actions. In Yonne, the assembly was more than once

105. A.N. C 178 C II 23 (Dordogne) 10 Sept.; C 178 C II 12 (Bouches-du-Rhône) 8 Sept.
106. A.N. C. 179 C II 54 (Morbihan) 3 Sept.
107. A.N. C 179 C II 46 (Lozère) 4 Sept.; C 180 C II 71 (Sarthe) 6 Sept.

incensed by the presumption and tactlessness of their (unnamed) visitors, one of whom was ill-advised enough to issue a warning against the election of "*des Nobles, des Prêtres et des hommes de loi.*" To this the president, Le Peletier de Saint Fargeau, icily replied: "qu'il avait eu le malheur de naître Noble, qu'il avait eu le bonheur d'être honoré de la confiance de ses concitoiens par la choix qu'ils viennent de faire de sa personne pour un de leurs Représentans . . ." (He might have added that he was also a former president of the Paris *parlement*.) It has already been noted that nearly all the *haute-voix* departments were especially anxious to avoid any risk that results might be influenced by the order of the voting. Two notably radical assemblies, those of Côte d'Or and Paris, also took precautions to see that important decisions were not taken by a minority of electors: in Côte d'Or, the moment for discussing the replacement of local officials was chosen precisely because the assembly was unusually well attended, and in Paris the hours of the sittings were designed to ensure that country electors could be present.[108]

Apart from Bouches-du-Rhône and Paris, very unusual assemblies which will be separately discussed, there seem to be signs of some *cabale* at work in Finistère, Loiret, Orne, Rhône-et-Loire, Somme, and Seine-et-Oise. In addition to these 6 cases, there were definite (and technically illegitimate) efforts to promote the election of Carra in Saône-et-Loire as well as in Creuse, and of Paine in Gironde, where he was not elected, as well as in Pas-de-Calais, where he was. It looks as though someone was working hard, though unsuccessfully, to get Priestley elected in Vendée, and amidst the general glorious confusion in Corsica, there is an indication that the perhaps diplomatic tertian fever which kept Paoli away from the elections did not entirely remove his hand from the controls.[109]

In 4 of the 6 departments in which there seems some evidence of *cabale*, this is to be found in the way in which the voting proceeded. In Rhône-et-Loire, where there were between eight and nine hundred electors and 15 deputies, plus 5 *suppléants*, to be elected, the whole of the voting was completed within 7 days. This could be explained by reference to the division of the electors into 6 *bureaux*, which would have speeded up the counting of votes; but this very division, which fragmented the assembly even in its places of voting, makes the electors' degree of apparent unanimity even harder to accept. Of the 20 men elected, only 6 went past the first ballot and only one to a third ballot, though 3 of the deputies chosen did not live in the department and one, Priestley, did not

108. A.N. C 180 C II 60 (Paris) 14 Sept., for the helpful elector, Lefebvre; C 180 C II 75 (Deux-Sèvres) 8 Sept.; C 180 C II 73 (Seine-et-Marne) 5 Sept.; C 181 C II 83 (Yonne) 6 Sept.; C 178 C II 20 (Côte d'Or) 9 Sept.; C 179 C II 60 (Paris) 4 Sept.

109. A.N. C 181 C II 79 (Vendée) 5 Sept.; C 178 C II 19 (Corse) 17 Sept. for the way in which previously vociferous criticism of the departmental administration was completely silenced by an injured reply sent by Paoli from his sick bed. For Carra, C 180 C II 70 (Saône-et-Loire) 5 Sept. and C 178 C II 22 (Creuse) 5 Sept.; for Paine, C 178 C II 32 (Gironde) 7 Sept., and C 180 C II 61 (Pas-de-Calais) 4–5 Sept.

even live in France. It hardly seems conceivable that this was an entirely spontaneous result.[110] In Orne, the assembly ran out of candidates very early and there was a string of third-ballot elections as it tried to decide among the relatively obscure; then the last 2 deputies, Carra and Gorsas, were suddenly elected on the first ballot, although the secretary apparently had no very clear idea who they were. (The president of the assembly was Dufriche-Valazé.)[111] In Loiret, the distribution of the votes is described in great detail and the assembly was evidently very much divided, slowly coming to a consensus over local candidates, though Condorcet had clearly some local fame. Then Brissot and Louvet suddently appeared from nowhere and swept the floor, to the exclusion of local men. The election of Louvet was particularly strange, since it involved giving him preference over 2 local candidates already elected as *suppléants.*[112] The allegations of *intrigue* in Seine-et-Oise have already been mentioned; it must be added that one of the effects of what went on, whatever it was, was to kill the chances of Goujon, the energetic and efficient *procureur-général-syndic*, who was said to be heading the poll at the time when the first storm arose, was in no way implicated in it, and yet was demoted to fifth *suppléant.*[113]

The other 2 cases are a little different. In Finistère, the Quimper *société populaire* petitioned for the introduction of *haute voix* and evidently had quite substantial support within the assembly; the *bureau*, however, seems to have made adroit use of a procedural device to stave off the discussion of this issue, and in the end secured a vote simply on the question of whether the petition should be discussed. The discussion was refused by 207 votes to 176. This episode is interesting partly because of the apparent techniques of the *bureau* (deputations were neatly introduced to divert attention at appropriate points), partly because of the strength of the opposition, partly because of the presence of a Breton-speaking element who seem very unlikely to have understood all that was going on, and partly because the name of every member of the *bureau* can be discovered among those from Finistère who were indicted for federalism in 1793.[114] Lastly, there is the strange case of Somme, one of the few departments

110. A.N. C 180 C II 68 (Rhône-et-Loire) 4–9 Sept.
111. A.N. C 180 C II 59 (Orne) 4–10 Sept. The secretary described Gorsas as "*homme de lettres demeurant a Paris*" and Carra as "*citoyen de Paris*" (ibid., 10 Sept.).
112. A.N. C 179 C II 43 (Loiret) 4–6 Sept.; 6 September for Brissot's very sudden election on the first ballot, and 8 September for Louvet's. The Loiret *procès-verbal* gives the distribution of votes in great detail.
113. A.D. Seine-et-Oise 1 M 361, 9 Sept., 17 Sept. Goujon also lost his seat as an elector (ibid., 12 Sept.) allegedly because of his repeated absences; his section's protest was overruled (16 Sept.), though other electors, notably Alquier, were similarly absent without being penalized.
114. A.N. C 178 C II 28 (Finistère) 4 Sept. See also J. Savina, "Les fédérés du Finistère pour la garde de la Convention," *La Révolution française* LXV (1913) for some background to this election. P. Levot, *Histoire de la ville et du port de Brest pendant la Terreur* (Brest, n.d.) has more light on the local situation and some revealing quotations; the names of those arrested in 1793 are in Levot, p. 424.

which had sent the Legislative Assembly a formal protest against 10 August and had held out as long as it could against recognizing the fall of the monarchy. On 17 August the Legislative understandably passed a decree directed against any departmental official, in any department, responsible for such protests. Someone in the Somme electoral assembly secured from Roland a copy of this decree, misrepresented it as applying to those responsible for departmental protests after 20 June, and on this ground persuaded the electors to cancel the election of Hourier-Eloi, who had been and still was the *procureur-général-syndic*, and Dufestel who had allegedly signed the June protest as a departmental official. These are the only cases in 1792 in which elections were actually canceled, and the cancellations did not stand, since Hourier-Eloi was later able to clear himself and Dufestel had never been an official. They might be explicable in terms of revolutionary enthusiasm—except that the behavior of the departmental administration in August, which was a much more serious matter, was never mentioned at all. The Somme election has other odd features, but this is the oddest. Those elected to fill the vacancies thus arbitrarily created were Hérault de Séchelles and Roland.[115]

Much more research would be needed before one could begin to know precisely what all this amounts to, but it has an interesting bearing on another question, that of the multiple elections of 1792. In all, 20 deputies were elected for more than one department. These were:

Albitte (Eure, Seine-Inférieure)
Barère (Hautes-Pyrénées, Seine-et-Oise)
Brissot (Eure, Eure-et-Loir, Loiret)
Camus (Haute-Loire, Seine-et-Oise)
Carra (Bouches-du-Rhône, Charente, Eure, Loir-et-Cher, Orne, Saône-et-Loire, Seine-et-Oise, Somme)
Cloots (Oise, Saône-et-Loire)
Condorcet (Aisne, Eure, Gironde, Loiret, Sarthe)
Jean de Bry (Aisne, Seine-et-Oise)
Dubois-Crancé (Ardennes, Bouches-du-Rhône, Isère, Var)
P.C.A. Goupilleau (Seine-et-Oise, Vendée)
Gorsas (Orne, Seine-et-Oise)
Grangeneuve (Gironde, Seine-et-Oise)
Hérault de Séchelles (Seine-et-Oise, Somme)
Lanthénas (Haute-Loire, Rhône-et-Loire)
Merlin de Thionville (Moselle, Somme)
Mercier (Loir-et-Cher, Seine-et-Oise)
Tom Paine (Oise, Pas-de-Calais, Puy-de-Dôme)
Priestley (Orne, Rhône-et-Loire)

115. A.N. C 180 C II 76 (Somme) 11 Sept., 13 Sept., 14 Sept. For the reinstatement of Hourier-Eloi and Dufestel, *Moniteur* XIV: 96 (session of 1 October). The *Moniteur* somewhat confuses the names and has Hourier as two people.

Robespierre *aîné* (Paris, Pas-de-Calais)

Sieyès (Gironde, Sarthe, Orne)

There were in all 54 offers of seats, made by 23 departments; but it will have been noticed that some departments had much more leaning toward these deputies than others, and that Orne, Eure, Loiret, Seine-et-Oise, and Somme made between them 22 of the 54 offers.

Who were these widely supported candidates? They may be roughly classified as journalists (Carra, Gorsas, Mercier) local celebrities (Lanthénas, perhaps Camus), men who happened to be *en mission* during the voting, or on military duty (Albitte, and, strikingly, Dubois-Crancé), foreigners profiting from very recent publicity (Cloots, Paine, Priestley—though Cloots was a French pamphleteer in his own right), and former or current deputies, a number of them also journalists. In a number of cases the reasons for the elections seem self-evident; but it does appear that the very widespread fame of the Girondins may have been a little exaggerated, in that in some instances their election seems to have been due to the efforts of a clique working on their behalf, rather than to their intrinsic appeal to the assembly as a whole. It is instructive to compare the circumstances of Grangeneuve's election in Gironde with those of his election, by "relative" majority only, in Seine-et-Oise. Carra was undoubtedly very well known and so was Condorcet, but rather special operations or influence in a limited number of departments did have a disproportionate effect on the apparent standing of some deputies.[116]

One slightly unexpected feature of these multiple elections is the apparent failure of politicians, as such, to attract widespread support. Condorcet was cited by those who elected him as a publicist or philosopher, without reference to his practical political activities: Boyer-Fonfrède, who alone of the electoral presidents of 1792 tended to behave rather like the cheer-leader at an American presidential convention, saw fit to refer to him as "*cet élève de l'école de Voltaire, cet ami de Payne....*"[117] Brissot, who had *Le Patriote Français* to help him, seems to have owed something also to the influence of his friends. Vergniaud seems to have been unknown outside Gironde. One cannot be dogmatic about this, since so few assemblies recorded the details of the voting, but let us consider the lively assembly in Béziers (Hérault), which obviously knew a good deal about the 1792 political scene and did note down the names of all those who got votes at every ballot. There was a good deal of steady feeling for Condorcet, though not enough for him to be elected, and some for Carra, and there was a scatter of tiny parcels of votes for men from both the Legislative and the Constituent—Thuriot, Lasource, Isnard, Pétion, Durand-Maillane, Grégoire, Sieyès, Rabaut-Saint-Etienne, and Robespierre, as well as for Cloots. Brissot was not mentioned at all, nor was any deputy from Gironde. The

116. A.N. C 180 C II 26 (Eure) 3 Sept.; and cf. pp. 164–65, 176–77, above.
117. A.N. C 178 C II 32 (Gironde) 7 Sept.

same sort of thing is true in the other departments outside Paris (Deux-Sèvres, Aude, Indre-et-Loire, and Gard) which kept some sort of detailed record, but these are much less interesting than Hérault, because their assemblies seem to have known much less about the deputies from the Legislative Assembly.[118]

Men elected in several departments were usually chosen about halfway down the list, which was naturally headed either by well-known local graduates of the Legislative, or by local officials. Despite Carra's eight departments, only his own Saône-et-Loire, which ranked him third, gave him higher than sixth place on the list. Condorcet could do no better than seventh anywhere, and the same sort of middle-to-lower rank went to most of the others. Brissot was second (on the second ballot) in Eure-et-Loir, but seventh in Eure and ninth in Loiret. Of the 20 deputies under review, only 5 were elected first in at least one of the departments which chose them: Albitte, Barère, Dubois-Crancé, Merlin de Thionville, and Robespierre. In each case it was an easy win on the first ballot, and in each case—coincidence or not, the fact is worth recording—the man concerned was later to back the Mountain.

Robespierre's status in this discussion does not look very impressive: two departments only, one of them Paris where he had made his revolutionary career, the other Pas-de-Calais where he had lived nearly all the rest of his life and with which he still kept in touch. Yet Robespierre is worth a second look, for in the 1792 elections he was unique. He was the only man in France who in two departments swept in at the head of the poll. His election in Paris is usually attributed to his control over the local political organization, but Pas-de-Calais is not so easy: he had been away from home for over three years, the radicals were by no means in control of the assembly, his political reputation was by no means an unqualified asset. Yet he was elected ahead of Carnot, a more recent departmental choice who might in any case have been expected to have had a far broader appeal. Carnot got more votes than Robespierre did; but a very large proportion of those who voted for him must still have put Robespierre first. This should be remembered when one is analyzing the basis of the standing in the Convention which Robespierre was later to achieve.[119]

And so to the two elections which came closest to Mortimer-Ternaux's stereotype of 1792: Paris and Bouches-du-Rhône. What was distinctive about these, and what, if anything, were the differences between them?

The similarities are in some ways very striking. Both were conducted *à haute voix*, both admitted and welcomed spectators, both were outspokenly republican, both ruthlessly excluded electors alleged to be sympathetic to the mon-

118. For the very interesting detail from Hérault (the Parisian record is as extensive) see, e.g., A.N. C 179 C II 33 (Hérault) 7 Sept.
119. A.N. C 180 C II 61 (Pas-de-Calais). For a comment on Carnot's very considerable appeal to the electors, M. Reinhard, *Le grand Carnot*, 2 vols. (Paris, 1950), I: 310. Cf. E. Lecesne, "L'élection des députés du Pas-de-Calais à la Convention nationale," *Mémoires de l'académie des sciences, lettres et arts d'Arras, 2ᵉ serie*, VIII.

archy. There are however some equally striking differences, some of them unexpected. It was Bouches-du-Rhône, not Paris, which made an explicit demand for the trial and execution of the king. It was Bouches-du-Rhône, not Paris, in which dissent over the choice of deputies was reduced to a minimum. Of the 12 Bouches-du-Rhône deputies, 8 were chosen by unanimous or near-unanimous vote, and two others got more than 90 percent support; only Moise Bayle and Rovère had to make some sort of fight for election, and even so they, like all the other deputies and all the *suppléants*, were elected on the first ballot. As we have seen, it was in Bouches-du-Rhône, not Paris, that spectators were directly invited to show their feelings over the results of the elections. The *procès-verbal* strongly suggests that proceedings were dominated by a Marseille/Avignon alliance, and that the *bureau*, with Barbaroux as president and Duprat as secretary, was in firm control throughout.[120]

In the Bouches-du-Rhône *procès-verbal* there is virtually no sign of disagreement within the assembly. In Paris, on the other hand, there were several periods of violent uproar which the man in the chair could not control. These may conceivably have represented protests against left-wing domination, but do at least suggest that the electors had more freedom to express their feelings than is sometimes implied. On 3 September someone produced an accusation against Robespierre himself. The ease with which he disposed of this does not alter the fact that it could be made and was listened to. Nor was the alleged "Jacobin" control in any sense complete. A courteous offer from the Club of the services of its *concierge* and *garçons* was unceremoniously rejected: the assembly kept on the Evêché *concierge*, and its *huissiers* were those of 1790-91. The *procès-verbal* also indicates that as far as the assembly was concerned, the chief attraction of the Jacobin Club was the space it provided for spectators. It would be difficult to judge how much influence these had, but the assembly did take some care to see that entry cards were provided for electors and that these did not get into the wrong hands.[121]

One interesting feature of the Parisian elections is the repeated concern for the participation of the electors from the cantons outside Paris, whose presence is often forgotten. The need for these men to make daily journeys to and from their homes seriously restricted the hours of the sittings, which by agreement did not begin till 9 A.M. and finished soon after 4 P.M. This seems to have been one main reason for the great length of the elections and was decided on, despite the admitted urgency, simply because of the rural element in the assembly, although sittings beginning early and ending late would surely have made the elections easier for a Parisian clique to manage. In fact, the voting was much more divided than in Bouches-du-Rhône. There seems to have been a solid left-wing core of

120. A.N. C 178 C II 12 (Bouches-du-Rhône) 4–9 Sept., for the quite extraordinary voting figures and the *provenance* of those elected.
121. A.N. C 180 C II 60 (Paris) 3 Sept. for the accusation; 4 Sept. for the Jacobin offer of staff, and for the entry cards.

about four hundred, attracting to itself more or less support, according to the popularity of the leading candidate. There were always fewer voters in the afternoon than in the morning, presumably because country electors were drifting home. With the exception of Robespierre, elected first and at a time when at least six sections, four of them radical, had not finished choosing their electors, and Philippe-Egalité elected last, all successful candidates got 40 percent or more *of the total number of possible votes*, and Danton, Collot, Manuel, Legendre, Billaud-Varenne, Desmoulins, and Raffron had majorities which were absolute, or nearly so, on any terms; but except for the elections of Danton and Collot, whose popularity hardly needs explaining, there was nothing to approach the Bouches-du-Rhône performance, and 5 elections went to the second ballot. As a rule, at each election there was someone with enough minority support to suggest that he had a fair chance of being chosen next; Augustin Robespierre, Thomas, and Philippe-Egalité, among others, were thus not last-minute candidates, but had been foreshadowed as possibilities for some little time.[122]

In Paris, as nowhere else, the choice of deputies was limited because the electors were continuously in touch with the results of elections elsewhere. Danton told the assembly on 6 September that Brissot, Pétion, and Delacroix had already been elected for Eure-et-Loir, and the next day it was decided that a list of the latest nominations should be posted daily in the hall. Of the 5 deputies not reelected for Paris, Brissot, Garran-Coulon, and Condorcet had all been given seats elsewhere by 6 September, and Hérault de Séchelles, elected for Seine-et-Oise on 13 September, drops completely out of the Parisian voting list at that point, which suggests that the electors were keeping a close eye on the news as it arrived.[123] Given Brissot's declared attitude to the monarchy at the end of July, and the tone of *Le Patriote Français* since mid-August, it seems unlikely that he had much chance of election, though he was mentioned on the very first ballot. Pétion was another matter and on the figures of 5 September was a real prospect. The only ex-Parisian with a bitter grievance over an explicit personal defeat was Kersaint; but it should be noted that his greatest success, on 8 September (236 votes against Desmoulins' 450) coincided with a dramatic rise in the number of voters, from about 700 to 936. At the next vote, allegedly influenced by remarks from Robespierre, the votes fell to 679, of which Kersaint got 36 and Desmoulins 465. Desmoulins was very nearly elected even on the high first ballot, and one cannot help wondering how far Kersaint's subsequent total loss of the promising support he had had before 8 September was affected by the character of the mysterious extra voters, who seem never to have been sighted again. Perhaps they were intimidated; but from what happened at their

122. Ibid., 4 Sept., for the hours of sitting and the reasons for them. The elections lasted from 4–19 Sept. and full details of the voting are given for every ballot.

123. Ibid., 6 Sept., for Danton's message; 13–14 Sept. for Hérault's sudden disappearance from the voting lists. The same thing happened to Tallien.

only appearance, it must have been plain that their cause was virtually hopeless.[124]

The Parisian elections had overall a strong flavor of *sans-culotte* radicalism unconnected with the Jacobin Club. The sections periodically recalled and replaced electors who had lost their support; and it was the majority in the assembly which overruled Robespierre and insisted that all signatories of the petition of 8,000 should be excluded, rather than merely those who had canvassed in its favor.[125] Both in Bouches-du-Rhône and in Paris it was resolved that the list of those elected should be submitted to the primary assemblies for approval, but whereas in Bouches-du-Rhône this seems to have been merely a paper proposal, in Paris at least two cantons and more than fourteen sections passed formal resolutions on the subject which were recorded in the electoral *procès-verbal*.[126] The revolution of 10 August had been after all a Parisian and not a Jacobin affair.

It should be remembered that in Paris, unlike Bouches-du-Rhône, the electors had little reason to respect or trust the Legislative Assembly. In any list of left-wing voting in the 1792 *appels-nominaux*, the Parisian delegation does not appear at the top, nor in the first ten, nor in the first half of the list. In point of radicalism, it ranked fifty-seventh out of eighty-three. Parisian disgust with the Legislative did not rest only on the behavior of Brissot and his friends but also on the fact that the most revolutionary city in France had in France's first constitutional legislature a delegation well to the right of those elected for Mayenne, Morbihan, or Corsica, not to speak of Finistère or Doubs. Of the 24 Parisian deputies, the total number voting steadily with the Left was 8, and this included 3 *suppléants*; among the 8 were Brissot and Kersaint, as well as Condorcet, who did not vote in the last 3 of the 7 *appels*. The vote on the Lafayette impeachment was 6 in favor, 8 against, 10 absent. Why should the Parisians not see this as an unimpressive performance, reflecting on the whole quality of the legislature? Moreover it was a performance by men elected on a property franchise, far removed from the ordinary electorate. Nevertheless, the Parisians did reelect 2 of their 1791 deputies who could be considered uncompromised and who had not been elected elsewhere—Dusaulx and Beauvais. It would be interesting to know just why Bouches-du-Rhône rejected Antonelle and Archier.

One last general point to be made about the electoral *procès-verbaux* concerns the later political attitude of those who in 1792 either profited by or were

124. Ibid., 7–8 Sept. Whatever the reason for Desmoulins's 450 votes on 8 Sept., it need not have been intimidation; the other 256 votes (excluding Kersaint's 230) are all over the place.

125. Ibid., 3 Sept.

126. A.N. C 178 C II 12 (Bouches-du-Rhône) 7 Sept.; C 180 C II 60 (Paris) 20–25 Sept., for ratifications, and 21 Sept. for Bondy section's objection to Philippe-Egalité. Note, 19 Sept., a resolution *censuring* Champs-Elysées's electors for their absence; maximum attendance was evidently desired, in Paris as elsewhere.

concerned with the "management" of individual elections. It seems likely that in Paris a left-wing delegation would have been chosen with or without Jacobin influence, and some of the formal safeguards over the voting are interesting; for example on 8 September, when only Robespierre, Danton, Collot, Manuel, and Billaud had been chosen, it was ruled that cantons and sections should be intermingled, to vote in random order.[127] Elsewhere, there is comparatively little sign that future Montagnards were much involved in or profited from the most evidently suspect maneuvers. Those who profited most frequently, and at times almost exclusively, from recognizable attempts to direct the voting were Girondins. Both in Rhône-et-Loire and in Bouches-du-Rhône, the delegation was made up of strikingly varied elements, but in both departments the future Montagnards came fairly low on the list and the more radical had trouble being elected.[128] This may imply only that the future Girondins were both better known and more popular, but in Bouches-du-Rhône the low place assigned to the department's most "patriotic" ex-Legislative deputies (who happened also to be future Montagnards) is interesting. In Loiret, Orne, and Seine-et-Oise the manipulations benefited well-known Girondins almost entirely. Though this may have been because they were patriots likely to be supported by any group of active republicans, Carra and Condorcet are the only members of the group for whom this seems a valid claim. Of course these operations were only the work of electoral supporters and do not reflect on the deputies themselves; but in general the "management" episodes and also the "irregularities" do personally involve the presence, in the *bureaux* of the assemblies concerned, of what looks like a disproportionate number of Girondins, both leaders and supporters: Barbaroux and Duprat in Bouches-du-Rhône, Dufriche-Valazé in Orne, Delecloy and Devérité in Somme (though they certainly had André Dumont as secretary), Blad and Gommaire in Finistère, and, for the "irregularities," Buzot in Eure and Lanjuinais and Defermon in Ille-et-Vilaine. This provides an interesting background for the later accusations of manipulation by the Convention's *bureau*, as well as for Girondin criticism of procedures in Paris.

VI

No attempt to re-create the mood of the 1792 assemblies can hope to be entirely successful: many of the *procès-verbaux* are but bare bones, and even the more detailed ones may do no more than hint at the surrounding atmosphere. (What was the "incident" which caused the Haute-Marne assembly to abandon its sitting altogether on the evening of 5 September? What was the 10 September riot in St. Calais [Sarthe] all about, and how were the *aristocrates* involved

127. A.N. C 180 C II 60 (Paris) 8 Sept.
128. A.N. C 178 C II 12 (Bouches-du-Rhône) 6–7 Sept., for the election of Granet and Gasparin (both L.A.) 5th and 7th, respectively, among 12 deputies; C 180 C II 68 (Rhône-et-Loire) 7–8 Sept. for Cusset and Noël Pointe at the bottom of the list.

in it persuaded to put on the *bonnet rouge* as a symbol of reconciliation?)[129] Nevertheless, however obscure the motives and feelings of the electors may be, they were free to choose what they wished to do and to record whatever they considered important, and a careful comparison of their proceedings sheds a surprising amount of light on the attitude which each was willing to adopt.

It is not possible to establish blanket criteria distinguishing the more conservative from the more radical assemblies; each assembly must be looked at not only for what it did, but for the situation in which it found itself at the time. The assemblies of Nord and Marne have much in common, although one sat for 43 days and the other transacted most of its business in 96 hours, and although one completely overhauled the departmental administration and the other did not so much as mention it. For the more obscure assemblies, which submitted little more than a minimal formal record, it is enlightening to look at the detail of this record with very special care. Sometimes it is simply ambiguous or totally unhelpful, but surprisingly often a reference to a local history will serve to develop and confirm a tentative inference drawn from such evidence as there is. Thus the assemblies of Allier and Hautes-Alpes each returned brief and at first sight very unrewarding reports of their activities. Each had had a wholeheartedly conservative delegation in 1791–92, so that neither had any deputies who could be reelected. Neither made any comment on the departmental administration. It is only when one comes to consider the position of a 1792 electoral assembly conducting its business in a hitherto placidly constitutionalist department that the possible significance of small details becomes clearer, and one can then observe that it was Allier, not Hautes-Alpes, which recognized and recorded the existence of constitutionalist primary assemblies and overruled them by majority vote; and that it was Allier, not Hautes-Alpes, in which the elections were vigorously fought out between rival candidates. In short, it was Allier, not Hautes-Alpes, which showed itself, even in a very bald record, as having some political vitality and willingness to assess the political situation as it actually was; and the local histories reveal Allier as a highly pragmatic department adjusting itself to the needs of the Republic in 1792–94, whereas Hautes-Alpes, as one historian has put it, was hardly touched by the Revolution.[130] Again, the uninformative record presented by Seine-Inférieure tells little until it is remembered that this was a department with one of the largest delegations in France, second only to Paris; that there was considerable local hostility to the Civil Constitution, and that the Seine-Inférieure delegation had been one of the most conservative in the whole Legislative Assembly. Under these circumstances, the ease

129. A.N. C 179 C II 41 (Haute-Loire) 5 Sept.; C 180 C II 71 (Sarthe) 10 Sept.
130. For light on Allier and Hautes-Alpes, L. Biernawski, *Un département sous la Révolution française: l'Allier de 1789 à l'an III* (Moulins, 1909), pp. 159–62, 165, 360–61; D. Greer, *The Incidence of the Emigration during the French Revolution* (Cambridge, Mass., 1951), p. 34 and *note* (comment by Barras and Fréron on Hautes-Alpes in 1793); and A.N. C 178 C II 3 (Allier) and C 178 C II 4 (Hautes-Alpes).

with which all the electors were accepted and the total uneventfulness of the elections supports the claim by one disillusioned elector that the Left in Seine-Inférieure had given up in despair.[131]

One cannot of course hope to deduce from the electoral record the exact position which the deputies elected would take up in a later period of political crisis. Even if the assembly's outlook can be clearly discerned, this did not bind its representatives; the issues of 1792–93 were hardly visible in the autumn of 1792; and, in any case, a sizable number of deputies were not in close touch with the assemblies which chose them. Yet all the same, outspokenly radical assemblies should not, theoretically, be saddled with a group of *à l'écart* deputies, nor should Hautes-Alpes (for instance) return a group of fervent Jacobins. What happens when the distribution of Montagnards, Girondins, and men from the Plain among the different departments is plotted on the map and looked at in the context of the electoral *procès-verbaux*?

The results of this exercise do seem to suggest that though it is still possible that the classification of the deputies may need modification in detail, in general it may not be too far from the truth. No one could be surprised that when all the men from Nord and Marne are gathered together into their respective delegations, these should prove to be overwhelmingly Montagnard, though it adds a neat touch that the Nord assembly realized as early as 4 October that it had made a mistake over Fockedey—who turned out to be its only antiregicide. Ariège, tucked away under the Pyrenees four hundred crow's-flight miles from Paris, had the most firmly regicide delegation in the whole of France, with not a single vote for mercy, and five Montagnards out of six deputies; its 1792 *procès-verbal* breathes an eloquent republicanism which accords well with the local historian's description of the elections as "*une magnifique démonstration démocratique*."[132] From the conservative Orne electors accepting a later-than-last-minute taking of the oath by a nonjuror, to the triumphant republicans of Dordogne; from the divided assembly of Pas-de-Calais to the naïveté of Hautes-Alpes (profoundly shocked in November by Serre's description of Paris); from the determined radicalism of Doubs to the dismayed irresolution of Gard, the electoral records, the local histories, and the subsequent behavior of the deputies fit, in a general way, extremely well.[133] No actively radical assembly, with the

---

131. A.N. C 180 C II 72 (Seine-Inférieure); P. Barrey, "Les élections à la Convention dans la Seine-Inférieure," *La Révolution Française* LXIV (1913): 140.

132. A.D. Nord L 755, 4 Oct. A.N. C 178 C II 8 (Ariège), and G. Arnaud, *Histoire de la Révolution dans l'Ariège* (Toulouse, 1904), p. 330.

133. A.N. C 180 C II 59 (Orne) 6 Sept. and 13 Sept., and P. Nicolle, "Le mouvement fédéraliste dans l'Orne en 1793," *Annales* XIII–XV (1936–38); A.N. C 178 C II 23 (Dordogne), and H. Labroue, *L'Esprit Public en Dordogne pendant La Révolution* (Paris, 1911), pp. 51–52; A.N. C 180 C II 61 (Pas-de-Calais); Reinhard, *Carnot*, and Lecesne, "L'élection des députés du Pas-du-Calais"; A.N. C 178 C II 4 (Hautes-Alpes) and T. Lemas, "Les assemblées électorales des Hautes-Alpes pendant la Révolution," *Bulletin de la Société des Etudes des Hautes-Alpes* IX (1890): 202–4; A.N. C 178 C II 24 (Doubs); A.N. C 178 C II 29 (Gard), and F. Rouvière, *Histoire de la Révolution Française dans le département du Gard*, 4 vols. (Nîmes, 1888), II: passim., e.g., pp. 331–34.

exception of that in Aisne, failed to elect a substantial number of Montagnards, and no apparently conservative assembly, with the exception of that in Allier, did do so. In Aisne, it is to be noted that the pro-Montagnard Quinette was elected at the head of the list, and that the men new to national politics were nearly all regicides; one can only speculate on what might have happened had Quinette's influence on the delegation not been removed in March 1793. In Allier, Forestier was the only one of the four supporters of the Jacobin régime who was openly committed to the Mountain, the others all being "attribution" Montagnards whose attitudes were nicely in line with the de facto republicanism of their departmental officials (chosen by the same electors) in the first half of 1793.[134] It might well be complained that some of the records are exiguous and that historians can say anything if they have little enough evidence, but the coincidences are too frequent to seem merely accidental. Consider the Meuse assembly, regathered in Châlons-sur-Marne after its precipitate departure from Goudrecourt, which showed admirable devotion to duty and even kept its temper and did as it was told when ordered by Roland, without notice, at the last minute, and when it was still a hundred miles from home, to replace the entire departmental *conseil-général.* Conscientious, yes; but if Roland in Paris could see the Meuse local officials as enough of a public menace to need peremptory removal, one would have expected at least some comment from the Meuse electors. None was offered, before, during, or after the elections. With such a background, can the political passivity of more than half the Meuse delegation under the Terror be entirely a matter of chance? [135]

At the time of the elections, the Montagnard/Girondin distinction did not of course exist, and in Bouches-du-Rhône and Eure, for example, the republican leadership was in the hands of men whose opposition to Parisian radicalism did not develop until later. One may, however, observe that whereas the most radical assemblies always elected some Montagnards, they did not by any means always elect Girondins, and that the most conservative assemblies elected a greater absolute number of Girondins than Montagnards. With the exception of that from Aisne, none of the 12 delegations in which the Gironde later had support from half or more than half the members was chosen by a radical-seeming assembly. Two particularly interesting bits of background are the conservatism of Seine-Inférieure, from which so many Girondin petitioners later came, and the lack of interest shown by the Somme assembly, which elected another great contingent of petitioners, in bringing the departmental officials to book for their behavior after 10 August. The Jura assembly, which chose 6 future Girondins among its 8 deputies, began by brushing aside a motion that the new Constitu-

134. A.N. C 178 C II 2 (Aisne) 4 Sept., and Appendix III; Biernawski, *L'Allier de 1789 à l'an III*, pp. 165, 360–61.
135. A.N. C 179 C II 53 (Meuse) 9–10 Sept. It was said on 10 September that as the departmental administration had apparently ceased to operate and the President and *pro-cureur-général-syndic* had fled under indictment, the newly elected *conseil-général* should make its way to Bar to take over as soon as possible. No other comment was recorded.

tion be ratified by the primary assemblies, and although it ended proceedings
with a series of explicitly republican resolutions, these were part of the aftermath of the last-minute news about Verdun, as a result of which the previously
completely outnumbered radicals seem to have taken the initiative and carried
their colleagues with them. But well before this happened the deputies had all
been chosen.[136]

Against its electoral background, the later pattern of parliamentary loyalties
looks plausible. This is the highest claim that can be made, because there is room
for error in at least three directions. First, although some check had been made
on the local history of thirty-odd departments, this could be no more than a
slight and arbitrary sampling, and may have been misleading; second, some of
the deputies may have been wrongly classified; third, and this anyhow is a very
probable explanation of a certain lack of detailed "fit," the assembly may have
mistaken its man, as Nord did with Fockedey, and perhaps Oise with Villette.
There is also the overriding fact of the distinctive experience available to the
deputies of the Legislative Assembly, and its possible effect on their later behavior. Nevertheless, department by department, the plausibility is there, and
makes it worth while to look at the distribution as a whole. How does it agree
with the standard generalizations on this subject?

Here, historians have been either very vague or deceptively precise: ranging
from Rudé's assertion that the Mountain was "weak in the provinces" and
Thompson's that the Girondins had "commercial constituencies" to Sydenham's
demonstration that the Girondins were scattered almost at random over France,
and Aulard's listing of departmental sympathies in considerable detail.[137]
Aulard's analysis interestingly suggests quite extensive Montagnard *strength* in
the provinces; he says also that in about one department in three, no Girondins
were elected at all.[138] Sagnac reiterates Aulard's points, with emphasis on
Montagnard strength and Girondin dispersal.[139] How do all these assertions
relate to the findings arising from the present study?

Aulard lists 8 Girondin-dominated departments (Gironde, Seine-Inférieure,
Somme, Aisne, Haute-Vienne, Ardèche, Jura, and Finistère). To these may be
added Hautes-Alpes, plus Côtes-du-Nord, Morbihan, Vosges, and Maine-et-Loire.
The total of 13 declines to 12 with the subtraction of Ardèche, whose 3 Girondins were outnumbered by 4 "committees" fence-sitters. At the other ex-

136. A.N. C 179 C II 38 (Jura) 8 Sept.; the deputies were chosen on 4–6 Sept. For
more about Jura, A. Sommier, *Histoire de la Révolution dans le Jura* (Paris, 1846) is
rewarding.
137. Rudé, *Revolutionary Europe* (London, 1967), p. 133; Thompson, *The French
Revolution*, p. 319; Sydenham, *The Girondins*, p. 183; Aulard, *Political History of the
French Revolution*, 4 vols. (New York, 1965), III: 42–43; Sagnac, *La Révolution
1789–1792* (Paris, 1920), p. 414.
138. Aulard, *Political History*, III: 40–42. This list, the only detailed one apart from
Sydenham's, has 165 names and gives the departments of origin.
139. Sagnac, *La Révolution 1789–1792*, p. 414, note 1.

Departmental delegations of 1793—political alignments.

treme, his 26 entirely non-Girondin delegations are reduced, via stray Girondins in Doubs, Loir-et-Cher, Seine-et-Marne, and Vienne, to 22 scattered widely from Ardennes to Hautes-Pyrénées.

At first sight the Girondins do look very dispersed indeed. A hundred and seventy-eight of them divided among 61 departments does not seem to allow for much concentration. A closer inspection however rather modifies this conclusion. Sixteen of the departments had only one Girondin each, and another 15 had only 2, so that 31 departments returned 46 deputies, and the remaining 30 between them elected 132, of whom 74, or more than 40 percent of the whole strength of the Gironde, came from the 11 departments of Aisne, Hautes-Alpes, Calvados, Eure, Finistère, Gironde, Jura, Maine-et-Loire, Seine-Inférieure, Somme, and Haute-Vienne. Another 24 Girondins were elected by Bouches-du-Rhône, Côtes-du-Nord, Eure-et-Loir, Ill-et-Vilaine, Vosges, and Morbihan. Seventeen departments thus produced more than half the Girondins in the Convention, and with the exception of Haute-Vienne, Vosges, and Jura, all were on or near the coast; only 2 were in central or north-eastern France. This suggests that there may have been some tendency toward geographical concentration, either among the members of the "inner sixty" or among those who backed them, or both. Western France, for instance, had evident Girondin sympathies, and the same was true of the south.

A line drawn so as to separate coastal, western, and southern departments from the rest of France might run from the Somme/Nord/Aisne boundary (Nord, on account of its long northern land frontier, being reckoned as a "northern" department) roughly south and west past Eure, Sarthe, Deux-Sèvres, and Charente to Gironde, along the southern border of Dordogne and Corrèze and thence roughly north-east to the junction of Ain and Isère on the Swiss border. Such a dividing line separates the metropolitan departments of France into two equal groups of 41 on either side. By an arithmetical accident, there are also 362 of our 730 deputies elected for each group of 41 departments.[140]

A look at the map shows that the deputies of the Plain, at least, were fairly equally divided. Both *en mission* and *à l'écart* deputies were very widely spread, and each group was as nearly as possible evenly split between the 2 areas. The "committees" deputies numbered 42 from north and east against 53 from south and west, a difference, but not a very striking one. The "inner sixty" too had no particular electoral locus. Though Gironde, Eure, Eure-et-Loir, Bouches-du-Rhône, Calvados, and Seine-et-Oise between them supplied 24 of the 58, the rest were to be found in ones and twos in 26 other departments, and the balance between south and west as against north and east was of the order of 32:25, hardly an impressive contrast.[141] This is reasonable enough, if the links between these deputies had grown up on a basis of personal liking and association among a number of groups of friends thrown together by their common parliamentary duties. But within the rank-and-file of the Gironde things were otherwise.

The clusters of sympathizers in Jura, Aisne, and Haute-Vienne, 17 men in all, numbered exactly half of all those the Gironde was able to collect in the whole of northern, central, and eastern France. There were 362 of our 730 deputies elected for this area, and including 25 members of the "inner sixty," only 59 of them altogether backed the Gironde. In the coastal, southern, and western de-

140. Seven of the "unclassified" deputies were elected for the coastal, western, and southern departments, and 12 for the north, east, and center. The 6 Corsican deputies (1 Girondin, 2 *à l'écart*, 3 Montagnards) make up the Convention's total of 749.
141. Twenty-five of 60, with the inclusion of Minvielle (Bouches-du-Rhône) and Bancal (Puy-de-Dôme).

partments the picture was entirely different. Hence came 86, or nearly three-quarters, of the Girondin rank-and-file. Only 9 of these 41 departments lacked at least one such deputy, and 12 departments had 3 or more. (The comparable figures for the north, center and east were 24 departments with no rank-and-file Girondins, and only 6 of the remaining 17 with more than one.) In Picardy, Brittany, and Normandy, mentioned by Aulard as sources of Girondin strength, this was greater than he supposed: the proportion of Girondin deputies ranged from 40 percent in Normandy through about 50 percent in Brittany to the very solid majority in old Picardy, now the department of Somme, where of 13 men elected in 1792, 10 became Girondin. In the Limousin too there were 8 Girondins in a total of 14 deputies. Only in Guyenne was the position weak: here the Girondin fortress in Gironde itself could not balance the apathy or downright hostility in Lot, Lot-et-Garonne, Landes, Gers, Aveyron, and Dordogne, and outside Gironde there were only 7 Girondins among 50 men elected. It looks as though Girondin opposition to the Mountain was not at all evenly spread over France, though, as one would expect, stray sympathizers could be found in many places. The bulk of it was quite strongly localized.

For example, those who petitioned against the expulsion of the Girondin leaders in June 1793 came far more from some areas than others. Excluding members of the "inner sixty" as likely to be moved more by personal considerations than anything else, there were 94 deputies who made more or less formal protest about the events of 31 May–2 June. Sixty of the 94 came from the 12 departments of Aisne, Hautes-Alpes, Jura, Maine-et-Loire, Seine-Inférieure, Somme, Haute-Vienne, Côtes-du-Nord, Drôme, Ille-et-Vilaine, Finistère, and Gers, and 45 came from the first 7 alone. Apart from those concerned in the group protests from Aisne, Jura, and Haute-Vienne, there were only 7 signatories who did not come from the southern, western, and coastal departments where the Gironde found so much of its support. From 40 of the 83 departments no deputies protested at all.[142]

Some of this locally concentrated parliamentary feeling for the Gironde came, one would think, from personal influence. In Aisne, Condorcet's department, it seems natural enough to find 7 of his fellow-members joining him to condemn 2 June, and the Girondins from Eure were closely associated with Buzot. Yet this is clearly only part of the story. In 3 departments with notable

---

142. See Sydenham, *The Girondins*, pp. 45–49. The number of Girondins in the present calculation is 177 (Chiappe was Corsican). The total of petitioners includes all those who seem to have been seen at the time as expressing formal sympathy with the Gironde, whether or not they were penalized for it (e.g., the C.P.S. treatment of the Hautes-Alpes deputies was selective). The Manche deputies, e.g., have thus been omitted (see ibid., p. 49 and note). Sydenham (ibid., p. 220) seems to imply that names are missing for Maine-et-Loire and Haute-Vienne, but I do not think this can be so; Delaunay *jeune* and Dandenac *jeune*, the only Maine-et-Loire possibilities, were away from Paris, and the attitude of all the Haute-Vienne deputies can be accounted for. Men from elsewhere might of course have signed.

concentration of petitioners, Hautes-Alpes, Somme, and Haute-Vienne, there were no local members of the "inner sixty" at all, and in Seine-Inférieure, which had, with Somme, more Girondins than any other department in France, there is little suggestion that Bailleul and Hardy were closely linked with the rest of the delegation. The predisposing factors, if there were any apart from a widespread feeling of outrage (but why among some deputies so much more than others?) must be looked for somewhere else.

It is not likely that there will be any pattern which covers all the men concerned; the Convention was too undisciplined, its members too individualistic for that. But some groupings of Girondin-oriented departments do emerge, beyond the obvious tendency of men who were simply conservative to emerge from conservative surroundings.

For one thing, it does seem worth noting that most of the departments with very heavy concentrations of Girondin petitioners seem to have been conservative places where the danger of active *counter*revolution (as distinct from a wish to limit the scope of the revolution in being) was fairly slight. Men from Hautes-Alpes, Jura, Seine-Inférieure, and Somme could urge a protest against Parisian intimidation of the Convention without taking the tremendous and unsuccessful gamble embarked on by the republicans among the federalists of Marseille and Toulon. Consider the case of Somme. Here in August 1792 the departmental authorities had delayed acceptance of 10 August as long as they dared, had indeed originally refused it, and had had to be sharply disciplined by the Legislative Assembly. Once brought to heel, however, the department stayed there; no royalists moved in to make successful capital of the officials' attempt to avoid being dragged further than they wanted to go; and the pattern was repeated in June/July 1793.[143] This strongly suggests that although the Somme revolutionaries would try to resist what they saw as undesirable extremes, there was no strong and active body of Somme counterrevolutionaries waiting to twist an antigovernment movement to its own ends. Delecloy putting up seditious posters in the streets of Amiens horrified the patriotic Jeanbon, and with the Austrians already besieging Valenciennes might well have done far more harm than he did, but the situation in Somme apparently did not make his behavior an immediate threat to the Republic, as the Committee of Public Safety tacitly recognized when Jeanbon's outraged report was quietly pigeon-holed. What was the point of making martyrs? —more especially when even Robespierre would himself have avoided 2 June if he could. It seems likely to be more than a coincidence that the *mass* parliamentary protests came from areas where such activity was not likely to provide, and in fact did not provide, a really serious public danger to the Revolution itself. The possible connection between the political situation in a given department and the sort of political attitude, vis-à-vis the Montagnard régime, which its representatives were willing to contemplate, seems at any rate worth investigating.

143. *Moniteur* XIII: 432; XVI: 636, 759.

Another approach to the Girondin problem, and one with broader implications, may be made if the geographical bias of Girondin support is considered in the context of Thompson's perhaps casual remark about "commercial constituencies." In the eighteenth century, down to the outbreak of revolution, the ports of France were rapidly expanding; in addition the coastal provinces of Picardy, Normandy, and Brittany included some of the most densely populated departments in the whole country. The response of deputies from coastal departments in the crisis of 1793 was a little unusual. With the exception of Vendée, there was not a single department along the Channel and Atlantic coasts from Pas-de-Calais to Basses-Pyrénées, or along the Mediterranean coast from Pyrénées-Orientales to the frontier of Savoy, which did not boast at least one Girondin deputy, and all but 2 had 2, 3, or more. The total was 77 Girondins from 20 departments, but it is the consistency which is interesting, in view of the patchiness elsewhere of concern for the Girondin cause. With the exception of Dunkirk in the far north-west and Rochefort in Vendée, all the major ports of France were in departments which showed a good deal of parliamentary sympathy for the Gironde, and a number of the ports themselves—Brest, Bordeaux, Marseille, Toulon, to take notorious examples—were sources of considerable anxiety to the Montagnard régime. The ports and coastal towns seem to be the best starting point for an enquiry into the connection, if there is a connection, between economic and social background and dislike, among deputies, of a radical republic; especially since in February/March 1793 the Republic became involved in a major maritime war.[144]

To look again at the general picture: there were of course some departments which elected delegations that were anti-Montagnard without being predominantly, or at all, pro-Girondin, and these included several of those listed by Sagnac as being, on account of their lack of Girondins, *exclusivement Montagnard.* For example, take the case of Isère, where in 1793 only prolonged and adroit manipulation by the Grenoble *société populaire* prevented the department from acting on the report of 2 of its conservative (though not actually Girondin) deputies, and becoming involved in federalist protest; how far the majority of the delegation would have wished this movement to go is uncertain, but it is obvious that the 2 Montagnards, Amar and Génissieu, were far to the left of their colleagues.[145] Of Sagnac's 26 "Montagnard" departments, only 13 in fact even had Montagnard majorities, and Lot-et-Garonne distinguished itself by electing a group of deputies so averse to committing themselves too far over the

144. Cf. perhaps the experiences of the little port of Granville, which in 1789 seems to have had no major grievances except of the most pedestrian, bread-and-butter kind. After 1789, the main results of revolution appeared to be an almost total collapse of maritime trade, hard times for everyone, and extensive black marketing: *"d'abord vivre."* Though not actively federalist, the port in 1793 sympathized wholeheartedly with the Gironde. C. de la Morandière, *Histoire de Granville* (Paris, 1966), pp. 263–64, 274 esp., and appendix for *cahiers.*

145. R. Tissot, *La société populaire de Grenoble pendant la Révolution* (Grenoble, 1910), for June–July 1793.

issues of 1793-94 that none would really become aligned with either of the factions; this department, engagingly reluctant to accept any of the inconvenient corollaries of revolutionary developments, was the only one in France whose entire delegation has been placed with the Plain.[146] Unlike the Gironde, the Mountain could not claim one department in France where every deputy was an avowed supporter.[147] In the provinces where the Gironde was strongest, that is in Picardy, Brittany, and Normandy, radical feeling was very muted indeed. From this it might appear that Montagnard strength, like Girondin, was strongly localized.

Yet when one looks at the map, it is not the concentration but the very wide dispersal of the Mountain that most catches the eye. The Mountain had a majority of the deputies in 18 departments from north, east, and center, from which came 122 Montagnards, and in 6 departments in south and east, from which came a total of 35. But these 24 departments between them returned only just over half of the Mountain's total strength. Against 22 departments without Girondins, there were only 4 which did not elect at least one Montagnard, all of them in the south: Hautes-Alpes, Ardèche, Lot-et-Garonne, Basses-Pyrénées. Ten departments, 3 of them in Brittany, had only one Montagnard, and 17 (4 from Normandy, one each from Brittany and Picardy) elected 2; the remaining 52 departments, Corsica included, elected 3 Montagnards or more. The pattern was an uneven one, but strong groups of Montagnards came from all over France: from Bouches-du-Rhône, Haute-Garonne, and Ariège in the south to Puy-de-Dôme and Dordogne in the center, Vendée on the Atlantic coast, and Doubs on the eastern frontier, to Marne east of Paris and Nord on the borders of the Austrian Netherlands. The Mountain was both stronger and weaker than Sagnac implies: stronger because even in predominantly conservative delegations like that from Aude there was usually a leavening of Montagnards, and weaker because it notably failed to dominate some of the provinces he includes as Montagnard territory. Alsace, Champagne and Burgundy, yes; here the proportion of Montagnard members averaged out at something between a half and two-thirds; but in Lorraine, despite a radical delegation from Moselle, and in Franche-Comté, despite 4 Montagnard deputies among the 6 from Doubs, the Mountain was heavily out-numbered. However, parliamentary weakness in one department was made up for by strength in another, and despite its overwhelming defeat in the west and its sweeping success in Paris and some (but not all) of the neighbouring departments, backing for the Mountain was less localized than that for the Gironde. Of the 299 Montagnards elected for metropolitan France, 114 came from southern, western and coastal departments and 185 from north,

146. For sidelights on the situation in Villeneuve, which in 1792 wanted to keep the monarchy, F. de Mazet, *La Révolution à Villeneuve-sur-Lot* (Delbergé, 1894), pp. 18-19, 61-62.

147. The varied opinions even in delegations with a very pronounced majority attitude suggest that many members had no hesitation in taking their own line.

center and east, a ratio of something like 38:62; without Paris, it was almost exactly 40:60.

Thus, while it is easy to understand a recoil by large numbers of local officials from the implications of the events of 2 June 1793, it may also be important to note that there were very few parts of France which lacked at least one local deputy of radical leanings, and more than 3 departments in 5 had 3 or more such men. During the recruiting missions which began in March 1793, when 72 departments were visited by Montagnards *en mission*, 48 of the 72 saw recruiting conducted by a Montagnard elected from the area. "The provinces" in their parliamentary representation cannot be said to have been predominantly Montagnard, but they were represented by men who were much more Montagnard than Girondin, and this meant that the radicals *en mission* were not in most cases carrying Parisian ideas into foreign territory; they were trying to guide the constituencies which had elected them in the direction in which they themselves had already begun to move. The greater the local contact, the wider the local knowledge, and the stronger the government's position. In these matters the Mountain's resources were, at least on paper, rather larger than is sometimes allowed.[148]

There was however another aspect to this question. We have already noticed that in the elections, the men at once most likely to be elected and least likely to be in close touch with their electors were, in general, the left wing of the Legislative Assembly. This raises two further possibilities. In the first place, if any substantial proportion of Montagnard deputies were ex-deputies of the Legislative, the Montagnard difficulties in the provinces would be increased, since it would be necessary not simply to strengthen the links existing in September 1792, but to restore any which might have been broken since September 1791. In the second place, it has not usually been supposed that any substantial number of ex-Legislative deputies did in fact back the Mountain. If the Mountain did draw substantial support from the Legislative, its character may need to be reassessed. Let us now look at the balance of political experience in the Convention and how it seems to have been shared among the various political groups.

---

148. For another side to this, note the course of events in Ardèche in December 1793. There was no local Montagnard to go *en mission*, and Reynaud (Haute-Loire) who was given the job was neatly hoodwinked by the local Right into arresting a number of *bons patriotes*: C. Jolivet, *La Révolution dans l'Ardèche 1788–1795* (Largentière, 1930), chap. XI. There was no Montagnard from Lot-et-Garonne either, and Paganel, a native *en mission*, was not overenthusiastic there in the revolutionary cause. F. De Mazet, *Villeneuve-sur-Lot*, pp. 61–62 and elsewhere.

CHAPTER 7

POLITICAL EXPERIENCE

Of all the legislatures of the revolutionary period, the Convention was the longest-lived. It sat without benefit even of by-elections for more than three stormy years, making up its dwindling numbers by calling on the *suppléants* elected in 1792, until some departments had exhausted their supply and all the candidates remaining had to be cast into a common pool from which names were drawn by lot as they were needed.[1] Although a number of those reelected in 1795 were *suppléants* fairly recently come to Paris, the majority were seasoned veterans of the Terror and the reaction, whose political experiences helped to shape the history of the Directory. When their parliamentary terms ended, many deputies were absorbed into the machinery of government, where some stayed in various capacities till 1814 or even 1815. Jeanbon Saint-André, dying in harness as a Napoleonic prefect fighting typhus in Mainz, is a reminder of the continuity of revolutionary and Napoleonic history.[2]

The so-called "act of amnesty" of January 1816, which exiled all the surviving regicides who had entered the imperial service as well as those who had taken an oath of Napoleonic loyalty during the Hundred Days, uprooted men well past middle age who had become part of the fabric of life in their local communities.[3] It is a measure of the Convention's conscious pride in itself and its achievement that the bitter divisions of its actual lifetime became, among survivors of the Restoration, not forgotten but comparatively unimportant. The better-off raised funds for the rescue of the indigent, and a man like Barras, who

1. Law of 5 *floréal* III (*Moniteur* XXIV: 278). For a full list of *suppléants* and their departments of origin, Appendix VIII, below.
2. Kuscinski, *Conventionnels*, p. 350. For Jeanbon's career as a whole, L. Lévy-Schneider, *Le conventionnel Jeanbon Saint-André* (Paris, 1901).
3. See for example the cases of Forestier, Oudot, and Ribéreau (Kuscinski, *Conventionnels*, pp. 261, 472, 524).

refused to contribute even though he himself was able to stay in Paris, fell even lower in his colleagues' estimation.[4]

It is very hard to judge what political prejudices and convictions any *conventionnel* brought with him to Paris to help determine the line of his future career. One can, however, isolate one possible formative influence: the sort of political experience he had already had at the time of his election in 1792.

I

Between 1789 and 1792 France offered an extraordinary range of opportunity to any man with political interests or an inclination toward public life. In local government, every administrative council for every governmental unit, from department down to commune, had to be elected, and so did departmental *procureurs*, town clerks and tax gatherers, judicial officials, the clergy, and the commanders of the National Guard. The defect of the system was that there might be more jobs than men willing and able to take them on. The advantage was that many deputies, before they reached Paris in 1791 or 1792, had had the chance to gain experience of public affairs in a more familiar setting. The self-denying ordinance which made ex-Constituents ineligible for the Legislative Assembly is usually condemned because it deprived France of the services of her only existing parliamentary politicians; it had, however, the effect of strengthening local political life by returning to it large numbers of ex-Constituents, some becoming judges and others members of departmental directories or town councils.[5] Three-quarters of the eighty-odd who returned a year later as members of the Convention came as old hands who had already been actively involved in revolutionary administration at two different levels. Conversely, since the Legislative Assembly had to be drawn from amongst those without experience in national politics, the most obvious candidates were the men elected over the two preceding years to run things at the local level, so that a very large proportion of the Assembly members who were reelected as *conventionnels* could also claim, by September 1792, both local and national experience. However misguided one may think some of the policies of the Convention to have been, the men who formed them should not have been unaware of problems of administration; the less so since the ex-deputies in the Convention were buttressed by a considerable number of newcomers who had had, if not national

4. Three who, having restored their own positions in France, went to great trouble on behalf of their exiled colleagues were Gleizal, Boissy d'Anglas, and Lanjuinais. Boissy and Gleizal, both from Ardèche, had taken a very cautious stand in 1793–94, and Lanjuinais, from Ille-et-Vilaine, was Girondin. Most of the exiles were naturally Montagnard. See Kuscinski, *Conventionnels*, pp. 298, 67, 370; also 34 (Barras).

5. Thus, to take random examples, Kervélégan became president of the Quimper court, Barère was chosen by his department as *juge au tribunal de cassation*, and Pierre-Louis Prieur resigned a judicial post in Paris to become a *substitut* to the Marne *procureur-général-syndic*; ibid., pp. 356, 24, 507.

experience, at least from one to three years' training in local government under revolutionary conditions.

The easiest way of classifying the kinds of political experience to the credit of the *conventionnels* in 1792 is by the scope of the governmental units in which they had worked. There are, first, the graduates of the Constituent and Legislative Assemblies, responsible for the whole of France; next come members of departmental directories and councils, then district officials, and finally those from the communes. This is rather a crude method; it equates parliamentary and administrative experience, and makes no allowance for differences in situation between one department and another (it may have been easier to administer Hautes-Alpes than Maine-et-Loire), nor for difference in size and complexity between one commune and another (to be a town councilor in Rugles or even in Evreux was not equivalent to holding the same office in Lyon or Bordeaux). It may, however, be justified on practical grounds, because of the interminable complications of drawing fine distinctions; and also, more importantly, because historians have made judgments about the political attitudes not only of parliamentarians but also of various categories of local officials, as such, in the year of the Terror, and it may be interesting to see whether those local officials who had been elected to the Convention showed any particular pattern of behavior. But before we go on to any discussion of the various groups suggested above, it seems necessary to consider whether other varieties of political experience should be included.

Does the term "local official" necessarily cover only administrators pure and simple, or should other elected persons be added to the list? What about judges, justices of the peace, clergy, and those in charge of the National Guard? All these held responsible positions, all had their share in the establishment and working of the new régime, yet none was an administrator in the ordinary sense, though the political importance of the clergy and the National Guard is self-evident and the number of ex-Constituents elected to judicial office in 1791 suggests political factors at work here as well. This sort of classification is bound to be arbitrary and to raise awkward questions about the status and significance of activity which is not in itself exactly political: for example, the acceptance of a revolutionary judgeship was felt by the family of Hérault de Séchelles to involve a scandalous commitment to the revolutionary cause,[6] but the function even of an elected judge is, after all, to apply the law, not to make it or take responsibility for it; in this sense judges are, perhaps, above politics—though possibly not so much so in a revolutionary era. The same kind of problem, in a more acute form, arises over the clergy. In the end a reasonable approach seemed to be (a) to treat elected National Guard commanders as local officials of the area to which their command applied, e.g., the Guard commander elected in, say, Saint-Dié would be reckoned as equivalent to a Saint-Dié communal official;

6. E. Dard, *Un épicurien sous la Terreur: Hérault de Séchelles* (Paris, 1907), p. 136.

(b) to provide a special category for judges and justices of the peace who had not served in other capacities—if they had done so, their parliamentary or administrative experience would take precedence, e.g., Barère has been treated as an ex-Constituent and not as a judge; and (c) not to count the clergy at all unless they had held some public office which was not ecclesiastical—e.g., Villar, consitutional bishop of Mayenne, was also president of the departmental directory and has therefore been included as a departmental official, and Thomas Lindet, constitutional bishop of Eure, has been included as an ex-Constituent. This decision on the clergy seemed unavoidable because, although acceptance of the Civil Constitution automatically signified *some* involvement in revolutionary politics, and the consequences might be very disagreeable, the degree of involvement intended is very hard to estimate either for the clergy themselves or for those electing them.

Finally, among those deputies who in 1792 had never before held formal public office, there were some who had had at least a good deal of informal political occupation. A category has therefore been provided for the political activists, men who had made a name for themselves by revolutionary journalism and/or by enthusiastic membership in revolutionary clubs. Journalistic and club activity implies political interest and perhaps some sophistication, and it seems justifiable to distinguish those concerned in it from men who, as far as can be seen, had taken no active interest at all in politics before their election to the Convention.

We have now eight categories of *conventionnel*, as follows: (1) ex-Constituents; (2) ex-members of the Legislative Assembly; (3), (4), and (5) ex-members of departmental, district and communal administrations, including National Guard commanders; (6) judges and justices of the peace without other post-1789 experience; (7) journalists and active members of revolutionary clubs, if they have not yet held public office; and (8) the completely inexperienced. What are the accepted generalizations about the numbers and political attitudes of deputies in these various categories?

In describing the previous experience of the *conventionnels*, modern historians seem to rely on the classification made by Pariset more than 50 years ago.[7] For the purpose of his analysis Pariset added to the 749 deputies elected in 1792 all the *suppléants* called up between 1792 and 1795, the colonial representatives who began to trickle in in 1793, and the deputies chosen early in 1793 to represent the new departments of Mont-Blanc, Mont-Terrible, and Alpes-Maritimes. These various additions, on his calculations (he did not specify the numbers in any category and made no claim to absolute accuracy) totaled 154; the total number of deputies who sat in the Convention at one stage or another of its history he therefore put at 903. He then listed various groups among the 903 in this manner:

7. G. Pariset, *La Révolution Française 1792-1799* (Paris, 1920), p. 7.

> 96 ex-Constituents
> 189 ex-members of the Legislative Assembly
> 245 lawyers
> 379 local government officials

and added the final comment that "the preponderance of lawyers and local officials is undeniable. They form by themselves more than two-thirds of the Convention (624 out of 903)."[8]

This procedure suggests certain problems. In the first place, any analysis of the Convention which is based on a classification of all the men who ever sat in it may seriously misrepresent its character at any given point in time. On Pariset's reckoning the total of 903 deputies includes 285 men from the Constituent and Legislative Assemblies. It seems probable that men of this standing would be elected, if they were elected at all, nearer the head of the poll than the foot of it, and that relatively few of them would be demoted to the rank of *suppléant*; thus the proportion of ex-deputies among the *suppléants* seems likely to be low. But a number of ex-deputies (Brissot, Vergniaud, Condorcet, Couthon, Robespierre, and many more) disappeared in the murderous feuds of 1793–94 or were excluded or eliminated in the reaction of 1794–95. If their replacements were men of local rather than national experience, this might make a significant difference to the balance of experience in the Convention as a whole.

In the second place, Pariset's statement in its existing form needs further clarification. From his adding together of "lawyers and local government officials" to make a total of "624 out of 903," one might assume that he was classifying all the deputies into groups of one kind or another. Yet on this basis, since he deals only with lawyers, local officials, and ex-deputies, the implication is that every *conventionnel* who was not an ex-deputy or a local official was a lawyer of some sort; which is not only improbable but manifestly untrue. When it is realized that many of his "local officials" were also probably lawyers, it becomes very hard to see how the argument has been constructed, and its arithmetic cannot be checked at all. It seems easier to avoid confusion by concentrating on an examination of the deputies' experience in public life, as such, leaving aside for the time being their professional background; more especially, as in eighteenth-century France the term "lawyer" can be so broadly applied as to be virtually meaningless, and Pariset does not discuss the way in which he has used it. If we therefore look only at his figures for ex-deputies, which are based on obvious criteria and can be checked with ease, we find that they imply that in 1792 men with experience in politics on a national level were heavily outnumbered by those who had had only local experience, or none at all. Or do they? . . . we are back again at the question of the composition of the Convention as it existed at any particular point in time.

8. Ibid.

The figures given by English historians for the political experience of the deputies seem to derive from Pariset's, but with baffling variations. For example, Goodwin, Hampson, and Sydenham all quote slightly different approximations to Pariset's figures for the ex-deputies, but use them as though *all* the ex-deputies were present *in 1792*; which may be somewhat misleading.[9] Mortimer-Ternaux and Kuscinski, who alone deal with the ex-deputies as individuals, give no total numbers, but provide material for conclusions about totals which conflict with each other as well as with the (differing) totals presented by everyone else.[10] It will therefore be necessary to establish (a) how many ex-deputies were chosen as titular *conventionnels* and how many as *suppléants*; and (b) whether any distortion is introduced by quoting figures for the whole period 1792-95 as though they reflect the balance of experience in the Convention in 1792. We shall also have to find out how many *conventionnels* belonged to each of the categories of local official, and here too it will be important to look both at the 1792 situation and at possible changes in it thereafter.

Historians have commented not only on the previous experience of the *conventionnels* but also on the relationship between their experience before they reached the Convention and the political attitudes they adopted after they entered it; the comment on this relationship has however been accompanied by surprisingly little discussion or documentation.

Other things being equal, the initial leadership among the *conventionnels* was most likely to come from the most experienced among them, whose prejudices might therefore be important. The ex-Constituents, though presumably by this time resigned to the Republic, had after all helped to create the constitution which had been destroyed by the mob on 10 August, and after their own experiences in 1789-91 they might also have reservations about Parisian extremism in politics. The much larger group of deputies carried over from the Legislative Assembly might also be expected to be a little prejudiced. They came from a body in which Brissot and his friends had been the leaders on the Left. The views of men so recently famous might well carry considerable weight with those coming with them into the Convention; in addition, as the best-publicized politicians in France, the Girondins might hope to be respected and perhaps followed by less seasoned deputies newly come up from the country. There was also the question of the effect on the rump of the Legislative Assembly, and on French public opinion in general, of the six-week interval between the fall of the monarchy and the opening of the Convention—an interval during which the undisciplined and insolent Parisian radicals had defied the national legislature,

---

9. A. Goodwin, *The French Revolution* (London, 1966), p. 139; N. Hampson, *A Social History of the French Revolution* (London, 1963), p. 155; M. J. Sydenham, *The Girondins* (London, 1961), p. 123.

10. Mortimer-Ternaux, *Histoire de la Terreur*, 6 vols. (Paris, 1864), IV: 457-67; A. Kuscinski, *Les Députés à l'Assemblée Législative* (Paris, 1900), passim.

and by their handling of the September massacres had shown what brutality they were willing to excuse.

With these factors in mind, we may consider Thompson's remarks on the *conventionnels* of 1792. "Nearly a hundred of these men remembered with what fear of popular violence they had removed from Versailles to Paris in October 1789, and with what dread of popular republicanism they had fired on the demonstrators of July '91. Nearly two hundred of them had fresh in mind the insurrection of August, and the September tyranny of the Commune. It was only three weeks since the prison massacre. There was too much that they could not or did not want to forget."[11]

Cobban seems to echo Thompson's views, but extends them to trace a direct connection between Assembly and Convention: "open conflict began after the Convention met between the two small factions which the Convention had inherited from the Legislative Assembly. On one side were the Brissotins and Rolandists, to whom a number of new members joined themselves; on the other, the Jacobin deputation from Paris, which became known as the Mountain."[12] Sydenham fills in the picture by claiming that the Girondin leaders, old and new, were supported by the "provincial lawyers and local officials" who "were as shocked as they by the Parisian massacres and shared their distrust of Paris";[13] a suggestion which links well enough with Mathiez's time-worn judgment on the behavior of local hierarchies in the summer of 1793, when the Girondin/Jacobin quarrel flared into civil war. "The rising," he writes, "was widespread rather than deep. It was essentially the work of departmental and district administrators, composed of rich property-owners. The communes, which were more popular in composition, showed themselves lukewarm or hostile. . . ."[14] Later research has modified this verdict without altogether rejecting it, but its implications for the Convention seem not to have been examined. Besides its several hundred ex-deputies, likely to be hostile to Paris (if the comments just cited are sound), the Convention included large numbers of local officials. Sydenham suggests that these men sympathized with the Gironde, and Mathiez says that there was a community of feeling, at least at the departmental and district levels, between such pro-Girondin deputies and those who had taken over their work at home.

Let us now look at the actual figures, to see how far they bear out these various judgments.

The analysis of the *conventionnels'* political experience which is set out below in Table 14 has been made under seven different headings. Column (i) is an analysis of the 730 men who have been classified according to their apparent political sympathies in 1793–94. All but three of these men sat from September

11. J. M. Thompson, *The French Revolution* (Oxford, 1943), p. 318.

12. A. Cobban, *History of Modern France*, 2 vols. (London, 1965), I: 203.

13. Sydenham, *The Girondins*, p. 124.

14. A. Mathiez, *The French Revolution* (New York, 1965), p. 336. For some modifications, Hampson, *Social History*, pp. 173–75.

Table 14. Membership of National Convention, 1792–95,
classified according to previous political experience

	(i) 1792 Classified 1793–94	(ii) Not Class-ified	(iii) Total Jan. 1793	(iv) Added 1793–95	(v) Total 1792–95	(vi) Losses 1793–95	(vii) Net Strength Oct. 1795
Former deputies							
Constituent Assembly	78	5	83	8	91	23	68
Legislative Assembly	191	3	194	1*	195	56	139*
Total former deputies	269	8	277	9*	286	79	207
Local officials							
Department	113	3	116	29	145	24	121
District	93	1	94	19	113	26	87
Commune	92	2	94	18	112	23	89
Total local officials	298	6	304	66	370	73	297
Others							
Judge or J. P.	59	2	61	10	71	8	63
Club member or journalist	36	2	38	3	41	21	20
No experience	68	1	69	58	127	15	112
Total others	163	5	168	71	239	44	195
Grand total	730	19	749	146	895	196	699*

*If de Varaigne is added, by 1795, 140 ex-Legislatives remained, among 700 deputies.

1792. Malhes the younger and Bertezène have been listed to replace Joseph Malhes and Tavernel, who both refused election; and Germignac, who died in December 1792, has been replaced by his *suppléant* Lafon. None of the three excluded ever really functioned as a deputy, and the three included in their stead all took their seats in January 1793. Column (ii) shows the deputies, elected in September 1792, who for various reasons were excluded from our political analysis, and column (iii) the Convention's total membership as it was in January 1793. Column (iv) shows the additional members who came in between January 1793 and October 1795, and column (v), for a comparison with Pariset's figures, the total membership over the three years. Column (vi) shows those who for one reason or another disappeared from the Convention by October 1795, including those members of the Left who were excluded in the spring and summer of 1795 but omitting those Girondins whose exclusion in 1793-94 was only temporary, and column (vii) the membership as it remained when the Convention finally dissolved at the end of October 1795. It was from those in this last column that the electors had to choose the five hundred ex-*conventionnels* who were to make up two-thirds of the first legislature of the Directory.

From Table 14 it appears that though Pariset's figures are very nearly accurate,[15] the impression given by them is in some ways misleading. The balance of experience suggested by them is much closer to the situation of October 1795 than to that of 1792. Almost all the old parliamentary hands of the Convention were elected at the outset, when they formed just about 37 percent of the total membership and were reasonably comparable in numbers, as they were vastly superior in standing and reputation, to the local officials. In 1792 only about one in five of the deputies lacked formal political experience, and fewer than one in eleven had played no previous part in public life. The developments of the next three years greatly changed the picture. Only a handful of former deputies arrived after the end of 1792. The *suppléants* and other new members were drawn almost equally from local office and from the ranks of those who had not previously held administrative posts, most of these latter being complete novices. On the other hand, 40 percent of those who were replaced or excluded in 1792-95 had graduated from the Constituent or Legislative Assembly, and more than three in five of the rest had held local office. Men whose Convention membership was their introduction to political responsibility, who formed less than 9 percent of the 1792 Convention, were 16 percent of the survivors of 1795. The changes of these years fell most heavily on the originally very large group from the Legislative (in 1792 towering over all the others) which was reduced by more than 28 percent, and on the small group of club enthusiasts and journalists, which was almost cut in half. The only other group to suffer appreciably was that of the ex-Constituents, whose numbers fell by 18 percent. The figures for local and judicial officials remained virtually unaltered, despite the reduction in the Convention's total size, and those for the totally inexperienced rose by nearly 80 percent. The net result was that in October 1795 the most experienced *conventionnels* were outnumbered by well over two to one. The discrepancy in 1792 was not nearly so great; perhaps at this stage the emphasis should fall not on the number of "lawyers and officials," but on the very solid block of former deputies and on the relatively insignificant number of those who were altogether new to public life.

So much for the general balance of experience among the deputies of 1792. What now of their political attitudes? Were the ex-deputies and the local officials as hostile to Paris, and by extension, to the Mountain, as historians seem to suggest? The figures in column (i) of Table 14 show the distribution of political experience among the deputies with whom this study is chiefly concerned. Table 15 is constructed to show the political attitudes adopted in 1793-94 by these men.

15. The figures given for the numbers of ex-deputies are different from those given by any of the historians who have been quoted. The conclusions reached are explained in Appendix I.

Table 15. Political attitudes in 1793–94
in relation to previous political experience

| | GIRONDE | | | PLAIN | | | | |
	"Inner sixty"	Other	Total	À l'écart	Committee	En mission	Mountain	Total
Constituent Assembly	9	15	24	14	12	3	25	78
Legislative Assembly	17	19*	36	16*	16*	10	113*	191
Department	9	16	25	25	24*	4	35*	113
District	6	20	26	15	14	5	33	93
Commune	7	25*	32	11	16	6	27*	92
Judge/JP	2	6	8	16*	8	5	22	59
Political activist	6	2	8	–	1	1	26*	36
No experience	2	17	19	21*	4	3	21	68
TOTAL	58	120	178	118	95	37	302	730

Note: This distribution can be assessed statistically in terms of the total in the bottom line, which shows the final balance of political sympathy in 1793–94 among our 730 deputies as a whole. The figures have been assessed at the 0.05 level of significance, meaning that if a result is considered significant there is only one possibility in twenty of its being due to chance. Small groups, being essentially unpredictable, often have no statistical significance, hence some apparent anomalies in the assessment of the table.
    *Significant deviations.

The most striking feature of Table 15 is the distribution of opinion amongst the Legislative Assembly deputies, which is utterly different, not only from that of the ex-Constituents, but also from that of almost every other group in the Convention. Apart from the political activists, few in number and in any case rather special in character, every other group gave about one-third of its strength to the Mountain. But with the Legislative deputies added the situation was transformed; just about three in five of these men were Montagnard. Furthermore, their proportion of *en mission* members was exactly the Convention's average, and though they had few "committees" members, they had equally few *à l'écart*; their energy was consistently directed toward the Mountain, not against it. It will also be observed that fewer than half of the Girondins from the Assembly had any close association with the Girondin leaders, though it might have been supposed that acquaintance already established in 1791–92 would have developed further in the autumn and winter of 1792–93. The Legislative members stand out as by far the Mountain's greatest source of strength. They were very much the largest group in the Convention as well as being, apart from the dedicated agitators, incomparably the most devoted to the Montagnard cause.

The main difference between most of the other groups lay in the variation of balance within each group between those who were prepared to give grudging tolerance to the Mountain and those who were not. The *en mission* deputies were so few, relatively speaking, (not much over 5 percent of all the deputies) that it is surprising to see men of varied political background represented amongst them in rough proportion to their representation in the Convention; the numbers are too small to have any statistical meaning but the consistency is interesting. Since the groups are very different in size, it is easier to compare the overall balance in each if the figures are converted to percentages, as in Table 16.

Table 16. Political attitudes in 1793–94 in relation to
previous political experience (percent)

| | GIRONDE | | | PLAIN | | | | |
	"Inner sixty"	Other	Total	À l'écart	Committee	En mission	Mountain	Total
Constituent Assembly	11.5	19.2	30.7	17.9	15.4	3.8	32.1	99.9
Legislative Assembly	8.9	9.9*	18.8	8.4*	8.4*	5.2	59.2*	100
Department	7.9	14.2	22.1	22.1	21.2*	3.5	30.9*	99.8
District	6.4	21.5	27.9	16.1	15.1	5.4	35.5	100
Commune	7.6	27.2*	34.8	11.9	17.4	6.5	29.3*	99.9
Judge/JP	3.4	10.2	13.6	27.1*	18.6	8.4	37.3	100
Political activist	16.6	5.5	22.1	–	2.8	2.8	72.3*	100
No experience	2.9	25.0	27.9	30.9*	5.9	4.4	30.9	100
% of whole Convention in political group	7.9	16.2	24.3	16.2	13.0	5.1	41.4	100

*Significant deviation.

It must, of course, be remembered that percentages may in themselves be very misleading, especially in the case of small groups where the placing of one or two individuals may considerably affect the result; the statistically significant figures in the tables are indicated with the same symbols as before.

We may take the *en mission* and Montagnard deputies together on one side, as actively assisting the Jacobin régime, and the Girondin and *à l'écart* deputies on the other, as actively or passively refusing cooperation. If the figures are added together Table 17 shows the result.

This confirms, among other things, several *negative* conclusions. The ex-deputies of the Convention were *not* alike, but markedly different in attitude. Among the local officials, those from the departments were *not* the most hostile to the Mountain; they were the best fence-sitters in the Convention; whereas the men from the communes were far more anti-Montagnard than Mathiez's comments suggest. The political novices were apparently *not* violent radicals swept into office in the autumn of 1792 by a surge of republican enthusiasm; they were the most conservative members of all. Looking at the situation as a whole, it would seem that in deciding the political future of France it was the distinc-

Table 17. General attitude toward the Jacobin régime (1793–94) of
deputies with different levels of experience (percent)

	Opposition	Support	Minimum co-operation (committees)
Constituent Assembly	48.6	35.9	15.4
Legislative Assembly	27.2	64.4*	8.4*
Department	44.2	34.4	21.2*
District	44.0	40.9	15.1
Commune	46.7	35.8	17.4
Judge/JP	30.7	45.7	18.6
Political activist	22.1	75.1*	2.8
No experience	58.8*	35.1	5.9
Convention overall	40.5	46.5	13.0

*Significant deviation.

tive outlook of the Legislative deputies which was crucial. These men were not
only strongly pro-Montagnard but also very numerous. (The political activists,
even more radical, were too few to exert much influence on the general outlook
of the Convention.) A last general conclusion might be that those who liked the
Mountain least were most likely to be found either among those deputies who
had had no experience whatever in national politics, or among those who had
had rather too much; but between one group and another, as can be seen from
Table 17, the balance between active and passive dislike fluctuated greatly.

II

If the groups are now examined individually, it does appear that Thompson
may be right in stressing the ex-Constituents' distrust of Paris. Their *à l'écart* and
Girondin members together make up just about half their total strength, and
next to the commune deputies they had the highest proportion of Girondins.
They also contributed nearly one-sixth of the membership of the "inner sixty,"
which proportionately recruited much better from the Constituent than from
the Legislative Assembly. Yet even so, more than one ex-Constituent in seven
was prepared to put up with the Mountain and more than one in three to give
active support. Pétion came from the Constituent, and Buzot, but so did Prieur
and Robespierre. It is the high proportion of *à l'écart* deputies, not far from one
in five, among men who must have had a strong political drive to come into the
Convention at all, that seems rather strange.

Were these men simply tired of politics by June 1793? If so, their later
history implies a swift recovery; eight of the 15 men concerned were active
Thermidorians, and all but one of the other 7 returned to revolutionary politics
under the Directory. As a group, the ex-Constituents were more consistently
interested in politics than were any other *conventionnels*. Among the 78 of
them, 62 had been continuously engaged in public life since 1789: after the
Constituent dissolved, 31 had become judges (53 of the 78 were lawyers) 23 had

held local offices, 5 were constitutional bishops, and 2 had taken to professional journalism. Of the remaining 16, 3 were in the armed services and had returned to duty, and the 13 who were in obscurity in 1791-92 included only 4 who were later *à l'écart* under the Terror. By the end of 1795, 11 of the 78 were dead and one, Barère, was sentenced to exile, but of the 66 survivors only 9 withdrew to private life. Whatever their political outlook, the other 57 battled on. This sort of persistent activity suggests that those *à l'écart* in 1793-94 were moved more by dislike for a particular régime than by waning interest in politics as such. The solitary complete drop-out from among the ex-Constituents, Denis Le Maréchal, makes this point perhaps rather too neatly. The parliamentary career which he abandoned in 1793 was not resumed until 1816, when he reappeared as a member of the *chambre introuvable* of Louis XVIII.[16]

As one might expect, most of the ex-Constituents had in 1789 been elected by the Third Estate, but not all of them. Seven (five of these in office in 1792 as constitutional bishops) had sat with the First Estate, and four with the *ci-devant noblesse*.[17] The kind of fervor which might be needed for political survival may perhaps be inferred from the alignment of these eleven members. Three of the bishops were Girondin, one bishop and one *curé* were Montagnard. Three of the nobles were Montagnard. One noble (Rochegude) and one bishop (Thibault) were of the "committees" group. Only one of the eleven, and he a *curé* (Colaud la Salcette), was *à l'écart*. One might conclude that whereas members of the erstwhile Third Estate could fade unobtrusively into the background during a period of crisis, those from the former privileged orders had, in order to stay in politics at all, a level of commitment which kept them permanently involved in some kind of responsible activity.

The comparatively small number of men who managed to make the parliamentary transition from 1789 to 1792 has already been noted. That there were any at all, however, gave the Convention a real continuity of experience in national politics which on the face of it was likely to be a considerable asset, and which distinguished it sharply from the Legislative Assembly of 1791.[18] For the first time, an elected body of Frenchmen was able to draw on the full range of revolutionary enthusiasm. But the striking difference between ex-Constituents and ex-Legislatives lay, of course, not only in the very different proportions of

16. Kuscinski, *Conventionnels*, p. 398.
17. Three other nobles from the Constituent were among the "unclassified" deputies; these were Philippe-Egalité, Sillery, and Le Peletier de Saint-Fargeau. All the other "unclassified" deputies were of the Third Estate.
18. The limited standing of the deputies of 1791 is suggested by the fact that only one of them seems to have been elected by more than one department. This was Lacombe-Saint-Michel, a professional soldier elected both by his own department (Tarn) and by Nord, where he was stationed in 1791. In a national sense the Legislative was an assembly of unknown men—more so, perhaps, than the Third Estate had been. For Lacombe's 1791 election, Kuscinski, *Législative*, p. 27; for his earlier career, Kuscinski, *Conventionnels*, p. 328.

them who were acceptable as *conventionnels* but in the political stance adopted by the majority in each group toward the problems of republican government.

The electoral verdict of 1792 was, in appearance at least, a vote of confidence in the left wing of the Legislative Assembly. It was so massive a vote that all the deputies receiving it could hardly be expected to have a common outlook in 1792–94, however firm their opposition to the king in 1792; 5 departments out of 6 could find at least one Legislative member they were willing to reelect, but the range of opinion in so large a section of the French electorate was naturally considerable, and it was at least improbable that men with backgrounds so diverse would show in the difficult, positive decisions of policy which had to be made by the Convention even the same degree of unanimity they had shown in the mainly negative decisions of 1792. They could well insist that the king was untrustworthy without being in any sense fervent Montagnards, as the record of the Gers delegation more than demonstrates.[19] Nevertheless, as we have seen, a high proportion of men from the Legislative did support the Mountain, and this was a considerable Montagnard asset. The Montagnard ex-Legislative members were not equally distributed throughout the 69 departments where they might have been found (for example, Charente-Inférieure had six of them, whereas 23 other departments, including Paris, had only one each) but they came altogether from 58 different departments scattered through the length and breadth of France, from Ardennes to Haute-Garonne, from Morbihan and Manche to Doubs, Drôme, Bouches-du-Rhône and Aveyron. During the Terror, 28 departments were revisited by one or more of their own ex-Legislative members *en mission* for the government of the Republic.

The exceptional political polarization of the Legislative members has already been noticed. Nearly 60 percent of them were Montagnard, and among those remaining opposition to the Mountain where it existed was direct rather than implicit. The proportion of men *à l'écart* was the lowest of that in any single group in the Convention. The nineteen Girondins not of the "inner sixty" comprised sixteen who signed addresses protesting against the decision of 2 June, two who were *en mission* in June and promptly embarked on highly questionable activities, and one who left Paris, for reasons unknown, immediately after 2 June, to join the refugees in Brittany.[20] Thus anyone in sympathy with the Gironde apparently carried his convictions into action. However, although the sympathizers were active they were not very numerous; among the June peti-

19. Gers held the parliamentary record for smooth transition from Legislative to Convention; of its 9 members, 6 were reelected. But despite its voting *à haute voix* and an apparently strong radical element, the Gers assembly of 1792 seems a mixed sort of body, which accepted at least one somewhat suspect elector and refused to discipline its delinquents (A.N. C 178 C II 31 [Gers] 4 Sept., 6 Sept.).

20. Coustard de Massy and Despinassy *en mission*; Giroust the unexplained fugitive. See Kuscinski, *Conventionnels*, pp. 204–5, 297. One of the two Maine-et-Loire deputies *en* (dubious) *mission* in Angers was the author of the report justifying Marat's impeachment; see P. M. Delaunay, *Rapport fait . . . sur les délits imputés a Marat. . .* (Paris, 1793).

tioners Legislative members were actually out-numbered by men newly arrived from the communes and nearly equaled by those with no political experience at all.

At the other end of the spectrum, among the Montagnards, there was about the same balance between open and tacit alignment. In opposition to Montagnard rule from the Legislative there were 16 men *à l'écart* and 37 Girondins;[21] in support of it were 76 men "sitting with the Mountain" or in the Jacobin Club, and 37 "Montagnards by attribution." In each case the proportion of the active to the less open supporters (though 24 of the "Montagnards by attribution" went *en mission*, which implied taking some responsibility) was something like two to one. But by any criterion the Legislative's contribution to the Mountain was formidable. Even if all the "Montagnards by attribution" are subtracted (and these were close to 20 percent of all the ex-Legislative deputies) there were still 40 percent whose Montagnard affiliations are indisputable. Those who might well have been most antagonized by the arrogance and the pretensions of Paris were apparently the least perturbed.

If this seems puzzling, it may be because the question of the Legislative's relationship with Paris has usually been looked at from the wrong point of view. The estrangement between the Girondins and the Commune arose largely from a switch in Girondin policy toward the king with which the majority of the Legislative's left wing need not necessarily have been in agreement. Paris dethroned the king after Brissot and his friends had begun to hesitate over his dethronement. It was possible to disapprove the Commune's behavior on various occasions after 10 August (as Cambon and Choudieu did) without regretting the lead given by Paris on 10 August, without sharing the Girondins' hostility to those who had taken the initiative out of their hands, and without developing the consistent distaste for Paris, its problems, and its attitudes, which was characteristic of, say, Guadet, after the Convention met. It is interesting that after 10 August the Girondins did not monopolize the formal leadership of the rump of the Assembly, as they were to monopolize that of the Convention in the first 4 months of its existence. The three last presidents of the Assembly, all elected after the king's fall, were Delacroix, Hérault de Séchelles, and Cambon, who were all to back the Mountain in 1793. Though Vergniaud took a leading role in the Assembly on 10 August, his presidency that day was unofficial and shared with a number of others, and when an election for a new vice-president was held in the afternoon, not he but Delacroix was elected with 332 votes out of 440.[22] The overwhelming support for Danton as minister of justice is also revealing; he got 222 votes out of 283, half as many again as Monge who was the next most

21. This number includes Bancal as one of the "inner sixty," though he was, of course, not involved in the final dispute.

22. Kuscinski, *Législative*, pp. 26–27. A ballot for the position on 8 August had proved abortive (*Moniteur* XIII: 358). Morlet, the president in office, did not appear in the Assembly at all until the afternoon of 10 August (Kuscinski, *Législative*, pp. 26–27).

popular ministerial choice.[23] On 10 August the leading Girondins were vociferously republican, and the reelection of Roland, Clavière, and Servan to the ministry was carried by acclamation.[24] Nevertheless, Vergniaud's reply to a group of Parisian petitioners, explaining to them why the Assembly could only suspend the king and must leave the formal deposition to the Convention, was no more than a justification and expressed no regret or feeling of frustration at the Assembly's limited powers.[25]

On 10 August and for some time thereafter, most of what was left of the Assembly was united in dealing with a frightening emergency. There was very little recrimination and little sign of any divergence of policy. Hindsight may, in any case, tempt one to exaggerate what were, at the time, only embryo differences in attitude. Yet even before 10 August it is possible to see some indication of future developments. On 26 July, for example, petitioners asked for the release of two men arrested, one for having attacked the king in a section meeting and the other for helping to publicize a left-wing newspaper. Duhem, Basire, and Grangeneuve all supported the petitioners. Basire's motion was carried, but with an amendment from Fauchet holding it in abeyance pending a report from the minister of justice. (Grangeneuve and Fauchet were later to be Girondin, the others Montagnard.) A week later the two men were still in jail and more petitioners appeared. This time support still came from the future Mountain, but there was silence from the Gironde, and the majority of deputies was willing to let the minister take his time. The pattern of action as between Mountain and Gironde was one which was to become familiar in 1793.[26]

In the days before the fall of the monarchy the behavior in the tribunes was very similar to that so bitterly criticized by the Girondins a few months later. It provoked in Rouyer a very similar reaction: "Si nous n'accoutumons pas le peuple à respecter la loi, bientôt nous serons obligés de la faire fléchir devant cette portioncule qui remplit nos tribunes . . . ."[27] His future colleagues of the Gironde were however not nearly as concerned in the matter as they naturally became when they were themselves the main target for popular demonstrations. On 9 August royalist deputies complained that they had been manhandled and insulted, in fact subjected to much greater indignity and even danger than the Girondins were ever to experience before 31 May, and claimed, as the Gironde was later to claim, that the legislature was being deprived of its freedom of debate. In the discussion that followed, although there was proper concern for the maintenance of order and respect, the Gironde was not much worried about

23. *Moniteur* XIII: 383. Votes: Monge 150, Lebrun 109, Grouvelle 91.
24. *Moniteur* XIII: 382.
25. *Moniteur* XIII: 382. Cf. his extraordinary attitude on 13 August, when he delivered a speech concerning the Convention's new quarters, and had a golden opportunity to pay tribute to Paris; instead he raised the possibility that in the future (sometime) the legislature might meet somewhere else. *Moniteur* XIII: 405–7.
26. *Moniteur* XIII: 248, 317.
27. *Moniteur* XIII: 296. This was on 31 July.

the grievances of the victims, being more interested in probing the causes of the popular ferment. "Le meilleur moyen de calmer toutes les inquiétudes, c'est d'aller tous d'un commun accord et avec cet enthousiasme du bien qu'inspire l'amour de la liberté, vers le bonheur public." So Isnard urged. Nine months later he had somewhat changed his tune. Choudieu did not change his; in 1792 as in 1793 he firmly directed attention toward "le salut d'Etat" as the overriding interest.[28]

The problem of popular attempts to influence public policy came up directly on 4 August, when the *Mauconseil* section presented a petition urging the deposition of the king. Rouyer wanted it rejected out of hand, Cambon as an alternative asked that it be reported on by a subcommittee, explaining that though he could not approve this sort of behavior, tact was called for—"*ne repoussons pas le peuple, mais éclairons-le* . . . ." Cambon's motion was carried. But later in the day, when Vergniaud reported the findings of the committee, the motion he put forward was, in effect, a chilly rebuke:

> L'assemblée nationale, considérant que la souveraineté appartient à tout le peuple, et non pas à une section du peuple, qu'il n'y aurait plus ni gouvernement ni constitution, qu'on serait livré à tous désordres de l'anarchie et des discordes civiles, si chaque citoyen ou chaque section isolée de l'empire pouvait délibérer qu'elle ne dégage lui-même de telle partie de son serment qui pourrait lui déplaire, et refuse obéissance . . . .

Despite the formal recognition of the "*amour ardent de la liberté*" of the petitioners, which embellished the motion fore and aft, the emphasis was much less on their patriotism than on their dangerous irresponsibility, and of course not at all on the merits of their case; and this only three days before the failure of the Lafayette impeachment gave final proof of the futility of Girondin initiatives. The denunciations to be heard in the Convention were already taking shape.[29]

After 10 August the Parisians had a new mouthpiece in the insurrectionary Commune, and friction between the national capital and the national legislature increased. The situation was similar to the one which was to develop after 20 September, in that Legislative deputies of all shades of opinion, like their *conventionnel* counterparts, were worried and enraged by Parisian presumption and insolence; but in the Legislative as in the Convention, some felt much more strongly than others. Three weeks after the fall of the monarchy there was an incident which threw a long shadow forward. On 30 August Girey-Dupré, of Brissot's *Le Patriote Français*, lodged a complaint with the Legislative over what he presented as the high-handed, indeed illegal, behavior of the Commune, which had called him up before it to explain some remarks which had appeared in the

---

28. *Moniteur* XIII: 373 (9 August).
29. *Moniteur* XIII: 327–28, 333. The significant thing here was not the Legislative majority's predictably hostile attitude toward the petitioners, but Vergniaud's apparent approval of the motion.

paper; he, of course, (he said) had refused to go. From this point on, everyone reported by the *Moniteur* as becoming involved in this affair behaved in a way exactly appropriate to his attitude in 1793. Girey-Dupré, while taking up a pose of outraged innocence, and beating the drum about the freedom of the press, managed to accuse the Commune of arrogance, unpopularity, usurpation of authority, and the misuse of power to serve private and/or sectional interest; the Commune replied that its actions, designed to forward a policy laid down by the Legislative itself, had been grossly and dangerously misrepresented in *Le Patriote Français* and that all that it had wished to do was to scotch the libel; Vergniaud, reporting for a subcommittee after what must have been an extremely hurried and flimsy investigation, was able to push through a decree rebuking the Commune before its side of the case had even been put forward; Charlier and Thuriot (two future Montagnards) vainly argued, the one that there might be something to be said on the Commune's side and the other that hasty action was at least ill-advised; and Cambon, not prepared to defend either side, clearly thought the whole business a storm in a tea-cup and tried to get the House to turn its attention to questions where there might be real danger of counterrevolution. It was the sort of squabble which the Convention was to see again and again, with all the protagonists playing appropriate roles.[30]

Between 30 August and 20 September the Girondin/Parisian estrangement widened, though there was neither time nor opportunity for most of the deputies to show where their sympathies lay. On the one hand, the general behavior of the Commune during and after the September massacres won few friends, and in fact might have been expected to attract widespread condemnation, especially during the last few days of the session when there were persistent reports that retiring deputies would be in danger of lynching as soon as their parliamentary immunity expired. These rumors were taken far more seriously than the actual threats and scufflings of the second week in August, and with good reason; after the massacres, no one could doubt the potential menace of mob action. Fuel was added to the flames as indignant local authorities reported back the receipt of the Commune's ill-advised circular describing the patriotic activity of 2–6 September and urging other municipalities to follow the Parisian lead.[31] By the third week of September, feeling in the Legislative about these and other matters was running high, and it was natural enough for leading Girondins to be vigorous in expressing it. On the other hand, however, there was

30. For examples of criticisms of the Commune's behavior by *Le Patriote Français*, see the numbers for 23 August and especially 24 August (p. 217). The real offense lay perhaps in the consistent refusal to appreciate either the purpose of the Commune's actions or the reason for its assumption of an authority independent of that of the Legislative Assembly, though this was the whole justification of the events of 10 August. For 30–31 August, *Moniteur* XIII: 575–76, 585–86, 588.

31. One such letter arrived from Amiens on 17 September (*Moniteur* XIII: 722). Its source (given the recent attitude of the Somme authorities) lends this letter a certain piquancy.

a certain difference in tone between Girondins making clear their opinion of Paris, and other deputies not extremists of the Left, who spoke on the same issues.

This difference was clearly illustrated on 17-18 September when, in the context of the above-mentioned rumors that plots were being hatched against anti-Parisian deputies, the activities of the Commune's *comité de surveillance* were put under investigation by a parliamentary subcommittee. On 17 September Vergniaud anticipated a more detailed survey to be made next day by the committee's *rapporteur*, to deliver a long and violent attack on Parisian subversiveness and intrigue. His speech was dominated throughout by the shades of the *septembriseurs*, with hardly a shadow of the sacrifice of 10 August; far from recollecting that the insurrectionary Commune had been created to serve the interest of the Revolution, he saw and presented its *comité de surveillance* as an instrument of illegal partisan tyranny.[32]

The *rapporteur* for the committee was J. Delaunay of Angers, whose speech and later report on the subject may instructively be compared with Vergniaud's oratory. Delaunay did not indulge in polemic, and directed his own attack much more firmly at counterrevolutionary conspiracy than at the alleged excesses of the Commune. The report which he ultimately presented to the Convention on 2 October drew attention to irregularities, but it also pointed out that the activity of the *comité* had been both necessary and salutary, stressed the fact that most of those arrested since 10 August had, on inspection, proved to be either ordinary criminals or self-evident counterrevolutionaries, and in conclusion suggested procedural improvements which would allow the *comité* to complete its work with proper safeguards.[33]

Now Delaunay was no hot-headed radical. After the Convention met, he moved only gradually away from the Girondins with whom he had until then been associated. As the Legislative's life drew to a close, he was still linked with the Gironde and had no apparent reason to feel any kindness toward the Commune.[34] Yet neither his speech of 18 September nor his report of 2 October followed the Girondin line on Paris, though their subject gave him every chance to do so. Instead, he presented as balanced a view as might reasonably have been hoped for. If Vergniaud may be said to prefigure the attitude of Girondin *conventionnels* from the Legislative, Delaunay may stand for a number of the Montagnards; for that mass of ex-Legislative opinion in the Convention which, while not Robespierrist, ended by accepting the logic which led to the Jacobin dictatorship.

32. *Moniteur* XIII: 728-29.
33. For the complete report, see J. Delaunay, *Rapport fait . . . sur les arrestations relatives à la révolution du 10 août 1792. . . (2 octobre 1792)* (Paris 1792); also *Moniteur* XIV: 107-8.
34. Kuscinski, *Conventionnels*, p. 193.

III

If the Legislative Assembly deputies were strikingly polarized toward the Mountain and the Gironde, and not much drawn toward the equivocation of the Plain, among local officials the Plain was a much more common refuge. The firm decision needed for factional alignments may have been harder for men who knew little of national politics before they were confronted with the suspicious and uncontrollable Paris of 1792-93. On the figures, it is tempting to associate increasing sympathy for the Gironde with narrowing political perspective, since the proportion of Girondins among local officials seems to rise as their administrative horizon contracts; 22 percent of those from the departments, nearly 29 percent of those from the districts, and more than one-third of those from the communes were Girondin. This may be a mere coincidence, but the number of Girondins from the communes was disproportionately high, and taken in conjunction with the conservative tendencies of the completely inexperienced it is at least suggestive. At any rate, the general distribution of political sympathies among the local officials who sat in the Convention suggests that large generalizations on this subject should be made with great caution.

Each group of local officials was of substantial size, and each had a different pattern of loyalties. The communal officials were the most "political," with a notably low proportion of men à l'écart; of the whole eight groups in the Convention they had proportionately the fewest Montagnards and the most Girondins. Theirs was an active opposition. The district officials had no outstanding sympathies, being curiously close to a Convention average from which every other group diverged far more widely. The departmental officials were the most cautious, the most inclined to a noncommittal middle way; they had fewer Montagnards than most other groups, but fewer Girondins as well.

This pattern of behavior among men involved in local affairs is not quite what might have been expected. According to Mathiez, the federalist revolts flickered out in the summer of 1793 because they could get no general support; because the "communes," "more popular in composition" were "lukewarm or hostile," and this outweighed the backing which the departments and districts "composed of rich property-owners" attempted to provide.[35] Hampson has qualified this view in two ways: first by pointing out that the poorer classes in the towns could be as conservative and prejudiced as the wealthy, so that where the revolts flared up, they might have genuine popular sympathy, and second, and for our purposes, more importantly, by claiming that as late as September 1793 the communal councils were believed by the radicals to be politically undependable because they were still dominated by the more prosperous elements in the community, these being the most likely (if left alone) to gravitate to the most

---

35. Mathiez, *The French Revolution*, p. 318.

responsible positions—"the 'natural' administrators of the country were the wealthy landowners and merchants who could only be excluded from power by the intervention of the Central Government or its agents."[36] The purges of 1793 which helped the *sans-culottes* to a temporary authority were, he says, based on the central government's distrust of the "silent hostility of local notables who had often declared for the Girondins."[37] All this suggests that the communal officials elected to the Convention in 1792 were *not* likely to be drawn from "popular" elements and should not be expected to show automatic feeling for the Mountain.

The deputies from the communes, one in three of them Girondin, do seem to lend some weight to this estimate of "silent hostility" from local notables, even if they also illustrate the deep divisions in revolutionary politics in 1793–94; one in three was Girondin, but three in ten were Montagnard; support for the Mountain, while on the low side, was not negligible. It seems certainly true that these deputies were drawn from the ranks of the "natural administrators" rather than from those of the *sans-culottes*. They were, of course, a mixed bag, from large towns and small, disturbed areas and quiet ones, but as one looks over the whole 94 of them certain patterns emerge. The great majority came from middle-sized country towns, and nearly two-fifths (36 out of 94) were lawyers. Of those in other occupations almost all were in the range from the reasonably comfortable to the well-to-do. Landowners, substantial farmers, army or naval officers, merchants, place-holders, civil servants, a few clergy, the inevitable doctors, the odd academic—few were wealthy, but hardly any were poor. The only two who apparently qualified in any sense as "men of the people" were Bernard des Sablons, a mason's son married to a *vigneron's* daughter, who worked in the fields until in 1790 he became a local official, and Jacques Chevalier, a poor farmer with many children. In general, the commune deputies were the type to stand fairly high in most local communities, the type to be accepted without difficulty by departmental electoral assemblies—but not, on the face of it, the type to take an exceptionally radical line in politics. Of course no conclusion can be drawn from so minute a sample of France's 44,000 communal councils, but the behavior of these deputies in the Convention is at least another salutary warning against generalization. The Convention held examples of very many types of administrators; perhaps, indeed, of most, except the Montagnard-inclined *sans-culottes*. Bernard and Chevalier backed the Gironde.

What now of what appears to be something of an anomaly: the fact that departmental officials, once seated in the Convention, were comparatively reluctant to support the Gironde, although it is a historical cliché that in June

36. Hampson, *Social History*, p. 211.
37. Ibid.

1793 the expelled Girondin leaders had their cause taken up by nearly three-quarters of the departmental administrations in France? [38] No explanation of this puzzle can rest on much more than guesswork, but one may point to certain differences in background and circumstance between those departmental members sitting in the Convention between September 1792 and June 1793 and those who in November 1792 were elected to fill their places at home. Some of the men who came to the Convention from the departments had first held office in 1790, and so had lived through the dismaying and unsettling crisis of the flight to Varennes. [39] A large number of others had been in office during the collapse of the monarchy in June–August 1792, and had seen many of their colleagues thoroughly discredited through having shown sympathy for the king after the demonstration of 20 June or (more rarely) even after 10 August. The general principle involved seems to have been accepted even in departments which were inherently conservative; it is revealing that Hautes-Alpes could find no one to elect above the district level, and that Orne, which also had no eligible ex-deputies and was desperate for candidates, discovered only two among the departmental officials. Departmental officials like Ménineau in Charente or Cayrol in Aude, who were elected but refused, could be counted on the fingers of one hand, whereas those who were simply passed over by the electors might in theory have numbered more than two thousand.

One result of this repudiation was that the balance of local officials in the Convention varied dramatically from that in the Legislative. In 1791, more departmental officials had been elected than district and commune officials combined; the respective figures were 282, 116, and 88. [40] In the Convention, as we have seen, the situation was very different; there were 116 departmental officials, and 94 each from districts and communes. The influx of ex-deputies had thinned the higher ranks of local officials, while allowing the communes a stronger voice than they had had before. [41] Another result was that the minority of departmental officials who came up to Paris in 1792 were a highly select group, aware not only of the importance of republicanism but also (one might reasonably conclude) of the dangers of committing themselves prematurely. Perhaps it is no wonder that more than one in 5, the highest proportion in any of our 8 groups, stuck to committee work under the Terror, or that a more than equal proportion quietly withdrew to the background. Of all the local government deputies, the departmental officials contributed the fewest signatures to

38. See, e.g., ibid., p. 184. G. Lefebvre, *The French Revolution, 1793–1799* (London, 1964), p. 56.
39. See, e.g., H. Pommeret, *L'esprit public dans le département des Côtes-du-Nord pendant la Révolution, 1789–1799* (Paris, 1921), pp. 140–42.
40. The balance was made up of 95 judges, 28 J.P.s, 137 without experience: total 746. (Figures derived from Kuscinski, *Législative*.)
41. The effect was repeated within the contingent of reelected deputies who reached the Convention from the Legislative.

the Girondin protests after 2 June 1793. It should be noticed, however, on the positive side, that they were used to carrying a certain amount of responsibility, and that once in Paris they could assess the Parisian situation for themselves. They might, like Chambon and Lidon, become furiously hostile to the Commune and personally antagonistic to Robespierre and Marat; but they might, alternatively, like Lebas, be pleasantly surprised at what they found. "Paris est plus tranquille qu'on ne me l'avait annoncé," he wrote on 21 September, "Le zèle qui porte les citoyens aux frontières n'est pas ralenti. On ne peut s'en faire une idée dans notre froid pays," and two months later: "Quels que soient les projets de ceux qui crient si fort aux agitateurs, il est certain que leur conduite n'est pas celle de vrais patriotes, et rassemble beaucoup à celle des feuillants . . . ." (27 November).[42] One is reminded of the experience of the Côtes-du-Nord *fédérés*, sent to Paris to protect the Convention, who, to the horror of the departmental directory which had dispatched them, ended by sharing the outlook of the *sans-culottes*.[43]

Back home in the departments, departmental officials who took office in November 1792 had less chance to be well informed and being largely new to office, had less experience of the dangers of trying to formulate policy during a major crisis. On the other hand, by the time they were elected the situation of the electoral assemblies who had to choose them, as they had had to choose the deputies in September, was somewhat altered, to the disadvantage of the radicals. In any one department the outcome of the November elections obviously depended to some extent on the ability of the radicals to maintain their enthusiasm once the military crisis had eased (as it did after Valmy) and the excitement of the Convention elections was over.[44] Moreover, in September 1792 the news of the prison massacres in Paris reached very few electoral assemblies, and those only at a time when the election of deputies had been virtually concluded. In the succeeding weeks anti-Parisian propaganda might be expected to make much more headway in the departments than it had had a chance to do in the three-week interval between 10 August and 2 September, when the Parisians could still be seen as republican heroes, if anyone thought of them at all. The Hautes-Alpes electoral assembly sitting in November was provided by Serre, one of the deputies sent to Paris two months before, with the most lurid description of his experiences and the general situation of the Convention. This had the desired effect, and as part of their official proceedings the

---

42. Stéfane-Pol, *Le Conventionnel Lebas* (Paris, 1900), pp. 28, 40.
43. H. Pommeret, *Côtes-du-Nord*, pp. 196–97.
44. The official date for the departmental elections (November) deterred some electoral assemblies from taking action in September over even very suspect administrations. The September assemblies had been summoned only to elect the Convention, and most of them stuck to the letter of the law. The dozen elections that were held were almost immediately legitimated by the Convention. For the sequel in Eure in 1793, A. Montier, "Le département de l'Eure et ses districts en juin 1793," *La Révolution Française* XXX (1896).

Hautes-Alpes electors signed an address embodying forthright condemnation of the *septembriseurs*: "vengeance terrible à ces agitateurs sanguinaires, qui ramanèrent, par les fureurs de l'anarchie, les jours affreux de la despotisme, si leurs têtes ne tombent sous la glaive de la loi!"[45]

Once elected, the new departmental officials knew about Parisian affairs only what they could gather from personal correspondence and a largely Girondin press, plus the official circulars which reached them in the course of business; and while Roland remained Minister of the Interior they might be certain of getting ministerial reports in which Paris would be put in the worst possible light.[46] The prejudices thus acquired early in one's administrative career were not lightly discarded, especially in view of the way in which the conduct of the king's trial might be reported. The effect even of the propaganda of August 1792 may be illustrated by the remark of an anonymous member from Allier in the Jacobin Club of Paris, in October 1792; he observed that it was only since coming to Paris that he realized who had actually carried out the revolution of 10 August, since the only papers circulating in his home town were *Le Patriote Français* and the *Chronique de Paris*, which gave all the credit to the Gironde.[47] In such circumstances, a high level of local conservatism is not hard to understand.

When we turn to the deputies who had come into the Convention from district office, there is even more temptation to facile conjecture. As far as social background goes, we are still dealing with "local notables." Again the *sans-culotte* element is hard to find, except perhaps for Roussel, son of a stone mason, and Boudin, son of a bootmaker, both of very moderate views, and four men whose occupation and background are unknown, only one of whom was Montagnard. In some ways the attitudes of men from the districts seem to call for little comment. In overall opposition to the Mountain, they rank almost exactly with the other two groups of local officials, and in support for the Gironde and in the extent of their withdrawal under the Terror they fall neatly between the other two. But here the neatness of the picture disappears. Why did the districts supply what looks like a disproportionate number of Montagnards, and why did only one district official in seven stay safely on the fence in the Committees of the Terror? Probably all that is really illustrated is the smallness of the sample, the slightness of the variations (which are not statistically significant) and the incalculability of revolutionary politics.

45. T. Lemas, "Les assemblées électorales du département des Hautes-Alpes pendant la Révolution," *Bulletin de la Société d'Etudes des Hautes-Alpes* IX (1890).

46. For Roland's correspondence, see L. de Cardenal, "Le bureau d'esprit public de Roland," *Annales* XV (1938): 172–73, and cf. his *Rapport du Ministre de l'intérieur à la convention nationale sur l'état de Paris; du 27 octobre 1792* (Paris, 1792).

47. A. Aulard, *La Société des Jacobins*, 6 vols. (Paris, 1889–97), IV: 372. Cf. the way Robespierre's speech on the *appel au peuple* was reported in *Le Patriote Français* (Robespierre, *Oeuvres*, ed. M. Boiloiseau et al. [Paris, 1958], IX: 201–2) and the one sentence quoted in the same journal from his speech of 29 March 1793 (ibid, p. 349).

These officials do not however quite fit a predictable pattern, and their behavior is not quite in line with the conventional view that district administrators shared with their departmental superiors a general anti-Montagnard prejudice.[48] Amongst local officials who reached the Convention, local solidarity was not predominant. Thirty-six departments sent both departmental and district officials, but there were only half a dozen departments in which the 2 groups agreed in their outlook. Considering their numbers, the district officials were quite widely scattered. They came altogether from 48 departments and the scatter was of points of view as well as of individuals; the 33 Montagnard deputies were from 26 departments, and those of the Plain were similarly dispersed. Only Girondin sympathy was slightly more concentrated, with two-thirds of the Girondins (18 out of 26) from 8 departments only. And so far as district officials took an independent line in the Convention, and a number of them did, they were slightly more likely to be Montagnard than Girondin.

Here it may be relevant to remember that because of its intermediate status in the administrative hierarchy, the official experience of these men had a flavor of its own. The districts were large enough to have a considerable sense of self-importance and in Loir-et-Cher, for example, there was friction between districts and department because the districts saw no reason to recognize that they were subordinate to the department's authority.[49] This independence could result in a complete refusal to accept the instructions or even to follow the lead of the departmental authorities in a major political crisis: thus in June 1793 the attempt of the Eure officials to rally the department for a march on Paris was utterly frustrated as all the districts, one after the other, flatly refused to have anything to do with the plan.[50] Or to take another unnerving instance of local independence, in November 1792 the Verdun district conducted the election of its officials with very dubious legality, since the Legislative Assembly had on 14 September declared the citizens of Verdun to be traitors to their country, and the department had urged that the elections be postponed pending further advice from Paris. The electors however pressed on, having no hesitation in choosing representatives who had been compromised by the events of the capitulation, and the new officials took up their duties at once, holding firmly to the view that no question of their fitness to do so could possibly arise. The department ultimately passed over the whole affair.[51] Revolutionary councils in general had a strong corporate ethos, the claim to private conscience was vigorously upheld, and districts were in a good position to assert their own right to pass judgment on departmental policy as well as on local or national affairs.

48. See, e.g., Thompson, *The French Revolution*, p. 366.
49. Cf. A. Bourgeois, "La Révolution en Loir-et-Cher," *L'Indépendant de Loir-et-Cher*, 16 December 1891.
50. A. Montier, "Le département de l'Eure et ses districts en juin 1793," *La Révolution Française* XXX (1896): passim.
51. E. Pionnier, *Essai sur l'histoire de la Révolution à Verdun 1789-1795* (Nancy, 1905), pp. 295-305.

This may be worth remembering, because in a district official, any natural independence could not but be reinforced by the natural tendency for him, in his 1790-92 capacity as a district official, to assert himself against his official superiors. We may take two examples of Montagnard district officials, one from a left-wing and one from a mainly conservative departmental delegation. Espert, the only official of any kind in the Ariège delegation, came from the district of Mirepoix, whose assembly had been for many months "the only administrative body [in Ariège] not to betray the Revolution" and had carried on a running fight with the departmental authorities in the interests of the democrats from the town of Pamiers. By 1792 the Ariège radicals were able to dominate the electoral assembly, but Espert had cut his political teeth in the struggle between district and department.[52] So too had Lejeune, from Issoudun in Indre. Unlike Espert, he was the only Montagnard elected from his department; like him, he came from an assertively independent environment.[53] Such factors are of course subsidiary, but so far as they helped to mould the character of parliamentary politics they cannot be quite ignored. The slightly radical balance among the district officials in the Convention can at least be said to have had some precedent in local experience.

IV

Whatever the level at which they had worked, the groups of local government deputies had at least two things in common: a shared experience of settling the functions and operating the machinery of a new administrative structure, and very similar proportions of men who openly or covertly resisted the leadership of the Mountain in 1793-94. There are no such unifying factors among our last three groups of deputies, the judicial members, the political activists, and those without previous political experience. These groups were quite dissimilar in the balance of their sympathies, and shared only a common ignorance of the burdens of formal political responsibility. All were small in size and diverse in character, and as samples are too limited to provide in themselves the basis for even the most tentative generalizations. They are however worth examining, partly because they seem to be so sharply differentiated in political attitude, and partly because such an examination may serve as a starting point for the raising of more general problems.

To take the judicial members first; any examination of these men as a group leads on to speculation about the character of the judiciary as a whole in the revolutionary period, and its point of view (if any) in politics. This matter was brought before the Convention itself almost as soon as it assembled. On 22 September 1792 Philippeaux demanded that the law be changed to make all

52. G. Arnaud, *Histoire de la Révolution dans l'Ariège*, (Toulouse, 1904), p. 331.
53. M. Bruneau, *Les débuts de la Révolution dans les départements du Cher et de l'Indre* (Paris, 1902), p. 265.

citizens eligible for election to the judiciary, on the ground that the majority of men hitherto elected to the Bench, all officially required to be experienced lawyers, had shown themselves to be also consistently reactionary: "dans la plupart, il suffit d'être patriote pour perdre un procès." Danton, in the same debate, attributed this regrettable situation to the fact that the judges concerned had had their professional training under the old régime, which had put its stamp on lawyers as a caste. "Tous les hommes de loi," he said gloomily "sont d'une aristocratie révoltante."[54] Since Danton was himself a lawyer and Philippeaux was a judge, their generalizations obviously had their limits and cannot be taken as adequate comment on the character of judicial *conventionnels*; apart from anything else, in the circumstances of 1792 the sort of judge under attack would have had very little hope of ever reaching the Convention. Yet even if the judicial *conventionnels* must be seen as a very questionable sample of the Bench as a whole, they might still have reflected the outlook of their profession, at least to the extent of being more cautious in their political views than the average of their colleagues. (Danton and Philippeaux, after all, were not being frivolous; they got a decree in the sense proposed.) Judges might also have purely professional reasons for taking a conservative line in the politics of 1793. The serious constitutional issues which were raised over both the trial of the king and the expulsion of the Girondins might well have had the effect of driving men professionally concerned with legal proprieties into either active or passive opposition to Montagnard policy.

The 59 deputies who have been grouped together as "judicial members" include 35 judges, who as noted above had to be practising lawyers, and 24 justices of the peace, who did not need legal training and were drawn, as in England, from a variety of sources; a good many, naturally enough, were local notaries or attorneys, some were landowners, some were merchants, and a few were doctors. The implication of Philippeaux's attack on the Bench of 1790-92 was that justices, chosen freely from the general public, were likely to be more liberal in attitude than the judges, drawn only from the legal profession. This conclusion can be tested in a very limited way by comparing in Table 18 the political sympathies of the judges and justices we have just mentioned. As far as these very meager figures go, they do little to support Philippeaux's argument. But the totals are in any case much too small to support any conclusion.

These were, of course, not the only judicial members in the Convention. Some of the ex-Constituents had sat on the Bench in 1791-92, and a number of deputies, having gone from Bench to Legislative Assembly, had then been re-elected to the Convention; in addition there were some judges and justices among the local officials. But there are not enough justices to enable further comparisons to be made. There were only 51 of them in the Convention altogether, including the 24 already analyzed above, and the remaining 27 are so

54. *Moniteur* XIV: 14.

Table 18. Judges and J.P.s (without other political experience)
divided according to political sympathy, 1793–94

	Judges	J.P.s	Total
Gironde	5	3	8
Plain			
à l'écart	11	5	16
Committees	4	4	8
en mission	3	2	5
Mountain	12	10	22
Total	35	24	59

widely scattered in political background and in attitude that further inspection seems unlikely to be very useful. The judges present rather a different case. Besides the 35 without experience, above, there were 75 others: 28 ex-Constituents, 31 from the Legislative Assembly, and 16 local government officials of various kinds. The local officials are too few in number and divided in experience to be worth examining, but the ex-Constituents and the Legislative deputies provide judicial groups approximately equal in size both to each other and to the inexperienced group with which they may be compared; these judges may also be compared with their nonjudicial fellows from the legislatures to which they had belonged. The comparative figures are shown in Table 19.

As far as the ex-Constituents are concerned, the correlation between judges and laymen is so surprisingly close that one is tempted to recall that half the laymen were lawyers anyhow; the proportion of legal talent in this group was extremely high. In the Legislative there is some apparent discrepancy, but not of significant proportions. Perhaps what comes out most clearly here is not the anti-Montagnard element among the Legislative's judges so much as the apparent effect on its members of the Legislative's brief year of office; by the standards of

Table 19. Political sympathies of judges in the Convention* as
compared with other deputies

	Constituent Assembly				Legislative Assembly				No experience			
	Judges		Others		Judges		Others		Judges		Others	
	No.	%	No.	%	No.	%	No.	%	No.	%	No.	%
Gironde	8	28.5	16	32.2	9	29.0	27	16.9	5	14.3	19	27.9
Plain												
à l'écart	6	21.4	9	18.0	3	9.7	13	8.1	11	31.4	21	30.9
Committees	3	10.7	8	16.0	1	3.3	15	9.4	4	11.4	4	5.9
en mission	2	7.1	1	2.0	2	6.4	8	5.0	3	8.6	3	4.4
Mountain	9	32.1	16	32.0	16	51.6	97	60.6	12	34.3	21	30.9
	28	100.0	50	100.0	31	100.0	160	100.0	35	100.0	68	100.0

*The percentages are inserted only to make comparisons easier; of course, with such small numbers they should not be taken seriously, but they serve to make gross differences of proportion more obvious, if these exist.

any large group of *conventionnels* other than their own former colleagues, the judges from the Legislative would rank as very radical indeed. If the three groups of judges are compared, the differences in their behavior are much easier to see than the similarities.

This seems about as far as this very sketchy evidence can take us. If the Convention's judges were conservative, they were not outstandingly so, and there are few signs of a judicial stampede from Montagnard rule. This stampede, if such it was, did not even come from a group with a predominance of lawyers; it came from a group with proportionately fewer lawyers than any other in the Convention.

This group, the most anti-Montagnard in the Convention by a clear margin, was made up of the men who in 1792 were entering public life for the first time. Three in every 10 of them withdrew again completely, as far as their parliamentary duties were concerned, under the Terror, and nearly another one in five[55] signed protests against the exclusion of the Girondins. That those who withdrew did so because they rejected the Mountain, rather than in response to the unwelcome responsibilities of power, is suggested by the fact that their retirement, for the most part, did not last very long. Twenty-one inexperienced deputies were *à l'écart* in 1793-94. One of these died late in 1794, and 3 others did not reappear, but the remaining 17 were all on the scene after Thermidor, and 13 of them were reelected in 1795. The Girondins in the group also stuck to their parliamentary careers, and 7 of the 10 who survived the Terror were later reelected. What we have here is apparently not a recovered preference for the private life which these men were so slow to abandon, but a startled recoil from the situation of the Convention in Paris in mid-1794.

Why did these deputies behave in so distinctive a manner—as distinctive in its way as the reaction of the men from the Legislative Assembly? They were political novices; were they perhaps markedly older than their fellows and more fixed in their ideas, or younger and more easily intimidated? No; one in three was over forty-five, two in three younger, which was almost exactly the Convention average. Was there something peculiar about the electorates which chose them? Did they come from very conservative departments, or ones where Girondin influence was strong? The evidence here is inconclusive. Though they came only from 44 of the 83 departments, and 18 departments elected 42 out of the total 68 of them, the pattern of distribution seems quite haphazard and does little to illuminate the general problem.

What about occupational background? Here the deficiency of lawyers is a teasing mystery. For what it is worth, the group had more than its quota of doctors (7 of the Convention's 45) and clergy (13 out of 55) but only 18 lawyers, of whom 13 were anti-Montagnard. Their judges excluded, every other group so far considered had a strong legal contingent ranging in size from about

---

55. This includes 2 members of the "inner sixty."

40 to well over 50 percent. But why should a lack of lawyers have given the group a conservative bias? As we shall later see, lawyers were no more radical than any other *conventionnels.* Leaving aside the lawyers, it might even be argued that the presence of a small *sans-culotte* and lower middle-class element (Noël Pointe the munition worker, Montégut once a grave digger, and several others risen from very humble origins) might have tipped the scales the other way. This suggestion however is unrewarding from the start, because not all these persons were Montagnard; Montégut was, and so was Noël Pointe, the archetype of the self-improving artisan with literary pretensions,[56] but Dufestel, a poor Somme farmer, was anti-Montagnard until in November 1793 he thankfully went home to care for his family, especially (he said) his 8 daughters.[57] Several others of much the same kind were conservative too. An occupational analysis raises further interesting questions, but provides no self-evident explanations.

One is driven back to the most obvious explanation, or part-explanation: that in facing the problem of Paris and the Republic in 1793, and in accepting the inevitability of Montagnard rule, political sophistication was a very important factor. The group in the Convention which found it easiest to support the Mountain was that drawn from the Legislative Assembly, made up of men who had seen the political crisis of August 1792 from close quarters, who could recognize better than most Frenchmen the debt of the Revolution to the revolutionary Commune, who were willing to admit the need for a firm hand, a clear policy and a dispassionate view of the facts in the even greater crisis of the spring of 1793. The mirror-image of their attitude was that of those deputies who in September 1792 could have known, on average, little more about national affairs than they could learn from the press, who had never carried public responsibility and were in no hurry to add to their burdens,[58] but who, because of their total unfamiliarity with the practical workings of revolutionary government, might be expected to be exceptionally vulnerable to anti-Parisian propaganda, and to be more aware of the dangers of Parisian extremism than of the need to take Paris into at least temporary partnership.

For comparison, we may consider the behavior of another group of deputies who also entered the Convention without the benefits of previous experience in revolutionary public duties. These were the 14 representatives of the new departments of Mont-Blanc, Mont-Terrible, and Alpes-Maritimes, who were admitted at

56. He wrote bad poetry, printed 2 speeches on the king's trial, and took pride in his workingclass background. See Noël Pointe, *Opinion sur le jugement du ci-devant roi des Français* (published fairly early; despite his disclaimers, he was plainly bursting to get into print) and *Discours . . . sur la discussion concernant le jugement de Louis Capet.*

57. Kuscinski, *Conventionnels,* p. 220.

58. Of these 68 deputies, 8 went *en mission* before June 1793, 6 being Montagnard and 2 Girondin. The Plain made no contribution. Under the Terror, 15 of the Montagnards were *en mission.* Five of the *à l'écart* members carried out missions after Thermidor. The total is 28.

various dates from 10 February to 23 May 1793. None of these men before he arrived could have had more than a remote and second-hand acquaintance with the intricacies of national politics. All were in time, though in three cases only just in time, for the crucial *appel* of 28 May 1793 on the reinstatement of the Commission of Twelve, in which the official vote was 279 in favor of the Commission and 238 against; allowing for irregularities on both sides, it was a fairly close thing. The new deputies supported the Commission by 8 votes to 4, with 2 absences. The 8 included the 3 unfortunate members from Alpes-Maritimes, who had been in Paris only 5 days. Nevertheless, all 3 were later persuaded to join the ranks of the June petitioners and had in due course to endure the consequences. It was of course possible for newcomers to the Convention to rush straight to the side of the Mountain (so Lemane behaved, at the same *appel*) but a wary or conservative response was more usual. This also can be illustrated by looking at the behavior of 2 deputies who reached Paris just before the voting on the fate of the king. Lafon (Corrèze), a justice from Beaulieu, arrived on 9 January, and Bertezène (Gard), making his début in public life, on 13 January. Lafon pleaded ignorance of the evidence and abstained throughout, an attitude which Kuscinski stigmatizes as transparent evasion, but which seems more likely elementary common sense.[59] Bertezène had no such inhibitions, though he had only one day to evaluate the situation; he voted with the Right throughout. Lafon later joined the "committees" deputies, where his caution properly placed him; Bertezène disappeared from parliamentary life throughout the Terror.[60] His initial reaction and later behavior were in key with the sympathies of nearly half of those who, like him, had no perspective against which to measure the events of 1793. Had the Convention been dominated by such unseasoned amateurs, it is hard to see how the Republic could have been held together.

The other side of the coin appears when we look at the last group on our list, the political activists of the clubs and the press. It has been necessary here to draw rather an arbitrary line. It seems probable that most men seriously considered for election in September 1792 would have had at least some connection with a local popular society, if there was one; but a distinction has been drawn between men who, if they engaged in club activity, remained in the background, and those who had been vigorous and conspicuous and gained some public reputation from what they had done. The former have been classed as politically inexperienced, the latter as political activists. In assessing journalistic activity, a similar sort of distinction has been made. In 1789–92 anyone interested in politics might well get himself into print, but a man has only been reckoned a political activist if his pamphleteering or newspaper work seems to have been a factor in his election.[61]

59. Kuscinski, *Conventionnels*, p. 362.
60. Ibid., p. 52.
61. So Dulaure, whose *Thermomètre du Jour* was well enough known by 1792 to get him elected for Puy-de-Dôme (Kuscinski, *Conventionnels*, p. 224).

Of the political activists, 12 were members for Paris. This was half of the whole Parisian delegation, and reflected the atmosphere in which the elections were conducted. The Parisian representatives were not however mere section leaders, in fact those among them who had become known for their club and organizational abilities were outnumbered by the journalists and publicists, such as Marat, Lavicomterie, Robert, Collot, Fréron, Desmoulins, and Laignelot. The club activists in the Convention, 18 in all, were certainly mainly Montagnard; apart from Thomas, the middle-aged Parisian mercer and antiregicide who has been placed with the "committees" group, and Hardy the Girondin doctor from Rouen, all backed the Mountain; but more than two-thirds of the Montagnards among them came from outside Paris. Eleven Montagnard club members from 83 departments is in itself a tiny number; but eleven Montagnards among only 12 non-Parisian club members may be a pointer to the resources of the Mountain in 1793. Many popular societies in the departments were far more sympathetic to the Gironde than to Paris in 1792-93, witness the attitude of the Orne societies, the Lons-le-Saulnier Jacobins, those of Villeneuve-sur-Lot and Nîmes, and the struggle of the National Café Club in Bordeaux against the Bordeaux Jacobin Club which was dominated by moderates.[62] But in 1793-94 victory was to go to the energetic and enthusiastic Left, and this victory may have been fore-shadowed in the political orientation of the enthusiasts who got themselves to the Convention in 1792.

The very presence of club members and journalists in the Convention is a reminder of a limited but significant change in the political atmosphere since 1791. Hampson says that *"on the whole,* a democratic electorate (in 1792) had returned the same sort of men that the active citizens had chosen in 1791."[63] The qualification allows him to pass over the fact that the butcher Legendre, the struggling playwright Laignelot, the incendiary pamphleteer Desmoulins were not at all the sort of people that a propertied Parisian electorate actually had chosen in 1791.[64] The Parisian case was exceptional in 1792, but it was not unique in choosing a new kind of deputy. In other areas, too, men were elected who at any earlier stage of the revolution would hardly have been considered. We have already noticed a few of the really poor; let us now look at two who might have been thought dangerous agitators. Cusset, a Lyons master weaver in a small way, was chosen for Rhône-et-Loire in the face of a letter to the electoral assembly claiming that, although patriotic enough, he was "trop incendiaire, désirant voir promener les têtes au bout des piques, quoiqu'il n'y en a pas à Lyon, parce qu'il mange l'argent des souscriptions faites pour les piques. Il ne paraît dans le Comité central que quand il a bien bu et c'est alors qu'il est le plus

---

62. Cf. P. Nicolle, "Le mouvement fédéraliste en Orne en 1793," *Annales* XIII (1936): 505; A. Sommier, *Histoire de la Révolution dans le Jura*, pp. 135-36; F. de Mazet, *La Révolution à Villeneuve-sur-Lot*, p. 82, and R. M. Brace, *Bordeaux and the Gironde*, p. 82.

63. *Social History*, p. 155; my italics.

64. Cf. remarks on p. 183 above, and Lefebvre, *Le Chute du Roi (Cours de la Sorbonne)*, p. 2.

abondant en motions . . ."[65] Nothing in his later history makes this description implausible. Yet the electoral officials did not make the letter public, and he was duly elected. In Marne, the wool-carder Armonville was probably carried to office largely by his popular backing in Reims, which made his coolness and moderation valuable public assets in the bloody rioting in the city during the elections.[66] That anyone at all who was known to be a public figure of this kind should have won recognition from a provincial electoral assembly was an indication of the sort of part that the *sans-culottes* were increasingly to play in the politics of 1793–94.

Of the political activists as a group, exactly half have been classified as journalists and half as club members. The group was strongly polarized in the political sense, with only 2 members from the Plain, 8 Girondins, and 26 Montagnards, 14 of whom were elected outside Paris. (See Table 20.)

Table 20. Club members and journalists: Political allegiance

	Club members			Journalists			Total
	Paris	Other	Total	Paris	Other	Total	Total
Gironde		1	1	none	7	7	8
Plain							
à l'écart		none			none		none
Committees	1	none	1		none		1
en mission		none			1	1	1
Mountain	5	11	16	7	3	10	26
Total	6	12	18	7	11	18	36

It will be seen that although, as has been noted, the club members were almost all Montagnard, the journalists had a considerable minority of Girondins. Moreover, the Girondin journalists were far more important than their mere number suggests. The 7 included Carra, elected for 8 departments, and Gorsas and Lanthénas, each elected for 2. If we add from amongst the ex-Legislative deputies, Brissot, elected for 3 departments, and Condorcet, elected for 5, the Girondin press becomes formidable. Of the 10 Montagnard journalists, only Marat could claim anything like equal notoriety, and outside Paris his reputation was an asset of very doubtful value. In the rest of the Convention the only really well-known Montagnard publicist was probably Robespierre, whose influence at this time may be measured by the fact that he was elected, outside Paris, only by his own department Pas-de-Calais. In the first months of the Convention, the Mountain could have used more, and more famous, journalists than it possessed. Neither the September massacres nor the Convention elections were needed to generate Girondin hostility to Parisian radicalism, as *Le Patriote Français* had

65. Kuscinski, *Conventionnels*, p. 165.
66. G. Laurent, "Un conventionnel ouvrier: Jean Baptiste Armonville," *Annales* I (1924): 242–49.

clearly shown, but they added to its bitterness, and this being so, the wide circulation of the Girondin papers and the accepted patriotism of their editors was an important matter.

The extreme pro-Montagnard sympathies of most of the activists need no further comment, but in the case of this particular group, political radicalism was not confined to those who supported the Mountain. The Girondin journalists were on political issues more ruthless than the average of their colleagues. In the king's trial, 5 opposed the *appel au peuple* and only 2 supported it. Only 2 favored the Marat impeachment, which Lanthénas opposed, and over the Commission of Twelve 3 of the 6 who were then in Paris did not come to vote. Five of the 7 were of the "inner sixty," which makes their recurring divergence from majority Girondin policy even more interesting. This did not prevent their anti-Parisian propaganda from being extremely effective, but it did bring them personally during critical votes more nearly into line with other activists in the Convention than might have been predicted. In other words, when hostility to Paris took the form of actual parliamentary action, the Girondin journalists could not always be relied on to act in accordance with their own apparent prejudices. As the political activists were a small but exceptional and highly radical minority in the Convention as a whole, so on critical issues such as the referendum the handful of Girondin journalist-activists were to the left of their own closest political associates.

V

The picture may now be considered from another viewpoint, to see what effect this distribution of loyalties had on the internal composition of the various political groups of 1793–94. In broad terms, nearly 80 percent of our 730 deputies had been officially involved in either parliamentary or local political life before 1792, with roughly similar numbers in either category: 269 ex-deputies, just about 37 percent of the 730, and 298 men, or 40.8 percent from the 3 levels of local governments combined. There were a further 95 (13 percent) who had been engaged in other kinds of public activity, and there were 68 (9.3 percent) who were, as far as can be seen, entirely inexperienced in revolutionary public affairs. However, as Table 15 has shown, this balance was not at all evenly maintained within the political groups, which differed as much in type of experience as they did in attitude toward the Jacobin régime. The range of contrast becomes easier to see if the figures are converted into histogram form, with the deputies grouped under 4 main headings: parliamentary experience, local government experience, other kinds of experience, and no experience at all.

From these diagrams it is possible to see at a glance how one may be misled by an average figure. The only political group which came near reflecting within its own ranks the balance of experience among the deputies as a whole was the

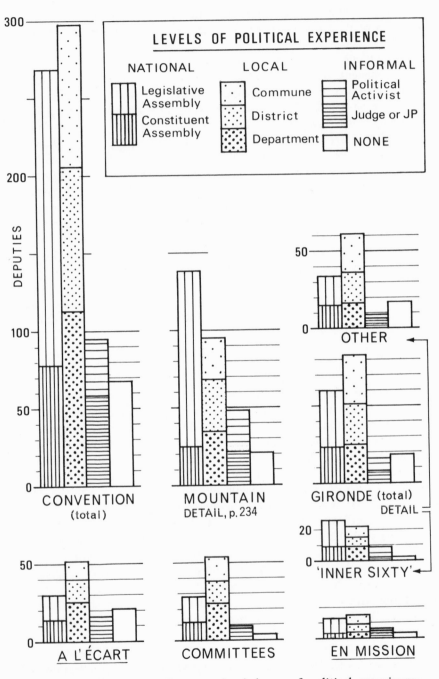

Fig. 1. Histogram to illustrate the balance of political experience within the political groups.

small group of *en mission* members, whose 37 deputies covered the whole range in proportions which made them, in sum, very nearly a microcosm of the whole Convention. And this group was so small that its character has no statistical significance! Each of the other groups had some peculiarity in the balance of its membership which marked it off both from all other groups and from the Convention as a whole. The Mountain, comprising 2 in 5 of all the deputies, might have been expected, far more than the *en mission* group, to be the Convention in miniature. Not only was this not the case, but the Mountain showed more numerous and more noticeable divergences from the Convention average than any other group. Statistically speaking, it had too few men from departmental office, too few from the communes, a barely adequate number without experience, and setting aside the political activists as a very small and very special category, it drew far too much support from the Legislative Assembly. It was the only group of *conventionnels* of which ex-parliamentarians were outstandingly the strongest component, being nearly half as numerous again as any other section.

The three groups of the Plain were quite different in composition. The *à l'écart* deputies had proportionately the fewest ex-deputies, a notably strong minority of political novices, and the highest proportion of judicial members of any group. More than 30 percent in all of those *à l'écart* had not carried political responsibility before 1792 and were apparently not attracted by it in 1793. There were no activists *à l'écart* at all; whatever the activists felt about the 1793 situation, and, after all, one in every three of them rejected the Mountain, their instinct did not lead them to stand aside. The largest contingent *à l'écart* was that from departmental office, and the smallest that from the communes—which would support the traditional view of the more radical attitude of communal officials, were it not that so many of those who remained politically active chose to back the Gironde rather than the Mountain.

Men *à l'écart* under the Terror were for that period political ciphers. The "committees" deputies, who were rather more than ciphers but who discreetly circumscribed their activities, offer an interesting contrast. Whereas the *à l'écart* members had a high proportion of inexperience, and possibly of timidity, the "committees" members were on average the *conventionnels* most accustomed to public life. More than 86 percent of them had previously been elected to political office, and the number of novices was negligible. The *level* of experience was, however, not quite so impressive, the ex-deputies being proportionately hardly more numerous than those in the *à l'écart* group. What distinguished the "committees" group was its very high proportion of local officials, who were an absolute majority of all its members, with men from departmental posts the outstanding contributors. When one considers that of the 95 "committees" deputies there were only 13 who had not held political office during one or more of the crises of 1790-92, and that the sympathies of the majority, as shown by their behavior in the 1793 *appels nominaux*, were conservative rather than radical, their restrained outlook in 1793-94 is not hard to understand.

The *en mission* group is so small that comment on it is difficult, except that its close approximation to the balance of experience in the whole body of members is amusing in view of the sort of commitment its members were willing to undertake toward the Montagnard régime: energetic support in 1793–94 without earlier consistent acceptance of the Montagnard line in politics. Its limited membership may be evidence of the difficulty of combining these two attitudes. It is interesting that its 10 members from the Legislative Assembly did not include a single regicide, though 8 of the 10 voted in the trial. A number of its deputies (Féraud, for one) had personal links with or sympathies for the Gironde which might well have got them into serious trouble, but which were overlooked in view of the useful work they were doing.

The range of background and political outlook among the *en mission* deputies does illustrate the variety of support which enabled the Republic to survive the crisis of 1793–94. Only about half a dozen of them ever showed much real enthusiasm for Montagnard ideas, even temporarily—there was more feeling for the Gironde than the Mountain—but all were willing to make at some point, and sometimes for a considerable time, an effort to do what they could to enforce government policy, possibly under very difficult conditions, although this combination of personal independence and major administrative responsibility might make them extremely and perhaps dangerously vulnerable to criticism. For example, Antiboul, with his colleague Bo, was captured by the federalists on the way to Corsica, in June 1793, and was detained in Marseille for a fortnight. Both men were interrogated at length by the rebels. After their release, Bo was able to restore his credit, but Antiboul was accused of unworthy conduct and executed with the Girondins at the end of October. Whatever the facts of events in Marseille, there was also between Bo and Antiboul a considerable difference in situation. Whereas Antiboul was undecided in politics, Bo had sat with the Mountain since September 1792; whereas Bo was a regicide, Antiboul had failed to reach any conclusion over the trial; whereas Bo was a left-wing graduate of the Legislative Assembly, Antiboul came from departmental office in Var, where there was serious trouble from federalists in 1793. (This might not have mattered so much if he had not tried in February 1793 to minimize its danger.) He was the only departmental official elected from Var who did not back the Mountain. In the overheated atmosphere of the autumn of 1793 it is not hard to see why he had little hope of establishing his innocence; yet there is no suggestion in Kuscinski's account that he was more than indiscreet. Other *en mission* deputies were luckier, but a high proportion had to defend themselves against political mistrust which might well have been fatal. There were 8 besides Antiboul who were in this position, or nearly one in 4 of the whole 37.

When one looks at the opposed "factions" of 1793, the Gironde and the Mountain, the apparent difference in internal structure is so striking and so unexpected that further analysis seems called for. The Gironde, after all, originated as a parliamentary group during the lifetime of the Legislative Assembly, from which nearly two hundred deputies passed straight into the Convention. Why were ex-deputies only a third of the total Girondin strength? Further, the figures indicate and the diagrams emphasize a major difference in political background between Girondin leaders and Girondin followers. What then about the Mountain? Here there was an obviously strong parliamentary element; the question is whether the ex-deputies were to be found only in one particular section of the Mountain, or whether they were more or less evenly distributed over the whole range of Montagnard attitudes. The figures work out as shown in Table 21.

Table 21. Montagnard political experience—detail*

| | Jacobin Club | Mountain | "By attribution" | | | No. in Convention |
			En mission	Committees	Total	
Const. Ass.	14	7	3	1	25	78
Leg. Ass.	47	29	24	13	113	191
Department	18	9	4	4	35	113
District	12	8	9	4	33	93
Commune	10	8	4	5	27	92
Judge/J.P.	10	4	5	3	22	59
Political activist	24	2	–	–	26	36
No experience	7	6	6	2	21	68
Total	142	73	55	32	302	730

*See also histogram illustrating these figures.

This, which might have established some similarity between Gironde and Mountain, merely emphasizes the contrast, which must now be explored.

In the "inner sixty," although the ex-deputies were not dominant, they were very important and were the largest single element. Two only of the "inner sixty" were novices, and the general level of experience was high. This is what one might expect of a group based on personal friendships and connections, in which the leading figures had been deeply engaged in politics for some time. The Girondin leaders, however, did not recruit a following of their own kind. Although there were certainly some ex-deputies among the rank and file of the Gironde, support came much more from local officials, who were an absolute majority of the whole. There was also a substantial number of men without any experience at all. Neither the ex-Constituents nor the ex-Legislatives were as sympathetic as might have been expected. Whatever the merits of the Girondin line in national politics, its proponents gathered their backers from among men who were far from their equals in political sophistication. They had more rank and file backing from among the 91 deputies (of our 730) from the communes than from among the 191 from the Legislative Assembly.

On the other hand, the parliamentary bias of the Mountain stands out as both clear and apparently general, though it varied a little from one section to another. The extreme at left and right, the members of the Jacobin Club and the

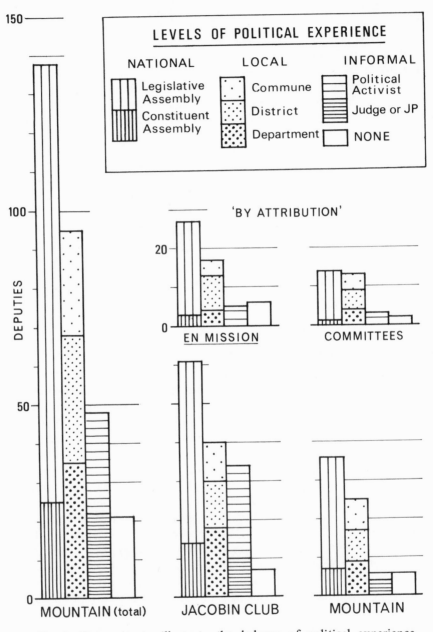

Fig 2. Histogram to illustrate the balance of political experience
among the Montagnards: detail.

"committees" section of the Montagnards "by attribution," had about the same proportion of ex-deputies; in both cases it was over 40 percent, above the Convention average, but below the average for the whole Mountain. In both the other sections just about half the members were ex-deputies. Political novices were nowhere at all significant. The figures also indicate that it was rare for a man who had not been engaged in political activity before he came to Paris in 1792 to join the Jacobin Club after he got there. The substantial contingent of comparatively inexperienced Club members was made up mainly of men who had already been engaged in newspaper work, or popular agitation, or both, before their election.[67] But the activists were a very small part of the whole strength of the Mountain, and overall it would be fair to say that as the level of political commitment went up, so did the number of Montagnard deputies; 21 without experience; 22 judicial members; 26 activists; 27, 33, and 35 from communes, districts, and departments; and 138 ex-deputies—with only the ex-Constituents spoiling the symmetry of the pattern. Even with the comparatively small levy from the Constituent, it is an impressive picture. The more one looks at the size of the parliamentary element in the Mountain the more astonishing it is; not far short of half the whole.

This situation was both strength and weakness to the Jacobin régime. On the credit side was an absolute majority of all the ex-deputies in our analysis, 138 of a total of 269, with the prestige which these men might be expected to command and the influence they and their friends and relatives could exert in departmental affairs. On the debit side was the fact that only just over half of the Convention's local officials were prepared even to tolerate the Mountain, and only one in three was a convinced supporter. This was the more serious because whereas the local officials had come into the Convention direct from local office, and had been actively and recently in touch with the electors who had sent them to Paris, much of the Mountain's formidable parliamentary strength came from the Legislative Assembly deputies who had been in Paris since October 1791, and had had at most only occasional and fleeting contact with their original or later constituents. The prestige and patriotism which had got them elected would not necessarily counterbalance a decline in influence at the local level when, for instance, the acceptance of controversial legislation was in question, or people in the departments were becoming alarmed by the drift of events in Paris. We have already seen how the correspondence of Birotteau, a district official from Pyrénées-Orientales, created difficulties for the deputies *en mission* in the spring of 1793. Goudelin, a Côtes-du-Nord departmental official, who in January 1793 wrote home regretfully describing how the Côtes-du-Nord *fédérés* had fallen under Parisian influence, obviously sympathized with the

____

67. The only men in this category I cannot find named in Aulard's records of the Club for the relevant period may well both have been members; both Audouin and Armonville spoke up bravely for the Mountain after Thermidor, and Armonville protested against the closing of the Club. See Kuscinski, *Conventionnels*, pp. 10, 12–13.

suspicion of Paris which had caused the department to send them;[68] whereas a deputy like Besson, tactfully explaining to *his* department of Doubs the proper attitude to take over the events of 31 May–2 June, was doing a useful and necessary job for the Mountain.[69] The problem, which would have been a difficult one in any case, was complicated by the Mountain's comparatively small share of ex-Constituents. Most of the ex-Constituents in the Convention had spent 1791–92 in some other form of public office, and had thus firmly entrenched themselves in the local political organizations; Thomas Lindet in Eure, Salle in Meurthe, and more briefly Pierre-Louis Prieur in Marne are examples of this process at work. But ex-Constituents as a group, more closely in touch with local opinion than the ex-Legislatives had much chance to be, were in the majority lukewarm or hostile to Montagnard rule; Rabaut Saint-Etienne was one such deputy, who in 1792–93 kept in touch with the *Société populaire* in Nîmes, his original 1789 electorate, and fanned its hostility to Paris;[70] and Durand-Maillane was another, urging the municipal officials of his birthplace to subscribe to Condorcet's *Chronique de Paris*.[71] The Montagnard body of 25 ex-Constituents had been for practical purposes further reduced because Dubois-Crancé and Chateauneuf-Randon returned to duty in the army in 1791, and Robespierre stayed in Paris instead of going home to Arras, where he might have been well employed in strengthening the radicals' somewhat uncertain hold on Pas-de-Calais.[72] This unevenness of Montagnard resources meant that its ex-deputies had fewer undisputed channels of influence in local affairs than their numbers would suggest. The point should not be pressed too far; Robert Lindet still headed the list of Eure *conventionnels* as far as local backing went, despite Buzot's leap to eminence in his absence;[73] but the difficulty was there, and increased that already created by the way in which the Convention's local officials had divided their allegiance.

Here again we come to the importance of *en mission* activity in the spring of 1793. "The Jacobins," says Thompson, "scattered over the provinces, and among the armies . . . had every opportunity to spread their opinions."[74] True enough. But it is also relevant that to begin with they were, in very many cases, at an artificial disadvantage. Consider Choudieu's position in Maine-et-Loire,

68. L. Dubreuil, *La Révolution dans le département des Côtes-du-Nord* (Paris, 1909), pp. 196–97.

69. A. Mathiez, "Lettres inédites du conventionnel Besson," *Annales révolutionnaires* XIV (1922): 145.

70. F. Rouvière, *Histoire de la Révolution française dans le Gard*. II: 180.

71. E. Vellay (ed.). "Neuf lettres de Durand-Maillane," *Annales* XIV (1937): 67–68.

72. Barère, as a newly-appointed judge, also spent almost all of 1791–92 away from home.

73. F. Evrard, "L'esprit public dans l'Eure, juillet-septembre 1792," *La Révolution française* LXVI (1914): 406. Cf. A.N. C178 CII 26 (Eure) 5 Sept.; Buzot got 490 votes of 591, Lindet 532 of 593.

74. J. M. Thompson, *The French Revolution*, p. 349.

where he was reelected at the head of the poll.[75] Choudieu and Delaunay, who came second, were both Montagnards. But they were followed by de Houlières, the third ex-Legislative, who was highly conservative until he resigned in mid-April 1793, and then by a mixed bag of four ex-Constituents, all anti-Montagnard, and four local officials, only one of whom had left-wing sympathies. After de Houlières' resignation he was replaced by yet another local official, Viger from Angers, who promptly became involved with the Gironde. The Left clearly had friends in Maine-et-Loire, but the opposition had, on the face of it, a very strong footing indeed; and both Choudieu and Delaunay spent 1791–92 away from home.[76] The 75 ex-Legislatives who were *en mission* in the spring of 1793 included 57 Montagnards who were in many areas badly needed to restore the links between the parliamentary Left and the electorate which had sent it back to office, but with which it had had little recent personal contact. Levasseur's trouble in Meurthe was partly caused by Salle's success, in 1791–92, making friends and consolidating his influence on the departmental directory, of which he had become a member after his return from the Constituent. Thompson points out, as others have done, that the Girondin maneuver of keeping up numbers in Paris by encouraging the dispersion of Montagnard strength into the departments ended by defeating its own ends.[77] It must also be said that the Girondins may have felt that little risk was involved. The Mountain had a lot of leeway to make up.

VI

From our analysis so far, it would seem that, with the partial exception of the Montagnards, there was little real homogeneity of background among men who in 1793–94 took a similar stand in politics. The Gironde, the Plain, and the Mountain, though drawing to different degrees on the range of experience the Convention had to offer, still covered the whole range. This being the case, there may be little point in enquiring how men from various levels of experience responded to the *appels nominaux*. Yet each of the political groups was internally divided on the issues raised by the *appels*, and since these issues might well have had special relevance for particular categories of deputy, it seems proper to ask whether, for instance, judges were more often to be found on the conservative side than the radical, whether they belonged to the Mountain or the Gironde. To illustrate the general issues raised: The demand for the *appel au peuple* was justified partly by objections to the supposed principles underlying

75. A. Meynier, *La Revellière-Lépeaux*, p. 307; cf. *Liste des citoyens députés à la Convention nationale* (Paris, 1792), 11, and A.N. 179 CII 47 (Maine-et-Loire), 4 Sept.

76. For the background and attitude of Maine-et-Loire deputies, see Appendices III–IV; for Viger, Kuscinski, *Conventionnels*, p. 606.

77. J. M. Thompson, *The French Revolution*, p. 349.

the conduct of the king's trial, objections which might have appealed particularly to the judicial deputies, and partly by hostility to the alleged presumption and illegal pressure of the Parisian Left, which might have appealed particularly to the local government deputies and the ex-deputies. The two *appels* of April and May were directly concerned with the problem of Parisian politics and, by inference, with the place of Paris in the new Republic; again the relevance for local government deputies seems apparent.

The voting on the *appel au peuple*, analyzed in terms of the political experience of the voters, was as presented in Table 22.

Table 22. Political experience and the trial of
Louis XVI*—the *appel au peuple*

	For	Against	Abstained	*En mission*	Absent	Total
Const. Ass.	41 (2)	38 (2)	–	4 (1)	–	83 (5)
Leg. Ass.	47 (1)	137 (2)	1	9	–	194 (3)
Department	52 (2)	60	–	2	2 (1)	116 (3)
District	42 (1)	46	4	2	–	94 (1)
Commune	44 (1)	46 (1)	1	1	2	94 (2)
Judge/J.P.	27 (1)	31 (1)	2	–	1	61 (2)
Political						
activist	3 (1)	31 (1)	1	2	1	38 (2)
No experience	30	36	1	–	2 (1)	69 (1)
Total	286 (9)	425 (7)	10	20 (1)	8 (2)	749 (19)

*For the sake of completeness, the deputies excluded from the political analysis have been included in these tables. Their numbers are shown in parentheses.

The conclusions already reached about the political importance of the Legislative Assembly deputies are here dramatically confirmed. The rest of the Convention voted against the referendum by 288 to 239, and most of the hostile majority, which in any case was not large, came from the political activists, without whom there was a margin of only 21 votes. Thus without the deputies of the Legislative, the decree would have suffered a clear but by no means humiliating defeat. But with the Legislative votes added, defeat became disaster. Their majority against was nearly twice as large as that of all the other groups combined. And these were the men who had served with Brissot, Vergniaud, and Gensonné through July, August, and September, who might have been expected to share their anger at Parisian insolence and Montagnard intransigence, who had lived through the days of the massacres and knew at first-hand the worst that could be said of the Commune. Girondin leadership was decisively repudiated by those who were in the best position to appreciate the reasoning behind it.

In other respects the result was a close thing. Table 22 shows the conservative instincts of the ex-Constituents, the only group with a favorable majority, and a marginal decision by the local officials to avoid a political gamble—a margin which delicately increases as the level of political responsibility rises. In view of the later behavior of the communal officials and the inexperienced deputies, their action on this occasion provokes speculation. The idea that the final decision on a crucial public issue should be entrusted to the people at large, speaking through their primary assemblies, was finally, if narrowly, rejected by those likely to have been most recently in touch with opinion at this level. The other line of argument which did not convince those who should have been attracted by it was the one which concentrated attention on the legal impropriety of the Convention's position, proposing the referendum as a way out. The judicial members who were new to politics were apparently not sufficiently impressed; and if we look further, at the whole total of 160 judges and justices among the *conventionnels*, the balance of opinion is very similar.[78] Judicial conservatism, if it existed, did not show itself here; the results for judges and justices were not significantly different.

If the referendum debate brought out the rancour of current political antagonisms, the controversy over the actual fate of the king aroused a different sort of bitterness, that between those who would and those who would not take responsibility for an irrevocable decision.[79] Whatever the complication of motive, the degree of rationalization on either side, it all narrowed in the end to an individual choice, publicly made—and made for most deputies twice—by an individual deputy. The overall result after the five exhausting days of 15-19 January is shown in Table 23.

Who was responsible for the death of Louis XVI? The answer seems quite clear. The 40 deputies who could not make up their minds where their duty lay had the decision taken out of their hands. If the men from the Legislative are excluded, the Convention had 204 members whose sympathies lay with the king from 14 January onward, plus another 66 who, after opposing the referendum, finally decided against the death penalty. Against mercy, there were 209 with no doubts, but the number who had backed the referendum and then decided on the death penalty was only 26. The margin for mercy was 35. Even if every one of the 33 waverers in this part of the Convention had opted for death, Louis would still have survived; remorselessness from the political activists was not

78. The vote among the whole body of judges and J.P.s was:

For	66
Against	83
Abstained	4
En mission	4
Absent	3
Total	160

79. Cf. Sébastien Mercier's later comment: "*une séparation presque absolue s'établit entre ceux qui avaient ou n'avaient pas voté la mort . . . les inimités s'enflammèrent, les haines s'accruèrent . . . enfin le supplice de Louis XVI menaçait tous ceux qui avaient voulu l'en préserver.*" (*Paris pendant la Révolution*, 2 vols. [Paris, 1862], I: 207-8.) While this is evidence from an antiregicide and exaggerates the fact—the Girondin regicides did not become hopelessly estranged from their friends who thought differently—it has a core of truth.

Table 23. Political experience and the trial of
Louis XVI—the trial as a whole

	For mercy			For severity			Un-decided	No vote	Total
	3 votes	2 votes	Total	3 votes	2 votes	Total			
Const. Ass.	38 (2)	7	45 (2)	31 (2)	2	33 (2)	2	3 (1)	83 (5)
Leg. Ass.	39 (1)	11	50 (1)	122 (2)	7	129 (2)	7	8	194 (3)
Department	38 (2)	16	54 (2)	39	10	49	10	3 (1)	116 (3)
District	35 (1)	9	44 (1)	34	7	41	6	3	94 (1)
Commune	38 (1)	13	51 (1)	31 (1)	5	36 (1)	5	2	94 (2)
Judge/J.P.	25 (1)	7	32 (1)	21	–	21	5	2	60 (1)
Political activist	3 (1)	4 (1)	7 (2)	29	–	29	1	1	38 (2)
No experience	27	10	37	24	2	26	4	2 (1)	69 (1)
Total	243 (9)	77 (1)	320 (10)	331 (5)	33	364 (5)	40	24 (3)	748 (18)*

*Caila can hardly be placed in the "no vote" category with ordinary absentees, since he did not live to see the voting to its end. On the evidence he would probably have been a regicide.

enough to outweigh the sympathetic majority elsewhere. But among those who had watched from close quarters his brief career as a constitutional monarch it was another story. Little more than a quarter of the Legislative's 194 representatives came out firmly for mercy, and the undecided were a mere handful of 7. The bulk of the Legislative stood implacably at one, and it was this implacability which brought the king to the guillotine.

Intimidated by Paris? A possibility. These were the men who knew best what a Parisian mob could do. But this is to assume that the more obscure deputies of the Legislative behaved as they did for reasons quite different from those ascribed to their more famous colleagues, and there is at least no evidence to support such an assumption. Brissot, Grangeneuve, Dusaulx, de Houlières, and others had no hesitation in defying Parisian opinion and sparing the king's life; on the other hand, there has never been any suggestion that Carnot, Lindet, or Couthon, let alone Gensonné, Ducos, Lasource, or Isnard were yielding to Paris in voting for death. Among less well-known names, the rock-like Legislative majority included Rouyer, so little intimidated by Paris that he had spent August and September in angrily denouncing the Commune, as he was to do in the Convention again and again. Another explanation better fits the facts. More than 6 in 10 of those *conventionnels* who had come from France's first constitutional legislature could see their king for a perjurer, and in the circumstances of 1792 looked past his perjury to find treason. Although they should have been among the most determined defenders of the 1791 constitution, they did not feel bound by an oath of loyalty which the king for his part had never honestly accepted. A Montagnard summed up for many of his fellows:

Faut-il juger le tyran Louis XVI?
Non, car il est *évident* qu'il est jugé.

A quelle peine sera-t-il condamné?

La raison, l'humanité, la justice, la loi, le ciel et la terre lui condamnent à *mort*.

Les représentans du peuple Français doivent-ils ordonner l'exécution du supplice?

Oui, le plutôt sera le mieux.

Si d'autres tyrans vouloient monter sur la trône, ou s'en partager les débris, que doivent faire de vrais républicains?

Les exterminer, ou *mourir*.[80]

Others laid more emphasis on legal formalities without questioning the conclusion. In the end, two-thirds of the Legislative's former deputies in the Convention accepted two simple truths: Louis was a traitor, and the penalty for treason was death.

Among their colleagues, only the political activists agreed. The deputies from every other kind of background in revolutionary public affairs found majorities of varying sizes in the king's favor, and only among the departmental and district members was he supported by less than half the total number. In view of later developments, it is interesting that the ex-Constituents, the completely inexperienced deputies, and the communal officials all had quite clear absolute majorities of antiregicides. The departmental officials were the most wary, with the lowest proportion of antiregicides and the highest proportion of indecision, plus more than one man in five who changed his mind after the referendum. Their caution was almost absurdly appropriate to what has already been said of their situation and experiences in 1791–92.

For the judicial members, whether judges or justices, it might be supposed that the trial, as a trial, posed special problems which were likely to be most acutely felt in its closing stages. The referendum, however justified, was largely a political expedient and might be dealt with on those terms. The sentencing of the king was different. The trial of a sovereign ruler on a capital charge, by a self-constituted court which had no judicial precedent or standing and which violated all the procedural conventions, could in some eyes be justified only if it too were treated as a matter of politics and not of justice, but however it might be treated there were uneasy consciences. To abandon technicalities in favor of an essentially imprecise "law of nature" was not an easy thing to do.[81] The judicial members, though somewhat conservative, were no more friendly to Louis than the ex-Constituents, in fact on their voting a little less, but as a group they were the most reluctant men in the Convention to commit themselves as

---

80. R. Gaston, *Opinion . . . sur le procès du dernier roi des Français.* This is the complete text.

81. Vadier, Montagnard by temperament and outlook, but also a trained lawyer and a 1791 judge, was not troubled over the justice of the death sentence, but he was seriously concerned about the form of the trial and only accepted it because it seemed politically unavoidable. See M. G. Vadier, *Seconde opinion . . . sur Louis Capet.*

regicides. Nor was this behavior limited to those judges and justices who were new to political life. The judicial members from all parts of the Convention showed a very similar pattern. Their voting was:

For mercy	3 votes 60 ⎱ 2 votes 20 ⎰	80
For severity	3 votes 57 ⎱ 2 votes 2 ⎰	59
Undecided		12
No vote		8
	Total	159*

*Originally 160. Caila was a judge from the department of Lot.

The differences from the voting of any but the Legislative Assembly are not large enough to be statistically significant, but the total of 159 judicial members *includes* 31 men from the Legislative, so that the result analyzed above might have been expected to be rather less moderate than it actually was. Here, if anywhere, is judicial caution. To investigate this matter of "revolutionary justice" and the judicial attitude to it in this particular instance would be a large task. It is interesting that although about a third of the Convention's judicial deputies felt strongly enough about the issues of the trial to publish their views in pamphlet form, fewer than one in seven of them ended by rejecting the form of the trial or repudiating some sort of judicial (as distinct from political) responsibility in it. The others were willing to accept responsibility, wherever their sympathies lay; but that did not make them willing participants in a decision from which there could be no appeal and no retreat.

The kind of dilemma in which many judges found themselves may be illustrated from the pamphlet published by Pardoux Bordas to explain the reasoning behind his three apparently contradictory votes. He had rejected the referendum as a danger to peace and public security and because he believed that the particular duty of dealing with the king lay only with the Convention. He had voted against the death sentence because on balance he believed it to be more dangerous to kill tyrants than to let them live; but on this the Convention had overruled him. He was willing to accept that verdict as no less honest than his own, and recognized an obligation to submit to it: "*à la loi faite, la soumission est un devoir. L'amour du bien public fut mon guide dans le voeu que j'émis. Le même sentiment a inspiré celui de la majorité,*"[82] and so, by accepting the majority

82. P. Bordas, *Précis des opinions prononcées à la tribune de la Convention . . . sur la peine à infliger à Louis XVI, et sur le sursis du Décret qui le condamne à la mort* (italics in quotation mine).

decision of the Convention as legally binding on the citizen, he rejected the reprieve. His scruples throughout, which were moral and practical rather than legalistic, were set nevertheless in a framework of assumption about the obligations of the citizen, and in this he resembled the majority of the articulate among his fellow judges, whether or not their conclusions agreed with his. The interest of his attitude derives from his position as an ex-member of the Legislative and a Montagnard from September 1792. If it was difficult for him to be unequivocally ruthless, how much more difficult for those who had neither his political experience nor, by January 1793, his explicit political commitment. It is in this way that the background of the deputies throws light on some of the considerations that were likely to weigh heavily in coming to political decisions. The deciding factor in the end probably was, and had to be, political attitude; but Bordas, like his fellow judges, was more exercised about some aspects of his duties than other deputies were likely to be.

One might finally say that, apart from the striking response of the ex-Legislatives, the most remarkable thing about the trial was the limited appeal which the antiregicides were able to make to the many special interests which should have been working in their favor. Allowing for the weight of anti-Parisian prejudice, the regicide vote amongst local officials was far heavier than might have been predicted. Here perhaps the most vigorous opponents of the death sentence fell into something of a trap, in that distrust of Paris was in itself as irrelevant a reason for opposing the death sentence as the wishes of Paris should have been to a decision to impose it; and the speeches suggest that even the least sophisticated of the deputies were doing their best to take their obligations seriously. There was clearly a strong conservative element among the local officials, most notably (as later events were to establish) among those from the communes; but there was a strong regicide element as well. In view of their later signs of sympathy with the Mountain, the narrow antiregicide majority from the districts is worth noting; among the local men they had proportionately the most regicides.

If there were many cross-currents in the voting on the trial, the *appels* of April and May are nearly impossible to evaluate in any useful sense. Too many deputies were absent, too many others away *en mission*, for any but the most self-evident conclusions to emerge. The figures are presented in Tables 24 and 25.

It would again appear from these figures that without the Legislative Assembly deputies—or had the Legislative deputies behaved similarly to most of their colleagues—the Republic's history in the spring of 1793 would have been very different. Both in April and in May the Legislative supplied between 30 and 35 percent of the left-wing votes *and* well over 40 percent of the deputies *en mission*; its members were outstandingly the most active and radical in the Convention. Theirs was the only sizable group which came anywhere near rejecting the Marat impeachment. The 15 Legislative abstainers were split

Table 24. Political experience and the impeachment of Marat, 13 April*

	For	Against	Abstained/ adjournment	*En mission*	Absent	Total
Const. Ass.	34	7	10	11	16	78
Leg. Ass.	36 (1)	30	15	56	54	191 (1)
Department	42	11	8	14	37	112
District	33	10	5	9	36	93
Commune	37	11	4	11	29 (1)	92 (1)
Judge/J.P.	14	5	5	10	25	59
Political activist	3	11	3	10	9	36
No experience	22	8	5	7	26	68
Total	221 (1)	93	55	128	232	729 (2)

*Kersaint (Legislative Assembly), Rebecqui (Department), and Manuel (Commune) had all resigned by the middle of April and have therefore been omitted. Of the nineteen "unclassified" deputies Mellinet (Commune) was the only one who certainly voted after the king's trial; he was absent on 13 April, but voted on 28 May. He died on 7 June. De Houlières (Legislative Assembly) is included as having voted on 13 April, and very likely did, but there is an element of doubt. The vote recorded for him (supporting the impeachment) probably fairly represents his views.

Table 25. Political experience and the reinstatement of the Commission of Twelve, 28 May

	For	Against	*En mission*	Abstained/ absent/ unknown	Total
Const. Ass.	36	13	12	17	78
Leg. Ass.	42	78	45	25	190
Department	53	23	13	23	112
District	47	30	7	9	93
Commune	42 (1)	26	9	15	93 (1)
Judge/J.P.	17	21	4	17	59
Political activist	5	19	3	9	36
No experience	27	17	5	19	68
Total	269 (1)	227	98	134	728 (1)

between 7 who took a Girondin line and 8 (6 of them Montagnard) who either rejected the proposal out of hand or would have nothing to do with it in its proposed form. The margin of feeling in favor of impeachment was thus one of 43 to 38, with 56 deputies, mostly Montagnard, out of Paris. By May some of the missing members had returned, rather more of those in Paris felt inclined to vote, and the Legislatives rejected the Commission of Twelve by nearly 2 votes to one. Elsewhere the Commission got in general fairly safe support, the exceptions coming of course from the political activists and, unexpectedly, from the judicial members, of whom about 30 percent did not bother to vote, thus allowing the minority of radicals to win a narrow victory. The solid vote against the Commission reflected the existence of persistent left-wing opinion from every level of experience, but without the strong lead from the Legislative Left the rest were soundly outnumbered. This *appel* also showed once again the divergence in outlook between Legislative and ex-Constituent deputies; with a dozen of their more active members away *en mission*, the ex-Constituents had proportionately the smallest left-wing vote of any group.

Politically, the *appels* of April and May are consistent with the diagnoses already made of future attitudes toward the Jacobin régime. The absences do however confuse the picture to some extent, in that the deputies *en mission* were on the average more radical than the average of the men who stayed in Paris, so that a group with a high proportion of *en mission* absentees in May might actually have more sympathy with the Mountain than the figures suggest. Next to the Legislatives, the group with proportionately the most men *en mission* in May was that of the ex-Constituents. This would imply that despite the activity of a number of ex-Constituents in opposition to the Mountain, as evinced by the *appels*, there was also a solid minority with rather different views. Between the king's death and the expulsion of the Girondins, the ex-Constituents were outranked only by the Legislatives and the activists in the proportion of men going into the departments—see Table 26.

Table 26. Deputies *en mission* 21 January–31 May 1793
in relation to political experience*

	Total no. of deputies	No. *en mission*
Const. Ass.	78	18
Leg. Ass.	191	75
Department	113	22
District	93	16
Commune	92	17
Judge/J.P.	59	11
Political activist	36	10
No experience	68	7
Total	730	176

*Note that among the Legislatives, both regicides and antiregicides went *en mission* in more than predictable numbers.

This was a portent for 1793–94. In the Convention the ex-deputies were the men with the greatest experience and the highest political standing, and it seems reasonable to conclude that those among them who were willing to accept responsibility should be entrusted with it at the highest level under the Terror. And so it turned out. The Committee of Public Safety, the most important executive authority in France during this period, was from April 1793 to the end of July 1794 numerically dominated by men from France's earlier legislatures. In all, down to 27 July 1794, 23 deputies were elected to the Committee for varying lengths of time. These can be split up as follows:

Constituent Assembly	5
Legislative Assembly	12
Department	1
Commune	2
Activists: journalist 1 ⎫ club 2 ⎭	3
	──
	23

The club agitators, Billaud-Varenne and Collot d'Herbois, were the only members who were not the free choice of the Convention itself, owing their seats mainly to the Parisian demonstration of 5 September 1793. At the time they entered the Committee it contained 3 ex-Constituents, 6 from the Legislative, and Saint-Just and Jeanbon, who had been delegates from their communes to Paris. After Thuriot (Legislative) resigned on 20 September, two-thirds of the "great" Committee in its final form consisted of former deputies. That this should have been so was a fitting reflection of the role played by such men since the first meeting of the Convention exactly a year before.[83]

83. The parliamentary history of the Convention needs further examination along these lines, particularly as far as its other committees are concerned. The names of the men elected to the Committee of Public Safety, and the dates of their service, are in Appendix IX, with some notes on the membership of the Committee of General Security.

CHAPTER 8

AGES AND PERSONAL BACKGROUND

The deputies of the Convention have now been examined, in their public lives, from three different points of view: as protagonists in the political struggles of 1792-94; as members of departmental contingents selected by the electoral assemblies of 1792; and as participants, to a greater or less degree, in the public affairs of the new France during the first three years of revolution. They were however individual citizens before they became politicians, and it is possible from Kuscinski's evidence to gather up some information about them simply as individuals: how old they were, the sort of environment they were settled in before the revolution began, what they did (or did not do) for a living, what happened to them when their parliamentary lives were over. Though necessarily sketchy, this material when analyzed may round out the picture a little, and give some tentative impression of the sort of man who was likely to become deeply involved in public life or to take up one or another particular attitude in politics.

I

The easiest of these matters to deal with is age: how old were the deputies when they were elected? Does it matter how old they were? Perhaps not. Yet in drawing up the Constitution of 1795, the Convention itself provided, for the first time in revolutionary history, a sizable gap between the age level required of the electors and that required of their representatives. In 1791 the minimum age for both had been 25. In 1792, the voting age dropped to 21 while the age for deputies remained at 25. The 1795 constitution widened the gap still further, restricting the membership of the Council of Elders to men of at least 40; furthermore, from 1799 all deputies were to be 30 or more, and from the outset the Directors, like the Elders, had to have reached 40. The age pattern in the

Convention itself seems therefore worth examining, for it seems at least possible that in deciding to emphasize maturity as a qualification for high responsibility, the men of 1795 may have been drawing to some extent on the lessons of their own experience.

If the 749 deputies of January 1793 are divided into 5-year groups according to their age at that date, beginning with those under 30 and ending with an amalgamated group of those who were 60 or more, the result is as shown in Table 27.

Table 27. Ages of deputies in the National Convention

	(i) included in political analysis	(ii) not included	Total
Under 30	50	1	51
30–34	116	4	120
35–39	169	2	171
40–44	153	3	156
45–49	105	2	107
50–54	66	3	69
55–59	47	4	51
60 plus	24	–	24
Total	730	19	749

It will be seen that the Convention was in no sense an elderly body and that the largest group in it was that of men in their later thirties, who comprised between one-fifth and one-quarter of all the members. If a line is to be drawn as Thompson draws it,[1] separating younger men from older, it seems proper to place it not at 50, as he does, but at 45; the numbers in the 35–39 and the 40–44 groups are not very different, but from the age of 45 onward the graph turns firmly and steadily downward. Almost exactly 60 percent of all the deputies were, at the end of 1792, between 30 and 45 years old (that is, born between the end of 1747 and the end of 1762). Those in their thirties were close to 40 percent of the whole, and two-thirds were under 45. On the other hand, a stipulation that one-third of France's legislators were to be aged 40 or more would have caused the Convention no inconvenience; the quota could have been met with something to spare; only about 45 percent were under 40.

Why then insert such a provision? Presumably because after the experience of 1792–95 it was felt wise to divide legislative responsibility, and an age qualification was a simple and uncontroversial way of distinguishing one house from the other. If, however, we look more closely at the situation in the Convention, there are indications that this separation of the older from the younger would have produced a different political orientation in the two groups. This can be seen if we compare the age pattern of the various political groups among our 730

1. J. M. Thompson, *The French Revolution* (Oxford, 1943), p. 312.

deputies, and is most evident if the figures (to be found in Appendix V) are converted in various ways into percentages, as in Table 28.

From this it seems that the most conservative members of the Convention were noticeably older than the average of their colleagues. As a group, the *à l'écart* deputies were moving well into middle age. Only one in three of them was under 40, more than 30 percent were 50 or more (against a Convention figure of under 20 percent) and one man only, Gouzy, was under 30.[2]

Table 28. Political groups 1793–94 divided
according to age (percentages)

	Under 30	Under 40	Under 45	30–45	Over 45	Over 50
Gironde						
"inner sixty"	13.8	56.8	77.5	63.7	22.4	6.9
Others	5.8	48.3	59.1	53.3	41.0	25.9
Plain						
à l'écart	.8	34.7	54.2	53.4	45.8	31.4
"Committees"	6.4	40.0	65.3	58.9	34.7	20.0
en mission	13.5	51.3	72.9	59.4	27.0	10.8
Mountain						
Jacobins	9.1	53.5	73.2	63.4	26.8	14.8
Mountain	9.6	52.1	69.9	60.3	30.0	13.7
Other	2.3	51.7	74.7	72.4	25.3	12.6
Mountain overall	7.3	52.3	72.5	65.2	27.5	13.9
Convention overall	6.8	45.9	66.8	60.0	33.2	18.8

It seems also that those most actively engaged in politics were on average the youngest *conventionnels*. Nearly three-quarters of the Montagnards, more than three-quarters of the "inner sixty," were under 45, and more than half of each were under 40.[3] But for the Gironde, unlike the Mountain, there was a sharp difference between leaders and followers. In the whole Convention, Brissot, Vergniaud, and their closer colleagues were a youthful group. But it seems that for some reason those who made up this comparatively small association of friends and acquaintances did not manage to capture the loyalty of their own contemporaries, but received instead either open or tacit sympathy from men a good deal older than themselves. Of the Girondin rank and file, one in 4 was 50 or more. If to these deputies are added those who were *à l'écart* in 1793/94, it appears that more than half of all the *conventionnels* over 50 had some distaste for Montagnard rule. Conversely, the 45 men from the "inner sixty" who were

2. For Gouzy, see Kuscinski, *Conventionnels*, p. 305.
3. The pattern is maintained if we add in the remaining two members of the "inner sixty," Bancal (42), and Minvielle (28).

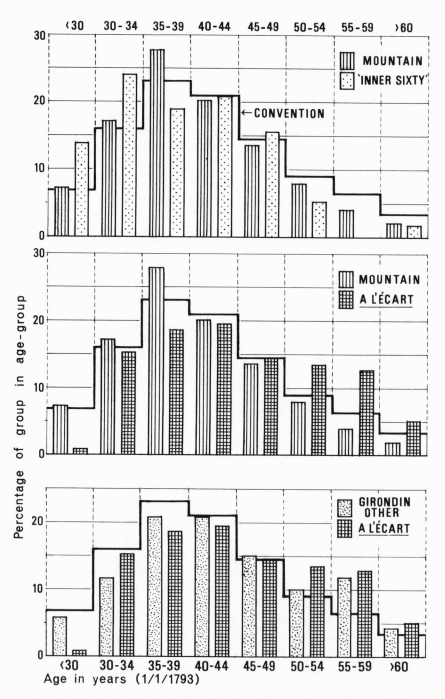

Fig. 3. Graphs to illustrate the different balance of age-groups within
the political groups.

under 45 found that the politically committed deputies of their own age group backed the Mountain by 3 to 1, and for men under 40 the proportions were even worse.

Of the 434 deputies who shouldered some sort of responsibility under the Terror, more than 7 in 10 were at most in their early forties.[4] The association, both at this time and later, between political activity and comparative youth can be illustrated in other ways. Between September 1792 and November 1795, 74 of our 730 deputies met unnatural death as a direct result of their involvement in politics: death by execution, suicide, maltreatment, lynching, the hardships of prison life or penal servitude, or—in the case of Marat—simple murder. Fifty-eight of the 74, or more than three-quarters, were under 45, and 42, or nearly 57 percent, were under 40. The total, just over 1 in 10 of the whole 730, included 1 in 5 of all those under 30. To take another example: by the end of 1795 the Convention had lost a further 66 members who had been excluded (and imprisoned, if they had stayed to be caught) because of their real or reputed enthusiasm for unfashionable political opinions. Of these men, 42, or more than 63 percent, were under 40, and 54, or more than 80 percent, were under 45. The younger men were more conspicuously involved in the complications, even if sometimes only the more sordid complications, of revolutionary politics, and paid the appropriate price. Before Thermidor that price was paid mainly by the Girondin leadership and the dissidents of the Mountain; after Thermidor it was paid almost entirely by those who still clung to Montagnard principles, or who had become too closely identified with the Montagnard régime. The "inner sixty" were young; the excluded Montagnards of 1795 were even younger.[5]

Thus, among the under-40's of our 730, 47 percent were Montagnard; among the over-40's fewer than 37 percent. By 1795 a number from both sides had, of course, disappeared, but the situation was controlled by the survivors (the new intake being lacking in influence as well as in experience) and these, as has been noted, were older rather than younger men, as well as professionally anti-Montagnard. By the end of 1795 the Mountain had lost, as well as its domination and more than one-third of its total strength, more than 40 percent of its younger members.[6] One can only guess how far the makers of the Constitution of the Year Three were aware of these things, but the stipulation that the

4. It need not be assumed that because the average expectation of life was lower in the eighteenth century than it is today, a *conventionnel* of, say, 45 was necessarily "older" than a man of that age and social standing would seem now. It might even be argued that anyone who then survived the perils of infancy and adolescence was naturally fairly tough, and if he did not have to undergo the hazards of working-class existence might survive almost indefinitely. Barère, it will be remembered, lived to be over 85; but he was well outdistanced by Denis Le Maréchal, dying at 96 in the town where he had been born in 1755.

5. Those excluded in 1795 came under fire for political views which they had adopted in 1793, or earlier; it is therefore their age in 1793, not 1795 which is relevant.

6. See Appendix VI for details of the Convention in late 1795.

executive of the new régime should be at least 40 can hardly be accidental. If this provision had been in force under the Terror, only Lindet, Carnot, Collot d'Herbois, and Jeanbon Saint-André could have held office on the "great" Committee, and Barère was the only one of the other 8 who would have qualified (with 6 weeks to spare) before the Convention dissolved. Lindet was the only one of the 12 who was over 45; the average age was just over 36.

In the end, however, whatever the survivors of the Convention may have thought about the age factor in politics, and about the best age for political leadership, is less important than the fact that the majority of the membership belonged to the second half of the eighteenth century, was educated in the full blaze of the Enlightenment, and reached early manhood during the political and economic crises of the seventies and eighties. In 1748, the publication year of *L'esprit des Lois*, when Voltaire was already 54 and on the eve of his great campaign for civil liberties, Robert Lindet was 2 years old. At the beginning of that year none of his future colleagues on the great Committee had yet been born; but neither had two-thirds of the men who ever became his fellow *conventionnels*.

II

Even if they were not yet established middle-aged citizens, with a minimum age of 25 in 1792 all the deputies of the Convention were mature enough to have entered by 1789 on some settled way of life, and most of them had done so. Apart from the relatively few whose background is not known, nearly all can be fitted into an occupational category of one kind or another. A handful of young men like Saint-Just or Laurenceot had been permanently distracted from completing their studies by the revolution or the outbreak of war, and can only by courtesy be placed with other members of their proposed professions, but these were exceptional. It is true that some *conventionnels* had led erratic lives, but virtually all the future deputies had in the year of the revolution some recognizable means of support, and only for a few was this entirely a private income, or the help of some generous relative. Most had had some vocational training. Many were lawyers, and others had legal qualifications they did not use; one in 14 was some sort of cleric; some were of the armed forces, on the active or retired list, some were civil servants, some were prosperous landowners or farmers (and a few were very poor ones), some were in trade, some were academics or journalists, three were professional artists, and one had been a grave-digger. Behind their public lives as politicians lay the private careers on which most had been well embarked before the coming of revolution twisted the future into fantastic shapes. Behind them all lay the accepted daily routine of the hundreds of communities of which they had been established members before they came, in 1789 or 1791 or 1792, to face the decisions of national politics in a Paris crucially different from the city that even the Parisians among them had once known.

It seems usually to be assumed, and is sometimes explicitly claimed, that there was no significant difference in social composition between the Third Estate of 1789, the Legislative Assembly of 1791, and the Convention of 1792.[7] It is common ground to all historians that the revolutionary assemblies all contained a very high proportion of lawyers and relatively few merchants or industrialists. This comparative dearth of men with a direct interest in the business world, noted by Jaurès with some surprise,[8] fits neatly into Cobban's recently presented thesis that the chief architects of revolution were the *"officiers* and the men of the liberal professions."[9] Like most recent historians, Cobban sees the Convention's membership as essentially homogeneous; Mathiez's assertion that the antagonism between Gironde and Mountain arose from social as well as political differences he dismisses as "pure supposition with little factual basis."[10]

All these assertions are very general, and recent histories give no detailed analysis of any revolutionary assembly. Cobban alone has attempted this for the Convention, but his figures, derived from Kuscinski, had a special problem in view, and in any case do not distinguish between *suppléants* and the titular deputies of 1792.[11] A more elaborate dissection of the *Dictionnaire* seems justified.

How useful is Kuscinski as a source? His information is fairly extensive, covering all but about 5 percent of the 1792 deputies. It is unfortunately not documented in detail, though it is often clear that a range of both official and private sources were consulted; on the other hand, an independent check of the 1795 property statements suggests that on the whole it may be reliable, though there are some puzzles which cannot at present be resolved. From internal evidence, Kuscinski was consciously careful and critical in dealing with problem cases, e.g., he makes it clear that F. P. Legendre, often described as an iron-master, was in fact mainly interested in the law.[12] His use of the terms *avocat* and more especially *negociant* may conceal ambiguities;[13] but for such men, evidence of family, education, environment, and apparent social position may be used to see that the picture which emerges has as much coherence as the evi-

7. See, e.g., N. Hampson, *A Social History of the French Revolution* (London, 1963), p. 155; cf. *ibid.*, pp. 60, 132–33.
8. J. Jaurès, *Histoire socialiste de la Révolution française*, 8 vols. (Paris, 1924), IV: 301–2.
9. A. Cobban, *Social interpretation of the French Revolution* (London, 1964), passim, esp. chap. VII.
10. Ibid., p. 65. Cf. A. Mathiez, *The French Revolution* (New York, 1965), p. 212.
11. A. Cobban, *Aspects of the French Revolution* (London, 1969), pp. 109–11.
12. *Conventionnels*, pp. 391–2.
13. Cf. Cobban, *Social Interpretation*, p. 57.

dence permits. Much more research will be needed before any final statements about the Convention's social make-up can be made, but the *Dictionnaire* contains enough material for at least tentative generalizations.

As a preliminary to an occupational analysis, we may ask a more general question. Hampson says that the deputies were overwhelmingly of the urban middle class.[14] Were they in fact "urban"? If so, in what sense?

Though most eighteenth-century Frenchmen naturally lived in the country, a recent demographic analysis has argued for the existence of 52 really large French towns, ranging in size from a group of about a dozen with 15 to 20,000 inhabitants, upwards through another dozen in each of the 20 to 25,000 and 25 to 35,000 categories, to 4 of 35 to 50,000, 5 of over 50,000 plus Lyon probably over 100,000, and finally Paris the incomparable with perhaps 550,000 citizens. Among these 52 large towns, only 33 were ranked among the departmental *chefs-lieux*, so that there were also another 50 *chefs-lieux* which, if not quite in the 15,000+ category, were regional centers and probably of quite respectable size.[15] Where had the deputies lived before they were elected? The level of their community experience may be relevant to any assessment of their original outlook as politicians. One would not expect a man with a "country lawyer's practice" in Clermont (Oise) to have quite the view of public problems held by one of the busiest barristers in Bordeaux,[16] and to be like Cassanyès a country barber-surgeon was not to be the equal of Dr. Marat in Paris or Dr. Hardy in Rouen. It may be interesting to see, both in general terms and within occupational groups, the balance of urban as against more rural experience in the Convention.

To classify the deputies by their places of residence, three categories have been adopted: (a) large towns (15,000+); (b) *chefs-lieux* not included in category (a), plus any other towns with 10,000+ inhabitants; (c) all other places. This somewhat crude method should indicate, very broadly, which deputies were "urban" in which sense, and may also allow some idea of whether men from larger towns showed in their political attitudes any noticeable variation from the norm. It may be objected that a town of 15,000+ is not really very large; but the standards of the eighteenth century were not those of the twentieth, and I have accepted this dividing line as reasonable.[17]

---

14. *Social History*, p. 155.

15. This sometimes led to anomalies. Reims was not the *chef-lieu* of Marne, despite its 30,000 citizens; that honor went to Châlons, which had fewer than 15,000 but not, apparently, so many fewer as to make its precedence absurd.

16. Bézard in Clermont, Grangeneuve in Bordeaux. Kuscinski, *Conventionnels*, pp. 55, 307–8.

17. R. Mols, *Introduction à la démographie historique d'Europe du XIVe au XVIIIe siècle*, 3 vols. (Gembloux, 1954–56) II: 514–16. Mols's account of the eighteenth-century French development of ports and industrial centers suggests, for these towns at least, a *bourgeoisie* rather less backward-looking than the one Cobban describes. Throughout the discussion below it might be of interest to remember that many of the "city deputies"

Kuscinski's information has been used to place deputies where they were more or less settled in 1789. If a man had spent his adult life in several places, choice has been made of the largest of these, provided he lived there for a considerable time, on the principle that this represents the broadest extension of his experience. Some men have been placed, failing other evidence, in the localities in which they were born and finally died. The moves arising from the dislocations or opportunities of the revolutionary years have been ignored; our concern is with the accumulated experience with which men entered the Revolution, rather than with the impact of highly abnormal circumstances. Half-a-dozen professional soldiers and sailors, the peripatetic Anacharsis Cloots who spent 1789 in Spain, and the Anglo-American Tom Paine have been omitted, because for professional or personal reasons they had failed to put down real roots in any French community. Otherwise the 1793 roll-call is complete.

The 749 deputies of January 1793 seem to have come from a total of at least 481 localities, as is shown in Table 29.

Table 29. Local origins of the deputies: Urban or rural

	No. of towns	No. of deputies
Very large towns— 15,000 inhabitants and upwards (33 of these *chefs-lieux* as well)	51	215
Chefs-lieux under 15,000 (mostly under 10,000) plus towns known to be of 10,000 or more	44	75
Other places	387	450
	481	740
Add deputies not assigned to localities		9
		749*

*For a detailed analysis see Appendix VI.

It would seem from the figures in Table 29 that the cities of France had a representation somewhat out of proportion to their share in the total population. Mols's estimates, at their most generous, provide for a combined population in his 52 such places of possibly two and one-half million, or about 10 percent of the population of France. But just on 30 percent of all the *conventionnels* were native or adopted sons of 51 of these cities. The number was

described came from such fast-growing towns. Concerning the size of "important" towns: Boston in 1776 had a population of about 16,000.

inflated by the inclusion of 54 Parisians, 20 sitting for Paris and 34 for other departments, but this only reflected the general trend; since Paris by herself had something approaching one-quarter of the total big-city population, she had approximately her fair share of the really urban deputies. When the *chefs-lieux* are added, it seems that France's more important towns supplied just about 40 percent of her parliamentary representation. Of the 52 cities listed by Mols, only one, Arles, did not have at least one representative and more than half had 3 or more. Of 56 other towns which became *chefs-lieux* in 1795, or had previously been chosen as interim capitals,[18] only 13 were unrepresented, and 20 had 2 or more deputies. The remaining 450 deputies in the analysis came from 387 different places, of which only 42 were represented more than once. At this point, however, we must make some slight reference to the extra impact of revolutionary political activity, and the extent to which it took men into environments markedly different from their own.

Among the men from large towns, departmental office is not a major consideration, since the *chef-lieu* was unlikely to be a place of significantly greater importance than the cities in which these deputies were already living. Parliamentary office was another matter; Paris was unlike anywhere else in France. Eighty of the men from cities, of whom 17 were Parisians, had sat in either the Constituent or the Legislative, and so had 34 of those from *chefs-lieux*. Of the 450 apparently more rural members, 168 had been deputies and 72 others had at least got as far as the department capital. Thus the 210 members, out of the Convention's 749, whose 1792 horizons had been limited in the main to the local scene were a solid minority, but they were a minority; more than 70 percent of the assembly in which they sat had by accident or design experienced environments rather more sophisticated.[19] It must also be added that most of the deputies from outside the cities and major towns either lived or worked in the solid market towns or traditional administrative centers with which France was so freely scattered. The future deputy isolated on his farm or estates or concerned only with village politics was extremely rare.

Nevertheless, local feeling was strong, and local rivalries were a factor contributing to the dispersal of political office among men from a number of widely spread local centers. The cities did not have things all their own way. Some accounts of the 1792 elections refer specifically to the care taken in arranging the electoral proceedings to balance the influence of all the districts, or to choose deputies so that all districts were represented and none need feel aggrieved.[20] In Seine-et-Marne, where there had been in 1789–90 a spirited and

18. List in J. H. Stewart, *A Documentary Survey of the French Revolution* (New York, 1951), pp. 139–41.
19. The 9 deputies not assigned to localities were all familiar with urban life, even if they were not settled anywhere in particular.
20. See, e.g., E. Lecesne, "L'élection des députés du Pas-de-Calais à la Convention," *Mémoires de l'académie des sciences, lettres et arts d'Arras, 2ᵉ série, VIII: 157;* L. Guillemaut, *La Révolution dans le Louhannais* (Louhans, 1903), p. 9.

complex battle over the (supposedly lucrative) location of the *chef-lieu*, the electors of 1792 returned their not very impressive collection of 11 deputies from 11 different localities.[21] Intense local rivalry tended to work against the interests of men from larger urban centers, whether because of local jealousies or from a desire to share offices out equally regardless of where those best qualified to hold them were likely to be found; and the electoral arrangements of 1792 gave these rivalries increased opportunity, since the elections were held by agreed rotation in the second town of the department and not in the *chef-lieu* as in 1791. Thus a major city which was also a *chef-lieu*, as 33 of the 52 were, had no chance of exerting direct influence on the elections.[22] The natural outcome was compromise. Smaller places were reasonably represented, although men from the merely village level were rare, but the numerical balance was toward the larger centers, perhaps both because of their economic and social importance and because of the greater political sophistication of their inhabitants. (In this respect, the record of the Bouches-du-Rhône election may be instructive.) Furthermore—and this cannot appear from bare totals, but only from a study of the political activity of the deputies—the men from really substantial towns were more influential as well as more numerous than they had any statistical right to be. If our 730 deputies are classified by place of origin as well as political sympathies, the result is shown in Table 30.

In this, with the really large towns we see the cumulative result of apparently slight discrepancies within the figures for other categories, and it looks as though there has been some force at work propelling men toward extremes. Both Mountain and Gironde are unexpectedly strong and both the *en mission* and the *à l'écart* groups unexpectedly weak. And within both Mountain and Gironde, the more definite the commitment, the higher the proportion of city-dwellers. The inclusion of 27 Parisians among the Montagnards of course raises the Montagnard urban total, but it should be noted that only 16 of these men were *elected* for Paris, and that among the 48 Parisians included in the whole analysis, 13 were Girondin; without them the Gironde too would have cut a poorer figure. With or without the Parisians, the Mountain got more than its share of city deputies, and so did the "inner sixty." The nucleus of the "inner sixty" in Vergniaud and his friends from Bordeaux and Brissot and his, largely from Paris, does not explain why the two groups should have found they had much in common, why other city deputies became involved with them (Barbaroux and Hardy, for example)—or why the Parisian delegation, composed entirely of city dwellers though not entirely of Parisians, should have found its Montagnard

21. Only 2 of the 11 members (Tellier, an ex-Constituent, and Bailly, a departmental official) had been in public life above the district level. For the 1789–90 struggle, see L. Barthoumeau, *La Formation du Département de Seine-et-Marne (1789–1790)* (Dijon, 1914), pp. 95–119.

22. Paris must of course be excluded from this judgment. Much naturally depended on whether the *chef-lieu* really was the most important center (e.g., Amiens) or merely the most conveniently placed (e.g., Cahors).

Table 30. Political sympathies, 1793–94,
and place of origin*

	Cities	Chefs-lieux not included under cities; and other towns of 10,000 +	Other places	Total
GIRONDE				
"Inner sixty"	28	7	23	58
Other	31	8	81 (3)	120 (3)
Total	59	15	104 (3)	178 (3)
PLAIN				
à l'écart	14	15	89	118
Committees	25	13	57	95
en mission	5	5	27	37
Total	44	33	168	250
MOUNTAIN				
Jacobins	61	18	64 (2)	142 (2)
Others	40	9	110 (4)	160 (4)
Total	101	27	174 (6)	302 (6)
Grand total	204	75	451 (9)	730 (9)
Excluded from political analysis	11	–	8	19
Convention total	215	75	459	749

*Figures in parentheses indicate deputies without a settled home in France. These have been included in the "other places" category to make clear the proportion of known city members in the total numbers of each political group.

majority working in association with men from other great towns, such as Duhem from Lille and Choudieu from Angers.

The political importance of the city deputies emerges in exaggerated focus if one looks at the background of the members of the great committees of the Terror. On the Committee of Public Safety, Hérault de Séchelles and Collot d'Herbois were native to Paris and Billaud-Varenne, born in La Rochelle and educated in Paris and Poitiers, had settled in Paris by 1789. Barère, with a legal career taking shape in Toulouse, had spent a year in Paris just before the revolution. Robespierre was a native and Carnot an adopted son of Arras, and Couthon had spent his life in Clermont-Ferrand. Prieur-Duvernois, born near Dijon, had, despite his career as an engineer officer, kept sufficiently in touch with Dijon politics to be president of its *société populaire* in the summer of 1791, just before his election to the Legislative.[23] All these places are among the 52 cities

23. L. Hugueney, *Les Clubs Dijonnais pendant la Révolution* (Dijon, 1905), p. 255.

in France.[24] Pierre-Louis Prieur was a lawyer from Châlons-sur-Marne, a departmental capital of considerable size and reputation, and Lindet and Jeanbon Saint-André came respectively from Bernay and Montauban, both important local centers; if it had not been for its geographical position, Montauban would probably have been *chef-lieu* of Lot, and in 1793 Bernay replaced Evreux for a time as *chef-lieu* of Eure. One only of the 12, Saint-Just from Blénancourt, was of comparatively rural origin, and even he had been educated in Soissons and Reims before his 1789 visit to Paris launched him into a wider world. The same point emerges, though not quite so dramatically, from the membership of the Committee of General Security. When this began to stabilize, at the end of October 1793, it contained 8 members from large cities, one from a *chef-lieu*, and 6 from other places; after Panis and Guffroy resigned, it had 7 city and 5 other members, plus Laloy from a *chef-lieu*.[25] The majority on the committee, like the greater committee almost in its entirety, represented in background and education not a cross-section of the widely dispersed French middle class, but rather various sections of that part of the middle class which was concentrated in France's largest centers of population.

A conclusion that the membership of the Convention was biased toward the growing cities rather than the towns and villages, and that active leadership came from the cities specifically rather than from towns generally, is not at all surprising. But it does raise further questions. The city deputies were more positive in their political attitudes than their colleagues; were they different in other ways as well?

III

If the deputies are classified according to occupation, and then divided into groups according to the places from which they came, the result is shown in Table 31.

Let us consider first the general occupational pattern in the Convention as a whole, as shown in the right-hand "total" column of Table 31.

The traditional spectacular number of lawyers is no myth. There they are, 357 of them; Thompson's 47 percent of the Convention[26] is almost exactly accurate. Of the 357, roughly 3 in every 8 would fall in Cobban's class of *officiers*.[27] This looks like a high proportion, but to determine whether the

24. But cf. R. R. Palmer, *Twelve Who Ruled* (Princeton, 1958), p. 17. "Except for Collot, who was born in Paris, and Hérault who lived there, these future rulers of France were all *provincials, used to small-town life*" (my italics). How small is a "small" town, and how large a "large" one?

25. See J. Guillaume, *Etudes Révolutionnaires, 2e série* (Paris, 1909), pp. 253–318 for the names; and also Appendix VI.

26. J. M. Thompson, *The French Revolution*, p. 312; though whether Thompson was talking about the Convention of 1792, or the whole body of deputies 1792–95, remains uncertain.

27. There were at least 21 notaries, 7 who had succeeded their fathers in a hereditary profession and 14 who had bought their practices or had them bought for them. The 1795 evidence suggests 1 or 2 more.

	Large cities	Chefs-lieux	Other places	Not classified (a) by origin	Not classified (b) politically	Total
Clergy[a]	19	7	29	–	–	55
Medicine	11	3	31	–	1	46
Army/Navy[b]	10	4	14	7	1	36
Business	19	4	43	–	1	67
Farming	2	–	36	–	–	38
Literary[c]	23	1	3	2	1	30
Academic	7	2	2	–	–	11
Artisan[d]	3	–	3	–	–	6
Clerk	3	–	–	–	–	3
Civil servant	10	5	36	–	–	51
Lawyer[e]						
(i) official post	32	19	94	–	7	152
(ii) private practice	57	28	116	–	4	205
Private means	3	1	5	–	2	11
Not known	5	1	30	–	2	38
Total	204	75	442	9	19	749

Notes on classification:

The occupations, save in a few cases where only 1789–92 information is available, are those of 1789. Official posts of revolutionary origin only have been ignored; the civil servants are those of 1789. If no occupation other than a revolutionary office is recorded, the deputy is classed as "not known." I should have liked to compare these findings with Cobban's much more expert handling of the same material (*Aspects of the French Revolution*, pp. 109–11), but could not do so, partly because he deals with the whole Convention without distinguishing original from later membership, partly because his approach to the lawyer/*officier* problem is different from mine, and partly because he seems to have mislaid 9 Protestant clergy, and it is not clear where he has put them; what I think is a slight error in his total does not account for this discrepancy. I have accepted Kuscinski's material as it stands, though from evidence in A.N. C353 C1838 (the statements of 1795) I think some amendments should be made; they probably would not affect the totals very much.

[a]*The clergy* include all men in orders in 1789, 46 Catholics and 9 Protestants, whether in parish work, in monasteries, chapters, etc., or teaching in church schools. Lay teachers in church schools have been entered as academics.

[b]*Army and navy* members include those on the retired list who had not adopted other occupations as well as those still serving or recalled because of the war. They do not include those who, like Laurenceot, were temporary volunteers, nor those like d'Aoust who resigned too early to be considered professionals.

[c]*The literary category* covers professional journalists, men of private means devoting themselves to letters, and a miscellany of other persons interested in the arts or learning, e.g., the artists David, Sergent, and Dulaure, the actor-manager Collot-d'Herbois, the chemist Guyton-Morveau.

[d]A division has been made between craftsmen and white-collar workers. There were few of either.

[e]The mass of *lawyers* has been summarily divided between those who had some sort of property in the law and those who had not. Category (i) includes those with ownership of official posts, and also notaries; category (ii) all the others. This might be further subdivided into *avocats au parlement*, other *avocats*, and other lawyers, and also to indicate those with substantial private means; but it seemed better to avoid a too minute and possibly meaningless complication. The simple *hommes de loi* were few, and so were the notaries. One anomaly is the inclusion of 4 *procureurs* in category (ii); they have been left there because this post seemed their sole source of income, and there was nothing quite like them in category (i) or among the civil servants. All the posts held by men in category (i) were bought, inherited, or acquired by patronage. The civil servant and *officier* categories probably overlap.

officier brand of lawyer was exceptionally interested in politics it would be necessary to undertake a detailed statistical survey of the whole eighteenth-century French legal profession—a daunting task. The ordinary *avocat* or *homme de loi* (Kuscinski uses both terms; the basis of the distinction is not always clear in a formal sense) was numerous, and so were the *avocats au parlement.* These were all professional lawyers to at least a considerable degree, not men whose qualifications, once earned, were no longer used; there were such men in the Convention, but they have not been reckoned as lawyers. The legal deputies ranged from Cambor-Borie, practising in a modest way in Sarlat in Dordogne, through Méaulle whose integrity had made him greatly respected in Chateaubriant, and old Rudel who at 73 had been 5 times mayor of Thiers, to Jean Mailhe, an *avocat au parlement* with an enviable Toulouse reputation. There were scholarship boys like the Robespierre brothers; there were brilliant intellects like Rouzet, the Toulouse tailor's son who became a teacher of law, and Vigneron, aged 42, who had been for nearly twenty years among the most distinguished *avocats* in Vesoul. Why were there so many of them? If it is argued that "the *officiers* and the men of the liberal professions" composed the "revolutionary bourgeoisie," then it should follow from these figures that, of middle-class Frenchmen actively interested in revolutionary politics, nearly every other man was a lawyer. Perhaps it may be enlightening to look later at one of the electorates which sent such men to Paris.

The rest of the Convention is indeed very largely composed of members of the "liberal professions," the clergy, oddly enough, being the most numerous. Among the 55 clerics there were, in addition to the 9 Protestants, 16 constitutional bishops. The next largest group of professional men, that of the 51 civil servants, serves as a reminder of what looks like a real change of balance between the Third Estate of 1789 and the Convention of 1792. The Convention was more varied in composition, less dominated by the bureaucratic legal element, than the Third Estate had been. The Third Estate had had 278 deputies in some sort of government office, many of whom must have been lawyers, and 166 lawyers in private practice, a total of 444 members out of 648, or nearly 69 percent.[28] The Convention, with a hundred more members, had a total of 357 lawyers, plus the 51 civil servants—408 in all, or under 55 percent. But the Third Estate reputedly contained only 31 representatives of all liberal professions outside the law and civil service. The Convention had a very solid medical contingent, plus a respectable number from the armed services and the world of letters. As a cross-section of the French intelligentsia, it was an improvement on the Third Estate; if its social composition was very much the same, its professional outlook was very much broader.

In view of the demands made on the Convention between 1792 and 1795, this change in composition, limited though it was, was potentially a great source of strength. The work of the Constituent Assembly had been primarily one of

28. These figures from R. R. Palmer, *The Age of the Democratic Revolution*, 2 vols. (Princeton, 1959–64), I: 478; I have not been able to check them.

constitutional and administrative reorganization, in which the skills of lawyers and bureaucrats would be much to the point. But if the Convention had not been able to establish the sovereign authority of the new Republic, to defeat its internal and external enemies, to keep it afloat through financial and economic crisis and in addition create an ad hoc administrative machine through which the necessary policies could be executed, any constitution it might have found time to draw up would hardly have had a chance to operate. To make a constitution (or two or three) it needed legal and philosophic expertise; to do all its other work it needed expertise in many other fields. It was the Republic's good fortune that so much was forthcoming. Dubois-Crancé's long report on the reorganization of the army, Kersaint's on the navy, are reminders that the Convention's professional soldiers and sailors had useful abilities. (The 31 soldiers included 5 engineers and a very experienced cartographer who established a most valuable collection of military maps.)[29] To see to supplies of wood and charcoal for Paris, there were a wood merchant, a forestry officer, and a man from the river-carrying trade; for advice on gun-founding, a large-scale ironmaster from Dampierre; for service on the Roads and Bridges Committee, a highway and canal engineer; to draw up the regulations on supply contracts, an official from the Navy Office; and so down a lengthy list. A doctor put in a report on the education of deaf-mutes, a mathematics professor reported on the new system of weights and measures and on the composition of elementary textbooks. The Convention harbored Guyton-Morveau, one of the most eminent chemists in France, whose interest in balloons led to the establishment of the first military balloon squadron in history and to his own personal attendance (in a balloon) at the battle of Fleurus.[30] And the lawyers did more than put the endless stream of decrees into presentable shape, or even organize the production of the paper to print them on. They were perhaps living proof of the general usefulness of the trained intelligence; as administrators of government policy they were versatile and ubiquitous. But their colleagues were as willing as they, and every major occupational category was represented *en mission* in roughly equal proportion. Between 1792 and the end of 1795, 405 of the original 749 *conventionnels* went to the provinces, and with one minor exception this massive levy fell equally right across the board; though it was possible to refuse a mission, surprisingly few men did.[31]

In carrying out their many jobs, the deputies were probably more effective because, no matter what their original background, so few of them were new to public responsibility. As we have already seen, 6 out of 7 had held some elective office, and one-third of the remainder had at least been conspicuously active in

29. *Moniteur* XV: 281–83; 22–6, for Dubois-Crancé and Kersaint; Kuscinski, *Conventionnels*, p. 100, for the cartographer, Calon.
30. This interest was shared by Second, who claimed to have found a method of steering balloons; but the claim was not substantiated. Kuscinski, *Conventionnels*, pp. 322–23, 560.
31. The figures were: clergy 31, medicine 26, army/navy 22, business 34, literary 8 (perhaps because a number of these men were journalists), academic 5, artisan 3, clerk 3, civil service 33, lawyer (i) 74 (ii) 121 (total 195), private means 8, not known 18.

club affairs or journalism. The average level of experience was high, and with the exception of the artisans and clerks (9 in all), every occupational group contained both ex-deputies and local officials, indeed 7 of the 12 had members from every level of government.[32] Despite their enormous numbers, the lawyers had extraordinarily few novices. Out of 357 lawyers a mere 18 were entirely new to public life, and only 7 of the remaining 339 had not held some sort of official post. It seems possible that the predominance of lawyers among deputies may have been but one reflection of their leading role in public affairs generally.

The Convention's weakness, in the eyes of some historians, lay not so much in inexperience or incapacity as in the narrow range of comprehension and sympathy to which it was restricted because its members were overwhelmingly professional in background and hence (by inference) in outlook.[33] Jaurès pointed out with concern the small number both of businessmen, which he found hard to understand, and *sans-culottes*, which was predictable in a middle-class assembly, but nevertheless unfortunate. The absence of commercial and industrial representatives meant, allegedly, that debates had a strong theoretical bias and those taking part in them had too little grasp of the practical consequences of the policies they were trying to formulate. Cobban sees this situation as a natural one, in that it was the professional men and not the commercial and industrial classes who were interested in the revolution and would therefore presumably dominate the parliamentary assembly, whose composition he sees as circumstantial evidence of this theory about the nature of the revolutionary *bourgeoisie*. There are thus several questions involved: the size of the nonprofessional groups in the Convention, whether or not these fairly reflect the amount of interest felt by their fellows in revolutionary politics, and whether it is necessary to conclude from the occupational background of the deputies any particular bias in practical problems of government.

From the figures, the deputies who were not *officiers* or lawyers or otherwise of the "liberal professions" were indeed a small minority; of the 694 *conventionnels* (among our 730) with known vocations, fewer than 1 in 5 had been engaged in agriculture, commerce, or industry. The disproportion is so striking that it is tempting to accept at once Cobban's conclusion that Frenchmen of this sort were simply not interested, except very indirectly, in revolutionary politics. At this point, however, it may be useful to turn from the "totals" column in the occupational table to a more detailed analysis.

IV

The dominant force in the Convention was the great mass of lawyers, so large in comparison with any other element that it was bound to establish the

32. There are altogether 14 categories listed, but the last 2—"private means" and "not known"—are of course not occupational in the ordinary sense. For the figures on deputies' experience in relation to their occupational background, see Appendix VI.

33. See, e.g., J. Jaurès, *Histoire socialiste*, IV: 300–2; J. M. Thompson, *The French Revolution*, pp. 312, 318–19; R. R. Palmer, *Twelve Who Ruled*, p. 17.

general "set" among the deputies unless counterbalanced by a very strong opposing trend in the rest of the membership. If we look to see where the deputies came from, we find that close to three-fifths of the lawyers, and about three-fifths of the whole body, came from outside the cities and important towns. Among the nonlegal deputies the distribution sometimes favored the larger centers, but it was very uneven and was pulled back toward the lawyers' average by the inevitable rural origin of the landowning/farming element. Though the lawyers carried a good deal of weight in the smaller places, they were proportionately most numerous as representatives of the *chefs-lieux*. The men from the really big cities were more varied; here were more doctors, more academics, and two-thirds of the Convention's tiny group of craftsmen and clerks. Men of letters were conspicuously urbanized, in fact two-thirds of their *conventionnels* had settled in Paris before 1789.[34] Only the cities had representatives from every occupational category. But when one looks at their figures, bearing in mind that these concentrations of 15,000 and more people had in most cases been expanding rapidly for two generations or more, a major puzzle presents itself: the apparently very limited political enthusiasm of members of the business community. Certainly more than one in four of the commercial and industrial deputies came from the cities; but nearly two-thirds came from small population centers, a figure above the Convention average, where one might have expected it to be below. For good or ill, it might have been assumed that the great cities would be both more politically aware and more conscious of their stake in politics than the smaller places, and the general pattern of membership suggests that this was the case, but one group of those most deeply involved in urban prosperity was content to leave politics very largely to others. The business classes' urban deputies, such as they were, were drawn mainly from the largest cities in France (25,000 inhabitants and upward) from which 14 of the 19 came, but most of the largest industrial centers and some of the most important ports had no members at all in the Convention who were directly concerned with their economic problems. Arras, Brest, Caen, Dieppe, Dijon, Lyon, Reims, Rouen, Toulouse, Troyes, even Montauban all had citizens as deputies, but these men did not come from their business communities: that is, unless one includes Armonville from Reims and Cusset from Lyon, both of whom were certainly connected with the textile trade. But both were artisans rather than businessmen in any larger sense.

In itself, the commercial and industrial membership of the Convention covered quite a broad spectrum. It may be divided into rough categories as shown in Table 32.

They were well scattered all over France. As it stands, the list is not such a bad sample of France's men of commerce, considering its brevity, and the

34. Only 4 of the 19 had been born there. Apparently Paris was more important as a magnet for intellectual activity than as an originating force.

Table 32. The commercial and industrial representatives

i) Transport and communications		
River-carrying trade	1	
Innkeeper/postmaster	1	
Postmaster	2	
Sea captain (retired)	2	
Shipowner	1	7
ii) Small business[a]		
Sale of combs and garters	1	
Butcher	1	
Corset-maker	1	
Draper and grocer	1	
Pharmacist	3	
Tanner	1	
Watchmaker	1	
Mercer	1	10
iii) Mercantile		
Furniture	1	
Groceries	1	
Spirits and salt	1	
Oil and grain[b]	1	
Slates	1	
Timber	1	
Wine	2	
Textiles (distribution)[c]	8	
Merchant, *négociant*, "in trade" unspecified[d]	22	38
iv) Industry		
Ironmaster	2	
Cask-maker	1	
Printer[e]	2	
Textiles (manufacturing)	3	
Unspecified (St. Etienne area)	1	9
v) Miscellaneous		
Mineral waters and mud baths (also owned a shop elsewhere)	1	
Public works contractor	1	
Industrial engineer (glass works)	1	3
		67

[a]The distribution between this and the next category is arbitrary and may be unjustified. One pharmacist, Opoix, was a learned man, and the tanner, Vermon, may have had a legal education (he became an imperial judge) as the mercer Thomas certainly did. (Kuscinski, *Conventionnels*, pp. 470, 603, 586). But all these people either came from small places or have a small "feel"—a purely subjective decision.

[b]Isnard, who also had manufacturing interests in silk and soap (ibid., p. 337).

[c]Unless a manufacturing interest is specified, those in the cloth trade have been left on the distribution side. The balance may need adjustment therefor.

[d]At least 10 of these came, like Isnard, from merchant families.

[e]Devérité seems to have been well off, and Vidalin knew enough about his trade to take responsibility for supervising the production of *assignats*. They have therefore been removed from category (ii). Kuscinski, ibid., pp. 206, 605.

perhaps rather numerous clothiers at least came from north, south, east, and west. But the puzzle of low numbers remains. Even allowing that it was the peculiar character of the Parisian elections in 1792 which caused the commerce of the capital to be represented by a mercer and a butcher, the fact remains that with the exceptions of Boscary and Monneron, *négociants*, one elected seventeenth and the other twenty-fourth out of 24, men of business do not seem to have been elected for Paris in 1791 either.[35] Why? Why was Bordeaux the only city in France to send as many as 3 merchants to Paris in September 1792? Why, when Poitiers had 6 citizens elected, were 5 of them lawyers and not one in trade? Why were both Le Havre's members lawyers, when in 1789 the electoral assembly of the Le Havre Third Estate had thought the merchants' *cahier* so important that it was reproduced in full? [36] And why—this seems strange indeed—were there proportionately fewer men of business elected in 1792 than in 1789? In 1789 there had been 85 among 648 deputies, yet the Convention could muster but 67 among 749.

As a move toward tentative explanation, we may consider what was required of a French revolutionary deputy. To accept election in 1789 had been to accept a responsibility which turned out to be far heavier and more prolonged than anyone had bargained for. France had no precedent for a legislative body which sat for more than two years without a break of any kind. No provision was made for the payment of members until 12 August 1789, when it was recognized that the job would not be finished quickly and that men might already have suffered a very burdensome absence from their ordinary occupations. The pay, substantial without being extravagant (it was a little more than that allowed in 1790 to a Paris *curé*)[37] was backdated to the end of April to cover the cost of the journey to Paris. By 1792 politics had ceased to be a highly unusual public duty and had become a career. Burke's reaction to the payment of members had been a sour prediction that this would attract the riffraff of the population seeking notoriety and an easy income.[38] Whatever the motives of the *conventionnels*—and Kuscinski does suggest that one at least owed his seat to the electors' momentary sympathy for his poverty and large family[39]—after the drafting of the 1791 constitution and the experiences of the Constituent they knew that they might have to accept a substantial interruption to their usual

35. Departmental list in Kuscinski, *Législative*, pp. 83–85; some detail on Pastoret, Cerutti, Gouvion, Quatremère, and Jean de Bry in *Biographie des Contemporains*, s.v. Thorillon and Treilh-Pardailhan I cannot find, but it does not seem very likely, given the character of the rest of the delegation, that they were in trade either.

36. N. Hampson, *Social History*, p. 62.

37. The Paris *curé*, like the Paris first episcopal vicar, was to be paid 6,000 livres a year. Deputies got 18 *livres* a day (6,570 *livres* p.a.) plus modest traveling allowances if *en mission* and, under the Convention, the uniform of a Representative of the People designed by David.

38. E. Burke, *Reflections on the Revolution in France* (London, 1910), p. 174.

39. Kuscinski, *Conventionnels*, p. 220; see also E. de Rouge, *Le conventionnel André Dumont* (Paris, 1911), p. 36, and the discussion of the Somme elections above, pp. 177–78.

way of life, and it seems fair to conclude that this in itself might narrow the possible range of candidates. Lawyers, traditionally prominent in the civil service, could after the session move into the new bureaucracy or the new judiciary, or they could hope to revive the practices temporarily forsaken. Civil servants could return to their former posts or find others of a like kind. Among the clergy of the Convention, a large number were to leave the priesthood or ministry before the session was over, an indication that a break with the past would not be too difficult. Men with business interests were more vulnerable. Most must have left someone else—a wife, a son, a relative—to manage their concerns. In Loiseau's case, at least, the responsibility was said to have been too heavy for the son who was left to carry it.[40] When Bidault was called up as a *suppléant*, in September 1793, he asked for a month's grace to try to put his affairs in order. He was lucky enough to have as a fellow townsman Robert Lindet, who recognized the public value of a firm employing many workers as well as supplying fabric for the army and used his influence with the Committee of Public Safety to get a manager appointed.[41] Such fortune could not be taken for granted, and simple self-interest, combined with the grave economic problems of the revolutionary years, may well have deterred many men from a parliamentary career. The bigger the business the harder to leave, and the less the attraction of a parliamentary salary.

This is speculation and there is no test that seems applicable. But it is enlightening to see what the *conventionnels* who sat on through 1793 did after their terms of parliamentary office were over. One hundred and twenty of them, for reasons sometimes but not always political, did not live long enough to have to decide; most of these died before the end of 1795, nearly all the rest during a further term in the legislature of the Directory, and the remaining few under the Consulate. More than two hundred of those who did survive their parliamentary careers then returned to private life without securing other government employment. This leaves just over four hundred men elected in 1792 who became public servants after they ceased to be deputies; 30 of these died between 1795 and 1805, and 307 of those remaining became in due course Napoleonic officials of one kind or another.

Even for politically discredited deputies, it was not too difficult to go into the public service, provided the disgrace was not extreme;[42] but the different occupational groups had very different proportions of men who ended in such

40. The business was that of innkeeper and postmaster. The too heavy responsibility may have been that of 7 sisters (Kuscinski, *Conventionnels*, p. 414). Putting in a substitute was only mandatory if the businesses were one's own; e.g., Boyer-Fonfrède came of a merchant family and Ducos was apparently still learning his job, so their worries were presumably fewer. But certainly some and probably most merchants in the Convention were less lucky than these 2, and all were older.

41. Kuscinski, *Conventionnels*, pp. 55–56.

42. For example Voulland and Dupin, both under decree of arrest in 1795, were both later appointed to official posts: Kuscinski, *Conventionnels*, pp. 610, 227.

posts. Of those surviving in 1795, two-thirds of the farmers went straight back to their properties, and about half the businessmen and the soldiers and sailors also resumed their earlier careers. But more than 70 percent of the lawyers became civil servants, with a large number going on to serve the Empire. For some reason, private life seems to have had less strong a backward pull on lawyers; and of course government service might have purely professional attractions—judgeships, for example. A legal career was not in itself difficult to resume, as Robert Lindet's example shows, but for lawyers more than for other deputies, parliamentary office and revolutionary or imperial public service might well seem merely variations on an old and familiar theme.[43] For what they are worth, the relevant figures are shown in Table 33.

Table 33. Deputies: Career after end of parliamentary term

	Died during or just after parlty. term	Govt. to 1805 or earlier	Place under Empire*	Total	Retired to priv. life	Total
Clergy	7	7	27	34	14	55
Medicine	6	9	14	23	16	45
Army/Navy	7	4	11	15	13	35
Business	16	6	19	25	25	66
Farming	7	4	7	11	20	38
Literary	9	4	8	12	8	29
Academic	3	1	4	5	3	11
Artisan	1	–	3	3	2	6
Clerk	–	–	3	3	–	3
Civil Service	7	6	26	32	12	51
Lawyers						
(i) official post	24	22	68	90	31	145
(ii) private						
practice	25	26	103	129	47	201
Private means	1	4	1	5	3	9
Not known	7	6	13	19	10	36
Total	120	99	307	406	204	730

*More detailed figures, including those for the deputies not politically classified, will be found in Appendix VI, together with a comment on the numbers of regicides and antiregicides who accepted Napoleonic office.

Table 33 makes no allowance for the considerable number of men who had already accepted paid office in government before September 1792. It will be seen that not quite one-quarter of those who held posts after 1795 did not serve the Empire. (Several men who died in 1805 have been left as imperial officials, as they were continuing in the jobs they already occupied and had apparently no thought of leaving.) But a very considerable majority, having opted for office, stayed on, though not necessarily in the same job; a large number of *conventionnels* changed their posts, perhaps several times, between the 1790s and 1814. Some of the judges were superannuated in the reorganization carried out in 1811.

43. Of the 25 businessmen who took government jobs, 3 certainly could not go back to life as before; for various reasons, the businesses owned by Douge, Haussmann and Lesage-Sénault had all collapsed (Kuscinski, *Conventionnels*, pp. 209, 326, 403). What others had to return to is not clear.

Neither the large legal element in the Convention nor its continued interest in public administration need be surprising. Even if opposition to the Crown before 1789 had not been centered in the *parlements*, who but lawyers should be most concerned and active in making and applying the law? Its implications are a different matter. It would be possible to assume, for example, that lawyers were so conspicuous among the leaders of the revolutionary movement *because* the revolutionary movement was so largely made up of lawyers, and here the composition of the Convention might be used, in Cobban's manner, as a telling piece of evidence.[44] Alternatively, one might argue that *because* lawyers were willing to become actively and continuously involved in public life, they offered themselves as convenient and, in view of their profession, suitable representatives for other persons no less interested in the revolution and its outcome, but less inclined toward a full-time and possibly permanent public career. Neither contention can be very easily tested, yet one needs to consider the matter, since even a very tentative conclusion would be relevant to the question of how far the deputies, being drawn so largely from one section of society, were cut off from the feelings and preferences of Frenchmen in general.

One rather crude check on the possible validity of either hypothesis might be carried out by looking at a departmental delegation with a very large proportion of lawyers, to see what sort of revolutionary movement is to be found in the community which elected it: whether there was on the one hand a movement in which lawyers and their grievances and ambitions played a dominating part, or on the other hand a movement largely influenced by nonlawyers which nevertheless allowed the election of a mainly legal group of deputies.

In 1792 the department of Lot chose perhaps the most "legal" delegation in the whole Convention: 6 *officiers*, 2 other lawyers, a doctor, and the Protestant pastor Jeanbon Saint-André—a delegation ready-made for Cobban's theory. And an examination of the situation in Lot seems to see the theory confirmed. In Lot, the outcome of the first 3 revolutionary years was a sharp decline in the relative position of Montauban, its largest (and only industrial) town, in favor of the far smaller center of Cahors; and those who apparently profited from this and played a large part in departmental politics were lawyers from outside Montauban. A lawyers' revolution, one might say, lay behind the choice of a "legal" delegation.

Yet the picture is not after all so simple. For a closer analysis reveals that it was Montauban, not Cahors, which in fact housed the department's most active revolutionaries, that Montauban's revolutionaries were both prominent and influential during the 1792 elections, and that their movement was squarely based on the social grievances of the predominantly Protestant *merchants and industrialists* of the town, with some support from Protestant workmen. The

44. Cobban, *Social Interpretation*, p. 61.

Convention elections were held under the very eyes of the Montauban revolutionaries, who took a considerable and at one point a decisive interest in their progress; but the character of the Montauban revolution cannot in any way be deduced from a mere inspection of the delegation selected. (The only Montaubanais to get a seat was Jeanbon himself.) The merchants secured no direct representation whatever, but they were nevertheless deeply involved in the revolutionary struggle from the outset, and a recent book relates the shifts in the balance of political authority in their town to conflicts between social groups with well-defined political attitudes; lawyers were no doubt concerned in these struggles, but nowhere do they appear as a significant *separate* group forwarding the Revolution.[45]

It is not easy, in Lot at least, to establish any consistent connection between the professional background of the deputies and that of the revolutionaries who interested themselves in the election. To generalize on this subject, it would be necessary to examine the social character of the revolutionary movement, and its relation to the choice of parliamentary representatives, department by department. An inquiry of this sort seems called for in Vendée, where a delegation of 6 lawyers, a constitutional cleric, a shipowner, a stock-jobber and one man of unknown background does not seem to reflect very well the multiple hostilities between town and *bocage* which according to Tilly were integral to the revolution in the northern part of the department; the clothiers especially do not appear at all; and the situation in the Maine-et-Loire delegation was similar.[46] Whatever one may conclude from analyzing the social composition of the Convention, one should be very wary of treating it as a sort of sample or cross-section of the membership of the revolutionary movement at large.

To return for a moment to the lawyers who formed so large a part of the Convention: another kind of difficulty is inherent in the designation of "lawyers" or even *officiers* as a separate *social* group. Apart from the immense variety within the profession, admitted by all historians, there is the larger problem of the relationship of the legal profession, or any other profession, to the community in which it operates. Lawyers were not a separate caste in eighteenth-century France. Many did come of legal families; Kuscinski refers to Jacques Forest as coming from a family of magistrates known in Roanne since the sixteenth century, and to the fact that the profession of notary had been hereditary in Gamon's family for two hundred years.[47] But in a society offering

45. For the fascinating development of the revolution in Montauban, L. Lévy-Schneider, *Jeanbon Saint-André*, and at greater length, D. Ligou, *Montauban à la fin de l'ancien régime et au début de la Révolution* (Paris, 1958). For the classic-type rural revolution in Lot, J. Viguier, "Les émeutes populaires dans le Quercy, en 1789 et 1790," *La Révolution française* XXI (1891); see also E. Sol, *La Révolution en Quercy* 4 vols. (Paris, 1929–32) vols. I–II esp. For the 1792 elections, A.N. C 179 C II 44 (Lot), 5–9 Sept. especially.

46. C. Tilly, *The Vendée* (Cambridge, Mass., 1964), passim.

47. *Conventionnels*, pp. 260, 277.

as many opportunities to the ambitious lawyer as the France of the *ancien régime* seemed to do, other parents might decide to put a boy to law. Among the total 357 lawyers of the Convention, Kuscinski gives the family background of 151, or about 42 percent, 64 *officiers* and 87 others. Seventy of the 151 had fathers who were not lawyers, and the range of paternal occupations was quite wide: doctor, soldier, merchant, *"bourgeois"* unspecified, cooper, coppersmith, eating-house proprietor. The family background of such men can hardly be disregarded altogether.[48] Then, on the purely professional side, there is the type of practice which each man established and the point of view he was accustomed to present. Bézard, as we have seen, had a country lawyer's practice in Oise. Dautriche had a rich revenue from the nobles and clergy of Charente-Inférieure. It is probably far too simple to see here much of the reason for Bézard's later joining the Mountain and Dautriche's the deputies *à l'écart*, but there may be something of a connection; the clue seems worth following up at least. Boilleau had a great local reputation in Yonne because he had secured the acquittal of a man accused of sacrilege; this tells us something both about Yonne and about Boilleau himself, who ended as one of the rare Girondin regicides. Jean Allafort was *avocat consultant* to the local farming population near Montion in Dordogne; it is hard to imagine his functioning as a deputy in complete indifference to their point of view, or their expecting him to do such a thing.[49] One could continue like this indefinitely. What sort of professional acquaintance was enjoyed in Bordeaux by Grangeneuve, one of the busiest barristers in the city, Gensonné, at 34 already high on the ladder, and Guadet, as renowned for his resourcefulness as for his legal knowledge? A number of their more important constituents may well have employed these men professionally. How far did such experience influence their preference for them as deputies? [50]

On this more personal level, a final question may be raised. In the Convention were 152 *officiers*, members of a professional group which according to Cobban, was drawn toward revolution because of its declining social and economic status.[51] Many of these *conventionnels* were obscure, but some were

48. The figures are:

	Officiers	*Practice only*	*Total*
Fathers lawyers	38	43	81
non-lawyers	26	44	70
Background unknown	88	118	206
Total	152	205	357

The higher proportion of *officiers* among the men of legal family seems probable enough.

49. Kuscinski, *Conventionnels*, p. 55 (Bézard), pp. 179–80 (Dautriche), p. 63 (Boilleau), p. 4 (Allafort).

50. On Grangeneuve, Gensonné, and Guadet, Kuscinski, *Conventionnels*, pp. 307, 289, 312. One might also consider the mixed environment of the many lawyers, like Jac, who owned much landed estate; ibid., p. 342.

51. This may be an unfair summary of his argument; but unless the range of men included as *officiers* is kept fairly wide, there are not enough of them in the Convention to be worth discussing. See however Cobban, *Social Interpretation*, pp. 59–60, 61.

very well-known revolutionaries indeed. It may be asked whether there was any apparent connection between their position and their activity as revolutionaries.

Fifty-five of the Convention's 152 *officiers* had bought or otherwise acquired their posts in 1780 or later, 13 of them, including Danton and Buzot, since the beginning of 1786. If their revolutionary feelings were inspired by the declining or disappointing status of the caste they had so recently joined, these feelings must have developed very rapidly, since 19 of the 55 sat in the Constituent and another dozen in the Legislative, and all but 2 of the rest were actively involved in revolutionary public affairs before 1792 at some lower level. Consider the 2 men mentioned above. In October 1786 Buzot was appointed *conseiller au bailliage et siège présidial*, Evreux. Less than three years later he was sitting on the extreme left in the Constituent, but the connection between his revolutionary opinions and the disillusionments resulting from his post as *conseiller* (if there were any) has yet to be established. In June 1787 Danton invested 78,000 *livres*, mostly if not entirely borrowed, in the post of *avocat au conseil du roi*. Though Lefebvre's careful calculations imply that Kuscinski may have over-estimated the return from this office, it seems likely that it may have brought in a substantial income, and highly improbable that it had much to do with the revolutionary views Danton began to display in July 1789.[52] The *officiers* of the 1780's included Choudieu and those of earlier years included Lindet, Kervélégan, Carrier, Cambacérès, Pétion, J. F. M. Goupilleau, the inflexibly scrupulous Noël, and Guyardin, who owed his *suppléant's* place in the Constituent to his reputation for integrity: in none of these instances does one find any suggestion that experiences as an *officier*, as such, were a source of resentment. The range of age was as broad as the range of office: in 1789 André Dumont was 24, perhaps too young to judge the value of the judicial post he had bought the previous year, and old Laboissière was 60, having held his office in the Agen *présidial* for more than 30 years. On a brief inspection, all that can be said about the importance of the *conventionnels'* status as *officiers* in deciding their political attitude is that the relationship is not obvious, and that for the best known among them no such relationship has yet been suggested by biographers. This is something which detailed biographical research may well establish, but which at present, for the Convention at least, can hardly be said to be proved.

To conclude a somewhat tedious and over-elaborate discussion: Cobban's thesis about the composition of the "revolutionary bourgeoisie" is buttressed only incidentally by reference to the revolutionary assemblies, and cannot be refuted merely by an analysis of the *conventionnels* and their background. Nevertheless, such an analysis is relevant to his argument, just as the problem of

52. See Kuscinski, *Conventionnels*, p. 96 (Buzot), and cf. ibid., p. 168, with G. Lefebvre, *Etudes sur la Révolution française* (Paris, 1954), pp. 32–33 and further. Danton's financial position, in which his investment in legal office was only one of the complications, may have laid him open to bribery as Lefebvre seems to believe, but he was not bribed to be a revolutionary any more than in 1793 he was bribed to be a regicide.

the "revolutionary bourgeoisie," which he has raised, is central to any theory about the motivating forces of revolutionary politics. Even so superficial an examination of the legal members of the Convention as this one has been suggests that a good deal of further research is called for. There let us leave the lawyers, and move on to less obtrusive groups.

V

As far as can be generally gathered from Kuscinski, the background of most of the rest of the *conventionnels* was much the same, in the social sense, as that of the lawyers: mostly middle-class, sometimes aristocratic, occasionally petty bourgeois, very occasionally moving to the fringes of the artisan/shopkeeper *sans-culotterie*.[53] For example, among the men of letters, who varied quite widely in income level and security, Tom Paine was the only man who had not had parents in sufficiently comfortable circumstances to provide him with a sound education of the eighteenth-century *collège* type.[54] Those deputies who, like Paine, had come up from below, seldom owed quite as much as he did to their own effort. A number of men from modest or accidentally impoverished homes had risen by attracting the patronage they needed from the local *curé*, from school authorities, from a philanthropic aristocrat or well-to-do bourgeois, or perhaps simply from relatives or friends. (Vergniaud was helped by his brother-in-law, Tallien by his father's employer the Comte de Bercy, Dupuis by the Duc de Rochefoucauld, Cassanyès by the *curé* of Canet.) The way up for a boy with brains but little money was most commonly through the church or the law, but paths to other careers remained open; Cassanyès, intended for the church, became a doctor, Brissot was encouraged into journalism by one of the friends concerned with his legal education, and four of the Convention's eleven academics were poor boys who had got the patronage they needed from the church without feeling obliged to take orders. More generally, too, there was a good deal of freedom in the choice of occupation. A surgeon's son might go to the bar, a boy intended by his family for the army or the church might take to medicine, and merchants might send their sons into any of the professions— indeed here was the biggest direct link between the world of commerce and that of the liberal professions. On the basis of our limited sample, it was much less common for sons of professional families to go into commerce, but this did happen too.[55] This variety in personal origins among members of any one

53. These comments are based on the information given by Kuscinski about family background, which covers about 40 percent of each of the occupational groups. The pattern is similar throughout.

54. For Paine, A. Aldridge, *Man of Reason* (London, 1960), pp. 14–15. Sergent, Collot d'Herbois, J. B. Louvet are samples of the rest; Kuscinski, *Conventionnels*, pp. 560, 145, 417, also p. 474 (Paine).

55. Ribet, described as ship-owner and *négociant* in Cherbourg, as well as an office-holder, was the son of a *conseiller du roi*, and Dubusc, a cloth manufacturer, was a doctor's son (Kuscinski, *Conventionnels*, pp. 524, 217).

occupational group meant that large numbers of deputies had some personal or family contact with interests and occupations different from their own, and that many professional men had family connections with the world of commerce quite apart from any links with it that they might develop from their own enterprise or the ordinary practice of their professions.

The Catholic clergy whose background is given by Kuscinski, 23 in all, or exactly half of the total of 46, exemplify in their own limited group the generally *bourgeois* character and the range of origins which was typical of most of the *conventionnels*, as well as the chances for advancement in social standing which had been both necessary and available for some of them. Seventeen of these clerics were of conventional, if varied, middle-class families; son of a cavalry lieutenant, son of a *marchand parcheminier*, 2 doctors' sons, 2 surgeons' sons,"of old bourgeois family" . . . etc. Two may have come from rather lower in the social scale; Châles was the son of a master-joiner in Chartres, and Chabot's father was a cook at the Rodez *collège* (but his godfather, François Rouquaymal, was a *notaire royal*, and anyhow his father was able to give him a good education). To balance these more fortunate 19, there were 4 from much humbler homes; Grégoire, son of a poor tailor, and Roux, son of a schoolmaster, both attracted clerical patronage, Audrein had parents *"peu aisés"* who nevertheless managed to educate him far enough for him to take orders, and Guiter, the seventh child of a poor family, apparently made his own way with some success—before 1789 he had become vicar of the cathedral church in Perpignan.[56] The eight Huguenots and one Lutheran who, with another 23 Catholics of unstated parentage, made up the clerical contingent, also seem to have been a solid *bourgeois* group. Like their Catholic colleagues, they were a little older than the Convention's average; only 2 of the 9 were under 40 and 5 were over 45.[57]

Of the 46 Catholics, 16 had been elected in 1791 to constitutional bishoprics. Three (Pocholle, Chabot, and Guiter) had effectively abandoned the priesthood by the time the Convention assembled, and 9 others were by that time more involved in public than in ecclesiastical affairs. Those who had been actively engaged in the establishment of the constitutional church provide an interesting sidelight on the sources from which its clergy were recruited. Two of the bishops, Fauchet and Grégoire, had made some stir in educated circles by their publications before 1789, and Fauchet's radicalism had cost him a prestigious post—though he did later acquire the wealthy abbey of Montfort in Brittany.[58] Lindet, Gay-Vernon, Huguet, Marbos, Royer, and Thibault, like Grégoire, went to their sees from country parishes. The rest of the bishops

56. Kuscinski, *Conventionnels*, p. 125 (Châles), p. 121 (Chabot), p. 308 (Grégoire), p. 537 (Roux), p. 13 (Audrein), and p. 319 (Guiter).
57. The figures for the Catholics are: Under 30, 1; under 40, 15, or almost exactly one-third (the Convention figure was nearly 46 percent); 40–45, 8; 45–50, 10; 50 plus, 12, or just over 25 percent (Convention, under 19 percent).
58. Kuscinski, *Conventionnels*, p. 251.

included Séguin and Cazeneuve, drawn from cathedral chapters, half a dozen priests who had been active mainly or largely as teachers (Audrein, Lalande, Massieu, Sanadon, Villar, Wandelaincourt), and Saurine, whose exact status in 1789 is not clear; he was in orders, had used a legacy to qualify as an *avocat*, had twice tangled with the authorities and left France for Spain, and on the eve of the Revolution, by backing the cause of reform, gained the notoriety which took him to the Constituent and then to the bishopric of Landes. The convention's dozen *curés* and episcopal vicars came from equally diverse sources: from teaching, from the canonry, from orders dissolved in 1790, from origins unknown; Roux alone was certainly at work in a parish in 1789.[59] Whatever view one takes of these deputies, they can hardly be seen as a fair cross-section of the French clergy whose attitudes were of such vital concern to the government of the Terror, and a glance at the group suggests the difficulty of being at once a priest and a revolutionary, the strains, dangers, and impossible dilemmas encountered by a cleric of advanced ideas. Yet the presence of these men in the Convention is an important part of the context of the decisions of Montagnards and Thermidorians on policy toward the church, because these were the men of God that the Convention could most closely observe. Their church might well be judged by their behavior. How did they stand, as clerics, Catholic and Protestant alike, at the end of their careers as deputies?

For Pocholle, Chabot, and Guiter the question is unnecessary, and for 2 Protestants and 2 Catholics (Lasource, Rabaut Saint-Etienne, Fauchet, and Simond) the guillotine cut off an answer; though Fauchet at least publicly proclaimed his faith to the end.[60] Four Protestants and 9 Catholics, of whom 7 had been constitutional bishops, returned to pastoral duties after they withdrew from politics. Three Protestants and 32 Catholics, including 8 bishops (one of them Thomas Lindet) abandoned the cloth; in most cases this decision was apparent by early 1794.[61] Such mass apostasy must have undermined any lingering respect for religious conviction in an assembly already overwhelmingly anticlerical. And there were political factors as well. Seven of the bishops were Girondin; one was *à l'écart*; 4 were uneasy members of the "committees" group; only 4 were Montagnard, and all of these left the church. Of the 9 Catholic *conventionnels* who remained true to their vows (10, if Fauchet is included) 5 were Girondin bishops, and one was Séguin, a bishop *à l'écart*. From the Montagnard point of view, the association between religion and counterrevolutionary feeling was easily made and was underlined by the attitude of the Montagnard

59. Kuscinski, *Conventionnels*, p. 308 (Grégoire), p. 412 (Lindet), p. 287 (Gay-Vernon), (Marbos), p. 543 (Royer), p. 584 (Thibault), pp. 560, 121 (Cazeneuve, Séguin); p. 13 (Audrein), p. 365 (Lalande), p. 439 (Massieu), p. 556 (Sanadon), p. 606 (Villar), p. 611 (Wandelaincourt), p. 557 (Saurine), p. 537 (Roux). For the bishops, see also P. Pisani, *Répertoire biographique de l'Episcopat constitutionnel (1791–1802)* (Paris, 1909).
60. Kuscinski, *Conventionnels*, p. 252; Pisani, *L'Episcopat constitutionnel*, p. 171.
61. Details in Appendix VII.

clerical deputies. One Montagnard, Coupé, did refuse to countenance clerical marriage and unhesitatingly accepted expulsion from the Jacobin Club rather than abandon his principles, but since he was in the process of leaving the church himself, his protest was not as effective as it might have been had he, like Grégoire, continued to wear his *soutane* throughout the Terror.[62] Only one of the 21 Montagnard priests was still in orders in 1795, and 3 of the 4 Montagnard pastors gave up their office as well. The moral hardly needs emphasis.

After the lawyers, the men of business, and the clergy, the most substantial group in the Convention was that of the civil servants; small enough in all conscience, an astonishing fall away from the solid block of 1789.[63] They varied a good deal both in social origin and in official status. Of those whose background is known, Courtois perhaps rose from the most lowly state, being a baker's son whose brilliant academic record presumably helped him on his way. In 1789 he was a tax collector at Arcis-sur-Aube. Hourier, who by 1789 had spent more than twenty years in a succession of government jobs, and Himbert, employed as a forester, also seem likely to have been of modest ancestry.[64]

Most of their colleagues however were very similar in stamp to the *officier* class of lawyer, in both social background and basic education. The bulk of the civil servants had rather dull-seeming jobs, 2 in 5 of them in some way connected with government revenues; though one would like to know why when 5 Navy Office representatives were elected, 3 of them very senior, there was no one from the War Office at all.[65] With the unrewarding exception of Basire, there were no very lively personalities among them, but their willingness to assume revolutionary responsibility after 1789, which was above the Convention's average, indicates that having entered the public service, they were prepared to continue in it, a conclusion confirmed by their choice of career after 1795.

The deputies with the highest average devotion to revolutionary public interest were, oddly enough, those from the land. There were only 38 of them altogether, an absurdly low number from an overwhelmingly agricultural society, but of the 38 only 4 had not been commune officials or better since 1789, and 18 had been deputies. Possibly in elections where town dwellers were apt to have an advantage, someone from the countryside had to be exceptionally well known to have much chance of election to the legislature; though it must also be remembered that 3 of these agriculturalists were poor men who took their first

62. Kuscinski, *Conventionnels*, pp. 155–56 (Coupé), p. 310 (Grégoire). The upholder of orthodoxy in the Lindet family was not Thomas but Robert, who was shocked at his brother's marriage (ibid., p. 412). See also ibid., pp. 345–46 for the Montagnard pastor, Jean Jay, and p. 461 for the priest, Monnel, who did not apostasize.

63. Though the criteria adopted may not be quite the same. But even if *officiers* and civil servants in the Convention are added together, the total is still only 203 out of 749.

64. Kuscinski, *Conventionnels*, pp. 157, 333, 333.

65. The presence of the Navy officials probably reflects the great public importance of naval administration in the naval ports from which all these deputies came.

step into politics with their election as deputies in 1791 or 1792.[66] It can hardly be claimed that any departmental delegation had a strongly agricultural bias, since the 38 deputies came from 30 different departments, but their small numbers meant that there was great patchiness in even such representation as there was; Normandy, Champagne, the Loire and Rhône valleys, the wine-growing areas of Bordeaux and Provence were left almost voiceless. How much this mattered will depend on one's view of the importance of direct as against "virtual" representation, and certainly there was no possibility in 1792 that the Catholic peasantry of Côtes-du-Nord, the reactionary seigneurs of Ardèche or their recalcitrant but otherwise conservative inferiors, or the flood-and-hail-bedeviled farmers and *vignerons* of Gard would have much influence in the national legislature, but the balance may have been tipped against rural interests even more in 1792 than in 1789.[67] Kuscinski's descriptions are too sketchy to allow any useful estimate of the types of farming represented. About all one can say is that a few of the group seem to have been really poor but most were fairly comfortable, that even allowing for the smallness of the sample the wine-growers seem badly represented, and that even if Arthur Young could not find many improving landlords in France, two of them reached the Convention.[68]

Those whose landholding gave rise to their most important single occupation were of course not the only landowners in the Convention, and here one comes up against Cobban's contention that the Revolution was the work of "the conservative landowning classes, large and small," which he buttresses with the assertion that all the revolutionary assemblies contained overwhelming majorities of landowners.[69] How many *conventionnels* did in fact own landed property?

66. The arguments are, of course, compatible; a nonentity from a rural area might seem a safe enough choice in a tricky political situation. It is hard to explain Dufestel's election on any but this sort of basis.

67. Palmer (*Age of the Democratic Revolution*, I: 478) says that 67 of the 648 deputies of the Third Estate "lived by the income or management of their own property, usually land." This is too vague to be very helpful, but if even half of these persons were genuinely of the landed interest the representation of 1789 was a shade better than that of 1792.

68. These were Lequinio from Morbihan, a qualified lawyer, son of a surgeon, who had a subsidy from the Breton Estates to help him with his land-clearing project at Ploeren; and Lauze de Perret, an extremely wealthy southerner who took enough interest in farming to work in the fields himself. The only *conventionnel* specified as a wine grower is Denis Roy from Argenteuil (Seine-et-Oise). I have included in the agricultural interest Précy who, as a bailiff from Aillant (Yonne), was the single member of a not unimportant managerial class. The men certainly poor were Jacques Chevalier, Duquesnoy, Dufestel; possibly also Boudin and Rongiès; Bonneval and d'Aoust, by contrast, were certainly rich. Kuscinski, *Conventionnels*, pp. 400, 197 (Lequinio, de Perret); p. 543 (Roy); p. 506 (Précy); pp. 137, 231, 220, 75, 535 (Chevalier, Duquesnoy, Dufestel, Boudin, Rongiès); pp. 71, 8 (Bonneval, d'Aoust). I have kept here entirely to Kuscinski's evidence, though it needs adjusting in a number of respects. The number of wealthy landowners was much larger than he implies, but he may not be too misleading over those whose *main* interest was the land, though even here he has probably missed some (e.g., Isoré).

69. Cobban, *Social Interpretation*, p. 170.

Supposing that a large number did so, what evidence is there that this was the most important determinant of their outlook on life?

So far as ownership of landed property is concerned, there is unfortunately no accessible evidence covering the membership of the 1792 Convention as a whole. Every deputy on leaving the Convention in 1795 was supposed to submit a statement setting out his financial position in 1789 (this was sometimes interpreted as meaning: at the point at which he had assumed national office) and in 1795. These statements are not ideal for the purpose in hand for several reasons. First, their primary purpose was to establish how far, if at all, the *conventionnels* were better off at the end of their period of office than they had been at the beginning; thus a considerable number contain merely an assessment of changes since 1789, with no indication of the exact situation at that date. Second, many *conventionnels*, including many leading Girondins and Montagnards, were either dead or under indictment in late 1795 and did not submit any statements at all; and third, even of those who were still about, either a number did not comply or their statements have not survived. Information of any kind is therefore available for well under half of our 730 deputies, and even when available it is by no means always of much value. Nevertheless, the general impressions drawn from it seem worth recording, such as they are.

The impression is that Cobban is both right in one way and misleading in others. He certainly seems to have been justified in his belief that *conventionnels* in general may have been landowners. Of the 321 of our deputies who put in financial statements, between one-half and two-thirds had a parcel or parcels of real estate in 1789; sometimes only a house to live in, but far more often a patch of vineyard, some *arpents* of arable land, a house or houses with a yard or a garden, a *métairie*, a bit of meadow, some woodland, or several or all of these; and a number of the younger deputies who had no such property expected to inherit it in due course from their parents. Some men had only a limited income from such sources, others had thousands of *livres*. The 10 wealthiest among the 321 were all landowners, though surprisingly enough it is here that the limited mercantile interest in the Convention becomes most conspicuous. These 10 all had capital assets which (they said) had been worth in 1789 200,000 *livres* or more. One of them, Desgrouas, had been a San Domingo planter, Dyzez had had much wealth in infeudated tithes, and 2 others had had very extensive landed estates; the other 6 derived most of their wealth from business interests, though they had a good deal of real estate as well.

Many deputies stated not only what they had, but how they had acquired it. Of those who did this, few owners of landed property had failed to gain a good deal, if not all, of it by inheritance or dowry from their own or their wives' parents and/or relatives. Sometimes it had been added to, but quite often such inheritance or share in the family property represented most of a man's estate and in a number of cases it was all he had. This real estate was not necessarily valued solely or even mainly as a source of income pure and simple, though this was of course a central consideration for the professional farmers. It seems often to have been seen as an inheritance to be passed on, rather than as an ordinary disposable capital investment. Lozeau, whose well-spread investments were all controlled with an eye to profit, seems to have felt a little self-conscious about his sensible and profitable operations in 1789-95, and justified them by saying that it was every citizen's duty to provide for his family. He may have been rationalizing a little—he had survived comfortably when others round him had been ruined, and he was obviously aware of it—but the feeling was commonly implied.

One indication of the general scale of values is that though many men complained of the inflation, the only one to complain bitterly that this had made the rents from his tenants valueless was Couturier, who was one of the professional farmers with an uncommon eye for rural financial realities. Nor was there any general move to buy national property, such as might have been expected if real estate had been of major interest as an investment. About 40 percent of the 321 deputies did buy such property, but many of the purchases were modest, and few either sank all their capital into them or borrowed large sums for the purpose. Very few took advantage of the inflation to pay off their debts—several refused to do this on the ground that it was dishonest—but many lost very heavily when the *rentes* which could have been put into land were repaid in worthless *assignats*. On the evidence of the 1795 statements, the compensation paid for the loss of an office was not a major factor in the purchase of national property; most sums received were small, quite often part was needed to pay off the cost of the office itself, and only in a tiny handful of cases does it seem to have enabled the purchase of land which would not otherwise have been bought.

Those who did buy land on a large scale were for the most part men who had owned a good deal of it in 1789. Marey was unusual in having the shrewdness to convert a considerable personal capital into extensive landed estate, but in doing so he was only adding to what he already had. Sixteen deputies put 50,000 *livres* or more into national property, but 8 of these, including Lozeau, found part or most of the price from selling holdings they had long possessed, and Creuzé-Dufresne said specifically that he had taken the chance to rearrange and consolidate his inherited estate. It should therefore be noted that in a number of cases, the acquisition of national property added less than might appear to the total of a man's investment in land; and further, that generalizations about the extent to which the "little man" improved his stake in the country through the sale of national property should take account not only of those who bought it directly but also of those who bought other parcels which were sold to enable such purchases to be made. And of course not everyone bought that could have done so. Of the 10 wealthy men mentioned above, 4 bought large amounts, one made a moderate and one a small purchase, and 4 bought nothing at all. The 4 large investors were all businessmen.

In nearly all cases, those deputies who put in detailed accounts could rightly claim that they were substantially worse off in 1795 than they had been in 1789, partly because inflation had made their salaries almost worthless and they had to borrow or live on their capital, and partly because investments not in land or in goods had been wiped out. They might reasonably have regretted that they had not taken advantage of the chance to buy church land, which would have been after all a patriotic gesture. But very few made this sort of comment.

From all this, what can be concluded which is relevant to Cobban's arguments? It may be suggested that though many *conventionnels* owned land, it cannot be demonstrated that this implied that the possession of landed property was for them a dominant concern. In the property statements, matters which might have been expected to loom very large in the minds of those with strong ties to the "rural interest"—for example requisitioning, or the operations of the *maximum*, which could with impunity have been attacked in 1795—do not appear at all, except when they are remarked on by men whose interest before and after 1789 clearly was farming and little else. To own property in the country was not to acquire the attitudes of a countryman. Nor was it necessarily, by contrast, to have the outlook of a capitalist investor. Much more research is called for, but the impression left by the 1795 statements is that in the minds of many deputies, landed property may have been valued not for what it returned but for what it represented—something in the way of security and an inheritance for one's children.[70]

If we move down to the next group on the list, the 46 doctors in the Convention are on the whole quite impressive. Their qualifications were various, ranging from Cassanyès's subdiplomate status as a country barber-surgeon to Hardy's Rouen M.D. and Salle's Ph.D. Seventeen had medical degrees from Paris, Reims, Toulouse, or Montpellier,[71] and more than half of the rest, at least, were well-educated and cultivated men. Eight had published learned works before the Revolution; Pressavin's had earned him membership of the Royal College of Surgeons in England. As a body of professional men, the doctors had had by 1792 less experience of public life than any other such group of *conventionnels*,

70. For all this, and information on pp. 289–90 below, see A.N. C 353 C 1838, where the returns are filed by departments. Information from 66 *suppléants* and 26 deputies from colonies and new departments is also included. I hope one day to analyze this material more adequately, but one difficulty in dealing with it is the number of men who specify their landed property without giving any indication of its value. The pressure of the 1795 inflation is clear; many men had sold their silver, jewelry, even their books to pay their household bills, and there were many to echo Bourgeois's rueful comment "*En un mot, rien dans les mains, rien dans les poches, et vive la République!*"

71. Montpellier was the most popular choice. These degrees were of of unequal reputation, but the trouble taken to acquire them suggests that they were valued by those who held them. All but a dozen of the medical deputies certainly had some formal qualification, and it seems likely that nearly all of them did. There were 6 surgeons besides Cassanyès, and these were not necessarily ill-educated; cf. Pressavin and Petit (Kuscinski, *Conventionnels*, pp. 506, 489).

perhaps because their professional obligations made it difficult for them to move far from home; they had an unusual proportion of communal officials, few representatives at higher levels of local government, and only 2 ex-Constituents. However, once elected to national office they could be extremely active and valuable. In its quality and range of interests this medical contingent is a reminder that Marat was not the only politically conscious practitioner of his time, and that eighteenth-century doctors could be as well aware as their successors of the social responsibilities of their calling. Petit pointed out to his colleagues that children must be fed before they could be educated, and tried to get money appropriated for this purpose; Calès published a shrewd pamphlet on the organization of health services in rural areas; Siblot, sent to Haute-Saône and Doubs on a recruiting mission, put in a report dealing with all aspects of government policy, including hospitals, prisons, pauperism, and library facilities; and Jouenne-Longchamp, who in 1795 reported on the education of deaf-mutes, spent his old age in exile in Brussels translating into French not only Jenner's treatise on inoculations but a book on the Lancaster method of teaching. The conservatism of many doctors was reflected in the high proportion, almost exactly one-third, who were *à l'écart* under the Terror, but this should not blind us to the large contribution of others (as of some of these men later) to the work of revolutionary government. The political nullity of a Joseph Fabre was more than balanced by the courage of Petit, one of the Girondins who continued to sit, whose anti-Jacobinism is a nice contrast to his radicalism in other directions.[72]

In one occupational group there was quite a large and interesting difference in family origin between some of the members and others. Twenty years before the outbreak of revolution it had been conceded that in the case of future army engineers plebeian birth might be overlooked, though the family of the prospective officer would have to come up to scratch in the matter of *vivant noblement*. Carnot was one of those who took advantage of this provision, as did also his younger brother.[73] The Convention contained altogether 5 army engineers, of whom 4 could be classified as *bourgeois* and the fifth, Prieur-Duvernois, could claim noble status only because his father had taken care to safeguard his prospects for promotion by getting a certificate of acceptable pedigree. By way of contrast, among the 21 infantry and artillery officers, men of noble birth out-numbered the commoners by 2 to one, and of the 4 naval officers 3 were noble; the single commoner was an engineer.[74] These were all deputies whose

72. Kuscinski, *Conventionnels*, pp. 489–90 (Petit), p. 99 (Calès), pp. 564–65 (Siblot), pp. 351–52 (Jouenne-Longchamp), p. 248 (Fabre).

73. On the new arrangement, the way it affected Carnot, and how his prospects later closed in, M. Reinhard, *Le Grand Carnot*, 2 vols. (Paris, 1950–52) I: 19–22.

74. The total number of nobles in the Convention is not easy to estimate from Kuscinski's evidence alone, but there were not 7 marquises (Hampson, *Social History*, p. 155) but 8–d'Aoust, Condorcet, Mailly, Rovère de Fontvielle, Sillery, Villette, Chateauneuf-Randon and Yzarn de Valady.

service careers were, or had been in 1789, intended as permanent. Twenty-three other *conventionnels* had been in the services for varying lengths of time before they retired either to live on private incomes or to other occupations, and among these the proportion of the nobly born was lower; the reasons for retirement are not usually stated, but it may be significant that Dufriche-Valazé, at least, gave up his post as lieutenant of grenadiers at the age of 22, when a royal ordinance excluding non-nobles from promotion wrecked his hopes forever.[75]

Though the vast majority of the Convention's service members had been officers, there were a few exceptions. Serre, whose occupation for the years immediately preceding the revolution is not stated, was a corporal of marines when he retired in 1785, and Drouet and Duquesnoy also served in the ranks for a time.[76] But by 1792 these men had long left such experience behind them. The common soldier can hardly be said to have figured personally among the deputies, and the National Guardsmen, of whom there were a number, were leaders rather than followers.

This exhausts the occupational categories of any size. Other groups were so small and/or so variegated that they really consisted of little more than scattered individuals. The lay academics, numbering fewer than a dozen, included three men who had been school principals (Gorsas had run his own school), three former professors from tertiary institutions, and five other teachers of various kinds. Only five of these men had ever held public office before, another possible indication that by 1792 the scope of public life was broadening. The election of 6 artisans and 3 clerks is yet a further bit of evidence in the same direction. None of these 9 had been chosen or, one feels, could have been chosen as a deputy before 1792, and 6 of the 9 had held no previous post of any kind at any level. The Convention's extremely mixed bag of men of letters was also largely inexperienced in the formal sense, though there was a clear division in its ranks between those who had been engaged in writing (or painting, or acting) for a living before 1789 and those who had not. Of the eleven *littérateurs* with private incomes, 6 had held parliamentary office before 1792, 3 in the Constituent and 3 in the Legislative; of the 19 others, Brissot and Dusaulx were the only ex-deputies—and Dusaulx was not self-supporting in quite the same sense as his fellows.[77] Thus 6 of the 8 ex-deputies among the men of letters (7, if Dusaulx is included) may reasonably be described as gentlemen amateurs, whereas the majority of those who came into politics for the first time in 1792 were professionals with a somewhat different contribution to make: the difference being, for the Gironde, that between Condorcet and Carra or Mercier, or, for the Mountain, that between Guyton-Morveau and Lavicomterie or Collot d'Herbois. With 23 of the 30 from cities, including 19 from Paris, the level of political commitment was naturally fairly high, some of the strength of the

75. Kuscinski, *Conventionnels*, p. 220.
76. Ibid., pp. 562, 200, 231.
77. He was secretary to the Duke of Orléans, and also had some money of his own. Kuscinski, *Conventionnels*, p. 235.

Gironde being reflected in its 11 supporters (including Louvet and La Revellière-Lépeaux as well as those already mentioned) against a perhaps less impressive Montagnard fourteen. Boissy d'Anglas found a refuge among the committee's deputies. Marey and Patrin, whose interests before the Revolution were scientific rather than literary or political, were complete novices in 1792 and apparently did not much like their new experiences; their à l'écart attitude under the Terror, though succeeded by a certain amount of activity in 1794–95, ended in complete withdrawal when their first parliamentary term was over. Andréi, the Opéra bouffe librettist, behaved in much the same way. But these were the exceptional cases; among the Convention's would-be intellectuals there were few political ciphers.

What, lastly, of the genuinely lower-class element, the sans-culotterie of which even Mathiez could find only 2 representatives? [78] Since this was by no means a unified class and the sans-culottes were of diverse social origins, they may be looked for in a variety of occupational categories: among the artisans obviously, but also among the small businessmen; and what of the small farmers? the clerks? what even of our corporal of marines? An additional difficulty is the possibility that a conventionnel might be poor and uneducated without necessarily sharing the political and social self-consciousness which, according to Soboul, was one of the hallmarks of the sans-culotte;[79] or he might meet every stipulation in September 1792 and yet demonstrate in the course of his parliamentary career that, though a Montagnard, he was moderate rather than radical.

A careful check reveals that if political outlook be for the time being set aside in favor of occupation, social background, and education as the main criteria,[80] Hampson's suggestion that Mathiez's 2 sans-culottes could be increased by another half-dozen[81] may still be an understatement. If we look first at the 6 deputies classified as artisans, we may accept without question, as Mathiez did, the munition-worker Noël Pointe and the wool-carder Armonville. To these may be added Cusset, the small silk weaver from Lyon, in every respect (including political) the revolutionary artisan par excellence; Montégut, once a grave-digger, later a municipal employee; Bernard des Sablons, a mason's son married to a vigneron's daughter, who worked in the fields until he achieved municipal office in 1790; and Boudin, a bootmaker's son who according to Kuscinski "se livrait à l'agriculture" at Meobecq until 1790.[82] From the ranks of

78. Cf. Jaurès, Histoire socialiste, IV: 302, note.
79. A. Soboul, Les sans-culottes parisiens en l'an II (La Roche-sur-Yon, 1958), e.g., pp. 1030–32, and pp. 408–9 for definition.
80. Cf. R. Cobb, "Revolutionary mentality in France in 1793–4," History XLII (1957).
81. Hampson, Social History, pp. 132–33.
82. Though he may have been too well-educated and too prosperous; he owned a farm (Kuscinski, Conventionnels, p. 75). But Noël Pointe was ostentatiously articulate, and prosperity was not in itself a disqualification. For Cusset, Montégut, and Bernard, ibid., pp. 165, 463, 51. Marcellin Béraud is a candidate, but I have left him out (with reservations) because he seems a little too comfortable (A.N. C 353 C 1838, Rhône-et-Loire).

those described as "farmers" we may perhaps take Rongiès, Dufestel (of the 11 children), Jacques Chevalier, and Duquesnoy.[83] All were comparatively poor and none had any social pretensions. From among the small businessmen come 2 postmasters, Drouet and Estadens, one the son of a wood merchant and the other the son of a locksmith; Battellier, a watchmaker, son of a lime-burner; perhaps the corset-maker Viquy; certainly the Paris butcher Legendre, "*sans éducation mais d'une caractère chaude*" who had been cabin boy and sailor, became a popular orator and helped to lead the attack on the Tuileries.[84] Who else? Possibly Robin, son of a postmaster, himself in the river-carrying trade at Nogent-sur-Seine; Maure, the Auxerre grocer, was probably too well off—though he was undoubtedly a fiery revolutionary, and what about Santerre after all? Lastly, from the white-collar workers, Moise Bayle, the Marseillais bookkeeper whom Barbaroux accused in 1793 of recruiting a following among the paupers of the city.[85] The total, excluding Maure, is sixteen.[86] Other marginal possibilities have been ruled out because of apparently *bourgeois*-type background and/or education.[87] None of the 16 potential *sans-culottes* had any real sign of education, except Noël Pointe's self-made flourish; only Legendre was well-to-do; few could do more than move on the fringe of *bourgeois* society. What however of their politics?

Here there is a split, and not on social or economic grounds as far as one can see. Four of the 16 (Estadens, Bernard, Chevalier, Dufestel) had Girondin leanings; Viquy was *à l'écart*; Boudin was of the "committees" group; the rest were Montagnard. The supporters of the Mountain, with the possible exception of Rongiès who went home late in 1793,[88] were admirably enthusiastic, though Legendre was perhaps a little on the moderate side. But does Bernard des Sablons cease to be a *sans-culotte* because he was terrified by the events of mid-1793? [89] The answer must be yes; this is a political category as well as a

83. See above, p. 277n. Rongiès had for reasons of convenience hyphenated his name with that of his birthplace; he violently objected when the secretaries, in the Legislative and later, addressed him as Flageac only, since this, he said, gave him "*la ridicule d'une noblesse dont il ne se targuait pas.*" Kuscinski, *Conventionnels*, p. 535.

84. Kuscinski, *Conventionnels*, pp. 220, 137, 231 (for the three farmers); 209, 247, 38, 609, 392. Cobban says (*Social Interpretation*, p. 147), that Legendre was "a ruffian, but a middle-class ruffian." If this is true, he was the only middle-class deputy without a decent education; and sailing before the mast in any capacity does not seem a very probable middle-class occupation for the period.

85. *Moniteur* XVI: 372.

86. For Robin, Maure, and Bayle see Kuscinski, *Conventionnels*, pp. 532, 442–44, 41. For some indications of Maure's dealings as a grocer, F. Molard, E. Duponteil, E. Drot (eds.) *Département de l'Yonne, Procès-verbaux . . . de 1790 à 1800*, III: 259, 261; IV: 202.

87. E.g., Tallien, Bouchereau, Thomas. Kuscinski, *Conventionnels*, pp. 574, 74, 586. Paine fortunately can be omitted as Anglo-American; what would one do with him otherwise?

88. "*Cet homme simple n'était pas fait pour la politique*" (Kuscinski, *Conventionnels*, p. 535). He said his wife was ill.

89. The letter in which he asked to be allowed to go—"*J'ai la bitude detre au grande hairre*"—is the best evidence of his background (Kuscinski, *Conventionnels*, p. 51).

social one. If the right political viewpoint is demanded, the Convention's *sans-culottes* dwindle to 10. The 6 excluded may however serve as evidence from within the Convention itself to support Hampson's assertion that resistance to Montagnard rule came in 1793 from the base as well as the apex of the social pyramid.[90]

Outside the occupational classifications altogether fall 49 deputies: 11 who either never had, or had never taken seriously, a permanent career, but could find private resources (their own or someone else's) on which to subsist without one, and 38 whose way of life before 1789 appears to be unknown.[91] The 11 who have been reckoned as of "private means" could in all cases but 3 be pushed into some sort of occupational category, the difficulty being their obvious and apparently complete abandonment of the occupation concerned. Six of them had served in the army; 2 were living on country estates; only Creuzé-Dufresne, a planter returned from San Domingo, Carpentier, on the evidence a wealthy Hazebrouck property owner, and the Duc d'Orléans, soon to be Philippe-Egalité, had no ready single focus of interest. The unifying factor among the 11 is that all can be seen as at something of a loose end on the eve of the Revolution: *"quelque peu désoeuvré"* as Kuscinski gently says of Barras. By 1791 all were actively engaged in politics, 2 (Orléans and Dubois-Crancé) as members of the Constituent Assembly, 2 more (Fréron and Villette) as journalists, and the rest at various levels of local administration. Orléans, as Philippe-Egalité, was executed and Villette died in 1793; of the remaining 9, 7 were Montagnards. The group is of some interest partly because of its small size—nearly all the *conventionnels* did either earn their livings, or add to their inherited incomes, or spend their leisure in the avowed pursuit of culture—and partly because of its uncompromising radicalism. In January 1793, 10 of the 11 voted against the referendum, and 9 unequivocally condemned the king. Under the Terror Creuzé-Dufresne alone was *à l'écart*. Each of the occupational groups we have looked at had at least some Girondins. Among the men of private means there were none at all.

What, finally, of the almost completely unknown? There were 38 such deputies. For just about half of them, 18 in all, Kuscinski gives some family or other background, and it follows the familiar pattern: son of a postal director, son of an infantry officer, son of a surgeon, of a notary, of a merchant; or of a "bourgeois family" unspecified. Four only of the 18 may have possibly been of humbler origin. Laurent, son of a schoolmaster; Plet-Beauprey, son of an inn-

90. *Social History*, p. 173.
91. Serre, of unknown occupation between 1785 and 1789, has been placed with the "armed services" because of his previous five years' service in the marines and a lack of information about his choice of an alternative, if any. Harmand has been placed with the lawyers on account of the legal education which apparently represented his final choice of vocation. These were arbitrary decisions. Some of the "unknown," e.g., Rameau, might be tentatively placed from the 1795 evidence (see Appendix IV) but I have let Kuscinski's evidence stand.

keeper; Roussel, son of a stonemason; Blondel, probably son of a baker; and these 4 sound another echo of conservative feeling from the lower social levels, in that not one of them was Montagnard.[92] Out of the 38 unknowns, 2, Blondel and Dugenne (after 1789 the local health officer in Sancerre)[93] were politically quite inexperienced in 1792. All the others had held office, in about 2 cases out of 3 at district level or above; but it was predominantly local office. The fact that there were no ex-Constituents and only 7 ex-Legislatives suggests the general obscurity of the men concerned, who as a group were also very strongly biased against the Mountain. One would like to know whether this merely reflects a greater concentration of scholarly interest upon Montagnards in general (hence a lower proportion of them in the "unknown" category) or whether the Mountain simply was more likely to recruit support from men of sufficient activity and prominence for their early careers to be more easily discoverable. This problem seems by nature insoluble, but the conservatism of the most socially obscure members of the Convention is at least a pleasing accompaniment to the conservatism of the most politically inexperienced.

What of Mathiez's claim that the antagonism between Mountain and Gironde was social as well as political?[94] As Cobban has pointed out, this claim has never been tested by any inspection of the Convention as a whole.[95] Whatever interests the *conventionnels* "represented," whatever the nature of the support attracted by the Girondin protest once it had been made, the struggle was parliamentary in its origins, and it is therefore surely in the Convention that any analysis of its social character should be begun.

An analysis of the Convention in terms of occupational background as well as political attitude produces the result in Table 34.

It seems that the Mountain had a wider range of support than any other political group: on the other hand, the number of Montagnards in the less usual occupations was so exceedingly small that it could hardly have affected general Montagnard attitudes unless the deputies concerned were extremely influential. Unfortunately they were very much of the rank and file. The medical profession had uncommonly little interest in the Gironde, but as it had no more than average interest in the Mountain either, with a very strong minority preferring to pull out of politics altogether, this does not take us far. The businessmen may have had a slight *penchant* for the Gironde, and a slight distaste for the Mountain, but the figures are small and this may have been a chance reaction. The "inner sixty" as it stands looks much more like what Sydenham says it was, a

92. Kuscinski, *Conventionnels*, pp. 378, 498, 537, 61. For Barras, Creuzé-Dufresne, Carpentier, Dubois-Crancé, see ibid., pp. 30, 163, 114, 212; also pp. 273, 608 (Fréron, Villette), and p. 239 (Orléans).

93. Kuscinski, *Conventionnels*, p. 221.

94. Mathiez, *The French Revolution*, p. 212. For the current rejection of this thesis, see, e.g., Hampson, *Social History*, pp. 157–58.

95. A. Cobban, *Social Interpretation*, p. 64.

Table 34. Deputies in National Convention—Occupations,
1789, and political sympathies, 1793–94

	GIRONDE			PLAIN			MOUNTAIN	
	"Inner sixty"	Other	Total	À l'écart	Committees	En mission		Total
Clergy	4	9	13	8	8	1	25	55
Medicine	5	2	7	15	3	2	18	45
Army/Navy	3	8	11	1	2	3	18	35
Business	8	11	19	10	11	4	22	66
Farming	2	10	12	7	1	1	17	38
Academic	2	–	2	1	2	–	6	11
Literary	7	4	11	3	1	–	14	29
Artisan	–	2	2	–	–	–	4	6
Clerk	–	1	1	–	–	–	2	3
Civil Service	2	14	16	4	8	3	20	51
Lawyer (i) Official post	7	25	32	17	25	8	63	145
(ii) private practice	17	27	44	42	25	11	79	201
Private means	–	–	–	1	1	–	7	9
Not known	1	7	8	9	8	4	7	36
Total	58	120	178	118	95	37	302	730

loose association of men of similar social background held together by personal friendships and similarities of taste. Petty bourgeois backing for the Gironde, such as it was, came from the floor of the Gironde, and not from the inner group. If the "inner sixty" has any flavor of its own at all, it is one of slight dilettantism, of dabbling in ideas rather than of vigorous pursuit of material ends. The pamphleteering Brissot, the able but idle Vergniaud, Ducos who felt he was "wasting his time" learning his family job as a man of commerce—these set the tone. The greatest Girondin protagonists of 1793 did not include Boyer-Fonfrède, who really did know something about the merchant marine, nor Kersaint with a store of naval expertise, nor even Grangeneuve with his thriving Bordeaux legal practice; they were, in the last weeks, Vergniaud, who had never taken his profession seriously, and Isnard, whose large and diversified inherited commercial interests seemed to survive absentee ownership.

About the Mountain even less can be concluded than about the Gironde. The range of occupations is so various that to put the emphasis on one point rather than another must be a matter of judgment about influence, which has little to do with statistics. Is the radical doctor Baudot more or less significant as a supporter than the radical grocer Maure or the chemist Guyton-Morveau or the archivist Basire? Perhaps the only historian who could take some comfort from these figures is Cobban, since the *officiers* certainly seem a little more inclined to the Mountain than the other lawyers. But the figures provide no decisive evidence, though the proportion of *officiers* to lawyers in the "inner sixty" arouses curiosity. No; from the totals in the occupational groups one must conclude that none of them was decisively committed in politics to any particular point of view. For Montagnards and Girondins both, such unity as there was apparently depended on similarity of viewpoint in politics, rather than on similarity of "interest" in the narrow sense. The most that one might say would perhaps be that because the Montagnard rallying point was the Jacobin Club and not Madame Dodun's salon or Dufriche-Valazé's diningroom, the Montagnards were more exposed than the Girondins to the point of view represented by Cusset or Noël Pointe, and even the most *bourgeois* may have broadened their outlook as a result. The Girondin leaders had no such regular meeting ground with humble sympathizers like Bernard des Sablons. But this is only to say again that figures are not everything.

Three other possible lines of approach remain. First: we have noticed that men from the cities were more positive in their choice of political allegiance than those from smaller places. The Gironde after all derived part of its leadership from Bordeaux and Marseille, and when the expelled deputies fled to raise rebellion, it was to Caën that they went. And it is in the cities that the greater *bourgeoisie* should have been most numerous and influential. The Mountain drew its support originally from Paris, but from what kind of Parisian and what kind of urban deputy generally? Were the city deputies who were divided in political allegiance divided in social background as well?

Table 35 does not seem very helpful either, in fact it even more strongly suggests that a quest for a social difference between opposing factions, if such a thing exists at all, must be directed toward the establishment of a difference in social level *within* occupations rather than a difference between them; there is no weighting in any particular direction on either side. Even so, it may well be fruitless. It is clear enough what may have distinguished Legendre from Duplantier, but what distinction, if any, can usefully be drawn between David and Dulaure, or for that matter between Saint-Just and Barbaroux? The table tells us that most of the Convention's *littérateurs* were city-dwellers, which is hardly news, and of divided views in politics, which is not news either. It shows the city men of business as the only group in the Convention symmetrically divided between the contending factions, with a tiny bunch of temporizers adroitly poised on the fulcrum of the see-saw; but there are not enough men of business to make this picture more than a basis for speculation. Once again the Mountain, as against the Gironde, is oddly strong in *officiers*, and one would like to know why; but the figures are very small and the problems probably illusory. The Girondin *littérateurs* were more numerous than the Girondin men of business, and better known than their Montagnard counterparts. There does not seem to be anything to support Mathiez's theory; but there is not much to refute it either, because the detailed enquiry which would put flesh on these bare bones has yet to be made, and where what should be relevant evidence is available it is contradictory. For example, the average standing of Girondin men of business was quite high, but the same may be said of the Montagnards, with the excep-

Table 35. Deputies from large towns*—Occupations,
places of residence, and political sympathies

	GIRONDE			PLAIN			MOUNTAIN			
	"Inner sixty"	Other	Total	À l'écart	Committees	En mission	Jac.	Oth.	Tot.	Total
Clergy	2	3	5	2	3	—	6	3	9	19
Medicine	2	1	3	1	—	—	6	1	7	11
Army/Navy	2	1	3	—	1	1	2	3	5	10
Business	4	4	8	—	3	—	4	4	8	19
Farming	—	1	1	—	—	—	1	—	1	2
Literary	6	3	9	2	1	—	10	1	11	23
Academic	2	—	2	1	1	—	2	1	3	7
Clerk	—	—	—	—	—	—	1	2	3	3
Artisan	—	1	1	—	—	—	2	—	2	3
Civil Service	—	3	3	—	2	—	2	3	5	10
Lawyer (i) official post	—	3	3	2	6	2	11	8	19	32
(ii) private practice	10	11	21	3	7	2	10	14	24	57
Private means	—	—	—	1	—	—	2	—	2	3
Not known	—	—	—	2	1	—	1	1	2	5
Total	28	31	59	14	25	5	60	41	101	204

*Comparable figures for chefs-lieux and for other places may be found in the complete table in Appendix VII.

tion of Legendre; how much or how little does he matter? Isnard was quite a wealthy man, but so was Le Cointre, the Montagnard textile merchant from Versailles.

Second, it might be argued that personal differences, or the lack of them, between leading Montagnards and Girondins in the Convention are to some extent beside the point, since the Girondins might have acted as spokesmen for social groups to which they themselves did not necessarily belong. (Here the legal activities of Grangeneuve, Guadet, and Gensonné might well be significant.) But along these lines, there is some possible relevant material from within the Convention itself which has been already referred to. The 1795 property statements are not much use for the leading figures of either Mountain or Gironde, because so many of these were missing in 1795 that any survey of the survivors may be seriously misleading, but they do conveniently seem to supply a certain amount of possible information about the rest of the Convention. Setting aside the leaders, can anything be learned about divergences between the followers on economic grounds?

The evidence here is of course limited, because only 321 of our deputies supplied statements of any kind. As far as it does go, it is unexpected in one direction and baffling in another.

If the expectation is that Girondins should be wealthier than Montagnards, the evidence of 1795—what there is of it—is to the contrary. Of the 10 wealthiest men thus disclosed, the leader, Marey (Côte d'Or), was à l'écart in 1793-94,

Ribet (Manche) was of the "committees" and Desgrouas (Orne) of the *en mission* group—and the 7 others were Montagnard! There was not a single Girondin. Of the 16 men who invested 50,000 or more *livres* in national property, 8 were from the Plain, again 7 (not entirely the same 7) were Montagnard, only one was Girondin. At the other end of the scale, although no Girondin could match the Montagnard Armonville's touching penury (all his 1789 posessions, he said, had not been worth 120 *livres* and he had always owed more than this) nearly one in 4, against the Mountain's 3 in 10, had a property income of less than 1,000 *livres* a year; a difference which on the face of it is not significant.

This however is not the whole story, because in 1795 some deputies were far more willing than others to make statements at all, and the Girondins were markedly less willing than any other group. Among the deputies still living and at liberty, the common rate of return was about 60 percent; for Montagnards, it was over 67 percent, not including submissions from half-a-dozen deputies (one of them Robert Lindet) who were actually under indictment or in jail. But fewer than 40 percent of the Girondins responded at all, and among those who did respond, a full third were so vague that no useful estimate of their financial position can be made. (The comparable figure here for all deputies was 20 percent and for Montagnards 13 percent.) Many had of course lost track of their affairs during the crisis of 1793–94, but this was now well in the past, and in any case is not the whole explanation; La Revellière-Lépeaux is only one of a number who simply disdained to give any estimate of 1789 position or income.

When to this large area of uncertainty is added the known fact that both Kervélégan and Isnard, whose property does not figure in the 1795 returns, were extremely well-to-do, it is apparent that no satisfying comparison between the economic situations of Mountain and Gironde can possibly be drawn, even tentatively, until much more information is available. The only comment which can be made is that the difference, if there turns out to be one, will not probably be a matter of stark contrast in affluence, nor will it be just a matter of Girondin mercantile interest versus Montagnard professional/*bourgeoisie*/*sans-culotte* alliance; for the 7 wealthy Montagnards were the lawyers Dyzez and Reynaud, the landowner/official Couturier, the iron-master Dornier—and the 3 merchants Le Cointre, Lesage-Sénault, and Champigny-Clément. Whatever the answer to this problem may be, it will have to be worked out outside the Convention, and it looks unlikely to be simple in any terms.

The third line of approach is geographical, a division of the deputies on a regional basis. We have noticed a tendency to geographical division among the deputies in general, with the Girondins being elected more commonly, though by no means wholly, in coastal, western, and southern departments, and the Montagnards more commonly, though by no means wholly, in the north, the center, and the east. Because the interest was in departmental delegations as such rather than in individuals, deputies were for this purpose classified according to the departments that elected them without regard to their own place of settlement in 1789; thus Brissot was counted for Eure-et-Loir and Jullien for Drôme, though on the eve of the revolution both were living in Paris. It will be interesting to see whether the same division of opinion, a largely coastal, western, and southern Gironde against a largely northern, eastern, and central Mountain, is revealed when the city deputies are placed not in their 1792 electorates but in their 1789 environments. Cities anywhere, one might argue, might have more in common with each other than have the rural backgrounds in which the individual cities are set; how far did Montagnard and Girondin emerge indiscriminately from city origins anywhere in France? Is the apparent pattern of regional difference blurred or accentuated in the more polemical city atmosphere? The Mountain is always said to have had its main stronghold in Paris, whereas the Girondins drew especially on the ports of Bordeaux and Marseille; it may therefore be worth while to divide the deputies from northern, eastern, and central cities into two groups, those from Paris and those from other places, and the deputies from southern, western, and coastal cities between those from ports and coastal towns and those from other places.

Though these figures are small, they are interesting. In general, Table 36 gives the same impression as the former figures for the regional allegiances of departmental delegations, but with more emphasis. The strong Girondin base in the ports is clear enough. Here the Mountain did worse than anywhere else, though in other southern and western cities it recovered remarkably well. Similarly the

Table 36. Deputies from large towns: Classified according to
geographical location* and political attitude

	GIRONDE			PLAIN			MOUNTAIN			
	"Inner sixty"	Other	Total	À l'écart	Committees	En mission	Jacobin	Other	Total	Total
(a) *Cities in coastal, southern, and western departments*										
Ports, coastal towns	12	13	25	3	7	2	6	10	16	53
Other	4	9	13	2	4	–	7	8	15	34
Total	16	22	38	5	11	2	13	18	31	87
(b) *Cities in northern, eastern, and central departments*										
Paris	9	4	13	2	4	2	24	3	27	48
Other	3	5	8	7	10	1	23	20	43	69
Total	12	9	21	9	14	3	47	23	70	117
Grand total	28	31	59	14	25	5	60	41	101	204

*The department of Nord, with a coastline as well as a long northern frontier, presents a special problem. In the analysis of departmental delegations it was reckoned a "northern" department. For present purposes, Dieppe has been placed as a port in category (a), but other cities (Arras, Lille, etc.), as "northern" in category (b).

Gironde got respectable support among deputies from Paris, something which may well represent a social split within the Parisian community, since the Girondin Parisians were nearly all elected outside the city by the assemblies of other departments and were on average, though not altogether, either socially superior to or socially more ambitious than the Montagnards. (This should not be pressed too far, but the Gironde had Kersaint as well as Condorcet, Dusaulx as well as de Bry, and no one from Paris quite in the Legendre category.) But backing for the Gironde from Parisians is not the most surprising feature of Table 36; after all Brissot had been elected for Paris in 1791. The strange thing is that the most Montagnard-orientated of the city deputies were not the Parisians, but the men from the other cities of the north, east, and center, who backed the Mountain by more than 3 to 2 to the virtual exclusion of the Gironde. Monestier from Clermont-Ferrand, Duhem from Lille, Rühl from Strasbourg, Delaguelle from Orléans, Prost from Besançon are examples from a long list. It is this repudiation of the Gironde which seems especially worth investigation. Support for the Mountain, among these city deputies, was not dramatically above the average for the whole northern/eastern/central area; but even allowing for the comparatively small number of Girondins from the area generally, the number from the cities was very low indeed.

Why this result? The deputies concerned were in no obvious way a special group, occupationally or otherwise; apart from the presence of a couple of artisans, they might have been any group of parliamentarians from anywhere in France. Their distribution of loyalties does not in itself constitute a new problem, except in so far as the apparent polarization of political feeling in city environments is a new problem, but it does sharply emphasize the problem already posed about a contrasting balance of political allegiance in north-eastern as against south-western France, and suggests that it is time that the political problems of the Republic were studied in a general geographical as well as social context.

* * * *

How much light is thrown on the political positions taken up by the *conventionnels* by a consideration of their personal backgrounds? What were their general characteristics? They were men in the prime of life, with the very young or the really elderly a small minority. Political leadership was in the hands of younger rather than older men, commonly in their thirties, who combined a variety of occupational backgrounds with maturity of judgment and considerable experience in public life. The rank and file of the Convention had also reasonable equipment for public affairs; most deputies were well educated and 6 out of 7 had held revolutionary public office before 1792. If the lines of political cleavage followed any social pattern, the pattern is not easily discerned by the casual observer. The contrast in sympathies between north and south, east and west, was relative not absolute; even in Paris the electors of 1792 chose two men who opposed the Mountain. To decide the basis of the contrast, if a general basis exists, the historian needs a number of comparative studies, and studies of urban revolutionary movements in particular, so that the deputies can be placed in the settings in which they began their political lives. If and when this sort of investigation is made, we may learn whether it was predictable or merely accidental that the *conventionnels* of central France as well as those from the invasion-threatened north and east were so often willing to accept Montagnard leadership.

The impact of foreign aggression is in itself inadequate to explain that rallying to a Jacobin republic which was so much commoner in some departmental delegations than in others: for different reasons, Aisne, Ardennes, Allier, and Basses-Pyrénées all fail to fit the pattern of behavior implied. If anti-Montagnard feeling in coastal areas is to be explained by the self-interest of the commercial ports, one needs to know why Bordeaux denied the Girondin fugitives even house-room at a time when Toulon was defying the national government. Personal rivalries, personal animosities must be part of the picture, but can hardly be the whole story. It may be that the search for general factors underlying any man's political choice is based on illusion, that every choice arose from an individual blend of experiences, but until we have an analysis of local revolutionary movements as a point of origin for revolutionary politicians, there is little basis for even informed guesswork. It has always been easy to generalize about urban radicalism and rural conservatism, as about the roots of counter-revolution in Brittany and the south. To explain the puzzling pattern of parliamentary loyalties in France's first republican assembly presents a more subtle challenge. Perhaps the quest is a vain one, but the evidence suggests that it may be worth pursuing.

CONCLUSION

The starting point of this study was the analysis of a body of basic general evidence about the deputies elected to the French National Convention in September 1792, to see whether such an analysis would throw any light on the current generalizations about political divisions within the Convention in the period centering around the expulsion of the Girondin leaders on 2 June 1793. The conclusions can only be tentative because the enquiry has been necessarily limited in its scope; yet because all the evidence examined has pointed, in its different ways, in the same general direction, these conclusions may at least suggest the lines along which future research might be directed.

The analysis of the evidence has involved at times a good deal of head-counting. This was inevitable, since the only way to test generalizations about "majorities" and "minorities" is to see how the Convention actually divided on the rare occasions when the views of its individual members were recorded in full, and generalizations about social character and political experience can be tested only by sorting out the facts, so far as they can be established. It should be unnecessary to repeat that no amount of head-counting can imply the existence of "parties" in any modern sense. However the deputies may be grouped by the historian, they remain individuals, and their Convention was a place of personal cliques and shifting loyalties, not of cohesive organization. Nevertheless, it has seemed possible to trace patterns of political behavior, with men tending to behave from January to June 1793 in a manner fairly consistent with their later behavior under the Jacobin régime. Moreover, groups of deputies differentiated on purely political grounds do appear, on further examination, to differ quite noticeably and unexpectedly in other ways as well.

As far as political divisions are concerned, the existence of a consistently right-wing element in the Convention seems undeniable, whatever label is attached to it. This right wing was overwhelmingly antiregicide, markedly anti-

Parisian, and progressively less active in politics from 21 January 1793 onwards, until under the Terror its members almost completely withdrew. The rest of what has been traditionally classed as the Plain was as divided and uncertain as its traditional reputation suggests, and after January 1793 only a minority of its members showed any inclination to take on major political responsibility.

The so-called "Gironde," though divided in attitude in the January–June period, was not so much so as has sometimes been claimed. Its members were far more active than those of the extreme right wing, and as far as the *appels nominaux* were concerned were, both in January and later, more agreed than the rest of the Plain. Those who were later to show active opposition to the events of 2 June formed the only section of the Convention which provided both consistent and convincing support for the initiatives against Paris that were put forward by those closely associated with Brissot and Vergniaud. The members of the "Gironde" in general were not only more strongly anti-Parisian but more strongly antiregicide than any other group in the Convention, apart from the extreme right wing.

There was also in the Convention an avowedly "Montagnard" and/or "Jacobin" element of quite substantial size. To this may perhaps be added a number of tacit sympathizers who have been classified as "Montagnards by attribution." These deputies certainly did not support the Gironde, as certainly did not share the views of the right wing, and can hardly be said to have shown the characteristics commonly associated with the Plain; if they were not in practice "Montagnard" it is difficult to know what else to call them. The "Mountain," as it has been defined, was by no means unanimous in support of Parisian radicalism, but since some deputies who were not at all pro-Parisian have been accepted as Montagnard by modern historians on other grounds, this is not in itself a major problem.

On the evidence considered, the attitude of "the Convention" toward "Paris" presents problems which need very careful definition. From the reception given to the various petitions presented by the Sections in the first half of 1793, it seems that none of the deputies really understood Parisian economic grievances, though some were more willing than others to admit their existence, and that only a section of the radical Left was willing to tolerate the Sections' strictures on the behavior of the Girondin deputies or to agree that a purge of the Convention might be necessary. (It should be noted in this connection that the suggestion implied in Robespierre's speech of 10 April, that the Convention should carry out a limited purge itself, had been raised by anti-Parisian petitioners before the end of 1792.) A large majority of deputies, including many who have been classed as Montagnard, resented any infringement of the Convention's sovereignty by pressure from the Sections, or indeed from anywhere else, and in this sense the Girondins certainly had "the Convention" on their side.

But to protect the Convention's integrity was one thing, to take action against "Paris" was another. There is no evidence that the Girondins had the support of a majority of their colleagues over either the impeachment of Marat or the reinstatement of the Commission of Twelve. On both occasions about three-quarters of the backing came from the Girondins themselves plus the firmly conservative deputies, who over the trial of the king had formed part of a demonstrable minority. So many deputies of all shades of opinion were absent from the Marat impeachment that it seems possible that this might be said to have been approved by default, if not actively sanctioned; but for the vote on the Commission of Twelve, most of the voluntary absentees were from the Convention's center and right wing, most of the compulsory absentees from the Left, and the voting was sufficiently close to make any claim of majority support for the verdict very dubious. In the general conduct of government affairs, which frequently and of necessity impinged on the problem of Paris versus the provinces, the main authority did not lie with the Gironde, but was entrusted by the Convention to other hands. The internal history of the Republic both before and after 2 June seems to make more sense if it is assumed that the Mountain was an important and significantly responsible minority, which was already very active in government before 2 June. It did not, of course, have a complete monopoly of activity or of office: witness Serre's presence as *rapporteur* for the *comité de guerre* on 16 May.[1] But the consistent domination by regicides, most of whom were Montagnard, of both *en mission* and executive committee appointments, in combination with their obvious importance in the day-to-day debates, is something that must now be recognized. It was after all the Jacobin régime which brought Paris to heel in 1794. It is conventional to say that there was comparatively little in common between demonstrators and politicians in May–June 1793, that the insurrection was used to solve a political problem; perhaps one should look rather more carefully at its aims, and at the unifying factor among those who accepted it. If this unifying factor was above all a feeling that the greatest threat to the Republic came from the counter-revolutionaries rather than from the Parisians, it can be perceived before as after 2 June; and the government of the Republic, before as after 2 June, was substantially in Montagnard hands, though the left wing of the Mountain was not as important as it later became.[2]

What can be said in general about the circumstances in which the deputies were elected, and the local backgrounds from which they emerged? The

1. *Moniteur* XVI: 400.
2. Of the twelve members of the "great" C.P.S., Barère and Lindet were first elected on 6–7 April, and Couthon, Saint-Just, and Hérault de Séchelles were added on 30 May. The apparent amalgam of types of Montagnard, and the incorporation of more left-wing elements, thus began *before* 31 May–2 June, and the formal evidence for the insurrection as a "Robespierrist" victory is not easy to find.

instinctive answer to this question is "Not very much"; not very much, that is, until we have numerous careful studies of local revolutionary movements and local public opinion, to extend and deepen the work begun by some of Aulard's students about 70 years ago. A few comments, however, seem to arise, even from the limited survey which has been undertaken here.

To begin with, however fine the local studies may turn out to be, they will have to be set in a general context if the evidence they provide is to be seen in proper perspective; to illustrate this point, one may note that Baumont's conclusions about the radicalism of the Oise electors might have been differently phrased had he known that the granting of unlimited powers to the deputies was requested by the Legislative Assembly and conceded by more than half the electoral assemblies in France, and that the departmental administration came under fire not only in Oise, but in nearly thirty other departments, including Calvados and Gard.[3] It is this general context which must serve to establish the possible significance, or otherwise, of the local incident. As for the elections themselves, it seems likely to be more than a coincidence that the pattern of radical-seeming assembly/radical-seeming delegation, and contrariwise, is so regularly repeated; and it is also at least interesting that the 28 departments whose addresses after 20 June, from all sources, showed only minority support for the king seem to have been unusually likely to record in their electoral minutes both the existence of monarchical feeling and the fact that it was overruled.[4] The apparently universal acceptance of the Legislative's version of 10 August seems important, and so does the complete ineffectiveness of the monarchists, even in remote and backward areas: Lozère, for instance, in which in the previous spring the counterrevolutionaries had even succeeded in driving the departmental administration out of the departmental capital. In assessing the atmosphere of the 1792 elections, held after all when the last symbol of royalist tradition had just been violently overthrown, it should at least be observed that it was at this time that the Lozère electoral assembly decided that it might be safe for the local officials to return to Mende, since the situation there had very much improved.[5]

Whatever the explanation for the results of the 1792 elections, there is no superficial evidence that the electors were generally intimidated. Unless for some reason there was a conspiracy of silence, the influence of spectators and popular clubs seems to have been overrated. Some of the *procès-verbaux* are very abbreviated, but a fair number, including some of uncertain literacy, show a

3. Cf. H. Baumont, "Les assemblées primaires et électorales de l'Oise en 1792," *La Révolution Française* XLIV (1904).

4. The information presented by Reinhard on the distribution of sympathy for the king after 20 June 1792 is very interesting. M. Reinhard, *La Chute de la Royauté* (Paris, 1969), maps pp. 509, 523; cf. also pp. 545, 593.

5. For the Lozère decision that Mende was once more comparatively safe for revolutionaries, see A.N. C 179 C II 46 (Lozère) 7 Sept.; for the earlier crisis, a long, untidy, indignant manuscript (of (?) March 1792) in A.N. F[19] 444 (Lozère).

touching pleasure in recording the minute details of procedure—with however no sign that any *société populaire* so much as communicated with the assembly, much less made its presence felt. Finally, the treatment of the retiring members of the Legislative Assembly deserves remark. Paris and Nord might be expected to discriminate among their former representatives, Dordogne had much less need to do so; but what inspired the electors of Indre, Isère, and (for heaven's sake) Pyrénées-Orientales, to abandon their entire delegations apparently without a second thought? And there were other departments not unlike these three. The rules generally governing reelection, if elastic at times, are nevertheless discernible, and they were observed with quite surprising regularity in very various places.

The evidence of the distribution of political sympathies as between deputies from different departments, like the evidence of political sympathies and divisions in the Convention at large, cannot at present be taken in any way as definitive, but it does seem to be interesting enough to justify further enquiry, if only because the most significant part of it relates to the Girondins whose political position after 2 June is reasonably clear. Why were deputies from coastal cities and departments apparently more than usually likely to be Girondin? Why were so few of the urban deputies of the north, east, and center attracted to the Gironde? How far, if at all, can similar regional differences be discerned for earlier or later legislatures? It seems time that someone wrote a modern history of revolutionary politics in Brittany and Normandy, and it is perhaps also time that someone looked at the urban politics of the Revolution from a point of view other than that of the *sans-culottes.*

The analysis of the personal background of the deputies could do no more than scratch the surface of so enormous a subject. As far as it goes, it offers in some ways few surprises, but it does raise questions about the relationship of personal background to attitude in Revolutionary politics which might well be further explored. One problem crying out for investigation is that brought up by Cobban, of the nature of the "revolutionary bourgeoisie" and the relationship between the men in office and those who elected them. It would, for example, be very interesting to know more about those people, other than *sans-culottes,* who took part in Parisian political life between 1789 and 1799. From this point of view, the local history of revolutionary movements is a field still awaiting exploitation.

It has not been possible to find much evidence to establish the existence of the social split between Mountain and Gironde on which Mathiez laid such stress. This does not necessarily mean that Mathiez was entirely wrong. Madame Dodun was after all the wife of a former director of the *Compagnie des Indes*; one would like to know her interest in entertaining the Girondins, and what other company she kept.[6] But as far as the Convention itself is concerned, the most

6. *Dictionnaire de Biographie Française* XI (Paris, 1967), p. 426.

important single concomitant of variations in political attitude seems to be not wealth, nor social status, nor local environment except in a restricted sense; it is experience of revolutionary public life and responsibility. The other discernible differences between political groups seem to fit in well enough with this one element of apparently exceptional importance.

The initially very tentative inquiry into these various possible differences turned out to be far more rewarding than had ever been expected. It was not foreseen that groups differentiated purely because of the political attitude of their members in 1793–94 would appear to differ so widely in other ways as well. It was probably predictable that the *à l'écart* deputies would be very markedly antiregicide, but not that they would tend also to be distinctly older, much less politically experienced, and less urbanized in their background than the leaders of either Mountain or Gironde. It was suspected that there might be differences between the "inner sixty" and their followers, but not that these would be so noticeable. The similarity of general character among the average of the various Montagnard groups was a little surprising; their age-grouping was less so, but the high average of political experience was a matter of astonishment, especially in view of the large numbers involved. In particular, the most startling conclusion to emerge from the whole study of the Convention was that the part played in it by the ex-deputies of the Legislative Assembly was crucial for the future of the Republic.

A large proportion of the ex-Legislatives in the Convention have been classified as Montagnard. This may turn out to be the wrong term for some of them, though it is hard to see what other can be used. However, whether Montagnard or not, they were in their voting, in their activity *en mission* and on the executive committees, and in their attitude to the Jacobin régime, unquestionably the most important left-wing influence in the Convention. The Legislative has long been treated as the vehicle of an aborted experiment, whose chief interest lay in the emergence of the Girondin threat to the monarchy and in the ineffectuality of the Feuillants. It now appears that the experience of its members was one of the major determinants in the creation of the Jacobin Republic. Any future history of 1791–92 must surely allow for the significance of this period as a nursery of the politicians of the Terror.

The evidence available on the extent and the sources of apparent *de facto* support for the Jacobin régime must sooner or later lead to the investigation of another problem about which modern historians have so far written very little. Why is it that we are so well informed about Girondin cliques and attitudes, while the shifts of political loyalty among those who actually helped to govern France during one of the most dramatic years in French history have never been subjected to close analysis? We have no parliamentary history of the Terror. We do not even know who may have been in Paris on 9 Thermidor. We do know that Jeanbon Saint-André and Pierre-Louis Prieur were not, and we know about the dissensions within the governing committees, but we know no more in detail about the identity of those who howled Robespierre down than we know of the personal and political background of the Thermidorians. The leaders, yes: but the leaders have long been known. Who were the followers, and what had they been doing under the Terror? What role did the *suppléants* of 1793-95 play in the Thermidorian régime?

The very existence of some of these problems has been obscured by the shadow of Robespierre himself, and it seems conceivable that ever since Thermidor, history has been written from a perspective distorted by the fears and hatreds of 1792-93. Why do the analyses of the Girondin feud with "Paris," on a political level, give so much space to Robespierre's plans and feelings, and virtually all the rest to *sans-culotte* grievances in general, with no consideration at all of Parisian attitudes to those who had so little sympathy for Paris? [7] It seems strange that so little is said about the possible significance of the March attack on the Girondin *printing-presses.* Why were Brissot and Gorsas singled out for popular violence? Rudé's discussion of the weeks preceding 31 May is understandably concentrated on the overwhelming problem of the food supply, but like Soboul's discussion of the preliminaries to and events of 4-5 September, this does have the effect of leaving the political demands of the insurgents hanging in a partial vacuum. In its only reference to the food question, the *Unité* section's deputation of 5 September asked for stricter enforcement of existing laws, and not for any further measures, whereas its demand for legislative and judicial action against counterrevolutionaries—including Brissot and the other imprisoned deputies—was detailed and explicit. As explicit, in fact, as the *Bonconseil* petition of 8 April.[8]

The *Bonconseil* petition has been presented as, and may in fact largely have been, the outcome of a Montagnard maneuver.[9] Yet this leaves the printing-press affair unexplained—whatever the truth of this, no one now argues that the Mountain was responsible for it—and it leaves untouched the question of *sans-culotte* feeling toward the Girondins, whatever this may have been. Perhaps Mathiez was right in implying that the *sans-culottes* really saw little difference between Mountain and Gironde until they were taught to do so.[10] Perhaps the events of 31 May-2 June were basically the product of a parliamentary feud, with *sans-culotte* discontents adroitly exploited by the Mountain toward the desired end. Yet from September onward *les assassins de septembre* had had to take the full weight of Girondin scorn and abuse, and what had been said about "Paris" during the king's trial can only have been deeply insulting to those who, unlike Grangeneuve's *modérés*, had laid their lives on the line on 10 August. There may be room for a fresh look at the Girondin/Parisian feud, to see it as more than a matter of Montagnard manipulation and not rooted solely in

7. Cf., e.g., Hampson, *Social History of the French Revolution* (London, 1963), p. 176.

8. G. Rudé, *The Crowd in the French Revolution* (Oxford, 1959), pp. 118-22; A. Soboul, *Les sans-culottes parisiens en l'an II* (La Roche-sur-Yon, 1958), pp. 151-75; and *Moniteur* XVII: 586-87 for the September petitions.

9. Rudé, supra, p. 120.

10. Mathiez, *La Vie Chère* (Paris, 1927), p. 177.

economic grievance: to see it, in short, from the point of view of the *sans-culottes* as revolutionaries, with their own views about the fall of the king and their own standards of republican behavior, and their own feelings about those who would call in troops from the provinces to see to the safety of the national government in Paris.

Robespierre as a symbol of the Jacobin régime casts a shadow of another kind. A symbol he became on 9 Thermidor, for obvious and valuable reason. "Is his grave not wide enough, that we may cast into it all our hatreds?" No grave in the Republic was wide enough for that. What was buried in Robespierre's grave was not hatred; it was the memory of the working alliances that had secured the Jacobin republic in 1793. The identification of 1793-94 with Robespierre's personal ascendancy has disguised the fact that very many of those who cooperated in government during that time were not in any sense Robespierrist. "Soyez unis," wrote Jeanbon to the Convention in January 1793, "et nous serons invincibles."[11] Although the unity never became a full reality, there was more of it in 1793 than men could admit in 1794—or than some would admit in after years, when the Terror had become acknowledged as the work of a Robespierrist *élite*, and much might be lost and nothing gained by proclaiming oneself a Montagnard. Yet what of the verdict of Barère and Levasseur, turning back in old age to the realities of that legendary year? Barère, who knew and emphasized the need for Robespierre's fall, said also that "he was a man without personal ambition, a Republican to his fingertips." Levasseur wrote: "Has one in fact ever believed or been able to believe that the Terror was the work of one man or a handful of men?"[12] Here were two men with no need to defend a terrorist who had been dead for a generation, who could have used his memory to excuse or explain away their own remote misdeeds. Instead, they shared in essentials the attitude of Lefiot, who would never retract his regicide vote: "j'ai toujours agi selon ma conscience, et je ne puis rétracter ce que ma conscience ne rétracte pas."[13] There was no need to be a Robespierrist to accept the verdict of January 1793, and the range of personality at work in the Committee of Public Safety, from Lindet and Carnot and Barère to Billaud and Collot, was a microcosm of that to be found shouldering the responsibilities of the Terror in the Convention at large. After Thermidor, it was wiser to forget, and there was never any later profit in remembering. But historians too have failed to remember what was forgotten in 1794, and have forgotten what Barère and Levasseur later chose to remember.

In considering the developments of the first 8 months of the Convention's history, it seems clear that the most revealing episode was the trial of Louis XVI. For whatever reasons, a high proportion of the personal decisions made by deputies during the voting on the trial turned out to be definitive. Nearly 79

11. Jeanbon Saint-André, *Opinion. . . sur le jugement du roi et l'appel au peuple.*
12. Quoted in G. Rudé (ed.), *Robespierre* (Englewood Cliffs, N.J., 1967), p. 121 (Barère), p. 115 (Levasseur).
13. Kuscinski, *Conventionnels*, p. 391.

percent of those who voted consistently in Louis's favor later opposed the Jacobin Republic, and 87 percent of the unrelenting regicides have been placed with the Mountain. As far as the political conflicts of 1792–93 are concerned, it has already been argued that after the trial there was nothing much to be added, and all that remained was to work out the logical implications of positions already taken up. Those who believed the proponents of the *appel au peuple* to be potential traitors were confirmed in this belief by Dumouriez's treason; those who believed that the Parisians were trying to "usurp the sovereignty" over the trial were confirmed in this belief when the Sections tried to interfere with the Convention's membership. The means used by the Gironde to find a counter-balance to Paris were in use before the *appel au peuple* as after, and if a condemnation of the Mountain were required, Gensonné had said on 29 December all that the Girondins were ever to say. The trial was not a diversion or a side-issue. It sliced right through the politics of the Republic, and showed the varying temper of the deputies' republicanism as nothing else was ever to do.

Sebastian Mercier has been quoted in another place as saying that the argument over the king's sentence divided the protagonists into two groups forever after; but the aftermath of the trial was not the Convention's only legacy to French politics. To study the Convention as a whole has been to realize the central importance of continuity in revolutionary history. If the experiences of the Legislative Assembly helped to shape the Jacobin Republic, so also the local experiences of men from Ariège or Vendée or Sarthe or Doubs must have added their weight to the scales. We need more local history; and we need a revision of the history of the Directory, written with a careful eye on its personal inheritance from the Convention. Of the 132 Girondins still about in 1795, 124 were reelected. What became of them later? "The Convention" of which more than two-thirds had to be re-elected was not the Convention of 1792, but a purged and inferior body from which more Montagnards than Girondins had been excluded. What influences were at work during the 1795 elections? Beside Lanjuinais's backing from 39 departments must be set the fact that Carnot was reelected for 9, and that the department of Nord (rejecting its Thermidorian Merlin) defiantly returned Robert Lindet who, being under decree of arrest, was technically ineligible to sit at all.[14] In range and quality of political experience, the Convention was quite impressive. It would be interesting to know how the Directory's legislatures compared with it.

A last word must be said about the deputies themselves. To live with them has been to understand Kuscinski's life-long devotion, and his gentle rebuke to Aulard for abandoning them to turn to the less rewarding history of Consulate and Empire.[15] They are too various for one ever to weary of them. The scamps and scoundrels have their own impudent attraction, as for example Drouet,

14. On the 1795 elections, cf. J. Suratteau, "Les élections de l'an IV," *Annales* XXIV (1952); although on the Convention evidence I would question some of his political assessments.

15. Aulard's introduction to Kuscinski, *Conventionnels*, p. II.

evading exile under a false name after 1816 and becoming the trusted servant of a local ultra-royalist, to whom he read the papers and thus kept up with the news; or Fréron, blandly explaining to the Convention the disappearance of 800,000 francs of taxes levied *en mission* by himself and Barras—"sur la route, leur voiture étant tombée dans une mare, le portefeuille avec les assignats s'y étaient perdus."[16] (And, truly, the money was never seen again.) Some deputies made fortunes out of the Revolution, like Laporte who was classed by Napoleon among *"les plus grands escrocs de l'Europe"*; many others lost nearly all they possessed. The Convention had sadists like Carrier, and other men like Chambon who walked out alone and unresisting to be lynched rather than be the cause of further bloodshed. Beside Barras, one may place Guezno who put up his deputy's medal as the price of a meal *en mission*, rather than pay the bill out of the Republic's pocket. Some men like Hentz were cool and efficient *en mission*; others resembled Beauvais, who looked at Toulon and moaned "Quelle crise horrible!"

In later years, some served the Empire faithfully (Albitte met his death in the retreat from Moscow) and some would never acknowledge it—Gourdan is said to have died of grief at its coming. Some deputies were royalist; Henry-Larivière went into voluntary exile in 1830, and Rouzet showed his royalism in another way when he eloped with the Duchess of Orléans in 1796. (With her for more than twenty years, he apparently finally married her; this action is said to have caused an Orléans family scandal.) After 1815, some found it easy to stay in France, some evaded exile, many accepted it, and several proudly refused invitations to return: "votre drapeau n'est pas le mien," said Laloy, "j'ai combattu pour le renverser; vaincu, je subis les conséquences de cet échec."[17] One is reminded of David's repeated refusal to paint a portrait of Wellington—"je ne peins que l'histoire"—and of Genevois's dying words to his servant: "Quand je serai mort et que les Bourbons auront été détrônés, tu viendras sur ma tombe, tu frapperas deux coups de canne et tu diras: Monsieur, nous les avons chassés!"[18] One hopes the servant did as he was asked; there were only six years to wait . . . The loyalty that led Saint-Just to share Robespierre's fate, and Soubrany to share Romme's; the treachery that allowed the *suppléant* David-Delisle to railroad Pierre-Nicolas Perrin to his death in the galleys on a false charge of peculation, so that his seat might fall vacant; the dignity that kept Vergniaud in Paris to face his enemies, and the adroitness that enabled Pelet after 1795 to serve every régime in turn; avarice, generosity, integrity and vice, the Convention had them all, and the stresses of the revolutionary years revealed each deputy for what he was. The history of the Convention, if it could ever be written, would be the history of the various responses of its members to challenges which few of them could ever have envisaged in September 1792.

    16. Kuscinski, *Conventionnels*, p. 275.
    17. Ibid., p. 366.
    18. Ibid., pp. 289, 181 (for David).

APPENDICES

THE EX-DEPUTIES IN THE CONVENTION

MEMBERS OF THE NATIONAL CONVENTION WITH PREVIOUS PARLIAMENTARY EXPERIENCE

i) *Those who sat in the Constituent Assembly.*
1792 electorate shown in parentheses.
Dates in parentheses are those at which men elected as *suppléants* took their seats.
  a) Men included in the political analysis

1. Albert (Haut-Rhin) (27/10/1790)
2. Alquier (Vendée)
3. Anthoine (Moselle)
4. Aoust (Nord)
5. Babey (Jura)
6. Barère (Hautes-Pyrénées)
7. Baucheton (Cher)
8. Bazoche (Meuse)
9. Bion (Vienne)
10. Boissy d'Anglas (Ardèche)
11. Bonnet (Aude)
12. Boussion (Lot-et-Garonne) (17/12/1789)
13. Buzot (Eure)
14. Chaillon (Loire-Inf.)
15. Chasset (Rhône-et-Loire)
16. Chateauneuf-Randon (Lozère)
17. Cochon de l'Apparent (Deux-Sèvres)
18. Colaud la Salcette (Drôme)
19. Couppé (Côtes-du-Nord)
20. Creuzé-Latouche (Vienne)
21. Cussy (Calvados)
22. Defermon (Ille-et-Vilaine)
23. Dubois-Crancé (Ardennes)
24. Dupont (Hautes-Pyrénées)
25. Durand-Maillane (Bouches-du-Rhône)
26. Dutrou-Bornier (Vienne)
27. Gauthier (Ain)
28. Girot-Pouzol (Puy-de-Dôme)
29. Goupilleau J.F. (Vendée)
30. Gourdan (Haute-Saône)
31. Grégoire (Loir-et-Cher)
32. Grenot (Jura)
33. Florent-Guiot (Côte d'Or)
34. Guyardin (Haute-Marne) (3/12/1789)
35. Jac (Gard)
36. Jary (Loire-Inf.)
37. Kervélégan (Finistère)
38. Lanjuinais (Ille-et-Vilaine)
39. La Revellière-Lépeaux (Maine-et-Loire)
40. Le Carlier (Aisne)
41. Leclerc (Maine-et-Loire)
42. Lemaignan (Maine-et-Loire) (21/10/1790)
43. Le Maréchal (Eure)
44. Lesterpt-Beauvais (Haute-Vienne)
45. Lindet T. (Eure)
46. Lofficial (Deux-Sèvres)
47. Mailly (Saône-et-Loire)
48. Marquis (Meuse)
49. Massieu (Oise)
50. Monnel (Haute-Marne)
51. Merlin de Douai (Nord)
52. Morin (Aude)
53. Nioche (Indre-et-Loire)
54. Palasne-Champeaux (Côtes-du-Nord)
55. Pémartin (Basses-Pyrénées)
56. Pérès (Haute-Garonne)

57. Pétion (Eure-et-Loire)
58. Pflieger (Haut-Rhin)
59. Pilastre (Maine-et-Loire)
    (13/11/1789)
60. Poulain (Marne)
61. Prieur P.L. (Marne)
62. Rabaut-Saint-Etienne (Aube)
63. Ramel-Nogaret (Aude)
64. Reubell (Haut-Rhin)
65. Robespierre M. (Paris)
66. Rochegude (Tarn)
    (10/2/1790)
67. Royer (Ain) (1/3/1790)

68. Saint-Martin (Ardèche)
    (4/12/1789)
69. Saliceti (Corse)
70. Salle (Meurthe)
71. Saurine (Landes)
72. Sieyès (Sarthe)
73. Tellier (Seine-et-Marne)
74. Thibault (Cantal)
75. Treilhard (Seine-et-Oise)
76. Vadier (Ariège)
77. Vernier (Jura)
78. Voulland (Gard)

b) Excluded because of withdrawal from politics by June 1793

1. Camus (Haute-Loire)
2. Egalité [Orléans] (Paris)
3. Le Peletier de Saint Fargeau (Yonne)
4. Sillery (Somme)
5. Verdollin (Basses-Alpes)

The position of Verdollin is uncertain. Kuscinski describes him as a *suppléant* (he was also elected as *député titulaire*, but by an irregular assembly) and gives no date for his entry to the Constituent. On the other hand, from the way Kuscinski writes it is possible to conclude that Verdollin did actually sit, and there is no description of any incompatible activity in 1789–91. See Kuscinski, *Conventionnels*, p. 597.

c) Elected as *suppléants* to the Convention, and called up at some date after January 1793

Deputy	Admitted to Convention	Deputy replaced
1. Chambon La Tour (Gard)	April 1793	Balla
2. Cherrier (Vosges)	13/10/1793	Noël
3. Cornilleau (Sarthe)*	28/3/1795	Philippeaux
4. Coupard (Côtes-du-Nord)*	7/10/1793	Couppé
5. Fricot (Vosges)	13/6/1795	Hugo
6. Guittard (Haut-Rhin)	27/4/1795	–
7. Lesterpt ainé (Haute-Vienne)	25/2/1795	not stated
8. Perès (Gers)	27/4/1795	–

*Kuscinski says (*Conventionnels*, p. 155) that Cornilleau was kept away from the Constituent by illness and that Coupard was *"député absent."* Their place on the list may therefore be reckoned as nominal, since the experience they gained from their election was apparently nil.

d) Elected as *suppléants* to the Constituent, but never sat

Deputy	Reason for not sitting
1. Cambacérès (Hérault)	Election invalidated
2. Cambon (Hérault)	,,

Deputy	Reason for not sitting
3. Chiappe (Corse)	Not called up
4. Fleury (Côtes-du-Nord)	,,
5. Ingrand (Vienne)	,,
6. Ruamps (Charente-Inf.)	,,
7. Sautereau (Nièvre)	,,

Of these, Ingrand, Cambon, and Sautereau were elected to, and sat in, the Legislative Assembly, and cannot be reckoned as members of the Constituent. For the other 4 men above, Kuscinski gives details of activities in 1789–91 which make it seem extremely improbable that they could have functioned as deputies during this period (*Conventionnels*, pp. 100, 137, 259, 543; and 103, 337, 558, for Cambon, Ingrand, and Sautereau). There were thus 8 ex-Constituents who were elected to the Convention, but did not sit until April 1793 or later, and 7 men who sat in the Convention from the outset, but who cannot be reckoned as ex-Constituents because in 1789–91 they were *suppléants* or rejected members who never took their seats. The total of ex-Constituents in the Convention in September 1792 is therefore the sum of those in category (a) and category (b): 78 + 5 = 83.

Mortimer-Ternaux (*Histoire de la Terreur*, IV: 457–61) gives a total of 77 ex-Constituents. He includes Enjubault (Mayenne) and Campmas (Tarn), neither of whom seems to have been elected (Kuscinski, *Conventionnels*, pp. 108, 243) and omits Bazoche, Bonnet, Dutrou-Bornier, Guyardin, Kervélégan, Le Carlier, Mailly, and Verdollin—total 8. The total of 77 is thus increased to 85, if Verdollin is accepted, less 2 errors = 83.

Pariset (*La Révolution 1792–1799*, p. 7) who seems to be followed by English historians, puts the total at 96. This would seem to be 83 plus 13 other deputies in categories (c) and (d) (excluding Cambacérès and Cambon?). Those in category (c) were certainly ex-Constituents, but it seems inaccurate to include them in any statement about the composition of the Convention *when it met*; Pariset does not do this, since he is concerned with totals, but Goodwin and others do. The deputies in category (d) cannot legitimately be considered ex-Constituents in any sense. Pariset's total ought therefore to be not 83 + 8 + 5 = 96, but 83 + 8 = 91.

ii) *Those who sat in the Legislative Assembly*
   a) Men included in the political analysis

1. Albitte (Seine-Inf.)
2. Arbogast (Haut-Rhin)
3. Audrein (Morbihan)
4. Auguis (Deux-Sèvres)
5. Azéma (Aude)
6. Basire (Côte d'Or)
7. Bassal (Seine-et-Oise)
8. Baudin (Ardennes)
9. Baudot (Saône-et-Loire)
   (10 July 1792)
10. Beauvais (Paris)
11. Belin (Aisne)
12. Bellegarde (Charente)
13. Bernard (Charente-Inf.)
14. Besson (Doubs)
15. Bissy (Mayenne)
16. Bo (Aveyron)
17. Bohan (Finistère)
18. Bonet de Meautry (Calvados)
19. Bonneval (Meurthe)
20. Bonnier d'Alco (Hérault)
21. Bordas (Haute-Vienne)
22. Borie (Corrèze)
23. Bréard (Charente-Inf.)
24. Brisson (Loir-et-Cher)
25. Brissot (Eure-et-Loir)
   (Paris)
26. Brival (Corrèze)

27. Calon (Oise)
28. Cambon (Hérault)
29. Cappin (Gers)
30. Carnot (Pas-de-Calais)
31. Carpentier (Nord)
32. Chabot (Loir-et-Cher)
33. Charlier (Marne)
34. Chazaud (Charente)
35. Chaudron-Rousseau
     (Haute-Marne)
36. Chédaneau (Charente)
37. Choudieu (Maine-et-Loire)
38. Clauzel (Ariège)
39. Cledel (Lot) (30/4/1792)
40. Cochet (Nord)
41. Condorcet (Aisne) (Paris)
42. Corbel (Morbihan)
43. Coupé (Oise)
44. Courtois (Aube)
45. Coustard (Loire-Inf.)
46. Couthon (Puy-de-Dôme)
47. Couturier (Moselle)
48. Curée (Hérault)
49. Dameron (Nièvre)
50. De Bry (Aisne)
51. Delacroix (Eure-et-Loir)
52. Delaunay J. (Maine-et-Loire)
53. Delcher (Haute-Loire)
54. Delmas (Haute-Garonne)
55. De Perret (Bouches-du-Rhône)
56. Descamps (Gers)
57. Despinassy (Var)
58. Deydier (Ain)
59. Dherbez-Latour (Basses-Alpes)
60. Du Bouchet (Rhône-et-Loire)
     (27/6/1792)
61. Du Bois du Bais (Calvados)
62. Dubreuil-Chambardel
     (Deux-Sèvres)
63. Ducos J.F. (Gironde)
64. Duhem (Nord)
65. Dupont (Indre-et-Loire)
66. Dupuy (Rhône-et-Loire)
67. Duquesnoy (Pas-de-Calais)
68. Dusaulx (Paris) (6/6/1792)
69. Duval (Ille-et-Vilaine)
70. Dyzez (Landes)
71. Eschassériaux J. (Charente-Inf.)
72. Esnuë-Lavallée (Mayenne)
73. Fauchet (Calvados)
74. Faye (Haute-Vienne)
75. Fiquet (Aisne)

76. Foucher (Cher)
77. François de la Primaudière
     (Sarthe)
78. Frécine (Loir-et-Cher)
79. Gamon (Ardèche) (15/3/1792)
80. Garran-Coulon (Loiret) [Paris]
81. Garrau (Gironde) (7/4/1792)
82. Gasparin (Bouches-du-Rhône)
83. Gaston (Ariège)
84. Gaudin (Vendée)
85. Gay-Vernon (Haute-Vienne)
86. Gelin (Saône-et-Loire)
87. Gensonné (Gironde)
88. Gentil (Loiret)
89. Olivier-Gérente (Drôme)
     [Louvèze]
90. Gertoux (Hautes-Pyrénées)
91. Gibergues (Puy-de-Dôme)
92. Giroust (Eure-et-Loir)
93. Gossuin (Nord)
94. Goupilleau P.C. (Vendée)
95. Gouzy (Tarn) (30/7/1792)
96. Granet (Bouches-du-Rhône)
97. Grangeneuve (Gironde)
98. Grosse-Durocher (Mayenne)
99. Guadet (Gironde)
100. Guimberteau (Charente)
101. Guyès (Creuse)
102. Guyton-Morveau (Côte-d'Or)
103. Haussmann (Seine-et-Oise)
104. Henry-Larivière (Calvados)
105. Hérault de Séchelles
      (Seine-et-Oise) [Paris]
106. Huguet (Creuse)
107. Ichon (Gers)
108. Ingrand (Vienne)
109. Isnard (Var)
110. Jagot (Ain)
111. Jard-Panvillier
      (Deux-Sèvres)
112. Jay (Gironde)
113. Kersaint (Seine-et-Oise)
      [Paris]
114. Laboissière (Lot)
115. Lacombe-Saint-Michel (Tarn)
116. Lacoste (Dordogne)
117. Laguire (Gers)
118. Laloy (Haute-Marne)
119. Lambert (Côte d'Or)
120. Laplaigne (Gers)
121. Laporte (Haut-Rhin)
122. Lasource (Tarn)

123. Lebreton (Ille-et-Vilaine)
124. Lecointe-Puyraveau
     (Deux-Sèvres)
125. Le Cointre (Seine-et-Oise)
126. Le Malliaud (Morbihan)
127. Lemoine de Villeneuve
     (Manche)
128. Lequinio (Morbihan)
129. Le Tourneur (Manche)
130. Le Vasseur (Meurthe)
131. Leyris (Gard)
132. Lindet R. (Eure)
133. Lomont (Calvados)
134. Louvet P.F. (Somme)
135. Loysel (Aisne)
136. Maignen (Vendée)
137. Maignet (Puy-de-Dôme)
138. Mailhe (Haute-Garonne)
139. Mallarmé (Meurthe)
140. Martineau (Vienne)
141. Masuyer (Saône-et-Loire)
142. Maulde (Charente)
     (22/8/1792)
143. Merlin de Thionville
     (Moselle)
144. Michaud (Doubs)
145. Monestier (Lozère)
146. Monnot (Doubs)
147. Maribon-Montaut (Gers)
148. Moreau (Meuse)
149. Morisson (Vendée)
150. Musset (Vendée)
151. Niou (Charente-Inf.)
152. Oudot (Côte d'Or)
153. Paganel (Lot-et-Garonne)
154. Perrin (Aube)
155. Pinet (Dordogne)
156. Piorry (Vienne)

157. Poisson (Manche)
158. Prieur-Duvernois
     (Côte d'Or)
159. Projean (Haute-Garonne)
160. Reverchon (Saône-et-Loire)
161. Reynaud (Haute-Loire)
162. Richard (Sarthe)
163. Ritter (Haut-Rhin)
164. Rivery (Somme)
165. Robin (Aube)
166. Romme (Puy-de-Dôme)
167. Rongiès (Haute-Loire)
168. Roubaud (Var)
169. Roux-Fazillac (Dordogne)
170. Rovère (Bouches-du-Rhône)
     [Vaucluse] (30/7/1792)
171. Rouyer (Hérault)
172. Ruamps (Charente-Inf.)
173. Rühl (Haut-Rhin)
174. Soubeyran de Saint-Prix
     (Ardèche)
175. Saladin (Somme)
176. Sallengros (Nord)
177. Salmon (Sarthe)
178. Sautayra (Drôme)
179. Sautereau (Nièvre)
180. Gervais-Sauvé (Manche)
181. Siblot (Haute-Saône)
182. Soubrany (Puy-de-Dôme)
183. Taillefer (Dordogne)
184. Thuriot (Marne)
185. Tocquot (Meuse)
186. Valdruche (Haute-Marne)
187. Vardon (Calvados)
188. Vergniaud (Gironde)
189. Vernerey (Doubs)
190. Vidalot (Lot-et-Garonne)
191. Viennet (Hérault)

Where two electorates have been shown, it indicates that for some reason the deputy concerned sat for different electorates in 1791 and 1792. Vaucluse and Louvèze, which were set up as electorates in 1792, were absorbed for the Convention elections by the departments of Bouches-du-Rhône and Drôme. The only Legislative deputies to be rejected by their original constituencies and reelected by others were the five from Paris—Brissot, Condorcet, Garran-Coulon, Hérault de Séchelles, and Kersaint.

   b) Excluded because of withdrawal from politics by June 1793
      1. De Houlières (Maine-et-Loire)
      2. Lamarque (Dordogne)
      3. Quinette (Aisne)
The total of these two categories is 191 + 3 = 194.

c) Elected as *suppléants* to the Convention, and called up at some date
after January 1793
Menuau (Maine-et-Loire), called up 28/9/1793 to replace Leclerc.
De Varaigne (Haute-Marne) called up by lot 5 *floréal?*

Mortimer-Ternaux (*Histoire de la Terreur*, IV: 461–67) gives a list of names.
He includes Tavernel (Gard) who was reelected but did not sit, and Germignac
(Corrèze) who sat only very briefly, being already mortally ill; he died on 18
December 1792, and his *suppléant* Lafon was admitted on 9 January 1793
(Kuscinski, *Conventionnels*, p. 292). Tavernel and Germignac have been omitted
from the list above. Mortimer-Ternaux omits Bonnier d'Alco, Maulde, and
Reverchon. His list, otherwise identical with my own, includes 193 names, which
with 3 additions and 2 deletions is brought to 194. His own stated total of 181
(p. 467) must be attributed, in default of other explanation, to imperfect arithmetic, excusable in view of the confusing way he sets out the names.
It is very hard to explain Pariset's figure of 189 for the number of ex-
Legislatives in the Convention. Was he excluding men who were not admitted to
the Legislative until late in the session? As can be seen from the list above, eight
suppléants were admitted to the Legislative in 1792. Rovère and Olivier-Gérente
were also admitted late, so that the total of those reelected in 1792 who had not
served a full term is 10. On Pariset's own criteria, the total number of ex-
Legislatives should be 194 + Germignac and Menuau = 196; if the late arrivals
are excluded, 196 − 10 = 186. But this treatment of Legislative *suppléants* is
inconsistent with his apparent treatment of Constituent *suppléants*, and in any
case does not produce the right total.
Kuscinski, in his *Les Députés à l'Assemblée législative de 1791*, identifies
196 men as *conventionnels*, though he does not give a total or a separate list of
names. He notes that Tavernel refused election, but includes Germignac, and also
Menuau, who as noted above was not called up until September 1793. His total
of deputies effectively sitting in January 1793 is therefore 194. He ignores de
Varaigne (Haute-Marne), Méricamp (Landes), and Rudler (Haut-Rhin) who were
all certainly chosen as *suppléants*; the reasons for believing de Varaigne may
perhaps have sat are set out below.
J. M. Thompson's engaging remark (*The French Revolution*, p. 312) about
the *conventionnel* who was travelling in Norway when elected, and never took
his seat, refers to Marey, and is libelous. Marey was in Norway at the time of his
election *to the Legislative Assembly*, and did not need to come home, being a
suppléant who was never required. He was reelected to and sat in the Convention. It may also be noted that old Lonqueue, Thompson's "oldest member,"
was not present in September 1792 as implied, being a *suppléant* who did not sit
until September 1793. The oldest deputy in 1792 was Rudel. It is not clear why
Rühl acted as the *président d'âge* on 20 September 1792 when he was only 57;
there were plenty of older men, including Dusaulx and Raffron from the Paris
delegation, both of whom seem likely to have been present and either of whom
could have given Rühl 10 years. If the report did not explicitly identify Rühl as
an ex-member of the Legislative, one would be tempted to think that the reporters simply got the name wrong, and that Rudel did have the honor which
would have come as a seventy-third birthday present; but this is conjecture, and
unsupported. He had at any rate belated recognition 3 years later, when he
presided over the first meeting of the Directory's legislature.
In identifying Nicolas Hentz as the Convention's youngest member, Kuscinski blundered, confusing the *conventionnel* Hentz with a younger cousin of the

same name; it can only be said in extenuation that Nicolas was an uncommon name among the deputies, and that to find 2 men named Nicolas Hentz living in the same area at the same time was hardly to be expected. There may well be other slips as bad, but the evidence I have come across suggests that these are unlikely to be extensive. But cf. G. Laurent, "Le plus jeune député de la Convention: Saint-Just ou Hentz?" *Annales* I (1924): 379–80; also the review of Kuscinski by Mathiez, *Annales Révolutionnaires* XII (1920), which despite its bias is not really damaging to any marked degree. One may I think assume that Mathiez would have been checking for errors since the book began to appear in 1916 and would have given them full publicity.

We may finally list those men who were elected to the Legislative Assembly as *suppléants*, did not sit, and finally sat in the Convention. Thirty-five of these were elected in 1792 as *députés titulaires*, and 5 were elected a second time as *suppléants* and were called up at various times from 31 August 1793 to 27 April 1795.

iii) *Elected as suppléants to the Legislative Assembly, but not called on to sit*

a) Sitting in the Convention from September 1792

1. Bailly (Seine-et-Marne)
2. Balland (Vosges)
3. Barrot (Lozère)
4. Beffroy (Aisne)
5. Marcellin-Béraud (Rhône-et-Loire)
6. Boissieu (Isère)
7. Bresson (Vosges)
8. Brunel (Hérault)
9. Dandenac M.F. (Maine-et-Loire)
10. Dechézeaux (Charente-Inf.)
11. Drouet (Marne)
12. DuBignon (Ille-et-Vilaine)
13. Duplantier (Gironde)
14. Espert (Ariège)
15. Izoard (Hautes-Alpes)
16. Jullien (Drôme)
17. Lozeau (Charente-Inf.)
18. Marec (Finistère)
19. Marey (Côte d'Or)
20. Martin (Somme)
21. Martinel (Drôme)
22. Mazade-Percin (Haute-Garonne)
23. Méaulle (Ille-et-Vilaine)
24. Meyer (Tarn)
25. Pellissier (Bouches-du-Rhône)
26. Penières-Delzors (Corrèze)
27. Pérard (Maine-et-Loire)
28. Plaichard-Choltière (Mayenne)
29. Pocholle (Seine-Inf.)
30. Porcher (Indre)
31. Ruault (Seine-Inf.)
32. Ruelle (Indre-et-Loire)
33. Serveau (Mayenne)
34. Turreau (Yonne)
35. Gillet (Morbihan)

b) Called up as *suppléants* to the Convention after January 1793

Deputy	Admitted to Convention	Deputy replaced
1. Alard (Haute Garonne)	3/8/1794	Julien
2. Champigny-Aubin (Indre-et-Loire)	26/9/1794	Dupont
3. Desgrouas (Charente-Inf.)	27/4/1795	—
4. Edouard (Côte d'Or)	15/5/1794	Basire
5. Eschassériaux R. (Charente-Inf.)	31/8/1793	Dechézeaux

A small insoluble problem about the Convention's membership arises from the inclusion in the *Dictionnaire* of 4 unexplained entries: BELVIALA. *Voir* Laporte; BENAZET. *Voir* Roquelory; BERNARDIN DE SAINT-PIERRE. *Voir* Saint-Pierre; and DE VARAIGNE. *Voir* Varaigne. None of these has any sequel. Were any of these men deputies?

Bernardin was not; he was elected for Loir-et-Cher, but refused the seat (A.N. C 179 C II 40 [Loir-et-Cher] 4 Sept., and letter annexed). The others were elected as *suppléants* for Lozère, Aude, and Haute-Marne respectively. They could have sat only as 5 *floréal* deputies, since there was no other suitable vacancy in any of the 3 delegations. One of them may have done so, since although Kuscinski says (*Conventionnels*, 23) that 12 men were called up on 5 *floréal*, his own details for the *suppléants* yield only 11 names for that date. But which one? The standard biographical dictionaries give no relevant information. De Varaigne is the only one of the 3 to appear in the *Table analytique*; unfortunately this entry duplicates that in the *Dictionnaire*, so that nothing can be learned from it, except perhaps that its existence makes him the marginally preferable candidate. If de Varaigne did sit, he brings the total of ex-Legislative *conventionnels* to 197. His full name was Pierre-Joseph-Bernard de Varaigne, and at the time of his election in 1791 he was *ingénieur en chef des ponts et chaussées*, Rhône-et-Loire, living in Lyon (Kuscinski, *Législative*, p. 130; cf. ibid., p. 75).

VOTING IN THE LEGISLATIVE ASSEMBLY
APPELS NOMINAUX OF 1792

For space reasons, it is impracticable to reprint the voting lists for the Legislative's *appels nominaux*, though these are very illuminating background for the 1792 elections if the deputies are re-sorted from the alphabetical Jacobin *Tableau comparatif* into their departmental delegations. As a sample, the voting of the Parisian deputies is reproduced below. The subjects of the *appels* are rather confusingly set out in the *Tableau comparatif*; for present purposes it need only be noted that (1) the Left had the initiative throughout; in general terms, a *oui* vote was a vote for the Left, a *non* vote, a vote for the monarchy; and (2) the last *appel*, on 7 August, was the final attempt to impeach Lafayette.

Paris	I	II	III	IV	V	VI	VII	Election result 1792
Beauvais	o	o	o	o	o	abs	o	Elected (16) (1791 15)
Bigot	n	n	n	n	n	abs	n	
Boscary	abs	o	n	n	resigned 5 June			
Brissot	o	o	o	o	o	o	o	Elected Eure-et-Loir (2), Eure, Loiret
Broussonet	o	o	o	o	abs	o	abs	
Cérutti	died 3 February							
Condorcet	o	o	o	o	abs	abs	abs	Elected Aisne (8) Eure, Gironde, Loiret, Sarthe
Crette	abs	n	abs	abs	abs	abs	abs	
De Bry	o	abs	abs	abs	abs	n	abs	
Fillassier	abs	n	abs	abs	abs	abs	abs	
Garran-Coulon	abs	abs	o	o	abs	abs	abs	Elected Loiret (2)
Godard	died 1 November 1791							
Gorguereau	abs	abs	n	abs	abs	n	n	
Gouvion	resigned 16 April; no record							
Hérault de Séchelles	o	o	o	o	n	o	o	Elected Seine-et-Oise (14), Somme
Lacépède	n	o	n	n	n	n	n	
Monneron	abs	n	resigned 31 March					
Mulot	abs	abs	abs	abs	abs	abs	abs	
Pastoret	abs	o	n	n	n	n	n	
Quatremère	n	n	n	n	abs	n	n	

315

Paris	I	II	III	IV	V	VI	VII	Election result 1792
Ramond	n	n	n	n	n	n	abs	
Robin	abs	abs	n	n	abs	abs	n	
Thorillon	abs	abs	n	n	n	abs	n	
Trulh-Pardailhon	n	abs	n	n	abs	n	n	

Suppléants

	I	II	III	IV	V	VI	VII	
Lacretelle	n	n	n	abs	abs	n	n	
Aléaume	voted from June				n	n	n	
Clavière	Minister 24 March; opted for ministry, 1 April							
Kersaint	from April				abs	o	o	Elected Seine-et-Oise (12)
De Moÿ	from April				o	o	o	
Dusaulx	from June				o	o	o	Elected (14)

THE VOTING IN THE *APPELS NOMINAUX* OF 1793

The deputies are listed in departments in the order in which they were called on to vote in the *appel* on the sentence, on 16–17 January 1793. This *appel* began with the department of Haute-Garonne, hence the dramatic impact of Mailhe's vote.

Symbols:

i) *Throughout voting*

o = *moderate* vote, i.e., for *appel au peuple*, for prison sentence, for reprieve, for impeachment of Marat, for reinstatement of Commission of 12.

x = *radical* vote, i.e., against *appel au peuple*, for death sentence, against reprieve, against Marat's impeachment, against the Commission of 12.

abs = absent. For the king's trial only, those who were ill are so identified.

abst = abstained from voting. For the Marat impeachment, this includes those who would not vote because they wanted the matter adjourned for further debate.

m = *en mission.* For the later *appels*, the record on this has to be checked carefully. The record of the *appel-nominal* must be compared with evidence from other sources; the pamphlet on the Marat impeachment is wildly inaccurate, with dozens of deputies listed as "absent" when they were actually *en mission.* None of the records seems wholly reliable. The editors of the *Archives parlementaires* note some of the errors made concerning the vote of 28 May, but there are other doubtful entries they do not mention.

Trial of Louis XVI

R = reprieve on specified conditions.
M = vote for Mailhe amendment.

Note that this list includes only those deputies who were sitting in January 1793; it does not include the *suppléants* who arrived later, nor the deputies for colonies or new departments, about a dozen of these latter having arrived by 28 May 1793.

ii) *For political groups*

The symbol preceding the name of each deputy indicates the political group to which he has been assigned.

Gironde   "inner sixty" = G
            sympathizers = g
            Those signing protests against 2 June 1793
            indicated by an asterisk.

A l'écart = E
"Committees" = C
En mission = m
Mountain   Montagnard ("sat with the Mountain," or equivalent) = M
            Jacobin Club of Paris, 1793/94 = MJ
            Montagnard "by attribution"–
            en mission 1793/94 = Mm
            committees 1793/94 = Mc
Not included in political analysis = O

		Trial of Louis XVI				Later appels	
		Guilt	*Appel*	Sen-tence	Re-prieve	Marat	Comm. of 12
Haute-Garonne							
C	Mailhe	x	x	M	o	*en mission*	
MJ	Delmas	x	x	x	x	x	x
Mm	Projean	x	x	x	x	*en mission*	
C	Perès	x	o	o	o	abs	o
M	Jullien	x	x	x	x	*en mission*	
Mm	Calès	x	x	x	x	abs	x
g*	Estadens	x	o	o	o	o	abs
C	Ayral	x	o	x	x	abs	o
Mm	De Sacy	x	x	M	x	abs	abs
g*	Rouzet	abst	o	o	o	abst	o
E	Drulhe	x	o	o	o	abs	abs
m	Mazade-Percin	x	o	o	o	*en mission*	
Gers							
g*	Laplaigne	x	x	x	x	abs	o
MJ	Maribon-Montaut	x	x	x	x	*en mission*	
g*	Descamps	x	x	x	x	abs	o
E	Cappin	x	o	o	o	abs	o
MJ	Barbeau-Dubarran	x	x	x	x	x	x
E	Laguire	x	x	x	x	abs	x
MJ	Ichon	x	x	x	x	*en mission*	
E	Bousquet	x	x	x	x	abs	abs
g*	Moysset	x	o	o	o	abs	o
Gironde							
G	Vergniaud	x	o	M	x	abs	o
G	Guadet	x	o	M	o	abst	o
G	Gensonné	x	o	x	x	abst	o
G	Grangeneuve	x	o	o	abst	o	o
MJ	Jay	x	x	x	x	x	x

		Trial of Louis XVI				Later appels	
		Guilt	*Appel*	Sen-tence	Re-prieve	Marat	Comm. of 12
G	Ducos	x	x	x	x	abst	o
M	Garrau	x	x	x	x	abs	x
G	Boyer-Fonfrède	x	x	x	x	o	o
g	Duplantier	x	x	M	x	abs	o
M	Deleyre	x	x	x	x	abs	o
G*	Lacaze	x	x	o	[ill]	o	abs
G	Bergoeing	x	o	o	o	o	abs
Hérault							
Mc	Cambon	x	x	x	x	abs	x
Mc	Bonnier d'Alco	x	x	x	x	abs	x
C	Curée	x	x	o	o	o	x
m	Viennet	x	o	o	o	o	o
G	Rouyer	x	o	x	x	*en mission*	
C	Cambacérès	x	x	R	o	abst	x
g	Brunel	x	o	o	o	*en mission*	
Mm	Fabre	x	x	x	x	x	m
C	Castilhon	x	o	o	o	o	o
Ille-et-Vilaine							
G	Lanjuinais	x	o	o	o	o	o
g*	Defermon	x	o	o	o	m	o
MJ	Duval	x	x	x	x	abs	abs
Mm	Sévestre	x	x	x	x	*en mission*	
Mc	Chaumont	x	x	x	x	abs	x
g*	Lebreton	x	x	o	x	o	abs
C	Du Bignon	x	x	o	x	o	x
g*	Obelin-Kergal	x	o	o	o	o	x
MJ	Beaugeard	x	x	x	x	x	x
E	Maurel	x	x	o	o	x	x
Indre							
E	Porcher	x	o	o	o	abs	o
C	Thabaud	x	x	M	x	abs	[unknown]
C	Pepin	x	o	o	x	abs	abs
C	Boudin	x	o	o	o	abs	o
MJ	Lejeune	x	x	x	x	m	x
g*	Derazey	x	o	o	o	o	o
Indre-et-Loire							
MJ	Nioche	x	x	x	x	x	m
Mc	Dupont	x	x	x	[ill]	x	x
MJ	Pottier	x	x	x	x	abs	x
g	Gardien	x	o	o	o	o	o
Mm	Ruelle	x	x	M	x	x	m
Mc	Champigny-Clément	x	x	M	x	x	x

		Trial of Louis XVI				Later appels	
		Guilt	*Appel*	Sen-tence	Re-prieve	Marat	Comm. of 12
MJ	Ysabeau	x	x	x	x	*en mission*	
m	Bodin	x	x	o	o	*en mission*	
Isère							
E	Baudran	x	x	x	x	abs	abs
E	Genevois	x	x	x	x	abs	abs
C	Servonat	x	o	o	o	o	o
MJ	Amar	x	x	x	x	abs	x
C	Prunelle-Lière	x	o	o	[ill]	x	abs
C	Réal	x	o	o	x	abs	o
E	Boissieu	x	x	o	x	abs	o
MJ	Génissieu	x	x	M	o	abst	o
C	Charrel	x	x	x	x	o	o
Jura							
g*	Vernier	x	o	o	o	o	abs
g*	Laurenceot	x	o	o	o	o	o
g*	Grenot	x	o	x	o	o	o
M	Prost	x	x	x	x	m	x
g*	Amyon	x	o	x	x	abst	o
G*	Babey	x	o	o	o	o	o
g*	Ferroux de Salins	x	o	x	o	o	o
C	Bonguiot	x	o	o	o	o	abs
Landes							
MJ	Dartigoeyte	x	x	x	x	*en mission*	
E	Lefranc	x	x	o	o	abs	o
E	Cadroy	x	x	o	o	abs	o
MJ	Ducos, P. R.	x	x	x	x	abs	x
Mm	Dyzez	x	x	x	x	x	x
g*	Saurine	x	o	o	o	o	o
Loir-et-Cher							
G	Grégoire	*en mission* throughout trial				abs	abs
MJ	Chabot	x	x	x	x	m	x
MJ	Brisson	x	x	x	x	x	x
Mm	Frécine	x	x	x	x	abs	x
C	Leclerc	x	x	o	o	o	o
Mc	Venaille	x	x	x	x	x	x
M	Foussedoire	x	x	x	x	abs	x
Haute-Loire							
Mm	Reynaud	x	x	x	x	x	x
MJ	Faure	x	x	x	x	abs	x
Mc	Delcher	x	x	x	x	*en mission*	

		Trial of Louis XVI				Later appels	
		Guilt	*Appel*	Sen-tence	Re-prieve	Marat	Comm. of 12
Mc	Rongiès	x	x	x	x	abs	x
g	Bonet de Treyches	. x	o	x	o	o	o
o	Camus		*en mission* throughout			[Austrian prisoner]	
g	Barthélemy	x	o	x	o	o	o
Loire-Inférieure							
Mm	Méaulle	x	x	x	x	x	x
g*	Lefebvre	x	o	o	o	abs	o
C	Chaillon	x	o	o	o	o	abs
o	Mellinet	x	o	o	o	abs	o
C	Villers	x	x	x	x	m	o
MJ	Fouché	x	x	x	x	abs	x
g*	Jary	x	o	o	o	o	abs
g	Coustard	x	o	o	o	o	m
Loiret							
E	Gentil	x	o	o	abst	abst	abs
C	Garran-Coulon	x	o	o	o	o	o
E	Lepage	x	o	o	o	abs	x
E	Pelé	x	x	o	o	abs	abs
C	Lombard-Lachaux	x	x	x	o	*en mission*	
E	Guérin	x	x	o	o	x	abs
MJ	Delaguelle	x	x	x	x	x	x
G	Louvet, J. B.	x	o	R	o	abst	o
MJ	Bourdon, L. J.	x	x	x	x	m	x
Lot							
C	Laboissière	x	x	M	o	abs	x
E	Cledel	x	x	x	x	abs	x
C	Sallèles	x	o	o	o	o	o
MJ	Jeanbon Saint-André	x	x	x	x	m	x
Mc	Monmayou	x	x	x	x	abs	x
Mm	Cavaignac	x	x	x	x	abst	m
E	Bouygues	x	o	o	o	o	o
o	Caila	x	x	[collapsed, d. 19 January]			
m	Delbrel	x	x	R	O	*en mission*	
C	Albouys	x	o	o	o	o	o
Lot-et-Garonne							
E	Vidalot	x	x	x	x	o	o
m	Laurent	x	o	o	o	abs	o
m	Paganel	x	x	M	o	m	x
E	Claverye	x	o	o	o	abs	o
o	Larroche	x	o	o	o	[on leave]	

		Trial of Louis XVI				Later appels	
		Guilt	*Appel*	Sen-tence	Re-prieve	Marat	Comm. of 12
C	Bouission	x	o	x	x	abs	o
E	Guyet-Laprade	x	o	o	o	o	o
E	Fournel	x	x	x	o	o	o
E	Noguères	x	o	o	o	o	o
Lozère							
C	Barrot	x	o	o	x	abst	o
M	Châteauneuf-Randon	x	x	x	x	x	x
Mm	Servière	x	x	R	[ill]	m	x
E	Pelet	*en mission* throughout trial				abs	abs
Mm	Monestier	x	x	R	x	x	abs
Maine-et-Loire							
MJ	Choudieu	x	x	x	x	*en mission*	
M	Delaunay, J.	x	x	x	x	abs	m
o	De Houlières	x	o	o	abs	o	[resigned]
g*	La Revellière-Lépeaux	x	x	x	x	o	o
g*	Pilastre	x	x	o	o	o	o
g*	Leclerc, J. B.	x	x	o	o	o	o
M	Dandenac, M. F.	x	x	o	o	abs	x
g*	Delaunay, P. M.	x	x	o	o	abs	m
M	Pérard	x	x	x	x	x	x
g*	Dandenac, J.	x	x	o	o	o	m
g*	Le Maignan	x	x	o	o	o	o
Manche							
E	Gervais-Sauvé	x	o	o	o	x	o
E	Poisson	x	o	o	o	o	o
MJ	Lemoine	x	x	x	x	x	x
C	Le Tourneur	x	o	x	x	*en mission*	
C	Ribet	x	o	R	o	abs	abs
C	Pinel	x	o	o	o	o	o
Mm	Le Carpentier	x	x	x	x	m	x
C	Havin	x	o	x	o	abs	o
E	Bonnesoeur-Bourginière	x	o	R	o	o	o
g	Engerran	x	o	o	o	o	o
C	Regnault-Bretel	x	x	o	o	abs	o
g*	Laurence	x	o	R	o	o	o
E	Hubert	x	o	x	o	o	o
Marne							
MJ	Prieur, P. L.	x	x	x	x	*en mission*	
M	Thuriot	x	x	x	x	m	x

		Trial of Louis XVI				Later appels	
		Guilt	*Appel*	Sen-tence	Re-prieve	Marat	Comm. of 12
Mc	Charlier	x	x	x	x	abst	x
M	Delacroix	x	x	x	x	abst	x
MJ	Deville	x	x	x	x	x	m
E	Poullain	x	o	o	o	o	o
MJ	Drouet	[ill]	[ill]	x	x	x	x
M	Armonville	x	x	x	x	x	x
E	Blanc	x	x	o	o	o	o
M	Battellier	x	x	x	x	x	x
	Haute-Marne						
M	Guyardin	x	x	x	x	x	x
Mc	Monnel	x	x	x	x	x	x
MJ	Roux	x	x	x	x	x	x
Mc	Valdruche	x	x	x	x	abs	x
MJ	Chaudron-Rousseau	x	x	x	x	*en mission*	
MJ	Laloy	x	x	x	x	x	x
C	Wandelaincourt	[abstained]		o	o	abs	o
	Mayenne						
m	Bissy	x	x	R	o	abs	x
Mm	Esnuë-Lavallée	x	x	x	x	abs	x
MJ	Grosse-Durocher	x	x	x	x	x	x
E	Enjubault	x	x	R	o	o	o
C	Serveau	x	x	R	o	o	o
C	Plaichard-Choltière	x	x	o	o	o	o
C	Villar	x	x	o	o	o	o
C	Lejeune	x	x	o	o	o	o
	Meurthe						
G	Salle	x	o	o	o	abst	o
M	Mallarmé	x	x	x	x	x	x
M	Le Vasseur	x	x	x	x	*en mission*	
G	Mollevaut	x	o	o	o	o	o
Mm	Bonneval	x	x	x	x	abs	x
C	Lalande	abst	o	o	o	abs	o
E	Michel	x	o	o	o	m	abs
C	Zangiacomi	x	o	o	o	o	o
	Meuse						
E	Moreau	x	o	o	o	o	o
E	Marquis	x	o	o	o	abs	o
E	Tocquot	x	o	o	o	o	o
Mc	Pons	x	x	x	x	abst	x

		Trial of Louis XVI				Later appels	
		Guilt	*Appel*	Sen-tence	Re-prieve	Marat	Comm. of 12
E	Roussel	x	o	o	o	o	o
E	Bazoche	x	o	o	o	o	o
C	Humbert	x	o	o	o	o	o
m	Harmand	x	x	o	x	abs	x
Morbihan							
C	Le Malliaud	x	x	o	x	*en mission*	
G	Lehardi	x	o	o	o	o	o
g*	Corbel	x	x	o	x	o	o
MJ	Lequinio	x	x	x	x	m	x
C	Audrein	x	o	M	o	o	abs
m	Gillet	x	x	o	x	abs	m
g	Michel	x	x	o	o	o	o
g*	Rouault	x	x	o	o	o	o
Moselle							
MJ	Merlin, A. C.	*en mission* throughout all voting					
MJ	Anthoine	x	x	x	x	m	abs
MJ	Couturier	*en mission* throughout early votes					x
MJ	Hentz	x	x	x	x	*en mission*	
g*	Blaux	x	x	o	o	m	o
M	Thirion	x	x	x	x	abst	x
C	Becker	x	x	o	o	abs	o
Mm	Bar	x	x	x	x	abst	x
Nièvre							
C	Sautereau	x	x	x	abs	abs	abs
Mm	Dameron	x	x	x	x	x	x
MJ	Lefiot	x	x	x	x	x	x
E	Guillerault	x	o	x	x	abs	o
Mm	Legendre	x	x	x	x	abs	x
MJ	Goyre-Laplanche	x	x	x	x	m	x
C	Jourdan	x	o	o	o	o	o
Nord							
M	Merlin, P. A.	x	x	x	x	abst	m
MJ	Duhem	x	x	x	x	*en mission*	
m	Gossuin	*en mission* throughout early votes					x
Mm	Cochet	x	x	x	x	abs	x
o	Fockedey	x	o	o	o	[resigned]	
MJ	Lesage-Sénault	x	x	x	x	m	x
C	Carpentier	x	x	x	x	o	abs
Mc	Sallengros	x	x	x	x	abst	x
Mm	Poultier	x	x	x	x	x	abs
MJ	d'Aoust	x	x	x	x	abs	x

		Trial of Louis XVI				Later appels	
		Guilt	*Appel*	Sen-tence	Re-prieve	Marat	Comm. of 12
Mc	Boyaval	x	x	x	x	abs	x
Mm	Briez	x	x	x	x	*en mission*	
Oise							
MJ	Coupé	x	x	x	x	abst	x
MJ	Calon	x	x	x	x	abst	x
MJ	Massieu	x	x	x	x	abst	x
o	Villette	x	x	o	o	abs	[d. 7 July]
m	Mathieu	x	x	x	x	o	o
MJ	Cloots	x	x	x	x	x	abs
m	Portiez	x	x	M	x	abs	o
m	Godefroy	*en mission* throughout early votes					x
Mc	Bézard	x	x	x	x	abs	x
MJ	Isoré	x	x	x	x	m	x
g*	Delamarre	x	o	o	o	o	o
MJ	Bourdon, F. L.	x	x	x	x	m	x
Orne							
G	Dufriche-Valazé	x	o	R	o	o	o
g	Bertrand de l'Hodiesnière	x	o	x	x	o	abs
E	Plet-Beauprey	x	o	R	o	*en mission*	
E	Duboë	x	o	o	o	o	o
g*	Dugué d'Assé	x	O	o	o	o	o
m	Desgrouas	x	o	x	x	abs	x
E	Thomas-Laprise	x	abst	R	o	abs	o
E	Fourmy	x	o	o	o	o	o
M	Dubois	x	x	x	x	abs	x
MJ	Collombel	x	x	x	x	x	x
Paris							
MJ	Robespierre, M.	x	x	x	x	x	x
MJ	Danton	*en mission*		x	x	abs	x
MJ	Collot d'Herbois	*en mission*		x	x	m	x
G	Manuel	x	o	o	[resigned]		
MJ	Billaud-Varenne	x	x	x	x	m	x
MJ	Desmoulins	x	x	x	x	x	abs
MJ	Marat	x	x	x	x	abs	x
MJ	Lavicomterie	x	x	x	x	x	x
MJ	Legendre	x	x	x	x	m	x
MJ	Raffron	x	x	x	x	abs	x
MJ	Panis	x	x	x	x	abs	x
MJ	Sergent	x	x	x	x	x	x

		Trial of Louis XVI				Later appels	
		Guilt	*Appel*	Sen-tence	Re-prieve	Marat	Comm. of 12
MJ	Robert	x	x	x	x	abs	abs
G*	Dusaulx	x	o	o	o	o	o
MJ	Fréron	x	x	x	x	*en mission*	
MJ	Beauvais	x	x	x	x	*en mission*	
MJ	Fabre d'Eglantine	x	x	x	x	abst	x
MJ	Osselin	x	x	x	x	abst	x
MJ	Robespierre, A.	x	x	x	x	x	x
MJ	David	x	x	x	x	x	x
MJ	Boucher	x	x	x	x	x	x
MJ	Laignelot	x	x	x	x	x	x
C	Thomas, J. J.	x	x	o	o	abst	abs
o	Egalité	x	x	x	x	[in prison]	

Pas-de-Calais

MJ	Duquesnoy	x	x	x	x	*en mission*	
M	Carnot	x	x	x	x	*en mission*	
MJ	Le Bas	x	x	x	x	x	abs
g	Paine	x	x	o	o	abs	abs
E	Personne	x	o	o	o	o	o
MJ	Guffroy	x	x	x	x	abs	x
m	Enlart	x	x	o	abs	abst	abs
Mm	Bollet	x	x	x	x	x	x
E	Magniez	x	o	o	o	x	o
g*	Daunou	x	x	o	o	abs	x
g*	Varlet	x	o	o	o	o	o

Puy-de-Dôme

MJ	Couthon	x	x	x	x	m	x
E	Gibergues	x	x	x	x	o	abs
MJ	Maignet	x	x	x	x	abs	m
MJ	Romme	x	x	x	x	x	m
M	Soubrany	x	x	x	x	abs	m
o	Bancal des Issarts	x	o	o	o	[Austrian prisoner]	
E	Girot-Pouzol	x	o	o	o	o	abs
Mc	Rudel	x	x	x	x	abs	x
M	Artaud-Blanval	x	x	x	x	abs	abs
MJ	Monestier	x	x	x	x	m	abs
g	Dulaure	x	x	x	x	abs	o
g	Laloue	x	o	x	x	o	o

Hautes-Pyrénées

MJ	Barère	x	x	x	x	abs	x
C	Dupont	x	o	R	o	o	o

		Trial of Louis XVI				Later appels	
		Guilt	*Appel*	Sen-tence	Re-prieve	Marat	Comm. of 12
E	Gertoux	x	x	o	o	o	o
E	Picqué	x	x	R	o	o	abs
m	Féraud	x	x	x	x	o	m
C	Lacrampe	x	o	x	x	o	abs
Basses-Pyrénées							
E	Sanadon	x	o	o	o	abs	o
m	Neveu	x	o	o	o	*en mission*	
E	Conte	x	o	o	o	o	o
E	Pémartin	x	x	o	o	o	o
G	Meillan	x	o	o	o	o	o
g*	Casenave	x	o	o	o	o	o
Pyrénées-Orientales							
g*	Guiter	x	o	o	o	o	o
E	Fabre	[ill(?) throughout trial]				abs	abs
G	Birotteau	x	o	R	o	o	o
M	Montégut	x	x	x	x	o	abs
M	Cassanyès	x	x	x	x	o	o
Haut-Rhin							
m	Reubell	*en mission* throughout all voting					
Mm	Ritter	x	x	x	x	*en mission*	
MJ	Laporte	x	x	x	x	x	m
C	Johannot	x	x	M	o	abs	abs
MJ	Pflieger	x	x	x	x	*en mission*	
E	Albert	x	o	o	o	o	o
C	Dubois	x	o	o	o	abs	o
Bas-Rhin							
M	Rühl	*en mission* throughout early votes					x
MJ	Laurent	x	x	x	x	*en mission*	
MJ	Bentabole	x	x	x	x	x	x
M	Dentzel	*en mission* throughout trial				abs	x
MJ	Louis	x	x	x	x	*en mission*	
m	Ehrmann	[ill throughout trial]				abs	abs
C	Arbogast	x	x	o	abst	abst	x
E	Christiani	x	x	o	o	abs	o
MJ	Simond	*en mission* throughout early votes					x
Rhône-et-Loire							
G*	Chasset	x	x	o	x	o	o
Mm	Dupuy	x	x	x	x	abst	x
E	Vitet	x	o	o	o	abs	abs
MJ	Du Bouchet	x	x	x	x	x	x
g	Marcellin-Béraud	x	o	o	o	abs	abs

		Trial of Louis XVI				Later appels	
		Guilt	*Appel*	Sen-tence	Re-prieve	Marat	Comm. of 12
MJ	Pressavin	x	x	x	x	m	x
E	Patrin	x	o	o	o	abs	abs
E	Moulin	x	x	R	o	o	o
E	Michet	x	o	o	x	o	o
E	Forest	x	o	o	o	o	abs
M	Noël Pointe	x	x	x	x	abs	x
MJ	Cusset	x	x	x	x	x	abs
Mm	Javogues	x	x	x	x	x	x
G	Lanthénas	x	x	R	x	x	abs
E	Fournier	x	o	o	o	abs	abs
Haute-Saône							
M	Gourdan	x	x	x	x	o	o
C	Vigneron	x	x	o	o	o	o
M	Siblot	x	x	M	x	m	o
E	Chauvier	x	x	o	x	o	o
E	Balivet	x	x	o	o	o	o
M	Dornier	x	x	x	x	o	o
E	Bolot	x	x	x	o	abs	abs
Saône-et-Loire							
M	Gelin	x	x	x	x	abs	abs
G*	Masuyer	x	x	x	x	o	o
G	Carra	x	x	x	x	*en mission*	
o	Guillermin	x	x	x	x	[d. 19 April]	
MJ	Reverchon	x	x	x	x	*en mission*	
Mm	Guillemardet	x	x	x	x	abs	x
MJ	Baudot	x	x	x	x	*en mission*	
E	Bertucat	x	o	o	o	x	o
MJ	Mailly	x	x	x	x	abs	abs
M	Moreau	x	x	x	x	abs	abs
C	Montgilbert	x	x	R	o	abs	abs
Sarthe							
MJ	Richard	x	x	x	x	*en mission*	
Mm	François-Primaudière	x	x	x	x	abs	x
g*	Salmon	x	x	o	o	o	o
MJ	Philippeaux	x	x	x	x	x	x
MJ	Boutrouë	x	x	x	x	x	x
MJ	Levasseur	x	x	x	x	x	x
g*	Chevalier	x	o	o	o	o	o
E	Froger-Plisson	x	x	x	x	o	o
E	Sieyès	x	x	x	x	abs	abs
Mm	Le Tourneur	x	x	x	x	abs	x

| | | Trial of Louis XVI | | | | *Later appels* | |
		Guilt	*Appel*	Sen-tence	Re-prieve	Marat	Comm. of 12
Seine-et-Marne							
Mc	Mauduyt	x	x	x	x	m	x
C	Bailly	x	o	o	o	o	abs
Mm	Tellier	x	x	x	x	abst	x
Mc	Cordier	x	x	x	x	x	x
E	Viquy	x	o	o	o	o	o
C	Geoffroy	x	o	o	o	o	o
g	Bernard	x	o	R	o	abst	o
C	Himbert	x	o	o	[ill]	abs	abs
C	Opoix	x	abst	o	o	abs	abs
E	Defrance	x	x	o	o	abs	abs
E	Bernier	x	o	o	o	o	abs
Seine-et-Oise							
MJ	Lecointre	x	x	x	x	abs	m
C	Haussmann	*en mission* throughout early votes					x
MJ	Bassal	x	x	x	x	abs	abs
m	Alquier	x	x	R	o	abs	abs
G	Gorsas	x	o	o	x	o	abs
M	Audouin	x	x	x	x	x	x
m	Treilhard	x	x	R	o	abs	abs
E	Roy	x	x	R	o	abs	o
MJ	Taillien	x	x	x	x	*en mission*	
M	Hérault de Séchelles	*en mission* throughout early votes					x
G	Mercier	x	x	o	o	o	o
G	Kersaint	x	o	o	[resigned]		
MJ	Chénier	x	x	x	x	abs	x
E	Dupuis	x	x	o	o	abs	o
Seine-Inférieure							
MJ	Albitte	x	x	x	x	x	m
Mm	Pocholle	x	x	x	x	m	x
G*	Hardy	x	abst	o	o	abs	o
E	Yger	x	o	o	o	abs	abs
g*	Hecquet	x	o	o	o	o	o
g*	Duval	x	o	o	o	*en mission*	
g*	Vincent	x	o	o	o	o	o
g*	Faure	x	o	o	o	abs	o
g*	Lefebvre	x	x	o	o	o	o
C	Blutel	x	o	o	o	abs	abs
g*	Bailleul	x	o	o	[ill]	o	abs
E	Mariette	x	o	o	o	*en mission*	
g*	Doublet	x	o	o	o	o	o
g*	Ruault	x	o	o	o	o	abs
E	Bourgois	x	o	o	o	o	o
g	Delahaye	x	o	o	o	o	abs

		Trial of Louis XVI				Later appels	
		Guilt	*Appel*	Sentence	Reprieve	Marat	Comm. of 12
Deux-Sèvres							
C	Lecointe-Puyraveau	x	o	x	x	abs	m
E	Jard-Panvillier	x	o	o	o	o	m
m	Auguis	x	x	o	o	*en mission*	
G	Duchastel	[ill]	[ill]	o	[ill]	o	o
Mc	Dubreuil-Chambardel	x	x	x	x	abs	x
C	Lofficial	x	o	o	o	o	o
MJ	Cochon	x	x	x	x	*en mission*	
Somme							
g*	Saladin	x	x	x	x	abs	x
g*	Rivery	x	o	o	o	abs	o
g*	Gantois	x	o	o	o	o	o
g*	Devérité	x	o	o	o	abs	o
g*	Asselin	x	x	o	o	abs	o
g*	Delecloy	x	o	R	o	abs	o
g*	Louvet, P. F.	x	o	o	o	abs	o
g*	Dufestel	x	o	o	o	o	o
o	Sillery	x	o	o	o	[in prison]	
g*	François	x	o	x	x	o	o
g*	Martin, J. B.	x	o	o	o	abs	abs
MJ	Dumont	x	x	x	x	x	x
Mc	Hourier-Eloi	x	x	x	x	abs	abs
Tarn							
G	Lasource	*en mission*		x	x	abst	x
Mm	Lacombe Saint-Michel	x	x	x	x	*en mission*	
E	Solomiac	x	x	o	o	abs	x
M	Campmas	x	x	x	x	x	x
E	Maruejouls	x	o	o	o	abs	o
o	Daubermesnil	[ill throughout trial—later on leave]					
E	Gouzy	x	o	R	o	o	o
C	Rochegude	x	o	o	o	m	o
E	Meyer	x	o	x	x	o	o
Var							
MJ	Escudier	x	x	x	x	x	x
M	Charbonnier	x	x	x	x	x	x
M	Ricord	x	x	x	x	x	x
G	Isnard	x	x	x	x	abst	o
G*	Despinassy	x	x	x	x	*en mission*	
M	Roubaud	x	x	x	x	*en mission*	
m	Antiboul	x	x	o	abst	x	abs
MJ	Barras	x	x	x	x	*en mission*	

		Trial of Louis XVI				Later appels	
		Guilt	*Appel*	Sentence	Reprieve	Marat	Comm. of 12
Vendée							
MJ	Goupilleau, J. F.	*en mission*		x	x	*en mission*	
MJ	Goupilleau, P. C.	x	x	x	x	*en mission*	
m	Gaudin	?	o	o	o	m	abs
Mc	Maignen	x	x	x	x	abs	abs
MJ	Fayau	x	x	x	x	m	x
m	Morisson	[abstained throughout trial]				abs	x
Mm	Musset	x	x	x	x	abs	abs
C	Girard	x	x	o	o	abs	x
Mc	Garos	x	x	x	x	abs	abs
Vienne							
Mc	Piorry	x	x	x	x	m	x
M	Ingrand	x	x	x	x	x	x
E	Dutrou-Bornier	x	o	o	o	o	o
E	Martineau	x	x	x	x	o	o
E	Bion	x	o	o	o	o	o
G	Creuzé-Latouche	x	o	o	o	o	abs
M	Thibaudeau	x	x	x	x	abs	m
E	Creuzé-Pascal [Dufresne]	x	o	o	o	o	m
Haute-Vienne							
g*	Lacroix	x	abst	o	o	abs	abs
g*	Lesterpt-Beauvais	x	x	R	o	o	o
M	Bordas	x	x	o	x	m	x
MJ	Gay-Vernon	x	x	x	x	x	x
g	Faye	x	o	o	o	o	o
g*	Rivaud	x	o	o	o	o	o
g*	Soulignac	x	o	o	o	o	o
Vosges							
g	Poulain-Grandprey	x	o	R	o	o	o
o	Hugo	[ill; never appeared]					
MJ	Perrin	x	x	x	x	m	x
G	Noël	[abstained throughout trial]				o	o
M	Jullien-Souhait	x	o	M	o	o	o
G*	Bresson	x	o	o	o	o	o
g	Couhey	x	o	o	o	o	o
C	Balland	x	o	o	o	o	o

		Trial of Louis XVI				*Later appels*	
		Guilt	*Appel*	Sen-tence	Re-prieve	Marat	Comm. of 12
Yonne							
MJ	Maure	x	x	x	x	abst	x
o	Le Peletier de Saint-Fargeau	x	x	x	x [murdered 20 January]		
Mm	Turreau de Linières	x	x	x	x	m	x
G	Boilleau	x	x	x	x	o	o
MJ	Précy	x	o	R	o	o	o
MJ	Bourbotte	x	x	x	x	*en mission*	
c	Hérard	x	o	x	x	o	o
MJ	Finot	x	x	x	x	abs	x
g*	Chastellain	x	o	o	o	o	o
Ain							
MJ	Deydier	x	x	x	x	x	x
MJ	Gauthier	x	x	x	x	abs	x
g*	Royer	x	o	o	o	o	o
M	Jagot	*en mission* throughout early votes					x
E	Mollet	x	o	o	o	abs	abs
MJ	Merlino	x	x	x	x	m	x
Aisne							
o	Quinette	x	x	x	x	[Austrian prisoner]	
g*	Jean de Bry	x	x	x	x	abs	abs
m	Beffroy	x	o	x	x	abs	abs
g*	Bouchereau	x	x	M	o	abs	abs
MJ	Saint-Just	x	x	x	x	m	x
g*	Belin	x	o	o	o	o	o
g*	Petit	x	o	x	x	abs	x
G	Condorcet	x	x	o	abst	abs	x
g*	Fiquet	x	o	o	o	abs	abs
g*	Le Carlier	x	x	x	x	abst	abs
g*	Loysel	x	o	R	o	o	abs
C	Dupin	x	x	o	x	abs	x
Allier							
E	Chevalier	x	o	[abstained]		o	o
Mc	Martel	x	x	x	x	x	abs
Mm	Petitjean	x	x	x	x	abs	x
MJ	Forestier	x	x	x	x	m	x
m	Beauchamp	*en mission* throughout all voting					
m	Giraud	x	x	R	[ill]	abs	x
Mm	Vidalin	x	x	x	m	abst	x
Hautes-Alpes							
g*	Barêty	x	o	o	o	o	o
g*	Borel	x	o	o	o	abs	abs

| | | Trial of Louis XVI | | | | Later appels | |
		Guilt	Appel	Sen-tence	Re-prieve	Marat	Comm. of 12
g*	Izoard	x	abst	o	o	abst	abs
g*	Serre	x	o	o	o	o	o
g*	Cazeneuve	x	o	o	o	o	o
Basses-Alpes							
o	Verdollin	x	o	o	o	[d. 16 April]	
E	Réguis	x	o	o	o	o	o
Mm	Dherbez-Latour	x	x	x	x	x	x
g*	Maisse	x	o	x	[ill]	abs	o
g*	Peyre	x	o	M	x	abs	o
E	Savornin	x	x	M	x	abs	abs
Ardèche							
C	Boissy d'Anglas	x	o	o	o	o	o
g*	Soubeyran de Saint-Prix	x	o	R	o	o	o
G	Gamon	x	o	R	o	o	o
C	Riffard de Saint-Martin	x	o	o	o	o	o
g*	Garilhe	x	o	o	o	o	o
C	Gleizal	x	x	R	o	m	o
C	Coren-Fustier	x	o	o	o	o	o
Ardennes							
E	Blondel	x	o	o	o	o	o
Mm	Ferry	x	x	x	x	en mission	
o	Mennesson	x	o	R	o	abs	abs
MJ	Dubois-Crancé	x	x	x	x	x	m
E	Vermon	x	o	R	o	abs	abs
Mc	Robert	x	x	x	x	abs	abs
E	Baudin	x	o	o	o	o	o
E	Thierret	x	o	o	o	abs	abs
Ariège							
MJ	Vadier	x	x	x	x	x	x
M	Clauzel	x	x	x	x	x	x
E	Campmartin	x	x	x	x	abs	o
M	Espert	x	x	x	x	abs	x
Mm	Lakanal	x	x	x	x	x	x
MJ	Gaston	x	x	x	x	m	x
Aube							
MJ	Courtois	x	x	x	x	x	m
Mm	Robin	x	x	x	x	abs	x

		Trial of Louis XVI				*Later appels*	
		Guilt	*Appel*	Sen-tence	Re-prieve	Marat	Comm. of 12
C	Perrin	x	o	o	o	o	o
m	Duval	x	x	o	o	o	abs
E	Bonnemain	x	o	o	o	o	o
E	Pierret	x	o	o	o	o	abs
E	Douge	x	o	o	o	o	o
M	Garnier	x	x	x	x	m	x?
G	Rabaut Saint-Etienne	x	o	o	o	o	abs
Aude							
M	Azéma	x	x	x	x	abs	abs
Mm	Bonnet	x	x	x	x	abst	m
C	Ramel-Nogaret	x	o	x	x	abst	abs
g*	Tournier	x	o	o	o	o	o
C	Marragon	x	o	x	x	abst	abs
g*	Periès	x	o	o	o	o	o
E	Morin	x	o	o	o	o	o
G	Girard	x	o	x	o	o	abs
Aveyron							
M	Bo	x	x	x	x	m	x
g*	St.-Martin-Valogne	x	o	o	o	o	o
E	Lobinhes	x	o	o	o	o	o
E	Bernard-Saint-Affrique	x	x	o	o	o	o
g*	Camboulas	x	x	x	x	abs	abs
Mc	Second	x	x	x	x	abs	abs
Mm	Lacombe	x	x	M	x	abs	x
M	Louchet	x	x	x	x	x	x
G	Yzarn de Valady	abst	o	o	o	abs	o
Bouches-du-Rhône							
G	Duprat	x	o	x	x	o	o
G	Rebecqui	x	o	x	x	[resigned 9 April]	
G	Barbaroux	x	o	x	x	o	o
M	Granet	x	x	x	x	x	x
E	Durand-Maillane	x	o	o	[ill]	abs	o
M	Gasparin	x	x	x	x	*en mission*	
MJ	Bayle	x	x	x	x	m	x?
MJ	Baille	x	x	x	x	abst	m
M	Rovère	x	x	x	x	m	x
G*	De Perret	x	o	o	o	abs	o

		Trial of Louis XVI				Later appels	
		Guilt	*Appel*	Sentence	Reprieve	Marat	Comm. of 12
m	Pelissier	x	x	x	x	abs	o
M	Laurens	x	x	x	x	x	x

Calvados

G	Fauchet	x	o	o	o	o	o
m	Du Bois du Bais	x	o	R	o	*en mission*	
E	Lomont	abst	o	o	o	o	abs
G	Henry-Larivière	abst	o	o	o	o	o
Mm	Bonnet de Meautry	x	x	M	x	abs	abs
C	Vardon	x	o	o	o	o	o
G	Doulcet de Pontécoulant	x	x	o	o	o	abs
C	Taveau	x	o	R	o	o	abs
C	Jouenne-Longchamp	x	o	M	x	o	o
C	Dumont	x	o	o	o	o	o
g	Cussy	x	o	o	o	o	o
M	Legot	x	o	o	o	abs	o
g*	Philippe-Delleville	x	o	o	o	o	o

Cantal

C	Thibault	x	o	o	o	m	o
MJ	Milhaud	x	x	x	x	x	m
E	Méjansac	x	o	o	[ill]	abs	o
MJ	Lacoste, J. B.	x	x	x	x	m	x
MJ	Carrier	x	x	x	x	abs	abs
m	Malhes, P.	[sat from 17 jan.]			abst	abs	x
m	Chabanon	x	o	o	o	abs	x
E	Peuvergne	x	o	o	o	abs	o

Charente

Mm	Bellegarde	x	x	x	x	*en mission*	
M	Guimberteau	x	x	x	x	*en mission*	
Mc	Chazaud	x	x	x	x	abs	x
C	Chédaneau	x	x	M	o	x	o
g*	Ribéreau	x	o	x	x	o	o
E	Devars	x	o	o	o	abst	o
C	Brun	x	o	x	x	abs	o
C	Crévelier	x	x	x	x	abs	o
m	Maulde	x	o	o	o	o	abs

Charente-Inférieure

MJ	Bernard	x	x	x	x	*en mission*	
Mm	Bréard	x	x	x	x	abs	x

		Trial of Louis XVI				Later appels	
		Guilt	*Appel*	Sen-tence	Re-prieve	Marat	Comm. of 12
MJ	Eschassériaux, J.	x	x	x	x	abs	x
MJ	Niou	x	x	x	x	*en mission*	
MJ	Ruamps	x	x	x	x	*en mission*	
MJ	Garnier	x	x	x	x	x	m
g*	Dechézeaux	x	x	o	x	abst	abs
C	Lozeau	x	x	x	x	abst	x
C	Giraud	x	x	o	o	abs	o
Mc	Vinet	x	x	x	x	abs	x
E	Dautriche	x	o	o	o	abs	abs
Cher							
C	Allasoeur	x	o	o	o	o	o
Mm	Foucher	x	x	x	m	abs	abs
C	Baucheton	x	o	o	o	o	o
Mc	Fauvre-Labrunerie	x	x	x	x	abs	x
E	Dugenne	x	o	o	o	o	o
C	Pelletier	x	o	o	o	abst	x
Corrèze							
MJ	Brival	x	x	x	x	x	x
M	Borie	x	x	x	x	m	x
C	Lafon	[abstained throughout trial]				abs	x
G	Chambon	x	o	x	abst	o	o
G	Lidon	x	o	M	x	o	abs
MJ	Lanot	x	x	x	x	x	x
g	Penières-Delzors	x	x	x	x	o	o
Corse							
M	Saliceti	x	x	x	x	*en mission*	
G	Chiappe	x	o	o	[ill]	o	o
MJ	Casa Bianca	x	x	o	o	abs	abs
E	Andréi	x	o	o	o	abs	abs
E	Bozi	x	o	o	abs	abs	abs
M	Moltedo	x	x	o	[ill]	abs	o
Côte d'Or							
MJ	Basire	x	x	x	x	m	x
Mm	Guyton-Morveau	x	x	x	x	abs	x
M	Prieur-Duvernois	x	x	x	x	*en mission*	
MJ	Oudot	x	x	x	x	abst	x
Mm	Florent-Guiot	x	x	x	x	abs	x
m	Lambert	x	o	o	[ill]	abs	abs

		Trial of Louis XVI				Later appels	
		Guilt	*Appel*	Sen-tence	Re-prieve	Marat	Comm. of 12
E	Marey	x	o	o	o	o	o
Mm	Trullard	x	x	x	x	*en mission*	
C	Rameau	x	x	o	o	abs	x
M	Berlier	x	x	x	x	abs	x
Côtes-du-Nord							
g*	Couppé	x	x	o	o	o	o
E	Palasne-Champeaux	x	o	o	o	o	abs
C	Gaultier	x	x	o	o	o	o
g	Guyomar	x	o	o	o	o	o
g*	Fleury	x	o	o	o	o	o
g*	Girault	x	o	o	o	abs	o
M	Loncle	x	x	x	x	o	abs
C	Goudelin	x	o	o	o	o	o
Creuse							
M	Huguet	x	o	M	x	abs	abs
E	Debourges	x	o	[abstained]		abs	o
E	Coutisson-Dumas	x	o	o	o	o	o
C	Guyès	x	o	x	x	x	x
C	Jorrand	x	o	o	x	o	o
E	Barailon	[abstained]		o	o	abs	abs
C	Texier	x	o	o	x	abs	abs
Dordogne							
o	Lamarque	x?	x	x	x	[Austrian prisoner]	
M	Pinet	x?	x	x	x	x	x
MJ	Lacoste	x?	x	x	x	*en mission*	
M	Roux-Fazillac	x	x	x	x	m	x
M	Taillefer	x	x	x	x	x	x
MJ	Peyssard	x	x	x	x	abs	x
M	Cambor-Borie	x	x	x	[ill]	abs	x
M	Allafort	x	o	x	x	abs	o
E	Meynard	abst	o	o	o	x	o
MJ	Bouquier	x	x	x	x	x	x
Doubs							
g*	Quirot	x	x	o	x	abs	o
M	Michaud	x	x	x	x	*en mission*	
E	Séguin	x	o	o	o	abs	o
Mc	Monnot	x	x	x	x	m	x
Mm	Vernerey	x	x	x	x	abs	x
Mm	Besson	x	x	x	x	abs	x

		Trial of Louis XVI				Later appels	
		Guilt	Appel	Sen-tence	Re-prieve	Marat	Comm. of 12
Drôme							
MJ	Jullien	x	x	x	x	abs	x
M	Sautayra	x	x	x	x	abs	abs
g*	Olivier-Gérente	x	o	o	o	abs	o
g*	Marbos	x	o	o	o	o	o
Mm	Boisset	x	x	x	x	abs?	x
E	Colaud la Salcette	x	o	o	o	abs	abs
M	Jacomin	x	x	x	x	abs	o
g*	Fayolle	x	x	o	o	o	o
E	Martinel	x	o	o	o	abs	abs
Eure							
G	Buzot	x	o	M	o	abst	o
M	Duroy	x	x	x	x	en mission	
M	Lindet, R.	x	x	x	x	x	x
g	Richou	x	o	o	o	o	o
E	Le Maréchal	x	o	o	o	o	abs
m	Topsent	[ill throughout trial]				abs	x
M	Bouillerot	x	x	x	x	x	x
G*	Vallée	x	o	o	o	abs	o
G*	Savary	x	o	o	o	abs	abs
g*	Dubusc	abst	o	o	o	o	abs
M	Lindet, T.	x	x	x	x	x	x
Eure-et-Loir							
MJ	Delacroix	en mission		x	x	x	x
G	Brissot	x	o	R	o	abs	o
G	Pétion	x	o	M	o	abst	o
g*	Giroust	abst	o	o	o	o	o
G	Lesage	x	o	M	o	en mission	
Mm	Loiseau	x	x	x	x	abs	x
E	Bourgois	x	o	[ill]	[ill]	abs	abs
MJ	Châles	x	x	x	x	m	x
Mm	Frémanger	x	x	x	x	x	x
Finistère							
g*	Bohan	x	o	x	o	abst	o
g*	Blad	x	o	R	x	o	o
m	Guezno	x	x	x	x	abs	o
C	Marec	x	o	o	x	abst	o
g*	Queinnec	x	o	o	o	o	o
g	Kervélégan	x	o	o	o	abst	o
Mc	Guermeur	x	x	x	x	en mission	
g	Gomaire	x	o	o	o	abst	o

		Trial of Louis XVI				_Later appels_	
		Guilt	_Appel_	Sen-tence	Re-prieve	Marat	Comm. of 12
Gard							
Mm	Leyris	x	x	x	x	x	m
E	Bertezène	x	o	R	o	abs	o
M	Voulland	x	x	x	x	m	x
g*	Aubry	x	o	R	o	o	o
C	Jac	x	o	R	o	abs	o
o	Balla	x	o	o	o	[resigned 2 April]	
g*	Rabaut-Pomier	x	o	R	o	o	abs
C	Chazal	x	o	M	o	o	o

THE MEMBERSHIP OF POLITICAL GROUPS

Showing department represented, occupation in 1789, and age on 1 January 1793.*

a) *The Gironde* [* = protest against 2 June 1793]

1. The "inner sixty"

Constituent Assembly

Babey, P. A. M.*	Jura	lawyer (i)	49
Buzot, F. N. L.	Eure	"	32
Chasset, C. A.*	Rhône-et-Loire	lawyer (ii)	47
Creuzé-Latouche, J. A.	Vienne	lawyer (i)	43
Grégoire, H.	Loir-et-Cher	cleric	42
Lanjuinais, J. D.	Ille-et-Vilaine	lawyer (ii)	37
Pétion, J.	Eure-et-Loir	lawyer (i)	36
Rabaut Saint-Etienne, J. P.	Aube	pastor	39
Salle, J. B.	Meurthe	doctor	33

Legislative Assembly

Brissot, J. P.	Eure-et-Loir	journalist	38
Condorcet, M. J. A. C. marquis de	Aisne	man of letters	49
De Perret, C. R. Lauze de*	Bouches-du-Rhône	landowner	45
Ducos, J. F.	Gironde	merchant	27
Dusaulx, J.*	Paris	man of letters	64
Fauchet, C.	Calvados	cleric	48
Gamon, F. J.	Ardèche	lawyer (i)?	25
Gensonné, A.	Gironde	lawyer (ii)	34
Grangeneuve, J. A. L. de	"	"	41
Gaudet, M. E.	"	"	37
Henry-Larivière, P. F. J.	Calvados	"	31
Isnard, H. M.	Var	merchant and manufacturer	34
Kersaint, A. G. S. Coetnempren, comte de	Seine-et-Oise	naval officer	51
Lasource, M. D. Alba *dit*	Tarn	pastor	29
Lidon, B. F.	Corrèze	arms manufacturer	40

*I have accepted Kustinski's statements on occupation, with reservations. A query indicates *either* that the position as given by Kuscinski is unclear, *or* that evidence supplied in 1795 by the man concerned does not quite accord with it. A number of deputies said by Kuscinski to have held offices before 1789 do not mention these in 1795; but they may have omitted or simply forgotten them. Evidence on notarial posts is also sometimes conflicting.

Masuyer, C. L.*	Saône-et-Loire	lawyer (ii)	40
Rouyer, J. P.	Hérault	"	31
Vergniaud, P. V.	Gironde	"	39

Department

Chambon, A. B. de	Corrèze	official	35
Chiappe, A.	Corse	"	32
Duprat, J.	Bouches-du-Rhône	silk merchant	32
Lacaze, J.*	Gironde	merchant	40
Meillan, A. J.	Basses-Pyrénées	commercial interests	44
Pontécoulant, L. G. le Doulcet de, comte	Calvados	soldier	28
Rebecqui, F. T.	Bouches-du-Rhône	merchant	48
Savary, L. J.*	Eure	lawyer (ii)	37

District

Birotteau, J. B. B. H.	Pyrénées-Orientales	lawyer (ii)	34
Bresson, J. B. M. F.*	Vosges	"	32
Dufriche-Valazé, C. E.	Orne	man of letters	41
Lehardi, C.	Morbihan	doctor	34
Noël, J. B.	Vosges	lawyer (i)	45
Vallée, J. N.*	Eure	"	38
Barbaroux, C. J. N.	Bouches-du-Rhône	lawyer (ii)	25
Bergoeing, F.	Gironde	surgeon	42
Boilleau, J.	Yonne	lawyer (ii)	41
Duchastel, G. S.	Deux-Sèvres	landowner	26
Girard, A. M. A.	Aude	not known	39

Commune

| Manuel, P. L. | Paris | academic | 39 |
| Mollevaut, E. | Meurthe | lawyer (ii) | 48 |

Judicial officials († = J. P.)

| Bailleul, J. C.*† | Seine-Inf. | lawyer (ii) | 30 |
| Lesage, D. T. | Eure-et-Loir | " | 34 |

Political activists

Carra, J. L.	Saône-et-Loire	man of letters (librarian)	50
Gorsas, A. J.	Seine-et-Oise	academic	40
Hardy, A. F.*	Seine-Inf.	doctor	44
Lanthénas, F. X.	Rhône-et-Loire	"	38
Louvet, J. B.	Loiret	author	32
Mercier, L. S.	Seine-et-Oise	"	52

No experience

| Boyer-Fonfrède, J. B. | Gironde | merchant | 27 |
| Yzarn de Valady, J. G. C. S. X. J. J. de Fraissinet, marquis de | Aveyron | soldier (ret.) | 26 |

2. *The supporters*

Constituent Assembly

Couppé, G. H.*	Côtes-du-Nord	lawyer (ii)	35
Cussy, G. de	Calvados	official	53
Defermon des Chapellières, J.*	Ille-et-Vilaine	"	40
Grenot, A.*	Jura	landowner	43
Jary, F. J.*	Loire-Inf.	farm-owner (also mining)	53
Kervélégan, A. B. F. Legoaze de	Finistère	lawyer (i)	44
La Revellière-Lépeaux, L. M.*	Maine-et-Loire	man of letters	39
Le Carlier, J. J. F. P.*	Aisne	lawyer (i)	40
Leclerc, J. B.*	Maine-et-Loire	"	36
Le Maignan, J. C.*	"	" ?	46
Lesterpt-Beauvais, B.*	Haute-Vienne	"	42
Pilastre de la Bradière, U. R.*	Maine-et-Loire	man of letters	41
Royer, J. B.*	Ain	cleric	59
Saurine, J. B. P.*	Landes	"	59
Vernier, T.*	Jura	lawyer (ii)	61

Legislative Assembly

Belin, J. F.*	Aisne	lawyer (i)	52
Bohan, A.*	Finistère	lawyer (ii)	42
Corbel, B. C.*	Morbihan	lawyer (i)	43
Coustard de Massy, A. P.	Loire-Inf.	soldier (ret.)	58
De Bry, J. A. A.*	Aisne	lawyer (i)	32
Descamps, B.*	Gers	lawyer (ii)	34
Despinassy, A. J. M.*	Var	soldier	35
Faye, G.*	Haute-Vienne	lawyer (i)	52
Fiquet, J. J.*	Aisne	not known (lawyer [ii] ?)	45
Gérente, J. F. O. de*	Drôme	lawyer (ii)	48
Giroust, J. C.	Eure-et-Loir	"	43
Laplaigne, A.*	Gers	"	46
Le Breton, R. P. F.*	Ille-et-Vilaine	"	43
Loysel, P.*	Aisne	industrial engineer	41
Louvet, P. F.*	Somme	lawyer (ii)	35
Rivery, L.*	"	merchant (also farmer)	50
Saladin, J. B. M.*	"	lawyer (ii)	40
Salmon, G. R. L.*	Sarthe	notary	28
Soubeyran de Saint-Prix, H.*	Ardèche	lawyer (ii)	36

Department

Bonet de Treyches, J. B.	Haute-Loire	lawyer (ii)	35
Casenave, A.*	Basses-Pyrénées	lawyer (i)	29
Delamarre, A.*	Oise	"	36
Delaunay, P. M.*	Maine-et-Loire	lawyer (ii)	37
Derazey, J. J. E.*	Indre	notary	43

Dubusc, C. F.*	Eure	manufacturer (cloth)	61
Dugué d'Assé, J. C.*	Orne	lawyer (ii)	43
Duplantier, J. P. F.	Gironde	merchant	28
Estadens, A.*	Haute-Garonne	postmaster	50
Gomaire, J. A.	Finistère	cleric	47
Guiter, J. A. S.*	Pyrénées-Or.	”	31
Laurence, A. F.*	Manche	lawyer (ii)	30
Moysset, J.*	Gers	official	66
Peyre, L. F.*	Basses-Alpes	not known	32
Poullain-Grandprey, J. C.	Vosges	lawyer (i)	48
Quirot, J. B.*	Doubs	lawyer (ii)	35

District

Barêty, P.*	Hautes-Alpes	notary	45
Bertrand de l'Hodiesnière, C. A.	Orne	lawyer (i)	36
Borel, H. M.*	Hautes-Alpes	merchant	36
Chastellain, J. C.*	Yonne	landowner	45
Doublet, P. P.*	Seine-Inf.	farmer	47
Fayolle, J. R.*	Drôme	official	46
François, L. F. A.*	Somme	” ?	36
Gantois, J. F.*	”	farmer	30
Gardien, J. F. M.	Indre-et-Loire	not known	37
Izoard, J. F. A.*	Hautes-Alpes	lawyer (i)	27
Lacroix, J. M.*	Haute-Vienne	notary	41
Maisse, M. F.*	Basses-Alpes	not known	36
Martin, J. B.*	Somme	landowner ?	58
Periès, J.*	Aude	not known	56
Ribéreau, J.*	Charente	lawyer (ii)	33
Richou, L. J.	Eure	lawyer (i)	44
Rouzet, J. M.*	Haute-Garonne	lawyer (ii)	49
Soulignac, J. B.*	Haute-Vienne	”	33
Tournier, J. L. G.*	Aude	not known	42
Vincent, P. C. V.*	Seine-Inf.	official	43

Commune

Asselin, E. B.*	Somme	notary	57
Bernard, C.	Seine-et-Marne	on the land (laborer ?)	35
Blad, C. A. A.*	Finistère	official	28
Blaux, N. F.*	Moselle	”	63
Brunel, I.	Hérault	”	50
Cazeneuve, I. de*	Hautes-Alpes	cleric	45
Chevalier, J.*	Sarthe	farmer	58
Dandenac, J.*	Maine-et-Loire	soldier	40
Devérité, L. A.*	Somme	printer (also legal post)	49
Fleury, H. M.*	Côtes-du-Nord	lawyer (ii)	38
Girault, C. J.*	” ”	official (ex-diplomat)	56

Guyomar, P. M. F.	Côtes-du-Nord	cloth merchant	35
Hecquet, C. R.*	Seine-Inf.	official	42
Le Febvre de la Chauvière, J. U. F. M. L. R.*	Loire-Inf.	doctor	35
Lefebvre, P. L. S.*	Seine-Inf.	official	40
Marbos, F.*	Drôme	cleric	53
Michel, G.	Morbihan	merchant	56
Penières-Delzors, J. A.	Corrèze	lawyer (ii)	26
Petit, E. M.*	Aisne	surgeon (also landowner)	53
Philippe-Delleville, J. F.*	Calvados	lawyer (i)	52
Rabaut-Pomier, J. A. R.*	Gard	pastor	48
Rivaud, F.*	Haute-Vienne	soldier (ret.)	38
Ruault, A. J.*	Seine-Inf.	cleric	47
Saint-Martin Valogne, C. Vaissière de	Aveyron	lawyer (i)	42
Varlet, C. Z. J.*	Pas-de-Calais	soldier (ret.) (engineer)	59

Judicial officials († = J. P.)

Béraud, M.†	Rhône-et-Loire	*graveur sur armes* ?	51
Couhey, F.	Vosges	lawyer (i)	40
Delecloy, J. B. J.*†	Somme	official	45
Faure, P. J. D. G.*	Seine-Inf.	lawyer (ii) (also owner of printery)	66
Garilhe, F. C. P. de*	Ardèche	lawyer (ii)	33
Obelin-Kergal, M. J. F.*	Ille-et-Vilaine	”	56

Political activists

| Dulaure, J. A. | Puy-de-Dôme | man of letters | 37 |
| Paine, T. | Pas-de-Calais | journalist | 55 |

No experience

Amyon, J. C.*	Jura	farmer	57
Aubry, F.*	Gard	soldier	45
Barthélemy, J. A.	Haute-Loire	lawyer (ii)	50
Bouchereau, A. F.*	Aisne	clerk (archivist)	36
Camboulas, S.*	Aveyron	in commerce	32
Daunou, P. C. F.*	Pas-de-Calais	cleric	31
Dechézeaux, P. C. D. G.*	Charente-Inf.	merchant	32
Delahaye, J. C. G.	Seine-Inf.	lawyer (i)	31
Dufestel, J. F.*	Somme	farmer	45
Duval, J. P.*	Seine-Inf.	lawyer (ii)	38
Engerran, J.	Manche	”	41
Ferroux, E. J.*	Jura	official ?	41
Laloue, J. R. de B. de	Puy-de-Dôme	soldier (ret.)	57
Laurenceot, J. H.*	Jura	law student	29
Queinnec, J.*	Finistère	farmer	37
Roüault, J. Y.*	Morbihan	lawyer (ii)	38
Serre, J.*	Hautes-Alpes	soldier (ret.)	30

b) The *à l'écart* deputies

Constituent Assembly

Albert, J. B.	Haut-Rhin	lawyer (i) ?	53
Bazoche, C. H.	Meuse	lawyer (i)	44
Bion, J. M.	Vienne	"	62
Colaud la Salcette, J. B.	Drôme	cleric	59
Durand-Maillane, P. T.	Bouches-du-Rhône	lawyer (ii)	63
Dutrou-Bornier, J. F.	Vienne	lawyer (i)	51
Girot-Pouzol, J. B.	Puy-de-Dôme	landowner	39
Le Maréchal, D.	Eure	commercial interests	37
Marquis, J. J.	Meuse	lawyer (ii)	45
Morin, F. A.	Aude	"	43
Palasne-Champeaux, J. F.	Côtes-du-Nord	lawyer (i)	56
Pémartin, J.	Basses-Pyrénées	lawyer (ii)	38
Poulain, J. B. C.	Marne	ironmaster	34
Sieyès, E. J.	Sarthe	cleric	44

Legislative Assembly

Baudin, P. C. L.	Ardennes	official	44
Cappin, J. E.	Gers	lawyer (ii)	32
Cledel, E.	Lot	doctor	57
Gentil, M.	Loiret	lawyer (ii)	33
Gertoux, B.	Hautes-Pyrénées	notary ?	48
Gibergues, P.	Puy-de-Dôme	cleric ?	52
Gouzy, J. P. L.	Tarn	lawyer (ii)	27
Jard-Panvillier, L. A.	Deux-Sèvres	doctor	35
Laguire, J.	Gers	not known	37
Lomont, C. J. B. Dubiche de	Calvados	lawyer (i)	44
Martineau, L. C.	Vienne	"	38
Moreau, J.	Meuse	"	50
Poisson, J.	Manche	"	46
Sauvé, G.	"	slate merchant	64
Tocquot, C. N.	Meuse	landowner	40
Vidalot, A.	Lot-et-Garonne	lawyer (ii)	58

Department

Andréi, A. F.	Corse	*littérateur*	59
Blanc, F. J.	Marne	wine-merchant	42
Boissieu, P. J. D.	Isère	official	38
Bonnesoeur-Bourginière, S. J. H.	Manche	lawyer (ii)	38
Bouygues, J. P.	Lot	"	37
Cadroy, P.	Landes	"	41
Chauvier, C. F. X.	Haute-Saône	doctor	44
Claverye, J. B. J.	Lot-et-Garonne	cleric	55
Conte, A.	Basses-Pyrénées	lawyer (ii)	55
Coutisson-Dumas, J. B.	Creuse	landowner	46
Debourges, J.	Creuse	lawyer (ii)	45
Douge, J. C.	Aube	wood business	57
Enjubault, M. E.	Mayenne	lawyer (i)	44

Fabre, J.	Pyrénées Or.	doctor	51
Froger-Plisson, L. J.	Sarthe	lawyer (ii)	40
Guyet-Laprade, P. J.	Lot-et-Garonne	soldier (? ret.)	36
Hubert, J. M.	Manche	lawyer (ii)	48
Lefranc, J. B.	Landes	,,	34
Martinel, J. M. P.	Drôme	,,	30
Méjansac, J.	Cantal	not known (notary?)	42
Meyer, J. B.	Tarn	lawyer (ii)	42
Pelet, J.	Lozère	,,	33
Plet-Beauprey, P. F. N.	Orne	not known	32
Séguin, P. C. A.	Doubs	cleric	51
Vitet, L.	Rhône-et-Loire	doctor (teaching)	56

District

Balivet, C. F.	Haute-Saône	lawyer (ii)	38
Chevalier, G.	Allier	lawyer (i)	57
Christiani, M. F. H.	Bas-Rhin	not known	32
Defrance, J. C.	Seine-et-Marne	Army doctor	50
Fournel, M. A.	Lot-et-Garonne	lawyer (ii)	34
Guillerault, J. G.	Nièvre	lawyer (i)	41
Magniez, A. G.	Pas-de-Calais	farmer	54
Maruejouls, P. S.	Tarn	landowner	60
Noguères, T.	Lot-et-Garonne	not known	53
Peuvergne, G.	Cantal	merchant	38
Pierret, J. N.	Aube	official	34
Réguis, C. L.	Basses-Alpes	,,	37
Roussel, C. J. de la Porte-Latine	Meuse	not known	43
Thomas-Laprise, C. J. E.	Orne	lawyer (ii)	33
Yger, J. B.	Seine-Inf.	lawyer (i)	37

Commune

Bertucat, M. M.	Saône-et-Loire	landowner	47
Bolot, C. A.	Haute-Saône	lawyer (ii); also private income	50
Bourgois, J. F. A.	Seine-Inf.	lawyer (ii)	51
Bousquet, F.	Gers	doctor	44
Campmartin, P.	Ariège	pharmacist	59
Creuzé-Pascal [Dufresne], M. P.	Vienne	private means	54
Genevois, L. B.	Isère	lawyer (ii)	41
Lobinhes, L.	Aveyron	doctor	53
Meynard, F.	Dordogne	lawyer (ii)	36
Moulin, M.	Rhône-et-Loire	cloth manufacturer	31
Viquy, J. N.	Seine-et-Marne	corset-maker	55

Judicial officials († = J. P.)

Baralion, J. F.†	Creuse	doctor	49
Baudran, M.	Isère	lawyer (ii)	41
Bonnemain, J. T.	Aube	,,	36
Bozi, J. B.	Corse	lawyer ?	46
Dautriche, J. S.	Charente-Inf.	lawyer (ii)	42
Devars, J.	Charente	,,	39

Duboë, P. F.	Orne	notary	43
Forest, J.	Rhône-et-Loire	lawyer ?	59
Fournier, A.[†]	"	notary	38
Mariette, J. C. L.[†]	Seine-Inf.	not known	32
Michel, P.	Meurthe	lawyer (ii)	37
Michet, A.	Rhône-et-Loire	"	48
Pelé, B. T.	Loiret	lawyer ?	60
Porcher, G. C.	Indre	doctor; also official post and legal education ?	40
Roy, D.[†]	Seine-et-Oise	wine-grower	49
Solomiac, P.	Tarn	lawyer ?	45

No experience

Bernard Saint-Affrique, L., Bernard, *dit*	Aveyron	pastor	46
Bernier, L. T. C.	Seine-et-Marne	lawyer (ii)	31
Bertezène, J. E.	Gard	"	33
Blondel, J.	Ardennes	not known	46
Bourgeois, N.	Eure-et-Loir	surgeon	39
Drulhe, P.	Haute-Garonne	cleric	38
Dugenne, F. E.	Cher	not known	55
Dupuis, C. F.	Seine-et-Oise	academic	50
Fourmy, J. D.	Orne	lawyer (ii)	51
Guérin, P.	Loiret	"	33
Lepage, L. P. N. M.	"	doctor	30
Marey, N. J.	Côte d'Or	man of letters	32
Maurel, J. F.	Ille-et-Vilaine	surgeon	51
Mollet, J. L. A.	Ain	lawyer (ii)	40
Patrin, E. L. M.	Rhône-et-Loire	man of letters	50
Personne, J. B.	Pas-de-Calais	lawyer (i)	43
Picqué, J. P.	Hautes-Pyrénées	doctor	46
Sanadon, B. J. B.	Basses-Pyrénées	cleric (teaching)	63
Savornin, M. A. J. L.	Basses-Alpes	lawyer (ii)	39
Thierret, C.	Ardennes	doctor	49
Vermon, A. J.	"	tanner (? legal education)	38

c) The "committees" deputies

Constituent Assembly

Baucheton, F.	Cher	lawyer (i)	43
Boissy d'Anglas, F. A.	Ardèche	man of letters	36
Boussion, P.	Lot-et-Garonne	doctor	39
Chaillon, E.	Loire-Inf.	lawyer (i)	56
Dupont, P. C. F.	Hautes-Pyrénées	" , also academic	52
Jac, J.	Gard	lawyer (i)	47
Lofficial, L. P.	Deux-Sèvres	"	41
Perès, E.	Haute-Garonne	lawyer (ii)	40
Ramel-Nogaret, D. V.	Aude	lawyer (i)	32
Rochegude, H. de P. de	Tarn	naval officer	51
Saint-Martin, F. J. Riffard	Ardèche	lawyer (i)	48
Thibault, A. A. M.	Cantal	cleric	45

Legislative Assembly

Arbogast, L. F. A.	Bas-Rhin	academic	33
Audrein, Y. M.	Morbihan	cleric (wide academic exp.)	51
Carpentier, A. F.	Nord	private means	53
Chédaneau, A. R. J. A. F.	Charente	official	32
Curée, J. F.	Hérault	not known	36
Garran-Coulon, J. P.	Loiret	lawyer (ii)	44
Guyès, J. F.	Creuse	lawyer (i)	31
Haussmann, N.	Seine-et-Oise	cloth manufacturer	32
Laboissière, J. B.	Lot	lawyer (i)	63
Le Malliaud, J. F.	Morbihan	"	39
Le Tourneur, E. F. L. H.	Manche	soldier	41
Lecointe-Puyraveau, M. M.	Deux-Sèvres	lawyer (ii)	28
Mailhe, J.	Haute-Garonne	"	42
Perrin, P. N.	Aube	merchant	41
Sautereau, J.	Nièvre	lawyer (ii)	51
Vardon, L. A. J.	Calvados	not known	41

Department

Ayral, B. L.	Haute-Garonne	merchant captain (ret.)	56
Bailly, E. L. B.	Seine-et-Marne	cleric (teaching)	32
Bonguiot, M. F.	Jura	lawyer (ii)	41
Dumont, L. P.	Calvados	"	27
Girard, C. J. E.	Vendée	lawyer (i)	60
Gleizal, C.	Ardèche	notary	31
Goudelin, G. J. P.	Côtes-du-Nord	lawyer (ii)	27
Johannot, J.	Haut-Rhin	in business	44
Jorrand, L.	Creuse	notary	36
Jourdan, J. B.	Nièvre	lawyer (i)	35
Lacrampe, J.	Hautes-Pyrénées	lawyer (ii)	35
Lejeune, R. F.	Mayenne	"	63
Lombard-Lachaux, P.	Loiret	pastor	48
Marec, P.	Finistère	official	33
Marragon, J. B.	Aude	"	51
Rameau, J.	Côte d'Or	not known (farmer?)	44
Regnault-Bretel, C. L. F.	Manche	lawyer (i)	50
Ribet, B. J. G. B.	Manche	commercial and shipping interests, also official post	46
Servonat, J. S.	Isère	notary	45
Taveau, L. J. N. F.	Calvados	not known	37
Thabaud, G.	Indre	official	37
Vigneron, C. B.	Haute-Saône	lawyer (ii)	42
Villar, N. G. L.	Mayenne	cleric (teaching)	44
Villers, F. T.	Loire-Inf.	cleric	43

District

Balland, C. A.	Vosges	lawyer (i)	31
Becker, J.	Moselle	shopkeeper and tithe-farmer	49

Boudin, J. A.	Indre	on the land	36
Brun, J.	Charente	official	66
Charrel, P. F.	Isère	lawyer (ii)	36
Crévelier, J.	Charente	academic	28
Giraud, M. A. A.	Charente-Inf.	lawyer (i)	44
Havin, E. L.	Manche	lawyer (ii)	37
Hérard, J. B.	Yonne	lawyer (i)	37
Humbert, S.	Meuse	"	42
Lozeau, P. A.	Charente-Inf.	salt and spirits merchant	34
Pinel, P. L.	Manche	not known	31
Réal, A.	Isère	lawyer (ii)	37
Serveau, F.	Mayenne	"	44

Commune

Blutel, C. A. E. R.	Seine-Inf.	lawyer (ii)	35
Castilhon, P.	Hérault	merchant	46
Du Bignon, F. M. J.	Ille-et-Vilaine	lawyer (ii)	38
Dubois, F. L. E.	Haut-Rhin	"	34
Gaultier, R. C.	Côtes-du-Nord	not known	40
Geoffroy, M. J.	Seine-et-Marne	furniture business	38
Himbert, L. A.	"	forestry officer	42
Jouenne-Longchamp, T. F. A.	Calvados	doctor	31
Montgilbert, F. A.	Saône-et-Loire	notary	45
Opoix, C.	Seine-et-Marne	pharmacist	47
Pelletier, J.	Cher	lawyer (i)	43
Pepin, S.	Indre	lawyer (ii)	46
Plaichard-Choltière, R. F.	Mayenne	doctor	52
Prunelle-Lière, L. J.	Isère	lawyer (ii)	44
Sallèles, J.	Lot	official	57
Zangiacomi, J.	Meurthe	lawyer (ii)	26

Judicial officials († = J. P.)

Albouys, B.	Lot	lawyer ?	42
Allasoeur, P.	Cher	lawyer (ii)	61
Barrot, J. A.	Lozère	"	39
Cambacérès, J. J. Régis de	Hérault	lawyer (i)	39
Coren-Fustier, S. J.†	Ardèche	lawyer (ii)	45
Lafon, P. R.†	Corrèze	not known	48
Le Clerc, C. N.	Loir-et-Cher	"	54
Texier, L. M.	Creuse	lawyer (i)	43

Political activist

Thomas, J. J.	Paris	mercer (also legal education)	44

No experience

Chazal, J. P.	Gard	lawyer (ii)	26
Dupin, A. S. O.	Aisne	official	48
Lalande, L. F.	Meurthe	cleric (teaching)	51
Wandelaincourt, A. H.	Haute-Marne	cleric	61

d) The *en mission* deputies

Constituent Assembly

Alquier, C. J. M.	Seine-et-Oise	lawyer (i)	40
Reubell, J. F.	Haut-Rhin	"	45
Treilhard, J. B.	Seine-et-Oise	"	50

Legislative Assembly

Auguis, P. J. M.	Deux-Sèvres	lawyer (i)	45
Bissy, J. F.	Mayenne	"	36
Du Bois du Bais, L. T.	Calvados	soldier (ret.)	49
Gaudin, J. M. J. F.	Vendée	ship-owner	37
Gossuin, C. J. E.	Nord	official	34
Lambert, C.	Côte d'Or	not known	57
Maulde, P. J.	Charente	lawyer (i)	34
Morisson, C. F. G.	Vendée	lawyer (ii)	41
Paganel, P.	Lot-et-Garonne	cleric	47
Viennet, J. J.	Hérault	soldier (ret.?)	58

Department

Antiboul, C. L.	Var	lawyer (ii)	40	
Beffroy, L. E.	Aisne	soldier	37	
Gillet, P. M.	Morbihan	official	26	?
Guezno, M. C.	Finistère	merchant	29	

District

Beauchamp, J.	Allier	official	31
Delbrel, P.	Lot	lawyer (i) ?	28
Enlart, N. F. M.	Pas-de-Calais	lawyer (ii)	32
Giraud, P. F. F. J.	Allier	landowner	47
Godefroy, C. F. M.	Oise	lawyer (ii)	37

Commune

Bodin, P. J. F.	Indre-et-Loire	doctor	44	
Chabanon, A. D.	Cantal	lawyer (ii)	35	
Desgrouas, C. F. G. M. E.	Orne	not known (estate in San Domingo)	45	
Féraud, J. B.	Hautes-Pyrénées	not known	33	?
Malhes, J. P.	Cantal	in business	44	
Mazade-Percin, J. B. D. de	Haute-Garonne	lawyer (i)	42	

Judicial official († = J. P.)

Duval, C.	Aube	lawyer (ii)	43
Ehrmann, J. F.	Haut-Rhin	"	35
Harmand, J. B.†	Meuse	lawyer ?	41
Laurent, A. J. B.	Lot-et-Garonne	not known	55
Neveu, E.	Basses-Pyrénées	lawyer (ii)	37

Political activist

Mathieu, J. B. C.	Oise	lawyer (ii)	29

No experience

Pellissier, M. D.	Bouches-du-Rhône	doctor	27
Portiez, L. F.	Oise	lawyer (ii)	27
Topsent, J. B. N.	Eure	merchant captain	37

e) *The Mountain*
   Symbols: as in Appendix III.

Constituent Assembly

Aoust, E. J. M. marquis de	Nord	landowner	51 MJ
Anthoine, F. P. N.	Moselle	lawyer (i)	34 MJ
Barère, B.	Hautes-Pyrénées	”	37 MJ
Bonnet, P. F. D.	Aude	lawyer (ii)	38 Mm
Chateauneuf-Randon, A., marquis de Joyeuse	Lozère	soldier (ret.)	35 M
Cochon de l'Apparent, C.	Deux Sèvres	lawyer (i)	42 MJ
Dubois-Crancé, E. L. A.	Ardennes	soldier (ret.)	45 MJ
Gauthier, A. F.	Ain	lawyer (ii)	40 MJ
Goupilleau, J. F. M.	Vendée	lawyer (i)	39 MJ
Gourdan, C. C.	Haute-Saône	”	48 M
Guiot, Florent	Côte d'Or	”	37 Mm
Guyardin, L.	Haute-Marne	”	34 M
Lindet, T.	Eure	cleric	49 M
Mailly, A. A. A. M. G. J. F. marquis de	Saône-et-Loire	lawyer (i)	50 MJ
Massieu, J. B.	Oise	cleric (teaching)	49 MJ
Merlin, P. A.	Nord	lawyer (i)	38 M
Monnel, S. E.	Haute-Marne	cleric	45 Mc
Nioche, P. C.	Indre-et-Loire	lawyer (i)	41 MJ
Pflieger, J. A.	Haut-Rhin	farmer	48 MJ
Prieur, P. L.	Marne	lawyer (ii)	36 MJ
Robespierre, M.	Paris	lawyer (i)	38 MJ
Saliceti, C.	Corse	lawyer (ii)	35 M
Tellier, A. C.	Seine-et-Marne	lawyer (i)	37 Mm
Vadier, M. G. A.	Ariège	landowner	56 MJ
Voulland, J. H.	Gard	lawyer (i)	41 M

Legislative Assembly

Albitte, A. L.	Seine-Inf.	lawyer (ii)	31 MJ
Azéma, L.	Aude	lawyer (i)	40 M
Basire, C.	Côte d'Or	clerk, state archives	31 MJ
Bassal, J.	Seine-et-Oise	cleric	40 MJ
Baudot, M. A.	Saône-et-Loire	doctor	27 MJ
Beauvais, C. N.	Paris	”	47 MJ
Bellegarde, A. D. de	Charente	had been soldier; post with comte d'Artois	54 Mm
Bernard, A. A.	Charente-Inf.	lawyer (ii)	41 MJ
Besson, A.	Doubs	lawyer (i)	34 Mm
Bo, J. B. J.	Aveyron	doctor	49 MJ

Bonet de Meautry, P. L.	Calvados	soldier	49 Mm
Bonneval, G.	Meurthe	landowner	54 Mm
Bonnier d'Alco, A. E. L. A.	Hérault	lawyer (i)	42 Mc
Bordas, P.	Haute-Vienne	lawyer (ii)	44 M
Borie, J.	Corrèze	"	36 M
Bréard, J. J.	Charente-Inf.	lawyer (i)	41 Mm
Brisson, M.	Loir-et-Cher	"	53 MJ
Brival, J.	Corrèze	"	41 MJ
Calon, E. N. de	Oise	soldier (ret.)	66 MJ
Cambon, P. J.	Hérault	cloth merchant	36 Mc
Carnot, L. N. M.	Pas-de-Calais	soldier	39 M
Chabot, F.	Loir-et-Cher	cleric	36 MJ
Charlier, L. J.	Marne	lawyer	38 Mc
Chaudron-Rousseau, G.	Haute-Marne	farmer	40 MJ
Chazaud, J. F. S.	Charente	lawyer (ii)	45 Mc
Choudieu, P. F.	Maine-et-Loire	lawyer (i)	31 MJ
Clauzel, J. B.	Ariège	small business	46 M
Cochet, H. J. L.	Nord	landowner ?	44 Mm
Coupé, J. M.	Oise	cleric	55? MJ
Courtois, E. B.	Aube	tax-collector	38 MJ
Couthon, G. A.	Puy-de-Dôme	lawyer (ii)	37 MJ
Couturier, J. P.	Moselle	official	51 MJ
Dameron, J. C.	Nièvre	lawyer (ii)	34 Mm
Delacroix, J. F.	Eure-et-Loir	"	39 MJ
Delaunay, J.	Maine-et-Loire	"	40 M
Delcher, E. J.	Haute-Loire	lawyer (i)	40 Mc
Delmas, J. F. B.	Haute-Garonne	soldier	41 MJ
Deydier, E.	Ain	lawyer (i)	49 MJ
Dherbez-Latour, P. J.	Basses-Alpes	lawyer (ii)	57 Mm
Du Bouchet, P.	Rhône-et-Loire	doctor	55 MJ
Dubreuil-Chambardel, P. J.	Deux-Sèvres	in trade, also owned land	64 Mc
Duhem, P. J.	Nord	doctor	34 MJ
Dupont, J. L.	Indre-et-Loire	cleric	37 Mc
Dupuy, J. B. C. H.	Rhône-et-Loire	lawyer (ii)	33 Mm
Duquesnoy, E. D. F. J.	Pas-de-Calais	farmer	43 MJ
Duval, C. F. M.	Ille-et-Vilaine	lawyer (i)	42 MJ
Dyzez, J.	Landes	"	50 Mm
Eschassériaux, J.	Charente-Inf.	"	39 MJ
Esnuë-Lavallée, F. J.	Mayenne	lawyer (ii)	41 Mm
Foucher, J.	Cher	lawyer (i) ?	39 Mm
François de la Primaudière, R.	Sarthe	official	41 Mm
Frécine, A. L.	Loir-et-Cher	lawyer (i)	41 Mm
Garrau, P. A.	Gironde	lawyer (ii)	30 M
Gasparin, T. A.	Bouches-du-Rhône	soldier	38 M
Gaston, R.	Ariège	lawyer (ii)	35 MJ
Gay-Vernon, L.	Haute-Vienne	cleric	44 MJ
Gelin, J. M.	Saône-et-Loire	lawyer (i) ?	51 M
Goupilleau, P. C.	Vendée	lawyer (ii)	43 MJ
Granet, F. C.	Bouches-du-Rhône	cooper (wealthy)	34 M

Grosse-Durocher, F.	Mayenne	landowner	46 MJ
Guimberteau, J.	Charente	lawyer (ii)	48 M
Guyton-Morveau, L. B.	Côte d'Or	*savant* (chemist)	55 Mm
Hérault de Séchelles, M. J.	Seine-et-Oise	lawyer (i)	33 M
Huguet, M. A.	Creuse	cleric	35 M
Ichon, P. L.	Gers	cleric (teaching)	35 MJ
Ingrand, F. P.	Vienne	lawyer (ii) ?	36 M
Jagot, G. M.	Ain	not known	42 M
Jay, J.	Gironde	pastor	49 MJ
Lacombe Saint-Michel, J. P.	Tarn	soldier	41
Lacoste, E.	Dordogne	doctor	47 MJ
Laloy, P. A.	Haute-Marne	lawyer (ii)	43 MJ
Laporte, F. S. C. D.	Haut-Rhin	"	32 MJ
Le Cointre, L.	Seine-et-Oise	cloth merchant	50 MJ
Lemoine de Villeneuve, J. A.	Manche	lawyer (i)	38 MJ
Lequinio, M. J.	Morbihan	landowner (also at the bar)	37 MJ
Le Vasseur, A. L.	Meurthe	official	46 M
Leyris, A. J.	Gard	not known	30 Mm
Lindet, J. B. R.	Eure	lawyer (i)	46 M
Maignen, F.	Vendée	farmer, stock-dealer	38 Mc
Maignet, E. C.	Puy-de-Dôme	lawyer (ii)	34 MJ
Mallarmé, F. R. A.	Meurthe	lawyer (i)	37 M
Merlin, A. C.	Moselle	lawyer (ii)	30 MJ
Michaud, J. B.	Doubs	"	33 M
Monestier, P. L.	Lozère	"	37 Mm
Monnot, J. F. C.	Doubs	"	49 Mc
Montaut, L. M. B. Maribon *dit*	Gers	soldier	38 MJ
Musset, J. M.	Vendée	cleric	43 Mm
Niou, J.	Charente-Inf.	naval engineer	43 MJ
Oudot, C. F.	Côte d'Or	lawyer (i)	37 MJ
Pinet, J.	Dordogne	landowner	38 M
Piorry, P. F.	Vienne	lawyer (ii) ?	34 Mc
Prieur-Duvernois, C. A.	Côte d'Or	soldier	29 M
Projean, J. E.	Haute-Garonne	lawyer (ii), also farm-owner	40 Mm
Reverchon, J.	Saône-et-Loire	wine-merchant	42 MJ
Reynaud, C. A. B.	Haute-Loire	lawyer (ii)	43 Mm
Richard, J. E.	Sarthe	"	31 MJ
Ritter, F. J.	Haut-Rhin	"	34 Mm
Robin, L. A. J.	Aube	river transport	35 Mm
Romme, G.	Puy-de-Dôme	academic	42 MJ
Rongiès, A. V.	Haute-Loire	small farmer	38 Mc
Roubaud, J. L.	Var	doctor	48 M
Roux-Fazillac, P.	Dordogne	soldier	46 M
Rovère de Fontvielle, J. S. F. X. A. marquis de	Bouches-du-Rhône	private means	44 M
Ruamps, P. C.	Charente-Inf.	farmer	42 MJ
Rühl, P. J.	Bas-Rhin	lawyer (i)	55 M

Sallengros, A. B. F.	Nord	lawyer (ii)	46 Mc
Sautayra, P. B.	Drôme	public works contractor	48 M
Siblot, C. F. B.	Haute-Saône	doctor	40 M
Soubrany, P. A.	Puy-de-Dôme	soldier (ret.)	40 M
Taillefer, J. G.	Dordogne	doctor	29 M
Thuriot, J. A.	Marne	lawyer (ii)	39 M
Valdruche, A. J. A.	Haute-Marne	doctor? (also landowner)	47 Mc
Vernerey, C. B. F.	Doubs	lawyer (ii)	42 Mm

Department

Baille, P. M.	Bouches-du-Rhône	not known	39 MJ
Barbeau du Barran, J. N.	Gers	lawyer (ii)	31 MJ
Barras, P. F. J. N.	Var	private means	37 MJ
Bayle, M. A. P. J.	Bouches-du-Rhône	book-keeper	37 MJ
Bentabole, P. F.	Bas-Rhin	lawyer (ii)	36 MJ
Berlier, T.	Côte d'Or	”	31 M
Bourbotte, P.	Yonne	not known	29 MJ
Boutrouë, L. M. S.	Sarthe	notary	35 MJ
Campmas, P. J. L.	Tarn	lawyer (ii)	36 M
Cavaignac, J. B.	Lot	”	30 Mm
Danton, G. J.	Paris	lawyer (i)	33 MJ
Delacroix, C.	Marne	”	51 M
Delaguelle, R. L.	Loiret	”	56 MJ
Deville, J. L.	Marne	lawyer (ii)	35 MJ
Dornier, C. P.	Haute-Saône	ironmaster	46 M
Fauvre-Labrunerie, C. B.	Cher	official	41 Mc
Fayau, J. P. M.	Vendée	not known	26 MJ
Foussedoire, A.	Loir-et-Cher	cleric	39 M
Garnier, J.	Charente-Inf.	lawyer (ii)	37 MJ
Hourier-Eloi, C. A.	Somme	official	39 Mc
Jacomin, J. J. H.	Drôme	lawyer (ii)	28 M
Julien, J.	Haute-Garonne	pastor	42 M
Laurent, C. H.	Bas-Rhin	doctor	51 MJ
Le Bas, P. F. J.	Pas-de-Calais	lawyer (ii)	28 MJ
Legendre, F. P.	Nièvre	” also small metal works	33 Mm
Louchet, L.	Aveyron	academic	37M
Louis, J. A.	Bas-Rhin	official	50 MJ
Maure, N. S.	Yonne	grocer	49 MJ
Monmayou, H. G. B. J.	Lot	lawyer (i)	36 Mc
Moreau, F. M.	Saône-et-Loire	public works engineer	28 M
Perrin, J. B.	Vosges	merchant	38 MJ
Petitjean, C. L.	Allier	lawyer (i)	44 Mm
Précy, J.	Yonne	bailiff	49 MJ
Turreau de Linières, L.	”	private means	28 Mm
Vinet, P. E.	Charente-Inf.	textile manufacturer	45 Mc

District

Allafort, J.	Dordogne	lawyer (ii)	51 M
Amar, J. P. A.	Isère	lawyer (i)	37 MJ
Boisset, J. A.	Drôme	official	44 Mm
Bouillerot-Demarsenne, A. J.	Eure	"	40 M
Boyaval, C. L. L.	Nord	lawyer (ii)	56 Mc
Briez, P. C. J.	"	lawyer (i)	33 Mm
Calès, J. M.	Haute-Garonne	doctor	35 Mm
Cassanyès, J. J. F.	Pyrénées-Or.	barber-surgeon?	34 M
Chaumont, J. F.	Ille-et-Vilaine	lawyer (ii)	48 Mc
Collombel, L. J.	Orne	official	54 MJ
Dandenac, M. F.	Maine-et-Loire	lawyer (ii)	42 M
Dartigoeyte, P. A.	Landes	"	29 MJ
Deleyre, A.	Gironde	man of letters	66 M
Dumont, A.	Somme	lawyer (i) ?	27 MJ
De Sacy, C. L. M.	Haute-Garonne	farmer	46 Mm
Du Roy, J. M.	Eure	lawyer (i)	39 M
Espert, J.	Ariège	not known	34 M
Fabre, C. D. C.	Hérault	lawyer (i)	30 Mm
Finot, E.	Yonne	"	44 MJ
Forestier, P. J.	Allier	lawyer (ii)	53 MJ
Frémanger, J.	Eure-et-Loir	lawyer (i)	31 Mm
Guffroy, A. B. J.	Pas-de-Calais	"	50 MJ
Isoré, J.	Oise	private means (farmer?)	34 MJ
Javogues, C.	Rhône-et-Loire	lawyer (ii)	33 Mm
Lefiot, J. A.	Nièvre	lawyer (i) ?	37 MJ
Lejeune, S. P.	Indre	lawyer (ii)	34 MJ
Lesage-Sénault, G. J. J.	Nord	merchant	53 MJ
Le Tourneur, E. P.	Sarthe	merchant draper	37 Mm
Levasseur, R.	"	doctor	45 MJ
Mauduyt, F. P. A.	Seine-et-Marne	private means	32 Mc
Pérard, C. F. J.	Maine-et-Loire	lawyer (ii)	32 M
Venaille, P. E.	Loir-et-Cher	official	39 Mc
Vidalin, E.	Allier	printer	49 Mm

Commune

Artaud-Blanval, J. A.	Puy-de-Dôme	farmer	49 M
Battellier, J. C.	Marne	watchmaker	35 M
Beaugeard, P. J. B.	Ille-et-Vilaine	lawyer (ii)	28 MJ
Bézard, F. S.	Oise	"	32 Mc
Bollet, P. A.	Pas-de-Calais	farmer	39 Mm
Cordier, M. M.	Seine-et-Marne	lawyer (ii)	43 Mc
Dentzel, G. F.	Bas-Rhin	Lutheran pastor	37 M
Garnier, A. M. C.	Aube	lawyer (ii)	50 M
Guermeur, J. T. M.	Finistère	"	42 Mc
Guillemardet, F. P. M. D.	Saône-et-Loire	doctor	27 Mm
Jeanbon, André, Saint-André, *dit*	Lot	pastor	43 MJ
Le Carpentier, J. B.	Manche	official	33 Mm

Legot, A.	Calvados	lawyer (ii)	45 M
Milhaud, E. J. B.	Cantal	soldier	26 MJ
Osselin, C. N.	Paris	lawyer (ii)	40 MJ
Panis, E. J.	"	"	35 MJ
Peyssard, J. P. Charles de	Dordogne	soldier (ret.)	37 MJ
Pocholle, P. P. A.	Seine-Inf.	cleric (teaching)	28 Mm
Pressavin, J. B.	Rhône-et-Loire	doctor	58 MJ
Ricord, J. F.	Var	notary	33 M
Robespierre, A. B. J.	Paris	lawyer (ii)	29 MJ
Rudel, C. A.	Puy-de-Dôme	"	73 Mc
Saint-Just, L. A. de	Aisne	law-student	25 MJ
Second, J. L.	Aveyron	official	49 Mc
Sergent, A. F.	Paris	artist	41 MJ
Souhait, J. J.	Vosges	lawyer (i)	33 M
Thibaudeau, A. C.	Vienne	lawyer (ii)	27 M

Judicial officials († = J. P.)

Bouquier, G.†	Dordogne	man of letters	53 MJ
Cambor-Borie, E.	"	lawyer (ii)	55 M
Ducos, P. R.	Landes	"	45 MJ
Dubois, L. T. J.	Orne	official	56 M
Escudier, J. F.†	Var	cloth merchant	33 MJ
Faure, B.	Haute-Loire	notary	46 MJ
Garos, L. J.	Vendée	lawyer (i)	53 Mc
Génissieu, J. J. V.	Isère	lawyer (ii)	41 MJ
Hentz, N. J.†	Moselle	official	39 MJ
Lacombe, J. H.†	Aveyron	lawyer (ii)	31 Mm
Lacoste, J. B.†	Cantal	"	39 MJ
Loiseau, J. F.†	Eure-et-Loir	innkeeper/post-master	41 Mm
Loncle, R. C.	Côtes-du-Nord	lawyer (ii)	39 M
Martel, P.†	Allier	lawyer (i)	44 Mc
Méaulle, J. N.	Loire-Inf.	lawyer (ii)	35 Mm
Merlino, J. M. F.	Ain	lawyer (i)	55 MJ
Philippeaux, P. N.	Sarthe	lawyer (ii)	36 MJ
Pons, P. L.	Meuse	"	33 Mc
Pottier, C. R.	Indre-et-Loire	"	37 MJ
Prost, C. C.	Jura	lawyer (i) ?	50 M
Ruelle, A.	Indre-et-Loire	lawyer?	38 Mm
Servière, L.	Lozère	merchant	33 Mm

Political activists

Armonville, J. B.	Marne	wool-carder	36 M
Audouin, J. P.	Seine-et-Oise	not known	28 M
Billaud-Varenne, J. N. B.	Paris	author (various)	36 MJ
Boucher, A. S.	Paris	lawyer (ii)	69 MJ
Bourdon, F. L.	Oise	lawyer (i)	34 MJ
Bourdon, L. J. J. L.	Loiret	"	38 MJ
Carrier, J. B.	Cantal	"	36 MJ
Chénier, M. J. de	Seine-et-Oise	author	28 MJ
Cloots, J. B. baron	Oise	man of letters	37 MJ
Collot d'Herbois, J. M.	Paris	actor-manager	43 MJ

Cusset, J. M.	Rhône-et-Loire	silk-weaver	33 MJ
David, J. L.	Paris	artist	44 MJ
Desmoulins, L. S. B. C.	Paris	journalist	32 MJ
Drouet, J. B.	Marne	postmaster	29 MJ
Fabre d'Eglantine, P. F. N.	Paris	author etc.	32 MJ
Fouché, J.	Loire-Inf.	academic	33 MJ
Fréron, S. J. M.	Paris	private means	38 MJ
Goyre-Laplanche, J. L.	Nièvre	cleric	37 MJ
Jullien, M. A.	Drôme	man of letters	48 MJ
Laignelot, J. F.	Paris	playwright	40 MJ
Lavicomterie, L. T. H. de	Paris	man of letters	46? MJ
Legendre, L.	Paris	butcher	40 MJ
Marat, J. P.	Paris	doctor	49 MJ
Robert, P. F. J.	Paris	lawyer (ii)	30 MJ
Simond, P.	Bas-Rhin	cleric	37 MJ
Tallien, J. L.	Seine-et-Oise	lawyer's clerk (wealthy wife)	25 MJ

No experience

Bar, J. E.	Moselle	lawyer (i)	43 Mm
Casa Bianca, L. G. de	Corse	naval officer	30 MJ
Châles, P. J. M.	Eure-et-Loir	cleric	39 MJ
Charbonnier, J. C.	Var	official	41 M
Champigny-Clément, R. J.	Indre-et-Loire	merchant	41 Mc
Ferry, C. J.	Ardennes	academic	36 Mm
Lakanal, J.	Ariège	cleric (teaching)	30 Mm
Lanot, A. J.	Corrèze	lawyer (ii)	35 MJ
Laurens, B.	Bouches-du-Rhône	surgeon	51 M
Moltedo, J. A. A.	Corse	cleric	41 M
Monestier, J. B. B.	Puy-de-Dôme	cleric	47 MJ
Montégut, E. F. S.	Pyrénées-Or.	laborer (grave-digger)	34 M
Pointe, Noël	Rhône-et-Loire	armourer	37 M
Poultier, F. M.	Nord	soldier? (varied and uncertain career)	39 Mm
Raffron, N.	Paris	academic	69 MJ
Robert, M.	Ardennes	lawyer (i)	54 Mc
Roux, L. F.	Haute-Marne	cleric	39 MJ
Sévestre, J. M. F.	Ille-et-Vilaine	clerk, civil service	39 Mm
Thirion, D.	Moselle	academic	29 M
Trullard, N.	Côte d'Or	soldier (ret.)	54 Mm
Ysabeau, C. A.	Indre-et-Loire	cleric (teaching)	38 MJ

f) *The deputies not politically classified*
(The reasons for exclusion from classification appear in the right-hand column.)

Constituent Assembly

Camus, A. G.	Haute-Loire	lawyer (i)	52 Austrian prisoner

Egalité, L. P. J. de Bourbon, duc d'Orléans	Paris	private means	45 under suspicion
Le Peletier de Saint- Fargeau, L. M.	Yonne	lawyer (i)	32 murdered 20 Jan.
Sillery, C. A. B., marquis de	Somme	soldier (ret.)	55 under suspicion
Verdollin, J.	Basses-Alpes	notary	54 died 16 April

Legislative Assembly

De Houlières, L. C. A.	Maine-et- Loire	man of letters	42 resigned 16 April
Lamarque, F.	Dordogne	lawyer (ii)	39 Austrian prisoner
Quinette, N. M.	Aisne	notary	30 ” ”

Department

Fockedey, J. J.	Nord	doctor	34 resigned 3 April
Hugo, J.	Vosges	notary	45 did not sit
Larroche, J. F. S.	Lot-et- Garonne	not known	29 on leave from 16 April

District

Mennesson, J. B. A. P.	Ardennes	lawyer (ii)	31 resigned 5 June

Commune

Guillermin, C. N.	Saône-et- Loire	not known	39 died 17 April
Mellinet, F.	Loire-Inf.	pharmacist	54 died 7 June

Political activist

Bancal des Issarts, J. H.	Puy-de-Dôme	lawyer (i)	42 Austrian prisoner
Villette, C., marquis de	Oise	soldier (ret.) (very rich)	56 died 7 July.

Judicial officials

Caila, J. B. E.	Lot	lawyer (i)	57 died 19 Jan.
Balla, J. F.	Gard	”	55 resigned 2 April

No experience

Daubermesnil, F. A. L.	Tarn	lawyer (ii)	44 ill; on leave Jan.–June

THE AGES OF THE DEPUTIES (1 JANUARY 1793)

i) *Political groups 1793–94 divided according to age*

	Under 30	30– 34	35– 39	40– 44	45– 49	50– 54	55– 59	60 plus	Total
Gironde									
"inner sixty"	8	14	11	12	9	3	–	1	58
Other	7	14	25	25	18	12	14	5	120
Total	15	28	36	37	27	15	14	6	178
Plain									
à l'écart	1	18	22	23	17	16	15	6	118
Committees	6	13	19	24	14	10	3	6	95
en mission	6	5	8	8	6	1	3	–	37
Total	13	36	49	55	37	27	21	12	250
Mountain									
Jacobin	13	20	43	27	18	12	6	3	142
Mountain	7	12	19	13	12	6	3	1	73
Other	2	20	22	21	11	6	3	2	87
Total	22	52	84	61	41	24	12	6	302
Conv. total	50	116	169	153	105	66	47	24	730

A table was also drawn up to show the age patterns of men with different levels of political experience, to see whether in particular the Legislative Assembly deputies had a divergent age pattern which could be related to the Montagnard pattern, above; but this showed only that ex-Constituents were a little older and activists a little younger than the average.

ii) *Change in age level 1792–95*

The age pattern of those who were members in October 1795 was almost identical with the pattern that would have obtained if all the members of January 1793 had continued in office. (No attempt was made to establish figures between these dates; the possible return did not seem likely to justify the effort involved.) The under-40 element of 1795, of course, included a significant proportion of comparatively inexperienced new members, the higher age groups having on average suffered least from changes. "Under 40" in this connection means "under 40 in 1792," the year in which nearly all the deputies were elected.

Age at 1/1/1793	Membership Jan. 1793	Admitted 1793–95	Dead, resigned, removed by Oct. 1795	Remaining Oct. 1795
Under 30	51	12	20 (3)	43 (9)
30–34	120	24	34 (1)	110 (23)

Age at 1/1/1793	Membership Jan. 1793	Admitted 1793–95	Dead, resigned, removed by Oct. 1795	Remaining Oct. 1795
35–39	171	39	55 (5)	155 (34)
40–44	156	34	37 (1)	153 (33)
45–49	107	18	26	99 (18)
50–54	69	11	13	67 (11)
55–59	51	6	9	48 (6)
60 plus	24	2	2 (1)	24 (1)
Total	749	146	196 (11)	699 (135)

Note: In this table, the figures in parentheses in columns (3) and (4) indicate the number of *suppléants* and new members included in the total.

This table also illustrates the disproportionate losses suffered by the younger members. Most of the losses among older members were from natural death or voluntary withdrawal; political executions were relatively few. The detail of the casualties is given below.

iii) *Age-groups affected by deaths, withdrawals, and removals 1792–95, in relation to political attitudes*

	Under 30	30–34	35–39	Total under 40	40–44	45	Total over 40	Total
GIRONDE								
"inner sixty"	6	6	7	19	7	8	15	34
Other	1	1	2	4	1	9	10	14
Total	7	7	9	23	8	17	25	48
PLAIN								
à l'écart	–	–	2	2	2	3	5	7
Committees	–	1	–	1	3	2	5	6
en mission	–	1	–	1	2	–	2	3
MOUNTAIN								
Jacobin	8	11	23	42	11	12	23	65
Mountain	1	4	10	15	6	3	9	24
Other	–	5	4	9	1	3	4	13
Total	9	20	37	66	18	18	36	102
Convention								
Total 1793	16	29	48	93	33	40	73	166 (of 730)
Suppléants/ unclassified	4	5	7	16	4	10	14	30
Total 1792–95	20	34	55	109	37	50	87	196

The Plain was thus very little affected, and the same is true of the rank-and-file of the Gironde. This is, of course, a distortion of the situation under the Terror, when 75 of the June petitioners were in prison and others from both groups were fugitive, but almost all of the survivors had returned to their seats by the end of 1794. The Mountain lost one-third of its strength, much of it during the 1795 reaction, and the "inner sixty" was reduced by more than half. The uneven incidence of the inroads on the Mountain is conspicuous; the greater the commitment the higher the proportion of casualties. The deaths among the younger members of the "inner sixty" would have been higher had not some of them (e.g., Louvet) evaded capture until it was safe to return; here again mere figures, unless unmanageably complicated, do not give the whole picture.

iv) By previous political experience

	Died during or just after parlty. term	Office to 1805				Napol- eonic office	Total office	No office	Total
		To 1799	To 1805	Died by 1805	Total				
Const. Ass.	16(+4)	2(+1)	4	4	10(+1)	30	40(+1)	22	78(+5)
Leg. Ass.	33	13	2	12	27	78(+2)	105(+2)	53(+1)	191(+3)
Department	16(+1)	3	3	2	8	45(+1)	53(+1)	44(+1)	113(+3)
District	18	15(+1)	2	1	18(+1)	36	54(+1)	21	93(+1)
Commune	14(+2)	7	3	5	15	39	54	24	92(+2)
Judge/J.P.	4(+1)	3	2	7	12	30(+1)	42(+1)	13	58(+2)
Political activist	14(+1)	–	–	1	1	16	17	5(+1)	36(+2)
No experience	5	3	–	5	8	33	41	22(+1)	68(+1)
Total	120(+9)	46(+2)	16	37	99(+2)	307(+4)	406(+6)	204(+4)	730(+19)

( ) = deputies not included in politcal classification

PERSONAL AND OCCUPATIONAL BACKGROUND

a) Political experience, place of origin, and political attitude 1793–94.

i) Deputies from large cities

| | *Gironde* | | | | *Plain* | | *Mountain* | | | |
	"Inner sixty"	Other	Total	À l'écart	Committees	En mission	Jacobin	Other	Total	Total
Constit. Ass.	2	8	10	–	5	2	5	2	7	24+4
Legisl. Ass.	12	3	15	2	6	1	12	14	26	50+2
Department	3	4	7	3	6	–	8	6	14	30+1
District	–	2	2	2	2	–	3	5	8	14
Commune	3	6	9	2	4	–	6	4	10	25+1
Judge/J.P.	1	2	3	1	1	1	3	1	4	10
Activist	6	1	7	–	1	1	19	2	21	30+2
None	1	5	6	4	–	–	4	7	11	21+1
Total	28	31	59	14	25	5	60	41	101	204+11

ii) Deputies from *chefs-lieux*

| | *Gironde* | | | | *Plain* | | *Mountain* | | | |
	"Inner sixty"	Other	Total	À l'écart	Committees	En mission	Jacobin	Other	Total	Total
Constit. Ass.	2	3	5	4	1	1	4	2	6	17
Legisl. Ass.	–	–	1	4	2	1	5	4	9	17
Department	1	2	3	3	2	–	4	1	5	13
District	3	–	3	1	3	–	–	–	–	7
Commune	–	2	2	1	4	1	2	1	3	11
Judge/J.P.	1	–	1	–	1	1	–	1	1	4
Activist	–	–	–	–	–	–	2	–	2	2
None	–	–	–	2	–	1	1	–	1	4
Total	7	8	15	15	13	5	18	9	27	75

iii) Deputies from other places, or without fixed settlement

	Gironde			Plain			Mountain			
	"Inner sixty"	Other	Total	À l'écart	Com-mittees	En mission	Jacobin	Other	Total	Total
Constit. Ass.	5	4	9	10	6	–	5	7	12	37+1
Legisl. Ass.	5	15	20	10	5	8	30	48	78	124+1
Department	5	10	15	19	16	4	6	10	16	70+2
District	3	18	21	12	9	5	9	16	25	72+1
Commune	4	17	21	8	8	5	2	13	15	57+1
Judge/J.P.	–	4	4	15	6	3	7	9	16	44+2
Activist	–	1	1	–	–	–	3	–	3	4
None	1	12	13	15	4	2	2	7	9	43
Total	23	81	104	89	57	27	64	110	174	451+8
Convention total	58	120	178	118	95	37	142	160	302	730+19

b) Occupations and places of residence with political attitudes 1793–94

i) Deputies from large towns

	Gironde			Plain			Mountain			
	"Inner sixty"	Other	Total	À l'écart	Com-mittees	En mission	Jacobin	Other	Total	Total
Clergy	2	3	5	2	3	–	6	3	9	19
Medicine	2	1	3	1	–	–	6	1	7	11
Army/Navy	2	1	3	–	1	1	2	3	5	10
Business	4	4	8	–	3	–	4	4	8	19
Farmer	–	1	1	–	–	–	1	–	1	2
Man of letters	6	3	9	2	1	–	10	1	11	23
Academic	2	–	2	1	1	–	2	1	3	7
Artisan	–	–	–	–	–	–	1	2	3	3
Clerk	–	1	1	–	–	–	2	–	2	3
Civil servant	–	3	3	–	2	–	2	3	5	10
Lawyer (i)	–	3	3	2	6	2	11	8	19	32
(ii)	10	11	21	3	7	2	10	14	24	57
Private means	–	–	–	1	–	–	2	–	2	3
Not known	–	–	–	2	1	–	1	1	2	5
Total	28	31	59	14	25	5	60	41	101	204

ii) Deputies from *chefs-lieux*

	Gironde			Plain			Mountain			
	"Inner sixty"	Other	Total	À l'écart	Com- mittees	En mission	Jacobin	Other	Total	*Total*
Clergy	—	4	4	1	—	—	2	—	2	7
Medicine	—	—	—	1	2	—	—	—	—	3
Army/Navy	—	—	—	—	—	—	2	2	4	4
Business	—	—	—	1	—	1	2	—	2	4
Farmer	—	—	—	—	—	—	—	—	—	—
Man of letters	1	—	1	—	—	—	—	—	—	1
Academic	—	—	—	—	—	—	—	2	2	2
Artisan	—	—	—	—	—	—	—	—	—	—
Clerk	—	—	—	—	—	—	—	—	—	—
Civil servant	—	—	—	—	4	—	—	1	1	5
Lawyer (i)	3	2	5	4	2	2	4	2	6	19
(ii)	3	2	5	7	5	2	7	2	9	28
Private means	—	—	—	—	—	—	1	—	1	1
Not known	—	—	—	1	—	—	—	—	—	1
Total	7	8	15	15	13	5	18	9	27	75

iii) Deputies from other places, or not classified

	Gironde			Plain			Mountain			
	"Inner sixty"	Other	Total	À l'écart	Com- mittees	En mission	Jacobin	Other	Total	*Total*
Clergy	2	2	4	5	5	1	6	8	14	29
Medicine	3	1	4	13	1	2	4	7	11	31
Army/Navy	1	7(2)	8(2)	1	1	2	3(1)	6(3)	9(4)	21(6)
Business	4	7	11	9	8	3	2	10	12	43
Farmer	2	9	11	7	1	1	8	8	16	36
Man of letters	—	1(1)	1(1)	1	—	—	2(1)	1	3(1)	5(2)
Academic	—	—	—	—	1	—	1	—	1	2
Artisan	—	2	2	—	—	—	—	1	1	3
Clerk	—	—	—	—	—	—	—	—	—	—
Civil servant	2	11	13	4	2	3	4	10	14	36
Lawyer (i)	4	20	24	11	17	4	15	23	38	94
(ii)	4	14	18	32	13	7	16	30	46	116
Private means	—	—	—	—	1	—	1	3	4	5
Not known	1	7	8	6	7	4	2	3	5	30
Total	23	81(3)	104(5)	89	57	27	64(2)	110(3)	174(5)	451(8)

Note: Figures in parentheses denote deputies with no fixed settlement.

iv) By previous political experience

	Died during or just after parlty. term	Office to 1805				Napoleonic office	Total office	No office	Total
		To 1799	To 1805	Died by 1805	Total				
Const. Ass.	16(+4)	2(+1)	4	4	10(+1)	30	40(+1)	22	78(+5)
Leg. Ass.	33	13	2	12	27	78(+2)	105(+2)	53(+1)	191(+3)
Department	16(+1)	3	3	2	8	45(+1)	53(+1)	44(+1)	113(+3)
District	18	15(+1)	2	1	18(+1)	36	54(+1)	21	93(+1)
Commune	14(+2)	7	3	5	15	39	54	24	92(+2)
Judge/J.P.	4(+1)	3	2	7	12	30(+1)	42(+1)	13	59(+2)
Political activist	14(+1)	–	–	1	1	16	17	5(+1)	36(+2)
No experience	5	3	–	5	8	33	41	22(+1)	68(+1)
Total	120(+9)	46(+2)	16	37	99(+2)	307(+4)	406(+6)	204(+4)	730(+19)

( ) = deputies not included in political classification

(c) Deputies: previous occupation and political experience 1789–92

	Parliamentary		Local govt.				No formal experience		
	Constituent Assembly	Legislative Assembly	Department	District	Commune	Judge/J.P.	Club, etc.	No experience	Total
Clergy	10	14	10	–	7	–	2	12	55
Medicine	2	12	5(1)	5	10	2	3	7	46(1)
Army/Navy	3(1)	18	3	–	5	–	–	7	36(1)
Business	2	16	18	7	12(1)	3	3	6	67(1)
Man of letters	3	5(1)	1	2	1	1	15	2	30(1)
Farming	6	12	2	9	5	1	–	3	38
Academic	–	2	1	1	1	–	2	4	11
Artisan	–	–	–	–	1	1	2	2	6
Clerk	–	–	1	–	–	–	1	1	3
Civil Service	1	9	12	11	10	3	–	5	51
Lawyer (i) Official post	42(3)	37	20(1)	24	8	13(2)	5(1)	3	152(7)
(ii) Practice	12	59(2)	32	24(1)	28	33	2	15(1)	205(4)
Private means	2(1)	2	2	2	1	–	2(1)	–	11(2)
No information	–	8	9(1)	9	5(1)	4	1	2	38(2)
Total	83(5)	194(3)	116(3)	94(1)	94(2)	61(2)	38(2)	69(1)	749(19)

Note: Figures in parentheses indicate deputies not included in the political analysis.

THE LATER CAREERS OF THE *CONVENTIONNELS*

About 41.5 percent of those who were members of the Convention in January 1793 ultimately became officials of one sort or another in the imperial bureaucracy. It is sometimes implied that this was the destiny of most of the surviving regicides. I have never seen any reference to the later careers of the antiregicides, who perhaps had far more freedom of choice. For a regicide, any viable alternative to a royalist restoration (which did in fact bring disaster to many in 1816) might offer a real temptation, even if it implied the abandonment of the republicanism of 1793.

In the eyes of the royalists, how many regicides were there, and what was their attitude to the Napoleonic régime?

There were 359 regicides among our 730 deputies, plus 5 from the 19 who had left the Convention by June 1793, a total of 364. I have excluded those who expressed their feelings by letter, being away *en mission* at the time. The royalist list of the *appels nominaux* notes these, but even Merlin who asked to have his vote counted was not allowed to share in the voting, and it seems unlikely that these men saw themselves as regicides in the same way as those who actually voted.

The antiregicides numbered 310 plus 10: 320, and those who did not vote at all 21 plus 4: 25. The remaining 40 deputies were undecided, and may be divided like this:

i)	against death sentence, against reprieve	22	
ii)	for death sentence, for reprieve	12	36
iii)	for death sentence, no vote on reprieve	2	
iv)	against death sentence, no vote on reprieve	4	
		40	

The royalists considered any man who had voted either for death or against the reprieve as a regicide, even if his voting was contradictory or he refused to confirm his verdict. Therefore all the men in groups (i)–(iii) were regicides, and the total number was 364 plus 36: 400, against 320 plus 4: 324 opposing death. The royalists also included all those who had voted the Mailhe amendment as regicides, whether or not they later supported a reprieve. This could of course be justified from the formulation of the amendment, but in considering how the later behavior of the deputies might be affected by their behavior in 1793, the relevant point is whether they themselves thought they might be considered regicide; and a man like, for example, Mailhe would not presumably have put himself in such a category. The Mailhe voters have therefore not been reckoned regicides unless they actually voted for death on 19 January. But compare E. Belhomme, *Les régicides* (Paris, 1893), pp. 37–38. For a later justification of a "reprieve" vote, addressed to a Restoration audience, see L. T. Dubois-Dubais, *Observations justificatifs sur les votes conditionnels . . .* (Paris, n.d.).

Not all these men lived long enough to have to consider their opinions of a new form of monarchy. Between 1793 and 1805 political feud, natural mortality, and accident eliminated about a quarter of the regicides and a rather smaller fraction of their opponents. In 1805 the survivors numbered 580, thus:

	Members 1793	Dead by 1805	Living 1805
Regicides	400	97	303
Antiregicides	324	67	257
No vote	25	5	20
	749	169	580

The 311 deputies who entered the Imperial service were:

	Number	% of survivors
Regicides	155	51.1
Antiregicides	146	56.6
No vote	10	50.0

The survivors of the 1793 Convention thus failed to show any overwhelming enthusiasm for Napoleon, though a considerable number were willing to accept him; and in this regard the regicides were proportionately not more, but less, conspicuous than the antiregicides.

It seems that a little more than half of these surviving *conventionnels* actively accepted the Empire. Almost exactly 2 in 5 of these men were ex-deputies of the Plain, which naturally had a higher survival capacity than either the Gironde or the Mountain (see figures below). It will be observed that the imperial officials included 67 Girondins of a possible 123, among them 15 of the 20 remaining of the "inner sixty"; 123 from the Plain out of 222; 117 from the Mountain's 228, and 4 of the remaining 10 unclassified. The Committee of Public Safety was represented by the prefect Jeanbon, who died in office in 1813, and Carnot, who retired from politics when the Tribunate was abolished in 1807. (His brief return in 1814–15 was more a patriotic gesture than an attempt to salvage the imperial régime as such.) Prieur-Duvernois was retired from the Army on a derisory pension in December 1801. Barère acted as a kind of undercover public opinion expert from 1803 to 1807, but it would be an exaggeration to describe him as a civil servant.*

---

*These details from Kuscinski, *Conventionnels*, pp. 350, 114, 510, 28, as a convenient source. Kuscinski is especially indignant about the treatment of Prieur "*quand les généraux de l'Empire étaient gorgés d'or*" (ibid., p. 510). The figures are different from Cobban's *Aspects of the French Revolution* (pp. 109–10), because I have considered only the deputies of January 1793; apart from this they should be the same as both are derived from Kuscinski.

Deputies—career after end of parliamentary term

i) By attitude in trial of Louis XVI

	Died during or just after parlty. term	Office to 1805				Napol- eonic office	Total office	No office	Total
		To 1799	To 1805	Died by 1805	Total				
Regicide	66+3	24	7	22	53	136+2	189+2	104	359
Anti- regicide	45+5	16+1	7	13	36	144+1	180+2	85+3	310
Undecided	5	4	2	2	8	18	26	9	40
No vote	4+1	2+1	–	–	2	9+1	11+2	6+1	21
Total	120	46	16	37	99	307	406	204+4 ·	730
Unclassified	9	2	–	–	–	4	6	4	19
Conv. total	129	48	16	37	99	311	412	208	749

ii) By occupation

	Died during or just after parlty. term	Office to 1805				Napol- eonic office	Total office	No office	Total
		To 1799	To 1805	died by 1805	Total				
Clergy	7	4	1	2	7	27	34	14	55
Medicine	6	5	1	3	9	14	23	16(+1)	45(+1)
Army/Navy	7(+1)	2	2	–	4	11	15	13	35(+1)
Business	16(+1)	–	1	5	6	19	25	25	66(+1)
Farming	7	2	–	2	4	7	11	20	38
Literary	9	–	2	2	4	8	12	8(+1)	29(+1)
Academic	3	–	1	–	1	4	5	3	11
Artisan	1	–	–	–	–	3	3	2	6
Clerk	–	–	–	–	–	3	3	–	3
Civil service	7	4	–	2	6	26	32	12	51
Lawyer i) official post	24(+3)	9(+1)	2	11	22	68(+2)	90(+3)	31(+1)	145(+7)
ii) private practice	25	13(+1)	6	7	26	103(+2)	129(+3)	47(+1)	201(+4)
Private means	1(+2)	2	–	2	4	1	5	3	9(+2)
Not known	7(+2)	5	–	1	6	13	19	10	36(+2)
Total	120(+9)	46(+2)	16	37	99(+2)	307(+4)	406(+6)	204(+4)	730(+19)

( ) = deputies not included in political classification.

iii) By political attitude 1793–94

	Died during or just after parlty. term	Office to 1805				Napol- eonic office	Total office	No office	Total
		To 1799	To 1805	Died by 1805	Total				
Gironde									
"inner sixty"	36	2	1	2	5	15	20	2	58
Other	13	6	2	4	12	52	64	43	120
Total	49	8	3	6	17	67	84	45	178
Plain									
à l'écart	5	5	1	4	10	55	65	49	119
Committees	11	5	6	4	15	47	62	21	94
en mission	3	5	1	1	7	21	28	6	37
Total	19	15	8	9	32	123	155	76	250
Mountain	52	23	5	22	50	117	167	83	302
Convention total	120	46	16	37	99	307	406	204	730

iv) By previous political experience

	Died during or just after parlty. term	Office to 1805				Napol- eonic office	Total office	No office	Total
		To 1799	To 1805	Died by 1805	Total				
Const. Ass.	16(+3)	2	4	4	10	30(+1)	40(+1)	22	78(+5)
Leg. Ass.	33	13	2	12	27	78(+2)	105(+2)	53(+1)	191(+3)
Department	16(+1)	3	3	2	8	45(+1)	53(+1)	44(+1)	113(+3)
District	18	15	2	1	18	36	54	21	93
Commune	14(+2)	7	3	5	15	39	54	24	92(+2)
Judge/J.P.	4(+1)	3	2	7	12	30	42	13(+1)	59(+2)
Political activist	14(+1)	–	–	1	1	16	17	5(+1)	36(+2)
No experience	5	3	–	5	8	33	41	22(+1)	68(+1)
Total	120	46	16	37	99	307	406	204(+6)	730(+19)

( ) = deputies not included in political classification

The clergy in the Convention

---

i) *Protestants*

Lasource
Rabaut Saint-Etienne   } executed 1793

Jean Jay
Bernard Saint-Affrique
Lombard-Lachaux
Rabaut-Pomier   } returned to practice as pastors

Dentzel
Jeanbon Saint-André
Julien   } abandoned the clerical life

ii) *Catholics*

1) *in 1792* Pocholle
             Chabot
             Guiter   } had already left the Church

Colaud la Salcette
Claverye
Moltedo
Foussedoire   } position uncertain
Paganel
Sieyès

All others had posts under the Civil Constitution of the Clergy.

2) *After 1792* + Fauchet
                   Simond   } executed 1793–94

+ Lalande
  Monnel
+ Séguin
+ Grégoire
+ Cazeneuve   } stayed in the Church
+ Royer
+ Saurine
+ Wandelaincourt
  Audrein

Bailly
Bassal
Châles
Claverye
Colaud la
    Salcette
Coupé
Daunou
Drulhe
Dupont
Foussedoire
Gibergues
Goyre-Laplanche
+ Huguet
Ichon
Gomaire
Lakanal
+ Lindet
+ Gay-Vernon
+ Massieu
Moltedo
Monestier
Musset
+ Marbos
Paganel
Roux
Ruault
+ Sanadon
Sieyès
+ Thibault
+ Villar
Villers
Ysabeau

abandoned the Church; Marbos not finally, but he did not go to Mass from 1792 until 1819, allegedly; on the other hand he was described in 1810 as "*un prêtre très chéri de ses paroissiens,*" so his status is a little doubtful. He held official (not clerical) posts under the Directory, the Empire, and the Restoration. See Kuscinski, *Conventionnels*, p. 435.

Summary

Of 55 clergy elected in 1792
    4 were executed in 1793–94

    4 Protestants
    9 Catholics   } continued as clerics

    3 Protestants
    32 Catholics   } abandoned the cloth; nearly all the Catholics apostasized

    3 Catholics had left the Church (effectively) by September 1792

Monnel was the only Montagnard priest to continue in orders.

Note: + = constitutional bishop.

THE *SUPPLÉANTS* AND NEW MEMBERS OF 1793-95

MEMBERS FOR NEW DEPARTMENTS

Alpes Maritimes: Blanqui, J. B.; Dabray, J. S.; Massa, R. C. **Mont-Blanc**: Balmain, J. A.; Carelli, F. J. B.; Dubouloz, J. M.; Dumaz, J. M. (*suppléant*); Duport, B. J. M.; Génin, J. P. (*suppléant*); Gentil, F.; Gumery, M.; Marcoz, J. B. P.; Marin, A. **Mont-Terrible**: Lemane, A.; Rougemont, I. (The last of these deputies, Génin, arrived on 7 August 1793.)

COLONIES

Guadaloupe: Dupuch, E. L.; Lion, P. J. (*suppléant*); Pautrizel, L. J. B. C. **Guiane**: Pomme, A. **Ile de France**: Gouly, N. B. L.; Serres, J. J. J. **Réunion**: Besnard, P. C. E.; Detchéverry, J. B. (*suppléant*). **Martinique**: Crassous, J. A.; Fourniols, M. (*suppléant*); Littée, J. **Saint-Domingue**: Bellery, J. B.; Boisson, J. G.; Dufay de la Tour, L. B.; Garnot, P. N.; Laforest, E. B. (*suppléant*); Mills, J. B. These members trickled in over a long period, from 10 April 1793 to 26 *vendémiaire* IV.

(For the new departments and the colonies (*suppléant*) indicates that the man concerned was replacing another who had refused the seat offered.)

SUPPLÉANTS

Aisne: Dormay, P. J.; Ferrand, A. **Allier**: Chabot, G. A.; Deléage, J. J. **Basses-Alpes**: Bouret, H. J. C. **Ardèche**: Thoulouse, J. J. **Ardennes**: Piette, J. B. **Ariège**: Bordes, I. J. **Aube**: David-Delisle, E. A.; Ludot, A. N. **Aveyron**: Rous, J. P. P. **Bouches-du-Rhône**: Bernard, M. A.; Le Blanc, J. B. B.; Minvielle, P. **Calvados**: Cosnard, P.; Lemoine, J. T. L. **Cantal**: Bertrand, A.; Mirande, N. **Charente-Inf.** *Desgraves, G.; Eschassériaux, R. **Corrèze**: Plazanet, T. A.; Rivière, P. **Corse**: Arrighi, J. M. **Côte d'Or**: Edouard, J. F.; *Sirugue, M. A. **Côtes-du-Nord**: Coupard, J. J.; *Toudic, B. **Creuse**: Faure, G. A. **Drôme**: Quiot, J. F. **Eure**: Bidault, L. M. G.; Francastel, M. P. A. **Eure-et-Loir**: Deronzières, L. A.; Lonqueue, L.; Maras, C. J. **Finistère**: Boissier, P. B. **Gard**: Chambon-Latour, P. B. **Haute-Garonne**: Alard, B.; Lespinasse, J. J. L. **Gers**: *Pérèz, J. **Gironde**: Ezemar, J. **Hérault**: Joubert, L. **Ille-et-Vilaine**: Tréhouart, B. T. **Indre-et-Loire**: Champigny-Aubin, L.; Potier, L. O. V. P.; Veau de Launay, P. L. A. **Isère**: Decomberousse, B. M. **Haute-Loire**: *Bardy, F.; Lemoyne-Vernon, J. C. **Loiret**: Gaillard, C. F. **Lot**: Blaviel, A. J.; Sartre, M. A. **Lot-et-Garonne**: Cabarroc, A. **Maine-et-Loire**: Menuau, H.; Talot, M. L.; Viger, L. F. S. **Haute-Marne**: *Varaigne, P. J. B. de (?) **Mayenne**: *Destriché, Y. M. **Meurthe**: Collombel, P.; Jacob, D. **Meuse**: Garnier, C. X. **Morbihan**: Bruë, J. B.; *Chaignart, V. F. M. **Moselle**: Karcher, H. **Nord**: *Derenty, F. M.; Mallet, C. P. **Orne**: Castaing, T. P. L. S.; Desrivières, J. G. **Paris**: Bourgain, D. G.; Boursault, J. F.; Desrues, P. F.; Fourcroy, A. F.; Rousseau, J.; Vaugeois, J. F. G. **Pas de Calais**: Du Broecq,

J. F.; Garnier, C. L. A. E.; Le Bon, J. **Puy-de-Dôme**: Jourde, G. A.; *Pacros, B. N. **Basses-Pyrénées**: Laa, A.; Vidal, J. **Hautes-Pyrénées**: Dauphole, J. P.; Guchan, P. **Pyrénées-Orientales**: Delcasso, D. L. **Bas-Rhin**: Grimmer, J. G. **Haut-Rhin**: *Guittard, J. B. **Rhône-et-Loire**: Boiron, J. B.; Noailly, P. **Saône-et-Loire**: Chamborre, J. B.; Jacob, C.; Millard, C. D.; Roberjot, C. **Sarthe**: Cornilleau, R.; Lehault, B. P. **Seine-Inférieure**: Albitte, J. L.; Lecomte, P.; Revel, F. B. **Seine-et-Marne**: *Bézout, E. L. **Seine-et-Oise**: Goujon, J. M. C. A.; Richaud, H.; Vénard, H. E. **Deux-Sèvres**: Chauvin-Hersant, F. A. **Somme**: Dequen, H. F.; Scellier, A. G.; Vasseur, L. J. A. **Tarn**: Deltel, J.; Terral, J.; Tridoulat, L. G. **Var**: Cruves, A. **Haute-Vienne**: Lesterpt, J. **Vosges**: Cherrier, J. C.; Fricot, F. F. **Yonne**: Jeannest la Noue, P. E. N.; Villetard, E. P. A.

*Indicates men called up on 5 *floréal* III. This list excludes Lafon, P. R. (Corrèze) who replaced Germignac (died 18 December 1792); strictly speaking therefore the total number of *suppléants* sitting 1792–95 was 115 (or with de Varaigne, 116). I have left it in the tables at 114 because Germignac hardly functioned as a deputy. Bertezène and P. Malhes, sometimes described as *suppléants*, were in fact titular members, since they replaced men who had refused the seats offered. Lafon took his seat on 7 January 1793. The first *suppléant* to arrive after that date was Villetard (Yonne; replacing Le Peletier) on 25 January 1793, and the last was Sartre (Lot) on 18 *thermidor* III (5 August 1795).

THE MEMBERSHIP OF THE EXECUTIVE COMMITTEE
OF THE TERROR 6 APRIL 1793–27 JULY 1794

i) *The Committee of Public Safety*
Constituent Assembly

Barère*†	6 April 1793 – 27 July 1794
Prieur P. L.*	10 July 1793 – 27 July 1794
Ramel	30 May–10 July 1793
Robespierre*	27 July 1793–27 July 1794
Treilhard†	6 April–22 June 1793

Legislative Assembly

Bréard†	6 April–5 June 1793
Cambon†	6 April–10 July 1793
Carnot*	14 August 1793–27 July 1794
Couthon*	30 May 1793–27 July 1794
Delacroix†	6 April–10 July 1793
Gasparin	10–27 July 1793
Guyton-Morveau†	6 April–10 July 1793
Hérault de Séchelles*	30 May 1793–January 1794 (resignation requested by letter, 31 December 1793)
Delmas†	6 April–10 July 1793
Prieur-Duvernois*	14 August 1793–27 July 1794
Thuriot	10 July–20 September 1793
Lindet R.*†	6 April–12 June 1793; 22 June 1793–27 July 1794

Department

Danton†	6 April–10 July 1793

District/Judicial

Commune

Saint-Just*	30 May 1793–27 July 1794
Jeanbon Saint-André*	12 June 1793–27 July 1794

Political activist

Billaud-Varenne*	6 September 1793–27 July 1794
Collot d'Herbois*	6 September 1793–27 July 1794
Mathieu	30 May–22 June 1793

Note: † = Committee of 6 April 1793
          * = "great" Committee

Summary

On Committee of 6 April	2 Constituent Assembly
	6 Legislative Assembly
	1 Department
On "great" Committee	3 Constituent Assembly
	5 Legislative Assembly
	2 Commune
	2 political activist

ii) *The Committee of General Security*

The membership of this committee was much more unstable than that of the Committee of Public Safety, and fluctuated considerably until it settled down in October 1793, with 2 ex-Constituents, 3 men from the Legislative, 4 departmental and 2 district officials, and 3 political activists, a total of 14 members. One district official and one activist resigned not long after, so that the Committee in its final form had 2 ex-Constituents, 3 Legislatives, and 5 local officials among its 12 members. Its early instability was partly due to a ruling, not always but frequently enforced, that any member going *en mission* was considered to have resigned. Between its first organization by the Convention in October 1792 and the collapse of the Jacobin régime at the end of July 1794, a total of 81 deputies held titular office on the Committee for periods ranging from about two weeks to a number of months. (The episode of 10–14 September 1793, when an effort to remove Chabot, Basire, and Julien from office produced some confusion, has been ignored). Of these 81 deputies, 36 served for fairly substantial lengths of time; these were:

Constituent Assembly: Vadier, Voulland. **Legislative Assembly**: Basire, Bassal, Barbeau-Dubarran, Brival, Alquier, Bernard (des Saintes), Chabot, Ingrand, Jagot, Elie Lacoste, Leyris, Lamarque, Maribon-Montaut, Pinet, Rovère, Ruamps, Rühl. **Department**: Bayle, Le Bas, Le Bon, Maure. **District**: Amar, A. Dumont, Guffroy. **Commune**: Méaulle. **Political activist**: Drouet, Laignelot, Lavicomterie, L. Legendre, David, Osselin, Panis, Tallien. **No experience**: Lanot.

The parliamentary bias was less pronounced after the beginning of June than earlier, and for whatever reason the flavor of intrigue surrounding elections to the C.G.S. was much stronger than for the C.P.S.; this caused Drouet and Maure to set on foot the agitation which in September 1793 finally removed Basire, Chabot, and Julien. Panis and Guffroy resigned, probably for political reasons, a little later (see Guillaume, II, 288–95, 308). In its early stages the C.G.S. was entirely dominated by ex-deputies from the Legislative; the decline of Legislative control coincides with the establishment of the C.P.S. in effective control of policy, and the greater importance of work *en mission*. On all this, and the membership generally, J. Guillaume, *Etudes Révolutionnaires* (IIe série [Paris, 1909] pp. 253–318). When the Gironde moved in for the only time to add men of its own choice to this committee (9–21 January 1793) the 15 deputies thus elected included only 6 ex-deputies, 3 from the Constituent and 3 from the Legislative (see Guillaume II, 274–75). The Committee of 17 October 1792–99 January 1793, to which the Girondins took such violent exception, included in a total of 30 members 22 men from the Legislative, 2 departmental and 2 communal officials, 3 political activists and one man without experience. The exact composition of the Committee of 9-21 January is not known, but it cannot have included, among 30 members, more than 17 men from the Legislative and 3 ex-Constituents (see ibid., 274-75; 267-68 for the October Committee). The Committee elected on 21 January, which the Girondins also much disliked, had 10 men from the Legislative, plus 2 activists; 5 of the 6 *suppléants* were also from the Legislative, and Drouet, an activist, was the sixth. (ibid., p. 277). Guillaume does not give details of political experience, but he seems very careful over names.

APPENDIX X

THE RESULTS OF THE *APPELS-NOMINAUX* OF 15-19 JANUARY 1793

These are discussed in detail in E. Seligman, *La Justice en France pendant la Révolution 1791-1793* (2nd. ed.; Paris, 1913). The confused expression of some of the votes requires interpretation, and no completely dependable record is available; but if the 37 special votes on guilt are carefully examined they divide between 9 who wanted to make their regicide position especially clear and 28 who wanted to express doubts of some sort about the form of the trial, without necessarily wanting to abstain entirely from the voting. Seligman discusses the problem of the abstentions (pp. 461-63) but his conclusions differ slightly from mine. I think it is clear that significant alterations were made in the totals of 17 January between the time they were originally announced in the Convention and the time they were officially published; not of a kind to affect the result, but of a kind which would meet the objections raised on the morning of 18 January. Cf. Seligman, pp. 468-82.

Note Seligman's reference (p. 607) to Salle's surviving notes of the vote on the sentence. A check of the *Moniteur*, which published this voting list a few days later, shows that Salle's *cahier* must have begun with the department of Ain, since this is the only way his figures can be made to fit. The *cahier* may represent notes made on 18 January; alternatively, Salle may simply have been making a *bordereau* copy from the original *cahier* and have begun in the middle, as Seligman (p. 478) says was done by the copyist getting the list ready for the press. The important thing seems to be that Salle's totals are in form exactly the same as those later published, but do not match those announced by Vergniaud on either 17 or 18 January, which remain inexplicable.

All that can be done with this material is to collate it, and make the most probable guess. The *Moniteur* is not entirely reliable; it confuses the votes of Beauchamp and Giraud (XV: 211), and includes a mythical vote from Péraldi, who was not even a deputy (not having been reelected from the Legislative)—a vote which cannot even result from mistaken identity, since all the Corsican deputies are accounted for.

No analysis, however elaborate, serves to explain the figure given on 17 January of 366 votes for death. The *Moniteur* gives four 17 January votes for death (Pétion, Lacombe, Blad, Fiquet) which are officially down as votes for reprieve or (Fiquet) for prison, and may therefore have been changed on 18 January; on the other hand the *Moniteur* has Champigny-Clément for mercy and the official record has him for death, so that he may have changed the other way. (Kuscinski, p. 128, has him for prison, but I have kept to the official version; he was otherwise a consistent radical.) And there is still Dumont's vote to be subtracted, which the secretaries certainly wrongly recorded as for mercy. Whatever one makes of all this, the arithmetic does not tally. But note (a) that no one, except possibly Champigny-Clément, seems to have changed from mercy to death between 17 and 18 January—and there were a number of votes which could have been reinterpreted—and (b) that several "indivisible" votes, notably Taveau's, were counted for mercy anyhow, whereas they should not have been counted at all.

Seligman is by far the best reference for the trial. A. Conte, *Sire, ils ont voté la mort* (Paris, 1966) is very detailed on 16-17 January, poor on the rest of the proceedings, almost undocumented and violently biased; he relies heavily on highly colored memoirs which he does not attempt to assess, and ignores the evidence to the point where he has apparently not even noticed that on 16 January Vergniaud was careful *not* to vote for death pure and simple.

BIBLIOGRAPHY

The compilation of an exhaustive bibliography on this subject would obviously be a lifetime occupation in itself; even the addition to an already lengthy book of the small selection of materials actually looked at would have taxed the patience of a generous publisher beyond reasonable limits. The bibliography has therefore been limited to (1) major primary sources; (2) the most useful general works on the Convention and the possible backgrounds of its members; and (3) a selection of specialist studies by way of example of what might be used. The only effort at comprehensiveness has been made in the case of the published speeches on the trial, of which no general list at present exists.

PRIMARY SOURCES

I. *Archival Sources*

The narrow approach adopted was rationalized by arguing that the *Archives Nationales* have very few series comprehensive enough to become part of the basis of a strictly comparative study. Two series which do meet this stipulation are noted below, together with other material which was sampled for further background.

i) *A.N. C 178 C II 1 (Ain)–C 181 C II 83 (Yonne)* has the *procès-verbaux* of the 1792 elections. I also looked at C 135–C 138 (the 1791 elections) but not with such care. A.N. F 1^c111 has the 1791 episcopal elections, and other material on church problems. I sampled some of the other Interior files (e.g., F 1^a, F^{19}) to widen my perspective a little; also some of the departmental L series files (Ain, Ardèche, Maine-et-Loire, and elsewhere). The full 1792 *procès-verbaux* missing from C 180 C II 74 (Seine-et-Oise) and C 179 C II 57 (Nord) are in A.D. Seine-et-Oise L 1 M 361 and A.D. Nord L 755.

ii) *A.N. C 353 C 1838* has the 1795 property statements. The limitations of this material have already been discussed. I made some use of F^7 (police records) but these are very uneven and often disappointing, though for any comprehensive study they would need to be minutely analyzed. For rewarding material and the use of it, cf. A. Soboul, "Sur les fortunes des Girondins," *Annales* XXVI (1954); for disappointing content, F^7 4753 (Kersaint).

II. *Proceedings in the Legislative Assembly and the Convention*

Procès-verbal de l'Assemblée nationale, séance permanente du vendredi 10 août 1792 (Paris, 1792).

Procès-verbal de la Convention nationale, imprimé par son ordre (72 v., Paris, 1792–an IV).

Convention nationale. Défense de Louis . . . par le citoyen de Sèze (Paris, 1792).

Appels nominaux . . . sur ces trois questions: 1. Louis Capet est-il coupable de conspiration contre la sureté générale de l'état? 2. Le Jugement de la Convention nationale contre Louis sera-t-il soumis à la ratification du peuple? 3. Y aura-t-il un sursis, oui ou non, à l'exécution du décret qui condamne Louis Capet? . . . (Paris, 1793).

Appel nominal . . . sur cette question: Quelle peine sera infligée à Louis? (Paris, 1793).

Liste comparative des cinq appels nominaux faits dans les séances des 15, 16, 17, 18 et 19 janvier 1793 . . . (Paris, 1793).

Appel nominal . . . 13–14 avril . . . a-t-il lieu à accusation contre Marat? . . . (Paris, 1793).

Archives parlementaires de 1797 à 1860 . . . première série (1787 à 1799) (72 v., Paris 1867–1892) LXV, 496–97, 520–41: *Appel nominal . . . "Le décret qui a cassé la Commission des Douze, sera-t-il rapporté, oui ou non? . . . (28 mai 1793).*

Exposition des motifs d'après lesquels l'Assemblée nationale a proclamé la convocation d'une Convention nationale (Paris, 1792).

Liste alphabétique de tous les conventionnels qui ont voté dans la séance permanente des 18 [sic] et 17 janvier 1793 (n.p., n.d.) (Royalist).

Liste des citoyens députés à la Convention nationale (Paris, 1792).

Tableau comparatif des sept appels nominaux fév. - 10 août 1792 (Paris, 1792).

Delaunay, P. M. *Rapport fait . . . sur les délits imputés à Marat* (Paris, 1793).

Appel nominal des 3 et 4 frimaire, l'an IIIe . . . sur cette question: y a-t-il lieu à accusation, oui ou non, contre Carrier, représentant du peuple? (Paris, an III).

Convention nationale. Le Pour et le Contre: recueil complet des opinions prononcées à l'assemblée nationale dans le procès de Louis XVI (Paris, l'an premier de la République). (As its title indicates, this has only the speeches actually delivered in the Convention, not necessarily in the order in which they were delivered.)

Porcelin de Roche-Tilhac. *Le Procès de Louis XVI*, 7 vols. (Paris, 1795). (This has many more speeches, but is not anything like complete.)

III. *Collections of documents*

The most important were obviously Aulard, A., *La Société des Jacobins: Recueil des documents*, 6 vols. (Paris, 1889–97) and Buchez, P. J. B. and Roux-Lavergne, P. C. *Histoire Parlementaire de la Révolution Francaise depuis 1789 jusqu'en 1815*, 40 vols. (Paris, 1834–38). Cf. also Lallement de Metz, G., *Choix des rapports, opinions et discours prononcés à la tribune nationale depuis 1789 jusqu'à ce jour*, 20 vols. (Paris, 1818–21).

IV. *Contemporary periodicals*

After the *Réimpression de l'ancien Moniteur*, 31 vols. (Paris, 1854), vols. 13–17 especially, I made most use of Brissot, J. P., *Le Patriote français, journal libre* (Paris, 1792–93); Condorcet, M. J., and others, *Chronique de Paris* (Paris, 1792–93); Gorsas, A. J., *Le Courrier des Départemens* (Paris, 1792–93); and Robespierre, M., *Le Défenseur de la Constitution*, in *Oeuvres complètes*, IV, ed. G. Laurent (Paris, 1939) and *Lettres à ses commettans*, in *Oeuvres complètes*, V, ed. G. Laurent (Paris, 1951).

V. *Correspondence, memoirs, speeches, etc.*

Although the use of these had to be highly selective, any listing of those consulted would be fairly lengthy. Roland's various reports (e.g., *Lettre ... à la Convention nationale du 30 septembre 1792; Lettre ... à la Convention nationale sur l'état de Paris, 27 octobre 1792*); and Delaunay, J., *Rapport ... sur les arrestations relatives à la révolution du 10 août 1792* (Paris, 1792), among many others, were useful for the Parisian problem. Some examples of the variety of available and highly relevant material: Clouet, P. R., "Lettres du conventionnel P. Vinet," *Annales* VII (1930); Daunou, P. C. F., *Mémoires sur la Convention nationale* (Paris, 1848); du Bois du Bais, L. T., *Observations justificatifs sur les votes conditionnels dans la malheureuse affaire du roi Louis XVI* (Paris, n.d.); Durand de Maillane, D. J., *Histoire de la Convention nationale* (Paris, 1825); Garat, D. J. *Mémoires sur la Révolution* (Paris, 1795); d'Héricault and Board, G., *Documents pour servir à l'histoire de la Révolution française*, 2 vols. (Paris, 1814); Soanen, H., "Lettres du conventionnel Rudel sur le procès de Louis XVI," *Annales* VIII (1931); Zivy, H., "Notes de Rabaut St. Etienne sur les premières séances de la Convention," *La Révolution Française* XLII (1902).

VI. *Pamphlets published by deputies on the trial of Louis XVI.*

This list includes *only* pamphlets by men who were members of the Convention at the time of the trial, and ignores the rest of the polemical literature on this subject, of which the royalists published a considerable proportion (cf., e.g., Laroque, *Les Bienfaits de Louis XVI* [7 jan. 1793]; Lefèvre, F. N., *Opinion sur le jugement et le procès de Louis XVI et de sa femme* [Paris, 1792]). It is as complete as I have been able to make it, though there must certainly be some omissions of pamphlets I cannot trace; J. F. Ducos's first speech is marked* to indicate that I have not been able yet to see this, the only copy being possibly available from the Cornell University collection. All deputies had the right to have their views printed at public expense and most used the

*Seventy-eight of the 83 departments had one or more deputies represented.

imprimerie nationale, though some of the more impatient resorted to their own printers. The place of publication is Paris, unless otherwise stated. Very few pamphlets are dated; where a date appears, this may be either that on which a speech was made or that on which it was printed. Not included among these trial pamphlets, but highly relevant to its author's own decision, is the pamphlet Le Peletier left with the printer immediately before he was murdered: Le Peletier de Saint-Fargeau, L. M., *De L'abrogation de la peine de mort.*

Albert, J. B., and Dubois, F. L. E. . . . *aux citoyens du département du Haut-Rhin, leurs commettans.*

Albouys, B. *Opinion. . . sur le jugement de Louis Capet, dernier roi des Français.*

———. *Opinion. . . sur la question, Si Louis Capet, dernier roi des Français, peut être jugé?*

Anthoine, F. P. N. *Opinion. . . sur le jugement de Louis, ci-devant roi des Français.*

Asselin, E. B. *Opinion. . . sur la question: Si le roi peut être jugé?*

———. *Complément de l'opinion. . . sur le procès de Louis XVI.*

———. *Mon dernier mot sur l'affaire de Louis XVI.*

Aubry, F. *Opinion. . . sur le jugement définitif de Louis Capet.*

Audouin, J. P. *Opinion . . . sur le jugement de Louis Capet, ci-devant roi des Français.*

Azema, M. *Opinion . . . sur le jugement de Louis Capet, dernier roi des Français* (1792).

Baille, P. M. *Opinion . . . sur le jugement de Louis XVI.*

Bailly, E. L. B. *Opinion . . . sur le jugement du dernier roi des Français.*

Balla, J. F. *Opinion . . . sur le ci-devant roi.*

Balland, C. A. *Opinion . . . sur la marche à suivre pour juger Louis Capet.*

———. *Opinion . . . sur les trois questions à savoir . . . .*

Bancal des Issarts, J. F. *Discours et projet de décret . . . sur Louis Capet et les circonstances actuelles.*

Barailon, J. F. *Considérations sur la nécessité d'ajourner le jugement de Louis Capet et de sa femme (14 jan. 1793).*

———. *Opinion . . .* (14 nov. 1792).

———. *Quelques réflexions . . .* (26 nov. 1792).

———. *Votations . . . dans les séances des 15, 16–17 et 19 janvier 1793.*

Barbaroux, C. J. M. *Opinion . . . sur les moyens de défense de Louis Capet, tirés de l'inviolabilité constitutionelle.*

Barère, B. *Discours . . . sur le jugement du procès de Louis Capet (4 jan. 1792)* (sic).

Barrot, J. A. *Opinion . . . sur le jugement de Louis XVI* (1793).

Baudin, P. C. L. *Opinion . . . sur le jugement qui doit décider du sort de Louis XVI.*

———. *Dernières réflexions . . . sur les questions relevantes au sort du ci-devant roi.*

Baudot, M. A. *Opinion . . . sur le jugement de Louis XVI.*

———. *Motifs . . . de J. M. Gelin et de M. A. Baudot contre l'appel au peuple dans le jugement de Louis seize* (7 jan. 1793).

Bayle, M. A. P. J. . . . *à ses collègues, sur le mode d'instruire la procédure du ci-devant roi.*

———. *Discours . . . contre l'appel au peuple et la proposition de faire confirmer le jugement . . . contre Louis Capet.*

Beauvais, C. N. *Opinion sur le jugement de Louis Capet, ci-devant roi des Français.*

_____. *Suite à l'opinion... sur le jugement de Louis XVI, ci-devant roi des Français.*

Becker, J. *Opinion... sur le ci-devant roi* (1793).

Beffroy, L. E. *Opinion... sur Louis le dernier.*

Bellegarde, A. D. de. *Opinion sur le procès de Louis Capet* (1793).

Bergoeing, F. *Opinion... sur le jugement de ci-devant roi.*

Berlier, T. *Opinion... sur la question de savoir si Louis XVI peut et doit être mis en jugement* (1792).

Bernard, A. A. B. *Opinion... sur le jugement de Louis Capet.*

Bernard Saint-Affrique, L. Bernard *dit. Opinion... sur le jugement de Louis Capet.*

Bertrand de L'Hodiesnière, C. A. *Opinion... sur Louis Capet.*

Bertucat, M. N. *Opinion... sur le jugement de Louis XVI.*

Besson, A. *Opinion... sur cette question: Quelle peine sera infligée à Louis Capet?*

_____. *Opinion... sur l'appel au peuple du jugement de Louis Capet.*

Bézard, F. S. *Opinion... sur le procès du ci-devant roi.*

_____. *Observations... sur l'état actuel du procès de Louis Capet, ci-devant roi de la Constitution* (12 déc. 1792).

_____. *Opinion motivée... sur la peine à infliger à Louis Capet* (17 jan. 1793).

Billaud-Varenne, J. N. B. *dit. Discours... sur le jugement de Louis Capet.*

Birotteau, J. B. B. H. *Opinion... sur le jugement de Louis le dernier.*

_____. *Discours... sur le jugement de Louis Capet* (29 déc. 1792).

Blutel, C. A. E. R. *Réflexions sur le jugement de Louis XVI.*

_____. *Suite des réflexions sur le jugement de Louis XVI* (6 jan. 1793).

_____. *Motifs énoncés sur la troisième question: Quelle peine Louis XVI a-t-il mérité?*

Bo, J. B. J. *Opinion... sur le jugement de Louis Capet.*

Bodin, F. J. F. *Mon opinion sur l'affaire de Louis Capet.*

Boilleau, J. *Opinion... contre l'appel au peuple sur le jugement de Louis Capet.*

_____. *Opinion... sur le procès du ci-devant roi.*

_____. *Opinion et jugement motivée... sur Louis le dernier.*

_____. *Opinion... relativement au sursis à l'exécution du jugement de Louis.*

Boisset, J. A. *Opinion... sur Louis XVI.*

Boissy d'Anglas, F. A. *Opinion... relativement à Louis.* (17 jan. 1793).

Bonnesoeur-Bourginière, S. J. H. *Opinion... sur le jugement de Louis XVI, dernier roi des Français.*

_____. *Opinion... sur la condamnation de Louis XVI, dernier roi des Français.*

Bordas, P. *Précis des opinions prononcées à la tribune de la Convention... sur la peine à infliger à Louis XVI, et sur le sursis du Décret qui le condamne à mort.*

Boucher, A. S. *A ceux de mes collègues qui ne sont qu'égarés.*

Bouchereau, A. F. *Opinion... sur cette question: Louis XVI peut-il être jugé?*

Bouquier, G. *Opinion... sur le jugement de Louis XVI.*

Bourbotte, P. *Opinion... sur le jugement de Louis Capet, dernier roi des Français.*

Bourdon, L. J. J. L. *Opinion... sur le jugement de Louis Capet, dit Louis XVI* (18 nov. 1792).

_____. *Seconde opinion... sur le jugement de Louis Capet.*

Bourgeois, N. *Opinion... sur le ci-devant roi et son jugement.*

Bousquet, F. *Opinion . . . sur le jugement du ci-devant roi.*

Boussion, P. *Opinion . . . sur le jugement de Louis Capet* (8 jan. 1793).

Briez, P. C. J. *Nouveau projet de décret sur l'affaire du ci-devant roi.*

_____. *Vues nouvelles sur l'affaire du ci-devant roi. Opinion . . . .*

Brissot, J. P. *Discours sur le procès de Louis . . .* (1 jan. 1793).

Brival, J. *Discours . . . sur le jugement de Louis Capet, dernier roi des Français.*

Brunel, I. *Opinion . . . sur l'affaire de Louis Capet* (30 nov. 1792).

Buzot, F. H. L. *Opinion . . . sur le jugement de Louis XVI.*

Cadroy, P. *Opinion . . . sur le jugement de Louis XVI* (16 jan. 1793).

Calès, J. M. *Opinion . . . sur le jugement de Louis XVI.*

Cambacérès, J. J. F. de. *Observations . . . sur le jugement de Louis XVI.*

Camus, A. G. *Opinion . . . sur les principes de la conduite à tenir . . . à l'égard du ci-devant roi et de sa famille.*

Cappin, J. E. *Observations . . . sur le jugement de Louis XVI, et sur la ratification par le peuple.*

Carra, J. L. *Discours contre la défense de Louis Capet, dernier roi des Francais* (3 jan. 1793).

_____. *Opinion . . . sur le jugement de Louis Capet, ci-devant roi.*

Casenave, A. *Opinion . . . sur le jugement de Louis XVI* (6 jan. 1793).

_____. *Opinion . . . sur le sursis à l'exécution du jugement de Louis XVI* (15 jan. 1793).

Cassanyès, J. J. F. *Opinion . . . sur le jugement de Louis Capet.*

Cavaignac, J. B. *Opinion . . . sur la question de savoir: si Louis XVI peut être jugé?*

_____. *Opinion . . . sur le jugement de Louis XVI* (Paris, 1833) (republished).

Chaillon, E. *Opinion . . . sur le jugement de Louis XVI* (16 jan. 1793).

Châles, P. J. M. *Opinion . . .* (14 jan. 1793).

Chasset, G. A. *Opinion sur l'affaire de Louis XVI.*

Chazal, J. P. *Opinion . . . dans l'affaire du ci-devant roi.*

Chénier, M. J. de. *Opinion . . . pour le jugement du ci-devant roi.*

Chevalier, J. *Opinion . . . sur l'affaire du ci-devant roi.*

Cledel, E. *Opinion . . . sur le jugement de Louis Capet.*

Cloots, J. B. *Harangue . . . à la Convention nationale . . . .*

Colaud la Salcette, J. B. *Opinion . . . sur les trois questions . . .* (17 jan. 1793).

Condorcet, M. J. A. N. C. de. *Opinion . . . sur le jugement de Louis XVI.*

_____. *Opinion . . . dans la séance du samedi 19 janvier.*

Conte, A. *Discours . . . contre le projet de décret . . . sur l'affaire de Louis XVI.*

_____. *Addition au mémoire . . . sur l'affaire de Louis XVI.*

Corbel, V. C. *Opinion . . . dans le jugement de Louis XVI, ci-devant roi des Français* (16 jan. 1793).

Coren-Fustier, S. J. *Opinion . . . sur la question de savoir si Louis XVI peut être jugé.*

Couhey, F. *Opinion . . . sur la peine à infliger à Louis Capet, ci-devant roi des Français.*

Couthon, G. A. *Opinion . . . sur le jugement de Louis Capet.*

Creuzé-Latouche, J. A. *Avis motivé . . . sur la peine à infliger à Louis Capet.*

Dandenac, J. *Opinion . . . dans l'affaire de Louis XVI.*

Dartigoeyte, P. A. *Opinion sur la question de savoir, si Louis XVI peut être jugé* (12 nov. 1792).

_____. *Opinion . . . sur cette question, Louis XVI peut-il être jugé?*

_____. *Opinion . . . sur la défense de Louis Capet* (3 jan. 1793).

Daunou, P. C. F. *Opinion . . . sur le jugement de Louis Capet.*
_____. *Considérations sur le procès de Louis XVI.*
_____. *Complément de l'opinion . . . sur l'affaire du ci-devant roi.*
Debourges, J. *Opinion . . . sur le jugement de Louis XVI* (17 jan. 1793).
De Bry, J. A. J. *Opinion . . . sur la question: Le ci-devant roi sera-t-il jugé?*
_____. *Sur les questions élevées dans l'affaire de Louis XVI du nom, ci-devant roi des Français* (7 jan. 1793).
Dechézeaux, P. C. D. G. *Encore une opinion sur le jugement de Louis XVI* (10 déc. 1792).
Delahaye, J. C. G. *Opinion . . . sur le jugement de Louis Capet.*
Delamarre, A. *Opinion . . . sur le jugement de Louis XVI* (16 jan. 1793).
Delbrel, P. *Opinion . . . sur les questions suivantes: Louis Capet peut-il être jugé? Par qui doit-il l'être?*
_____. *Observations sur la question de savoir si la Convention doit renvoyer aux assemblées primaires la ratification de l'application de la peine à prononcer contre Louis Capet.*
Delcher, E. J. *Opinion . . . sur Louis Capet.*
Delecloy, J. B. J. *Opinion . . . sur le mode de juger Louis Capet.*
Deleyre, A. *Opinion . . . sur la question du jugement de Louis XVI.*
_____. *Opinion . . . contre l'appel au peuple, sur le jugement de Louis XVI.*
De Sacy, C. L. M. *Opinion . . . sur Louis XVI et sur ses défenses.*
Descamps, B. *Opinion . . . ou le cri de la vérité et de la justice dans la decision à prononcer sur l'affaire de Capet.*
Desmoulins, L. S. B. C. *Opinion . . . sur le jugement de Louis XVI.*
_____. *Discours . . . sur la question de l'appel au peuple.*
Devérité, L. A. *Mon opinion sur le jugement de Louis XVI* (15 déc. 1792).
Dherbez-Latour, P. J. *Opinion . . . sur la peine à infliger au dernier roi des Français* (17 jan. 1793).
Drouet, J. B. *Opinion . . . sur le procès de Louis XVI.*
Du Bignon, F. M. J. *Opinion . . . sur le procès de Louis XVI.*
_____. *Réflexions sur le jugement de Louis XVI.*
Duboë, P. F. *Motifs des opinions . . . dans le jugement de Louis Bourbon, dernier roi des Français.*
Dubois, F. L. E. *See* Albert, J. E.
Dubois-Crancé, E. L. A. *Opinion . . . sur Louis XVI.* This was also printed at Melun, 1792, as were a number of other pamphlets; a Melun printer seems to have developed a special interest in the trial.
Duchastel, G. S. *Opinion . . . sur cette question: Quelle est la peine que le peuple français doit infliger à Louis?*
_____. *Réflexions . . . sur la manière dont les questions ont été posées dans l'affaire de Louis* (14 jan. 1793).
Ducos, J. F. *Motifs . . . dans le jugement de Louis Bourbon, ci-devant roi.*
_____. *Opinion . . . sur le jugement de Louis XVI.*
Ducos, P. R. *Opinion . . . sur cette question: Louis XVI peut-il être jugé? doit-il être jugé par la Convention nationale?*
_____. *Opinion . . . sur le jugement de Louis XVI.*
Dufriche-Valazé, C. E. *Opinion . . . sur le jugement de Louis Capet.*
_____. *Rapport . . . sur les crimes du ci-devant roi* (6 nov. 1792).
Dugenne, F. E. *Opinion . . . sur le jugement de Louis Capet.*
Dugué-d'Assé, J. C. *Opinion . . . sur le jugement de Louis XVI.*

_____. *Suite importante de l'opinion . . . sur le jugement de Louis XVI.*

Dulaure, J. A. *Opinion . . . sur le jugement du ci-devant roi.*

Dumont, A. *Discours . . . sur le procès de Louis XVI.*

Dumont, L. P. *L. Ph. Dumont . . . opinant sur cette question: "Quelle peine infligera-t-on à Louis XVI, ci-devant roi des Français? "*

Dupont, P. C. F. *Opinion . . . sur le jugement de Louis le dernier.*

Durand-Maillane, P. T. *Opinion . . . et ses motifs dans le jugement de Louis Capet* (3 jan. 1793).

_____. *Opinion . . . sur les trois questions posées pour le jugement de Louis XVI, et leurs motifs* (16 jan. 1793).

Dusaulx, J. *Opinion . . . sur le jugement de Louis Capet.*

Duval, C. F. M. *Coup d'oeil sur la conduite de Louis XVI.*

Engerran, J. *Résumé sur l'affaire de Louis Capet.*

Enlart, N. F. M. *Opinion . . . sur le jugement de Louis XVI.*

Fabre, C. D. C. *Opinion . . . sur le jugement de Louis Capet.*

Fabre d'Eglantine, P. P. N. *Opinion . . . sur l'appel au peuple.*

Fauchet, C. *Opinion . . . sur le jugement du ci-devant roi.*

_____. *Suite de l'opinion . . . sur le jugement du ci-devant roi.*

Faure, B. *Opinion . . . sur Louis le tyran.*

Faure, P. J. D. G. *Opinion . . . sur le procès du roi.*

_____. *Opinion . . . sur le jugement du roi.*

_____. *. . . à la Convention.*

Fayau, J. P. M. *Opinion . . . sur le jugement de Louis Capet, ci-devant roi des Français.*

Féraud, J. B. *Opinion . . . sur Louis Capet.*

Ferroux, E. J. *Opinion . . . sur le jugement de Louis XVI.*

Finot, E. *Opinion . . . sur le jugement du ci-devant roi.*

Fockedey, J. J. *Opinion . . . sur le jugement de Louis XVI.*

Fouché, J. *Réflexions . . . sur le jugement de Louis Capet.*

Fourmy, J. D. *Opinion et projet de décret . . . sur la question de savoir si Louis XVI sera jugé.*

François, L. F. A. *Discours . . . sur l'article premier du Projet de Décret: Louis XVI peut-il être jugé?*

Gamon, F. J. *Opinion . . . sur la question de savoir s'il est de l'intérêt du peuple de surseoir l'exécution du jugement qui condamne Louis à mort.*

_____. *Projet de décret . . . dans l'affaire de Louis Capet.*

Garilhe, F. C. P. de. *Motifs . . . sur cette question: à quelle peine Louis XVI, ci-devant roi des Français, sera-t-il condamné?*

Garnier, J. *Opinion . . . sur la manière d'instruire le procès de Louis Capet.*

_____. *Opinion . . . contre le mesure de renvoi au peuple du jugement de Louis XVI.*

Garran-Coulon, J. P. *. . . sur le jugement de Louis XVI.*

Gaston, R. *Opinion . . . sur le procès du dernier roi des Français.*

Gaudin, J. M. J. F. *Opinion . . . sur le jugement de Louis.*

Gelin, J. M. *Motifs de J. M. Gelin et de M. A. Baudot . . . contre l'appel au peuple dans le jugement de Louis seize* (7 jan. 1793).

Genevois, L. B. *Le procès de Louis XVI . . . .*

_____. *Sur Louis Capet . . . .*

Gensonné, A. *Opinion . . . sur le jugement de Louis.*

Gertoux, B. *Opinion . . . sur la forme de jugement de Louis XVI.*

Girard, A. M. A. *Discours . . . prononcé le 17 janvier 1793.*

_____. *Essai rapide . . . sur le procès de Louis Capet.*

Girault, C. J. *Opinion . . . sur le jugement de Louis XVI.*

Girot-Pouzol, J. B. *Motifs de l'opinion . . . sur le jugement de Louis Capet.*

Gleizal, C. *Projets et décrets proposés . . . sur la peine à infliger à Louis Capet* (26 déc. 1792).

Goudelin, G. J. P. *Opinion . . . sur la défense et le jugement de Louis Capet.*

_____. *Opinion . . . prononcée . . . le 17 janvier 1793.*

Goyre-Laplanche, J. L. *Opinion . . . sur le procès de Louis le dernier.*

Grégoire, H. *Opinion . . . concernant le jugement de Louis XVI* (15 nov. 1792).

Guadet, M. E. *Opinion . . . sur le jugement de Louis, ci-devant roi des Français.*

Guffroy, A. B. J. *Discours . . . sur ce que la Nation doit faire du ci-devant roi.*

_____. *2ᵉ discours . . . sur la punition de Louis Capet.*

_____. *Discours . . . contre le sursis à l'arrête de mort du tyran* (20 jan. 1793).

Guillermin, C. N. *Quelques réflexions . . . sur le procès de Louis Capet.*

_____. *Réfutation de plusieurs objections de Salles et de Vergniaud sur le procès de Louis Capet.*

Guiot, Florent, *Motion d'ordre proposée . . . sur l'article premier du projet de décret: Louis XVI peut être jugé.*

Guiter, J. A. S. *Discours . . . sur la question suivante: Louis XVI peut-il être mis en jugement?*

_____. *Discours . . . sur les mesures à prendre pour l'intérêt de la République, en jugeant Louis Capet.*

Guyomar, P. M. A. *Opinion . . . concernant le jugement de Louis Capet.*

Guyton-Morveau, L. B. *Opinion . . . dans l'affaire de Louis Capet, dernier roi des Français.*

Harmand, J. B. *Opinion . . . sur le jugement de Louis XVI.*

_____. *Opinion . . . sur l'espèce de peine méritée par Louis XVI.*

Hentz, N. J. *Opinion . . . sur le procès du ci-devant roi.*

_____. *Réflexions . . . sur l'appel au peuple.*

Ichon, P. L. *Discours . . . sur l'affaire de Louis XVI.*

_____. *Discours . . . sur le jugement de Louis XVI.*

Izoard, J. F. A. *Voeux . . . sur les trois questions . . .* (17–18 jan. 1793).

Jary, F. J. *Opinion . . . sur le jugement de Louis XVI* (16 jan. 1793).

Jeanbon, André, Saint-André dit. *Opinion . . . sur cette question: Louis XVI peut-il être jugé?*

_____. *Opinion . . . sur le jugement du Roi, et l'appel au peuple.*

Jouenne-Longchamp, T. F. A. *Opinion . . . sur le jugement de Louis Capet* (16 jan. 1793).

Jourdan, J. B. *Sur la peine à infliger à Louis XVI.*

Julien, J. *Opinion . . . sur le procès de Louis Capet, ci-devant roi des Français.*

Jullien, M. A. *Opinion . . . sur le jugement de Louis XVI.*

Kersaint, A. G. S. C. de. *Opinion . . . sur cette question: Quel parti la Convention nationale doit-elle prendre touchant le ci-devant roi et sa famille?*

_____. *Seconde opinion . . . sur le jugement du ci-devant roi.*

Laboissière, J. B. *Opinion . . . concernant l'affaire du ci-devant roi.*

_____. *Résultat des differentes opinions prononcées à la Convention nationale . . . .*

Lacombe Saint-Michel, J. P. *Opinion . . . sur le jugement de Louis.*

Lacoste, J. B. *Discours . . . sur le jugement de Louis XVI.*

Lafon, P. A. *Déclaration faite . . . concernant les motifs qui l'ont porté à ne pas opiner sur les questions relatives au Jugement de Louis Capet* (16 jan. 1793).

Lakanal, J. *Opinion . . . sur la question de savoir: Si Louis XVI peut être jugé?*

Lambert, C. *Opinion . . . sur le jugement de Louis XVI* (23 déc. 1792).

_____. *Opinion . . . sur le mode de jugement de Louis seize.*

_____. *Supplément à l'opinion . . . sur le mode de justice de Louis seize.*

_____. *Opinion . . . sur le jugement de Louis XVI . . .* (17 jan. 1793).

Lanjuinais, J. D. *Opinion . . . sur Louis le dernier* (31 déc. 1792).

Lanthénas, F. X. *Motifs des opinions . . . sur le jugement de Louis.*

La Revellière-Lépeaux, L. M. *Opinion . . . sur la question de l'appel au peuple du jugement de Louis* (7 jan. 1793).

_____. *Opinion . . . sur la question de savoir si Louis XVI peut être mis en jugement* (1 déc. 1792).

Lavicomterie, L. T. H. de. *Réflexions . . . sur le procès criminel du ci-devant roi.*

_____. *L'appel au peuple est un paradoxe.*

Le Breton, R. P. F. *Opinion . . .* (15 jan. 1973).

Le Carpentier, J. B. *Opinion . . . sur l'affaire de Louis XVI* (30 nov. 1792).

_____. *Discours . . . sur le jugement définitif de Louis Capet* (6 jan. 1793).

Le Clerc, C. N. *Opinion . . . sur le sort de Louis Capet.*

Le Clerc, J. B. *Opinion . . . sur le jugement de Louis XVI.*

Lecointe-Puyraveau, M. M. *Opinion . . . sur Louis Capet* (27 nov. 1792).

_____. *Opinion . . . sur les propositions relatives au mode de jugement de Louis Capet.*

Le Cointre, L. *Opinion . . . sur le jugement de Louis Capet.*

Lejeune, S. P. *Opinion . . . sur Louis Capet, ci-devant roi des Français.*

Le Maréchal, D. *Déclaration et opinions . . . sur les trois questions . . . .*

Le Peletier de Saint-Fargeau, L. M. *Opinion . . . sur le jugement de Louis XVI, ci-devant roi des Français.*

_____. *Opinion . . . sur le jugement du ci-devant roi des Français.*

Lequinio, M. J. *Opinion . . . sur le jugement de Louis XVI* (3 déc. 1792).

_____. *Opinion . . . sur la défense de Louis XVI* (27 déc. 1792).

Lesterpt-Beauvais, B. *Précis de l'opinion . . . sur la peine à infliger à Louis Capet.*

Lindet, J. B. R. *Attentat et crimes de Louis, dernier roi des Français.*

Lindet, R. T. *Opinion . . . sur l'affaire de Louis Capet.*

Loiseau, J. F. *Opinion . . . sur le jugement du ci-devant roi* (19 déc. 1792).

Louchet, L. *Opinion . . . sur le procès de Louis XVI.* (30 nov. 1792).

_____. *Deuxième opinion . . . sur le procès de Louis XVI* (8 jan. 1793).

Louvet, J. B. *Opinion . . . contre la défense de Louis Capet, et pour l'appel au peuple.*

Louvet, P. F. *Opinion . . . sur l'affaire du ci-devant roi.*

_____. *Suite de l'opinion . . . sur l'affaire du ci-devant roi.*

Lozeau, P. A. *Opinion . . . sur le jugement de Louis Capet, ou réfutation du défenseur de Louis, et du système de l'appel au peuple.*

Mailhe, J. *Rapport et projet de décret . . . au nom du comité de législation . . .* (7 nov. 1792).

Manuel, J. *Opinion . . . pour le jugement de Louis XVI.*

Marat, J. P. *Discours . . . sur la défense de Louis XVI.*

_____. *Opinion . . . sur le jugement de l'ex-monarque.*

Marec, P. *Opinion . . . sur l'appel au peuple du jugement du ci-devant roi* (19 déc. 1792).

_____. *Supplément à l'opinion . . . sur l'appel au peuple du jugement du ci-devant roi.*

Marey, N. J. *Opinion . . . sur le jugement de Louis XVI.*

Massieu, J. B. *Opinion . . . sur le jugement de Louis XVI* (1 déc. 1792).

Masuyer, C. L. *Un mot sur Louis le traître, ou le dernier, et sa famille.*
Maulde, P. J. *Opinion . . . sur le jugement de Louis le dernier.*
Maure, N. S. *Un mot sur l'affaire de Louis XVI.*
Mazade-Percin, J. B. D. de. *Opinion sur l'affaire de Louis Capet* [no. 1] (3 déc. 1792).
_____. *Opinion . . . sur l'affaire de Louis Capet* [no. 2].
_____. *Opinion . . . sur l'affaire de Louis Capet* [no. 3] (16 jan. 1793).
Méaulle, J. N. *Discours . . . sur le jugement de Louis XVI.*
_____. *Opinion . . . sur l'appel au peuple.*
Mellinet, F. *Discours . . . sur la question suivante: Louis XVI peut-il être jugé?* (1 déc. 1792).
Mennesson, J. B. A. P. *Mon avis sur le jugement du dernier roi.*
_____. *Mon dernier mot sur le jugement de Louis* (16 jan. 1793).
Mercier, L. S. *Opinion . . . sur Louis Capet.*
Merlin, A. C. *Lettre . . . au président de la Convention nationale* (6 jan. 1793).
Merlin, P. A. *Opinion . . . sur le procès de Louis XVI.*
Meynard, F. *Opinion . . . concernant le procès de Louis XVI.*
_____. *Suite de l'opinion . . . sur le procès de Louis XVI.*
Michet, A. *Observations sur le procès de Louis XVI.*
Milhaud, E. J. B. *Opinion . . . sur le jugement de Louis Capet, dit Louis XVI.*
Mollevaut, E. *Opinion . . . sur cette question: Quelle peine sera infligée à Louis?* (16 jan. 1793).
_____. *Opinion . . . sur le sursis au décret de mort prononcé contre Louis Capet.*
Monmayou, H. G. B. J. *Opinion . . . sur le jugement du ci-vant roi.*
Montgilbert, F. A. *Opinion . . . sur le jugement de Louis XVI.*
_____. *Motion d'ordre . . .*
Moreau, F. M. *Opinion sur la jugement du ci-devant roi* (31 déc. 1792).
Morisson, C. F. G. *Opinion . . . concernant le jugement de Louis XVI* (13 nov. 1792).
_____. *Seconde opinion . . . concernant le jugement de Louis XVI.*
_____. *Troisième opinion . . . sur le jugement de Louis XVI.*
Neveu, E. *Opinion . . . sur le jugement de Louis XVI* (17 jan. 1793).
Nioche, P. G. *Opinion . . . sur ces deux questions: Louis XVI peut-il être jugê? Le sera-t-il par la Convention Nationale?*
_____. *Opinion . . . sur la question de savoir si le jugement de Louis Capet doit être renvoyé à la ratification des Assemblées primaires?*
_____. *Opinion . . . sur la question de savoir, quelle peine sera infligée à Louis Capet?*
Osselin, C. N. *Discours sur l'inviolabilité.*
_____. *Opinion . . . sur l'appel au peuple du jugement de Louis Capet (3ᵉ discours).*
_____. *Quatrième discours contre le sursis proposé à l'exécution du jugement de Louis.*
Oudot, C. F. *Opinion . . . sur le jugement de Louis XVI.*
Paganel, P. *Opinion . . . sur le jugement du ci-devant roi.*
Paine, T. *Opinion . . . concernant le jugement de Louis XVI.*
_____. *Opinion . . . sur l'affaire de Louis Capet.*
Pellissier, M. D. *Opinion . . . sur le jugement de Louis XVI.*
Pémartin, J. *Opinion . . . sur l'affaire de Louis Capet.*
_____. *Raisons de mon opinion . . . sur l'affaire de Louis XVI* (16 & 17 jan. 1793).
Penières-Delzors, J. A. *Opinion . . . sur le jugement de Louis XVI.*

Pepin, S. *Opinion . . . sur le procès de Louis Capet.*
Pérard, C. F. J. *Opinion . . . sur le jugement de Louis XVI.*
Personne, J. B. *Opinion . . . dans l'affaire ou procès de Louis.*
Pétion, J. *Discours sur l'affaire du roi.*
———. *Opinion . . . sur le roi.*
———. *Opinion . . . sur la question s'il existe ou non une Convention nationale.*
Petit, E. M. *Opinion . . . sur le jugement de Louis Capet, dernier roi des Français*
    [no. 1].
———. *Opinion . . . sur le jugement de Louis Capet, dernier roi des Français*
    [no. 2].
Petitjean, C. L. *Un mot et quelques observations . . . .*
Philippeaux, P. N. *Opinion . . . sur le jugement de Louis XVI.*
Pinet, J. *Réflexions sur le jugement de Louis Capet.*
Plet-Beauprey, P. F. N. *Opinion . . . sur la peine à infliger à Louis Capet* (18 jan.
    1793).
Pointe, N. *Opinion . . . sur le jugement du ci-devant roi des Français.*
———. *Discours . . . sur la discussion concernant le jugement de Louis.*
Pons, P. L. *Opinion . . . sur l'inviolabilité de Louis Capet.*
Porcher, G. C. *Opinion . . . sur cette question: Quelle est la peine à infliger à
    Louis Capet?*
Portiez, L. F. *Opinion . . . sur cette question: Le roi des Français était-il
    jugeable?*
Pottier, C. A. *Opinion . . . sur le jugement de Louis XVI.*
Poullain-Grandprey, J. C. *Opinion . . . sur le jugement de Louis XVI.*
———. *Opinion . . . sur cette question: Le jugement qui sera prononcé par la
    Convention nationale, sera-t-il soumis à la ratification du peuple?*
Poultier, F. M. *Opinion . . . sur le procès du ci-devant roi.*
———. *. . . sur le supplice de Louis Capet.*
Pressavin, J. B. *Opinion . . . sur le procès du roi.*
Prieur, P. L. *Opinion . . . sur le jugement de Louis Capet.*
Prost, C. C. *Discours . . . sur l'inviolabilité de Louis XVI.*
———. *Discours . . . sur le jugement de Louis XVI* (29 déc. 1792).
Prunelle-Lière, L. J. *Opinion . . . concernant le jugement de Louis XVI.*
———. *Suite de l'opinion . . . concernant le jugement de Louis XVI.*
Quinette, N. M. *Projet de décret sur le jugement de Louis XVI* (6 déc. 1792).
———. *Opinion . . . sur le jugement de Louis Capet.*
———. *Complément des décrets . . . dans l'affaire de Louis Capet.*
Rabaut-Pomier, J. A. Rabaut *dit, Opinion . . . sur cette question: La Convention
    nationale, doit-elle renvoyer à la sanction du peuple, le jugement qu'elle pro-
    noncera sur Louis Capet?*
———. *Suite de l'opinion . . .*
Rabaut Saint-Etienne, J. P. Rabaut *dit. Opinion concernant le procès de Louis
    XVI* (28 déc. 1792).
Raffron, N. *Sentiment . . . sur le jugement de Louis XVI* (16 déc. 1792).
Rameau, J. *Et moi, non . . . .*
Ramel-Nogaret, D. V. *Que doit faire la Convention nationale sur la procès de
    Louis Capet?*
Réal, A. *Motifs . . . dans le jugement de Louis Capet.*
Reynaud, C. A. B. *Opinion . . . sur le jugement de Louis Capet.*
Ribet, B. J. G. B. *Opinion . . . sur le jugement de Louis Capet, dernier roi des
    Français.*

Ricord, J. F. *Opinion . . . sur le sort de Louis XVI.*

———. *Opinion . . . concernant le jugement de Louis XVI.*

Rivaud, F. *Opinion . . . sur le jugement de Louis XVI.*

Robert, P. F. J. *Opinion . . . concernant le jugement de Louis XVI.* (13 nov. 1792).

———. *Suite de l'opinion . . . sur le jugement et les crimes du ci-devant roi.*

———. *3ᵉ opinion . . . sur le jugement de Louis Capet.*

Robespierre, A. B. J. *Opinion . . . sur le procès de Louis XVI.*

Robespierre, M. *Opinion . . . sur le jugement de Louis XVI.*

———. *Seconde discours . . . sur le jugement de Louis Capet.*

Roussel, C. J. de la P.–L. *Opinion . . . sur le jugement du roi.*

Roux, L. F. *Opinion . . . sur le jugement de Louis Capet* (12 jan. 1793).

Rouzet, J. M. *Opinion . . . concernant le jugement de Louis XVI* (15 nov. 1792).

———. *Suite de l'opinion . . . concernant le jugement de Louis XVI* (1 déc. 1792).

———. *Avis définitif . . . dans le jugement de Louis XVI* (27 déc. 1792).

Roy, D. *Opinion . . . sur le sort du dernier roi des Français.*

Rudel, C. A. *Opinion . . . sur le jugement de Louis Capet.*

Saint-Just, L. A., de. *Discours . . . sur Louis XVI* (26 déc.1792).

———. *Opinion concernant le jugement de Louis XVI* (13 nov. 1792). (Nismes, 1792).

Saint-Martin, F. J. Riffard. *Opinion . . .* (17 jan. 1793).

———. *Opinion . . . dans l'affaire du ci-devant roi.*

Salle, J. B. *Déclaration . . . dans l'affaire du ci-devant roi.*

———. *Opinion . . . dans l'affaire du ci-devant roi.*

Salmon, C. P. L. *Opinion . . . sur cette question: Quelle peine sera infligée à Louis Capet?* (17 jan. 1793).

Saurine, J. B. P. *Opinion . . . au moment du troisième appel nominal . . . .*

Savary, L. J. *Opinion . . . sur le jugement du ci-devant roi.*

Second, J. L. *Opinion . . . dans le jugement à mort de Louis XVI.*

———. *Opinion politique et constitutionelle . . . sur le jugement de Louis, et contre l'appel au peuple.*

Séguin, P. C. A. *Opinion . . . sur le jugement de Louis XVI* (16 jan. 1793).

Sergent, A. F. *Opinion . . . sur la jugement de Louis Capet.*

———. *Opinion . . . prononcée . . . au troisième appel nominal . . . .*

Serre, J. *Opinion . . . contre l'inviolabilité du roi.*

———. *Opinion . . . sur la question suivante: La mort de Louis intéresse-t-elle le salut de la république?* (27 déc. 1792).

Sévestre, J. M. F. *Opinion . . . sur le jugement de Louis Capet* (1 déc. 1792).

Soulignac, J. B. *Précis de l'opinion . . . sur cette question: Quelle peine sera infligée à Louis?*

Tallien, J. L. *Projets de décrets concernant Louis Capet . . . .*

Thibaudeau, A. G. *Opinion . . . sur le jugement de Louis XVI* (1 déc. 1792).

———. *Opinion . . . sur la question de savoir si le jugement de Louis Capet doit être remis à la ratification du peuple* (31 déc. 1792).

Thibault, A. A. M. *Opinion . . . sur le jugement de Louis XVI.*

Thirion, D. *Opinion . . . sur le procès du ci-devant roi Louis Capet.*

Thomas, J. J. *Opinion . . . sur le jugement de Louis XVI.*

———. *Supplément à l'opinion . . . sur le jugement de Louis Capet.*

Thuriot, J. A. *Opinion . . . sur le proposition de surseoir à l'exécution du decret de mort prononcé contre Louis Capet.*

Tocquot, C. N. *Déclaration . . . sur le sursis du jugement de Louis Capet.*
Turreau de Linières, L. *Opinion . . . sur Capet.*
———. *Motifs . . . dans le jugement de Capet.*
Vadier, M. G. A. *Opinion . . . concernant Louis XVI.*
———. *Seconde opinion . . . sur Louis Capet.*
Vardon, L. A. J. *Opinion . . .* (17 jan. 1793).
Vergniaud, P. V. *Opinion . . . sur le jugement de Louis XVI.*
Vermon, A. J. *Réclamation sur le vote qui lui est attribué dans l'appel nominal . . . sur cette question: Quelle peine sera infligée à Louis?* (3 fév. 1793).
Vernier, T. *Opinion . . . sur le jugement du dernier roi des Français.*
Viennet, J. J. *Opinion . . . sur le jugement de Louis.*
———. *Réponse à la question sur la peine à infliger à Louis XVI.*
Viquy, J. N. *Opinion . . .* (16 jan. 1793).
Wandelaincourt, A. H. *Opinion . . . sur le jugement de Louis Capet.*

SECONDARY SOURCES

Among the *standard bibliographies* special mention should be made of Walter, G., *Repertoire de l'histoire de la Révolution française; travaux publiés de 1800 à 1940*, Vol. I: *Personnes* (Paris, 1941); Vol. II: *Lieux* (Paris, 1951), which was invaluable for a first access to local history, as well as for other purposes. For *general reference* on the *conventionnels* and their possible background, I used: Arnault, A. V., and others, *Biographie nouvelle des contemporains*, 20 vols. (Paris, 1820); Beltau, J., and others, *Dictionnaire de Biographie française* (Paris, 1933–in progress); Franklin, A., *Dictionnaire historique des arts, métiers et professions exercés dans Paris depuis le treizième siècle* (Paris, 1906); Marion, M., *Dictionnaire des institutions de la France aux XVIIe et XVIIIe siècles* (Paris, 1923); and Mols, R., *Introduction à la démographie historique de l'Europe du XIVe au XVIIIe siècle*, 3 vols. (Gembloux, 1954–56).

The *general histories* of the Revolution most consulted are cited in the foot-notes. With biographies, as with memoirs, the list becomes too long; but I would cite especially Lévy-Schneider, L., *Le Conventionnel Jeanbon Saint-André* (Paris, 1901), for its fascinating picture of the local situation in Montauban as well as of Jeanbon himself. A good biography of Louis XVI is very badly needed.

For *local history* the field is again enormous. Most of the older histories are right-wing in flavor. About seventy years ago Aulard's students seem to have been put to work in this area; the standard of their work varies, but Bruneau, M., *Les Débuts de la Révolution dans les Départements du Cher et de l'Indre* (Paris, 1902) and Labroue, H., *L'Esprit Public en Dordogne pendant la Révolution* (Paris, 1911) are fair examples from this period. The first-rate books now being published (e.g., Hufton, O., *Bayeux in the late Eighteenth Century* (London, 1968) are on a smaller scale. For some reason, material seems to be more plentiful on counterrevolutionary than on revolutionary areas.

The only modern works dealing with groups of *conventionnels* are Sydenham, M. J., *The Girondins* (London, 1961); and Melchior-Bonnet, B., *Les Girondins* (Paris, 1969). Many specialist sources have been cited in footnotes. I note particularly, for their usefulness in various ways, Belhomme, E., *Les Régicides* (Paris, 1893); Dodu, G., *Le Parlementarisme et les Parlementaires sous la Révolution* (Paris, 1911); Gaulot, P., *Les grandes journées révolutionnaires* (Paris, 1877) (reprints, accurately, the entire voting of 15–19 January 1793); Pisani, P., *Repertoire biographique de l'épiscopat constitutionnel 1791–1802* (Paris, 1909); Reinhard, M., *La Chute de la Royauté* (Paris, 1969); and of course Kuscinski, A., *Les Députés à l'Assemblée Législative de 1791* (Paris, 1900); and *Dictionnaire des Conventionnels*, 4 vols., (Paris, 1916–19). For the trial, as noted, E. Seligman, *La Justice en France pendant la Révolution 1791–1793*, 2nd ed., (Paris, 1913), and for important comparative purposes, Wedgwood, C. V., *The Trial of Charles I* (London, 1967).

The standard specialist periodicals are of course *La Révolution Française* and the *Annales Historiques de la Révolution Française* (from 1908 to 1923, the *Annales Révolutionnaires*); but the *Revue Historique de la Révolution Française* (Paris, 1910–22) is worth glancing through. Local general periodicals are innumerable; for an example of what may be found in this area, cf., Coüard, E., and Lorin, F., "Les élections à l'Assemblée législative dans le département de Seine-et-Oise," *Mémoires de la Société Archéologique de Rambouillet* XX (1908). I made no pretense of even an attempt to survey these, but simply used what I happened to encounter, which was a surprising amount.

INDEX